SECOND EDITION

COLLECTIVE BARGAINING & LABOR RELATIONS

E. EDWARD HERMAN
University of Cincinnati

ALFRED KUHN
Late of the
University of Cincinnati

RONALD L. SEEBER
New York State School
of Industrial and Labor Relations
Cornell University

PRENTICE-HALL, INC., *Englewood Cliffs, New Jersey 07632*

Library of Congress Cataloging-in-Publication Data

Herman, E. Edward, (date)
    Collective bargaining and labor relations

    Bibliography: p.
    Includes index.
    1. Collective bargaining—United States.
2. Industrial relations—United States. I. Kuhn, Alfred,
(Date). II. Seeber, Ronald Leroy. III. Title.
HD6508.H43 1987   331.89′0973   86-20515
ISBN 0-13-140575-6

Editorial/production supervision and interior design: NANCY G. FOLLENDER
Cover design: 20/20 SERVICES
Manufacturing buyer: HARRY P. BAISLEY

Printed in the United States of America

10 9 8 7 6 5 4 3 2 1

ISBN 0-13-140575-6 01

Prentice-Hall International (UK) Limited, *London*
Prentice-Hall of Australia Pty. Limited, *Sydney*
Prentice-Hall Canada Inc., *Toronto*
Prentice-Hall Hispanoamericana, S.A., *Mexico*
Prentice-Hall of India Private Limited, *New Delhi*
Prentice-Hall of Japan, Inc., *Tokyo*
Prentice-Hall of Southeast Asia Pte. Ltd., *Singapore*
Editora Prentice-Hall do Brasil, Ltda., *Rio de Janeiro*

This book is dedicated to our parents and wives
and our children
Diane, Robert, David, Jeffrey, Henry, and *Brent*

"He that flies from his own family has far to travel."
(Longe fuit, quisquis suos fugit.)

PETRONIUS, **SATYRICON, SEC. 43**

This book is a tribute to the co-author of the first edition of this text, the late Alfred Kuhn. At his memorial service the following message from Kenneth Boulding and Lawrence Senesch was read: "Our joy in his life will long outlive our grief in his passing for his mind will live on in his works and speak to us for many years to come."

CONTENTS

Part III
The Framework of Collective Bargaining

Part VII
Special Topics

ARBITRATION CASES   523

BIBLIOGRAPHY   582

GLOSSARY   606

INDEX   611

PREFACE

The second edition of *Collective Bargaining and Labor Relations* has been significantly revised and updated. The book reflects the major changes that have taken place in the labor relations arena. We have written a number of totally new chapters and sections.

The field of collective bargaining and labor relations is very dynamic and in a constant state of motion. Since our first edition, there has been a major change in the industrial relations climate in the United States. Economic fluctuations, new technologies, foreign competition, a second term republican administration in Washington all had an impact on the U.S. labor scene. In the revised edition we have attempted to capture the effect of some of these changes. We have updated all our statistical material as well as our comprehensive bibliography. We also incorporated in our text recent research findings on subjects covered in this book.

PRODUCT DIFFERENTIATION

In view of the variety of texts in labor relations and collective bargaining it is necessary to explain what makes this book different. The book provides an in-depth coverage of a number of areas that are either omitted or underemphasized in other texts; specifically the reader is directed to the following chapters: "The Question of the Bargaining Unit," "Preparation for Bargaining," "Costing of Labor Contracts," the four chapters on the bargaining process, and "Management and Union Security," "Concessions and the Future of Collective Bargaining," the bargaining simulation, and recent arbitration cases addressing current issues.

The chapter on bargaining units provides a comprehensive coverage of different types of units. It examines the certified and the negotiation unit; it looks at the unit of direct impact. It reviews the role and the significance of NLRB decisions. It discusses single employer, multi-employer and craft bargaining units. It evaluates coordinated bargaining. It also discusses at some length the concept of a bargaining structure.

The chapter "Preparation for Bargaining" provides a detailed coverage of all aspects of preparations for negotiations. It addresses such issues as formulation of proposals, bargaining books, tactical moves, sources of data, and bargaining procedures.

The subject of "Costing of Labor Contracts" is usually neglected in collective bargaining courses and in the past has been absent from most texts. In our view the knowledge of costing of contracts is a major challenge confronting labor relations managers. The advent of computers and the increasing number of sophisticated, quantitatively trained specialists occupying managerial positions is conducive to shifting many industrial relations decisions away from labor relations personnel to actuaries, accountants, economists and finance experts, most of whom lack background in labor relations. To prevent such a shift in responsibilities, labor relations staffs will require better understanding of finance and costing. The purpose of the costing chapter is to familiarize the reader with various aspects of costing.

The four chapters on the bargaining process attempt to give the reader the best of two very different worlds: On the one hand, the practical aspects of negotiations and impasse resolution are presented. On the other, the theoretical rigor of the bargaining models of Kuhn and Walton and McKersie are offered. This reflects our thinking that it is not possible to understand fully the collective bargaining process and the various social interactions embodied in that process without an understanding of both vantage points. The chapters "The Negotiation Process," "Bargaining Theory and Bargaining Power," "The Application of the Bargaining Theory Model," and "Impasse: Resolution and Regulation" attempt to provide such an understanding.

The subject of management and union security is discussed in some depth in Chapter 15. The topic is important in itself and it also provides crucial insights into the broader nature of collective bargaining. In addition, we have included a chapter devoted to concessions bargaining. To some extent, concessions have revolved around management's freedom to change methods of production and these are significant in the context of management and union security.

The bargaining simulation is a helpful supplement to bargaining course. The simulation has been successfully tested on students with and without background in labor relations as well as on professional managers from large corporations, some of whom have had negotiation experience. The results with the various groups have been excellent, and highly recommend the simulation as a teaching tool. The simulation, as contrasted with most other simulations on the market, is so structured that it is never out-of-date. The worksheets accompanying it permit the instructor and students to utilize the latest published data for simulation purposes. In our view, negotiations do not end when a settlement is reached and an agreement is signed. Collective bargaining is a continuous process consisting of contract negotiations administration and interpretation. In the last section of the book we have included recent arbitration cases which illustrate some of the issues emerging during the administrative phase of the contract. The arbitration awards for these cases are included in the Instructor's Manual.

So far we have discussed the subjects that we have included, and which are usually omitted from or lightly covered in other texts. This raises the question—what was the trade-off? The answer is we left out most of wage theory which is extensively treated in some texts. Here we concur with Dunlop that "an industrial relations system is not a subsidiary part of an economic system, but is rather a separate and a distinctive subsystem of the society."* Our book attends mainly to labor relations, labor law, and collective bargaining topics, with only a few relatively pragmatic aspects of wages discussed in Chapter 13.

Every author has to make hard choices of what to include. We feel that the advantages of intensive coverage of the areas presented here outweigh those of an encyclopedic volume with briefer coverage of more numerous topics.

Most chapters of this text are self-contained, thus giving instructors the flexibility to use chapters in the sequence which will best meet their needs. This text, together with some supplementary readings, meets the needs of the usual two semester or three quarter course. By omitting some chapters the instructor can use the text for two quarter, one semester, and one quarter courses.

This volume is designed for both undergraduate and beginning graduate students in industrial relations and collective bargaining, and many of its chapters should be distinctly useful for practitioners in the field as well. It should be a fully adequate text without supplementation, though particular teachers may want to add their own selection of readings.

ORGANIZATION

Part I, Chapter 1, discusses development and growth of the labor movement. Without it, there would be no collective bargaining and thus, no need for this text. The chapter reviews the emergence of the first unions, examines different types of unions, and discusses national unions, the Knights of Labor, the development of the American Federation of Labor, left-wing unionism, the IWW, the CIO and the separation and reunion of the AFL-CIO. Employer reaction to unionism and its impact on development of unions is also evaluated. We also look at the continuing forces behind the labor movement and their potential impact on the future size and shape of the labor movement.

Part II, Chapters 2–4, of our text covers evaluation of the legal framework for collective bargaining.

Chapter 2 discusses the period of opposition, the Conspiracy Doctrine, the injunction, the Sherman Act, and the Clayton Act. The chapter also covers the period of support: the Norris-LaGuardia Act and the Wagner Act. Other statutes covered are

---

*John T. Dunlop, *Industrial Relation Systems* (New York: Holt, 1958), p. 5.

the Taft-Hartley Act, the Landrum Griffin Act of 1959, the 1974 Health-Care Amendments, and attempts at labor law reform.

Chapter 3 evaluates the effects of the law on bargaining power, union and management security, and attitudes toward bargaining. It examines the legal status of primary strikes, lockouts, secondary boycotts, and picketing. The chapter also reviews regulation of bargaining tactics, mediation, and arbitration. It also addresses union organizing of new members by examining the regulations of election campaigns.

Chapter 4 concludes Part II. It is addressed to the employment discrimination law and its relation to collective bargaining. The chapter traces the development of legal protection against discrimination. It discusses different sources of protection and remedies for discrimination. It also discusses the effects of the law on negotiated seniority provisions and grievance and arbitration procedures.

Part III, Chapters 5–6, discusses the framework of collective bargaining which consists of unions, employers, and employees within various kinds of bargaining units. The two chapters in this part discuss the union employer organizational structure and bargaining units.

Chapter 5 covers the union institution. It looks at the local, national, and international union and at the structure of the AFL-CIO Federation. It also examines democracy in unions and problems associated with it. The chapter also reviews the organizational structure of employees. It evaluates the environment of the firm; it looks at the multi-national firms and at employer associations. It also discusses the internal aspects of the organization, different types of management, and the impact of all these factors on collective bargaining.

Chapter 6 of Part III covers the bargaining unit. It outlines different types of units and discusses the significance of NLRB decisions regarding determination of units. It also examines the effects of unions and employers on the dimension of units. Specifically, the chapter looks at craft and multi-employer units and at coordinated and coalition bargaining.

Part IV, Chapters 7–8, covers preparation for bargaining and costing of labor contracts.

In the preparation for bargaining chapter the following topics are covered: the composition, size and selection of teams of union and management negotiators, the preparation of bargaining data, the value of economic data, the importance of bargaining books, formulation of management and union demands, tactical preparation for bargaining, and bargaining procedures.

Every provision of the contract can have cost implications. Part of the preparation process is to establish costing procedures and methodology to be used during bargaining. These topics are covered in Part IV. Chapter 8 examines issues related to costing of labor contracts. The chapter reviews the components of the compensation package. Data used for costing of contracts are outlined. Various methods of costing of wages and fringe benefits are analyzed and critically evaluated. Factors influencing dimension of management financial offers are reviewed. Concepts such as elasticity of demand, present value, and discounted cash flow models are discussed and their implications for costing examined.

Part V, Chapters 9–12, covers the bargaining process, negotiations, bargaining theory and bargaining power, the application of the theory, and impasse resolution.

Chapter 9 provides a practical foundation of the basis of negotiation process. It reviews bargaining procedures during the different stages of the bargaining process and evaluates elementary strategy and tactics of bargaining.

Chapter 10 represents a theoretical compliment to the practical material presented in Chapter 9. A review of bargaining theory is presented, followed by an extensive review of two major theoretical works: Alfred Kuhn's development of materials on transactions and power, and Walton and McKersie's development of a behavioral theory of labor negotiations.

Whereas Chapter 10 provides a general theoretical framework of transactions and of power and bargaining power, Chapter 11 is specifically geared to the application of the theory to a model of negotiations. The model evaluates the impact of a potential strike threat on the thinking and behavior of negotiators at the bargaining table.

Chapter 12 looks at the level and importance of strike activity in the United States. Recognizing that a bargaining impasse is at the center of all overt conflict, we conclude this chapter and section with a look at the various methods of impasse resolution.

Part VI, Chapters 13–15, is directed toward the content of collective bargaining: Chapter 13 addresses the issue of wage determination and secondary effects of collective bargaining. Product market competition as a determinant of wages is reviewed. Occupational, interindustry, geographic, union-nonunion, and interfirm-intrafirm differentials are examined. The wage determination criteria are evaluated. The chapter also addresses itself to the secondary effects of collective bargaining. Drawing on the institutional work of Schlichter, Healy and Livernash and the recent studies of Kochan and of Freeman and Medoff, the impact of bargaining on management behavior and workers is assessed.

The next chapter in Part VI covers employee benefits. It discusses such topics as: wage employment guarantees, supplementary unemployment benefits, severance pay, pension plans, health care plans, vacations, and holidays.

The management and union security chapter covers the relationship between unions and management. It examines the problems of survival and allocation of prerogatives. It discusses interest and ability* in the making of decisions. It also evaluates the concept of secure versus insecure management and its effect on collective bargaining. The chapter addresses itself to the question of how much and what kinds of security are necessary for the union to function properly. The chapter evaluates the relationship among the union function, union responsibility, union security, and the state of labor relations. The chapter reviews various forms of union security and also examines management attitudes and workers' reactions to the issue of union security.

Part VII, Chapters 16–18, is the last part of our text. It presents three chapters on special topics in collective bargaining and concludes with a look at concession bargaining and the future of industrial relations in the United States.

Chapter 16 discusses the nature and meaning of plant government, the judicial process in plant government, and the grievance procedure. Substantial attention is given to the functioning of the grievance procedure and the arbitration process. Chapter 17 is concerned with developments in the public sector. The chapter reviews the growth of collective bargaining in the public sector. It covers federal, state, and local legislation governing public employees. It examines administrative agencies, unfair labor practices, determinations of bargaining units, elections, and certification procedures. Other issues addressed by this chapter are: the process and scope of bargaining in the public sector, union security, the right to strike, and the future of collective bargaining in the public sector.

Chapter 18 concludes the book with a look at the concession bargaining era of the early 1980s. The causes, content, and potential long-term impact of concession bargaining are discussed. The chapter ends with a look toward the future of labor-management relations in the United States.

The text contains a revised collective bargaining simulation, which is based on an actual case. The simulation contains background on the company, on the union, financial data, sources of additional external data, present contract terms, instructions for negotiations, worksheets, role profiles, and evaluations questionnaires. An instructor's simulation manual is available to adopters of this book.

The book also includes actual arbitration cases covering labor contract interpretation issues. The cases cover such topics as discharge, ability versus seniority, assignment of work outside bargaining units, involvement in work slowdowns, refusals to take lie detector tests, conspiracies to steal, drinking and lunch hour intoxication, bumping rights, and demotions.

ACKNOWLEDGMENTS

We wish to express our appreciation to those who have assisted us in making this volume possible, especially to many of our graduate students who served as research assistants for varying periods. Their tireless hours spent in searching for data are greatly appreciated. We wish especially too acknowledge the contributions of Judi Peddersen and Eileen Kelly—Judi for her major contributions in the preparation, evaluation, and update of Chapter 4 of this edition (the Intersection of Discrimination Law with the Process of Collective Bargaining) and both Judi Peddersen and Eileen Kelly for their extensive work on the chapter on Collective Bargaining in the Public Sector.

We are grateful for the research assistance of Cheryl M. Byrne, Carol L. Haberman, Sandra L. High, Paul J. Molini, Jr., William E. Moore, Sharon Stout, and David Walsh. Our thanks also go to all those students who responded in their class comments to earlier versions of this text. We should also like to thank our publisher's reviewers, who have read and commented comprehensively on the manuscript. Many of their comments have been reflected in this volume. Appreciation is also acknowledged to our publishers, particularly to Alison Reeves, Acquisitions Editor—Management and Industrial Relations, and Nancy G. Follender, Production Editor—Business and Economics, for their assistance, cooperation, and work in preparing this volume for publication.

Contributions from colleagues and friends are also acknowledged, especially Howard M. Leftwich, John M. Wagner, and Louis J. Manchise. Our thanks to Douglas M. Yeager for co-authoring the earlier version of the collective bargaining simulation included here and to Philip R. Dankert, Collection Development Librarian at Cornell University, for the preparation of a glossary and an extensive labor relations and collective bargaining bibliography. We are indebted to our secretaries for coping with a large volume of material and for their effort in typing and retyping the manuscript, particularly to Susan Burns, Cindy Barsman, Melissa Harrington, Ann Herson, Joyce Orzino, and Debbie Woolston. All provided excellent secretarial and typing assistance, frequently under difficult conditions.

SUGGESTED OUTLINE FOR A ONE-QUARTER OR ONE-SEMESTER COURSE

There are two main types of one-quarter or one-semester courses for which an instructor might wish to use significantly less than the entire book. One would be for a course in labor relations, or labor relations and collective bargaining; strongly recommended for this purpose would be Chapters 1, 2, 5, 6, 7, 9, 15, 16, and 18. Chapter 3 should be added if the instructor wishes somewhat more attention to labor law than is found in Chapter 2. Chapters 12 and 17 might also be added if the instructor prefers more attention to impasse resolution and to public sector bargaining, respectively. A second type would be a quarter or semester course focused more specifically on collective bargaining for students who have already taken an introductory course in labor and who may be expected to study labor law separately. Recommended for this purpose would be Chapters 5 through 16 and Chapter 18. Chapter 5 on union and employer institutions might be omitted if this material has already been covered in a prior course, and Chapter 4 might be added if the instructor has a special interest in employment discrimination.

DEVELOPMENT AND GROWTH OF THE LABOR MOVEMENT*

The development, growth, and survival of an institution such as the labor movement depends on several conditions. First, there must be some initial and continuing urge to seek new modes of behavior. Second, experimentation with new methods must take place. Except by lucky accident, satisfactory solutions to problems will not be found on the first trial. Third, those particular experiments that show significant degrees of success must be continued and repeated, and the failures must be discontinued.

The Industrial Revolution created unsatisfactory consequences that lasted a long time, and the succeeding century or so witnessed many exploratory activities by American working people as they tried to find some "better way."

In this spirit the following discussion is not so much a "history" of the American labor movement as a selection, in largely chronological order, of the experiments and experiences from which American unions learned certain lessons. It is those lessons that have shaped the structure and behavior of the labor movement as we know it today. The legal aspects of labor history are largely omitted from this chapter and appear in a separate chapter.

---

*The use of masculine pronouns throughout this text is not of sexist intent, but simpler to read and more appropriate to the particular subject matter as it is discussed in its early days. The authors recognize the increased numbers of women in the work force, and trust that the readers will bear in mind that all cases described in this book apply equally to both men and women.

BARGAINING APPROACH VS. OWNERSHIP APPROACH

Prior to the Industrial Revolution, nonagricultural production took place very largely through a craft system, regulated by a guild in each major craft. Importantly, once people completed their apprenticeships and became journeymen workers, they owned their own tools and had considerable freedom to move to different shops or to set up shop for themselves. After the Industrial Revolution people had to work with machines, not tools. For all practical purposes workers lost the freedom to own their tools or to become their own bosses.

Following this loss of ownership of the tools of production, workers saw two possible remedies to their plight. One was to accept the loss of ownership and seek to bargain better terms from the new owners—an alternative called the bargaining approach. The other was to seek to regain ownership of the tools—called the ownership approach. But individual workers had little or no bargaining power under the new industrial system. Hence successful bargaining required collective action. Individual workers also lacked the financial resources to own the new machines. Hence ownership would also have to be done collectively. Thus either approach seemed to require collective action and led workers to form unions.

Job Orientation vs. Class Orientation

To the extent that workers think of their problems as tied mainly to their own job, industry, or firm and seek solutions at that level, their thinking is said to be job oriented and their programs job wide in scope. Other problems are faced by workers in many crafts and industries. All receive their incomes mainly from wages rather than from interest, rents, or dividends. The fear of unemployment is widespread, and few jobs are wholly safe from technological change, the relocation of a plant, or an administrative shakeup. All workers take orders rather than give them; all know that displeasing the boss may be serious; and most know the difficulties of trying to live on a modest income. Off-the-job differences between boss and workers *are* apparent in most industries. Although it is not possible to draw a precise line between them, workers do not doubt that there *are* two groups and that they live in different worlds. To the extent that workers feel that their problems and the solution to them are common to all workers but are different from the problems of employers, workers are class oriented, and their programs are class wide in scope. They also can then be said to display *employee consciousness*. Employees and unions can, of course, think in terms of both job and class at the same time and pursue programs at both levels. The real question is: Which dominates their thinking and commands their major efforts?

This distinction is not confined to workers. Associations of doctors, lawyers, personnel managers, or teachers reflect a job orientation, as do trade associations. On the other hand, the United States Chamber of Commerce and the National Association of Manufacturers reflect a class orientation, since they unite employers regardless of job or industry in an effort to deal with problems of interest to all employers.

Four Groups of Reactions

The thinking and behavior of unions can be classified into four approaches: job-oriented bargaining, class-oriented bargaining, job-oriented ownership, and class-oriented ownership. Although these four categories are not entirely satisfactory for describing all types of behavior, nevertheless they provide a useful framework in which to view the various experiments of the labor movement during its first century or so, and they seem to provide a more workable set of categories than Commons' two-way distinction between job-conscious and class-conscious unions.[1] Let us illustrate the terms. A union following the job-oriented bargaining approach will seek concessions for its members from their employers. It may also strive to improve the economic position of the industry or occupation.

Workers following a class-oriented bargaining approach would tend to form a single, strongly centralized union through which all workers would deal simultaneously with all employers, at least on major issues. Class-oriented bargainers may also use political or other pressures to get concessions from private employers. Minimum-wage legislation, unemployment compensation, social security, and worker's compensation (as they are financed in the United States) illustrate the use of government as an aid in extracting concessions from private employers for the benefit of all workers. There is also a class-oriented interest in laws that regulate collective bargaining, since they affect bargaining power, and hence concessions, for many different unions.

Job-oriented workers may also follow the ownership approach. They might, for example, purchase the plant in which they work and operate it as a producer cooperative. Or they might advocate public ownership of their own firm or industry, without desiring public ownership of other firms or industries. Class-oriented unions following the ownership approach may advocate public ownership of important industries, and perhaps of all industry, through socialism or communism or their variants.

HISTORICAL DEVELOPMENT
OF THE AMERICAN LABOR MOVEMENT

In Europe at the start of the Industrial Revolution, labor was plentiful, while land and capital were scarce. In America land was plentiful, while labor and capital were comparatively scarce. With land plentiful and agriculture unmechanized, dissatisfied wage workers in America had more opportunity than their European counterparts to leave their jobs and carve out homesteads. Although the obstacles were often formidable, self-employment was a feasible alternative to wage employment to a greater degree and for a longer time here than in Europe. Individual bargaining power was greater in America, and the need for unions was smaller. Accordingly, unions did not start as soon or with as much vigor as in Europe. And when they did get under way, they placed greater confidence in bargaining and less in ownership. The fact that American workers had not lived through the transition from the feudal to the industrial system did not, however, seriously mitigate the impact of industrialization when it finally arrived. For many years after the Industrial Revolution, to one who lived by selling his labor, the market system meant "sell or die."

The First Unions

Strikes and "labor disturbances" in America are considerably older than unions, going back as far as 1636. The "Company of Shoemakers" was granted a charter by the Colony of the Massachusetts Bay in 1648, and the coopers were granted a charter at the same time, the former, at least, operating after the fashion of a guild rather than a union, with powers to maintain quality but not to raise prices.[2] Journeyman tailors struck successfully in New York in 1768, and journeyman printers demanded and received a wage increase in New York in 1778. Although many other such isolated actions are recorded, the first union (that is, a continuous association) was that of the shoemakers in Philadelphia in 1792. In 1793 and 1794, respectively, the carpenters and shoemakers formed organizations in Boston. In 1794 the printers organized in New York, as did those of Philadelphia in 1802. During the next fifteen years, unions of one or more of the trades already mentioned, plus those of bakers, tailors, and others, were formed in most important cities in the United States. Some succeeded in getting wage increases, some got hours reduced to ten a day, and some prevented their employers from hiring journeymen from other towns at cut rates. These early unions were all confined to skilled trades. As will be noted in the next chapter, some interesting legal cases arose during this period, notably the Cordwainers (shoemakers) case in 1806.

At that time the Industrial Revolution had not yet had any important effect on the American scene, but a widening market did put pressure on wage rates. When most commodities were produced for local consumption and were sold directly at the shop, the master could pay a fair wage and charge a price to cover it. But by this period some goods were being purchased by merchants in large volume from those employers who would sell at the lowest price. The merchants then shipped them to distant points for sale. Producers were thus put into direct competition with other producers in distant places, and they were forced by the merchant to bid against one another. Employers were then under greater pressure to cut wages. Thus, extension of the market increased the workers' urge for unions as a means of self-defense.

Although "the colonists did not establish many societies modeled on the English guilds . . . a number were organized and thrived."[3] And nowhere, apparently, except in Scandinavia, did a guild evolve into a trade union. As organizations reflecting the unity of work and ownership, the guilds died a natural death when work and ownership were separated. Unions and trade associations are the present organizations that represent the now separated interests of workers and owners, respectively.

This "first round" of unionism in the United States lasted from about 1790 to 1815 and was local in nature. All traces of unions as collective bargaining agencies disappeared during the depression that followed the War of 1812, although a few survived as social and beneficial organizations. From this first round, American workers learned that job-oriented collective bargaining with an employer can produce immediate and significant gains. They learned at the same time that depression can be lethal, at least to a locally based union.

A Different Type of Union

The Declaration of Independence had said that all men are created equal and that life, liberty, and the pursuit of happiness are inalienable rights. But an apparent discrepancy between these brave words and the facts of life had brought much discontent. By the late 1820s, this feeling came to a head in the election of Andrew Jackson and the ensuing "era of the common man." The thinking of the time was largely class wide.

Workingmen then suffered many difficulties now long forgotten. They could be imprisoned for debt. They could rarely get an education for themselves or their children. They were paid in a variety of currencies of changing and uncertain value. They often worked 14 to 16 hours a day, and they held a low priority among other creditors if an employer happened to go bankrupt while owing them wages. Problems of this kind could be approached only through politics, not by bargaining with employers. In consequence, a variety of working people's parties were formed; they achieved notable success during the 1820s and 1830s in bringing free public education, banking reform, mechanics' lien laws, the elimination of imprisonment for debt, and the political franchise for those who did not own property.

A number of local, job-wide craft unions formed during this "second round" were able to improve the conditions of the worker at his job, as had the unions of the first round. But above and beyond them were a variety of unions that tried to encompass workers of various kinds in a local, or regional, class-wide organization. The broad class coverage of unions founded during this period was useful for attacking the particular problems of the moment. But the membership was too diverse to hold together once those aims were accomplished. Most of these "unions" disappeared in the early 1830s, when it was found that they were unable to do much successful bargaining with employers. Their legacy was a conviction that class-based organizations can be effective in dealing with certain kinds of broad problems, but that they are ineffective in the bread-and-butter issues of getting specific concessions from employers. With the exception of some limited ventures into the field of producer cooperatives, the ownership approach was largely absent from this period.

The Appearance of National Unions

Partly because of the inability of the class-based unions to deal satisfactorily with employers, a third wave of unions got under way in 1834, building upon and adding to the group of unions that had been started in the preceding years. These were organized on the same craft base as the first round of unions and grew rapidly to a total of about 300,000 members—a rather impressive number, considering the size of the population. Within two years, each major city displayed from a half-dozen to more than fifty different craft unions. Many bargained successfully on wages and hours.

Because the widening of the market was now accentuated by the wide development of canals and railroads, the workers in a local union in one city often found their wages limited by the wages received by similar workers in other cities. They therefore started to combine into national craft unions to prevent competitive wage-cutting. The National Trades Union was formed in New York in 1834. It was a notable achievement for its time, presaging much that was to happen later, even though this particular organization apparently lasted only two or three years. Despite their wide geographic scope, such national unions were job oriented in that they confined their attention to a single type of worker.

Some awareness of class-wide problems was reflected in the joining together of unions of different crafts at the local level into a city central, presently known also as a central labor union or central labor council. In 1834 an attempt was made to form a federation of national unions to deal with broader problems, but the federation lasted only a few months. The federations at the local level and the attempted federation at the national level did not represent an abandonment of job-oriented unionism, however. The individual local and national unions retained their independence and strength; the federation activities supplemented rather than supplanted the individual unions.

The depression and panic of 1837 hit suddenly and lasted for more than a decade. With it, virtually the entire labor movement collapsed—national, city central, and local. The disappearance of these unions was attributable to adverse surrounding conditions; their performance, while they lasted, was good. This was part of the record from which later leaders learned their lessons.

The Ownership Approach in Action

The psychological state induced by the depression, along with the scarcity of jobs to be bargained about and the active interest of a group of intellectuals, produced a strong wave of humanitarian schemes centering on the *cooperative communities* recommended by the Englishman Robert Owen or the Frenchman François Fourier. Although about fifty of these communities were started, all were eventually abandoned. Poor financing and heavy fixed charges accounted for many failures. Lack of managerial ability, internal dissension, and lack of common sense helped dissolve others. The refusal of private business (which thought them subversive) to sell them materials assisted the collapse of several.

The ineffectiveness of bargaining during this depressed period led to another variation on the ownership theme. Starting with a worker-owned shoe factory in Philadelphia in 1836, *producer cooperatives* multiplied during the forties and fifties, especially after a wave of unsuccessful strikes in 1851 and 1852. These ventures lasted about as long as their half brothers, the cooperative communities; most became insolvent, and those that were successful took in hired employees and gradually lost their cooperative identity. They succeeded mainly in sapping the energies and funds of the unions that sponsored them, leaving the unions ill prepared to bargain collectively when that task again presented itself.

At the same time another movement, not subject to the same defect, got well under way under the sponsorship of unions and other sympathizers. This was the *consumer cooperative*. Run in the interests of its customers, the consumer cooperative has the single-minded objective of producing at lowest cost, with no undue concern for the welfare of its employees. In fact, the employees of a cooperative might themselves organize to bargain collectively with its management. The Civil War largely destroyed the movement, and except for farm cooperatives, credit unions, and miscellaneous other cooperatives, this institution has not fulfilled its early promise in the United States. It is interesting to note that agricultural cooperatives have been more successful than other types of cooperatives. In England and Scandinavia, however, cooperatives have become a potent economic force and are closely allied to the union movement. The experiences with both consumer and producer cooperatives are detailed by Perlman.[4]

It is symptomatic of the later development of trade unionism in this country that, even during periods of deep disillusion over the prospects of collective bargaining, the attempts to use the ownership approach were usually limited in scope and individualistic in nature. They involved only small groups, banded together to make their way cooperatively in a free and uncontrolled economy. These groups assumed that the worker had the opportunity to improve his lot if only he would use the proper method. Each group tried to improve the well-being of its own members within the existing system but did not work toward uprooting the system.

During the period from roughly 1830 to 1850, the major exceptions to this general tendency were the doctrines of Thomas Skidmore and George Henry Evans. Early in this period, Skidmore advocated the equal division of all wealth among all citizens, along with the provision that it be passed on in equal shares to each succeeding generation. Later in this period, his ideological successor Evans proposed merely the equal division of land. He later softened his program, asking only that government lands in the West be available free to small settlers, not gobbled up by wealthy speculators.

These two movements originated among intellectuals, not workers. They were not heavily espoused by unions, for the community at large registered strong disapproval of tampering with the ownership of property. However, most working people did support the move for homestead laws, which would permit them to acquire unsettled lands at little or no cost. The agrarian and homestead movement was the focal point of working-class efforts during much of the nineteenth century. Once again, we note how abundant land diluted the urge for unions.

All in all, experience up to this point indicated (1) the success of narrowly conceived craft unions bargaining with their employers over mundane affairs of daily existence; (2) the success of political action for class-wide objectives, but the impermanence of an organization based primarily on such objectives and accepting a heterogeneous membership; (3) the failure of cooperative communities and cooperative enterprises from internal and apparently inherent weaknesses, as well as their high cost to unions; and (4) the strong objection from the community at large to schemes that threatened property rights. Experience also led to a general distrust by workers of intellectuals and all their works. As to "heroic" long-run goals, the prospective task of subduing the West was heroic enough to subvert the notion of remolding the whole society under workers' control long before that notion moved from the field of thought to effective action.

The Arrival of Permanent Unions and Federations

The Industrial Revolution in the United States may be dated roughly from 1840. By 1850 it was beginning to have real impact, with railroads, steelmaking, factories, and a rapid growth of employees in manufacturing industries. By 1850 prosperity had returned, bringing with it improved prospects of gains through bargaining. Once again came a wave of new unions—the fourth—this time with stronger emphasis on national organizations. Collective bargaining became firmly established in a number of industries. Indeed, some of the unions established during the early 1850s have operated continuously ever since. The typographers, for example, celebrated their centennial in 1952 as the oldest continuous union.

Many of these unions were killed off by the depression of 1857, and some others by the turbulent conditions of the early Civil War years. During the later years of the war, however, a high demand for labor combined with a rapid inflation, in which real wages dropped by about a third, to produce a new drive for unionism. Again there appeared a multitude of locals, city centrals, and national unions, along with a quasi-federation called the National Labor Union, which started in 1866 and lasted six years. By 1870 some thirty national unions were in existence. Most dated from the Civil War, but some had lived through from the previous decade.

There is no need to trace the ups and downs of the labor movement during the next few decades. Industrialism was on the march. Big business was beginning to hit its stride. Workers were still confused and divided over how to protect their interests. Each era of prosperity brought renewed emphasis on bargaining, which produced tangible gains. Each depression brought renewed emphasis on ownership, which produced confusion and depleted treasuries. During the last decades of the nineteenth century, the Iron Molders alone, under W. H. Sylvis, established at least ten cooperative foundries. Similar enterprises were set up by unions in a score of other fields. Like the cooperatives of the forties these too failed, leaving the sponsoring unions disillusioned and penniless. Although a few unions (mainly in railroads, building, printing, and machining) held rather closely to straight collective bargaining, most unions wandered regularly into other activities. During the 1870s and thereafter, the goal of unionism was further confused by the introduction of a Marxist-socialist element that actively struggled for but never gained control of the American labor movement.

The Knights of Labor

Amid the confusion of the seventies and eighties, two attempts at federation stand out, one temporary and one permanent. The Knights of Labor was formed in Philadelphia in 1869. It remained a small and secret organization for almost fifteen years, when a combination of circumstances brought a rapid increase to about two-thirds of a million members. Under the leadership of Terrence V. Powderly, it accepted unskilled labor, the self-employed, and, indeed, virtually any gainfully employed people except gamblers, saloonkeepers, bankers, and a few other groups. The Knights hoped to improve the lot of working people through legislation, land reform, banking reform, producers' cooperatives, and an attack on monopoly. It did not officially approve of strikes, although it did conduct some successful ones, notably one against the Wabash Railroad, a part of the financial empire of Jay Gould. Gould's capitulation in 1886 marked the high point of this organization.

In due time, it was discovered that so diffuse an organization could not concentrate adequately on the particular needs of any of its component groups. In fact, the needs of some conflicted directly with those of others. In addition, members of craft unions that had affiliated with the Knights were faced with a dual loyalty and double expense. By 1887 the membership and influence of the Knights had started to decline.

The American Federation of Labor

Meanwhile the craft unions had started a new organization, the American Federation of Labor. Growing out of an organization started in 1881, the AFL was founded in 1886. It soon became and has since remained a significant American labor organization, now known as the AFL−CIO. The federation was molded by the personality and beliefs of Samuel Gompers, who remained president for all but one year until his death in 1924. Despite Samuel Gompers's opposition to the Knights of Labor and friction between the Knights and the AFL, the interaction between the two organizations probably contributed to the development of the AFL. Though Gompers was heavily steeped in, and partially sympathetic toward, socialism, he was convinced by previous events that strong and permanent unions could exist in the United States only if they stuck to job-oriented bargaining. According to Gompers, the unit of union structure must be a group of people having closely similar interests, which meant to him that they must belong to the same craft. They must eschew ownership ideas, since these attack the prevailing concept of property and can generate powerful public resistance. Unions must make contracts with employers and scrupulously abide by them, just as do suppliers of other employer needs. Although they must not hesitate to strike, unions must largely accept the world of business as it is and in turn be businesslike in dealing with employers. If the basic union of organization is to have the desired homogeneous membership, the importance and independence of the individual unions must be preserved. The federation must remain a loose agency of coordination with little real power. Gompers put great emphasis on the autonomy of the separate national unions and on the strict preservation of their jurisdictional lines. Because it was a loose and relatively weak federation, the importance of the AFL lay not so much in its actions as in the philosophy it gave the union movement.

It was recognized that, since government could inhibit the ability of unions to exist, grow, and strike, unions must pay attention to politics. But this attention should be confined to supporting candidates who espouse labor's aims, rather than becoming a permanent attachment to a political party. Government help should not be sought in the economic sphere, since such action would encourage the interference of government and end in the public control of unions. By attending mainly to strong unionization, not politics, labor, it was felt, could bargain satisfactory conditions from private employers.

By the end of the nineteenth century the frontier had closed, and the nation was rapidly becoming urbanized and industrialized. These circumstances cut off a progressively larger and larger portion of the population from any source of income except wages, and finally brought the full impact of the Industrial Revolution to the United States. The accelerated growth of the AFL, from 250,000 members in 1897 to 1.6 million in 1904 and to more than 2 million in 1914, attests to the fact that many American workers felt the need for some protective device and accepted the trade union for this purpose. Membership, however, was still confined largely to the building trades, railroads, and coal mines. The last included the only substantial group of unionized unskilled and semiskilled labor in the nation.

During World War I, organized labor received official recognition, to which it had long aspired but had not been accustomed. A War Labor Board was established to settle union-management disputes that might interfere with the war effort. By this act the government openly accepted unions as the "official" agent for workers. Labor representatives were also included on several government boards dealing with manpower and mobilization. Organized labor acquired new status and dignity on the American scene.

Left-Wing Unionism

The job-oriented bargaining approach of Gompers was by no mean unchallenged. Founded in 1876 on principles of Marxist socialism, the Socialist Labor Party in 1889 came under the strong leadership of Daniel de Leon, who undertook to bring the AFL back to its "true historic mission"—as the Marxists saw it—of socialism.

The depression, unemployment, and strike defeats of 1893 and 1894 seemed to support the socialist arguments that job-oriented bargaining was useless and that class-oriented ownership should be tried. At the AFL convention of 1894, a resolution that the AFL go on record as favoring "collective ownership by the people of all the means of production and distribution" was defeated by political maneuvering rather than by lack of support. That same year, Gompers was defeated for the presidency by a western coal miner, the socialist John McBride. Following Gompers' return to office by a narrow margin in 1895, the socialists became convinced that they would have to work mainly outside the federation, though not without some boring from within. Then, as subsequently, the socialists were concentrated heavily in New York City, with additional major groups in Milwaukee and Chicago, and some lesser ones in Reading (Pa.) and Bridgeport (Conn.).

The IWW

The settlers and miners of the early West were hard-fisted and direct acting. The new-blown capitalists' dealings with labor were often ruthless and primitive. The mines, lumber camps, docks, and, in part, farms employed many unskilled workers, often in remote areas without family or community life, where "the company" was the whole of life. Such conditions are common sources of militance.

Dissatisfied with the conservative methods of the AFL and its lack of interest in their problems, the Western Federation of Miners left it in 1897. By 1905, with the help of the Socialists, they had established a new federation. This they called the Industrial Workers of the World—more commonly known as the IWW, or "Wobblies." Under the colorful and militant leadership (although not the initial presidency) of "Big Bill" Haywood, the IWW very competently stirred up and capitalized upon discontent. The IWW succeeded in winning several important strikes. But after winning a strike, the union would bound off to some new trouble spot instead of staying to build a lasting union structure. Its behavior was so erratic, in fact, that within several years it was abandoned by both the Socialists and the Western Federation of Miners. In due time, the IWW turned more conservative than the AFL itself and lost all significance as a separate organization. (In 1953 the Bureau of Labor Statistics listed only twenty-two locals with a total membership of 16,500, and by 1961 the IWW was no longer listed—although one source reports some scattered outposts, based mainly on nostalgia.) A brief resurgent interest in IWW philosophy and organization was experienced in the late sixties and early seventies, particularly among young radicals on college campuses. The IWW is still in existence today, and continues to publish its newspaper, the *Industrial Worker*. In the April 1984 issue it printed its regular feature, the IWW Directory for North America, in which it has listed branches, names of delegates, and box office numbers in three Canadian provinces and in twenty-four states.[5]

In its effect on public opinion, the IWW followed in the footsteps of the Molly Maguires.[6] The anthracite miners of eastern Pennsylvania faced a highly intransigent and authoritarian group of coal companies, particularly the "captive" mines of the Reading Railroad Company under the presidency of Franklin Gowen. The "Mollies'" technique for achieving justice for miners in the 1870s took the eminently direct form of murdering company officials. Their violence came to a head in the railroad strikes of 1877.

The so-called Haymarket Riot in Chicago in 1886 also received much public attention. Seven policemen were killed by the explosion of a bomb toward the end of a rather dreary meeting, held in Haymarket Square in connection with the aftermath of a strike at the McCormick Reaper Works. Four anarchists were eventually hanged, and one committed suicide before the execution; unions received much extremely bad publicity from the incident—though it was the opinion of many persons then, and apparently of nearly all serious students now, that no really admissible evidence was ever adduced at the trial as to who did, in fact, throw the bomb.[7]

The lesson learned from these developments was that any violence or radical ideology associated with unions or strikes will be magnified in the press and will greatly increase the difficulties and reduce the effectiveness of the labor movement. This reinforced the conviction that straight bargaining unionism, with no touch of radicalism and without violence, was the only way to command the public acceptance necessary for union survival in the United States.

Employer Opposition

The rapid increase in union membership from 1897 to 1904 stimulated employers into an opposition movement that was probably as well organized as the labor movement itself and perhaps more single-minded in its purpose. Starting in 1903, the

National Association of Manufacturers (NAM) vigorously promulgated what it called "the open shop" as the standard "American plan" for dealing with employees. Although an open shop, strictly defined, is open on equal terms to union and nonunion employees, the "open shop" of the association was closed completely to union members. Policies similar to those of the NAM were followed by the trade associations in several industries. These groups maintained employer "strike funds" to assist companies suffering from strikes, and "blacklists" of union members to assure that they would not be hired anywhere in the industry. Sometimes they brought pressure against firms in their industries, in a sort of secondary boycott, if they showed an inclination to deal with a union.

A period of about twenty years, starting shortly after the turn of the century, was marked by intense antagonism and considerable violence in many areas, particularly in the mining industry. Many employers maintained substantial arsenals of weapons, or acquired them when a strike seemed likely. They also employed company guards who were prepared to use the weapons. In addition, they often hired professional strikebreakers supplied by "detective" agencies, and tended to call out the national guard more or less automatically whenever a strike was called. A typical pattern was for the courts to respond with an injunction against the strike and for the governor to respond with the militia. The coal mines in West Virginia and Colorado and the copper mines of northern Michigan were scenes of some bloody fights. Notable was the "Ludlow Massacre" in 1914 in connection with the Rockefeller-owned Colorado Fuel and Iron Company installation at Ludlow, Colorado. A total of fifty people were killed over a ten-day period in what was virtually open warfare. A typical management reaction during this period was a flat refusal to deal with a union or even to acknowledge its existence.

However, by no means all employers of the period were opposed to unions. During the 1890s and early 1900s, widespread agreements between unions and employers were reached in the stove, glass container, and building trades, and in newspaper publishing, brass polishing, coal mining, pottery, overalls manufacturing, railroads, and Great Lakes shipping industries. Many of these agreements continued for decades. A notable experiment in a cooperative attitude was made by the National Civic Federation, which was started in 1900 as a result of the turmoil of the 1890s. Its cardinal premise was that labor and capital are interdependent. The organization probably helped to pave the way for the acceptance of unions.

Organized employer opposition, however, probably accounted for the slower rate of union growth after 1904. After an upsurge in union membership during World War I, employers used new devices to reinforce their opposition to unions. One was to eliminate the desire for unionization by treating their employees better. Another tactic was to "join" that part of the union movement that they could not "lick." Employee associations—so-called company unions—were formed, financed, and guided by employers.

The continued open shop movement, the "personnel offensive," and company unions,[8] along with persistent charges of union radicalism and several court decisions described in Chapter 2, all had a depressing effect on union membership. Economic conditions contributed to the same result. The stability of the 1920s provided no burning issues about which to rally workers, and the severe unemployment of the early thirties was more than unions could offer to cure. Gompers' leadership was inadequate during his later years, and that of William Green, elected as a compromise candidate in 1924 to replace him, was hardly better. The AFL was decaying from its own lack of strength, and its conspicuous failure to attempt to organize the rapidly growing steel, automobile, rubber, and petroleum industries made its weakness even more apparent. The combination of events carried union membership steadily downward from a total of 5 million in 1920 to less than 3 million in 1933. Even the boom of the late twenties had not brought the customary increase in membership. There was suspicion in informed circles that unionism was entering a permanent eclipse.

UNIONS TAKE ON THEIR PRESENT DIMENSION

The demise of unions that seemed imminent at the beginning of the depression of the 1930s obviously did not occur. Whereas previous depressions had diminished or destroyed union strength, this one brought sweeping changes in legislation and government attitudes. These changes, combined with events within labor itself, started a burst of unprecedented union growth. Because of lessons learned during the preceding century, this wave of growth was largely unencumbered by excursions into producer or consumer cooperatives, class-wide unionism, or socialism. The movement concentrated instead on organizing for collective bargaining.

The Norris–LaGuardia Act of 1932, the National Industrial Recovery Act (NIRA) of 1933, and the Wagner Act of 1935 protected and encouraged union organization. They also created an atmosphere in which unions seemed respectable, even desirable, to government and much of the public. Unions took quick advantage of this new environment to recruit members, and workers responded avidly.

THE CIO AND A SPLIT LABOR MOVEMENT

During the early thirties a long-smoldering debate came to a head in the AFL over the amount of its organizing activity and the structure of union organization. The United Mine Workers under the redoubtable John L. Lewis, the Amalgamated Clothing Workers under Sidney Hillman, the International Ladies' Garment Workers under David Dubinsky, the Textile Workers under Emil Rieve, and several other AFL unions felt that the only feasible organization for mass production industries was the "industrial union," in which all types of workers within a given plant belong to the same union. They thought that the then largely unorganized major industries, such as the automobile, radio, rubber, and steel industries, should be unionized on that basis.

The AFL hierarchy were not averse to having new unions in these fields or to having them organized initially on an industrial basis. But they insisted that the charters be so drawn that the machinists, carpenters, electricians, and the like would later be divided into the separate craft unions, which held long-established control of the AFL. This procedure was entirely unacceptable to the proponents of industrial unionism.

Furthermore, the AFL had never done much organizing as a federation, since it left such actions largely to its constituent unions. But the workers in the mass production industries were mainly semiskilled operatives who did not fall within any of the skilled crafts and whom the craft unions were notably uninterested in organizing. In 1935, in an effort to get more action, the dissatisfied unions formed a Committee for Industrial Organization (CIO), under the initial chairmanship of John L. Lewis, to encourage and assist unionization of the mass production industries *within* the AFL. Such assistance seemed necessary because the greater ease of replacing unskilled employees and the militancy of the large employers in mass production industries had long frustrated the employees' unaided efforts to unionize.

The action of the CIO group was interpreted by the AFL Executive Committee as "dual unionism"—the cardinal sin of splitting labor. After some maneuvering on both sides, the CIO was suspended from the AFL in 1936. Refusing to repent, it was expelled in 1938. The AFL and the CIO subsequently developed an intense rivalry, in which the AFL finally engaged in strong drives to organize some of the mass production fields before the CIO could get them. Although it thus gained considerable membership, the AFL did not foreclose the CIO's drive, which captured the industries it was most concerned about.

Which force was the more important is impossible to tell; but, between them, the two forces—the new attitude of government toward organized labor and the organizational rivalry within the labor movement—produced a rapid increase in union membership. From a desperate low of .9 million in 1900 to 3.6 million in 1934, it rose to almost 8 million by 1939, and to 17 million by 1955, the year of the AFL−CIO merger. Union membership peaked at about 22 million in 1980 and by 1982 it declined to slightly under 20 million. The latest status of union membership is discussed in more detail in a latter part of this chapter.[9]

Unions Come to Steel and Autos

The introduction of unions into two important industries presents an interesting contrast on both the union and management fronts. In the steel industry the Amalgamated Association of Iron, Steel, and Tin Workers had tried for some forty years before 1930 to represent the workers. It never got a foothold in more than a small part of the industry. It engaged in several very bitter strikes, largely defensive and unsuccessful. As a result, very few steelworkers, who were of mixed national origin, were easily aroused by rosy promises. Following the passage of the NIRA and the Wagner Act, steel companies tried to siphon off the pressure of the new union ferment by forming company unions. Knowing the history of the situation, the Steel Workers Organizing Committee (SWOC, subsequently the United Steelworkers of America) of the CIO pursued a cautious educational program designed to lure the company unions into the CIO. The campaign was widely successful. One of the early supporters of the SWOC was John L. Lewis of the United Mine Workers Union. He made a significant contribution toward the formation of SWOC. Acknowledging defeat in the same quiet way the union had gained its victory, Myron C. Taylor, chairman of the board of United States Steel Corporation, signed an agreement with SWOC. This agreement recognized the union as representing its members and granted a forty-hour week, time and a half for overtime, and a 10-cent-an-hour increase in wages. Many small steel companies followed suit shortly. But "Little Steel" (the three or four firms next in size to United States Steel) fought to keep the union out and capitulated only after two or three years of bitter struggle. Except in "Little Steel," the advent of unionism to the steel industry was marked by restraint, nonviolence, and relative good will on both sides.

In the automobile industry, which is much younger than steel as a mass production industry, workers were acutely conscious of many complaints. These included the speedup of assembly lines, alternating seasons of overtime and layoff, and lack of seniority (each laid-off worker was rehired each year as a new employee). The auto workers were ripe for unionization, which was severely resisted by managements. But they did not like the AFL's idea of dividing them into craft unions, and the craft unions themselves were reluctant to admit a group of semiskilled workers who might outvote the skilled. The auto workers' enthusiasm was not dampened by sobering memories of unsuccessful strikes.

In the automobile industry, both management and labor contrasted with Big Steel. Moreover, the industry consisted mainly of three large and well financed companies that had apparently resolved to avoid unionization at all costs. The stage was set for a bitter battle. Extravagant demands, sit-down strikes,[10] mass picketing, and assorted violence and intimidation by workers accompanied the purchase of tear gas and armaments and the hiring of strikebreaking thugs and spies by management. The parent CIO alternately rejoiced over this exuberant response to its organizing call and despaired over the unruly growth and behavior of the United Auto Workers (UAW), which created unfavorable public reaction. Some of the auto strikes were considered premature by the CIO, which nevertheless could not abandon them. The advent of unions in the automobile industry involved bitter fighting, starting in the main Chevrolet plant of General Motors in 1937, proceeding to the Chrysler Corporation, and ending with Ford in 1941.

Along the way, the UAW used numerous sit-down strikes. In plant after plant, the workers would put down their tools but not leave the workplace. The sit-down not only brought work to a halt by the regular employees, but it also kept possible strikebreakers from entering the plant to replace them. Although many sit-downs were short, others continued for long periods, as food and blankets were provided by sympathizers from outside. Their success was assisted by the fact that Governor Frank Murphy of Michigan was sympathetic to the labor movement and rejected requests to use the police powers of the state to remove the strikers. Managements took a dim view of this situation, which to them constituted illegal trespass as well as strike action, a position later upheld in the courts.

Among the auto makers, Ford Motor Company was best equipped organizationally and technically to fight battles at this level. The famed Ford Service Department, headed by one Harry Bennett, was a sort of combination intelligence agency and goon squad, which also infiltrated its operatives into some officerships of the union. When UAW officers Walter Reuther and Richard Frankensteen recognized the relative weakness of the union, they concentrated their organizing attempts on propagandizing. One of the efforts was to recruit blacks into the union, since the company imported many from the South to use as strikebreakers without their knowledge of how they were being used, while Henry Ford used his personal connections with black preachers to have them discourage blacks from joining the union. Bennett also utilized muscular "loyal" blacks as "guards," amply equipped with blackjacks and other weapons.

Union propaganda efforts were inhibited by local regulations prohibiting the distribution of leaflets. In the famous "Battle of the Overpass," while trying to distribute literature, Reuther and Frankensteen were severely beaten by "indignant, loyal workers," who, as photographs revealed, were carrying handcuffs in their pockets.[11]

Meanwhile, both the CIO and the AFL were also organizing such fields as transportation, public utilities, nonferrous metals, chemicals, and petroleum. They were also recruiting white-collar and professional workers in both private industry and government. By the beginning of World War II, the great bulk of mining, manufacturing, and transportation firms were dealing with unions. Thus, in the eight years from 1933 to 1941, unionism was transformed from a sick and declining institution representing only a few industries to a vigorous one firmly established in nearly every major industry. By 1941 unions had signed up a large proportion of the workers who could be considered "readily organizable." From then until the mid-1950s, their growth was just about equal to the growth in the size of the labor force. Thereafter it declined relative to the labor force.

Reunion in New York

By the end of World War II, many of the differences that had led to the separation of the CIO from the AFL had either disappeared or diminished in importance. Both groups recognized the importance of both craft and industrial unions, and the AFL had acquired some industrial affiliates. It appeared that organizing, political affairs, education, research, and some other activities could be carried on more expeditiously by a single all-inclusive organization. Raiding, in which one union tries to take away another union's members, had been a frequent source of friction, both within and between the two federations. When Philip Murray, president of the CIO, and William Green, president of the AFL, died within two weeks of each other in late 1952, they were replaced by Walter Reuther and George Meany, both of whom felt strongly the need for a reunited labor movement. They shortly negotiated a workable no-raiding agreement between the two federations and achieved closer cooperation in other activities. By the spring of 1955 they were able to conclude a merger agreement; by summer they had forged a new constitution; and in December each federation held a convention in New York City and adopted the merger agreement. Thereupon the first convention of the merged AFL–CIO was convened, and it adopted the new constitution.

The quarter century since the reunification of the AFL and the CIO can perhaps best be described as a holding operation. George Meany was made the first president of the AFL−CIO and remained president till he retired for reasons of health in late 1979 at the age of eighty-five; he died shortly thereafter. He was replaced by Lane Kirkland, long his second in command, who was fifty-seven at the time. It is interesting to observe that over the years, Kirkland represented labor on various boards and commissions; as a result he probably developed long-standing personal relationships with persons at the top of the American corporate structure.[12]

During this quarter century of merged federation, the United Mineworkers and the Teamsters remained outside the federation. The Auto Workers joined them in independent status in 1968, to a substantial extent because of what it viewed as the ultraconservative stance of the federation, particularly with respect to foreign policy, and because of the federation's strong reluctance to work with representatives from labor organizations in the communist and Third World blocs.

While president of the UAW, Walter Reuther had sought to give the American labor movement a substantially more aggressive stance than did George Meany and the AFL group in the federation, and particularly to work out a more flexible and imaginative relationship between labor of various nations and the large multinational corporations. In 1969 Reuther had the UAW join with the Teamsters in an organization they called the Alliance for Labor Action (ALA), with the possible eventual aim of developing a rival and more liberal federation. The ALA lasted only until Reuther's premature death in the crash of a private plane in 1970. The UAW reaffiliated with the AFL−CIO on July 1, 1981.[13]

The main structural change following the AFL−CIO merger brought a somewhat enhanced role for the Industrial Union Department and a series of mergers of member unions. Many of these mergers brought together formerly separate AFL and CIO unions covering the same fields. Some other mergers simply brought together related types of employees, without reference to their former federation. Mergers still continue elsewhere, mainly reflecting certain economies of scale. Other aspects of more recent developments are discussed in connection with particular problems in later chapters on union structure, bargaining structure, legal problems, negotiations, and union and management security.

CONTINUING FORCES BEHIND
THE LABOR MOVEMENT

We have now examined the main forces that started the labor movement and brought it to roughly its present size and shape in the United States. Will the forces that formed the movement in the past continue to prevail? Or will some others become dominant in a way that will dramatically reshape unionism? The sensible answer is, of course, that nobody knows, given the complexities and uncertainties of contemporary life. Besides, the question can perhaps be answered better at the end of the book than at the beginning. But since we are dealing with the forces that molded the union movement we may pause for a few observations. We will break them into two main parts, though the two are considerably interrelated. The first will deal with the forces that cause a labor union, or a union movement, to reach out for members. The second will deal with the impulses toward unionization within employees, either to initiate it for themselves or to respond favorably to an attempt from existing unions to bring them in.

The forces within unions that make them reach out are both pragmatic and philosophical. The pragmatic involves calculations much like those of a business selling the service of representation. "If we invest X thousands of dollars in an organizing drive in ABC Manufacturing Company, how many members can we get, and how much net revenue can we derive from them in dues, adjusted for the probability that the organizing effort may fail?" In recent years unions have lost an increasing fraction of representation elections, and they are becoming more reluctant to spend the money on new recruitment. For example, as late as the mid-1960s, unions won 60 percent of their representation elections. But by 1978 the percentage had dropped to 46.[14] The effect is cumulative, in that the smaller the number of new recruits, the smaller the base from which to finance subsequent expansion drives. We cannot tell yet whether the trend will snowball, or whether it will be reversed in the near future.

A philosophical factor is a crusading or ideological drive within the union establishment. This was important for many organizers during the nineteenth century. During the 1930s, particularly within the CIO, the union movement was seen as a glorious, heroic agent of reform, helping to remove poverty and enhance the dignity of working life. The idealism of many union leaders released vast energy and sacrifice. But the bright glow of a reform movement dims once it is institutionalized and most of its daily work is done by hired hands. Furthermore, the dedication that spurs the founders of a movement rarely carries into the next generation, and the American labor movement is now nearly two generations beyond the 1930s. Besides, it has long been evident that some leaders of unions can be just as prone to favoritisms and venalities as anyone else, as notably occurred in the Teamsters and in the East Coast Longshoremen's unions. Like any other organization, the union develops its vested interests, which it then strives to protect. Barring some unforeseen upheaval, it seems unlikely that the large self-sacrificing dedication of a half century ago will soon reappear. To both leaders and members, the appeal will have to be more pragmatic.

As to the response of potential members, it was long thought that employee consciousness was a prerequisite for widespread acceptance of unions. One had to feel one was in the working class to stay, and probably one's children as well. Striving to improve the working-class life would then seem the only sensible course. It would make people willing to join a union and thereby presumably kill the chance of rising into management. Why not, if the chance of rising seems pretty small anyway? Professional, paraprofessional, and technical people, by contrast, along with most white-collar workers, had typically thought of themselves as upwardly mobile. Hence, they did not want to spoil their chances of rising by joining a union. They also tended to have more job security than workers in the shop and were made to feel close to management.

That pattern of thought has changed substantially. As it turned out, in the shop, a worker who displays leadership traits as a shop steward or union president might be quite promotable into supervision. And after union shops became widespread, management could hardly hold union membership against an employee, since the employer had signed the contract that forced him or her to join. In due time, unionized shop workers won more advantages than the office workers, to whom unions then started looking much less reprehensible. Office workers, meanwhile, came to realize that most of *them* didn't rise into management either. Thus, while the idealism that had given a strong positive thrust to unionization died down, so did the stigma that had been such a negative force outside the shop. The new aura of acceptability was augmented when in recent decades it has become virtually the standard "American way" to join pressure groups to advance one's cause. Thus, even many professional and technical people nowadays do not feel it demeaning to join a union. And if it looks like money-grubbing—well, who *doesn't* do *that?*

As a consequence of the above forces, most recent growth in the labor movement has occurred among technical, professional, sales, routine white-collar, and related occupations, especially within the public sector, while membership in the traditional blue-collar jobs has declined. Described by industry rather than occupation, the increases are in insurance, real estate, education, retailing, banking, government, and the like, while the declines are mainly in manufacturing and mining. These are also, of course, the relatively growing and declining sectors of the economy, respectively. For example, two large industrial unions, the Auto Workers and the Steelworkers, have obviously lost members as the number of employees in automobile and steel companies has declined, partly in consequence of automation. Furthermore, there has been a substantial and steady migration of industry to the sunbelt, where widespread right-to-work laws may impede unionization of the workers there who "replace" the unionized ones left behind in the North and the East.

The Need for a "Lawyer"

Quite aside from any economic benefit of unionization, many persons have a quite personal need for someone to speak for them in dealing with their employer. First, some people are rather inarticulate. They feel they lose arguments not because they are wrong but because they cannot argue as well as the management people with superior verbal skills. Second, there are now thousands of public laws and regulations that affect working life, not to mention rules made by the management. Since management hires specialists to know all these things, employees often feel that they also need a specialist to speak for them. Third, most worker grievances are really complaints that the boss has done something wrong. Yet the boss is the one to whom a complaint must normally go, and the employees may fear the boss will hold it against them if they complain. It is then degrading and humiliating to have to accept a boss' conclusion that you are wrong just because you fear for your job if you protest it. The union provides a third-party "attorney" who can present your complaint impersonally. It can also assure you that you will not be disciplined for the mere act of protesting. These needs parallel those for a lawyer and for due process in other areas of life, and exist whether or not the individual has any interest in collective bargaining over economic matters. Thus far, no device has been found that performs this function so well for employees as a union. It is something like a law firm hired jointly by all the employees.

A union, especially if it is large, also gives employees both the feeling and some of the reality of power. The union can take the employee's case right through to top management, or outside through various agencies and on up to the Supreme Court, if need be. Union presidents may consult with the president. They can be photographed at the White House. They can testify before congressional committees. Such things convey a vicarious sense of importance to members. In some places, like coal towns, the union is an encompassing social institution, a way of life, somewhat comparable to the church in much of the Spanish-speaking world, and to be thrown out of it is much like excommunication. To some, the union is also a philosophy that rationalizes one's life, just as "Free enterprise" and "What's good for business is good for the country" help rationalize the pursuit of self-interest by business. "Solidarity" and "More purchasing power for workers is good for the economy" do the same for the worker. The Chamber of Commerce and a host of trade and other employer organizations publicize these legitimizing slogans for business. Unions are about the only organization that does it for workers. On both sides, the slogans and related rationale provide a sense of identity, of affiliation, and of worthwhileness in the larger scene. Though the magnitude of this effect varies greatly from person to person, and is probably unconscious for most, its role in holding people in the union movement is not insignificant.

At a more pragmatic level, the many offices and posts of a union offer the possibility for some to achieve positions of relative prestige and power without having to leave the ambit of working-class life.

Since many union members in the United States must join a union to keep their jobs, compulsory membership might seem a potent force for recruiting members. Actually, it does little more than assure that when one union member leaves a job his replacement will also join. Compulsory membership itself would increase membership if employment is increasing in companies that have union shops. But that effect is not significant, since the areas where the union shop is most strongly established have had declining employment over the years. Thus, for membership to increase significantly, it is necessary to unionize previously nonunion plants.

The increasing frequency of having both wife and husband hold jobs could have a psychological impact on readiness to join unions, in two contrary directions. One is that possible loss of a job does not hold the same terror to one of two income earners as it does to the sole breadwinner. Hence, employees may have more courage in talking back to the boss as individuals, and they may feel less need for the "lawyer" function described above. The opposite effect would be to make employees less fearful of offending the boss by joining. For most of the nation, the latter reaction will probably dominate. For the antiunion "sunbelt" states, the former may do so.

For reasons that will be clearer after we discuss labor legislation and employer "weapons," the state of the law and of employer resistance may have much to do with the rate of union growth. In fact, it is distinctly possible that the slow rate of union growth in the past decade is attributable to increased skill and determination by employers to avoid unionization, along with the increased inability of legal processes to provide workers and unions the level of protection they had had from the late 1930s through the 1950s. In fact, after remaining discreetly neutral during various battles over labor legislation ever since World War II, a number of the very large American corporations joined the traditionally activist smaller businesses represented by the Chamber of Commerce and the National Association of Manufacturers in successfully fighting the Labor Law Reform Bill in 1978. Certainly, too, the general mood of public sympathy for unions that prevailed from three to five decades ago has largely been lost. For example, the psychological effects may be subtle but strong when one knows he is much less likely than decades ago to get a smile and a warm handshake when identifying himself as an organizer for the union or when announcing that he has just signed a membership card. These things could turn around again, but we have no way of knowing.

Along another dimension, the mounting level of imports and the growth of multinational corporations are presenting unions with much the same problem they faced in the widening of the market in the early 1800s. But the solution is much less simple.

UNION MEMBERSHIP

According to a recent article in the *Monthly Labor Review* by Larry J. Adams,[15] between 1980 and 1984 unions lost 2.7 million members from the ranks of employed wage and salary (EWS) workers. This drop is particularly serious for unions, because it took place during a period of growth of the nation's work force. Although the total U.S. work force grew in the 1980–84 period, a decline in employment in some highly unionized industries, foreign competition, deregulation of the transportation industries, competition from nonunion firms, and recession in the "smokestack" industries all led to a major reduction of employment in the heavily unionized sector. The economic recovery that followed the 1981–1982 recession benefited industries and occupations with low levels of unionization and not the industries that have been the basis of traditional union strength.

According to the Bureau of Labor Statistics[16] (BLS), in May of 1980 unions represented 20,095,000 of (EWS) workers; this total does not include the 2,282,000, or the 11 percent, of union members who were self-employed, unemployed, retired, laid off, or not counted as EWS workers on other grounds. When these excluded categories are counted, the 1980 total rises to 22,377,000. By 1984 the total union membership of EWS workers had declined to 17,417,000; there are no available 1984 BLS statistics on union membership of persons who are excluded from the reported totals of unionized EWS workers. One could apply the 11 percent figure from 1980 to the 17,417,000 total of 1984 and assume or guess that the total 1984 union membership was actually 11 percent higher than the above total, or 19,333,000.

Another statistic that represents bad news for unions is the proportions of all EWS workers who are unionized. In 1980, 23 percent of all EWS workers were union members. By the end of September of 1984, this total declined to 19.1 percent.[17]

Until 1980 the BLS published a biennial publication entitled *The Directory of*

National Unions and Employee Associations. The publication of the directory, which contained statistical data on labor unions, was discontinued with the 1980 issue. The Bureau of National Affairs (BNA) filled the vacuum left by the BLS and began publishing the *Directory of U.S. Labor Organizations.* In its 1984–85 edition, the BNA reports that membership in U.S. labor organizations declined from 21,248,000, or 25.7% of the civilian labor force (CLF), in 1970 to 19,763,000, or 17.9% of the CLF, in 1982.[18] (see Table 1–1.) The Adams data just discussed highlight the recent steep downward membership trends confronting the labor movement. In a February 1985 report by the AFL–CIO Committee on the Evolution of Work, this problem was recognized. The report states that "the proportion of workers who are eligible to join a union and who in fact belong to a union has fallen from close to 45 percent to under 28 percent since 1954."[19] To assess and evaluate the issues facing labor unions and come up with some potential answers, the AFL–CIO Executive Committee created the Committee on the Evolution of Work. Recently, the committee issued a number of recommendations addressing such topics as: "New Methods of Advancing the Interests of Workers," "Increasing Member's Participation in Their Union," "Improving the Labor Movement's Communication," "Improving Organizing Activity," and "Proposing Structural Changes to Enhance the Labor Movement's Overall Effectiveness."

TABLE 1–1.   U.S. LABOR ORGANIZATION MEMBERSHIP, 1970–82[1]

(In thousands)

Year	Membership	Civilian Labor Force[2]	
		Number	Percent Members
1970	21,248	82,771	25.7
1971	21,327	84,382	25.3
1972	21,657	87,034	24.9
1973	22,276	89,429	24.9
1974	22,809	91,949	24.8
1975	22,361	93,775	23.8
1976	22,662	96,158	23.6
1977	22,456	99,009	22.7
1978	22,757	102,251	22.3
1979	22,579	104,962	21.5
1980	22,366	106,940	20.9
1981	—	—	—
1982	19,763	110,204	17.9

[1] *Includes active members reported by unions, but excludes Canadian members.*
[2] *Revised from "Total Labor Force" classification in Table 2 of the 1982–83 edition of the directory.*
— = Data not available.

SOURCE: Directory of U.S. Labor Organizations, 1984–85 Edition, Courtney D. Gifford, Staff Editor, Daily Labor Report, The Bureau of National Affairs, Inc. Washington, D.C. p. 2 and Bureau of Labor Statistics. Handbook of Labor Statistics, December 1983 (Bulletin 2175).

THE OUTLOOK FOR THE LABOR MOVEMENT
IN THE EIGHTIES AND THE NINETIES

The reasons for union growth and union decline are complex and difficult to analyze. Industrial relations literature concerned with these topics can be divided into two major schools: the saturationist school under the leadership of Daniel Bell, and the historical school headed by Irving Bernstein.[20] According to the saturationists, union membership "is a predictable function of known structural qualities in the economy." This school claims that there is a limit to the labor force that unions can organize. Some groups within the labor force have a higher potential for unionization than others, and thus structural changes of the labor force could have an adverse effect on unionization. The historical school stresses the unpredictable nature of union organizing. Williams[21] states that the writers in this group claim that union growth "proceeds at the modest trend pace" punctuated with a "burst of growth at irregular intervals"; the potential for unionization is not based on a "readily indentifiable group" but "social mores, laws and economic pressures." An evaluation of both positions suggest that the "truth" probably incorporates elements of both schools. Structural changes of the labor force, economic fluctuations, deregulation, growth of the high-technology and service industries, geographic moves of industry, larger proportion of women workers in the labor force, changes from unskilled to more highly skilled and from blue-collar to white- and technological-collar workers, changing attitudes of workers toward unions, employers questioning legitimacy of unions, changes in legislative interpretations, new legislation, election, transfer of power from Democrats to Republicans, and shifts in public opinion are all factors that influence the level of unionization.

Union growth depends on the willingness of the unorganized to join unions and of the organized worker to stay in the union. One of the best articles on the subject, titled *Why Workers Join Unions*, was written by E. Wight Bakke in 1945. He states:

> The worker reacts favorably to union membership in proportion to the strength of his belief that this step will reduce his frustrations and anxieties and will further his opportunities relevant to the achievement of his standards of successful living. He reacts unfavorably in proportion to the strength of his belief that this step will increase his frustrations and anxieties and will reduce his opportunities relevant to the achievement of such standards.[22]

The employment shifts of the last few decades away from those industries and occupations in which unions traditionally enjoyed a high level of support and the sophisticated level of antiunion activity by employers pose major challenges to the future of the labor movement. Organizing tactics and slogans appropriate during the 1930s may have relatively little appeal to today's work force. It is claimed by some writers that presently many union members are "solidly middle class," better educated and informed, and more affluent than their predecessors. Many own homes rather than rent and are more concerned with taxes and schools and with sending their kids to college than with union positions on equal rights amendments, social programs, and consumer protection legislation. They are critical of union leaders who advocate increases in social spending. Some blame unions more than business for inflation. Some promanagement spokespersons claim that "the leaders of organized labor are out of touch with their membership . . . [and that] union members today are more independent and less beholden to the unions for their economic survival . . . [and that] many union officials have difficulty relating to the new workforce."[23]

The challenges confronting unions come not only from occupational and industrial shifts in employment but also from minorities, women, and youth who object to "the rigidities of the union command structure, work rules and seniority systems."[24] The future growth of the union movement may depend on its ability to adapt its organizing strategies to the work force of the 1980s and 1990s. Labor's challenge is to persuade unorganized workers that unionism can offer economic betterment and job security and protection from arbitrary actions by employers. To accomplish this, unions may have to redefine their goals and convince space-age workers that they left behind the nineteenth century. Labor may have to recast programs to appeal to the needs of women and the younger and better educated work force.[25] Many of these workers value flexibility, recognition, individuality, and independence. Some of these characteristics may be in conflict with the traditional nature of the labor movement.[26]

John Schidman writes, "Demographic changes in the labor force will force organized labor to face the challenge of a restructured internal membership and the restructuring of appeals to the unorganized."[27] The success of future organizational activities of unions would require that the labor movement reassess its structure, role, and function and adapt it to the needs of the eighties and nineties.

SUMMARY

For numerous reasons, unions actively seek to recruit and hold members. In doing so, they appeal to a wide variety of social, psychological, and economic motives of workers for wanting to join unions. Between the forces driving workers toward unions and the institutional forces reaching out of the unions to pull them in, a powerful union movement has been created in the United States. These forces have been strong enough to cause most of the growth in union membership long after the first impact of the Industrial Revolution wore off. What the future will hold is not known. It seems unlikely, however, that the union movement will shrivel away in the near future. For the present, it seems advisable to understand and to learn to deal with unions in their present form.

If so, we must still attend to what the AFL under Gompers and most of subsequent unionism have learned from the lessons of history. The aftermath of the Industrial Revolution provided the urge for workers' self-defense through organization. A substantial number of such experiments showed that the ownership approach on a job-oriented basis is simply not workable. The local unions of the Jacksonian era, the Knights of Labor, and several other experiments not described in this text demonstrated that the class-wide union is ineffective in bargaining and has poor survival value in the United States. Political activities succeeded in a number of cases, but labor organizations based primarily on them disappeared. Therefore, political action must be included in labor's kit of tools. But it must be a supplemental activity of unions whose primary aim is more stable. Class-based ownership has never been tried in the United States and therefore cannot be judged as feasible or not. But moves in this direction generated intense opposition from the community and less than wild enthusiasm among the workers. Furthermore, they usually brought ideological splits and intense rivalry within the unions. Hence, whatever their other alleged merits, socialist aims could be the death of American trade unions.

By contrast, the goal of getting "more" through bargaining is immediate, tangible, and extraordinarily permanent. Hence, it seems likely that dealings between employers and unionized employees will be the norm for at least a fifth of our work force for some time, albeit with changes of emphasis, which reflect the sharpening mood of the New Right and the increasingly multinational nature of America's major employers. It also seems likely that in the future, as in the past, settlements reached in the unionized sector of the economy will be conspicuous pattern setters for the rest of it. If so, unionization will carry much more weight than its relative size would indicate.

NOTES

[1]In reading elsewhere on the subject of unions, the student will often encounter the terms *job conscious* and *class conscious. Job consciousness* is nearly equivalent to what we have termed the "job-oriented bargaining approach"; and the term *class consciousness* may be equated with what we have termed the "class-oriented ownership approach." Although the serious student of labor should certainly be aware of the terms *job conscious* and *class conscious*, we have largely avoided them because they fail to distinguish between the scope of the group with which the worker identifies himself and the kind of action he wishes to take to protect his interest. For example, they fail to cover adequately either class-wide bargaining activities or job-oriented ownership proposals.

The term *class conscious* carries a Marxist connotation, whereas *class oriented* and *class wide* do not. In addition, the traditional terminology has been confused by some authors, who consider class consciousness to be a prerequisite of *any* labor union movement—a usage clearly inconsistent with the Marxist implications of the term. Later in this chapter, by referring to this prerequisite condition as *employee consciousness*, we have tried to deal with the prerequisite conditions for unions without clashing with existing terminology.

[2]John R. Commons, "American Shoemakers, 1648–1895," from *Labor and Administration* (New York: Macmillan, 1913), reprinted in Richard L. Rowan (ed.), *Readings in Labor Economics and Labor Relations* (Homewood, Ill.: Irwin, 3rd edition 1976), pp. 88–100.

[3]Philip Taft, *Organized Labor in American History* (New York: Harper & Row, 1964), p. 2.

[4]Selig Perlman, *A History of Trade Unionism in the United States* (New York: Macmillan, 1922), pp. 31ff.

[5]See *Directory of Labor Unions in the United States, 1953*, Bulletin 1127 (Washington, D.C.: U.S. Department of Labor, 1953), Bureau of Labor Statistics, p. 21; *ibid.*, 1961, Bulletin 1320; Joyce L. Kornbluh (ed.), *Rebel Voices: An IWW Anthology* (Ann Arbor: University of Michigan Press, 1964); Gibbs M. Smith, *Labor Martyr Joe Hill* (New York: Grosset and Dunlap, 1969); and Fred Thompson and Patrick Murfin, *The IWW: Its First 70 Years* (Chicago: IWW, November 1976). *Industrial Worker*, 81, No. 4, Washington, D.C. 7.

[6]Details on the "Mollies" can be found in Wayne G. Broehl, Jr., *The Molly Maguires* (Cambridge, Mass.: Harvard University Press, 1964). This volume has the rare distinction of being an academic work for which the author has been able to sell movie rights—as reported in *Monthly Labor Review*, 88, no. 4 (April 1965), 449.

[7]Almost all histories of the American labor movement include a discussion of the Haymarket Riot. A convenient recent one is Taft, *op. cit*, pp. 130–35.

[8]These are to be distinguished from independent unions that cover only a single company but are not dominated by the employer.

[9]The figures from 1900 through 1953 are from Irving Bernstein, "Growth of American Unions," *American Economic Review* (June 1954), p. 303ff. The 1955 figure is from Bureau of Labor Statistics Releases, *Union Membership 1960*, (November 1961), p. 1. The 1980 and the 1982 figures are from *Directory of U.S. Labor Organizations 1984–85 Edition*, Courtney D. Gifford, (ed.) Staff Editor, Daily Labor Report, The Bureau of National Affairs, Inc., Washington, D.C., p. 62.

[10]In order to make sure strikebreakers do not enter the plant and operate it, the strikers in a sit-down strike refuse to leave the plant instead of refusing to enter it. Food and bedding are sent in from the outside by sympathizers.

[11]In this connection, consult August Meier and Elliot Rudwich, *Black Detroit and the Rise of the UAW* (New York: Oxford University Press, 1979), especially pp. 39f.

[12]*The Nation*, January 19, 1980, pp. 37f.

[13]Proceedings of the 14th Constitutional Convention of the AFL–CIO New York, New York, 1981 p. 58. *The American Almanac of Jobs and Salaries*, John W. Wright (New York: Avon, 1982), p. 578.

[14]Thomas Ferguson and Joel Rogers, "Labor Law Reform and its Enemies," *The Nation*, January 6, 1979, p. 1.

[15]Larry T. Adams, "Changing Employment Patterns of Organized Workers," *Monthly Labor Review* (February 1985), pp. 25–31.

[16]*Ibid.*

[17]*Ibid.*

[18]Courtney D. Gifford (ed.), *Directory of U.S. Labor Organizations 1984–85 Edition* (Washington, D.C.: The Bureau of National Affairs, Inc., 1984).

[19]*The Changing Situation of Workers and Their Unions*, A Report by the AFL–CIO Committee on the Evolution of Work, February 1985, pp. 5–34.

[20]Daniel Bell, "The Next American Labor Movement," *Fortune*, April 1954, p. 120ff.; Irving Bernstein, "The Growth of American Unions," *American Economic Review*, Vol. 44, June 1954, pp. 301–18. Source: Myron Roomkin and Hervey A. Juris, "Unions in the Traditional Sectors: The Mid-life Passage of the Labor Movement," *Industrial Relations Research Association Series: Proceedings of the Thirty-First Annual Meeting*, 1978, p. 216.

[21]C. Glyn Williams, "The State of American Unionism," Business and Economic Review, 24, no. 6 (May 1978), 3–6.

[22]E. Wight Bakke, "Why Workers Join Unions," *Personnel*, 22, no. 1 (July 1945), 37.

[23]*Nation's Business*, April 1979, p. 32.

[24]A. H. Raskin, "Big Labor Strives to Break Out of Its Rut," *Fortune*, August 27, 1979, p. 33.

[25]A. H. Raskin, "Management Comes Out Swinging," *Industrial Relations Research Association Series, Proceeding of the Thirty-First Annual Meeting* 1978, *op. cit.*, pp. 223–32.

[26]P. J. Pestillo, "Learning to Live Without the Union," *Industrial Relations Research Association Series*, 1978, *op. cit.*, pp. 233–39.

[27]John Schmidman, *Unions in Post-Industrial Society* (University Park and London: Pennsylvania State University Press, 1979), p. 98.

THE EVOLUTION OF THE LEGAL FRAMEWORK FOR COLLECTIVE BARGAINING IN THE PRIVATE SECTOR

There can be little doubt, as we review their history, that our laws regarding unions and collective bargaining and the attitudes of those who formed those laws have made a deep impression on the development and present status of collective bargaining. In the United States, the mainstream of organized labor has shown a strong acceptance of private enterprise in general and of management security within the area of collective bargaining. This is in marked contrast to the expectations of labor in much of the rest of the world.

Presumably, the willingness of labor to stick with the present approach will depend upon the ability of that approach to provide labor with bargaining power reasonably equal to that of management. However, if labor's bargaining power should become too great, it could destroy private enterprise by curtailing incentive and distorting basic economic relationships. It is the purpose of this chapter and the next to describe and evaluate public policy with respect to unions and collective bargaining.

All divisions into historical periods are arbitrary, and this one is no exception. For convenience, however, the history of public policy toward unions and collective bargaining will be divided into four periods. The first is the *period of opposition*, which may be dated roughly from 1800 to 1932. The second, the *transition toward acceptance*, overlaps it, starting about the time of World War I and extending also to 1932. The *period of support* starts with the Norris–LaGuardia Act in 1932 and extends to the passage of the Taft–Hartley Act in 1947. The *period of control* runs from 1947 to the present.

THE PERIOD OF OPPOSITION TO UNIONS

The Conspiracy Doctrine

Complaints of employers against unions started coming into the courts long before any legislation had been passed on the subject. Nevertheless, judges felt obligated to make decisions, which they did on the basis of their consciences (or prejudices) and precedents borrowed from other subjects. Such common law decisions constituted the whole of the legal attitude toward unions during most of the nineteenth century. During most of this period judges came mainly from the upper middle classes, whose consciences often placed unionization on a par with gambling and wife-beating. Hence, with a virtually clear field to choose from, they selected precedents detrimental to unions, chief of which was the conspiracy doctrine.[1]

The first instance of a union's being brought to court and its members fined was that of the Philadelphia Cordwainers in 1806, to which the conspiracy doctrine was applied. The essence of the doctrine is that what is legal for one person becomes an illegal conspiracy if several persons join together for the same purpose. The doctrine was stated clearly in the Hatters case in 1823, where a strike sought to get an employer to discharge a man who was working for "knocked-down wages." The strikers were found guilty, on the ground that

> journeymen confederating and refusing to work, unless for certain wages, may be indicted for conspiracy—for the offence consists in the conspiracy and not in the refusal; and all conspiracies are illegal though the subject matter of them may be lawful—The gist of the conspiracy is the unlawful confederation, and the act is complete when the confederacy is made, and any act done in pursuit of it is a constituent part of the offense.[2]

The Supreme Court of New York used similar words in 1835. "The conspiracy in this case was not to commit an offense . . . .: the raising of wages is no offense—the conspiracy is the offense."[3]

It would be an exaggeration to say that unions themselves were illegal and that their mere existence was prohibited. They were taken to court only for specific actions against employers or fellow workers, and only the union activity, not the union itself, was held illegal. But when it is considered that the main reason for union existence is to bargain collectively, that it is the fact of collectivity, not the bargaining, that is illegal, and that "the act is complete when the confederacy is made," the distinction becomes almost meaningless.

The bias of this doctrine against unions is plain, for the same line of reasoning was conspicuously *not* applied in other areas. Capitalists were permitted to join together in the joint-stock company, the forerunner of the modern corporation. Voters and candidates for public office were allowed to "conspire" to get control of the government through political parties. "Conspiracy" to do many things was evident on all sides, but only with respect to unions did the common law find it illegal. As the defense attorney in the original Cordwainers' case put it:

> Dancing is very fashionable and a very pleasing recreation; though according to the principle of my learned friends, a country dance would be criminal, a cotillion unlawful,

even a minuet a conspiracy; and nothing but a horn pipe or a solo would be stepped with impunity![4]

He added that to seek help in putting out the fire in one's house would be a conspiracy, and the city could be destroyed "or those who put out the blaze must be consumed in the flames of the common law."[5]

In partial justification of the use of the conspiracy doctrine, it may be observed that the economy was still close enough to a handicraft system that the banding together of workers to raise their wages closely resembled a monopoly agreement by craftsmen to fix the price of their product and was strongly at odds with the new *laissez-faire* philosophy of the age, particularly when the tactic used was a tight closed shop. As the Recorder's charge to the jury put it at the end of the trial in the first case: "A combination of workmen to raise their wages may be considered in a two fold point of view: one is to benefit themselves . . . the other is to injure those who do not join their society. The rule of law condemns both."[6]

In 1842 the conspiracy doctrine was considerably softened by a decision of Chief Justice Shaw of the Massachusetts Supreme Court. Judge Shaw ruled that the conspiracy could not be prosecuted unless either its aims or its methods were illegal in themselves.

This decision stopped only temporarily the use of the conspiracy doctrine against unions, and there were more conspiracy cases during the second half of the century than during the first half.[7] This was legally possible despite the Shaw decision because the decision had not come out of the United States Supreme Court, and judges in future cases therefore had just as much right to apply the older precedents as the newer one.

Although the conspiracy doctrine undoubtedly slowed the development of an organized labor movement, it would be a mistake to attribute too great an importance to it. Although conspiracy cases were fairly numerous, the penalties were seldom large enough to be a serious deterrent. As was seen in Chapter 1, unions did progress during the period, and the main causes of their periodic rise and fall seemed quite independent of the law. The doctrine of conspiracy persisted, however, as a partial basis of decisions until about 1930.

The Injunction

As noted in Chapter 1, by the 1880s unions had begun to take on pretty much their present form and philosophy. The AFL was under way and was doing effective bargaining in some trades. Although the Knights of Labor had folded, it was evident that labor was on the march, and employers were alert for an effective method to combat it. This they found in the labor injunction, first used in England in 1868 and first copied in this country sometime during the rail strikes of the 1870s. Since it was more effective than the conspiracy doctrine, use of the latter declined.

The injunction is a legal device with many uses other than in labor disputes. It is an order issued by a judge at the request of one party directing a second party to refrain from some specified act. Its most obvious use is to prevent irreparable damage, as to prevent me from cutting down a magnificent tree you claim is on your side of the property line until there has been a full investigation to determine who is right. In business and labor relations "irreparable" tends to mean something that could not be made good by a money payment that is within the capacity of the offender to pay.

A full-fledged injunction goes through three stages—a temporary restraining order, a temporary injunction, and a permanent injunction.[8] The first may be issued by a judge on the basis of an *ex parte* hearing—that is, with only one of the affected parties present. Within a few days both parties will be heard, and either the complaint will be dismissed or a temporary injunction will be issued. If the parties cannot settle the dispute under the temporary injunction, the court may make it permanent and forbid forever the enjoined act. Because of the temporary nature of the strike, permanent antistrike injunctions rarely occur in labor disputes. The temporary restraining order is usually sufficient.

Four aspects of the injunction make it a particularly effective weapon for employers and a particularly heinous one for unions when used against strikes. First, the judge has full discretion whether to issue the restraining order or not—without having to hear the union's side at all. Because of the bias already described, judges often tended to enjoin strikes upon the slightest pretext when asked to do so by an employer. The exercise of the bias was facilitated by a second factor—the very great breadth of meaning given to the term *property* by the courts. The "property" that could be protected by an injunction came to include, not only tangible goods and buildings, but such intangibles as good will, right of access, and eventually, the right to operate one's business without interference. Under such broad definitions almost any strike was potentially enjoinable.

A third aspect of the injunction was the method of levying penalties. Unlike violation of a law, where minimum and maximum penalties are often specified by the law itself, violation of an injunction constitutes contempt of court. The penalty lies in the discretion of the judge who issued the order and whose temper is usually not improved by having his or her personal orders disobeyed.

Finally, the notion that an injunction preserves the status quo until a fuller determination of the situation can be made simply does not apply in a strike. A strike is a dynamic thing, and a strike enjoined is a strike being lost, particularly when it is an organizing strike called by an incipient union trying to get established in a plant. The stamp of illegality often had a further inhibiting effect on those who were not confirmed and fighting unionists.

The impact of the injunction during its heyday (roughly 1880 to 1932) cannot be appreciated unless it is put in the context of the times. There was then no legal protection of the right to join a union, and employers could freely fire anyone who participated in a strike or gave evidence of sympathy for the union. A lost strike often meant lost jobs for all participants. Hence, solidarity, as evidenced by an uncrossed picket line, was crucial. But the court order prohibited picketing, if nothing else.

The Sherman Act is Added

In 1890 the courts received from Congress an important new basis for injunctions, the Sherman Antitrust Act. There is much controversy over whether Congress intended the law to apply to unions, which are not explicitly mentioned in the statute.

In 1908, however, in the case of *Loew* v. *Lawler,* the Supreme Court ruled that the Sherman Act made "every contract, combination, or conspiracy in restraint of trade illegal," whether of business, farmers, or labor.[9] By 1928 unions had been prosecuted 83 times under the act, constituting 18 percent of all the cases brought under the act.[10]

One of the most important cases on record, and one that indicated the need for some restriction in the use of the injunction, was that of the Pullman strike in 1894. During the winter of 1893−94, the Pullman Palace Car Company, near Chicago, instituted a wage reduction. In March its employees joined the American Railway Union, a new industrial union under the presidency of Euguene V. Debs, designed to include all workers connected with railways. In May the Pullman workers went on strike. After trying unsuccessfully to get the Pullman Company to arbitrate, the American Railway Union voted to stop handling all Pullman cars on the railroads. The railroad companies continued to make up their trains with Pullman cars included, so that the boycott of Pullman cars shortly became a railway strike.

Within a few days, the attorney general of the United States obtained from the Chicago circuit court an injunction based on the Sherman Act and on the obstruction of the mails. It enjoined the union, its officers, and "all other persons whomsoever" from "in any way or manner interfering with" the business of the railroads entering Chicago, carrying United States mail, or engaging in interstate commerce. It forbade "compelling or *inducing or attempting to* compel or *induce* by threats, intimidation, *persuasion,* force of violence, any of the employees . . . to refuse or fail to perform any of their duties as employees."[11] Many other restrictions were added, but the simple substance was that no one was allowed to strike or in any way, directly or indirectly, to assist the strike. Debs and several other union leaders were later jailed for contempt. The strike was marked by considerable violence and the presence of federal troops sent in by President Cleveland. After about two weeks, the strike was broken and the violence was ended.

A sidelight illustrates the mood of the times. The original dispute involved only the Pullman Company and its employees who manufactured Pullman cars. Pullman cars on the trains were operated by the Pullman Company, not by the railroads, and the refusal of railroad employees to handle trains with Pullman cars in them was directed at the Pullman Company, not at the railroads. It apparently did not occur to the authorities to ask the railroad companies simply to omit the Pullman cars from their trains. In that case the trains and the mails would have run, and the whole affair would have been confined to a simple strike against the Pullman Company.

The Abortive Clayton Act

Apparently in order to restrain judges from their continued application of the Sherman Act against unions, the Clayton Act, which in 1914 amended the Sherman Act, included this provision:

SECTION 6: That the labor of a human being is not a commodity. Nothing contained in the anti-trust laws shall be construed to forbid the existence and operation of labor, agricultural, or horticultural organizations, or to forbid or restrain individual members of such organizations from lawfully carrying out the legitimate objects thereof; nor shall such organizations, or the members thereof be held or construed to be illegal combinations or conspiracies in restraint of trade under the anti-trust laws.

In its Section 20, the Clayton Act also restricted the use of injunctions by federal courts to cases where "necessary to prevent irreparable injury to property, or to the property right . . . for which there is no adequate remedy at law." In view of what subsequently occurred, it is worth quoting the last paragraph of Section 20 in full:

> And no such restraining order or injunction shall prohibit any person or persons, whether singly or in concert, from terminating any relation of employment, or from ceasing to perform any work or labor, or from recommending, advising, or persuading others by peaceful means so to do; or from attending at any place where any such person or persons may lawfully be, for the purpose of peacefully obtaining or communicating information, or from peacefully persuading any person to work or to abstain from working; or from ceasing to patronize or to employ any party to such dispute, or from recommending, advising, or persuading others by peaceful and lawful means so to do; from paying or giving to, or withholding from, any person engaged in such a dispute, any strike benefits or other moneys or things of value; or from peaceably assembling in a lawful manner, and for lawful purposes; or from doing any act or thing which might lawfully be done in the absence of such dispute by any party thereto; nor shall any of the acts specified in this paragraph be considered or held to be violations of any law of the United States.

Sections 6 and 20 together seem to provide unequivocally that a union itself, a strike, and any peaceful activity to organize or assist a strike is not to be considered a conspiracy in restraint of trade under the antitrust laws and is not under any circumstance to be enjoined by a federal court, except to prevent damage that the union could not, by the payment of damages or otherwise, make good. The Clayton Act was widely hailed as the "Magna Carta of labor."

One would think from reading the Clayton Act that the use of injunctions in general and injunctions under the Sherman Act in particular would come to an end in labor disputes, except for cases plainly involving irreparable injury to property. The reverse actually occurred.

The tortuous argument by which the Supreme Court negated the wording of the law went as follows. The Clayton Act (said the Court) covers only *peaceful* activities by unions. But (the Court added, in a clause of questionable accuracy) the courts had never prohibited peaceful activities. Hence, the Clayton Act did not change anything. Since the act did not change anything, the courts could continue to apply all the precedents previously developed.

The upshot of the matter was that, whereas injunctions under the Sherman Act had theretofore been confined to secondary boycotts and sympathy strikes, after the Clayton Act they came to be applied to ordinary primary strikes. The only advantage of the Clayton Act to unions was that the union itself could not be condemned as a conspiracy in restraint of trade, a matter not seriously in question in any event.[12]

Unions were also significantly restricted in their tactics, even under those circumstances when strikes were legal. In 1921, the Supreme Court restricted the use of peaceful picketing in *American Steel Foundries* v. *Tri-City Central Trades Coun-*

cil.[13] In this case the court set a precedent, thereafter followed by most state courts, in which picketing by more than one person at a worksite gate was considered unlawful.

The case that seems to have held the greatest potentiality for completely thwarting the actions of organized labor was that of the *Hitchman Coal and Coke Company* v. *Mitchell.*[14] The case started in 1907, well before the passage of the Clayton Act, but was not decided by the Supreme Court until 1917. The employees of Hitchman Coal had been induced to sign *yellow-dog contracts*, agreeing that they would not join a union while employed there. The Supreme Court upheld the enforceability of such contracts and approved an injunction against all organizing activity on the ground that any organizing efforts constituted an inducement to breach the contract.[15] The decision constituted a massive potential for blocking unionization, since under it an employer could make it illegal for anyone even to ask an employee to join a union. Though the decision did not actually have such a sweeping effect, along with other judicial attitudes toward organized labor it apparently did contribute substantially to the decline in union membership and influence during the 1920s. Only the more important federal cases have been described here; injunctions by state and local courts in purely routine strikes were continuing with mounting frequency from 1880 to about 1935.

Summary of the Period of Opposition

Several observations summarized the period of opposition and its effects. First, unions found the law, as applied, strongly against them from around 1800, when unions first appeared, until the era of the New Deal in the 1930s. The opposition was effectuated through the conspiracy doctrine, the injunction, and a particular type of application of the Sherman Act. During this period, the law placed no restrictions on employer efforts to prevent or destroy unions.

Second, unions found more favor in the legislative branch of the government than in the judicial; the difference between the language of the Clayton Act and the court decisions under it is an important case in point.

Third, unions developed an almost psychotic opposition to the use of injunctions in labor disputes and a deeply ingrained fear of any legislation restricting union activities. The reaction to the injunction had obvious grounds. After all, the original public sentiment behind the Sherman Act was directed toward restraining employers, not unions. Justice Brandeis, in his dissent in the *Bedford Cut Stone* case, pointed out that the court under the Sherman Act had made rulings that permitted one corporation to control 50 percent of the steel industry and another to control virtually the whole of the shoe machinery industry, while under the same act it had denied "to members of a small craft of workingmen the right to cooperate in simply refraining from work, when that course was the only means of self protection against a combination of militant and powerful employers."[16]

THE TRANSITION TOWARD ACCEPTANCE

Prior to World War I, several states enacted legislation recognizing the right of employees to organize. But these laws were of little avail, and most were thrown out by the courts. An important example was a law passed in 1903 in Kansas outlawing the yellow-dog contract, which was overruled by the Supreme Court of the United States in 1915. The federal Erdman Act of 1898, dealing with the settlement of labor disputes on the railroads, prohibited yellow-dog contracts in that industry. In 1908 the Supreme Court ruled it unconstitutional, as a violation of the Fifth Amendment.[17] Justice Holmes dissented, the basis of his reasoning (here as in a number of other cases) being that the court majority had assumed that the bargaining power of employers and individual workmen is equal, and that this assumption was contrary to fact.

Some occurrences on the administrative front also presaged the development of a new policy. Late in World War I the federal government established a War Labor Conference Board, consisting of five management, five labor, and two public representatives to plan for the handling of labor problems. This board recommended the creation of a National War Labor Board and certain guiding principles for labor relations. Among other principles, the War Labor Conference Board included the following:

> Right to organize—1. The right of workers to organize in trade unions and to bargain collectively through chosen representatives, is recognized and affirmed. This right shall not be denied, abridged, or interfered with by employers in any manner whatsoever.[18]

No provisions were established for enforcing the principle and meanwhile the Supreme Court continued to deny it, as in the *Hitchman and Kansas* decision. The shortage of labor, however, did give bargaining power to employees, and union membership grew apace during the war period.

Several boards were set up to handle labor disputes, and later the National War Labor Board took over the same function. The mere fact that union leaders could appear before such government boards as recognized spokesmen for organized employees was in itself a marked advance. From 1917 to 1920 the railroads were operated by the government. Under its policy of strict nondiscrimination between union and nonunion employees union membership increased considerably. In 1919 President Wilson called a conference of labor and management leaders to try to work toward a peaceful settlement of postwar disputes, but the conference split on the employers' refusal to recognize the desirability of collective bargaining. It is interesting to note that a similar conference called by President Truman after World War II accepted the principle of collective bargaining without question but split on the management-security issue.

In 1920 the railroads were returned to private hands. But the principle of nondiscrimination continued, and in 1926 it was made permanent by the passage of the Railway Labor Act. This was the first time that the government declared unqualifiedly the right of private employees to join (or not to join) unions without interference from their employers and also provided a mechanism for enforcing this right. It should be noted, however, that the railroad industry stood alone in its development of a means of dealing neutrally with the issues of unionization and collective bargaining. Throughout the decade of the 1920s, the remainder of private industry continued to use the courts as a primary vehicle in its drive against unionism.

Meanwhile, in response to a series of adverse court decisions, unions were pressing strongly for some restriction of injunctions. In 1928 both major political parties endorsed such a limitation, and in 1930 the Supreme Court upheld the pertinent sections of the Railway Labor Act by ordering the Texas and New Orleans Railroad to bargain with the Brotherhood of Railway Clerks instead of with a company-dominated union. The late 1920s clearly portended a reversal of the legal status of unions that had prevailed since the *Cordwainers* case in 1806.

Although the period from roughly 1900 to 1932 was one of transition toward the acceptance of unions, actual restrictions on union activities were proceeding with mounting intensity. The tide of change visible by World War I did not actually arrive until 1932.

THE PERIOD OF SUPPORT

The Norris–LaGuardia Act

In 1932 Congress finally accomplished what it had apparently intended in 1914 in the Clayton Act. In some nine carefully worded paragraphs, the Norris–LaGuardia Act denied to federal courts the right to forbid strikes, peaceful picketing, or other actions not illegal in themselves, such as publicizing the strike or raising and disbursing funds in its support. Labor injunctions were not entirely outlawed, but the conditions of their use were drastically limited. The yellow-dog contract was made unenforceable.

Because the courts had often circumvented the Clayton Act by declaring a particular action not to be a "labor dispute," that term was carefully defined. To make doubly sure that the courts would not interpret the law out of existence, a preamble stated that unorganized workers are "commonly helpless" in dealing with employers, and that "full freedom of association [and] self-organization" are necessary. Although some lower courts continued to issue injunctions such as before, the Supreme Court eventually sustained the Norris–LaGuardia Act in a series of cases.[19] By 1947 some 16 states, including most important industrial ones, had passed laws roughly similar to the Norris Act.[20] On the other hand, many states passed no such laws, and state courts continued to issue injunctions on much the old terms. The full potential of the Norris–LaGuardia Act was never to be felt, however, due to further legal developments that would continue the period of support for trade unionism.

The Wagner Act—High Point of Support

The National Industrial Recovery Act of 1933 laid the way for the Wagner Act a few years later. Its primary purpose was to block the downward spiral of wages and prices through codes of fair competition. As part of an effort to stabilize wages, unionization was encouraged through Section 7(a) of the NIRA, which contained the central provision of the later Wagner Act but without the latter's safeguards and administrative machinery. The National Industrial Recovery Act was declared unconstitutional on May 27, 1935, in the case of *A. L. Schechter Poultry Corp.* v. *United States.*[21]

The Wagner Act, whose official title was the National Labor Relations Act,[22] passed Congress in 1935 in a strong antibusiness atmosphere. Its central provisions are still part of our basic labor legislation and seem likely to remain so for many years. Hence the remainder of this chapter has contemporary, rather than merely historical, significance.

The Wagner Act was monolithic, in the sense that it contained only one central idea, with all other parts in direct support of it. This central purpose was stated succinctly in Section 7:

> Employees shall have the right to self-organization, to form, join, or assist labor organiza-
> tions, to bargain collectively through representatives of their own choosing, and to engage
> in concerted activities, for the purpose of collective bargaining or other mutual aid or
> protection.

The "right to bargain collectively" is the core of the law. The phrase "through representatives of their own choosing" brought to labor the prerequisite of meaningful bargaining—that each side must have complete unilateral control over the selection and control of its own "attorneys" in a dispute, with no interference or control whatsoever by the opposing party. The law did not make a parallel statement of management's right to select its own representatives, because management's freedom on that score had not been seriously challenged by unions.

Experience had made it clear that a bare statement of workers' rights to organize would be meaningless, since employers possessed effective devices for preventing organization. Therefore, the law listed five *unfair labor practices* in which employers were not allowed to engage. Prohibition of the first three prevented the employer from exercising influence on the employees' choice regarding unionization. The first denied the employer the freedom "to interfere with, restrain, or coerce employees in the exercise of the rights guaranteed in Section 7." The second made it unfair "to dominate or interfere with the formation or administration of any labor organization or contribute financial support to it," which is another way of saying that company unions are improper. The third prevented an employer from discriminating between union and nonunion employees in such a way as to encourage or discourage the joining of unions. An exception permitted closed or union shops.

The listing of a fourth unfair labor practice was necessary if the first three prohibitions were to be enforced; it prevented an employer from discriminating against anyone who filed charges or gave testimony under the act. Regulation of a final unfair practice was necessary if the previous ones were to have any meaning. It prohibited an employer from refusing to recognize and bargain collectively with the representatives selected by his employees—the "good faith bargaining" requirement.

Two additional things remained to be done. One was to provide a mechanism for determining the employees' choice of bargaining representative. This was accomplished in Section 9 through a government-supervised secret-ballot election. In it the employees could choose between union and no union, or between two or more unions in the event of such a contest. Less formal methods, such as a card check of union members, could be used if both sides were satisfied as to their accuracy. The majority choice prevailed, and a union so selected became the exclusive representative of all employees in the bargaining unit. By this simple technique, the law largely substituted peaceful persuasion and the ballot box for the violence and bitterness of the typical organizing strike—a major contribution of the law.

Finally, a National Labor Relations Board was established to enforce the law. Much of its work was delegated to regional boards, which conducted hearings and decided on charges of unfair labor practices, subject to appeal to the national board, and from there to the federal courts.

The law was essentially remedial rather than punitive. A finding of guilt was handled by an order to cease and desist rather than by a penalty on the employer. The board could petition the courts for an enforcing order if the employer did not comply; further noncompliance then became contempt of court. An employee who had been discriminatorily fired could be ordered reinstated with back pay. This provision, too, was essentially remedial, not punitive.

The change in government attitude reflected in the Wagner Act can be gathered from the preamble: "It is . . . declared to be the policy of the United States to . . . [encourage] the practice and procedure of collective bargaining." The law certainly had an encouraging effect, and there can be little doubt that the Wagner Act was largely responsible for the rapid rise of unions during the following decade.

Needless to say, the law was not viewed with joy by employers, particularly since the protections and guarantees accorded unions and employees were not accompanied by any restrictions on union activity or any protections for employers. The National Association of Manufacturers, in particular, conducted an intense campaign in which it alleged that the law was unconstitutional and advised its members to disregard it.

The psychological effect of the Wagner Act upon workers was felt immediately, as union organizers tried to make them feel that the "government wants you to join." Real enforcement did not begin until the Supreme Court accepted the law as constitutional in 1937,[23] though its impact was widened by a number of states that passed "little Wagner Acts" to cover intrastate commerce. Employers immediately started a campaign to change the law, either by repeal or by making it more balanced.

Because of widespread misconception, it is important to note that the Wagner Act did *not* deal in any way with bargaining disputes between an employer and a union. The same is essentially true for its successor, the Taft—Hartley Act, though the latter does require the parties to notify the Federal Mediation and Conciliation Service of an impasse in bargaining. The National Labor Relations Board did not (and does not) conciliate or arbitrate labor disputes, provide people who will do so, or deal with strikes over bargaining issues. The board under the Wagner Act merely settled questions of representation and handled cases in which an employer tried to interfere with the existence or independence of a union. It did, however, have to rule on whether or not certain issues were bargainable in order to enforce the requirement that employers bargain. This issue of the scope of bargaining will be taken up in subsequent chapters. On the whole, the Wagner Act did not regulate bargaining or the outcome of bargaining. It prepared the way for collective bargaining by guaranteeing the existence of both of the parties to the process, assuming that the process could then go forward without assistance or intervention.

A Diversionary Gambit on Labels.   It is usually pointless to quibble about the names of things. However, it may help in understanding several pieces of legislation if the terms *prolabor* and *antilabor* are clarified. For example, the Norris—LaGuardia Act was generally thought of as prolabor, and its statement that labor should have full freedom to organize seems to support that view. Yet the law did not *assist* unions or employees in the exercise of those rights. It merely ceased the federal government's assistance in fighting unions.

The Wagner Act was clearly one-sided. It protected unions from employers but not employers from unions and therein reflected the antibusiness atmosphere of the day. But it also reflected the underlying reality that up to that time the need of unions for protection from employers was intense, whereas employers had displayed considerable competence in defending themselves. The subsequent developments that changed this situation are examined in the next section.

There is also little doubt that the original board was prounion. Given a choice in electoral units, it would rather consistently draw the boundaries (that is, gerrymander) in order to favor a prounion vote. And its strictness in proscribing unfair labor practices left many employers feeling that their tongues had been glued and their hands roped in their attempts to deal with unions. Whether this prounion action by government was an appropriate counterbalance to its long assistance to employers can be answered by each according to his or her own predilection.

THE TRANSITION TO TAFT—HARTLEY

The Wagner Act was not long destined to remain our basic labor legislation. Two broad reasons led to its amendment by the Taft—Harley Act in 1947, at the tender age of twelve.

The Wagner Act was inherently not a whole labor policy. It was passed after a long period of intense antiunion activity by managements, assisted by government. Unions were weak and much in need of protection from militant employers, who barred no holds in fighting them. The Wagner Act had a single purpose—to protect employees and unions from employers, by identifying a series of "protected activities" and then preventing employers from violating them.

The Wagner Act was clearly a product of its time and reflected the bad image that then surrounded management. But the law made no provision for the conditions it created. By restricting employer interference with the formation of unions, under an administration sympathetic to labor, the law enabled many mass-based unions to grow from fledglings to large and powerful organizations quite able to defend their own existences. The labor movement as a whole grew from 4 million in 1935 to roughly 16 million in 1948, testifying to the impact of the Wagner Act. Some labor leaders developed more skill in acquiring power than in using it wisely, but the Wagner Act made no provision for controlling the results. For example, the law gave no protection to the employer, the public, or even the employees in a fight between two unions. The Wagner Act had furthered the practice of collective bargaining by requiring an employer to bargain with a union of his or her employees, but it made no provision for a union's refusing to bargain and trying to force conditions unilaterally on an employer. Nor did the law provide for workers caught in a dictatorial union. These and other problems made it clear that the Wagner Act was not adequate as a complete, permanent labor policy.

A second major reason for revision was the vocal and vituperative criticism of the law and unions by business and the press. Employers had always objected loudly that the act was one-sided. During World War II numerous strikes occurred. The vast majority were short, total time lost from strikes was low, and many were wildcats called in violation of union orders. Nevertheless, the press contrasted the safety and comfort of strikers with the conditions of soldiers in foxholes and exaggerated the injury done by the strikes.

At the end of the war, pent-up energies had to be released. Many employer-union relationships barely begun before the war had been thrown into the lap of the War Labor Board for the duration, with strikes, serious bargaining, and major wage adjustments held in suspension. These parties now had to test each other's strengths and intentions, while inflation added tension. A wave of strikes during the first year of peace was inevitable. But goods were short on all sides, and every strike seemed to tighten the shortage. Employers and newspapers reported how "union monopolies" were throttling the economy and demanded that "something be done." As the law on the books at the time, the Wagner Act took the blame for the mountain of strikes, despite their probable inevitability.

Given that *some* changes in the law were needed, labor leaders virtually guaranteed drastic modifications by adamantly rejecting minor ones while Congress was still sympathetic to labor. By the time the Republicans got control of both houses of the Congress in 1946, it was too late for minor concessions. As Representative Fred Hartley, sponsor of the bill in the House of Representatives, made clear, it was the intent of its framers "to reverse the basic direction of our national labor policy," and the mood of the Congress was about as strongly antiunion as the Wagner Act Congress had been prounion. The Taft—Hartley Act, officially the Labor-Management Relations Act of 1947, was passed over the veto of President Truman, who objected to the reversal of policy, though he had earlier approved strong legislation for curtailing public emergency strikes.

In contrast to the single-minded Wagner Act, the Taft—Hartley Act is complex. Its complexity resides largely in additions to the Wagner Act, since much of the original Wagner Act still remains unchanged in Taft—Hartley. While the Wagner Act protected employees and unions from employers, Taft—Hartley seeks to protect employees, unions, management, and the public from the acts of both unions and management. And, while the Wagner Act attempted to regulate only the relationship between unions and management, its successor also regulates some aspects of the labor contract, some internal affairs of unions, and other activities. In scope and framework, the law is capable of being a balanced labor policy. Whether or not it is so in fact, it unquestioningly ushered in the era of control, as we shall see.

In 1959 Congress passed the Landrum—Griffin Act, which consisted of two major parts. One was the Labor-Management Reporting and Disclosure Act, which will be discussed separately later in this chapter. The other was a series of amendments to the Taft–Hartley Act, which will be incorporated into the discussion of that law just below.

THE PERIOD OF CONTROL: TAFT–HARTLEY AND MISCELLANEOUS LEGISLATION

The Taft–Hartley Act ushered in the period of control, which seems a reasonably accurate name for the period ever since the Act's passage in 1947. Other legislation discussed in the rest of this chapter also seems to fall properly under the heading of "control." The 1974 health care amendments will also be discussed. Attention will be given to decisions by the National Labor Relations Board and the courts, since shifts in interpretations have often been as important as if the law had been changed.

Basic Conditions of Collective Bargaining

Protection of the Right to Organize and Bargain.   In its preamble and statement of policy, Taft–Hartley retains the language of the Wagner Act in stating that it is the policy of the United States to encourage the practice and procedures of collective bargaining. To clarify an important distinction, the encouragement of collective bargaining is not the same as having government take sides to strengthen the bargaining power of union or management in a fight between them after collective bargaining already exists. The law accepts the major implication of this statement of policy by recognizing (1) that collective bargaining presumes the existence of unions and (2) that employers have considerable power and desire to prevent or destroy unions (and therefore collective bargaining), which power they will often exercise unless they are restrained. The Taft–Hartley Act therefore retains the Wagner Act's Section 7 guarantee that employees "shall have the right to self-organization, to form, join, or assist labor organizations, to bargain collectively through representatives of their own choosing, and to engage in other concerted activities for the purpose of collective bargaining." Except for one change affecting union security, the law then repeats from the Wagner Act the five unfair labor practices that employers are prohibited from using to fight the existence of unions. To the extent that these five provisions (Section 8[a]) are enforced, they assure that employees can have unions and be represented by them if they so desire—as discussed in the preceding section. As we will discuss later, Section 7 adds that employees shall have the right to refrain from union activities.

The law's coverage is not universal, in that it specifically excludes groups of labor on the basis of the occupation or the industry in which they work. This exclusion of coverage of the protections of the Taft–Hartley Act therefore serves to discourage collective bargaining by these groups. The act explicitly excludes agricultural and domestic labor, supervisors in all industries, and all levels of government employees. The AFL–CIO has sought to extend the law to cover agricultural employees, whose employers in most states are free to use the wide range of "union-busting" devices of pre–Wagner Act days. An important exception is California, where in 1975 the

California Agricultural Labor Relations Act established mechanisms for conducting representation elections for field workers. Nearly a decade of relative peace has followed in California after years of dispute between the United Farm Workers (UFW), the Teamsters, and the agricultural employers. Despite this success, it is unlikely that the Taft–Hartley Act will be expanded to cover agricultural labor in the near future.

Government workers, as will be seen in a later chapter, have not been denied collective bargaining rights despite their absence from Taft–Hartley coverage. In the 1960s and 1970s, the federal government and most states passed separate enabling legislation making the exclusion of government workers nearly insignificant.

As federal law, Taft–Hartley can apply only to interstate commerce. However, the term is interpreted very broadly, so that almost any business can be brought within the law if the board so chooses. Since many states do not similarly protect the right to organize, such protection is largely nonexistent where not provided by federal law. In practice, the board confines its jurisdiction to firms that do more than $50,000 to $500,000 in business per year, depending on the industry. Thus, in states that do not have enabling legislation, employees in smaller firms not covered by Taft–Hartley have no legal protection of the right to organize. Even in states that do have their own legislation, the right may be tenuous, as enforcement provisions and procedures are not well developed in the states.

Taft–Hartley acknowledges that recognition of a union by an employer is a prerequisite of collective bargaining and requires employers to deal with unions that represent a majority of employees. In support of this requirement, each side must bargain with the other in good faith and reduce the agreement to writing if the other side so desires. The law, of course, does not require either side to make concessions. But it does require that each give reasons for its position and make some counterproposals. In addition, an employer cannot discharge workers for making bargaining demands.

Protection of Mutual Independence in Bargaining.   Meaningful collective bargaining requires that each side maintain complete independence in selecting and instructing its bargaining representatives. The five unfair labor practices prohibited to employers give unions and employees this basic protection, thereby accepting an important implication of collective bargaining. But a "free speech" clause of the law, as presently interpreted, destroys some of this protection.

The Wagner Act had said nothing about an employer's freedom of speech. The board had consistently prohibited open threats by employers and sometimes even ruled against statements mildly disapproving of unionization if, under the circumstances, the statements might reasonably lead workers to expect reprisals. As unions grew stronger, the board had allowed employers more freedom if their speech would not create fear of reprisal.

Because the full implication of this section is often not recognized, we will state it very flatly. Collective bargaining presupposes *independent* selection of bargaining representatives on both sides, and Section 7 of the law assures employees the right to representatives "of their own choosing." The law means that it is none of the employer's business whether his or her employees unionize or not and, if they do, what union they select. This does not mean that the employer has no *interest* in the matter. Obviously he or she has, and, given the chance, the employer would presumably help employees to select either no union or a weak one. But the law insists that it would be improper for him or her to participate in this choice, in the same sense that it would be improper for one party in a lawsuit to determine which attorney, if any, should represent the other party.

At the same time, information possessed by the employer that would be useful to the employees in deciding whether to unionize should not be withheld. The problem, then, is to prohibit employer statements that coerce but to allow those that inform or persuade, even if the latter are clearly antiunion. This is not an easy distinction to enforce. To be consistent, the law must, of course, also protect the employer's independence from the union in the opposite direction—a matter to be discussed below.

Section 8(c) of the Taft–Hartley Act specifically provides employers full freedom of speech unless their expression "contains threat of reprisal or force or promise of benefit." This provision deals mainly with words rather than their effect—with instruments rather than results. Prior to 1953, the board gave much attention to the probable coercive effects of what an employer said. Under the Eisenhower administration, the board tended to protect employer speech at the expense of employee independence. For example, it refused to set aside a representation election lost by the union, although the employer argued strongly against the union in a meeting several days before the election, on company time and property, with all workers requested to attend. Prounion spokesmen were not allowed to reply.[24] The company also enforced a "no-solicitation" rule, which prevented employees or the union from seeking support or membership on company property. As of 1965, the board considered it consistent with an atmosphere conducive to a free election for an employer to give a preelection speech on company time and property to massed assemblies of employees if it is more than twenty-four hours before an election, and if the employer has no rule prohibiting the union from soliciting off-duty workers on company premises.

Then, in 1969, the U.S. Supreme Court spoke to the issue of preelection speeches in *NLRB* v. *Gissel Packing Co.*[25] The court attempted to harmonize both the employer and employee interest in free and full disclosure of information with the employee interest in an uncoerced decision on collective bargaining by establishing a rather high standard for employer campaign communications. It encouraged advance assessment of the validity of employer "predictions" and "opinions." In 1971, the Second Circuit Court of Appeals stated in *Bausch and Lomb, Inc.* v. *NLRB* that minimal "chilling" of employer and union speeches by setting aside an election for misrepresentations is outbalanced by the interests of employees in free, fair, and informed representation elections.[26] *Gissel's* high standards were applied in a 1972 case. In it, the NLRB set aside an election because the likelihood of the employer's statements that a union victory would induce the company's major customer to deal elsewhere could not be demonstrated.[27]

Nor have the courts or the board ignored the matter of a union's intrusive threats and promises during an election campaign, for such are outlawed as much as are the employer's. Indeed, in a 1973 case, *NLRB* v. *Savair Manufacturing Co.,*[28] the Supreme Court set aside the union's narrow election victory because the waiver of initiation fees was conditioned on joining immediately and not after the election. This waiver was analogized to the grant of gifts or benefits by union or employer while an election was pending. In August 1978 the NLRB held, in the *Associated Milk Producers* case,[29] that the informal, antiunion remarks that a supervisor made to employees individually did not become a speech to a massed assembly merely because he made the remarks to every employee. The comments in question were made on the same day as the election, yet they were not considered to violate the 1965 *Peerless Plywood* rule, and the election results were sustained.

The employer's freedom of speech seems to conflict in principle with the free and voluntary choice of bargaining representatives by employees and to require a choice between two freedoms. There are at least three related grounds on which this amount of restriction is not inconsistent with the First Amendment. First, freedom of speech deals with the transmission of ideas and ceases to be protected when it is so closely related with illegal action as not to be separable from the action. Second, freedom of speech does not include the right credibly to threaten harm. And third, the First Amendment has been interpreted as allowing the regulation of false or fraudulent statements in connection with contractual relations. Hence, if an employer should threaten, say, to discharge any employees who join the union, either the employer is lying or he or she is acknowledging illegal intent. The presumed appropriate balance, which the board in general seeks to maintain, is to prohibit obvious coercion of the employee choice, while otherwise allowing freedom of speech to the employer.

Apparently on the grounds that it would look more like an order than a suggestion, an employer will be considered to have influenced an election improperly if he interviews a substantial number of employees individually or in small groups, away from their workplace and at a location that the employees regard as the "locus of managerial authority"—even if his remarks are free of threats or promises. On the other side, under certain circumstances an election may be declared invalid if the union engages in serious misrepresentations under conditions where they cannot be countered effectively.

One kind of employer influence on the workers' selection of a bargaining representative can arise from the limitation on "economic strikers' " right to vote in a representation election, in Section 9(c)(3). To deal first with the original provisions of the law, if employees strike to improve their welfare (i.e., an "economic" strike in contrast to a strike against an unfair labor practice by the employer), the employer may hire permanent replacements for the strikers. If a representation election is held while the strike is in progress, the strikers cannot vote, but their replacements can. Since presumably the employer would hire only replacements who were reasonably sure to vote against the union, this technique permits an employer to exert an important and perhaps a compelling voice in the choice between union and no union. It also seems to conflict with Section 8(a)(3), which states:

> It shall be an unfair labor practice for an employer by discrimination in regard to hire or tenure of employment or any term or condition of employment to encourage or discourage membership in any labor organization.

This section was modified in 1959 to allow economic strikers (and their replacements) to vote in an election held within a year of the beginning of the strike. This change softens the provision. But, since elections under these circumstances are often called at the initiative of the employer, the change sometimes encourages the employer to postpone the election and drag out settlement of the strike. Strikes under these circumstances often last more than a year.

On the other side, the law in Section 8(b)(1) makes it an unfair labor practice for a union to "restrain or coerce . . . an employer in the selection of his representatives for the purposes of collective bargaining or the adjustment of grievances." It is also unfair for the union to engage in or encourage a strike or boycott to push an employer into an employer association, which presumably would then be his bargaining representative. Both these provisions help preserve the independence of the employer in selecting his bargaining representative. Neither is of great practical import, as the practices they deal with are not frequent.

It is an unfair practice for a union to coerce employees in their selection of a bargaining representative or, except under a union security clause, to attempt to cause an employer to discriminate between union and nonunion workers. In addition, a union may not try to influence workers' freedom of choice by striking to force an employer to recognize one union when another is already duly certified. These are all reasonable rules for sound collective bargaining and outlaw abuses that had been frequent under the Wagner Act.

The extreme difficulty of this issue can best be presented by the examination of a recent series of NLRB decisions. In 1977, the Board held in *Shopping Kart Food Market* that it would no longer probe into the truth of statements made during an election campaign.[30] In 1978, the NLRB reversed itself and reverted to the prior policy of the regulation of campaign speech in *General Knit of California*.[31] In 1982, the Board again reversed itself and chose the freedom-of-speech path in *Midland National Life Insurance*.[32] Each of these policy changes directly followed the appointment of a board member whose view differed with the existing precedent. One would have to view this issue as not permanently decided!

Exclusive Representation

Representation rights under Taft–Hartley remain substantially unchanged from the Wagner Act, in that the bargaining agent designated by majority vote is the exclusive representative of the whole bargaining unit. This provision is essential to meaningful collective bargaining and connotes its acceptance. The representation election also largely eliminates the strike for recognition.

All in all, the Taft–Hartley Act and the board apparently accept and effectively protect the most important prerequisites of collective bargaining in numerous cases that actually come up for decision.

Lesser Conditions of Collective Bargaining

Several lesser conditions of the law show doubtful acceptance of collective bargaining. Taft–Hartley emphasizes the rights of individual workers as against the organized group. In Section 9(a), which establishes the principle of exclusive representation, the law pauses to establish the right of any individual to present a grievance to the employer and have it settled without the intervention of the union, so long as the settlement does not violate the contract. And Section 7(a) guarantees the right of employees to refrain both from joining unions (except under a union shop) and from engaging in "other concerted activities."

The rules for representation elections have been changed by the board in a way that makes election of a union less likely than before. In a three-way vote between union A, union B, and no union, if no one choice receives a clear majority, a runoff election is necessary. Under the original board rules, if the nonunion vote constituted a minority of the total votes, the board ruled that a majority wanted union representation and then conducted a runoff election between the two unions. Under present rules, the two highest contenders in the first vote are placed on the final ballot. The final results can be no union, even if a majority voted for *some* union in the initial election. Although this change lessens the likelihood of union representation, it may well be a fairer measure of employees' desires.

In Section 301(a), either employer or union may sue the other for breach of contract. In the opinion of many experts, disputes under the contract are most effectively settled by accommodation or arbitration, not by lawsuit. For a long time, this section of Taft–Hartley had little effect. Except for a temporary furor resulting in waiver clauses when the law was first passed, companies and unions notably disregarded the provision. Subsequently, however, this provision has had major effects on the scope and enforceability of arbitration clauses, as demonstrated by *Lincoln Mills** and subsequent cases.

Administration and Enforcement

The organization and techniques for enforcing the Taft–Hartley Act are similar to those described earlier for the Wagner Act but with several modifications. Although the National Labor Relations Board retains the basic responsibility for administering the act, the president, the attorney general, the courts, and special boards may become involved in special cases, particularly in public emergency strikes. Taft–Hartley, unlike the Wagner Act, also requires that courtroom rules of evidence apply in hearings on unfair labor practices, and thereby makes administration of the law somewhat more cumbersome. Taken as a whole, the shortcomings of the law—and labor considers them major—lie mainly in enforcement. The complaint is that protective action by the board is so slow and the nonpunitive remedies are of so little deterrent effect on employers that millions of workers are effactually denied protection of the law. An award of back pay following long infringement can nevertheless be substantial, and a potential deterrent. For example, in late 1979 the NLRB awarded employees of American Cyanamid Company $12 million in back pay, on grounds that many had been illegally locked out by the company for some three years. That amount

---

*353 U.S. 448 (1957) 1 L.ed. 2d 972.

was net of other earnings for those employees, the company's potential total liability being over $25 million.

MISCELLANEOUS EFFECTS OF LEGISLATION

Political Action

The Federal Corrupt Practices Act is amended by Section 313 of the Taft–Hartley Act, which makes it illegal for "any labor organization to make a political contribution or expenditure in connection with any [federal] election," primary, convention, or caucus, or for any candidate or party to accept such a contribution. The same rule also applies to corporations.

Union papers often use their pages to endorse or denounce candidates and issues, and other court cases have ruled it not illegal for a person on union salary to engage in political work. In 1957, however, the Supreme Court upheld an indictment of the Auto Workers for financing an electioneering television broadcast out of general union funds. The majority opinion did not deal with the constitutional issue; the minority considered the law a violation of freedom of speech.[33] It has also been ruled that, under a union shop, if a member requests it, the union can be required to refund that fraction of his dues that would be spent for political activity.

As described in a later chapter, the more overt types of political activity are carried on by COPE, the AFL–CIO's Committee on Political Education. Since COPE collects its funds independently of union dues and assessments and does not engage in collective bargaining, it is not a labor organization under the act and is not subject to it. Certainly, the law has not thus far taken unions out of politics and will not do so unless amended or more strictly enforced.

Considering that the law prohibits any "expenditure in connection with" an election, it is difficult to imagine how such a law could be enforceable or constitutional if interpreted literally. But so long as the law is loosely enforced, as it has been, the underlying controversy is avoided. Some proponents argue that, since the law covers corporations as well as unions, it should be strongly enforced against unions to bring the two sides into balance. This argument is difficult to accept, since the presumed equality between corporations and unions is only superficial. The Federal Election Campaign Act of 1971 and amendments of 1974 and 1976, as well as the Federal Elections Commission ruling in Sun-PAK,[34] have all allowed for a proliferation of corporate PACs (political action committees). From 1974 to 1980, the number of corporate PACs increased by 1200 percent, and in the 1980 elections, business groups outspent labor groups by almost three to one. While unions are the only significant channel through which workers can make their political influence felt, employers have numberless avenues for doing so.

Theoretically, workers hold the ace in the game of politics, with many more votes. To date, this advantage has been more potential than real. Though union political activity has not been seriously hampered by Taft–Hartley, workers have shown little inclination to vote in disciplined fashion along lines recommended by their leaders. Readiness to follow their leaders in strictly union matters has not thus far carried over into the broad political field. Whether this fact represents resistance by workers to political guidance from unions or greater exposure to employer opinion in the mass media is hard to tell.

Jurisdictional Disputes

In the broadest sense, a jurisdictional dispute may take either of two forms. One is a contest between two unions as to which shall represent a group of workers, and the other is a contest over the assignment of particular work to one union or the other. The latter is the more common meaning, but a strike or boycott in support of either type is an unfair labor practice under Sections 8(b)(4)(C) and (D) of Taft–Hartley. An employer is particularly helpless in the face of a jurisdictional strike, since to satisfy one union automatically antagonizes the other. Jurisdictional fights involving work assignments are most common in craft unions, particularly in the building trades, where repeated changes in methods and materials make the boundary lines between crafts necessarily impermanent. By contrast, disputes over representation rights occur in both craft and industrial unions. The raiding of other unions by the Teamsters and the Mineworkers represents some of the more aggravated cases.

Legal restrictions on jurisdictional disputes certainly seem justified. Perhaps the law has indirectly encouraged a workable result, having led the parties to develop techniques for settling such disputes within the labor movement by discussion, conference, and, if necessary, binding arbitration. Although jurisdictional strikes have by no means been eliminated, they have declined to a small fraction of their earlier level.

Supervisors

Under the Taft–Hartley Act, supervisors are permitted to join unions, but they are not protected in their right to do so. That is, they may legally be disciplined by their companies if they join. The result has been the almost complete disappearance of supervisors' unions, which had become fairly numerous in the late 1930s and early 1940s.

Other Provisions of the Law

Section 305 of the Taft–Hartley Act makes it unlawful for employees of the government or of wholly owned government corporations to strike, and anyone who does so is to be discharged forthwith. The employee forfeits civil service status and is ineligible for reemployment by the government for three years. And for private employees under a union shop, the union may not charge initiation fees "which the board finds excessive or discriminatory."

Sections 206 through 210 of the Taft–Hartley Act allow for government intervention in certain "national emergency disputes." It was believed by the framers of the act that certain strikes would be so serious in their effect that every attempt should be made to avoid them. This part of the act provides the president with the power to intervene in disputes which "imperil the national health or safety." These procedures will be more fully examined in a later chapter on conflict.

THE LABOR-MANAGEMENT REPORTING
AND DISCLOSURE ACT, 1959

On September 14, 1959, President Eisenhower signed the Landrum−Griffin Act into law. As noted, it consists of two major parts. One is a series of amendments to the Taft−Hartley Act, already discussed. The other is the Labor-Management Reporting and Disclosure Act (LMRDA), which we will now examine. Compared to the Kennedy−Ives, Kennedy−Ervin, Shelley, and Elliot bills, which had also been introduced to cover much the same ground, the Labor-Management Reporting and Disclosure Act was considered a relatively "tough" labor law.

The law grew out of the recommendations of the McClellan Committee for eliminating the corruption and racketeering found in certain unions. Through the newspapers and television, employers put on an intense, dramatic, and highly coordinated campaign, which left the general impression that the sins of some parts of some five or six unions characterized all unions. By contrast, the union campaign was conflicting and disorganized. Some unions opposed any legislation and some wanted limited legislation, whereas the former CIO unions supported fairly strict legislation. There was also disagreement as to whether the law should cover the Railway Labor Act unions, which it does.

Provisions of LMRDA

We will first describe the law's provisions and then its rationale and effects. The law contains seven titles. Title I is entitled "Bill of Rights". It asserts that "every member of a labor organization shall have equal rights and privileges within such organization" to nominate, vote, attend meetings, and participate. These equal rights are subject, however, to "reasonable rules," such as those denying apprentices or emeritus members full rights. Title I asserts freedom of speech and criticism about any candidate or policy, again subject to "reasonable rules" about responsibility to the organization and to its legal and contractual obligations. Dues, initiation fees, and assessments may not be raised except by secret ballot or other processes that assure membership consent. No labor organization is to limit the right of any member to institute any action in a court or administrative agency, provided that he may first be required to exhaust reasonable procedures (not to exceed four months) within the union before he may sue it, and provided that he or she does not accept employer help. Except for nonpayment of dues, a member may not be fined, suspended, expelled, or otherwise disciplined until after a full and fair hearing, preceded by written charges and time to prepare his defense. The union must also, on request, provide a copy of any union-management agreement to any member affected by the agreement. Any provisions of a union constitution or bylaws in conflict with Title I are void.

Title II requires a variety of reports from each union, to be filed with the secretary of labor. Each union must also make the same information available to any member who asks and must permit examination of union records for verification. Each officer is to report any investments or transactions that (briefly interpreted) involve a conflict of interest.

Title II also requires employers to report (1) direct or indirect payments or loans to unions or to their officers or employees, (2) expenditures whose purpose is to interfere with or coerce employees in their rights to organize or bargain collectively, or expenditures to spy on such activities, and (3) any payments to either employees or outside groups (such as a labor relations consultant) to get them to try to influence employees for or against unionization and collective bargaining. Persons who receive payments for such purpose must also so report.

Title III deals with trusteeships. Any trusteeship established by a union over any subordinate body, as by a national union over a local, must be reported within thirty days, and semiannually thereafter, with details and reasons. The purpose of the trusteeship must be legal, such as to remedy financial malpractice or undemocratic procedures, and it must be handled in accordance with the union's constitution and bylaws.

Title IV provides that elections in unions must be fair, open, honest, reasonably frequent, and secret. Complaints of improprieties may be filed with the secretary if the plaintiff has unsuccessfully sought satisfaction within the union. The secretary can take reasonable remedial action, including a government supervised reelection. Challenged elections are presumed valid pending final decision. Officers of local unions must stand for election not less than every three years, those of intermediate bodies every four years, and those of national unions every five years.

Title V deals with two "Safeguards for Labor Organizations." The first makes it an affirmative obligation of persons handling union funds to use them solely for the welfare of the members, subject to recovery suits by members and fine or imprisonment for improper conversion. The second prohibits any member of the Communist Party from being an officer or nonroutine employee (such as organizer) during or within five years after termination of membership. This section was declared unconstitutional in 1964 as violating the First and Fifth amendments.[35] For five years after conviction or end of imprisonment, it denies the same posts to persons convicted of most major felonies or "conspiracy to commit any such crimes."

Title VI covers "Miscellaneous Provisions," while Title VII consists of the Taft–Hartley amendments, which need not be elaborated here.

Enforcement Provisions

Title I, the Bill of Rights, is enforceable solely through suit by an aggrieved party in a federal district court. Willful false reporting or failure to report under Title II is subject both to criminal penalties and to civil suit by the secretary of labor. Title III on trusteeships is subject to the same criminal and civil actions. Violation of election provisions of Title IV is subject only to remedial action by the secretary, though he has recourse to the courts to assure compliance. Violation of the safeguards of Title V is subject only to criminal penalties.

Implementing LMRDA

Promptly after passage of the law, the secretary of labor created a Bureau of Labor-Management Reports (BLMR) within the department to handle the law. The bureau has concentrated heavily on educational efforts designed for prevention rather than prosecution. The many detailed reports required by the law, coupled with possible criminal penalties, brought fears of harassment. The bureau, while insistent, has been fair and helpful, and these fears have apparently been calmed. In 1963 the bureau was joined with another to become the Office of Labor-Management and Welfare-Pension Reports (LMWPR), which now administers both the Reporting and Disclosure Act and the Welfare and Pension Plans Disclosure Act. The passage of the ERISA in 1974 caused the creation of another agency, the Office of Labor-Management Standards Enforcement (LMSE), to administer the LMRDA.

The total number of complaints of violations reaching the secretary has remained relatively constant since the first year of the act. Numerous changes have been made in union constitutions and bylaws at various levels to conform to the provisions of the act. Many violations have been purely technical; yet others have been substantive.

Complaints about elections have been more frequent in large unions. However, complaints about the absence of the secret ballot are most common in small ones. Presumably, these reflect a practice common to small organizations of voting an unopposed slate by acclamation. If nominating procedures have been proper, LMSE will no longer enforce the secret-ballot requirement in an unopposed election unless write-ins are allowed.[36] The secretary has filed about twenty-five actions per year for violations of election requirements from the beginning of the act.[37] Over 150 subpoenas per year were issued to obtain documents or testimony of witnesses.[38] Meanwhile, unions were charged with a total of 115 violations of the reporting requirements. Prior to 1969, only nine employer and twelve labor relations consultant violations were filed, and there have been none since 1969.[39] Approximately sixty individuals per year have been charged or indicted on criminal charges under the act, mostly for embezzlement, theft, or conversion. Over 75 percent have been convicted.[40] There were other criminal violations involving false reporting. Before reaching any conclusions about criminal behavior in unions, the reader is cautioned to examine these statistics in light of the fact that there are over 50,000 separate union organizations in the United States.

Some Broader Observations About LMRDA

Certainly, honest elections are to be desired, and the law has almost unquestionably raised the quota of them. There was, however, little apparent reason to believe that prior to the act, election malfeasance occurred in more than a tiny fraction of cases. Aside from elections, trusteeships, and the disqualifications for officeholding, the provisions of the law are predominantly procedural, not substantive. The election and trustee provisions have almost certainly had desirable results, of a sort that most leaders approve. Although it has assisted the removal of some undesirables, the restrictions on officeholding are more doubtful.

To pursue the question of procedure versus substance: The law, for example, does not require a strike vote. It merely requires that the union's rules about strike votes, *if there are any*, be properly implemented. The law does not prevent a union from disciplining a member for revealing union business if the rules provide that he or she may not reveal it. It merely says that the member may not be disciplined for such action without a fair hearing. Both the Department of Labor and the courts have been reluctant to decide that a union's rules are not "reasonable," and "reasonableness" is all the law requires. This arrangement reflects the basic philosophy of the LMRDA, which is to assure union members certain democratic processes and to leave the rest to them.

There is some suspicion of a two-way lack of realism in the law. One was an exaggerated belief that most union members were held in the iron grip of union bosses. The other was that, if given the weapons of democracy, they would throw the rascals out and live happily ever after under grass-roots control. The overall view seems to be that the LMRDA has had a conspicuous influence in a tiny number of cases and moderate influence in a moderate number of cases, but that its total impact has been and will remain peripheral. The student of organizations is apt to conclude that, no matter what the laws, unions are likely to remain essentially bureaucratic rather than either dictatorial or democratic—and not because they are unions but because they are large organizations. All this does not mean that wishes of members will be systematically ignored. It means that members' wishes will be implemented by the bureaucrat's keeping his ear to the ground, not by being voted out of office, although the latter also occurs from time to time. If the bureaucrat's ear is good, the process can be effective, presumably supplemented from time to time by the "engineering of consent."

THE 1974 HEALTH CARE AMENDMENTS

On August 25, 1974, the Taft–Hartley Act was extended to private, nonprofit hospitals, whose employees may now utilize all the representational and collective bargaining mechanisms available to other private sector workers since 1935. Because of the nature of health care, special dispute-settlement procedures were provided, in which the Congress sought to balance the rights of employees to bargain against the right of the public to uninterrupted health care. The special status thus accorded to health care institutions seemingly calls for special treatment by the board and the courts.

Because employees in nonprofit hospitals had previously been denied Taft–Hartley protection, hospital administrators had no legal obligation to recognize or deal with any employee organization. The extent to which the law fosters collective bargaining is seen in some subsequent results. The 1974 through 1981 Annual Reports of the National Labor Relations Board reveal that nearly 5000 representation elections have been held in the health services industry since the passage of the amendments.[41] Although private, nonprofit hospitals are only a part of the industry, the significant escalation of organizational activity in this sector can be attributed to the amendments. Unions won 55 percent of the elections in the health sector, as compared to an overall win rate of under 47 percent during this period. It is clear that the continued growth of the health industry coupled with the relative success of union organizational efforts in this sector will provide for interesting union-management relations in the future. We can conclude that the amendments have already had, and will continue to have, a significant effect on the industry.

THE CURRENT SITUATION: ATTEMPTS
AT LABOR LAW REFORM

Bills to amend the National Labor Relations Act and to alter the jurisdiction, procedures, or remedies of the NLRB have been introduced at every session of Congress for
more than forty years. Only a few received serious attention, and even fewer reached
the floor. As a result, the NLRA has been amended only a few times since it was passed
in 1935.

In July 1977, President Carter proposed a bill, "The Labor Law Reform Bill of
1977" (LLRB). It was strongly supported by organized labor and strongly opposed by
business. "Its stated purpose is to reduce delays in scheduling representation elections
and deciding unfair labor practice cases and to strengthen remedies for violations of the
NLRA's substantive provisions."[42] The bill passed the House largely intact in late
1977 but was blocked by a Senate filibuster in 1978. In 1985 the bill was generally
considered to be dead, though the concerns with which it dealt are not.

NATURE OF THE CONTROVERSY

The large corporations have adapted comfortably, if reluctantly, to the institution of
unionism, particularly high-technology, capital-intensive corporations to which labor
is a small fraction of cost. But smaller employers, particularly in the South and
Southwest, bitterly oppose unionization and—in an atmosphere that supports right-to-
work laws, which place limitations on union security clauses—have thus far widely
succeeded in avoiding it. On the other side, unions have firmly organized and live in
reciprocal accommodation with the large corporations, albeit with some special problems about multinationals. But they report feeling utterly stymied by the many
relatively small (compared to GM, GE, Exxon, and so on) employers who allegedly
violate the law so blatantly that their employees are afraid to assert their legal rights.
Unions cite the older case of the Kohler Company and the more-recent one of the J.P.
Stevens Company as "proving" that an adamant employer can keep board orders
against it tied up in legal processes for ten to fifteen years, meanwhile continuing to
accrue additional violations. During the whole time the company may engage in
practices repeatedly reaffirmed by the board and the courts to be gross and willfull
violations. Meanwhile, the company may continue to receive what the union con-
strues as subsidies in the form of large government contracts, gained in part because
their violations of the law enabled them to underbid unionized competitors. In the
end, claims labor, the costs of the remedial-only awards are so small that the company
has in effect been rewarded by the government for its violations. Only stiff punitive
damages, claim the unions, can prevent such employer behavior. On the general
principle that "justice delayed is justice denied," the unions claim that unless the
board also speeds its processing of cases, millions of workers will continue to receive no
meaningful protection from the law.

The outside observer may see the Chamber of Commerce and the National

Association of Manufacturers, which spearheaded the opposition to LLRB, as hewing close to the line that the NAM first adopted around the turn of the century. For the most part they simply do not like unions, and if the government sees fit to protect them, then the protection should at least be kept to a minimum. Increasingly candid reference to their goal as a "union-free environment" leaves the position of some firms unmistakably clear. This stance differs sharply from that of many large corporations, which see no realistic likelihood of ever being nonunion again, and presumably do not want to reenact the costly warfare of the thirties. Therefore, they "actively" stay out of the fight, as they did with the many right-to-work votes of the 1950s. Nevertheless, one analysis suggests that they were closer to getting into this fight than has been their custom.[43]

Perhaps because they prefer not to state their opposition to unions flatly, the small employers focused their objections to the LLRB mainly on such grounds as that the law would change the remedial philosophy of the law, possibly deter the exercise of employers' legitimate right to oppose unions, reduce employer motivation toward voluntary compliance, and perhaps slow or leave unaffected the pace of processing complaints. The employer opposition also expressed concern for the plight of unorganized workers, who might have less protection under the LLRB from coercion by a union or who might be subject to union arguments without a reasonable opportunity to hear counterarguments by management.

Both sides presumably understand clearly that the intent of the LLRB, as well as its probable effect, is to increase the power of labor relative to that of smaller employers by making it much less easy for the employers to avoid unionization. Whatever their rationalizations, the positions of the parties toward the bill follow logically.

NOTES

[1]A substantial portion of English–American law consists of rulings made by judges in particular cases rather than laws passed by legislatures. Any judicial decision tends to establish a precedent and, in fact, normally constitutes the law with respect to the situation it covers until a contrary decision is rendered in a similar case or until legislation creates a new rule. The body of precedent thus established constitutes the *common law*, or judge-made law, and judges tend to follow these precedents until there arises some compelling reason to deviate. When a new kind of a case arises, covered by neither legislation nor closely related precedent, the judge will normally seek guidance either in a parallel relationship from a different field or in some general principle of law.

The conspiracy doctrine, as applied to unions in the United States, was actually borrowed from prior English decisions of a similar nature. It reflected the economic belief that wages were set by the market and that a union could only distort proper relationships. It also, of course, protected merchants and manufacturers, who were the dominant class of the time. Furthermore, American judges were aware that property owners could vote while propertyless workers could not.

[2]*People* v. *Trequier et al.*, 1 Wheeler's Criminal Cases, 1942 (1823).

[3]*People* v. *Fisher et al.*, 14 Wendell 10 (1835).

[4]"The Philadelphia Cordwainers, 1806," in John R. Commons et al. (eds.), *A Documentary History of American Industrial Society* (Cleveland: Arthur H. Clark, 1910), vol. 3, p. 183.

[5]*Ibid.*

[6]*Ibid.*, p. 233.

[7]Edwin E. Witte, "Early American Labor Cases," *Yale Law Journal*, 1926, vol. 5, p. 827.

[8]The terminology regarding these stages is not fully standardized. Hence, the reader may not find them called by the same names elsewhere.

[9]208 U.S. 274 (1908); 52 L.ed. 488.

[10]Edward Berman, *Labor and the Sherman Act* (New York: Harper, 1930), p. 4.

[11]*In re Debs*, 64 Fed. 724, 726 (1893). Emphasis added.

[12]The intent of the Congress in passing sections 6 and 20 of the Clayton Act may not have been as clear as the language of its paragraphs seems to indicate. In this connection, the reader should consult Gregory, *Labor and the Law* (New York: Norton, 1946), pp. 158–74, especially p. 170ff. It is difficult to believe, however, that the majority in Congress were aware of the subtleties that, Gregory reports, some crafty lawyers had used in wording the law. If they were not, the Congress as a whole must have intended the law to be taken at its face value. See also *Duplex* v. *Deering*, 254 U.S. 443 (1921), 65 L.ed. 349.

[13]257 U.S. 184, 209 (1921).

[14]245 U.S. 229 (1917).

[15]The student will find a somewhat more extended though still brief description of the surrounding circumstances of this decision in Fred Witney, *Government and Collective Bargaining* (Philadelphia: Lippincott, 1951), pp. 57–60.

[16]*Bedford Cut Stone Co. v. Journeymen Stonecutters' Association of North America*, 274 U.S. 37 (1927).

[17]*Adair* v. *United States*, 208 U.S. 161 (1908).

[18]*National War Labor Board*, Bulletin 287 (Washington, D.C.: U.S. Department of Labor, Bureau of Labor Statistics), p. 32.

[19]The basic validation of the law arose in the case of *Senn* v. *Tile Layers' Protective Union* under Wisconsin's "Little Norris–LaGuardia Act." See Gregory, *op cit.*, pp. 338f.

[20]*Complete Labor Equipment*, Vol. 3, *State Labor Laws* (New York: Prentice–Hall).

[21]295 U.S. 495 (1935).

[22]49 Stat. 449 (1935).

[23]In the case of *NLRB* v. *Jones & Laughlin Steel Corporation*, 301 U.S. 1 (1937), by a five-to-four decision.

[24]*Livingston Shirt Corporation*, 33 LRRM 1156.

[25]*NLRB* v. *Gissel Packing Co.*, 395 U.S. 575 (1969).

[26]*Bausch & Lomb, Inc.* v. *NLRB*, 451 F. 2d 873 (2d Cir., 1971).

[27]*Blaser Tool & Mold Co.*, 196 NLRB 374 (1972).

[28]*NLRB* v. *Savair Mfg. Co.*, 414 U.S. 270 (1973).

[29]*Associated Milk Producers*, NLRB, 1978, 99 LRRM 1212.

[30]*Shopping Kart Food Market*, 228 NLRB 190 (1977).

[31]*General Knit of California*, 239 NLRB 101 (1978).

[32]*Midland National Life Insurance Co.*, 263 NLRB 24 (1982).

[33]32 U.S. 567.

[34]Edwin Epstein, "An Irony of Electoral Reform," *Regulation*, Vol. 3, No. 3 (Washington, D.C.: American Enterprise Institute, May-June 1979).

[35]*Brown* v. *U.S.*, CA9, June 19, 1964, 56 LRRM 2593.

[36]*Monthly Labor Review*, January 1965, pp. 3–7.

[37]*Compliance, Enforcement and Reporting in 1976 and 1977*, U.S. Department of Labor, Labor-Management Services Administration (LMSA), p. 3.

[38]*Compliance, Enforcement and Reporting in 1975*, U.S. Department of Labor, Labor-Management Services Administration (LMSA), p. 18.

[39]*Compliance, Enforcement and Reporting in 1976 and 1977*, U.S. Department of Labor, Labor-Management Services Administration (LMSA), p. 3.

[40]*Ibid.*, p. 3.

[41]Thirty-Ninth through Forty-Sixth Annual Reports of the National Labor Relations Board, Table 16.

[42]*Proposed Amendments to the National Labor Relations Act* (Washington, D.C.: American Enterprise Institute for Public Policy Research, 1978), p. 1.

[43]Thomas Ferguson and Joel Rogers, "Labor Law Reform and Its Enemies," *The Nation*, January 6–13, 1979.

SOME EFFECTS OF THE LAW:

on Bargaining Power, Union and Management Security, Attitudes Toward Bargaining, Union Organization of New Members

The preceding chapter traced the history of the law regarding unions and unionization in the United States. For nearly 130 years the government was strongly supportive of employers in their efforts to fight and prevent unions, though strong unionization did develop and became accepted during that period in a number of industries. Under the Wagner Act the government was distinctly prounion, strongly protecting the rights of workers to organize and of unions to use numerous tactics against employers, while sharply restricting the rights of employers to fight back. Taft—Hartley restored some balance to this relationship after 1947, at least roughly countering restrictions on employers with parallel restrictions on unions.

We have already drawn the distinction between "procollective bargaining" and "prounion" positions, and this chapter continues to operate within that distinction. As to the former, we recognize that Taft—Hartley continues the Wagner Act's position of encouraging collective bargaining and also continues its protections in the forms of employee rights to organize and employer obligations to bargain.

This chapter first addresses the issue of the impact of the law upon employee's rights to organize. Does the law itself, the interpretations of the law by the NLRB, and the actions of the agency affect the outcomes of representation and decertification elections?

The present chapter also focuses on the question of bargaining power, as follows. Assuming that collective bargaining has been established and contin-ues under protection of the law, within that context does Taft–Hartley tend to push bargaining power toward employers or toward unions? Because of the complexities and partially contradictory aspects of the law and its enforcement some answers are clearer for some sections of the law taken one at a time than they are for the overall effect. We also ask whether or not the law seems to foster "mature" bargaining. The more technical discussions of bargaining power in later chapters will be necessary for understanding the details of negotiations. A general intuitive understanding of power will suffice for the present chapter. We must also recognize that in many respects the interpretations and applica-tions of the law by the board and the courts do much more to determine the actual impact of the law than does the wording of the law itself.

The law makes no attempt to define power or bargaining power or to regulate it as such. But it does regulate many things that nevertheless affect bargaining power.

Like the Wagner Act, Taft–Hartley, in its "Findings and Policies" section, recognizes "the inequality of bargaining power between employees who do not possess full freedom of association or actual liberty of contract, and employers who are organized in the corporate or other forms of ownership association." The "Findings" make clear that a major purpose of the act is (or was) to help rectify this discrepancy in bargaining power

> by encouraging the practice and procedure of collective bargaining and by protect-ing the exercise by workers of full freedom of association, self organization, and designation of representatives of their own choosing, for the purpose of negotiat-ing the terms and conditions of their employment.

In this statement the law follows the more realistic judges of the past, such as Holmes and Cardozo, who cut through legalisms and frankly recognized that the paraphernalia of organized labor dealt with bargaining power and had to be appraised in that light.

THE REGULATION OF CERTIFICATION CAMPAIGNS

Organizational campaigns by unions are a substantial, and continuing, effort. Over 7500 certification elections and nearly 1000 decertification elections are conducted each year by the NLRB[1] (see Table 3–1). The role of the NLRB in these many election campaigns is to provide an atmosphere in which the employees' rights to organize are delicately balanced against the employer's rights of free speech. The NLRB has promulgated, through many case decisions, a set of rules that guide employer and union behavior during election campaigns.

The NLRB, as was stated in Chapter 2, has at times regulated the content of

TABLE 3.1

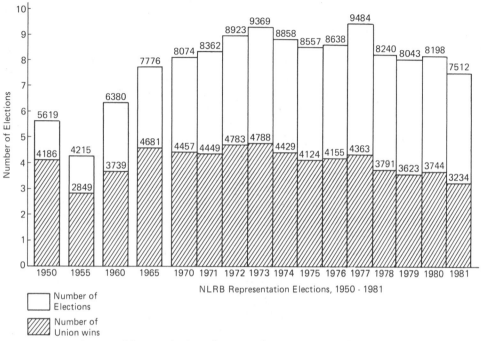

NLRB Representation Elections, 1950 - 1981

☐ Number of Elections

▨ Number of Union wins

SOURCE: *Annual Reports* of the Natonal Labor Relations Board.

employer and union communications. This has been done to prevent deliberate lies and misstatements of fact from influencing employee choice in union representation. Although under current policy the board does not engage in such regulation, in the past it has set aside the results of elections based upon both employer and union lies.[2] The question at issue here is whether the current NLRB tilt toward free speech (even the freedom to lie) has a tendency to favor employers or unions in their efforts to influence employee choice. It is not a simple question, and no statistical evidence yet exists to support a conclusion on either side. The policy certainly produces one undesirable outcome. Campaigns in which distortions and outright lies can occur are probably less likely to focus on the issue of whether employees wish to participate in collective bargaining.

Section 8(c) of Taft–Hartley permits dissemination of information during campaigns, as long as no threat of reprisal or promise of benefit is made. Cases involving threats of reprisal have primarily rested upon issues of direct economic consequence to employees, such as a statement by an employer that the workplace would be closed in the event of a union victory in the election.[3] Likewise, the promise of benefit has been construed as direct economic benefit. Employers' promises are distinguished from unions' promises, since the employer, assuming a union loss, has the unilateral power to change conditions, whereas the union has the power only to negotiate changes.

An area of substantive rule is the issue of relative equality of access to employees for the purpose of campaigning. "Captive-audience" speeches, where employees are involuntarily assembled on work time for the purpose of employer speeches, are commonly held during certification campaigns. They are a protected form of employer free speech, provided that the union has alternative means to communicate with employees.[4] The NLRB has consistently refused to allow unions any sort of "equal time" to respond to employer captive-audience speeches.[5] They have, however, adopted rules to allow unions full opportunity to contact all eligible voters by means of a names-and-addresses policy.[6] Within seven days following the scheduling of an election by the Board, the employer must furnish to the board the names and addresses of all employees eligible to vote in the certification election. This list is then turned over to the union leadership for their use. This policy was adopted as a counterbalance to the captive-audience policies already in place, thus granting unions a potentially effective organizing tool.

A final area worth mentioning is that of the indirect effect of NLRB procedure. A union organizing campaign is a fragile mixture of fact and emotion, and the timing of various events can affect the outcome of any campaign. Recent research by Roomkin and Block has shown that the longer the period of time between the petition for election and the actual election, the more likely the union will lose.[7] Since challenges to proposed bargaining units and other legal matters often result in exactly the kind of delay that Roomkin and Block test, it has been suggested that NLRB procedure itself may not be entirely neutral. Although it would be difficult to alter the procedures enough to make a difference in election outcomes, that was in part the intent of the 1977 Labor Law Reform debate. It is unlikely, however, that change will come about in the near future.

THE REGULATION OF BARGAINING TACTICS

Legal Status of the Primary Strike and Lockout

Section 7 of the National Labor Relations Act states: "Employees shall have the right to self organization . . . to bargain collectively and . . . to engage in other concerted activities for the purpose of collective bargaining or other mutual aid or protection." Section 13 adds, "Nothing in this Act, except as specifically provided herein, shall be construed so as either to interfere with or impede or diminish in any way the right to strike, or to affect the limitations or qualifications on that right." Together these two sections provide the fundamental protection of the right to strike. In fact, despite the restrictions and injunctions of earlier years, the right to strike against one's own employer to extract concessions has generally been recognized ever since the demise of the conspiracy doctrine. The right of the employer to operate during an economic strike if he can, either with nonstriking regular employees, or with newly hired replacements, has also been recognized.

The direct primary strike, peacefully conducted, is lawful under the common-law doctrine that "the deliberate commission of harm on another is unlawful unless it is justified,"[8] justification normally consisting of the pursuit of self-interest. The methods of pursuing self-interest are normally legal unless specifically outlawed, as are physical violence, coercion, or business monopoly.

The Norris—LaGuardia Act protects most strikes from federal injunction. In the *Apex Hosiery Company* case in 1940, the federal Supreme Court ruled that interruption of the flow of commodities in interstate commerce by a strike did not violate the Sherman Act, even though the union's purpose was to eliminate nonunion competition in the production of hosiery. The ruling reversed the *Coronado* case of 1925, in which the Supreme Court ruled that an organizing strike in the Coronado mines violated the Sherman Act because it intended to interrupt the flow of coal from these mines until they were organized. Together, the common-law doctrine of the pursuit of self-interest, Norris—LaGuardia, the *Apex* case, and Taft—Hartley legalize the primary strike.

The Law and Bargaining Power in Primary Strikes

If we are to diagnose the law's effect on bargaining power, we must first establish some reference point from which deviations can be measured. Any such standard is necessarily subjective and arbitrary, since bargaining power is a matter of degree and there is no such thing as a "correct" amount on either side. While remaining aware of the arbitrary judgment involved, for want of something better we will establish the effective primary strike as a "standard" power relationship in collective bargaining. An effective primary strike is one in which essentially all productive activities cease in an organization because essentially all employees stay away from work and are not replaced. "Essentially all" allows for certain emergency operations to continue. Such a strike contains no inherent power bias toward either side, and is accepted by the law.

With respect to the partial strike, however, the board and the courts have vacillated between giving the bargaining advantage to the employer and being neutral. Through a slowdown, the union can exert pressure on the employer at little or no cost to employees. And by operating during a strike, the employer may bring costs to the strikers without commensurate loss to himself. The freedom of employers to turn a strike into a partial strike by recruiting strikebreakers has consistently been fully protected, though it significantly reduces the bargaining power of the strikers. Legal and societal protection should be differentiated here. The attitudes of potential replacements and the attitude of the community toward a strike exert much influence on whether the legal right can actually be exercised.

But the freedom of employees to conduct a partial strike in the form of a slowdown was for some years ruled unlawful by both the courts and the board.[9] (The decisions by both authorities were made on grounds other than bargaining power.) The board had also ruled as unlawful an off-again-on-again partial strike. We are speaking, of course, of strikes after a contract has expired; those under a contract would normally be subject to the no-strike clause.

So long as these partial tactics were legal for employers but illegal for unions, bargaining power was shifted toward employers. Since 1960, however, slowdowns, extended rest periods, and "quickie" strikes have all been ruled to be economic pressures that are not in themselves evidence of bad faith in bargaining.[10] There are, of course, certain "stipulations" in interpreting this decision. The Supreme Court continues to counsel caution in condemning as unprotected stoppages that are "part and parcel" of proper collective bargaining. Yet even if "quickie" stoppages are treated as protected activity, the employer is not wholly deprived of recourse to self-help. In a 1972 case, the NLRB held that a single unannounced walkout would be presumed protected. However, the employees would be subject to discharge

> when and only when the evidence demonstrates that the stoppage is part of a plan or pattern of intermittent action which is inconsistent with a genuine strike or genuine performance by employees of the work normally expected of them by the employer.[11]

On this aspect of bargaining power, the law may now be regarded as formally neutral.

The Law and Lockouts

In a simple sense, the lockout is the management counterpart of the strike. But its actual use is less than simple. Generally speaking, a lockout used to destroy or prevent unionization is proscribed as an unfair labor practice. On the other hand, equality of treatment would suggest that lockouts used solely for bargaining power be allowed under the same circumstances as are strikes.

Apparently, the board now clearly allows nonstruck firms in an employer association to lock out employees so as to avoid whipsawing by a union that strikes only one firm (or a few firms) in the association. The employer may also attempt to operate with temporary replacements, just as he might in a strike. But for some reason, the board for years was not consistent about single employers who wanted to close down in a fashion tantamount to an employer-initiated strike. Whenever the employer is not allowed to lock out following a contract expiration, bargaining power is shifted to the union. Even though mutuality of pressure remains, as in a strike, such a rule permits the union to terminate the relationship at moments disadvantageous to the employer, but prevents the employer from terminating at moments disadvantageous to the union. Now, however, it is essentially correct to say simply that an employer may lock out in defense of a legitimate bargaining position, and that no bias inheres in this position of the board.

The Law and Secondary Boycotts

A boycott is a concerted withholding of some relationship with another party, typically a refusal to conduct certain kinds of business with an employer. It is *primary* if conducted directly at the party with whom one has a dispute. It is *secondary* if it is conducted indirectly at the primary party through action against some other "third" party. Boycotts that withhold labor are usually called strikes instead of boycotts; hence "boycott" normally refers only to the withholding of purchases or sales of commodities. The law on the subject does not use the terms *boycott* or *secondary boycott* or define those terms. The law merely describes certain kinds of behaviors that are regulated. Hence all references to boycotts below represent the simplifying language of this volume, not the language of the law itself.

Boycotts have a long and stormy legal history. It is substantially accurate to say that prior to the New Deal all boycotts by labor were illegal, except those conducted against their own employer. The reverse attitude reached its zenith in the *Hutcheson* case in 1941. There the carpenters organized an effective primary and secondary boycott of Anheuser-Busch beer after the company had assigned the installation of new equipment to machinists instead of carpenters. Although the boycott substantially injured the company, the Supreme Court ruled that the union could not be sued (or, by implication, enjoined), in a wording that sought to harmonize the Sherman, Clayton, and Norris–LaGuardia Acts. If given this legal protection of a secondary boycott in support of the jurisdictional dispute, then seemingly any nonviolent tactic was allowable. Employers felt helpless and infuriated. The *Hutcheson* decision also took unions out from under the Sherman Act in the way apparently intended by the Clayton Act.

Instead of seeking a middle ground between the pre-New Deal and the *Hutcheson* position, the Taft–Hartley Act returned by pendulum swing virtually to the former position. In Section 8(b)(4), the act places rather sweeping prohibitions on secondary boycotts by unions under the general justification of protecting nonparticipants, and some sizable loopholes in the prohibition were plugged in the 1959 revisions of the law. The law, however, places no restrictions on actions by employers which have the effect of a secondary pressure, whether the actions are directed against unions or against other employers.

With boycotts, as with free speech, it would seem that a law cannot rationally regulate instruments of power without regard to the strength of the instruments and to the conditions and results of their use. The Taft–Hartley Act shows no such regard in its rather sweeping prohibition of secondary boycotts. The general logic of the prohibition is to protect a neutral employer from becoming enmeshed in a dispute to which he is not a party, an objective certainly valid in itself. But the wide scope of the prohibition raises questions. For example, is it always and necessarily preferable to protect the secondary employer from a boycott, no matter how small the harm to him from allowing the boycott or how large the harm to the union from prohibiting it? Here it seems important to inquire when and where secondary boycotts are employed and for what purposes, what effect they have on bargaining power, and how much harm they do to secondary employers.

It would seem reasonable that if the purpose of a boycott is illegal or clearly undesirable, public policy should prohibit it. If its purpose, for example, is to force employees out of one union and into another, if it seeks monopoly by forcing an employer to handle or to cease handling certain goods, if it tries to control the employer's selection of a bargaining representative or to influence the employer's political activities or to support racketeering, there would seem to be little doubt about the reasonableness of outlawing the boycott.

However, if the boycott is used in support of (or instead of) an organizing strike in the primary plant by employees who want a union, the answer is much more difficult. Employees might lack the power either to unionize or to bargain in certain small firms where the workers are easily replaced and where the shutting off of supplies or sales through a secondary boycott might be their only source of power. To prohibit secondary boycotts here is to deny collective bargaining, and it is an open question as to which it is preferable to protect the secondary employer (as present law does) or the ability to organize. The relative harm done to each group would seem to have a bearing on the question.

A still thornier question arises when a union exerts pressure on an employer to recognize a union that an "uncoerced majority" of his own employees does not want. If the pressure is successful, the employees are forced into a union against their will—a seemingly undesirable act. But if the rest of the industry is organized, the nonunion firm may be forcing down wages in the other firms. The question then arises as to whether it is desirable that the law prohibit the only device by which union firms can protect their own wage standards. The answer is not easy, though present law clearly sides with the nonunion firm and against both employees and employers in the unionized firms. The issue sometimes merges with that of appropriate bargaining units, a complication we will not go into here.

The extent to which the secondary employer is hurt by a boycott and whether he is in fact an "innocent bystander" can be examined simultaneously in a hypothetical case. We will do this in the framework of a secondary boycott instituted in support of a primary economic strike, with no questions of representation or illegal objectives intertwined. Suppose that employer A operates a bakery and that B is a dealer in bakery supplies who provides A's ingredients. A's bakers strike for higher wages. If the strike is effective, A stops baking. It is then a matter of indifference to both the strikers and to A whether B can ship ingredients to the bakery, since none will be processed. No secondary pressures on B will be attempted; they would not shut down the bakery more completely and are therefore superfluous.

But suppose also that A decides to operate during the strike and does so with reasonable success. That is, the primary strike is ineffective. The strikers now post pickets at B's plant to induce B or B's employees to stop shipments to A. If B does stop, on either his or her own or the employees' initiative, meanwhile continuing to ship to all other customers, two important facts should be observed: (1) the loss of business by B is no greater than if the strike against A were effective, in which case B would also lose A's patronage during the strike, and (2) the pressure on A is no greater than that of an effective primary strike. If the effective strike is the standard power relationship, then a secondary boycott in support of an ineffective primary strike shifts bargaining power toward the standard, not away from it. At the same time, it brings no greater hardship to the secondary employer than an effective primary strike would bring. Unless it is desirable for other reasons to shift bargaining power in favor of employers, the prohibition of secondary boycotts in such cases does not seem justified. It would seem reasonable, however, to enjoin the boycott of B if it sought to stop B's deliveries to any customer other than A.

As for the alleged "neutral" status of secondary employers, the courts and legislators have never faced up to the fact that in a less than fully effective strike, suppliers and customers of primary employers cannot help taking sides. For example, if B stops shipping to A or permits his or her employees to do so, B helps the strikers at A to convert an ineffective strike into an effective one. But if B continues shipments, he or she helps A to break the strike, whether this is the intention or not. Since B must choose, he faces possible retaliatory action from the side he does not favor. The present law influences this choice consistently in support of the employer. For the law protects B from retaliatory action by the bakers' union, but not by the bakery—say, through cancellation of future patronage. In fact, B has no effective legal protection, even if all bakeries together deliberately boycott B out of business for siding with the union. To outlaw the secondary pressure by unions in support of an ineffective primary strike is always to support the employer at exactly the time when employee bargaining power is below standard. It might seem that the law should either permit certain secondary boycotts in support of legal primary strikes or justify its proemployer bias.

Another instance in which the secondary employer may not be innocent occurs when the employer accepts "farmed-out work" from a struck primary employer—work which, but for the strike, would have been done by the primary employer. The law views this as an "ally" relationship, and the rulings seem to be clear that the union may picket the secondary employer under these circumstances. The employees of the secondary employer, however, are apparently not free from disciplinary action by their own employer if they refuse to handle "struck work," under Section 8(b)(4)(B) —though the legal status of this situation is not entirely clear.

Several other aspects of the law seem to push bargaining power toward employers. In addition to being made unfair labor practices, subject to cease-and-desist orders, like employer unfair labor practices, secondary pressures by unions are also made unlawful acts, subject to suit in federal court. According to Section 303, if the employer can prove loss, he "shall recover the damages by him sustained and the cost of the suit." The suit may be entered "without respect to the amount in controversy," which means that the court may not dismiss the suit as inconsequential.

In addition, if an employer files a charge that a union is engaged in a secondary boycott or certain other unfair practices and if the board "has reasonable cause to believe such charge is true," it *must* apply for a temporary restraining order pending resolution of the dispute before the board. Further, by Section 10(1), the preliminary investigation of such cases "shall be made forthwith and given priority over all other cases." This means that if an office of the board is processing unfair-labor practice charges against an employer and the employer then files secondary boycott charges against the union, the office must give priority attention to the charges against the union. The 1959 amendments mitigated this situation slightly, but not significantly, and these provisions have real effect in determining the priorities.

Under Section 303 damage suits for unfair labor practices work in one direction only. The employer can legally recover any damage, however slight, caused by union unfair practices. But, except under unusual circumstances, if unfair practices by the employer destroy the union or deplete its treasury, the employer can only be required to cease and desist, without penalty. He is liable only for back wages to employees injured by an unfair labor practice.

Picketing

Picketing is an adjunct to other organizational or bargaining tactics rather than a tactic in itself. This is not intended to suggest that picketing is unimportant. It is true that under a full-fledged accommodation approach, the employer accepts the strike as a two-edged pressure and stops production until a settlement is reached. But employers who use conflict or power bargaining continue to operate, and the strike may be ineffective without a convincing picket line. A picket line can use the persuasive method of making the "scab" feel like a peculiarly low creature or the coercive methods of making such a person fear for his safety or of physically preventing his passage. Seasoned unionists will stay off the job until ordered back by their leaders; for them a picket line is not essential. It is the raw union member and the nonmember who may be converted from a strikebreaker to a striker by a healthy-looking picket line. Thus, the picket line becomes important and so does the law concerning it where (1) the employer tries to avoid the mutual nature of the strike pressure, and (2) the union is weak and undisciplined.

Thus, picketing resembles the secondary boycott in its relation to power. It is unimportant where the union is strong but may be crucial where the union is weak. Hence restriction of picketing, as of secondary tactics, hurts weak unions without affecting strong ones—in bona fide primary strikes. Hence, too, the restriction of picketing (other than to prevent acts illegal in themselves) probably pushes bargaining power away from "standard" rather than toward it.

The Legality of Picketing

Picketing in general was illegal before the Norris–LaGuardia Act, based on the assumption that "peaceful" and "picketing" are contradictory terms. It was both illegal and enjoinable by federal courts under the *American Steel Foundries* decision of 1921 except under great restriction, such as a single picket.[12] Both peaceful and violent picketing had been outlawed by the courts in several industrial states. Peaceful picketing was lawful in some other industrial states but was circumscribed as to number of persons allowed and minimum distances between them. Even in states that declared picketing to be legal, however, federal courts could often take jurisdiction and enjoin it. During the 1920s, a number of liberal judges nevertheless protected peaceful picketing by refusing to enjoin it if the pickets could show that they were defending their self-interest.

Under Norris–LaGuardia, picketing was clearly legalized unless violent, reaching the high point of protection in the *Hutcheson* case cited above. In the early 1930s several states passed laws patterned on Norris–LaGuardia, to provide the same protection in state courts. In 1940 the federal Supreme Court, in *Thornhill v. Alabama*,[13] virtually identified peaceful picketing with protected speech under the First Amendment.

Subsequent decisions and legislation have moved far from the *Thornhill* position. Between 1938 and 1947 numerous state and local antipicketing laws were enacted, outlawing anything from outright violence (which was always illegal) to the mere presence (in Texas) of more than one picket at each plant entrance, with no pickets closer together than 50 feet.

Under Taft–Hartley and most state laws, peaceful picketing in support of a primary strike is legal. "Mass" picketing is not permitted by the board, even if no violence is involved, "mass" being interpreted to mean the blocking of passage. However, relying on the police powers of the state, the courts have often enjoined picketing involving more than just a few people, even when no violence, threats, or actual blockage is involved. The reason given is that large numbers of pickets create a presumption of danger. How many pickets constitute mass picketing has not been defined for this purpose and seems to depend on the judge in the individual case.

The Taft—Hartley Act gives strikebreakers and strikers equal protection through the combination of Section 7 and 8(b)(1). The former guarantees not only the right to organize and strike but also "the right to refrain from any and all such activities," and the latter section makes it unfair for a union "to restrain or coerce employees in the exercise of the rights guaranteed in Section 7." Unions that engage in illegal picketing may be enjoined, and individuals who participate may be fired without reinstatement rights. It is no defense that the unlawful picketing is a self-defense against an egregious employer's unfair practice. As a practical matter, however, it is often difficult for an employer to sustain a discharge based on improper conduct on a picket line and even harder to hold a union responsible for it as an entity. In consequence employers may not actually receive the level of protection against improper picketing that the provisions of the law seem to call for.

A portion of Section 8(b) of Taft—Hartley provides that it is not unlawful for a person to refuse to cross a picket line of an employer other than his own, in the event of a strike there which has been ratified or approved by the properly certified union.

Like other tactics, picketing can influence the existence or security of a union as well as its bargaining power. In the hotel, restaurant, and other industries composed of many small firms, it is common to find a nonunion establishment picketed by workers from other firms in an effort to unionize it. The practice is known as "stranger picketing." It has been clearly outlawed in some states but clearly accepted in others if the pickets can show an economic interest in the outcome. More recently, certain courts have acknowledged that even unions which lack members among the employees of the picketed company are not necessarily "strangers" who have no economic interest in organization there.[14]

Under Section 8(b)(7) of Taft—Hartley, it is unfair for a union to picket for a recognitional object for more than 30 days without petitioning for a representation election.

Unions sometimes try to enlist consumer boycotts in their support, particularly against employers who refuse to recognize or bargain with the union. Conspicuous examples in recent years have been the boycott campaigns against Farrah slacks., J. P. Stevens products, and grapes or lettuce from nonunion farms in California. In such cases it is essentially correct to say that any such boycott is legal so long as it does not involve picketing. To illustrate, a newspaper campaign might be organized urging consumers to stop *all* purchases from a department store or chain in the hope of inducing it to stop handling a particular, single boycotted item. However, if pickets walk around the store, their signs may refer only to the single item being boycotted. In that case the boycott is technically primary, even though it is carried on at the premises of a merchandiser several steps removed from the source, since it is directed at the primary producer. If effective at that level its result is substantially the same as would be achieved by an effective strike against the primary producer, in which case the store would have none of the struck merchandise to sell.

Picketing in Secondary Boycotts

Except in the period between the *Hutcheson* and *Thornhill* decisions in 1940 and the passage of the Taft–Hartley Act and related state laws in 1946 and 1947, picketing in connection with secondary boycotts has almost always been illegal and enjoinable. The Taft–Hartley Act, in Section 8(b)(4), makes it an unfair labor practice for a union to engage in a secondary boycott or to "induce or encourage" one, and the general position of the law has been that if a secondary boycott is itself illegal, so is picketing in support of it.

All in all, the law and decisions about picketing are confused. One possible approach is that peaceful picketing is a form of communication, which should be scrupulously protected under the First Amendment. The other is that in a society conditioned not to cross picket lines, picketing is more than speech; it is a form of coercion, even if peaceful and unfrightening. At the time of the *Thornhill* decision, one could peacefully picket almost anything in which an interest could be demonstrated. Now one must give great attention to intent, actual effects, and public policy toward the thing picketed, so that a person had better not throw up a picket line without a lawyer by his or her side—or, better still, the judge. As with secondary boycotts themselves, we have gone almost full circle from great restriction of secondary boycott picketing to no restriction (if peaceful) and back to great restriction. Judges on the bench differ widely from one another, but the currently recognized precedent is the Supreme Court's 1976 decision in *Hudgens v NLRB*. Succinctly, the Court held that where striking employees picketed a retail establishment (the primary employer) located within the mall of a large shopping center (the secondary employer), the rights and liabilities must be determined exclusively under the criteria of the NLRA and without reference to the First Amendment. Thus, the pickets had no constitutional right to be immune from threats of prosecution for trespass, since such constitutional protection was available against private landowners only when their property assumed all of the attributes of a municipality.[15]

An interesting complication concerns *common situs picketing*. To clarify by example, suppose that the primary employer is a supplier of ready-mixed concrete whose plant is struck and being picketed. The question then arises whether picket lines may also be placed at a distant construction site where the company's concrete is being poured, the construction site being the location of a secondary employer who has no dispute with his own employees. The standards have been established in the *Moore Dry Dock* case, and can be summarized by saying that such picketing is allowed if it is clearly confined to the times and locations of the primary employer's operations and is clearly identified as being directed against the primary, not the secondary, employer.

The common situs issue was raised in Congress in 1975 when a bill was passed allowing unions to picket all the contractors at a construction site when there was a dispute with just one of the contractors. President Ford, after earlier indicating that he would sign the legislation, vetoed the bill, thus ending prospects for legislative clarification of this issue.

MEDIATION AND ARBITRATION

Several details of the mutual requirement to bargain in good faith are spelled out in Section 8(d) of Taft—Hartley. Either side wishing to terminate or modify the contract must give sixty days' advance notice. If agreement is not reached after thirty days, the party desiring termination or modification must so inform the Federal Mediation and Conciliation Service and any comparable state agency. The existing contract remains in effect until the end of the sixty days or the end of the contract, whichever is later, with no strikes or lockouts permitted. Any employee who strikes during the period loses his or her status as an employee—that is, the employer may discharge or otherwise discipline the employee, who has no recourse under the law.

This section has several effects upon bargaining power. First, the Conciliation Service may take the initiative in trying to enter a dispute, whether requested by the parties or not. As a result, there have been occasional complaints that the service gets into disputes it should stay out of. Either one or both of two results may occur: (1) a significant realignment of bargaining power may follow entrance of the mediator, or (2) the parties may not bother to bargain seriously until the mediator arrives. If the mediator stays out until invited by both sides, neither unwanted result is likely.

The above conditions reflect difficulties of mediation, not criticisms of the law or the service, which has done an excellent job and has remained acceptable to both unions and managements through many years in a difficult role. The service was created originally in 1913, as part of the Department of Labor. To remove the possible taint of bias, the Taft—Hartley Act made it an independent agency. The mediation provision of the Taft—Hartley Act contains no inherent or consistent bias in either direction.

In the *Lincoln Mills* case, however,[16] the courts threw the government's weight far in the opposite direction by widening automatically all arbitration clauses to a degree many unions may not have achieved in negotiations. When supplemented by the *Warrior and Gulf* case,[17] the Court ruled that a dispute on any topic is to be construed as arbitrable unless the contract explicitly indicates that it is not.

The final provision of this section is roughly evenhanded in the way it has been applied. The law makes it improper for a strike or lockout to occur during the notification period. The strike is made unlawful. And although a lockout is not specifically made unlawful, the board has at times awarded employees wages lost on account of such a lockout.

EFFECTS OF THE LAW ON UNION AND MANAGEMENT SECURITY

Union and management security are defined in later chapters in terms of each organization's ability to perform its institutional function, and absence of undue interference in that performance. Current legislation has certain effects on the security of unions and managements, and the purpose of this section is to explore those effects briefly.

The Assurance of Union Existence

The most fundamental conditions of union security are that the union exist and be accorded representation rights. By making raiding more difficult, the law makes a union's continued existence more secure, and by requiring the employer to recognize and bargain in good faith with a certified union, the law establishes representation rights. Those two points were discussed earlier. Furthermore, short-term security of the union's representation status is assured in the provision that a new representation election may not be held sooner than one year after a valid election has been conducted (Section 9(c)(3)), and a union's status is also assured for the life of a current contract, which normally runs for at least a year and which might run for three years or more. Regarding the more direct union security devices of compulsory membership or dues payment, current legislation ranges from permissive to prohibitive. At no time in our history has membership or dues payment been required by law.

The union shop is permitted under Section 8(a)(3) of Taft–Hartley. A new employee must be allowed thirty days after hiring, or after the effective date of the contract, to join the union, with a special provision of only seven days in the construction industry. Because union security, or even any collective bargaining at all, is difficult on any basis except a closed shop in such short-term employment as that involving stevedores, construction workers, and some musicians (see Chapter 15 on union security), subterfuge forms of the closed shop have developed there with the knowledge and cooperation of employers. If such places have union hiring halls, these are "required" by law to handle union and nonunion people alike. But seniority clauses are widespread. Since they give preferred position to longer-term employees, who are nearly always union members, the practical effect is that of a closed shop.

Under Section 8(a)(3) of the original (1947) Taft–Hartley Act, a union shop could be negotiated with an employer only if approved by a majority of those bargaining unit members voting in an NLRB election held under Section 9(e). Even an overwhelmingly affirmative vote did not automatically provide the union shop, however. It merely allowed the union to negotiate on the subject. Under the original Section 9(e)(2), following a petition of 30 percent or more of the bargaining unit a union shop deauthorization election could be held, and if a majority voted against the union shop it was mandatorily eliminated, under Section 8(a)(3). The 1951 amendments to Taft–Hartley eliminated the union shop authorization elections but retained deauthorization elections. According to Dworkin and Extejt, the operation of this clause has been neglected by researchers for almost twenty years.[18] From 1953 through 1978, the board has received 3,403 deauthorization petitions and conducted 1,629 elections, with roughly 60 percent of the polls resulting in deauthorization.[19] A vote resulting in deauthorization is much more common in small bargaining units than in large ones. Though such elections have been occurring with increasing frequency in recent years, they still constitute a small fraction of all NLRB elections.[20] As with decertification elections on the question of representation, the overall impact remains small.[21]

In 1956, 25 states had laws regulating union security in some way. By 1965 the number had dropped to 19, and only one state (Louisiana in 1976) has since adopted a right-to-work law. Right-to-work laws remain a subject of considerable interest in many states, however. In recent years, referendums and legislative initiatives on the question have appeared in many states. Most of these state laws prohibit all types of formal union security.

The prohibition of closed and union shops is logical if it is concluded that compulsory membership or dues payment improperly violates individual freedom. However, most of these state laws also prohibit maintenance of membership. Since maintenance of membership only holds an employee to a commitment that he has individually and voluntarily assumed and from which he can periodically escape, it is difficult to avoid a conclusion that the laws are intended more to weaken unions than to protect the rights of workers.

It is often felt that such laws restrict only unions. As we shall see in our later chapter on management security, some managements feel that union security is of value to them as well. Hence, a prohibition of union security can constitute a restriction on management as well as on unions. The main drive for such legislation has traditionally come more from small- and medium-sized firms rather than from the industrial giants.

Whatever the merits of the laws themselves, the "right-to-work" label misrepresents the issue. To start with one extreme, it requires considerable stretching of terms to imagine that anyone's "right to work" is curtailed by maintenance of membership. At the other extreme, one's freedom to hold a given job *is* infringed, if not destroyed, if union membership is both required for a job *and* is unavailable.

It is clear that a closed shop, or even a union shop, taken in conjunction with a closed union interferes with the right to work, and that the combination is presumably contrary to sound policy. The distortion arises when the right to work is presumed to be denied by a union shop when union membership is readily available and dues are reasonable. Then the employer is free to hire any worker, and any worker is free to hold any job. The only "right" that is infringed is the worker's "right not to pay dues"—a phrase that hardly has the propaganda appeal of "right to work."

The obvious effect of such laws is to reduce or eliminate a union's formal assurance that its membership and dues income will remain steady at high levels of bargaining unit membership. The possible consequences of such continued insecurity are traced in Chapter 15. However, when we attempt to trace the actual effects of right-to-work laws, as contrasted to the "logical" effects, they do not show up at all clearly. Lumsden and Petersen review both the earlier statistical studies and the stated impressions of employers, employees, and unions, and report a general conclusion that the laws apparently have little effect.[22]

Our general conclusion, therefore, with regard to states which have adopted right-to-work laws is that they hold significantly different attitudes regarding unionization than do the remainder of the states but that no evidence exists of any significant impact on unionization of the actual right-to-work laws themselves.[23]

The authors conclude, "Thus, we align ourselves with prevailing suspicions that the battle for right-to-work laws is one of symbol rather than substance."[24] Since attitudes toward unionization do seem to have some effect, we face the chicken-egg question whether in certain states the attitudes produce the legislation or the legislation reinforces the attitudes. There is probably some of both.

State vs. Federal Laws on Union Security

Section 14(b) of Taft–Hartley establishes a relationship between state and federal law that creates a bias against union security. Any type of union security that is permissible under federal law, such as union shop and maintenance of membership, is nevertheless illegal if prohibited by state law, since the latter is then controlling. At the same time, any type of union security that is permissible under state law, as is the closed shop in many states, is nevertheless illegal if prohibited by federal law, which is then controlling. Although the mid-sixties and the immediate post-Nixon years produced congresses presumed to be strongly sympathetic to organized labor, all attempts to repeal Section 14(b) failed, and none seems likely to succeed in the near future.

Dues checkoff is allowed by Taft–Hartley and by most states if individually authorized in writing by each employee. Section 9 of Taft–Hartley also provides some union security in that representation rights of a union cannot be challenged for a year after a union is certified. At the same time, the law weakens union security by providing for decertification elections on petition of 30 percent or more of employees, or on petition of an employer faced with demands for recognition from two or more unions. Under Section 302, employers are prohibited from financing dissident employees in seeking decertification elections or in suing the union, though the employer might do so indirectly through an "outside" organization, such as a right-to-work committee. The "economic-strikers" provision can also reduce the security of a union, particularly one whose status is precarious to begin with.

The Union's Ability to Function

In normal operation, the union has two major responsibilities: one to formulate and effectuate bargaining strategy, and the other to uphold its side of the contract. Chapter 5 will describe how the discharge of both responsibilities requires some degree of internal discipline. Although a union can exert some discipline through social pressure, its most compelling formal disciplinary power would lie in making membership a condition for holding the job. In all states that prohibit union security, unions thus lack this type of formal disciplinary power. Although the Taft–Hartley Act permits union security, it destroys the power that normally goes with it. Even under a union shop, according to Section 8(a)(3), an employer may not discharge a worker for nonmembership unless he fails "to tender the periodic dues and the initiation fees uniformly required as a condition of acquiring or retaining membership." Nor, according to Section 8(b)(2), may a union try to make an employer do so. By these provisions, union security was reduced to nothing more than assured income. For some years union discipline was so effectively destroyed under the law and board rulings that a union could not even enforce a fine for a deliberate attempt to break the union, much less for nonattendance at union meetings.[25] In this respect, Taft—Hartley seemed to seek two contradictory things—to make unions more "responsible" by making them suable for unfair practices and breach of contract while simultaneously denying them the instruments through which responsibility is achieved and effectuated. However, since 1970 the board has held that there is no violation of the act for a union to fine members for crossing a picket line or for strikebreaking, and the courts may enforce such a fine if the individual does not pay it. These provisions now substantially enhance the disciplinary powers of a union over its members.

Under Sections 301 and 303 of Taft—Hartley, both sides are explicitly suable for breach of contract. Both sides have shown sense enough not to use this provision. A typical management position is:

> When a husband and wife get to the point where they have to settle their differences in court, the marriage is already dead. When we get to the point where we carry on our industrial relations in the courts, we'd better look for a new industrial-relations manager.

Management Security

Neither state nor federal laws deal with management security as such, though some affect it indirectly. Management representatives have for years wanted the law to state which issues are bargainable and which are not. Such a law would greatly limit management security if its list of bargainable issues were very broad. Managers who advocate such a list, of course, want it to be narrow, in which case management security would, in effect, be provided by law, or at least be greatly enhanced. A "management clause" is neither required nor restricted by law, though it is assisted insofar as it has been ruled to be a mandatory issue about which a union may not refuse to bargain. State laws help in one way to enforce management clauses, in that they make unenforceable any arbitration decision that exceeds the arbitrator's authority and that thereby invades decision areas reserved to management.

The ultimate degree of management security lies in keeping unions from forming. By outlawing the major devices by which companies destroy unions, the law also limits this highest degree of security. Although the law otherwise does not formally interfere with management security, the board has added steadily to the list of issues over which management may not refuse to bargain. In consequence, many managements feel their security has been substantially invaded by board rulings.

In one sense, it is probably impossible to protect management security significantly by law—as by stating that some issues are nonbargainable. Such a list naively assumes that bargaining issues are separable; in fact, the law would prove unenforceable whenever an employer found it more to his advantage to bargain on an issue than not to bargain.

In short, the law has very definite effects on the kinds of provisions that can be used to establish union security—but a rather uncertain effect on management security.

ATTITUDES TOWARD BARGAINING

The general atmosphere in which a relation takes place may be one of the most important determinants of its outcomes. Hence, the effect of the law on the general attitudes of the parties toward collective bargaining may be one of its most important effects. To assist evaluation of that effect, and because the distinctions are useful elsewhere in this volume, we will devote the present section to a way of categorizing attitudes toward bargaining. For convenience, we will base our characterizations on a shortened and modified version of the attitudes described by Selekman.[26] The present shortened version of Selekman's "Varieties" includes conflict, power, accommodation, and cooperative relationships, as follows. Although the general tone of a relationship is necessarily the consequence of behaviors on both sides of the bargaining fence, the main determinant is the attitudes of management, which constitutes the force in charge of the organization. The four types sometimes represent four successive stages of development of a given relationship. But a given relation can start at any stage, shift in either direction, or stay in a given pattern indefinitely.

Conflict

In the conflict relation, management strongly opposes the very existence of the union. It does more or less everything it can to prevent or eliminate unionization, and need not necessarily confine its opposition to legal means. The company may subtly or blatantly blacklist or discriminate against union sympathizers, spurn union representatives, hire labor spies, engage professional strikebreakers, threaten to move the plant, utilize massive and some scurrilous publicity against the union, seek to mass public and/or private police at union demonstrations, and organize "citizens' committees" of local residents and businesses to oppose unionism.

If a union manages to organize a plant despite such efforts, management will deal with it because it must. But it will make no secret of its desire to eliminate the union. The employer will refuse any union security, try to discredit the union, and confine bargaining to the narrowest possible scope. If there is a strike, management will try to break the union as well as the strike. This attitude, widespread during the early days of unionism, was exemplified during the fifties by the Kohler company of Kohler, Wisconsin, and in the seventies by the J. P. Stevens textile firm. The conflict attitude is more characteristic of small- and medium-sized firms than of large ones and is more widely found in the Sunbelt and the Midwest than elsewhere in the nation.

Power Bargaining

The difference between conflict and power bargaining is roughly that between cold war and peaceful but competitive coexistence. As in conflict relations, management also sees the union as an undesirable obstruction between itself and its employees. But it concludes that the union is there to stay, and ceases open attempts to destroy it. Under pressure, management might even grant union security, and possibly recognize that security for the union is not necessarily bad for management. It will nevertheless view union security as an unjustified boost to union power and an invasion of the individual's "right to work." Management will try to keep the union weak and defensive. Both sides will push their bargaining power to the full, sometimes shortsightedly. Although the company would not hire professional strikebreakers, it will try to operate during a strike, possibly hire new employees to replace strikers, and appeal to union members over the heads of their leaders to return to work or accept a management-proposed contract.

The union may build large strike funds, engender antagonism toward the employer among members and the public, enlist political pressures, or strike in blatant disregard of the public interest. Typically, each side attempts to demonstrate that it cannot be "pushed around," while personal relations are likely to be strident and caustic, and may impugn the motives or integrity of the opponent.

Accommodation Bargaining

In the accommodation approach, management does not necessarily *like* unions or assist in their expansion. But it accepts them as legitimate and seeks the best possible relationship with them. Perhaps most important, management views the union as a *channel* for dealing with employees rather than an *obstacle* to employee relations, and tries to figure how best to use that channel. Management will not bypass the union leaders by going over their heads in appeals to the membership, any more than management would expect the union to try to go over the heads of company executives to the stockholders. For example, job evaluation, merit rating, recreation plans, and other actions that directly affect employees will be handled through the union.

In the accommodation spirit, management does not belittle the union, and might even refer to its cooperative attitude as a factor in the company's success, recognizing that high loyalty to the union often goes hand in hand with high loyalty to the company.[27] Both sides accept that a tough relationship in which both throw their weight around benefits neither in the long run and can be psychologically and financially costly indeed.

Two points in the accommodation approach are notable. First, neither side challenges the essential security of the other. The second affects the conduct of a strike. Instead of viewing the strike as a rough struggle in which the union tries to keep bargaining unit employees out of the plant while the company tries to get them in, management simply closes down production when a strike is called. Not only does this approach eliminate confrontations on the picket line, it in fact reduces the role of picketing to information only. It also tacitly acknowledges that the union is the source of authority from which employees receive their instructions about bargaining strategies, and does not seek to abrogate any of that authority to management any more than it expects supervisors to take their instructions about the strike from the union. In similar spirit the union will seek to prevent the strike from working undue hardship, as when the Steelworkers bank and tend furnaces during a strike to keep their expensive linings from cracking or transportation workers keep materials flowing to hospitals or other crucial locations. In accommodation, the parties do not eliminate warfare or particularly shift advantage within it. But they do limit its scope and reduce it casualties.

Cooperation and Summary of Attitudes

The cooperative approach brings the union and its members directly into the process of improving productivity and morale. It is more than a simple suggestion system. On the part of the union, it requires recognition that both sides can benefit from superior production and a willingness to utilize the knowledge that workers acquire about a job because they are closer to it than anyone else. On the part of management, it requires abandoning the attitude that workers "are not paid to think" and an unqualified commitment that improvements initiated by workers will not lead to layoffs or paycuts for anyone. For most of this volume, we will be concerned with the power and the accommodation approaches. Cooperation in the sense described here is relatively rare, and the conflict approach is perhaps more accurately referred to as collective fighting than as collective bargaining. At the same time, unions and managements do engage in many activities that are cooperative in the broad sense of the term. Joint efforts to improve the quality of working life, including job enrichment, may not only make life on the job more satisfying for employees. They may also improve productivity and morale substantially in the long run. Joint safety efforts certainly can simultaneously protect workers and reduce costs to employers, and they are widespread. Many fringe benefits are complex, like health and retirement benefits. These are often worked out through a joint effort to find the best solution rather than through a contest of power. It is not impossible that in due time there might be joint efforts to study the environmental impact of certain production products or processes, though it would seem that the public might need representation as a third party in any such venture. Whether American unions will ever move seriously toward codetermination, the European practice of having unions represented directly in the corporate board of directors, is yet to be seen, and is discussed in more detail in Chapter 15.

DOES THE LAW FOSTER "MATURE" BARGAINING?

As expressed in present legislation, what type of bargaining relationship does public policy tend to foster: conflict, power, accommodation, or cooperation? Because of the complexity of the law, any brief answer will oversimplify. Nevertheless, there are respects in which both the federal and the state laws seem mildly oriented toward conflict and power bargaining rather than toward accommodation or cooperation. For example, the law furthers the conflict and power relation by discouraging mutual acceptance of the strike pressure. On the employer side the law assists employers who seek to avoid the mutual pressure of the strike, in that the law limits the number of peaceful pickets, gives as much protection to strikebreakers as to strikers, and protects employers against secondary pressures if they attempt to break a strike. On the union side the law provides very wide immunity to consumer boycotts against employers, no matter how remotely they may be connected to the dispute in question. On both sides the law protects the kinds of partial strikes that seek to impose a cost on the opponent without having to endure some cost for oneself. This is not to suggest that the law or board should rule differently in these situations, but merely to identify the probable consequences of protecting certain kinds of activities.

In fact, by giving protection to the rights of strikebreakers during a bona fide primary contract strike the law may endorse an anomaly, which has received scant attention. Section 9(a) clearly states that the representative selected by the majority of the employees shall be the *exclusive* representative of all employees in the bargaining unit for purposes of collective bargaining. Now, if, following a contract expiration, an employer operates during a contract strike and some members of the bargaining unit continue to work, those employees are then working on terms negotiated individually between themselves and the employer, which terms have conspicuously *not* been accepted by their collective representative, the union. In addition, striker replacements may be hired during the strike and be paid rates specifically rejected by the union, though not rates that have not been offered to the union by the employer. Certainly the union is not the exclusive representative of replacements and is not really their representative at all. Thus the law requires employees in a bargaining unit to conform to terms agreed to by the union so long as a contract is in effect, while simultaneously guaranteeing their right not to conform between contracts. The anomaly is that whenever a contract has terminated and is not yet renewed the law allows the exclusive representation status of the union to lapse at the precise moment the union is engaging in the central function for which it is legally designated as exclusive representative—namely, collective bargaining. After the bargaining is finished and a new contract is signed, the exclusive representative status is restored.

In the 1980s, trends developed that are indicative of the great state of flux of the U.S. industrial relations system. On one hand, more and more employers chose to fight unions with every weapon available to them, even including the bankruptcy laws.[28] Thus if we looked at only those situations, we might conclude that collective bargaining is becoming more conflict-centered. On the other hand, a significant amount of union-employer cooperation began in other sectors of the economy. Likewise, if we looked at only those cases, we might conclude that there is a trend toward accommodation and cooperation. The fact that these two trends occurred at the same time only underscores the statement at the beginning of this section: Because of the complexity of the law no simple answer describes the effect of our public policy.

SUMMARY

The total legislation concerning union-management relations is too complex to permit easy summary. Instead, we will take a bird's-eye view of the conditions in which collective bargaining lives and has grown.

Mostly through the courts, the law actively helped to restrain unions and their bargaining tactics for nearly 130 years from the Cordwainers case in 1806 until 1932. During the following fifteen years both the existence and the bargaining tactics of unions were strongly protected, at least within the federal jurisdiction. In the first ten of those fifteen years, many unions grew rapidly, in a rough-and-tumble development. Just as unions and managements reached a point where their relationship might have matured, World War II intervened. It made many aspects of labor relations highly abnormal and, through wage stabilization and the disputes machinery of the War Labor Board, took much of the relationship out of the hands of the parties and gave it to the government.

In the immediate postwar period, the Taft—Hartley Act and a series of state laws reversed the direction of labor policy. Taft—Hartley is a detailed, complex, and occasionally contradictory instrument. Almost forty years after its passage, some of its sections have not been tested or clarified in the courts.

Clearly, the Wagner Act needed amending, and employers and the public needed some protection from union abuses that had arisen after 1935. But, taken as a whole, Taft—Hartley was passed in an atmosphere of wanting to "get unions" rather than to create an equitable system of industrial relations. Although there had been serious complaints that unions were both corrupt and too powerful, it was not until twelve years after Taft—Hartley, with the Labor-Management Reporting and Disclosure Act, that the Congress enacted legislation aimed at "cleaning up" unions without necessarily weakening them.

The overall effect of the law leaves somewhat of an ambiguity. The Taft—Hartley additions to Wagner were passed in an aura of complaint about the overweening power of the big unions—the Teamsters, Steelworkers, Auto Workers, Mineworkers, and the like. The law has had little effect on the power of those unions, though their power probably has been diminished by such developments as automation, employer associations, declining employment, and more-sophisticated bargaining by employers, all of which were also possible under the Wagner Act. By contrast, the law has markedly increased the ability of employers to weaken or avoid unions in the areas of the private economy where unions were comparatively small, weak, or absent to begin with— though this effect is probably attributable far more to difficulties of enforcement than to specific provisions of the law, and probably affects the ability of unions to exist far more than it affects their bargaining power if they *do* exist. Meanwhile, unionization has been expanding rapidly among public employees at state and local levels, even in those states that provide no significant protection at all of the right to organize, and that prohibit strikes. Contradictory effects like these make it risky to guess what the effects would have been if different laws had been passed.

Viewed overall, the most civilizing aspect of the law is its provision that questions of representation are to be settled by a secret ballot of the affected employees, not by a fight between workers and employer with no holds barred. By further making any union thus selected the exclusive representative of the employees in the bargaining unit the law has removed an important source of friction in the form of fighting among unions within a bargaining unit. Finally, the requirement of bargaining in good faith is another major civilizing aspect of the law, particularly as the requirement has been broadened over the years. All of these provisions help foster an accommodation rather than a power or conflict relationship. For strict accuracy, however, it should be noted that these are all contributions of the original Wagner Act, not of the Taft—Hartley additions passed in 1947 and later years. Many extensions of application have nevertheless come in the post-Wagner Act period.

NOTES

[1]*Forty-Seventh Annual Report of the National Labor Relations Board*, for the Fiscal Year ended September 30, 1982, Table 11.

[2]*Midland National Life Insurance Co.*, 263 NLRB 24 (1982); *General Knit of California*, 239 NLRB 101 (1978).

[3]*Standard Knitting Mills, Inc.*, 172 NLRB 1122 (1968).

[4]*Livingston Shirt*, 107 NLRB 400 (1953).

[5]Except in some cases when the employer has committed unfair practices. *See Montgomery Ward & Co., Inc.*, 145 NLRB 846 (1964).

[6]*Excelsior Underwear, Inc.*, 156 NLRB 1236 (1966).

[7]Roomkin, Myron and Richard Block, "Case Processing Time and Outcome of Elections: Some Empirical Evidence," *University of Illinois Law Review*, 1 (1981), pp. 75–97.

[8]Charles O. Gregory, *Labor and the Law* (New York: Norton, 1946), p. 108.

[9]25 LRRM 806 and 26 LRRM 1493.

[10]*NLRB v. Insurance Agents' International Union*, 361 U.S. 477.

[11]*Polytech, Inc.* 195 NLRB 695 (1972), 321.

[12]257 U.S. 184 (1921).

[13]310 U.S. 88 (1940).

[14]Robert A. Gorman, *Basic Text on Labor Law: Unionization and Collective Bargaining* (St. Paul, Minn.: West, 1976), p. 220.

[15]"Labor Picketing on Private Property and the Vexation of Logan Valley: The Nixon Court Responds in *Hudgens v. NLRB*," *Capital University Law Review*, Vol. 6, No. 235, 1976; and Robert Gorman, *Basic Text on Labor Law: Unionization and Collective Bargaining* (St. Paul, Minn.: West, 1976).

[16]*Textile Workers v. Lincoln Mills*, 353 U.S. 448.

[17]*United Steelworkers of America v. Warrior and Gulf Navigation Company*, 363 U.S. 574 (1960).

[18]James B. Dworkin and Marian M. Extejt, "The union-shop deauthorization poll: a new look after 20 years," *Monthly Labor Review* (November 1979), pp. 36–40.

[19]*Ibid.*, p. 38.

[20]*Ibid.*, p. 39.

[21]Anderson, John C., Charles A. O'Reilly III, and Gloria Busman, "Union Decertification in the U.S.: 1947–1977," *Industrial Relations*, 19 (Winter 1980), pp. 100–107.

[22]Keith Lumsden and Craig Peterson, "The Effect of Right-to-Work Laws on Unionization in the United States," *Journal of Political Economy* (October 1975), pp. 1237–48.

[23]*Ibid.*, p. 1247.

[24]*Ibid.*, p. 1248.

[25]*Bloomingdales and William P. Ward v. Distributive, Processing, and Office Workers of America (Independent)*, 33 LRRM 1093.

[26]Benjamin H. Selekman, "Varieties of Labor Relations," *Harvard Business Review* (March 1949), pp. 175–99. Descriptions of these attitudes also appear in the Introduction of Benjamin Selekman, Sylvia K. Selekman, and Stephen H. Fuller, *Problems in Labor Relations* (New York: McGraw-Hill, 1950), and subsequent editions.

[27]For studies indicating that loyalties to company *and* union tend to go up and down together, see Ross Stagner, W.E. Chalmers, and Milton Derber, "Guttman-Type Scales for Union and Management Attitudes Toward Each Other," *Journal of Applied Psychology* (October 1958), p. 299.

[28]Many firms, including Continental Air Lines and Wilson Foods, in the early 1980s have used the bankruptcy provision to fundamentally alter their relationships with their unions.

THE INTERSECTION OF DISCRIMINATION LAW WITH THE PROCESS OF COLLECTIVE BARGAINING

4

Racial, ethnic, and sex discrimination have been pervasive in American life throughout the history of our society. Our country found itself divided into Civil War over slavery, and throughout the twentieth century protests over this issue have erupted into sometimes violent clashes. Perhaps no concern today is more central to the eradication of discrimination than the operation of race-blind and sex-blind labor markets. While the national commitment to the end of discrimination has continuously grown throughout this century, only in the past twenty years has our society been willing to commit the efforts and resources of our government to this task. There have been a wide variety of suggestions on how to end labor market discrimination. Of course, many of those efforts intersect with the operation and goals of our collective bargaining system, sometimes in direct conflict. It is to this topic that this chapter is addressed. We do this by first describing several major laws and executive orders designed to combat employment discrimination. According to one authority, "perhaps no other area of law has such overlapping, competing, complementary, conflicting sets of statutory, executive, administrative, judicial, contractual remedies"[1] as does employment discrimination law. We then shift the focus to an attempt to sort out the relationships between the laws and collective bargaining, particularly with respect to hiring, seniority (with its transfer, promotion and layoff implications), and discharge. Finally, we examine some of the procedural dilemmas confronting a discriminatee when a union or collective bargaining agreement is involved.

THE DEVELOPMENT OF LEGAL PROTECTION
AGAINST EMPLOYMENT DISCRIMINATION

Historically, under common law, employers had been relatively free to establish terms and conditions of employment. Likewise, labor unions were insulated from government interference under common law. An employer's complete freedom of action was first limited with the protection of organizational rights of employees by the Railway Labor Act of 1926 (amended in 1934) and the National Labor Relations Act (1935). These laws prohibited employers from discriminating against employees or applicants because of their union or organizational activity. In addition, they permitted unions to become bilaterally involved with the employer in setting terms and conditions of employment. Then, in 1938, the Fair Labor Standards Act restrained employers in their ability to make wage determinations. These statutes were extensively amended during the 1940s and 1950s, yet no restraints were placed on the employer's prerogative to discriminate on the basis of race, sex, religion, or national origin. In 1959, when the Landrum–Griffin Act was passed, restrictions were placed on unions such that their members could no longer be disciplined for exercising free speech. Nothing, however, in the law prohibited unions from engaging in invidious exclusionary policies.

The first concrete efforts to combat discrimination in employment were directed against *racial* discrimination. Their origins were in labor law. During the Wagner Act years, the National Labor Relations Board refused to establish bargaining units on the basis of racial lines and refused, in some instances, to certify unions that engaged in discriminatory practices. One year before the landmark Supreme Court case, *Steele* v. *Louisville and Nashville Railroad Co.*, The NLRB declared (in 1943):

> We entertain grave doubts whether a union which discriminatorily denied membership to employees on the basis of race may nevertheless bargain as the exclusive representative in an appropriate unit composed in part of members of the excluded race.[2]

This logic apparently set the stage for the 1944 *Steele* decision, according to which a labor organization, under Section 9(a) of the Wagner Act, had the duty to provide "fair representation" for all employees in an exclusive bargaining unit.[3]

In 1962 the NLRB held for the first time that a union commits an unfair labor practice when it violates its duty of fair representation (*Miranda Fuel Co.*).[4] This opinion was, however, substantially reversed by the Second Circuit Court of Appeals. Then, in 1964, the board ruled in the *Hughes Tool Company* case that a refusal to process an employee's grievance solely for reasons of race and constituted a violation of the duty of fair representation as derived from the obligation to bargain. This board decision was not controlled by the *Miranda* reversal in the court of appeals but by a Supreme Court opinion in yet another case (*Galveston Maritime Assn.*).[5] In *Galveston*, the High Court did not resolve whether violation of the duty of fair representation was an unfair labor practice. On the basis of this decision, the NLRB assumed that it had the authority to rule on the issue and implied that the employer (in *Hughes*) had an obligation under Section 8(a)(5) of Taft–Hartley not to enter into contracts permitting invidious discrimination.

The water was still muddy. Then, in 1966, in *Local 12, Rubber Workers* v. *NLRB*, the Fifth Circuit Court of Appeals held that "the duty of fair representation was implicit in the exclusive representation requirement of Section 9(a) of the act. . . . as guaranteed in Section 7."[6] As a result of this decision, the board could thereafter invoke unfair labor practice charges against both unions and employers when dealing with racial discrimination cases.

Discrimination on the basis of race, sex, and national origin remained a major national problem, and pressure for relief continued to build in the late 1950s and early 1960s. Despite the attempts by the National Labor Relations Board and the courts to alleviate some forms of blatant racial discrimination, it was clear that no entirely satisfactory solution was to be found there. Even if the NLRB and the courts pursued their present course, the remedies would protect only victims of *racial* discrimination in *unionized* employment situations. It was clear that if broader issues of employment discrimination were to be addressed, the relief would need to impact upon much wider labor markets. In the mid-1960s, Congress finally began to face the issue of employment discrimination by passing the Equal Pay Act of 1963 and Title VII of the Civil Rights Act of 1964. The Equal Pay Act, enacted as an amendment to the Fair Labor Standards Act of 1938 (FLSA), prohibits the payment of unequal wages for equal work because of sex.[7] The act protects all employees covered by the minimum wage and overtime provisions of the FLSA. For their part, unions are prohibited from causing or attempting to cause discrimination in violation of the statute. Several courts have held that unions are not liable for damages under the Equal Pay Act. Defenses (of unequal pay) based on seniority systems have not been extensively litigated. A differential based on the date of hire is justified on a seniority basis as long as it is applied uniformly. Thus, the standard to be applied in determining the equality of jobs under the Equal Pay Act remains the "substantially equal" test: this standard embodies the middle course between a requirement that the jobs in question be exactly alike and a requirement that they merely be comparable.[8] Since 1974, coverage has been extended to employees of government agencies. It should be noted here that "equal pay for equal work" is not the same legal argument as that of "comparable worth." Equal-pay provisions require that two workers performing exactly the same task be paid the same rate of pay. Comparable worth is a concept embodying the notion that equal pay should be provided for workers whose duties and responsibilities are equal even though performed in different occupations. A number of cases are in various stages within the federal court system over this principle at this writing.[9]

In *County of Washington* v. *Gunther*, a closely divided Supreme Court held that the Bennett Amendment to Title VII (which permits an employer to differentiate on the basis of sex in paying wages, "if such differentiation is authorized by the Equal Pay Act") incorporated into Title VII the four specific affirmative defenses contained in the Equal Pay Act. Thus, "substantial equality of jobs is not an element of a prima facie Title VII case for sex-based wage discrimination.[10] The comparable worth lawsuit may be based on any or all of the three general theories of Title VII discrimination: (1) disparate treatment, (2) perpetuating the effect of post discrimination and (3) adverse impact. In practice, there is very little conflict between the Equal Pay Act and the collective bargaining process, since most labor agreements establish and grant wage rates based on the job classification such that women are paid exactly the same rate as men. In addition, the Equal Pay Act exempts pay differences based upon a seniority system, a system which measures earnings by quantity or quality of production, a merit system, or "any other factor than sex."

Title VII of the Civil Rights Act of 1964, which became effective on July 1, 1965, was the product of an epic legislative struggle. It embodies many contradictory and conflicting provisions of both a substantive and procedural nature. As amended in 1972, the statute prohibits employers, unions, employment agencies, and state employment services from discriminating on the basis of race, color, sex, religion, or national origin in virtually all phases of the employment process.[11] It has become the cornerstone of employment discrimination law. The 1972 amendments broadened coverage to encompass any company with fifteen or more employees, as well as government employees who had been excluded under the original act. Title VII established its own administrative agency, the Equal Employment Opportunity Commission (EEOC), but placed severe limitations on its authority since the EEOC could not initiate legal action in the federal courts. The EEOC's lack of enforcement powers during its first seven years limited its role to investigation, persuasion, and conciliation. Since 1972, the agency has had the power to bring civil actions against private parties in federal district court to remedy violations of Title VII. Under Title VII, two developing areas of concern involve the protection of females from toxic substances and sexual harassment.

Almost simultaneously with Title VII came a vigorous new executive order program for government contractors and subcontractors: "affirmative action" was the order of the day. Executive Order (E.O.) 11246, as amended* required all contracts with covered contractors to contain specific agreements regarding nondiscrimination on the basis of race, color, national origin, or sex in employment. Contractors who have more than fifty employees and contracts of over $50,000 must develop affirmative action compliance programs. The heart of Executive Order 11246 is the requirement that an employer take affirmative action to recruit, hire and promote women and minorities whenever those groups are "underutilized" in the employer's work force, without regard to whether the employer has discriminated against those groups in the past. The executive order covers about 300,000 contractors, employing approximately 41,000,000 employees, or about one-third of the national work force. The executive order has collateral consequences for labor organizations and employment agencies. The application of sanctions for noncompliance with E.O. 11246, as by debarment from procuring federal contracts, has been extremely rare.

Passage of the Age Discrimination in Employment Act of 1967 represented an attempt to remedy unemployment and/or arbitrary exclusion from employment opportunities of persons aged forty to sixty-five. In 1978, the upper age limit was raised to seventy, effective January 1, 1979. Two groups of employees, however, are exempt from coverage and may still face compulsory retirement at age sixty-five: persons employed "in a bona fide executive or a high policy making position" entitled to a

---

*Executive Order 11246 was issued in September 1965. Executive Order 11375, issued in October 1967, amended E.O. 11246 to prohibit sex discrimination. E.O. 11246 was again amended in October 1978 by E.O. 12086.

minimum of $44,000 in retirement income and persons "serving under a contract of unlimited tenure . . . at an institution of higher education." Under the 1978 amendments, the latter group was exempt only until July 1, 1982. The act proscribes all forms of employment discrimination against the protected age group, not just hiring preferences. In addition to acts of discrimination, the statute prohibits publishing notices or advertisements indicating a preference, limitation, or discrimination based on age. Under the current regulation, the ADEA is not applicable to age limitations restricting entrance in bona fide apprenticeship programs.

The ADEA is a hybrid of Title VII and the Fair Labor Standards Act (FLSA) of 1938; the prohibitions in the ADEA generally follow Title VII, but the remedies are those of the FLSA.[12] Section 4(f) (2) of the ADEA, as amended in 1978, provides that it is not unlawful to observe the terms of a bona fide seniority system which is not a subterfuge to evade the purposes of the Act, *except* that no such seniority system shall require or permit involuntary retirement of any employee under the age of seventy on the basis of age. Because seniority systems generally tend to favor rather than disfavor older workers, there have been few age cases challenging terminations on the basis of bona fide seniority systems.

Congress passed the Rehabilitation Act of 1973 to protect handicapped individuals from discrimination in employment. According to the act, a handicapped person is defined as any individual with a physical or mental disability which constitutes or results in a substantial handicap to employment and who can reasonably be expected to benefit in terms of employability from vocational rehabilitation services.[13]

Organizations holding any federal contracts in excess of $2,500 with any federal agency must include an obligation to take "affirmative action" to employ and advance qualified handicapped persons. There is no requirement of goals and timetables; affirmative action in the handicapped context is centered largely on self-evaluation, advertisement, and use of vocational rehabilitation programs. The contracting employer must make "reasonable accommodation to the physical and mental limitations of an employee or applicant." Discrimination is permitted only if an employer can show that such accommodation would cause undue hardship in the conduct of his business. Conflict between this act and the collective bargaining process may arise when an employer's attempt to make "reasonable accommodation" for a handicapped employee or prospective employee runs counter to certain provisions (such as seniority and job assignment) of the collective bargaining agreement. When such an agreement prohibits an employer from taking certain steps of accommodation, it has been held to constitute a legitimate business reason.[14]

The Vietnam Era Veterans' Readjustment Assistant Act of 1974 requires companies holding government contracts of $10,000 or more and their subcontractors to take affirmative action to employ and advance both the disabled and nondisabled veterans of the Vietnam era. This encompasses veterans who spent any time on active duty for a period of more than 180 days between August 5, 1964, and May 7, 1975. Goals and timetables under this act were eliminated, as they were under the Rehabilitation Act of 1973. Nothing in the law requires a company to hire anyone but the most qualified applicant(s). Thus, among persons otherwise equally qualified, veterans are to be given preference. Since late 1978, the newly reorganized Office of Federal Contract

Compliance Programs (OFCCP) has been empowered to ensure compliance of both the handicapped and veterans' affirmative action requirements. The handling of individual complaints, however, is under the jurisdiction of individual state agencies and the Department of Labor.

During the late sixties, the Supreme Court resurrected two statutes passed during the post–Civil War period. The Civil Rights Act of 1866 (42 U.S.C. 1981) clearly prohibits discrimination on the basis of race. For over a century, it was presumed that the statute was based on the Fourteenth Amendment, and therefore afforded protection only against the actions of government entities or private entities sufficiently involved in the government to be clothed with state action. In 1968 the Supreme Court, in *Jones* v. *Alfred H. Mayer Company*[15], held that a companion provision of this act was based upon the Thirteenth Amendment, as well as the Fourteenth, and therefore reached private as well as state action. Thus, according to a 1976 Supreme Court decision, this statute precludes private employment discrimination on account of race or color, and is applicable to whites as well as blacks.[16] The Civil Rights Act of 1871 (42 U.S.C. 1983) was broader in scope, declaring as discriminatory those actions which were based on race, religion, sex, or national origin.[17] There is, however, some question as to whether the same degree of protection is provided against each of these forms of discrimination. Along with Section 1981, Section 1983 continues to be used in federal litigation.

THE RELATIONSHIP BETWEEN DIFFERENT SOURCES OF PROTECTION AGAINST EMPLOYMENT DISCRIMINATION

The rights created by the various statutes and by Executive Order 11246 are largely independent. They supplement rather than supplant one another. An individual may invoke the protection provided by one or more of the statutes in the same proceeding (e.g., Title VII and Section 1981 or Title VII and the National Labor Relations Act). Furthermore, he or she may concurrently institute different proceedings under different statutes, or under the Executive Order, involving the same practices. Thus, for a single act, the employer may be found guilty of multiple violations. In certain instances, as will be discussed in the *Alexander* v. *Gardner-Denver* case,* a person may institute successive proceedings under different statutes, or under the Executive Order, seeking relief in the later proceedings which was not granted earlier. The availability of independent rights and remedies to combat employment discrimination has been anything but accidental. Congress specifically recognized this independence and explicitly endorsed a multiforum cause-of-action approach for persons alleging discrimination. In this light, Congress also attempted to preserve, rather than displace, the state agencies that enforced state fair employment practices legislation along with whatever rights against employment discrimination had developed or would develop under existing labor legislation.

---

*The Supreme Court held that a prior adverse arbitration award did not foreclose suit under Title VII on the issue of race discrimination.

As we explore the issues throughout this chapter, it will become apparent that there is conflict between nondiscrimination efforts in employment and the collective bargaining process.

REMEDIES AVAILABLE IN EMPLOYMENT DISCRIMINATION CASES

Once the federal courts find unlawful employment discrimination, they may grant relief to either (or both) the identifiable or the unidentifiable victims of the discrimination. In keeping with the remedial purposes of Title VII, courts have ordered back pay, reinstatement of discharged employees, admission to union membership to those denied it, and seniority adjustments. The courts have also issued "quota" hiring and promotion orders benefiting persons *other than* identifiable victims. This remedy remains controversial in terms of contentions of reverse discrimination, despite the 1979 Supreme Court decision in the *Weber* v. *Kaiser Aluminum* case, distinguishable because of the nonmandatory nature of its "quota" system. The most persuasive argument justifying the reverse discrimination which inevitably occurs whenever a mandatory hiring quota is imposed is that quota orders actually achieve significant integration of work forces in which there were severe statistical imbalances caused by past discrimination. To date, very few courts have ordered promotion quotas, as distinct from those involved in hiring cases. The reason for this reluctance is rather obvious: The identifiable victims of the (potential) reverse discrimination are, almost certainly, majority group members with long-term service with the employer. Thus, the disruptions to internal labor relations would probably be severe. (For case histories see latter section on reverse discrimination.)

According to the Supreme Court, the Title VII back-pay provision was expressly modeled on the back-pay provision of the National Labor Relations Act.* This remedy has never been closely contested by the courts as an appropriate remedy for individual plaintiffs once discrimination is found. Back-pay awards reflect total lost earnings less any interim earnings. Fringe benefits have been included in many back-pay awards. Most awards withhold taxes but include interest in computing the award under Title VII.

Despite these guidelines, the methods of computing how much back pay is due may be exceedingly complex, and the complexity is multiplied in a class action where there are numerous plaintiffs. In calculating class-wide back-pay awards, the Fifth Circuit, in *Pettway* v. *American Cast Iron Pipe Co.*, set forth two dominant principles of computing back pay, namely: "(1) unrealistic exactitude is not required, (2) uncertainties in determining what an employee would have earned but for the discrimination should be resolved against the discriminating employer."[18] The court in *Pettway* suggested a method of compensation described as a "formula of comparability or representative earnings formula," whereby

---

*Back pay is also available in actions brought under sections 1981 and 1983.

approximations are based on a group of employees, not injured by the discrimination, comparable in size, ability, and length of employment . . . to the class of plaintiffs.[19]

This proposal has some exceedingly important implications for the nondiscrimination—collective bargaining conflict. Suppose a class of minority discriminatees are awarded back-pay remedies. They return or continue to work in a bargaining unit dominated numerically, as well as politically and socially, by Caucasians, most of whom are aware of the outcome of the recent litigation. As word spreads about the back-pay award, a substantial amount of friction and resentment builds up, doing little to ameliorate the already existing racial conflict. In the single-employee case, the conflict may be even further exacerbated.

"Front pay," a corollary of back pay, is compensation for the period between the date of the higher court order and the date when (potential) employees finally achieve their "rightful place." To date, this remedy has been granted in only a few cases.

Neither compensatory nor punitive damages are recoverable under Title VII. Yet in *Stamps* v. *Detroit Edison Co.*,[20] a district court found that certain racially discriminatory policies had been deliberately pursued, and it imposed punitive damages in excess of $4 million. This case is an exception and there remains a strong divergence of opinion as to whether punitive damages are recoverable under the statute, with no definitive appellate decision having been rendered to date.

An extensive and consistent line of authority holds that a union is jointly liable with an employer for discrimination caused in whole or in part by the provisions of the collective bargaining agreement, regardless of the union's good faith, lack of intention to discriminate, or justifiable reliance on judicial authority, and that this joint liability requires the union to share in the back-pay award, if any. Suppose, however, that a union acquiesces in employer discrimination *not* based on provisions of a collective bargaining agreement. Does it still assume any joint liability? The weight of authority, as of this writing, indicates that such acquiesence is sufficient to establish liability.

We have to this point described the most important features of antidiscrimination laws and the variety of remedies available to those discriminated against. Some of the conflicts between collective bargaining and the within-groups pressures created by antidiscrimination law as well as remedies have been suggested.

The conflict between the granting of relief in employment discrimination cases, be it in the form of back (or front) pay or retroactive (or adjusted) seniority or any of the other available remedies, and the collective bargaining process is rather obvious. To whatever extent a discriminatee is granted relief, nonprotected members of the bargaining unit may resent the outcome. Thus, there is also conflict with the people represented by the bargaining process as well as with the bargaining outcomes themselves. We now describe in more detail the most important features of the conflict between collective bargaining and discrimination law.

HIRING DISCRIMINATION

Overt discrimination in hiring has been diminished considerably in recent years. At present, conflicts arise primarily in the *placement* of protected class employees in a unionized setting to the extent that such placements clash with seniority.

Discrimination overtly based on an individual's race, color, religion, sex, or national origin is an unlawful employment practice unless legally justified by a bona fide occupational qualification (BFOQ) in cases of hiring or employing individuals. For example, it is legal to stipulate that a teacher in a religious school or college be of a particular faith, even though this requirement excludes others, since it is a BFOQ. In no event can race be used as a BFOQ for any job or for any reason. Unlawful discrimination also exists if, despite the presence of a neutral basis for an employer's action (such as in a refusal-to-hire situation), the asserted basis is a pretext for a status-based motive. In the landmark case, *Griggs* v. *Duke Power Co.*, The Supreme Court held that high school education and standardized intelligence test requirements had been unlawfully used as conditions of employment in jobs from which blacks had been excluded prior to the effective date of Title VII.[21] The *effects* or consequences of both requirements, not simply the motivation, relate to propriety of the standard, became the critical deciding factors in establishing discrimination.

The act does not require that any person be hired simply because he or she was formerly the subject of discrimination or because he or she is a member of a minority group. Certain standards designed to remove artificial, arbitrary, and unnecessary barriers to employment have been established in recent years regarding the content of both applications for employment and interviews. Questions which may have a "disparate impact" on minorities or women simply may not be asked. An employment practice has a "disparate impact" if it results in a disproportionately adverse effect on members of protected classes. In 1972, a circuit court ruled, in *Gregory* v. *Litton Systems, Inc.*, that a corporate policy of excluding from employment persons with a record of a number of arrests without convictions was unlawful because, as in *Griggs*, of its disproportionately adverse effect on blacks.[22]

In general, however, there are few possible conflicts between remedies for hiring discrimination and collective bargaining. In most employment situations, the employer completely controls the hiring process, and collective bargaining has generally not eroded this employer prerogative. The conflicts between affirmative action hiring requirements and hiring halls in referral unions are readily apparent. The tendency to perpetuate a predominantly white male membership has been strong in many construction unions. The point of attack for those wishing to end this practice, however, has been apprenticeship programs—the means by which the workers in the trade acquire their training and their eventual status as full-fledged journeypersons.

Two cases are worth noting in this area. In *Asbestos Workers, Local 53* v. *Vogler*,[23] the court held that a local union which required, among other things, a familial connection between new and existing members was discriminating against minorities. In *Hameed* v. *Ironworkers' Local 396*,[24] the Eighth Circuit Court held that a requirement of a high school diploma as a condition for eligibility to apprenticeship programs to be discriminatory as well, since it could not be established as a necessary requirement for successful completion of the program. Apart from these situations, however, there is relatively little tangible conflict between hiring procedures and the collective bargaining process other than the obvious clash between affirmative action placement commitments and seniority provisions.

THE CONFLICT BETWEEN NEGOTIATED SENIORITY PROVISIONS AND TITLE VII OF THE CIVIL RIGHTS ACTS OF 1964

Nature and Scope of the Conflict

The crux of the equal employment opportunity—seniority conflict is that the "last fired, first fired" and "last hired, last eligible for promotion or transfer" principles, which are the basis of contractual seniority, usually work to the disadvantage of minorities and females. These parties are often the victims of past exclusion from integrated seniority rosters, thus leaving them with fewer years of service. During recessions and periods of high unemployment, seniority inevitably clashes with the principle of equal employment opportunity.

In *Griggs* v. *Duke Power Co.*, The Supreme Court brought this conflict to the surface. The Court ruled that discrimination could be established based on the *consequences* of given events even for "acts, neutral on their face, and neutral even in terms of their intent."[25] Herein arises the current problem of accommodating the seniority of white males accumulated under circumstances of exclusion or limitations upon the employment of blacks and other minorities.

Judicial Interpretation of the Seniority—Equal Employment Opportunity Conflict

Much of the controversy in recent years has centered on interpretation of Section 703(h) of Title VII. The courts have come almost full circle in their interpretation of what constitutes a bona fide seniority system and the extent, if any, to which such a system must be bent to accommodate the rights of certain protected classes. A limited view of the scope of the Court's remedial authority in seniority cases generally prevailed until 1977, when the *Franks* v. *Bowman* decision, discussed later, was rendered.

The stage for judicial interpretation of seniority was set in 1968 in *Quarles* v. *Philip Morris, Inc.*[26] In this case, a federal district court in Virginia interpreted Title VII to permit judicial invasion of "job" or "departmental" seniority found to be discriminatory. The court in *Quarles* defined a "bona fide seniority system" under Title VII to exclude systems which perpetuated the present effects of past discrimination. The remedy was to establish a system in which an employee transferred from one department to another would carry to the new department seniority computed from the date hired. A similar case before a federal appellate court in 1969 was *Local 189, United Papermakers & Paperworkers* v. *the United States*.[27] Here again the Court ruled that it was not the intent of Title VII to make incumbent white employees suffer for the past discriminatory acts of their employer. Title VII did not permit grants of retroactive seniority or bumping privileges to injured black employees. Thus, plant-wide seniority could be asserted only with respect to job vacancies and not with respect to presently filled jobs.

The following three cases represent the next phase of judicial interpretation of the seniority provisions: *Waters* v. *Wisconsin Steel Works*,[28] *Jersey Central Power* *and Light Co. v. IBEW Local 327,*[29] and *Meadows v. Ford Motor Co.*[30] In the *Waters* case, the appeals court held that the last hired, first fired seniority system was not itself discriminatory, and that it did not perpetuate prior racial discrimination in violation of Title VII. Altering the rights earned by length of service would, the court reasoned, be placing the burden of past discrimination created by the employer upon the shoulders of innocent white employees. In *Jersey Central Power*, the court of appeals had to determine the relationship between two agreements whose terms were inconsistent, namely, a conciliation agreement entered into by the EEOC and the employer modifying the seniority system to implement what the parties believed to be the "rightful place" doctrine* and the collective bargaining agreement. The court ruled that the latter should prevail to determine the order of layoffs despite a disproportionately adverse impact on minorities and women. In *Meadows*, the appeals court ruled that a class of women had been discriminated against in hiring at a new truck plant. It held that both back pay and date of application (retroactive) seniority were permissible remedies under Title VII once hiring discrimination had been established. The court observed that the burden of retroactive pay falls upon the party who violated the law, whereas the burden of retroactive seniority is borne by employees who are innocent of any wrongdoing.

A further major but relatively short-lived breakthrough for protected classes on the question of seniority occurred in a 1976 Supreme Court decision in *Franks v. Bowman Transportation Co.*[31] *Franks* involved a class action suit alleging racially discriminatory employment practices in the hire, transfer, and discharge of over-the-road (OTR) truck drivers. In its decision, the Supreme Court held that retroactive "fictional" seniority was an appropriate remedy for discrimination against individuals *after* the effective date of Title VII. The Court held that the award of retroactive seniority was necessary to provide make-whole relief for those employees who applied for transfers. In its decision, the Court ruled that the award of retroactive seniority to victims of hiring discrimination after the effective data of Title VII did not deprive other employees of "indefeasibly vested rights" conferred by the collective bargaining agreement.

The next stage in judicial interpretation of the status of seniority provisions took place in 1977 in a well-known and surprising Supreme Court decision rendered in *International Brotherhood of Teamsters v. United States.*[32] In this case, the Court held that seniority systems that lock in the effects of past discrimination are *immune* under Title VII, even when the employer's preact discrimination results in whites having greater existing seniority rights than blacks. The union did not, in the High Court's opinion, violate the law in agreeing to and maintaining the seniority system. The Supreme Court concluded that employees who suffered only preact discrimination were not entitled to any relief, and that no one could be granted any retroactive seniority prior to the effective date of Title VII. Since the government had proved that the company had also engaged in postact racially discriminatory practices, the Court

---

*This is a remedial doctrine intended to correct for the "rightful place" which, in the absence of any prior discrimination, would have been accorded to members of the protected class.

held that retroactive seniority to the date of such discrimination could be accorded members of the affected class.

Two other relevant seniority decisions were handed down during the same 1977 Supreme Court session, *United Air Lines, Inc.* v. *Evans*[33] and *East Texas Motor Freight System, Inc.* v. *Rodriguez.*[34] In *Evans*, the Court held that if a seniority system were neutral in its operation, the mere fact that it perpetuated the effects of a past discriminatory act did not establish a violation of Title VII. This decision was even more restrictive than *Teamsters* of the rights of incumbent minorities or females. In the *Rodriguez* case, the issue was whether a transfer policy requiring that a city driver resign his job and forfeit all seniority in order to be eligible for a line driver's job was discriminatory. The Court thus held that since the plaintiffs were admittedly not qualified for the positions sought, they could not challenge the seniority system on the grounds that such practices perpetuated past discrimination.

In the landmark 1971 Supreme Court decision, *Griggs* v. *Duke Power Co.*, it had been decreed that the disparate impact of discriminatory practices and devices violated Title VII unless saved by business necessity. With the 1977 "trilogy" (*International Brotherhood of Teamsters* v. *United States, United Air Lines* v. *Evans* and *East Texas Motor Freight System* v. *Rodriquez*), the Supreme Court established a more restrictive set of rules in cases involving seniority conflicts. Thus, the Court has "resolved" the controversy over the interpretation of Section 703(h) by declaring that, absent a discriminatory purpose, the routine operation of the seniority system cannot be an unlawful employment practice under the act, *even if the system has some discriminatory consequences*. To be actionable, the seniority system must have been designed with an intent to discriminate or to lock in other discrimination.[35] This rule has now been applied to seniority cases affecting race, national origin, sex, and religion.

Post-*Teamsters* court decisions have utilized the standards set out in *Teamsters* to determine whether or not seniority systems were designed, maintained or manipulated to discriminate. Some of the standards extracted from *Teamsters* follow:

1. whether the seniority system operates to discourage all employees equally from transferring between seniority units
2. whether the seniority units are in the same or separate bargaining units
3. whether the seniority system had its genesis in racial discrimination
4. whether the system was negotiated and has been maintained free from any illegal purpose.

In 1982, the Supreme Court held, in a case alleging both racial and sexual discrimination, *American Tobacco Co.* v. *Patterson*, that 703(h) applies to seniority systems adopted after the effective date of Title VII, as well as those adopted prior thereto. Reiterating its analysis in *Teamsters*, the Court held that ". . . to be cognizable, a claim that a seniority system has a discriminatory impact must be accompanied by proof of a discriminatory purpose."[36]

Employees laid off in reverse order of seniority would now appear to have no Title VII claim unless they filed a timely charge protesting the original hiring, transfer or promotion discrimination.

A case connecting both the seniority and hiring issues was decided in 1984. In *Firefighters Local Union No. 1784* v. *Stotts*,[37] the Supreme Court held that when a bona fide seniority system comes into conflict with a consent decree during times requiring layoffs, the seniority rights are to be considered preeminent. In brief, the City of Memphis entered into a consent decree in 1980 in which the city agreed to adopt the long term goal of making the proportion of blacks in each of its fire department classifications approximately equal to the proportion of blacks in Memphis. When budget deficits precipitated the need for layoffs in 1981, the city laid off workers on the basis of seniority, in accordance with its collective bargaining agreement with the firefighters. The Supreme Court agreed that the seniority system was bona fide and allowed the layoffs to occur, in effect minimizing any impact the original consent decree would have.

It is well-settled that normal Title VII standards, as well as an "intent" requirement[38] apply to both Title VII and Section 1981[39] disparate treatment promotion cases. Length of service requirements continue to be scrutinized to determine if they perpetuate the effects of past discrimination.[40] Experience level is also a factor in determining relative qualifications of employees even apart from a bona fide seniority system.[41] Courts have generally accepted the use of subjective criteria in promotions to upper level or professional positions. The practice is scrutinized much more closely, however, in blue-collar or low-level promotions. Courts continue to enjoin illegal promotion practices, but they are rather divided on the propriety of quotas to remedy discrimination in promotion.

BEYOND TITLE VII: ALTERNATIVE APPROACHES FOR COMBATING EMPLOYMENT DISCRIMINATION ON SENIORITY-RELATED ISSUES

Teamsters and related cases were decided solely under Title VII of the Civil Rights Act of 1964 as amended. It is certainly worth arguing that if present effects of past discrimination "telescoped by seniority systems" offend other legal principles, they may still be litigated and disposed of under those laws. We turn now to duty of fair representation issues, to Executive Order 11246 and related administrative action, and to state laws and executive orders as each pertains to combating employment discrimination on seniority-related issues.

Duty of Fair Representation Issues

As discussed earlier, the duty of fair representation first emerged in the 1944 Supreme Court decision in *Steele* v. *Louisville and Nashville Railroad*. If a union refuses to renegotiate or reconsider a seniority provision containing a non-transfer lock-in, even if the status of blacks and whites has been determined by a pre-act discrimination in placement, it might be subject to a suit by minority employees for breach of the duty of fair representation. Since the doctrine of fair representation is independent of Title VII, litigation under this theory would not be foreclosed by the recent seniority decisions.

Executive Order 11246 and Related Administrative Action

One effect of the Supreme Court seniority decisions is to attach even more importance to affirmative action under E.O. 11246 and other measures that embrace the affirmative action concept. Several courts of appeals have already recognized that E.O. 11246 clearly stands on a different footing than Title VII and is not controlled by the act. The conflict inherent in implementing affirmative action programs is rather apparent. Suppose that a company has been affirmative in its hiring practices and has hired sufficient numbers of women applicants to meet its annual goals. After hiring the women, the company may want to place them in particular job vacancies. It is at this juncture that affirmative action may clash directly with the terms of a collective bargaining, whereby vacant positions are allocated on the basis of seniority.

State Laws and Executive Orders

Several governors have in recent years issued Executive Orders similar to E.O. 11246. To the extent that such orders may require redress to the victims of present effects of pre-act discrimination, manifest in present seniority provisions, nothing in the recent Supreme Court seniority decisions suggests that those orders would be illegal under Title VII.

THE DISCHARGE ISSUE

Discharge cases account for a large share of the charges filed with the EEOC against private employers.[42] Such cases also represent a high percentage of Title VII court actions. We shall devote some time to a discussion of the discharge issue, primarily as it interfaces or conflicts with the collective bargaining process.

The majority of discharge cases are disparate treatment cases. The courts continue to apply the order and allocation of proof principles established in *McDonnell Douglas Corp.* v. *Green*[43] and *Texas Department of Community Affairs* v. *Burdine*[44] to discharge cases.

In an overwhelming percentage of Title VII discharge decisions rendered by the EEOC and the courts, employers (defendants) prevail primarily because the employees (plaintiffs), and frequently their attorneys, totally misunderstand the legal principles and burden-of-proof requirements of the Title VII discharge action. The basic principle is that an employer "has the right to discharge an employee for good reason, bad reason, or no reason absent discrimination."[45] The principle is based upon Sections 703(a) and 706(g) of Title VII. They prohibit discharge because of race, color, religion, sex, or national origin (703(a)) but reinstatement by a court is prohibited if the discharge occurred for any reason other than discrimination (706(g)).

The burden of proof is particularly onerous in the single-employee discharge case. The plaintiff must meet the initial burden of proving that he or she was a member of the protected class, that he or she was discharged, and that disparate treatment has occurred. The employer meets the initial burden of rebuttal by giving a legitimate, nondiscriminatory reason for the discharge. The final burden then falls on the plaintiff to demonstrate that the reason given by the employer for the discharge "was in fact pretext."[46] Since there is virtually no employee for whom an employer cannot find a valid, objective reason for discharge, the employee usually finds it extremely difficult to show that the reason given was "pretextual" unless he or she focuses on employment patterns broader than his or her individual case.

The particular reasons for a discharge vary significantly; yet there are certain common threads that run through many discharge cases. Several courts have relied on evidence pertaining to an employer's overall policies in evaluating a particular discharge. One critical factor is whether or not the discharged employee was given repeated warnings and an opportunity to improve. Additionally, an employer's deviation from normal patterns and practices is frequently determinative. For example, in *Lowry* v. *Whitaker Cable Corp,*[47] contrary to company policy, a black employee was given a warning slip within the first six days, denied a locker routinely given to other employees, and labeled a voluntary quit despite an actual termination. The court held that it was highly improbable that these three circumstances could have occurred in the plaintiff's situation in a period of 19 days in the absence of racial discrimination.

Since it is extremely difficult to win a single-employee discharge case under Title VII, many competent plaintiff's attorneys generally try to bring such cases as class actions, provided that they can meet certain procedural requirements.

To evaluate the relative level of conflict between the collective bargaining process and the nondiscrimination protection afforded by Title VII for an employee pursuing reinstatement following a discharge requires a double-pronged approach. If the union takes the grievance and pursues it in earnest, there is essentially no conflict since the grievant can only be accorded full relief once. If the grievant simultaneously or concurrently pursues his Title VII rights by filing charges with the EEOC or a state agency, then the only conflicts that might arise are the procedural ones described in the next section of this chapter. Conflict is minimal compared to the situation in which the union either refuses outright to take a grievance for reinstatement or accepts the grievance but accords it little or no priority. The grievant may then file charges with the EEOC against both the company and the union, alleging that his or her discharge was motivated by discrimination.

On balance, most of the conflicts between the collective bargaining machinery and nondiscrimination law on the issue of discharging an employee are procedural, rather than substantive.

GRIEVANCE AND ARBITRATION PROCEDURES VS. TITLE VII: THE INHERENT CONFLICT AND SOME PLAUSIBLE SOLUTIONS

Title VII of the Civil Rights Act of 1964 exemplifies the possible conflict between a national policy which attempts to eliminate employment discrimination and a federal labor policy which emphasizes the private settlement of industrial disputes through grievance arbitration procedure.* This conflict is illustrated when a discriminatory act by an employer or union constitutes a violation of both Title VII and the terms of a collective bargaining agreement.

Prior to the landmark decision on the issue of pursuing multiple forums in seeking remedies for alleged discrimination in employment, *Alexander* v. *Gardner-Denver Co.*,[48] an individual discriminated against had to pursue *either* a contractual (grievance/ arbitration) *or* a statutory remedy.

In a 1970 case, *Dewey* v. *Reynolds Metals Co.*,[49] the Sixth Circuit Court of Appeals reviewed a lower court's ruling in a religious discrimination case. It ruled that an arbitrator's decision was final and that an employee should not be able to relitigate his or her grievance in courts. The court reasoned that to give employees the recourse to both arbitration and the federal courts would "sound the death knell" for arbitration clauses in labor contracts.

When the Supreme Court began to hear the *Gardner—Denver* case, it was faced with decisions from the lower courts which had adopted the rationale of *Dewey*, namely that an employee was bound by an arbitrator's decision. In *Gardner—Denver*, the Supreme Court was confronted with determining under what circumstances, if any, an employee's statutory right to a trial *de novo*** under Title VII is precluded by a prior submission of his or her claim to binding arbitration. The Court acknowledged the absence of any express authority in Title VII about the relationship between federal courts and the grievance-arbitration machinery. The Court reasoned, "The clear inference is that Title VII was designed to supplement, rather than supplant, existing laws and institutions related to employment discrimination."[50] It held that the relationship between forums is complementary, "since consideration of the claim by both forums may promote the policies underlying each."[51]

The Court thus held that an arbitral award would not bar a concurrent or subsequent suit in federal court alleging a violation of Title VII rights, but that when an arbitrator had given "full consideration to an employee's Title VII rights," a court could accord the decision "great weight."[52]

Gardner—Denver does not require that an individual utilize both the arbitral forum and the courts for processing discrimination claims. Thus, employees may bypass the grievance procedure entirely and begin Title VII lawsuits, or they may proceed in the arbitral forum without ever resorting to the federal courts. Should the employee be uncertain of how to proceed with a discrimination charge, he or she is protected, since *Gardner—Denver* holds that there can be no prospective waiver of an employee's rights under Title VII.

Courts that have considered the issue of arbitral authority subsequent to *Gardner—Denver* have not always resolved the issue consistently with that decision. In a 1975 case, *Southbridge Plastics Division* v. *Rubber Workers Local 759*,[53] a federal district court granted the employer an injunction against the union processing the

---

*Virtually all of the 160,000-plus collective bargaining contracts currently in force contain a grievance procedure for disputes arising during the term of the contract. In 95 percent of the procedures, arbitration is the final step.

**Anew, afresh; a second time—*Black's Law Dictionary*

grievances of the employees to arbitration. The employees were alleging that a layoff was in violation of the collective bargaining agreement. The union then refused to sign the agreement and initiated grievances when several senior males were not given preference in shift assignments. Southbridge refused to arbitrate; it reasoned that if the arbitrator's decision were favorable to the union members, the company would be required to reassign female employees, contrary to Title VII and the EEOC conciliation agreement. The court decided that

> *no useful purpose would be served by requiring arbitration of the grievances* filed by the union members.[54]

The *Southbridge* solution of denying the union access to arbitration "encourages employers to attempt to extricate themselves from the inevitable dilemma of defending actions in two forums, a solution arguably neither warranted nor contemplated by *Alexander* (v. *Gardner−Denver*)."[55]

Another case decided since *Gardner−Denver*, *Goodyear Tire and Rubber Co.* v. *Rubber Workers Local 200*,[56] involved arbitral authority and Title VII−type issues. Goodyear filed an action in state court seeking to vacate an arbitrator's award granted pursuant to the terms of the collective bargaining agreement. The company and the union were parties to two agreements, one covering collective bargaining, the other, pensions. The union challenged provisions in each agreement, applying different standards to maternity disability from those applied to other types of disability caused by illness or injury. An arbitrator sustained the grievance with regard to the payment of disability benefits under the pension agreement, which contained a clause providing that its provisions could be modified where necessitated by federal or state statute or regulation. The company contended that the arbitrator had exceeded his legal powers by asserting that the EEOC guidelines* were federal regulations. The Ohio Supreme Court ruled that the company was correct. The court found the decision of the arbitrator to be ambiguous, and it even implied that the arbitrator *may* have exceeded his authority, yet it enforced the award.

As indicated by these last two court decisions, there is disagreement as to the arbitrator's authority in deciding a Title VII violation. The major difficulty of trying to apply the law to resolve Title VII−type grievances is that one must recognize that under current court interpretations, decisions of arbitrators are not necessarily final. Under the *Gardner-Denver* decision, arbitration awards can be appealed through the courts when Title VII rights are at issue.

Although *Gardner−Denver* mandates that the courts grant a statutory remedy in addition to, and not as a substitute for, any contractual remedy granted by an arbitrator, the court in *Southbridge* effectively made just such a substitution. The

---

*The specific guideline regarding employment policies relating to pregnancy and childbirth is 29 C.F.R.§1604.10(b)(1976). It provides that disabilities caused or contributed by pregnancy or related conditions must be treated in the same manner as other temporary disabilities for purposes of benefits, privileges, and leave. As of October 31, 1978, Title VII was amended along these lines—the guideline is now statutory law.

Goodyear decision, on the other hand, is reasonably consistent with the *Gardner–Denver* implications.

There are a number of advantages in utilizing the arbitral forum. In the first instance, considering the time and expense necessary to process a Title VII–type grievance, the use of arbitration would relieve the EEOC and the federal courts of a substantial backlog. Additionally, arbitration satisfies the common desire of both management and labor to avoid the adverse publicity of a Title VII suit. Also, the arbitration procedure may be of therapeutic value to the individual employee in the broad context of democratic self-government in grievance matters.

The *Gardner-Denver* decision failed to consider the possibility that an employer, or union, might limit grievance or arbitration mechanisms to those grievances that do not involve a discrimination issue. This would be an unfortunate outcome for various reasons. It may well be a separate violation of Title VII to remove discrimination claims from the grievance procedure. Additionally, such action would likely have a severe impact on minorities by making it more difficult to remedy employment-based discrimination for the individual employee. Additionally, a segregation syndrome might likely result:

> An artificial and coercive kind of segregation would arise between discrimination and nondiscrimination complaints. Minority grievants would no longer file their charges with shop stewards and union representatives would therefore be able to very neatly wash their hands of all such problems and encourage resort to another forum. This would undermine a principle promoted by Title VII and other labor legislation, i.e., that the parties themselves are best able to resolve their own problems and should do so on a voluntary basis. Moreover, it would encourage unions and employers to believe that discrimination is not their own problem—and that, unlike other grievances, could be ignored.[57]

Professor Harry T. Edwards of Harvard Law School has proposed a "two-track arbitration system," the need for which has arisen from a complex of conflicting interests, for handling Title VII cases.[58] Employers and unions, along with individual employee–grievants, want the relatively speedy and inexpensive resolution of disputes that arbitration has traditionally supplied. Employers do not want to be subjected to litigation in several forums on the same claim. Unions want to make certain that they comply with their duties of fair representation. Employees who believe they have been subjected to discrimination want full relief. All the while, the EEOC and the courts must guide the development of public policy and precedent under Title VII.

Professor Edwards' proposal seeks to reconcile these conflicting interests. It would permit arbitration of certain cases that implicate Title VII rights in which the grievance alleges an act that is potentially a violation of both the collective bargaining contract *and* of Title VII. It would specifically, however, exclude the following grievances from arbitration: (1) those alleging only a breach of law, (2) those charging both the union and employer with discrimination, (3) those seeking a reformation of the contract, (4) those claiming inconsistency between the collective bargaining agreement and a court or administrative order, (5) those constituting a class action, or (6) those involving unsettled areas of law. These criteria should screen the scope of inquiry, limiting the jurisdiction of the arbitrator in a way designed to minimize or eliminate the necessity of court review.

The collective bargaining agreement could establish a special procedure for handling cases that survive the screening criteria. Specifically, it could establish for the life of the contract a panel of lawyer-arbitrators with expertise about Title VII. Employees would be able to opt to use the special procedure if they agreed not to file charges with the EEOC or in court until arbitration ended. The collective bargaining agreement would require arbitrators, when they find employment discrimination, to award a full remedy. If employees filed charged with the EEOC or in court, the employer would be able to decline or withdraw from, arbitration. Procedural safeguards would be enhanced. Professor Edwards contends that if this procedure were followed carefully, it could minimize the incentive for an employee to relitigate in court. Additionally, in keeping with the *Gardner—Denver* decision, the court would be likely to accord "great weight" to the arbitral award. Should an employee choose to avoid the special procedure and go directly to court, at least the problem of multiple forums will have been eliminated.

Professor Edwards recognizes several potential problems of this two-tract system, but believes they are outweighed by the benefits of arbitration—speed and relatively inexpensive dispute resolution—and by its safeguards of societal, employer, union, and employee interests.

Nearly two decades after the passage of Title VII, the procedural conflicts inherent in instances where a union member seeks to assert both contractual and statutory rights in charging employment discrimination have yet to be fully resolved. It is hoped that during the eighties more innovative and expeditious solutions will be proposed and accepted, both by the federal courts and by all parties to the disputes.

THE IMPACT OF EQUAL OPPORTUNITY LAW ON COLLECTIVE BARGAINING

The most obvious impact of nondiscrimination legislation and regulations during the past fifteen years has been the continuing trend toward government presence in both the substantive and procedural aspects of incorporating equal opportunity remedies in the workplace. Out of this presence is emerging a whole new set of relationships as the collective bargaining process may conflict with federal and state laws. Before assessing the overall situation since 1964, let us highlight some conflicts between equal opportunity laws or regulations and the collective bargaining process. The major conflicts emerge not in negotiating the collective bargaining agreement, which usually contains a nondiscrimination clause, but in *administering* the agreement.

The most apparent conflict involves seniority. Suppose, for example, that a company seeks to make "reasonable accommodation" under the Rehabilitation Act by hiring a diabetic, assessing his or her physical limitations, and placing him or her, with appropriate restrictions, on a job in an industrial setting. The union is understandably upset that a new employee may be given placement or transfer opportunities "at the expense of" other members of the bargaining unit with greater seniority. On another issue, discharge, the seniority conflict is also readily apparent. Suppose the EEOC or the courts find a discharge (or other termination) a violation of Title VII and order a full remedy, including back pay and seniority relief. The discriminatee returns to the job with the "extra" seniority which, even though not in violation of the contract, engenders resentment from co-workers, particularly those whose seniority is diminished by the award. A similar situation is created when discriminatory hiring practices are found and some person or class of persons is awarded retroactive seniority, as in *Franks* v. *Bowman Transportation Co.* Other seniority-related conflicts are also apparent in the area of layoffs and recalls, where clashes with affirmative action goals and timetables under the Executive Order are commonplace.

Apart from seniority, there are other conflicts between affirmative action requirements, government guidelines, and certain provisions of collective bargaining agreements. Consider the following example: An organization decides to increase the number of skilled tradespeople by instituting a formal apprenticeship program for 15 positions in six different trades. Advertising in the local newspaper and posting notices at the facility yield approximately 2000 applications. The collective bargaining agreement stipulates that for each *three* in a particular trade, *two* must be filled from the bargaining unit. Thus, to the extent that there are only two openings per trade, the applications from the general labor market languish. This constraint points up a potential conflict with affirmative action requirements for obtaining certain percentages of minorities and females in the skilled trades where they are conspicuously absent.

Union liability is easily seen in the case of a union committeeperson, who after acting in reasonably "good faith" in civil rights terms, abandons as without apparent merit a grievance filed by a minority employee. He may then find the union subject not only of an unfair labor practice but also of a Title VII charge.

The foregoing examples illustrate how many of the remedies devised to eliminate prohibited employment discrimination through federal legislation and executive orders have made, and will continue to make, significant inroads on traditional notions about the collective bargaining process. Let us now review three developments which reflect this most vividly: (1) the restructuring of discriminatory seniority systems and contract provisions; (2) the role of labor arbitration as the mechanism for resolving labor disputes where discrimination has been alleged; and (3) the increasing resistance to the NLRB's traditional noncommittal role in discrimination cases.

Court decisions restructuring discriminatory seniority systems have generally attempted to strike a balance between the rights of employees adversely affected by past discrimination and the expectations of those not disadvantaged. In the process, they have frequently ignored the impact of any imposed remedy on the institution of free collective bargaining. Such restructuring has generally been based on the "rightful place" remedy, whereby employees adversely affected by past discrimination are accorded the seniority rights they would have enjoyed but for the discrimination. Theoretically, this is to be accomplished without depriving other employees of their jobs or accumulated seniority rights. But, as noted herein in connection with job security, seniority is a set of relative priorities, and to raise one priority necessarily lowers some other one. Hence, in layoff and recall, the "rightful place" remedy has been extremely controversial. If recalls under this remedy are based on plant- or company-wide seniority alone, an employee who had been a victim of past discrimination might be recalled to a job he had never before held in preference to the incumbent at the time of layoff.

The most noteworthy impact of the extensively restructured contract provisions called for by court and agency seniority remedies is the conflict with the conventional policy against interference of this type with the terms of the collective bargaining agreement. The congressional history surrounding the passage of Section 8(d) of the NLRA, for instance, indicates a clear intent to keep the NLRB from sitting in judgment on the substantive terms of such agreements, except when those terms violate an express statutory provision. The provisions of the Norris—LaGuardia Act expressing a policy against federal court interference in "labor disputes" were declared inapplicable by Congress in the formulation of Title VII remedies.*

Perhaps even more significant than the substantive restructuring of seniority clauses is the identifiable trend toward government presence in the *procedures* established to resolve disputes under such restructured provisions. Thus, there has developed an apparent distrust of traditional grievance and arbitration procedures regarding resolution of discrimination claims. This has been exemplified in recent years by the imposition of extracontractual complaint resolving mechanisms in a series of steel industry cases, as well as by the Supreme Court's decision in *Alexander* v. *Gardner—Denver.* That case resolved the debate over the proper role of labor arbitration in the area of employment discrimination claims by declaring that arbitral determinations need not preclude, or be deferred to in, subsequent Title VII actions.

Thus far, we have said little about the role of the NLRB in handling discrimination charges. The fact is that increasingly the NLRB has been facing issues of race and sex discrimination in employment when exercising its authority in representation and unfair labor practice proceedings. It has, however, been extremely reluctant to assert its authority where civil rights violations have been alleged. This trend seems to be changing, however, as during the past few years we have been witnessing an attempt by several federal appellate courts to pressure the board to exercise its power in combating employment discrimination. The enactment of Title VII and a rediscovery of the applicability of Section 1981 of the Civil Rights Act of 1866 have added new dimensions to the Duty of Fair Representation (DFR) doctrine. A plaintiff who feels victimized by a union's breach of its DFR may thus consider proceeding under Taft-Hartley by filing a charge with the NLRB or a lawsuit under the Taft-Hartley Act, and/or proceeding under Title VII or #1981 of the Civil Rights Act of 1866, or both.[59]

Another area of increasing importance concerns the union role in enforcing Title VII and other equal employment opportunity laws. Among both local and international unions, in and outside the AFL—CIO, there is considerable variation in sentiment about equal opportunity policy. Industrial unions generally feel that they should not be held responsible for discrimination since they are not responsible for hiring, or for management policies and decisions that may historically have restricted the upward mobility of minorities and women. These feelings aside, the EEOC and the courts have rather consistently held that unions are responsible for both inclusions and omissions in contract provisions negotiated by them as the sole bargaining agent, and for fair representation of all bargaining unit members under those agreements.

---

*42 U.S.C.A.§20003-5(h) (1974).

By express provisions of Title VII, a union is liable for its own discrimination against its members, applicants for membership, the employees it represents, and other persons over whom it exercises direct or indirect control with respect to employment opportunities or status. When it acts in the role of an employer, a union is also subject to liability under employment discrimination laws. A union is normally held jointly liable with an employer under Title VII, Section 1981 and Section 1983 of the Civil Rights Act of 1871 for discrimination caused by provisions of a collective bargaining agreement.[60] There is precedent for holding a union jointly liable with an employer under the Age Discrimination in Employment Act. Unions are not, however, liable for discrimination under the Equal Pay Act. A union is unquestionably liable and may be forced to pay full back pay when it takes the initial action and induces an employer to discriminate. Unions may also be liable under Title VII for acquiescing in employer actions which are not based on provisions of a collective bargaining agreement.[61]

In the final analysis, unions, like employers, will have to face legal responsibilities in combating employment discrimination. A real peril to unions is the developing impact of financial liability. It is apparent that a union can use two methods concurrently to protect itself against discrimination charges and to minimize the danger of financial liability. These are (1) initiating an affirmative action plan, with or without employer cooperation, including bringing Title VII issues to the bargaining table and, if necessary, to the courts, and (2) modifying its current collective bargaining agreement to better accommodate a grievance-arbitration procedure that can adequately handle discrimination grievances.

REVERSE DISCRIMINATION

> There is, perhaps, no other area of employment law that so brings the tensions inherent in Title VII into focus as that called 'reverse discrimination.'[62]

Reverse discrimination will be considered here only in the context of affirmative action. In *Regents of the University of California* v. *Bakke*,[63] the Supreme Court addressed the legality under Title VI of the Civil Rights Act of 1964 and the Equal Protection Clause of a medical school admissions program which set aside a fixed number of places for minorities. The Bakke decision yielded two separate majority opinions: (1) Bakke was improperly denied admission to the medical school on racial grounds, because race may not be the sole criterion for a preference, at least absent a judicial, legislative or administrative finding of past discrimination by the institution, (2) even absent a finding of prior discrimination, race may be given some consideration in an admissions process as part of a school's exercise of First Amendment rights to create a diverse student body.

United Steelworkers of American v. *Weber*[64] was the first reverse discrimination case to come before the Supreme Court under Title VII. The issue in *Weber* was whether a voluntary, collectively-bargained selection ratio for craft trainees was permissible under Title VII. Kaiser Aluminum and the Steelworkers had negotiated a plan whereby for every two training vacancies, one black and one white employee were to be selected from race-segregated lists ranked in seniority order. The Supreme Court reversed the lower federal courts and found the Kaiser-Steelworkers plan valid under Title VII.

Fullilove v. *Klutznick*[65] involved a direct constitutional challenge to a congressional enactment which required that minority business enterprises (MBE) be awarded at least 10 percent of certain construction funds. Several contractors sought declaratory and injunctive relief, alleging that the MBE preference was unconstitutional on its face. The issue again (as in Weber) fragmented the court. Finally, a six-member majority of the Supreme Court approved the 10 percent MBE set-aside because it was deemed equitable and reasonably necessary to redress identified discrimination.

The courts in post-Weber decisions generally have upheld action taken pursuant to a formal affirmative action plan against claims of reverse discrimination where the plan (1) is remedial (in response to a conspicuous racial imbalance in the employer's work force or a finding of discrimination); (2) is reasonably related to the remedial purpose; (3) does not unnecessarily trammel the interests of white employees; and (4) does not continue beyond a period reasonably required to eliminate the conspicuous imbalance or correct the discrimination. The reluctance of the judiciary to discourage affirmative action was reaffirmed in *Setser* v. *Novack Investment Co.*[66]

SUMMARY

In the last ten years the scope of employment litigation has increased immensely. Not only are there available to employees, former employees and applicants for employment the remedies of Title VII (of the Civil Rights Act of 1964, as amended), the Civil Rights Acts of 1866 and 1871 (42 U. S. C. #1981 and #1983) and the Age Discrimination in Employment Act (ADEA), but increasing litigation has developed under the Equal Pay Act and under a variety of state common law theories, including actions based on breach of employment contracts and actions based upon the torts of wrongful discharge. In addition, several states have adopted statutes limiting the employment-at-will doctrine. Common law claims may permit jury trials and subject defendants to awards of compensatory and even punitive damages. Nevertheless, particularly in times of high unemployment, the need and desire of workers to create job security, if necessary through the vehicle of discrimination claims and related litigation, and the increasing willingness of state legislatures and courts to re-examine the employment-at-will doctrine indicates that employment litigation will continue to expand in the foreseeable future.[67]

Looking to the future, certain new directions in collective bargaining seem to be emerging. In at least one case, a district court has recognized the validity of tripartite agreements in which unions, employers and a government agency acting on behalf of minority or female employees agreed to maintain specific proportions of such protected classes in a work force after completion of layoffs. Moreover, the court declared that the provision of the tripartite agreement should prevail if and when they were found to be inconsistent with seniority provisions in the collective bargaining agreement. Even though this decision was later reversed on appeal, it suggests the extent to which collective bargaining may possibly be altered, both substantively and procedurally, by equal opportunity remedies.

In addition to government involvement in the collective bargaining process, the 1970s and early 1980s have been a time for considerably more participation of minorities, females, and protected classes in the process. These groups have organized as pressure groups within their unions and have brought the bargaining process to bear as a force against discrimination. With the ever increasing integration of the work force, it seems clear that more efforts will be directed by protected classes to air their concerns through traditional union channels.

A NOTE ON OTHER WORKPLACE LAWS

Although this chapter to this point has dealt exclusively with employment discrimination and its intersection with the collective bargaining process, there are other labor or workplace laws which intersect in a parallel fashion. The Fair Labor Standards Act (FLRA), the Employee Retirement and Income Security Act (ERISA), and the Occupational Safety and Health Act (OSHA) are all federal labor laws which regulate terms and conditions of employment that are mandatory topics of collective bargaining. The FLRA and ERISA establish minimum standards for wages, hours, and pension plans, which are nearly always improved upon by collectively bargained provisions. Only clauses in opposition to these laws (such as a wage under the national minimum) would provide for a conflict. The case of OSHA is somewhat different, however. Many unions and managements, following the passage of OSHA, negotiated contractual provisions that created joint labor-management safety committees. These committees were designed to act in concert with the OSHA law by allowing the two sides to monitor the workplace jointly. A recent analysis by Larry Drapkin reveals that in doing so, unions have sometimes exposed themselves to legal liability for some health and safety activity.[68] Interestingly enough, this legal liability has arisen under tort law rather than duty of fair representation cases. It is another area of law which warrants close attention over the next few years.

NOTES

[1]Mack A. Player, *Federal Law of Employment Discrimination in a Nutshell* (St. Paul, Minn.: West, 1976), p. 7.

[2]*Bethlehem—Alameda Shipyards, Inc.*, 53 NLRB 1016 (1943).

[3]*Steele* v. *Louisville and Nashville Railroad,* 323 U.S. 197 (1944).

[4]*Miranda Fuel Company,* 140 NLRB 181 (1962), enf. denied 326 F. 2d 172 (CA 2, 1963).

[5]*Local 1367, International Longshoremen's Assn.* (Galveston Maritime Assn.), 148 NLRB 897 (1964), enf. 368 F. 2d 1010 (CA 5, 1966), cert. denied, 389 U.S. 837 (1967).

[6]*Local 12, Rubber Workers* v. *NLRB*, 368 F. 2d 12 (CA 5, 1966) cert. denied, 389 U.S. 837 (1967).

[7]77 Stat. 56, 29 U.S.C. §206(d) (1970).

[8]*Thompson* v. *Sawyer*, 678 F. 2d 257, 293, 298 FEP 1614, 1645 (D.C. Cir 1982).

[9]For a good review of all of the economic, social, and legal components of the issue of comparable worth, see Michael Evan Gold, *A Dialogue on Comparable Worth* (Ithaca, New York: ILR Press, Cornell University, 1983).

[10]452 U.S. 161, 25 FEP 1521 (1981).

[11]78 Stat. 253 (1964), as amended 86 Stat. 103 (1972). 42 U.S.C. §2000 e-e17.

[12]Lineberger, "Recent Developments in Age Discrimination," American Business Law Journal, Vol. 17, 1979, p. 363, cited in Barbara L. Schlei and Paul Grossman, *Employment Discrimination Law, Second Edition* (Washington, D.C.: The Bureau of National Affairs, 1983), p. 485.

[13]41 CFR 60-741.2.

[14]*Daubert* v. *United States Postal Service*, 31 FEP 459 (D. Colo. 1982).

[15]*Jones* v. *Alfred H. Mayer Co.*, 392 U.S. 409 (1968).

[16]*McDonald* v. *Santa Fe Trail Transportation Co.*, 427 U.S. 273 (1976).

[17]Judicial interpretations of the applicability of the statutes to these issues have been made, respectively, in the following cases: *Cypress* v. *Newport News General and Nonsectarian Hospital Assn.*, 375 F. 2d 648 (4th Cir., 1967); *Spence* v. *Bailey*, 325 F. Supp. 601 (W.D. Tenn., 1971), aff'd. 465 F. 2d 797 (6th Cir., 1972); *Reed* v. *Reed*, 404 U.S. 71 (1971); *Korematsu* v. *United States*, 323 U.S. 214 (1944).

[18]494 F. 2d 211 (1974).

[19]*Id.*, at 262.

[20]365 F. Supp. 87 (E.D. Mich., 1973).

[21]*Griggs* v. *Duke Power Co.*, 401 U.S. 424 (1971).

[22]*Gregory* v. *Litton Sys., Inc.*, 472 F.2d 631, 5 FEP 267 (9th Circuit, 1972).

[23]407 F.2d 1047, 1 FEP 577 (5th Circuit, 1969).

[24]637 F.2d 506, 24 FEP 352 (8th Circuit, 1980).

[25]*Griggs* v. *Duke Power Co.*, 401 U.S. 424 (1971).

[26]279 F. Supp. 505 (E.D. Va., 1968).

[27]416 F.2d 980 (5th Cir., 1969), cert. denied, 397 U.S. 919 (1970).

[28]*Waters* v. *Wisconsin Steel Works*, 427 F. 2d 476 (7th Cir., 1970), cert. denied, 400 U.S. 911 (1970).

[29]508 F. 2d 687 (3rd Cir., 1975), cert. granted, 425 U.S. 987 (1976) (judgment vacated and case remanded to court of appeals).

[30]510 F. 2d 939 (6th Cir., 1975), cert. denied, 425 U.S. 998 (1976).

[31]424 U.S. 747 (1976).

[32]*International Brotherhood of Teamsters* v. *United States*, 431 U.S. 324 (1977).

[33]*United Air Lines, Inc.* v. *Evans*, 431 U.S. 553, 52 L. Ed. 2d 571 1977.

[34]431 U.S. 395 (1977).

[35]See *Franks* v. *Bowman Transportation Co.*, 424 U.S. 747, 762−66 (1976). See also case cited in footnote 27.

[36]456 U.S. 69, 28 FEP 716 (1982).

[37]34 FEP 1702 (1984).

[38]*United States Postal Service Bd. of Governors* v. *Aikens*, 460 U.S. 711, 31 FEP 609 (1983); *Trout* v. *Lehman*, 702 F. 2d 1094, 31 FEP 286 (D.C. Cir. 1983); *Wilmore* v. *City of Washington*, 699 F. 2d 667, 31 FEP 2 (3rd Cir., 1983).

[39]*Hill* v. *K-Mart Corp.*, 699 F. 2d 776, 31 FEP 269 (5th Cir. 1983); *Metrocare* v. *Washington Metro. Area Transit Authority*, 679 F. 2d 922, 29 FEP 1585 (D.C. Cir. 1982); *Payne* v. *Travenol Laboratories, Inc.*, 679 F. 2d 798, 28 FEP 1212 (5th Cir.) cert. denied 459 U.S. 1038 (1982); *Pouncy* v. *Prudential Insurance Co.*, 688 F. 2d 795, 28 FEP 121 (5th Cir. 1982).

[40]*Payne* v. *Travenol Laboratories, Inc. supra*, Note 39; *Jackson* v. *Seaboard Coast Line R.R.*, 678 F. 2d 992, 1016−17, 29 FEP 442, 463 (11th Cir. 1982); *Williams* v. *Hoffmeister*, 520 F. Supp. 521, 27 FEP 783 (E.D. Tenn., 1981).

[41]*Paxton* v. *Union Nat'l. Bank*, 688 F. 2d 552, 29 FEP 1233 (8th Cir. 1982), cert. denied, 460 U.S. 1083 (1983).

[42]Over half of the charges filed in fiscal 1980 were discharge cases. See "Analysis of Charge Receipts," *EEOC Annual Report*, 1980.

[43]411 U.S. 792, 5 FEP 965 (1973).

[44]450 U.S. 248, 25 FEP 113 (1981).

[45]*Tims* v. *Board of Education of McNeil, Arkansas*, 452 F. 2d 551, 552, 4 FEP 127, 128 (8th Cir., 1971) (1981 case).

[46]*McDonnell Douglas Corp.* v. *Green*, 411 U.S. 804, 5 FEP at 970 (1972). (Although *McDonnell Douglas* was not technically a discharge but rather a refusal to reinstate or rehire case, the burden of proof requirement contained therein has normally been applied to the single-employee discharge cases.)

[47]348 F. Supp. 202, 5 FEP 409 (W.D. Mo., 1972), aff'd. 472 F. 2d 1210, 5 FEP 612 (8th Cir., 1973).

[48]415 U.S. 36 (1974).

[49]429 F. 2d 324, 2 FEP Cases 687 (1970).

[50]415 U.S. 36, at 48−49.

[51]*Id.*, at 50−51.

[52]*Id.*, at 60, n. 21.

[53]403 F. Supp. 1183 (N.D. Miss., 1975).

[54]*Id.*, at 1188.

[55]Marvin Hill, Jr., "The Authority of a Labor Arbitrator to Decide Legal Issues Under a Collective Bargaining Contract: The Situation After Alexander v. Gardner-Denver," *Indiana Law Review*, Vol. 10, No. 5, 1977, p. 924.

[56]42 Ohio St. 2d 516, 330 N.E. 2d 703 (1975).

[57]Address of William B. Gould before the Society of Professionals in Dispute Resolution, *Daily Labor Report*, No. 204, October 23, 1973, p. E-1, as cited in Marvin Hill, Jr. and Anthony V. Sinicropi, "Excluding Discrimination Grievances from Grievance and Arbitration Procedures: A Legal Analysis," *Arbitration Journal*, Vol. 33, No. 1, March 1978, p. 20.

[58]Harry T. Edwards, "Labor Arbitration at the Crossroads: The 'Common Law of the Shop' v. External Law," *Arbitration Journal*, Vol. 32, No. 2, 1977, pp. 88–90.

[59]*Causey* v. *Ford Motor Co.*, 516 F. 2d 416, 425, n.12, 10 FEP 1493, 1500 (5th Cir. 1975).

[60]*McDaniel* v. *Essex Int'l., Inc*, 696 F. 2d 34, 30 FEP 831 (6th Cir. 1982); *Jackson* v. *Seaboard Coast Line R.R. Co.*, 678 F. 2d 992, 29 FEP 442 (11th Cir. 1982); *Lyon* v. *Temple Univ.*, 543 F. Supp. 1372, 30 FEP 1030 (E.D. Pa. 1982).

[61]*Macklin* v. *Spector Freight Systems, Inc.*, 478 F. 2d 979, 989, 5 FEP 994, 1001 (D.C. Cir. 1973).

[62]Schlei and Grossman, *op. cit.*, p. 775.

[63]438 U.S. 265, 17 FEP 1000 (1978).

[64]443 U.S. 193, 20 FEP 1 (1979).

[65]448 U.S. 448 (1980).

[66]657 F. 2d 962, 26 FEP 513 (8th Cir.) (en banc), *cert. denied*, 454 U.S. 1064 (1981).

[67]Mark S. Dichter and Paul Weiner, *Employment Litigation and Its Alternatives* (Litigation and Administrative Practice Series, Litigation Course Handbook Series, Number 243). New York: Practising Law Institute, 1984.

[68]Larry C. Drapkin and Morris E. Davis, "Health and Safety Provisions in Union Contracts: Power or Liability?" *Minnesota Law Review*, 65 (April 1981).

THE UNION AND THE EMPLOYER ORGANIZATIONAL STRUCTURE

Like business firms and ships, unions come in various sizes, shapes, and ages, which make for differences in behavior. It is the purpose of this chapter to examine some of those differences.

The organizational base of unions is laid in job-oriented units, whose main function is bargaining with employers. A superstructure, the federation deals with certain class-wide problems like social security or laws regulating bargaining. But it exercises somewhat tenuous control over the constituent unions.

PART I

UNION STRUCTURE

The Membership Base: Craft, Industrial, and Related Types of Unions

Pure craft and pure industrial unions are rare in the United States. Almost every union represents either a compromise or an extension of its basic principle of organization, and some are simply hodgepodge aggregations. Incidentally, some organizations that are called unions are not really unions at all. Despite improvements in their tools and materials, some occupations are still essentially preindustrial. For example, barbers and master plumbers create the whole of their "product" by themselves. Each owns his own tools and is free to work as an employee or to set up shop for himself. Unions of such persons are simultaneously craft and industrial, though they are regularly referred to as "craft." Their primary function is to set the price of their product to the public, not the price of their wage to an employer; they are in reality guilds rather than unions, whatever we may call them. Bricklayers, carpenters, electricians, paperhangers, and other building craftsmen fall into the same category when they do repairs or construction for individual householders.

More common are unions that combine several related crafts, generally known as *amalgamated craft unions*. Examples include the Brotherhood of Boilermakers, Iron Ship Builders, Blacksmiths, Forgers, and Helpers; and the Plasterers' and Cement Masons' International Association of the United States and Canada. Such unions retain the essential orientation of craft unionism. However, if a particular industry employs only a limited number of different skills, an amalgamation of the unions covering those skills may result in an industrial union or a close approximation of it. For example, much of the men's clothing industry was organized originally into separate craft unions of stitchers, pressers, cutters, trimmers, and so on. When these crafts were combined into the Amalgamated Clothing and Textile Workers Union (ACTWU), they became a true industrial union. The ACTWU and the International Ladies' Garment Workers' Union (ILGWU) typically bargain as a complete industrial union for all organized employees in a given company. The United Steelworkers of America do the same in many of their plants.

If industrial unions extend their coverage, they become *multi-industrial*. The names of several illustrate such extension: the Gas, Coke, and Chemical Workers (subsequently merged into the Oil, Chemical, and Atomic Workers); the United Automobile, Aircraft, and Agricultural Implement Workers (generally known as the UAW); and the United Rubber, Cork, Linoleum, and Plastic Workers (URW). Unions often extend their jurisdiction without changing their names to match. For example, the ACTWU includes workers in retailing, cleaning and dyeing, and laundries; and the Teamsters (International Brotherhood of Teamsters, Chauffeurs, Warehousemen, and Helpers of America) includes many brewery workers and retail clerks, among others. The International Brotherhood of Electrical Workers is a hybrid; it is definitely a craft union in the building trades and an industrial union in electrical manufacturing.

Amalgamations often reflect obvious relations, as between plumbers and steam-fitters or gas and coke workers. The relationships on which other amalgamations are based are less obvious. The machinist in a factory presumably has a choice between a craft union of machinists and an industrial union of factory workers. He may have no practical choice, however, if an industrial union organizes the rest of the plant but the machinists have no locals in the area. And his choice may be eliminated if the National Labor Relations Board, on the basis of a hearing, decides that all shop workers in the plant constitute an appropriate bargaining unit and, after an election, certifies the industrial union as the exclusive bargaining representative. If he has a free choice, he may choose the union with the most vigorous leaders rather than the one that seems abstractly more logical. In many cases, the union selected is simply the one that got there first or conducted the most effective campaign. Many brewery workers, dairy workers, and retail clerks belong to the Teamsters because the Teamsters had already organized the drivers in their firms and were ready, willing, and able to organize the workers inside the plant. Small clothing firms in coal-mining towns have sometimes been represented by the United Mine Workers "because it was there." A special case was the "catchall" District 50 of the United Mine Workers, which sought members in diverse fields, including steel, automobiles, chemicals, clothing, retailing, textiles, and construction. District 50 is now affiliated with the United Steelworkers, but has retained its "catchall" characteristics, thereby resembling a *general union.* That type is common in Europe but is rather rare in the United States, except for District 50 and some segments of the Teamsters union. Any one local of either union, however, is likely to have only one job-oriented group within it. Viewed broadly, rather than following any rigid formal patterns, unions in many respects organize in the directions and areas that seem most likely to bring them members and to organize the unorganized.

A difficult jurisdictional problem may arise during the transition from a craft operation to an industrial one. Under older construction techniques, carpenters were carpenters and plasterers were plasterers. But in many present buildings the walls consist of machine-made panels. In installing such a wall, the distinction between a "carpenter" and a "plasterer" may have to be made on some niggling basis—such as whether the panel is nailed or cemented into place. In many respects building construction has ceased to be a group of crafts and has become an industry, and many of its difficult problems of technology and of industrial relations may never be adequately solved unless industrial unions supplant the craft ones presently there. In recent years, the unions in the building trades have tried to get more concerted action in dealing with large construction firms. This coordination approaches industrial unionization in fact if not in form. Meanwhile, such jobs as steamfitter, stone mason, and electrician retain much of their original requirements of skill in all kinds of construction, and nearly all building crafts retain their identity in small construction and in repair and maintenance.

The Local Union

Nearly all union structure in the United States is built on the basic local unit. If we include only those affiliated with the AFL–CIO—which is a federation, not a union—in 1983, there were 96 national and international unions. The federation's total membership as of June 30, 1983, was 13,758,000. In 1981 there were 49,400 local unions.[1] The local is normally confined to a geographic area small enough for all members to attend a single meeting. This may mean ten locals of a given union in a large city or only one local for the whole of a sparsely populated county. In industrial unions, a local usually covers a single plant or a number of small plants. It may carry the employer's name, as the "Oldsmobile local." Occasionally, ethnic groups formed separate locals, as in the case of Italian and Jewish locals of clothing workers in New York City. In the South, in the past, locals of some unions were based on race. A local may have as few as a dozen members, while the largest, Local 600 of the UAW covering the River Rouge plant of the Ford Motor Company, has about 20,000 members.

Unlike management, a union is structured as a formally constituted, democratic organization, with ultimate power vested in its members. The bylaws of each local define the number, terms, duties, election, and salary (if any) of local officers. They also cover procedural matters, such as calling and terminating strikes, ratifying contracts, selecting convention delegates, frequency of meetings, auditing, dues, fees, and other details. Many locals elect or appoint a business agent to do the detailed work. In larger locals, the president and/or the secretary-treasurer may be full-time officers, with salary, office, and staff. Salaries of local officers vary considerably from union to union but tend to run about even with the top rates received on the job by the union members. Membership meetings, plus referendums, constitute the legislative branch, and the officers, the executive. Some locals have an executive board to make certain interim decisions between meetings. The bylaws specify dues, assessments, initiation fees, or fines.

The president, vice-president, and secretary-treasurer perform the duties normal to those offices and are elected by the members of the local. In a small local the officers may serve as negotiators of a contract, though a staff representative from the national union or its appropriate district is the usual principal negotiator. In that case, it is typically the function of the officers to inform the district representative of the special problems and desires of the local membership. It is often their additional function to "sell" the membership on the nature of the possible contract gains, as contrasted with what they would like or think they ought to have. The president normally participates in a final effort to settle grievances before they go to arbitration.

Shop stewards are normally elected, supposedly in sufficient numbers so they can consult with employees who have or think they have a grievance, and they usually accompany an aggrieved employee in presenting a grievance to the supervisor at the initial step of the grievance procedure. Because they are presumably familiar with any grievance from its inception, they usually follow the grievance through all of its steps, including being present and probably testifying at an arbitration of the grievance. There is also a grievance committee, usually elected, who sit with management representatives in an effort to resolve grievances. In unions that operate a hiring hall, as is often the case with the longshoremen, building trades, and musicians, some person(s) must also be in charge of keeping records of members and of referring them to jobs when requests are received.

In unions of nonfactory workers, including construction workers, hotel and restaurant workers, barbers and beauticians, and others who work in scattered small groups, the primary work of the local is done by a *business agent*, who may be elected or appointed and is nearly always paid. He may negotiate contracts, settle grievances, preserve jurisdictions, recruit new members, and handle correspondence and accounting. Sometimes he virtually *is* the local union. Among longshoremen on the dock, the *walking delegate* performs this function.

Initiation fees, which represent a union member's initial financial obligation, are required by most unions and may be set either by the national organization or by an individual local subject to limits in the national constitution. Monthly dues are required by all labor organizations; some apply a single rate, whereas others utilize a varying rate structure, often a percentage of the earnings. The maximum dues payment among unions is usually determined by local units. Most unions exempt unemployed members from paying dues, a smaller percentage exempt retirees, workers temporarily laid off, and apprentices. Per capita taxes, which are contributions by local affiliates of national unions to the parent organization, are required almost uniformly.[2]

The International Union

Locals are normally affiliated directly with a *national union* (or *international*, if the union has locals in Canada) and pay per capita dues to it. Each local is bound by the international constitution as a condition of holding its charter. Legislative power is vested in the *convention*, which is normally held every year or two. Most delegates represent locals on a per capita basis. Some are selected at large and some from city, state, or district bodies, which will be described shortly. The convention selects an executive board to carry on the legislative function between conventions, and the board may in turn have an executive committee to function between meetings of the full board. International officers are usually elected either by the convention or by referendum and normally include a president, vice-president, and secretary-treasurer, all on a full-time basis. Salaries of international presidents of major selected unions range from $40,000 to over $100,000[3] a year, plus expenses. The officers may hire a staff of as many as several hundred persons. Members of the executive board usually have specific personal assignments, such as organization and membership, contacts with locals, economic policy, political action, negotiations, and public relations.

There may also be district, state, county, or city divisions of an international union, known as joint boards, county councils, state councils, and the like. They coordinate the work of locals within their area. They also link the international and the local, breaking down the administrative task of the international into more convenient units. In some unions, each member of the executive board is responsible for some geographic area. The organizational levels between the local and the international are normally secondary in importance, although (especially in industries of numerous small firms, such as clothing or building construction) the joint board or local trades council sometimes does the real collective bargaining. The district may also be important.

Elections of Union Officers

Under Title IV, Section 401, of the Labor-Management Reporting and Disclosure Act "every national or international labor organization, . . . shall elect its officers not less often than once every five years . . . Every local labor organization shall elect its officers not less often than once every three years. Officers of intermediate bodies such as general committees, system boards, joint boards, or joint councils, shall be elected not less often than once every four years." The statute also outlines the procedures that have to be followed during such elections.

The Whole Union

The thing referred to as "a union" is normally the totality of the national or international office, state or regional offices, if any, plus all the locals. It is difficult to make generalizations about behavior or structure, because of the many differences among unions. In industries or companies that operate on a national scale, the national officers of the union do most of the important negotiating with employers, as has traditionally been the case with the United Automobile Workers, the United Steel-workers of America, and the United Mineworkers. By contrast, where there is little or no competition among geographically separated firms, negotiations with employers are usually carried on by the officers of the local union. If a regional or national representative participates in negotiations, his function may be more to provide experience and negotiating skill than to influence the outcome toward any national pattern. Negotiations in building trades, transit companies, bakeries, and laundries are normally conducted at the local level by the local union.

Creation of new local unions is the principal purpose of organizing activities, which are relatively expensive. It is customary for salaries and expenses of organizers to be paid by the regional or national union. Whereas workers in some other industrial nations take unionization for granted and do not wait to be recruited, American workers usually do not form a union until they feel an explicit need for one. An organizer's typical first move is therefore to uncover and publicize grievances and dissatisfactions in order to create resentment against the employer and a felt need for a union. If and when the plant is organized, the actual process of negotiating contracts and of processing grievances may be left to the local union.

THE AFL−CIO FEDERATION—FORMAL STRUCTURE*

Since December 1955, the AFL−CIO federation has operated as a single unit. Any national union that accepts the principles and objectives of the federation can apply for and presumably obtain membership in it. A local union may affiliate directly with the federation if there is no national union in its field, and it is then known as a *federal union*.

It should be clearly understood that the AFL−CIO is *not a union*, nor were the separate federations before it. It does not engage in collective bargaining, nor can an individual join it except indirectly as a member of an affiliated union. The function of the AFL−CIO is to bring about organized cooperation of the constituent unions on behalf of labor as a whole. It has been found advantageous, for example, to pool forces for lobbying and electioneering. The central body is highly useful for settling jurisdictional disputes between national unions and has worked out reasonably successful procedures for this purpose. When the government asks labor to name representatives to some board or commission, the federation makes the selection in the name of all labor. Policies regarding emergency wage controls, minimum wage legislation, social security, immigration, or tariffs can be executed better by a central organization. A variety of periodicals and pamphlets is turned out by the federation covering news of interest to labor as a whole. In brief, the federation carries on the class-wide functions

---

*See Figure 5-1.

FIGURE 5.1

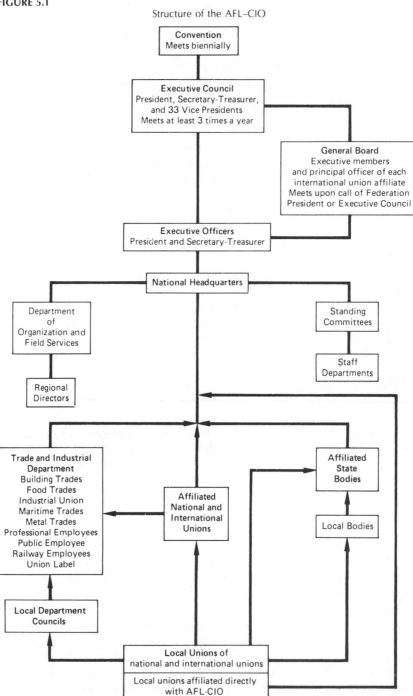

Structure of the AFL–CIO

SOURCE: *Directory of National Unions and Employee Associations, 1977*, Bulletin 2044 (Washington D.C.: U.S. Department of Labor, Bureau of Labor Statistics, 1979), p. 2. See also Directory of U.S. Labor Organizations, 1984–85 Edition, Courtney D. Gifford, Staff Editor, The Bureau of National Affairs, Inc., Washington, D.C., 1984. p. 6.

of the labor movement. Some money and effort for organizing drives also come from the federation. The AFL–CIO receives its income from a per capita tax on the affiliated unions.

The top governing body of the federation is the biennial convention, which technically has final authority in virtually all matters, including broad policy, acceptance or expulsion of affiliated unions, and selection of federation officers. In actuality, the top officers make the decisions on most matters; their power and prestige are unlikely to be overruled or even openly challenged in the convention. Disagreement among officers is normally ironed out in private. The officers consist of a president, a secretary-treasurer, and thirty-three vice-presidents, who jointly constitute the Executive Council. The thirty-five officers must all be members of affiliated unions; most are officers thereof. The officers together constitute the Executive Council, which is the governing body of the federation between conventions.

The General Board, consisting of the Executive Council plus the principal officer of each affiliated union, meets at least once a year and decides any matters of policy referred to it by the council. The AFL–CIO pays the expenses of the council but no salaries. The merged federation, like the former separate federation, seems to be continuing the prior practice of reelecting its top officers till death or retirement. Although generous retirement pay might make it easier to achieve flexibility by "kicking a person upstairs" into early retirement, there are thus far no signs that it will be used this way. Figure 5–1 shows the structure of the AFL–CIO federation and its affiliate unions.

Subject to some qualification, the federation is loose; any member union can withdraw if it feels that the advantages of freedom outweigh those of affiliation. The UAW, for example, was in the AFL–CIO until 1955, disaffiliated from the AFL–CIO in 1968 and rejoined the Federation in 1981. Although the federation has little power over its constituent unions, the constitution permits it to be more demanding than the AFL had been with respect to such things as racial discrimination.

Some international unions with headquarters in the United States, like the UAW, have many members in Canada. In 1981 about 45% of total union membership in Canada belonged to U.S. international unions.[4]

Both the CIO and AFL had established city, state, and district councils, nearly all of which have now been merged into single AFL–CIO bodies. Not all these mergers of intermediate bodies have worked well, and cooperation is far from full. In New Jersey, for example, the former CIO group of unions pulled out of the state federation in mid-1964 in a dispute over some officerships and formed the independent Industrial Union Council. After the dispute was settled, however, they rejoined the main body in 1965. Conversely, cooperation at the local level may be close between federation and nonfederation unions, as is often the case with AFL–CIO unions and the unaffiliated Teamsters.

The major functions of the federation are reflected in its list of standing committees—on legislation, civil rights, political education, ethical practices (dealing with corruption and communism), international affairs, education (within the unions as well as in the nation in general), social security, economic policy, community services, housing, research, public relations, safety and occupational health, veteran's affairs, organization, and inter-American affairs. Provisions are also made for discouraging the raiding of one union by another and for settling jurisdictional disputes.

The AFL–CIO also has subdivisions called departments, which coordinate groups of unions that have related problems. There is one department each for building trades, food trades, industrial union, maritime trades, metal trades, professional employees, and union label. These departments are, in effect, subfederations. Each has its constitution and officers, accepts or rejects unions for membership, and collects its own per capita tax. A national union may belong to more than one department but need not join any. If only a portion of the union's membership is qualified for affiliation, the union may affiliate with respect to that fraction. Tables 5–1 and 5–2 provide statistical data of membership of national unions, large unions, and local affiliates.

Among the AFL–CIO departments, the Industrial Union Department (IUD) has special significance. In 1955, the former CIO entered the merged federation almost intact as the IUD. It brought along its president and secretary-treasurer (Walter Reuther and James B. Carey, respectively) and its $1.25 million treasury. Some thirty-five former AFL unions joined the IUD for all or part of their membership. The IUD carries considerable weight in the AFL–CIO but by no means dominates it. An important function of the IUD is to coordinate bargaining strategies of two or more unions that deal with the same employer.

The AFL–CIO and Member Unions

The AFL–CIO constitution gives the organization more formal control over its member unions than did the constitution of the AFL, and in this respect the new

TABLE 5.1 MEMBERSHIP OF NATIONAL UNIONS, 1983

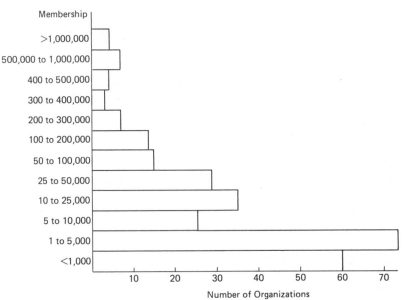

SOURCE: Leo Troy and Neil Sheflin, *U.S. Union Sourcebook* (West Orange, N.J.: IRDIS, 1985), pp. 3–8.

TABLE 5.2 LARGE UNIONS AND LOCAL AFFILIATES

Union	Members (1982)	Number of Local Bodies
Teamsters (IBT)	1,800,000	770
National Education Association (NEA)	1,641,354	12,300
Steelworkers (USW)	1,200,000	5,100
Auto Workers (UAW)	1,140,370	1,485
Food and Commercial (UFCW)	1,079,213	770
State, County (AFSCME)	950,000	3,000
Electrical (IBEW)	883,000	1,433
Service Employees (SEIU)	700,000	350
Carpenters (CJA)	679,000	1,744*
Machinists (IAM)	655,221	1,735
Communication Workers (CWA)	650,000	900
Teachers (AFT)	573,644	2,200
Laborers (LIUNA)	450,442	820
Clothing and Textile Workers (ACTWU)	400,000	1,255*
Hotel, Restaurant (HERE)	375,000	220
Plumbers (PPF)	353,127	491*
Operating Engineers (IUOE)	345,000	181*
Ladies Garment Workers (ILGWU)	276,000	401
Paperworkers (UPIU)	263,695	1,217
Musicians (AFM)	260,000	580
Retail (RWDSU)	250,000	300

Derived from Appendix A of same report.

SOURCE: Courtney O. Gifford, *Directory of U.S. Labor Organizations*, 1984–85 Edition (Washington, D.C.: BNA, 1984), Parts I and III.

federation more nearly resembles the old CIO. The original federations reflected their respective histories; the AFL grew from a merger of existing unions, whereas the large unions—steel, autos, and rubber—were themselves created by the CIO. Three areas in which the AFL–CIO has sought increased influence are jurisdictional disputes, corruption and communism, and civil rights.

In regard to the methods of enforcement, although the federation can set standards of behavior for member unions, it cannot replace their officers, change their rules, discipline their members, or curtail their incomes. Its ultimate disciplinary power lies solely in suspension or expulsion. But, although the AFL–CIO is important to the labor movement as a whole, an individual union may suffer little from nonaffiliation. For example, if the federation successfully lobbies for an increased minimum wage, an expelled union benefits as much as a member union. There may be some loss of prestige, but this is hardly important to a strong, functioning union. The United Mine Workers, in fact, may have enhanced prestige from its voluntary independent status. If there has been any weakening of the Teamsters by expulsion, it doesn't show; the expulsion may have hurt the federation more than the Teamsters. The Teamsters were expelled from the federation in 1957.

However, if the federation can charter a new union that could successfully raid the expelled one, it wields a solid club. For example, in 1949 the CIO expelled the United Electrical Workers (UE) for alleged communist domination. It then chartered a new union, the International Union of Electrical, Radio, and Machine Workers

(IUE), which eventually captured much of the original membership. By contrast, after expelling the International Longshoremen's Association (ILA) for corruption, the AFL was almost totally unsuccessful in recruiting its members into the replacement union. Eventually, however, the combined efforts of the AFL–CIO, the federal government, the state of New York, the city of New York, the Waterfront Commission, and assorted other agencies cleaned up the union enough to get it back into the federation. Corruption was also eliminated in several smaller unions following actual or threatened expulsion. Probably the main effect of the federation's action in these cases was to strengthen the position of the reform groups *within* the affected unions. On the whole, as a combined effect of the disciplinary actions by the federation, the Ethical Practices Code of the federation, and the law, corruption seems to have dropped to a minor level within AFL–CIO unions.

The Teamsters is a different matter, however. The federation felt that it was hopeless even to try to establish a rival union. And by expelling the Teamsters, the AFL–CIO gave up *all* formal authority over it.

Race, Communism, and Jurisdiction

No union may be a member of the AFL–CIO if its constitution or bylaws contain racially discriminatory provisions. The federation also attempts to exert influence over its affiliated unions in several other areas. The separate actions of the AFL and CIO in removing communist elements were sufficiently successful that, in the Communist Control Act of 1954, Congress declared affiliation with either federation (and by implication the AFL–CIO) to be *prima facie* evidence of noncommunist control.

Jurisdictional problems take two forms. The first is work assignment: Should the metal molding on a wooden cabinet be installed by the metalworkers (because it is metal) or by the carpenters (because it is on a wooden object)? The second is representation rights: Is the Auto Workers or the Machinists the appropriate union to organize a machine shop of the Ford Motor Company?

At the 1961 convention of the AFL–CIO a new section, "The Settlement of Internal Disputes," was added to the constitution. It became effective in 1962 and requires affiliates to respect the established collective bargaining and work relationships of every other affiliate. In the event of a dispute, the case goes to a mediator selected from a panel of mediators from within the labor movement. If he or she cannot settle the dispute within fourteen days, it is referred to an impartial umpire selected from a panel of "prominent and respected persons," whose decision can be appealed to the Executive Council for a final ruling. Penalties on a union that does not comply with the final decision include loss of right to use the appeals machinery, possible suspension, and assistance by the federation to the other union.

Miscellaneous Union Organizations

The *Directory of National Unions and Employee Associations* in its 1980 edition lists three organizations which either behave as a federation or have some characteristics of a federation; for example, they issue charters to and maintain a formal affiliation among autonomous labor organizations. These three are: The Assembly of Governmental Employees (AGE), the National Federation of Independent Unions (NFIU), and the Telecommunications International Union (TIU).[5]

According to the 1980 *Directory of National Unions*, in 1978 sixty-six national or international unions were not affiliated with the AFL−CIO. There is also a fair number of local unions that never affiliated with either a national or international union or a federation. Usually such unions are confined to a single establishment, employer, or locality. Although the AFL−CIO is considered by many to be the official voice of the labor movement, there are organizations, some very large ones, that do not belong to the Federation. The two largest independent unions are the International Brotherhood of Teamsters with 1.8 million members and the National Education Association with 1.6 million members.[6]

DEMOCRACY IN UNIONS

Some Problems of Democracy in General

Democracy in its ideal state requires many things: informed citizens, intelligent awareness of one's own self-interest, awareness of the rights of others, willingness to accept wise leadership, and a mechanism that informs leaders of the wishes of the electorate and replaces those leaders if they do not respond. The technical apparatus of democracy includes secret ballots, freedom to oppose, and a judicial system that protects individuals and restrains officials.

Anyone who has observed democratic organizations at close range, particularly private ones, knows that a vast gulf often exists between the ideal and the actual. Reluctance to attend meetings, impatience with the business part of the meeting, unwillingness to serve on committees, and the greater readiness to criticize leaders than to help them—these things are observed almost anywhere that democratic organizations operate. Often, they reflect a feeling that the "business" is unimportant or that the member does not understand it well enough to cast an intelligent vote. When important discussions do reach the floor, many members hesitate to speak, some get off the subject, and others cannot be heard. Officers get reelected because no one wants to hurt their feelings, or because they pull the strings, and decisions gravitate to those who will make them. In organizations other than governments, the unopposed slate, elected by acclamation, is common.

In government, voters often know little about the candidates. Some citizens shrink from politics as from a loathsome disease, and others are indifferent. Though the issues may seem important, they also often seem unfamiliar and hopelessly complex. Many persons never bother to vote. The nonparticipation of most corporate stockholders is too well known to deserve comment. Much the same may be said for professional, charitable, fraternal, and civic organizations.

These inadequacies appear even where people are honest and sincere, and are greatly aggravated if leaders or voters are self-seeking or dishonest. Unions are spared none of these difficulties and add a few of their own. In the following pages we will raise the questions: How much democracy is there in unions? How much ought there to be? What can be done to eliminate the discrepancies? Incidentally, except at the stockholder level, these questions do not arise on the management side; the basic structure of management is authoritarian, with power flowing down from the top.

The legal response to concerns about union democracy was the enactment of the Labor-Management Reporting and Disclosure Act of 1959. The act is discussed in more detail in Chapter 2.

Special Problems of Democracy in Unions

Plant Government versus Union Government.   Democracy is concerned with making government responsive to those governed. A complication arises at the outset in unions. What the employee is really concerned about is his plant government—the set of rules and regulations, wages, and conditions in his job. If the union, in conjunction with management, creates a good plant government, the member may care little about how the union itself is run. That is, the member may see himself or herself less as a participant in the union than as a customer buying a service from it, and if the service is good he or she may not care whether the "supplier" is honest or democratic.

Solidarity and the External Nature of the Union's Problems.   The union itself does not provide for the member's wants but merely bargains for him or her with a third party, the employer. In many organizations disagreement and criticism about internal matters are allowed, even encouraged. But in conflict with outsiders, the factions are expected to close into a solid front. This expectation is heightened during negotiations and is greatest during a strike. At a strike rally, the union leader is both chairman of a discussion group and captain of an army. Experience shows that he or she is more vulnerable if lack of toughness loses a strike even if victory comes from suppressing dissent. For the union's most important business, the ground rules are not those of domestic policy, but of foreign policy during war, when dissent is made to seem treasonous.

All this does not mean that democratic practices are absent but merely that they face special obstacles. Instead of the traditional year, many union contracts now run for two or three years and greatly increase the noncrisis periods between negotiations. Furthermore, union security provisions now place the existence of many unions out of jeopardy and improve the conditions for tolerating dissent.

The Absence of Conflict over Policy.   The major business of democratic government is to accommodate disagreements over policy, whereas questions of means tend to be left to elected leaders and their appointees. Contests over candidates are often policy contests in disguise.

The union's main policy has traditionally been simple and uncontested—*more.* The rest are mainly technical questions—how much to ask, when and whether to strike, whether to act tough or reasonable. But these are really matters of technical competence, not policy, and we normally do not select technical competence by elections. However, this factor should not be exaggerated. A large union with diverse membership may have many policy conflicts over bargaining goals.

Management Reactions and Democracy.   Another condition that militates against rank-and-file control is management's preference. Although employers often accuse unions of being undemocratic, much of this criticism, however, arises from a simple desire to find fault with unionism. When an employer is actually dealing with a union, he or she generally prefers one with strong leadership. He or she wants to deal with representatives on a "businesslike basis" and is annoyed if they must repeatedly go back to the members. On details, an employer may prefer to talk things over with the business agent, reach a conclusion, and know that "that's that." By contrast, democratic processes "rock the boat," as is nicely sensed in an important business magazine: "A new union administration—always a topic of nervous interest among businessmen."[7]

The Psychology and Politics of Leadership.   Union members distrust leaders who have not come up through the ranks. David MacDonald, president of the Steelworkers, was an apparent notable exception, having been the hired secretary of the former president. But even he was defeated in 1965 by a rank-and-filer, I. W. Abel. In addition, election to a salaried union post brings a sharp change in the quality of life. Time is now spent in offices, conference rooms, planes, and hotels, not in the dirt and noise of the mill. The leader's income is probably larger and more regular, with an expense account added. Many of his contacts are now with people of higher status— the officers of the company, the higher officials of the union, the school board, the community chest, and the city council. Though he or she may tell the members how much simpler life was at the bench, he or she may resist returning.

Meanwhile, the leader acquires experience at a difficult and demanding job. The cost of on-the-job training for union leaders are probably as high as for corporate executives, particularly when the issues in bargaining are as complex as pensions, job evaluations, health plans, and automation. Union members see no more logic in discarding experienced executives every few years than does a corporate board of directors. Besides, the corporation probably has a larger pool to draw from. "Effective union leaders are relatively scarce; and experienced, proven union leaders not in office are even scarcer."[8] This is one reason the leader is normally returned election after election, often without opposition, at least at the national level. Turnover of local officers is often quite high.

A notable exception is the International Typographical Union (ITU), which has operated a two-party system (the only union to have one) during most of its long history.[9] The reasons are unique and seem to include several instances of forebearance by leaders who could probably have eliminated opposition if they had so desired. In 1984 the ITU and Teamsters leadership concluded a merger agreement subject to rank-and-file approval. Because of election irregularities of ITU officers in 1983, the first election was reversed. Another election was conducted in August of 1985. During that election the proposal to merge with the Teamsters was defeated.[10] A suggestion of two permanent parties would usually be called dual unionism, one of the nastiest epithets in the union movement. With this exception, there is no permanently organized opposition to the incumbent officers of American unions. At the national-union level, the president traditionally held much the same position as did the presidents of the United States within their own parties, where a president's position as head of the party was normally unchallenged so long as he or she was president, and defeat would come only from the opposition party. That relation still generally holds, though there have been increasing exceptions in both spheres. The techniques of holding power are standard and well known—patronage, prestige, constitutional authority, constant publicity, and the seduction of potential rivals into useful but invisible posts. As both chief of state and party secretary, a competent president of an international union can normally hold on till death or retirement.

Democracy cannot be measured quantitatively, and it is difficult to say how large a fraction of the labor movement actually represses it, as contrasted to the fractions in which democracy merely meets with obstacles or functions reasonably well.

Some past abuses have been flagrant. William Hutcheson was elected president of the Carpenters for life and appointed his son Maurice to replace him when he retired in 1953. At one point, James Caesar Petrillo was not only elected president of the Musicians for life but was granted authority to change the union constitution at will. However, when opposition later became strong, he *was* replaced and the constitution was normalized. While president of the United Mine Workers, John L. Lewis held dissident locals in line by ousting their elected presidents and replacing them with his trustees. Well-grounded fears for physical safety have quieted occasional rivals in the Teamsters, Mineworkers, International Longshoremen, and scattered other unions.

Petty tyrants crop up in union offices (even among supervisors, office managers, or corporate executives), and some have fined, expelled, or denied jobs to members who criticized them. Historically, the task of protecting workers from management so greatly overshadowed that of protecting them from the union that little thought was given to the latter—though many leaders have worked hard to protect members' rights. Managements may criticize dictatorial leadership. But the kind of labor leader most in need of the criticism could fend it off with, "Whatever management criticizes must be good for the workers."

At least until recently, the internal procedures for protecting members against improper discipline from the union itself have been woefully inadequate. For example, under the bylaws, a member who appealed his discipline for criticizing the president of a local union might find the president sitting as judge. Other appeals procedures, though not essentially unfair, were often so cumbersome that only a masochist would use them. The international convention is the court of final appeal in most unions. But this body may meet only every two or three years and is too large and unwieldy to handle essentially judicial matters.

Public Review Boards.   One minor union, the Upholsterers, and one major one, the United Automobile Workers, have established public review boards. That of the UAW is the better known, though basically it was copied in 1957 from the Upholsterers' plan of 1953, shortly after the publicity given to malfeasance and racketeering in the Teamsters Union by the McClellan Select Committee of the United States Senate. Its establishment can be interpreted in part as a move to erase the smear Hoffa had left on the whole American labor movement. It was also in part a frank recognition that the protection of members' rights was not all it could be, even in this union, which had a long-standing reputation for clean living and strong membership participation.

The UAW Public Review Board consists of seven distinguished citizens not connected with the union. The board members are proposed by the international president, with the approval of the International Executive Board, to the delegates of each constitutional convention of the union. Acting jointly with the Appeals Committee of the Constitutional Convention, they have the "authority and duty to make final and binding decisions" on cases brought before them from aggrieved members of subordinate bodies of the union. During the calendar year of 1984 the board decided 49 appeals, and there were 18 appeals pending as of December 31, 1984. The 1984 cost to the UAW of operating the board was $633,744. To cut down on costs the board held some meetings on Saturday; also, some sessions were conducted through long-distance conference calls instead of personal meetings.[11]

Some apprehension existed over the creation of the body, because it is highly unusual for a private organization to give to outsiders final and binding authority over internal matters, and the courts are traditionally reluctant to deal with internal matters of private organizations. While agreeing that the board is a healthy thing, some union officers feel it has been too concerned with technicalities rather than substance of fairness. At the present time, it seems unlikely that it will be abolished or that other unions will copy it.

PART II

THE EMPLOYER ORGANIZATIONAL STRUCTURE

In this section we examine management as an organization—as a system, for those who want to sound more up-to-date. In the preceding section we did the same for the union organization. But we may immediately note an important difference. Although there is wide disagreement as to whether any particular plant needs such a thing as a union organization, no one, not even the union, seriously questions the need for a management. This difference is discussed in more detail in Chapter 15.

Many forces, both inside the organization and outside in its environment, determine how its management will feel toward and deal with its employees—how the management will feel initially about the prospect of having its employees organize into a union and how the management will deal with a union if and when one is organized. In some organizations employers employ sophisticated methods to avoid unionization. The discussion of this subject is postponed to a later chapter on union and management security.

We look first at some of the larger relations of the firm with its environment. On one side are the input relations, in which the firm takes in such things as labor, materials, and capital from its environment. On the other side are the output relations, in which the firm releases such things as manufactured products, services, advertising, wages, and other payments to its environment. Speaking broadly, the study of these input and output relations falls mainly within the subject matter of economics.

Second, and by contrast, we look at relationships inside the firm. These involve feelings and aspirations, likes and dislikes, and flows of information within the company. The internal politics and organizational structure of the firm are also relevant. In present-day terminology, this second group of forces would be thought of as "behavioral" rather than economic. Though many of these relations, both economic and behavioral, are reasonably universal, the analysis will reflect mainly the way they occur in the United States today. In short, economics does much to explain the day-to-day human relationships of the employee on the job.

The contrast between the *intrasystem* and the *intersystem* aspects of a business firm are a clear indication of the reasons why a competent understanding of labor relations requires interdisciplinary knowledge. The subject of labor relations stands, so to speak, with one foot in market analysis and the other in behavioral sciences and related disciplines.

THE ENVIRONMENT AND CONSTRAINTS OF THE FIRM

The Private Profit Economy

There has been increasing dispute in recent decades whether firms seek to maximize profits, as economists generally have argued (or at least find convenient for their models), or whether they "satisfice" profits, as argued by Herbert Simon and others who view firms through the eyes of organization theory. We need not settle this point to be reasonably confident that over any extended period the management of a firm must see to it that its income equals or exceeds its expenditures. Although the relation may not be quite as widely recognized there, the same is true for most government bureaus, nonprofit service organizations, and labor unions viewed as employers, not to mention individual colleges or departments within a university. True, in these cases the income may come from taxation or contributions rather than from sale of products. And the "revenue" may take the form of a budget allocation rather than a return on sales, the budget allocation being achieved through persuading higher levels of administration rather than persuading customers. Yet the imperative of keeping expenditures within budget constraints may be no less binding. In fact, in this respect the whole of a nonprofit organization may operate under much the same logic as does a subdivision with a profit firm.

Within the United States, both sides to collective bargaining operate under a limited contractual relationship. Unlike some relations in Japan, Latin America, and Eastern Europe, the employer has no responsibility for the economic welfare of the employee or the employee's family beyond payment of the contracted wage and related fringe benefits for as long as the employee continues to perform satisfactorily and is needed by the employer. Nor has the employee any responsibility for the economic welfare of the employer beyond the satisfactory performance of specified tasks. In particular, and unlike the situation in the areas mentioned, the employer has no obligation to keep an employee on the payroll unless it is considered to be in the economic interests of the firm to do so. The situation is softened somewhat by various employee security provisions under union contracts. But overall, neither the law nor the customs of our country obligate an employer to retain employees who are not needed.

Numerous kinds of regulations may affect employers in their relations with employees. For example, public utilities may need utility commission permission before passing increased wage costs to consumers in increased utility bills, and safety regulations might require larger crews of employees than the employer thinks are necessary. These regulations may affect the *level* at which the employer will be seeking to balance costs and incomes. But they do not remove the imperative of keeping them balanced.

The Input Side

Cost structure refers to the percentage of total costs that go to particular inputs, such as wages, materials, power, advertising, and the like. In some industries, labor constitutes a high percentage of total cost. It has been high in such industries as construction, transit, handmade pottery, education, and service. On the other hand, in some highly automated, capital-intensive industries like the refining of petroleum, labor costs may represent a very small proportion of total costs. Needless to say, managements are under greater pressure to avoid large wage increases in labor-intensive rather than capital-intensive industries.

An employer also has a *labor structure*, which means the numbers and ratios of different types of employees. Some industries employ only one or a few dominant types. The trucking industry employs mainly drivers; the nonrail transit industry employs mainly driver-salespeople; the clothing industry employs people with a few skills related to cutting, stitching, and pressing; and an orchestra employs musicians almost exclusively. Even an industry as complex as building construction is dominated by representatives of less than a dozen specific crafts. By contrast, a large manufacturing plant making complex items includes much unskilled and semiskilled labor whose abilities can be used just as easily to put together ships as automobiles, radios as pumps. In addition, there exist a variety of skilled jobs in manufacturing, with a sprinkling from nearly every occupation. For example, firms in steel, automobiles, chemicals, textiles, or paper all include their quotas of drafters, electricians, carpenters, machinists, crane operators, truck drivers, plumbers, and many others—if not for production, then at least for maintenance work. Illustrative of the scope of skills employed in large modern industry is a steel plant that has several agricultural economists on its staff, because some of its waste products contain ingredients for fertilizers.

The homogeneous group of employees poses a different set of problems to management from that posed by the occupationally cosmopolitan group. The plant with only a few types of labor has a simple wage structure. It is easy to make comparisons with what competing employers are paying for the same kinds of labor, and for competitive reasons it is important that they pay about the same.

The large plant with a variety of workers may find it more important to maintain proper differentials among the jobs within its own plant than to pay the same as other plants. These differences are important for keeping status structures and lines of promotion clear and for motivating employees to train themselves for higher positions. Furthermore, it is difficult to compare general wage levels of two firms that include many kinds of employees in widely differing proportions. The total (or the average) wage measures the employer's labor cost. An employer can bargain effectively over his total (or average) wage bill only if he bargains simultaneously with all employees. If the employer were to deal with different groups separately, he might deal most generously with those who hold "bottleneck" jobs and whose actions could seriously curtail output of the whole plant. Or he or she might treat best those who negotiate first and put the real "squeeze" on the later groups in order to keep the total wage bill within a given amount. In either event, severe discontent of some groups will almost certainly follow. Both strategically and practically, employers in mass production industries generally find it preferable to deal with a single union for all employees rather than with a separate union for each group. Therefore, they tend to prefer a single union of the industrial type, though there are some notable exceptions, as we shall see. The urge is not nearly so strong with employers who hire only one or a few different kinds of labor.

Even people who have worked in other circumstances tend to think of organized workers mainly in terms of factory work, or perhaps in terms of an office, where a reasonably fixed number of people work in essentially unchanging work places for a regular work week of approximately forty hours. As Dunlop[12] has made abundantly clear, many other circumstances prevail, and they are worth reviewing. In the airlines, railroads, and over-the-road bus and truck transportation, employees eat and sleep away from home much of the time, and their associated costs must be provided or paid for by the employer. These industries also face scheduling problems in getting employees to their homes from time to time, either as part of their work runs or with "deadhead" transportation provided. The work of local bus drivers is concentrated in the first part of the morning and the last part of the afternoon, and raises questions as to whether they should be paid for the largely unusable time in between. Construction workers are often employed a month here, two days there, a week somewhere else, sometimes by the same construction firm and sometimes by different ones. Hence union-management contracts are nearly useless unless they encompass essentially all employers with whom a given individual is likely to work. In addition, provisions must be made about pay for days when they report to work and then are sent home because of bad weather. And to be feasible, such fringe benefits as vacations and pensions must be negotiated on a multiemployer basis.

Lumberjacks in logging camps typically live for extended periods in facilities provided by their employer, and their contracts may need to deal with quality of food and beds, sanitation, transportation out of camp, medical care, or even the number of movies per week. Migrant farm workers have much the same problem, but in more severe form because they change employers much more often. Construction engineers may be moved by their employer from coast to coast or to foreign nations at perhaps two-to-five-year intervals. Aprons, outer clothing, safety goggles, hard hats, and tools are required in many jobs, and decisions must be negotiated about who is to pay for them and how often they are to be cleaned or replaced. The role of tips as part of pay must be arranged for many service workers, as must be the role of royalties for those whose recorded commercials or artistic performances are replayed many times. Garment workers are subject to strongly seasonal employment, circus performers face some very special problems, as do movie actors and technicians when working on location. Finally, teachers may need to negotiate about academic freedom or free tuition for their families. In short, although this volume will deal mostly with the more obvious types of relationships, it should be kept in mind that the subject matter of collective bargaining contracts is tremendously varied.

The Output Side

The output of a firm is in its product, and the main problem on the output side is the state of competition in the product market. Many small-to-medium-sized firms are found in such industries as clothing, construction, trucking, and retailing. Competition is vigorous and often breaks out in price-cutting. Prices tend to run close to costs, leaving little margin for profit. Each firm is extremely reluctant to agree to anything that might raise its costs above its competitors', and the pressure to get costs below that level is strong. Since many of these industries tend to have fairly high labor costs, wage-cutting is an obvious way to reduce costs. In addition, it is easy for new firms to enter the industry or old ones to move to low-wage areas. Under these circumstances, employers may desire some stabilizing force to keep competitors from getting a cost advantage based solely on wage-cutting. The labor union is the only device now legally able to do this. Despite objections to some specific actions of the union, an employer in this kind of industry will often recognize that a strong union covering all his competitors may benefit him as well as his employees. The union, if it is to stabilize wage rates in such an industry, must be large. In fact, it will almost necessarily be more powerful than any single employer and may be stronger than all of them combined. It may be able to win from employers virtually anything the industry is able to give, in which case the only way the union can get "more" is to make the industry more prosperous. Union leaders may therefore become interested in reducing costs, increasing sales, and generally improving the welfare of employers. Employer willingness to accept the union's stabilizing effects on costs is thus augmented by the fact that union leaders may view the problems of the industry in much the same light as does management. Where industries consist of many comparatively small employers, it is common for them to form an employer association and engage in multiemployer bargaining. This type of bargaining is examined in more detail in our bargaining unit chapter.

In short, when management sells its output in an environment of vigorous competition among many small firms, it tends to resist unionization less if the union is strong, if the union covers all important competitors, and if all competing firms can bargain simultaneously through a single employer association. Although the union tends to dominate this relationship, it also tends to show restraint, which grows out of its understanding of the economic limitations of the industry.

At the opposite end are the industrial giants, whose profits sometimes run to eight to ten figures. Their product markets are more likely to be characterized by price leadership by dominant firms as in automobiles, steel, cigarettes, and cereals. Though with occasional exceptions, uniformity of wage rates among competing firms of this sort is less pressing than in the price-competitive industries. And because their differences are often more important than their similarities, the industrial giants usually bargain singly, sometimes dealing separately with a variety of different unions. These firms are large enough so that bargaining between any one of them and even a large union is by no means one-sided. It does not follow that large companies in the same industry sign widely different labor contracts. The method of establishing labor conditions is somewhat similar to price leadership.

THE ENVIRONMENT AND MANAGEMENT THINKING

The above discussion of the management's relation to its environment on the input and output sides is by no means comprehensive. Obviously, such additional factors as rate of growth, rate of technological change, seasonal and cyclical regularity or irregularity, antitrust policy, foreign competition, and government policy—to mention only a few—will have consequences on a firm or industry. These need not be detailed. However, a consequence is that, more than almost anything else, management wants flexibility and freedom of action to adapt to the vicissitudes of organizational life.

SOME INTERNAL ASPECTS OF THE FIRM

There are many ways a firm must adjust to the input and output side of its environment. But the firm itself is a complex arrangement of people, machines, materials, and money. A great deal of the work of management, and certainly of the personnel function, is concerned with people. They must be located, recruited, trained, placed, and evaluated. They must also be motivated, and induced to work with their tasks and with each other. As products and processes change, the methods and content of jobs must be modified and redescribed, and their relative rates of pay must be reevaluated. Any change in product or process may also change the relative numbers of different skills that the firm employs. A major change in job mix may require months of advance planning so that new employees can be recruited or existing employees can be retrained. An orderly reduction in force must also be planned long in advance to minimize hardship to employees, avoid penalty rates for unemployment compensation, hold down severance costs, and stay within the constraints of the seniority rules and affirmative action guidelines—to mention only the more conspicuous considerations. Many of these adjustments can be facilitated by specialists, who may be either hired or engaged as consultants. For example, industrial engineers are specialists in arranging physical layouts and muscular movements for optimum efficiency. Other specialists deal in such areas as job evaluation, merit rating, recruitment, employee testing, interviewing, and employee record keeping. To say that there are specialists in these areas does not require merely that experienced people be available. It also requires large bodies of knowledge stored in libraries, in computer memories, taught in university courses, and acquired through numerous experiments for evaluating different methods of doing things.

As a consequence, managements, at least in large firms, have access to a large body of expertise about the effective use of human beings in production. Among many other things, this knowledge covers the differences in effect between authoritarian and democratic supervision, the effective use of grievance procedures, the strengths and weaknesses of participative decision making, job narrowing, and job enrichment, and ways to reduce turnover. To list these areas does not mean that we have precise knowledge about all of them in which high confidence can be placed. But it does mean that there are reasonably systematic methods of learning about them.

One consequence is a potential battle over numerous details. While recognizing the importance of individual differences, management tends to think that there are known or knowable ways of making the most effective use of human beings as factors of production. Unions seem to thwart the related moves that management considers sensible in dealing with its employees. For one thing the union objective, insofar as it has one in this area, is to make work life more satisfactory for employees. This goal may or may not coincide with the most effective use of human beings as factors of production. Second, it is unlikely that union officers or negotiators will have anything approaching the expertise available to management on this score. This fact may leave the union representatives feeling defensive on such matters, possibly leading to the kind of aggressive response that sometimes arises from insecurity. Third, union leaders and members observe the way business firms make use of applied psychology in their advertising to mold consumer perceptions into seeing the advantages but not the disadvantages of the products they sell. These observations are not reassuring about the possibility that management's professional use of applied psychology in the workplace does not have a parallel "brainwashing" purpose of shifting workers' loyalties from the union to management. Management's assurance that the various experts are objective and impartial in dealing with employees is apt to be met with the stereotypical, "The company's payin' them, ain't they?"

This aspect of the relationship sometimes goes a step farther. Not only can management acquire expert help in dealing with employees, it now seems worthwhile for some to acquire ultrasophisticated advice in handling the union itself. This may include evasions of the law through minute knowledge of its loopholes and technicalities. An example might be for management "accidentally" to delay delivery of certain information in ways that will hamstring the union's preparation for negotiations and then to be "understandingly patient" while union attorneys frustratedly try to find whether they can compel delivery of the information from the company. The ultrasophistication may lie in making such moves seem utterly natural and legal, certainly not subject to prosecution, and then generously offering the requested materials at an inconveniently late date as a gesture of good will. The union representatives may thus be left "off base" because they cannot be sure whether management's behavior involved an honest mistake or a very clever bargaining ploy.

By virtue of its function, management may view employees mainly as a factor of production, even though some employers, especially small ones, will have deep concern for their employees as persons. The "science" of personnel got under way about the time of World War I. A substantial motive for it was a self-conscious desire to handle the employee-as-human-being aspect so well that the desire for unions would be avoided. This historical background adds to union suspicions about personnel science. On the other hand, once professionals have been hired to deal with the human side of workers, and take that job seriously, the personnel department can find itself sharply at odds with production departments from time to time, when production sees a tendency of personnel to "coddle" employees. Among other things, in a nonunion plant the personnel department is likely to be the division designated to receive employee complaints and act as a sort of an "attorney" for the employee in dealing with line supervision.

Top management can view this situation in at least two ways. One is to believe that its own personnel function can protect the human interest of employees better than the union can, for the simple reason that the personnel department is professionally better informed about such matters. A management with this view will tend to see unionization as the effort of an outside group to do poorly what the personnel department can do better. It will also probably believe that the union does not really care about the employees, but only about the power of the union and its officers. Other managements may look at things differently. They may conclude that the employee can never fully trust the personnel department, since it is bought and paid for by management. Such a management recognizes inherent limits on its own ability to deal with the human interests of the employees and accepts the desirability, or at least the reasonableness, of an organization bought and paid for by the employees to speak for them in such matters.

In short, one management may see the union as basically a frustrating *obstacle* to the relationship between company and employee. Another may see it as the appropriate *channel* for that relationship, and may even see the union as partially providing a free personnel department.

WHY THE DIFFERENCE? SOME TYPES OF MANAGEMENT

It is, of course, not possible to know the precise causes of management reactions. But it is possible to observe some of the more obvious sources of these attitudes. We will describe two.

The Small Individual Enterprise.   To illustrate one extreme type of management, we may imagine a well-established, successful small enterprise such as might be found in retailing, wholesaling, small manufacturing, trucking, real estate, or a wide variety of other industries. The enterpriser's success was probably the result of a lifetime of worries, sacrifices, near bankruptcies, baffling decisions involving both money and ethics, grueling work, and ulcers. It may have been the fruit of the owner's being caught up in some "crazy" idea in which he alone had faith—plus the persistence to make it work. For many years this person may have been founder, investor, president, foreman, machinist, advertising manager, and office helper, doubling as maintenance person on weekends. Before starting a business, he may have worked for someone else, receiving wages, salary, or commission. He may have disliked having to take orders based on decisions he had not helped to make, and it probably had made him wince to think of the way someone else stood with a hand on the valve that controlled the flow of income. At great personal sacrifice and with a risk he could only vaguely guess at, he started in business for himself.

The plant may be more familiar to this person than home and more important in his or her thinking. The employees may be better known than his or her family and their welfare may be more important. He or she may always have treated them as well as the condition of the business permitted—often better. As the number of employees grew to 10, 20, 50, 100, the employer continued to have as much interest in and affection for them as his or her spreading attention permitted.

To such a person, the idea that the employees should form a union to bargain, or even strike, and ask to participate in the making of a decision about which he or she knows so much more than they can ever know is utterly shattering. "It is *my* plant" (and "my" may be spoken with pleading rather than arrogance) in a sense and to a degree that no one else can ever appreciate. The employer feels unionization to be the utter antithesis of everything he has built and stood for. It introduces "outsiders" between him and the employees and threatens to embitter a relationship that had always seemed good. The owner is dismayed that the employees feel that he has not treated them as well as possible.

Business dealings have shown him that many people are shrewd in their selfishness, ready to take advantage of a technicality. The owner may have disagreed with their ethics, but he understood their motives. Unions, on the other hand, often seemed to pursue tactics that are not only costly to employers but make no economic sense to the union or its members. The employer knows how to protect himself against the "shrewd operator" but is baffled and frightened by the prospect of dealing with the unpredictable actions of a union that does not even seem to pursue a rational self-interest. In addition, the union seems to threaten the freedom to manage his own firm according to a personal concept of what is right and wise—a freedom that may be the most cherished thing in his life.

If this enterpriser is forced to deal with a union, he will probably feel bitter about it for many years—perhaps till his or her death. The owner will be angry at the union, and also at himself, feeling inescapably that the failure was somehow his or her own. He or she will be slow to adjust to the new method of operation. It will be long before it is accepted as an accomplished fact, and it will probably never really be understood. He may even liquidate the business rather than deal with a union or strike out blindly at the union. With the arrogance that sometimes goes with the self-made entrepreneur, the owner's anger and retaliatory actions against the union may know no bounds. Such a successful, small individual enterprise represents one extreme situation into which a union may be introduced.

The Large Corporation.   Despite the obvious contrast in size between the small individual enterprise and the large corporation, size is probably one of the less important differences. The ownership and structure of the large corporation tend to give it a different outlook and philosophy in its reaction to unions.

Pride of ownership is likely to be small or nonexistent. The enterprise may be owned collectively by hundreds of thousands of stockholders. It may be almost completely "inside" controlled, in which case hired management has superseded ownership as the controlling force. Unlike the income of the proprietor-owner of the small enterprise, the salaries of the corporation officers are charged to the company as expenses, not paid out of profits—although profit-sharing plans often tie some considerable part of the officials' incomes to profits. Since the officers are themselves employees, they have an important psychological bond with the rank and file.

Officers of a corporation have normally come up through the ranks. They have learned to take orders as well as give them and have often had to accept and effectuate policies that they themselves disapproved of. They have observed that neither the world nor their firm fell to ashes when their judgment was overruled. To people trained in this school, the union is merely one more pressure among the dozens to which they have already adapted. While any new pressure may mean another headache or ulcer, they assume that they can learn to live with it.

The division of labor within the large corporation simplifies the problem, and the obvious way to deal with the union is to create a new vice-presidency, replete with staff and office, to handle labor relations. Although this statement oversimplifies, something rather like this has happened in many large American corporations in recent decades. A budget appropriation is made for the department, some dividends are withheld for the contingency of a strike, and the enterprise goes on.

When the problem of labor relations is assignable to a special department as a staff function, it takes on a psychological quality quite different from that in the individual enterprise. It becomes a technical problem to be investigated, pondered, and, if possible, solved. It is usually interesting, often frustrating, certainly challenging. In brief, the task of dealing with the union becomes professionalized. The union creates a job to be done, not an insult to be vindicated.

This professionalization creates an additional psychological reaction. In the absence of unions, departments of industrial relations would have been long delayed and might still be nonexistent in many firms. In a very real sense, the employees in such departments owe their jobs to unions and must recognize, at least subconsciously, that the disappearance of unions would threaten their personal security. Perhaps one of the miscellaneous forces tending to perpetuate unions is that a professional arm of management has a vested interest in their continuance.

Intermediate Types.   The two pictures just drawn represent extremes. Actual cases demonstrate a tremendous variety of reactions. Some individual proprietors have actually welcomed unions, while some corporation officers display fierce proprietary interest and take personal offense at unionization. Emotional biases picked up from parents or friends often add complications, as do the convictions of some that unions will destroy the economy. The important point is that some managements view unionization as a challenge and an interference. Others see it as a reasonable expression of workers' desire for representation and take the union in stride. Still others show mixed and intermediate reactions. In general, however, the large corporation is probably better equipped psychologically and organizationally to make this adjustment than is the individual enterprise or the closely held corporation. The North-South contrast in employer attitudes toward unions may partly reflect this difference.

Every management, however, knows the need for discipline, and it is a rare one that does not see in unionization at least a potential, and at worst an impossible, obstacle to prompt and effective disciplinary action. But, as we shall see later, management may also find through the union a better grievance procedure than management alone can provide.

COMPLEX ORGANIZATIONAL STRUCTURES

One generally thinks of an employer as being in some particular industry and as being an independently acting unit. Actually, the world shows many variations. Among other possible ones, we discuss joint bargaining by multiple employers (multiple employer bargaining), firms that cross industries (conglomerates), and firms that cross national boundaries (multinationals). The first of these is discussed in the chapter on the bargaining unit. Conglomerates and multinationals are discussed next.

Conglomerate Mergers and Collective Bargaining

Despite the passage of the Celler–Kefauver Amendment to Section 7 of the Clayton Act in 1950, and its presumed intent of giving the FTC and the Department of Justice the weapons necessary for restraining all types of anticompetitive and conglomerate mergers, available data suggests that such mergers have been flourishing during the last two decades.[13]

Although the literature in both economics and law contains conflicting reports as to the overall desirability of conglomerate mergers, many labor relations experts and union officials feel that this restructuring of industry has shifted bargaining power to management. Their common arguments include (1) the claim that a conglomerate can "whipsaw" unions as it shifts production among plants when one is struck, and (2) the "deep pockets" argument that because of imperfections in the capital market, firms with greater capital reserves can more easily absorb the costs of a strike.[14]

Recognizing the possible deleterious effects of sustained conglomerate growth without countervailing union tactics, the AFL–CIO formed a special committee of the Industrial Union Department in 1964, charged with the development of *coalition bargaining* between a single firm and a combination of several different international unions. Coalition bargaining is discussed in more detail in the chapter on the bargaining unit.

A recent study indicates that the rationale behind coalition bargaining may be based on faulty assumptions about conglomerate bargaining leverage.[15] Hendricks mentions that the sole purpose of conglomerates is not to reduce labor costs, and that the impact of conglomerates on union power, if measured by wage level, appears to have been neutral.[16] Moreover, according to Hendricks, the union coalition response to conglomerate mergers has been motivated by various factors other than that of power shifts. Hendricks believes that scale economies in providing fringe benefits, and workers' concern over wage variation among member firms of a conglomerate can explain the real impetus behind coalition bargaining. For example, following a conglomerate merger workers may initiate wage comparisons among themselves which were never contemplated in the past. Equity theory holds that employees are concerned with the *perceived* fairness of pay, based on an individual's comparison between (1) his or her own input into the job and pay, and (2) the inputs and pay of others doing comparable work. Consequently, dissatisfaction from a perception of inequitable pay might partially explain the push behind coalition bargaining.

Regardless of the effect of conglomerate mergers on bargaining power, it might seem preferable public policy to allow the structure of collective bargaining to adapt to the changing environment as it has done so often in the past.

Multinationals and Industrial Relations

Although not all trade unions are ideologically opposed to multinational corporations (MNC), organized labor has typically perceived them as a distinct threat to unions and their members. The MNC presents many potential problems for unions. Levison and Maddox state the MNC because "its transnational decision-making capacity gives management a potential advantage over local labor" in such areas as: (1) depletion of union membership and transfer of job opportunities to foreign operations; (2) shipping production from nonstriking countries to customers in a striking country; (3) threatening to move or to reduce domestic production and to expand foreign operations; (4) covering losses from domestic strikes through profits from foreign operations; (5) weakening the bargaining authority of domestic managers because of complex decision-making structures; (6) difficulties in obtaining financial data for purposes of negotiations; and (7) finally, labor relations practices of MNCs may differ considerably from existing practices of local unions. All these factors weaken the bargaining power of labor unions.[17]

Labor's response to the continuing growth of the multinational corporation has ranged from innovative collective bargaining to support of legislation to make life less favorable for the multinationals. Political affiliation, ideological orientation, union structure and bargaining experiences, perceived threats of multinationals, and union labor market influence have generally dictated the choice or choices of strategy. To counteract the bargaining power of the MNCs, unions try to cooperate on an international scale. Such cooperation may take a variety of forms: gathering and distribution of data, international consultations, and lobbying for protective legislation.[18]

Transnational bargaining is another potential response of unions to the MNC. Available evidence indicates, however, that this response to the multinational corporation has had very limited success. Except for Canadian–United States accords between some auto firms and the UAW and multinational union agreements with the Belgian Glaverbel Glass Company and BSN–Gervais Danone in France, transnational bargaining is hampered by conflicting approaches to collective bargaining among trade unions. It is also hampered by uncertainty about the enforceability of transnational labor contracts; the preference for regional, company, and plant agreements by European trade unions; and outright opposition to transnational collective bargaining by such federations as the AFL–CIO and the Communist-led World Federation of Trade Unions. Still another union approach to the MNC is the call for endorsement of international fair labor standards, but this approach has also suffered from a lack of labor unity, in addition to objections that such standards would apply only to employers of multinationals. The lack of unity is exemplified by a World Federation of Trade Unions reference to international codes of conduct as "an illusion about changing the nature of capitalism," while another federation, the International Confederation of Free Trade Unions, strongly favors their adoption.[19]

Direct negotiation with multinational corporations in host countries, along with innovative techniques like European codetermination between management and workers, appears to offer trade unions some opportunity to countervail the power of multinationals.

Unless international labor reaches some consensus about optimal strategy and unless innovative techniques produce significant results, trade unions will presumably rely on conventional weapons. These include union organizing attempts in countries that have rudimentary industrial relations policies, pressure on multinational corporate headquarters to bargain with "source unions," limitations on overtime to prevent crossnational shifts in production during a strike, and consumer boycotts.

To put it mildly, the task of unions in dealing successfully with truly multinational corporations is several orders of magnitude more difficult than dealing with managements in conventional intranational relations. For example, even some powerful and well established American unions have faced almost insuperable difficulties in extending union conditions from the Snowbelt to the Sunbelt within the United States. When we add differences in cultures, laws, currencies, taxes, languages, ideologies, and other conditions, taken in conjunction with the fact that the international trade union structure has nowhere near the cohesion possessed by a multinational corporation, it is not surprising that unions feel rather discouraged at their prospects.

SUMMARY

The purpose of this chapter is to review the major components of the organizational structure of unions and employers.

The first part of the chapter discusses union structure. Subjects considered are: membership base of unions with particular attention to craft and industrial unions; the functions and operation of local and international unions, and the structure of the AFL–CIO Federation. In one section the special problems of democracy in unions are explored. The topics covered are plant government versus union government, solidarity and the external nature of the union's problems, the absence of conflict over policy, management reactions and democracy, the psychology and politics of union leadership and the structure and operation of the United Auto Worker's Public Review Board.

The second part of this chapter covers the organizational structure of employers. The environment and constraints to which an employer may be exposed are analyzed.

The input and output side of an employer's enterprise and its impact on labor relations are evaluated. Topics surveyed in this section are: labor-intensive versus capital-intensive industries, the labor structure and the number and ratios of different occupational groups employed by firms, the size and location of employment, the output of companies and the state of competition in their product market, and ways in which employers can respond and make adjustments to the input and output sides of their environment.

The chapter also surveys different types of management and their attitudes towards unions. It looks at the small individual enterprise as well as at the large corporation. The reactions and philosophies towards unions of different types of firms are reviewed and interpreted. The final part of the chapter considers the effect of conglomerates, mergers and multinationals on labor relations.

NOTES

[1] *Directory of U.S. Labor Organizations 1982–83 and 1984–85 Editions*, Courtney D. Gifford (ed.) (Washington, D.C.: The Bureau of National Affairs, Inc.), pp. 5–6.

[2] Charles W. Hickman, "Labor Organizations Fees and Dues," *Monthly Labor Review*, 100, 5, (May 1977).

[3] John W. Wright, *The American Almanac of Jobs and Salaries* (New York: Avon Publishers, 1982), p. 603.

[4] *Directory of Labour Organizations in Canada* (Government of Canada: Labour Data Branch, Central Analytical Services, Department of Labour, 1981), pp. 11, 15.

[5] *Directory of National Unions and Employee Associations, 1980*, U.S. Department of Labor, Bureau of Labor Statistics, September 1980, (Bulletin 2079), p. 4.

[6] *Ibid.; The Bureau of National Affairs 1984–85 Directory, op. cit.*, pp. 3, 5.

[7] *Business Week*, August 28, 1965, p. 82.

[8] Benson Soffer, "Collective Bargaining and Federal Regulation of Union Government," in Martin S. Estey, Philip Taft, and Martin Wagners (eds.), *Regulating Union Government* (New York: Harper & Row, for Industrial Relations Research Association, 1964), p. 103.

[9] A detailed study of the union is that of Seymour Lipset, Martin Trow, and James Coleman, *Union Democracy* (New York: Free Press of Glencoe, 1956).

[10] "Union Election Reversed Over Vote Violations," *The Cincinnati Enquirer*, Sunday, May 6, 1984, p. A-15. *Arbitration Times* (Fall 1985), p. 3.

[11] *Twenty-seventh Annual Report of the Public Review Board International Union, UAW*, to the membership of the United Automobile, Aerospace and Agricultural Implement Workers of America, 1984 p. 10.

[12] John T. Dunlop, *Industrial Relations Systems* (New York: Holt, 1958).

[13] Wallace Hendricks, "Conglomerate Mergers and Collective Bargaining," *Industrial Relations*, 15, no. 1 (February 1976).

[14] *Ibid.*, p. 77.

[15] *Ibid.*, pp. 75–85.

[16] *Ibid.*, p. 85.

[17]Donald L. Levison, Jr. and Robert C. Maddox, "Multinational Corporations and Labor Relations: Changes in the Wind?" *Personnel* (May-June 1982), pp. 70−77.

[18]*Ibid.*

[19]Robert F. Banks and Jack Stieber, *Multinationals, Unions, and Labor Relations in Industrialized Countries* (New York: Cornell University, New York State School of Industrial and Labor Relations, 1977), p. 11; "Easier Said than Done," *The Economist* (October 15, 1977), p. 90.

THE QUESTION OF THE BARGAINING UNIT

6

The term "Bargaining unit" is relatively new. It acquired prominence with the enactment of the National Labor Relations Act (Wagner of 1935). According to Chamberlain, "The pre-1933 literature would reveal virtually no discussion of and very little reference to the concept of a bargaining unit."[1] The *idea* of a bargaining unit, however, is not new. It predates labor legislation and the NLRB, and has been in existence as long as collective bargaining. The appearance of collective bargaining invariably poses the question as to who should be the employees that the labor organization is to represent in bargaining. In other words, what should the appropriate bargaining unit be? The ingredients necessary for collective bargaining are the presence of a labor organization, an employer, and "a defined group of employees"[2] on whose behalf the labor organization is to negotiate. A review of nineteenth-century labor contracts reveals that these agreements referred specifically to groups of employees whom the unions represent in bargaining.[3]

TYPES OF BARGAINING UNITS

The Range of Possibilities. *Bargaining unit* carries several connotations. Dunlop classifies bargaining units into three categories: the election unit, the negotiation unit, and the unit of direct impact. The *election unit* is the unit that the NLRB certifies for collective bargaining, commonly referred to as the "appropriate bargaining unit." According to Dunlop, "The country was done a great disservice when the Wagner Act called the unit for a certification election, the bargaining unit."[4] Cox et al. also state that the certified unit "might more accurately be denoted as the appropriate election unit."[5] Dunlop's *negotiation unit* refers "to the constituency of the people who actually bargain across the table."[6] *The unit of direct impact* is the unit directly affected by the outcome of particular negotiations;

 Certified bargaining units or *election units* differ in scope of coverage. Three main categories are: the single-employer, single-location unit, the single-employer, multilocation unit, and the multiemployer unit. Each of these units in turn may include differing clusters of jobs or job classifications.

 The single-employer, single-location unit can cover all workers eligible for certification in a single establishment,[7] or any particular category of employees such as craft, clerical, professional, production and maintenance, or any other specific classification of employees that the NLRB finds eligible for separate certification.

 Multilocation units encompass employees who work in a number of plants, stores, or offices of a single employer, in either the same or different towns. Any of the classifications of employees discussed in the previous paragraph could constitute such a unit.

 Multiemployer bargaining units embrace the employees of a number of employers and are discussed later in this chapter. The multiemployer unit can cover all employees eligible for certification,[8] or any one of the categories discussed in the previous paragraphs.

 The negotiating unit can be subdivided into two categories and their variations. First, each category could extend to more than one union, as illustrated by coalition bargaining, discussed later in this chapter. Second, a negotiating unit could consist of one or more certified units, or noncertified units, or a combination of certified and noncertified units created by voluntary arrangements between the parties without the assistance of the NLRB.

 The unit of direct impact extends beyond the boundaries of certified and negotiating units. It may cover more than one industry, as when settlements by auto companies have a direct impact on auto parts companies. Such pattern relationships also exist in the rubber industry, in steel fabrication,[9] and in a variety of other industries. The concept of a unit of direct impact is not limited to the private sector. In the case of municipal bargaining, terms agreed upon by a large municipality would have a direct effect on neighboring communities. Furthermore, a negotiating unit in the public sector may be directly affected by negotiations in the private sector, and possibly the reverse may take place. Unlike the single-cell amoeba which is an independent entity, industrial relations systems are highly interdependent, and every agreement may eventually have some impact on every other negotiating unit.

 The major difference between the unit of direct impact and the certified unit or negotiating unit is that the former is more of a theoretical conceptualization without clearly defined boundaries, whereas the latter units are formally defined either by the parties or by the NLRB.

Statistics

According to a 1980 Bureau of Labor Statistics (BLS) study of Characteristics of Major Collective Bargaining Agreements covering 1000 workers or more, January 1, 1980 (see Table 6–1), out of the 1550 agreements covering 6,593,800 workers, 924 covering 3,754,200 were with single employers. This is further broken down into single and multiplant units. There were 2,607,100 workers who were covered by 463 single-employer agreements and who bargained on a multiplant basis; the others bargained on a single-plant basis. A significant proportion of workers included under major collective agreements are covered by multiemployer contracts: 2,839,600 workers, 626 agreements. Most of these multiemployer units were in nonmanufacturing. Out of the total of 750 manufacturing agreements for 3,025,150 workers, only 105 for 444,600 workers were for multiemployer units; the picture was quite different in nonmanufacturing, where out of 800 agreements for 3,568,650 workers, 521 agreements for 2,395,000 workers covered multiemployer units.[10]

THE NLRB AND THE APPROPRIATE BARGAINING UNIT

Viewed in broad perspective, the size and composition of bargaining units tend to reflect certain pervasive competitive, organizational, and historical forces. For example, producers of steel in Birmingham and Chicago are in competition with one another and with foreign imports, whereas building contractors in those two cities are not. Over-the-road truckers face different bargaining and representation problems than do local police and firemen, and a union that represents the staff employees of the United Steel Workers could hardly function with the same kind of organizational units representing workers in hundreds of scattered coal mines. In a general way, the shape of bargaining units under varying circumstances reflects certain basic realities to which unions, managements, and the legal process almost inescapably bow.

It is nevertheless true that circumstances often allow considerable discretion in the selection of bargaining units, in which case the law, and notably the NLRB, may be a crucial determinant. Section 9(b) of the National Labor Relations Act (NLRA) requires the NLRB to determine in each representation case whether "in order to assure to employees the fullest freedom in exercising the rights guaranteed by this act, the unit appropriate for the purpose of collective bargaining shall be the employer unit, craft unit, plant unit, or subdivision thereof." The statute provides the NLRB with broad discretionary authority in determining the appropriateness of bargaining units. The only limitation on the board's authority relates to professional, craft, and guard employees. Specifically, in cases affecting professional employees, the board is not allowed to include both professional and nonprofessional employees in the same bargaining unit "unless a majority of such professional employees vote for inclusion in such unit" (Section 9(b)(1), NLRA). In craft certification cases, the board is prohibited from deciding "that any craft unit is inappropriate for such purposes on the ground that a different unit has been established by a prior Board determination" (Section 9(b)(2),

TABLE 6.1 EMPLOYER UNIT BY INDUSTRY

(Agreements covering 1,000 workers or more, January 1, 1980)

| Industry | All Agreements | | Single Employer | | | | | | Multiemployer Unit | |
| | | | Total | | Single Plant | | Multiplant | | | |
	Agreements	Workers	Agreements	Workers	Agreements	Workers	Agreements	Workers	Agreements	Workers
ALL INDUSTRIES	1,550	6,593,800	924	3,754,200	461	1,147,100	463	2,607,100	626	2,839,600
MANUFACTURING	750	3,025,150	645	2,580,550	397	1,008,350	248	1,572,200	105	444,600
Food, kindred products	79	234,200	50	103,850	29	48,350	21	55,500	29	130,350
Apparel	31	207,900	6	16,050	2	4,500	4	11,550	25	191,850
Other Manufacturing Industries	640	2,583,050	589	2,460,650	366	955,500	223	1,505,150	51	122,400
NONMANUFACTURING ..	800	3,568,650	279	1,173,650	64	138,750	215	1,034,900	521	2,395,000
Transportation[1]	62	469,550	18	70,700	5	6,250	13	64,450	44	398,850
Mining, crude petroleum, and natural gas	16	169,050	12	23,050	9	12,950	3	10,100	4	146,000
Retail trade	123	405,200	65	172,800	14	25,350	51	147,450	58	232,400
Services	66	323,450	19	69,150	9	23,000	10	46,150	47	254,300
Construction	327	1,195,000	3	4,050	1	1,200	2	2,850	324	1,190,950
Other Nonmanufacturing Industries	206	1,006,400	162	833,900	26	70,000	136	736,900	44	172,500

[1]Excludes railroads and airlines.

SOURCE: *Characteristics of Major Collective Bargaining Agreements*, (Washington, D.C. Department of Labor, Bureau of Labor Statistics, 1981), p. 19.

NLRA). And in guard certification cases, the board is not permitted to certify guards in the same units as nonguards. In addition, no labor organization can be certified as a representative of guards if it is affiliated or "admits to membership employees other than guards" (Section 9(b)(3), NLRA). Another limitation on the board's authority is found in Section 9(c)(5), which states that "in determining whether a unit is appropriate for the purposes specified in subsection (b) the extent to which the employees have organized shall not be controlling."

The NLRB classifies bargaining unit issues according to type, scope, and composition. To elaborate, the Fifteenth Annual Report of the NLRB states that the basic unit determination issues confronted by the board are:[11]

1. The type of the unit, i.e., whether an industrial unit embracing a general class such as production and maintenance employees or a smaller group within the general category is proper;

2. The scope of the unit, i.e., whether it should be a multiemployer, multiplant, plant wide, or some smaller departmental unit; and

3. The composition of the unit; i.e., whether the unit should include "fringe" groups such as clerks, technical and professional employees, and so on. To some extent the composition of bargaining units may be specifically limited by section 2(3) of the act which exempts certain classes of employees, such as agricultural and domestic workers, from its operations.[12]

Prior to the Wagner Act of 1935, many labor disputes arose over refusal of employers to recognize labor unions. The certification process largely eliminated this source of conflict. Unless an employer voluntarily agrees to recognize a union, before a union can be elected and certified as a representative of a group of employees, the NLRB must determine the appropriate bargaining unit that the union is to represent. Dunlop notes that "determination of the bargaining unit is the most significant responsibility exercised by the National Labor Relations Board for the future of collective bargaining,"[13] and Bok remarks "that unit determination may profoundly affect labor management relations and constitute a heavy proportion of the work of the NLRB."[14] Gorman states that "unit determination is at the heart of our system of collective bargaining and has a most pervasive impact upon industrial relations."[15]

Since the Labor Management Relations Act provides few guidelines for unit determination, the board has developed its own standards. These now are: mutuality or community of interest, geography or physical proximity, employers' administrative or territorial divisions, functional integration, interchange of employees, bargaining history, employee desires, and extent of organization.[16] Other criteria that the board sometimes applies are: "organization and representation of employees,"[17] "similarity of duties, skills, interest and working conditions of the employees,"[18] "similarity in the scale and manner of determining earnings . . . common supervision and determination of labor relations policy."[19]

In a study of the NLRB and the appropriate bargaining unit, Abodeely states that

The NLRB has properly identified a number of factors germane to determining an appropriate bargaining unit. The problem lies with the Board's application of these factors. The inconsistent case-to-case manner in which the Board uses the individual factors invites speculation that the Board is using the factors to support rather than to reach its determinations.[20]

Thus, in the final analysis, value judgments of board members may be the most important criterion that determines appropriateness of bargaining units.

The role of the NLRB in determining bargaining units needs clarification in several respects. First, although charged with determining appropriateness of bargaining units, the board is not required to seek and certify the "most appropriate or optimal unit." Thus, the board theoretically has broad discretion. Second, the unit is based on "jobs or job classifications"[21] and not on specific individuals employed in these classifications. Thus, turnover of employees does not change the legal status of a unit. Third, membership in the unit and in the union are not necessarily the same. Employees in the bargaining unit need not be members of the union, except under a union shop or related union security provision. Under Section 9(a) of the NLRA, labor organizations "selected for the purpose of collective bargaining by the majority of the employees in a unit . . . shall be the exclusive representatives of all the employees in such unit." Thus, it is possible for a union to be elected as the representative of a group of employees, the majority of whom may not belong to it, and conceivably none might belong. The union would still have the legal obligation to bargain for and fairly represent all employees in the unit, regardless of their union affiliation.

Certification of an appropriate bargaining unit by the NLRB creates a legally recognized unit around which vested interest of unions and employers evolve. Unions defend the boundaries of the legal unit against both employers and competing unions.

In most instances, employers and incumbent unions try to guard the unit against invasion by other unions, particularly if there is a threat of fragmentation of the existing bargaining structure. Employers are also protective of the status quo if the incumbent union seeks to expand its jurisdiction. However, defense of the legal unit by both sides does not imply that the unit is frozen. Dunlop notes that two-thirds of "employees covered by collective bargaining agreements are in situations where the actual negotiation area represented by the people sitting at the bargaining table is different from the area covered by the NLRB certifications."[22] Wellington and Winter state that, "Unit determination plays a large role in both the private and public sectors in influencing which, if any, union will be chosen as a bargaining representative, the power structure of bargaining, the ability of various groups of employees to affect directly the terms and conditions of their employment, and the peacefulness and effectiveness of the bargaining relationships."[23]

The Significance of NLRB Decisions

In evaluating the NLRB's actions, the question could be raised as to the significance of the dimension of bargaining units determined by the board.

From the union's point of view, board decisions are often crucial. Whether the board establishes a single- or a multilocation election unit can make the difference between winning or losing a certification election and bargaining rights. For example, unions long encountered difficulties winning certification elections among units of multiple retail stores. Things changed dramatically in favor of unions with the *Save-On Drugs, Inc*. case,[24] in which the NLRB recognized the easier-to-organize single store as an appropriate unit for certification.

These NLRB policies are also significant for management. Employers may favor large multilocation units in which it would be difficult for a union to organize and obtain a majority. Managements may also want to include in such units antiunion employees. Thus, in proposing the boundaries of bargaining units, the parties obviously take opposing positions.

Jack Barbash states that "the regulation of process leads almost inevitably to the regulation of substance." The importance of the NLRB's authority to determine the appropriateness of bargaining units is apparent from the following statement by Barbash: "The NLRB's early support of more inclusive units accelerated the ascendancy of industrial unionism, exemplified . . . in steel, coal and electrical products." The certification process not only acts as a catalyst to collective bargaining, but it also influences collective bargaining outcomes. The existence of certification machinery eliminates the recognition dispute and transfers the determination of the initial bargaining unit from the bargaining parties to the NLRB. Although the parties have the freedom to expand units established by the NLRB, these initial NLRB units are the basic building blocks upon which the parties, through bargaining, can build more elaborate structures. However, the bargaining units that the NLRB determines as appropriate are not necessarily the same as those the parties would have established, sometimes through power confrontations, had there been no certification machinery. Bargaining outcomes are affected by the bargaining power held by each party; this power in turn is influenced by the dimensions of bargaining units. Since the NLRB is the major force in determining dimensions of initial units, it follows that NLRB decisions would have an impact on bargaining outcomes.[25]

In recent years some authors have expressed the view that too much effort is wasted by the parties, the NLRB and the courts in searching "for that elusive concept: an 'appropriate bargaining unit' tailor made for each individual case." Subrin suggests that a significant amount of energy could be conserved if the NLRB were to utilize a rule making approach in determination of appropriateness of bargaining units. Under rule making the board could develop standards with clearly understood reasons which would make outcomes fairly predictable. Subrin, as director of the Office of Representation Appeals of the NLRB, had a firsthand opportunity to observe the problems encountered in searching for the appropriate bargaining unit. Although the Subrin proposal for rule making has many advantages, because of too many conflicting and vested interests it is very doubtful whether this approach will be translated into reality in the foreseeable future.[26]

UNIONS AND THE DIMENSION OF BARGAINING UNITS

The initiative in forming bargaining units is usually taken by labor organizations; they present to management or to the NLRB their version of an appropriate unit. The unit favored by a labor organization may be confined to a single employer or subdivision thereof or it may cover multiple employers. Some considerations that influence the union's preference about type, scope, and composition of units are as follows: first, the union's existing bargaining unit structure, pattern of organization, jurisdictional mandate in its charter, and the relative bargaining power of the unit under consideration. Second, the union's probability of success for gaining recognition, which depends in turn on such factors as past certification practices of the NLRB, desires of employees, and attitudes of employers. Third, the administrative, competitive, and operational structure of the firm, including degree of centralization of its industrial relations activities, scope of its product market, size of the labor force and number and size of firms in the industry, product similarity among firms in the industry, intensity of competition, state of technology, and relationship of some of these elements to the unit under consideration.

EMPLOYERS AND THE DIMENSION OF BARGAINING UNITS

In responding to the union initiative, the same factors that influence union policies are also taken into account by employers, but typically with opposite preferences. For whereas unions measure success by the frequency of recognition as bargaining agents, employers measure success by their ability to keep unions out, and either party's potential for victory often hinges on the dimension of the bargaining units.

Under the NLRA, an employer is free to recognize and bargain with a labor organization without its being certified as a representative of some group of employees. Under such voluntary recognition, the unit that emerges is essentially determined through bargaining. Because of NLRB policies and court decisions, employers have selected formal election and certification over voluntary methods in determining representation rights. More specifically, in the fifties and sixties, under the *Joy Silk Mills* doctrine, employers could be found guilty of an antilabor practice if they refused to bargain with a union that proved its majority status through valid authorization cards. But under a 1972 NLRB policy, endorsed by the Supreme Court in *Linden Lumber Division, Summer and Company* v. *NLRB*, employers in representation cases can insist on formal election and certification without risking charges.[27]

The certification machinery provides employers with an opportunity to counter the union initiative in proposing bargaining units. When a union petitions for certification, employers are notified and allowed to respond. The response may be acceptance, rejection, or proposed modification. Although the NLRB is not legally obliged to receive management proposals, employer arguments are thoroughly reviewed, the weight given to them depending on the circumstances of each case.

The importance attached to management views by the NLRB may be influenced by the composition of the board. NLRB members are presidential appointees, and those appointed by Republican presidents may be more promanagement than those appointed by Democrats. Thus, which side has the upper hand in certification cases may depend on the board's political coloration at the moment.

THE BARGAINING STRUCTURE

The variety of bargaining units, in terms of definitions and range of possibilities, that can be found in labor relations systems can be included under the common heading designated as "bargaining structure." Arnold R. Weber[28] states that the term *bargaining structure* incorporates "a multiplicity of units tied together in a complicated network of relationships by social, legal, administrative and economic factors." In his view, the structure "may be described by the scope of the units of which it is comprised and the system of decision making adopted by the parties on both sides of the bargaining table." Many factors determine the bargaining structure. According to Weber, these can be classified as "market factors, the nature of bargaining issues, representational factors, governmental policies and power tactics in the bargaining process."

Market Factors

Both employers and unions take into account the market context when devising the dimension of bargaining structures. Employers have been sensitive to competitive pressures when developing appropriate boundaries for bargaining structures. Weber states that unions have tried to shape "bargaining structures that are co-extensive with the specific market(s) encompassed by their jurisdiction." A distinction can be drawn between the approaches of industrial and craft unions in determining appropriate bargaining structures. For industrial unions, usually, output or "the scope of the product market" is important. For craft unions, inputs or "labor market considerations" are of greater significance.

The Bargaining Issues and Structure

Bargaining issues can be classified as market wide, company wide, or local. Weber points out that wages have "market-wide implications," fringe benefits like pensions and insurance plans usually have "company-wide" implications. And issues such as safety, work rules, and washup times are related to local working conditions and are usually treated at the local level. The structures of collective bargaining that emerge in various industries reflect the nature and significance of the issues to be negotiated. Thus, in some industries, issues such as wages and major fringe benefits are negotiated at the national level and local issues are left to local bargaining. The bargaining structure in the automobile industry is an example of such a dual approach. Weber states that when "the important issues are market wide in nature, such as wages, there will be strong pressures for expanding the scope of the negotiating unit and centralizing decision-making power within the unit to avoid variations among plants or firms. Conversely, demand for decentralized or even fractionalized bargaining are likely to develop when local problems are paramount."

Representational Factors

Individual firms or unions are sometimes willing to enter into comprehensive alliances in order to increase their bargaining power. Weber points out that "the formation of the common front inevitably involves a partial relinquishing of individual group goals." The cost of a "common front" normally is a reduction of local autonomy. A smaller employer in a multiemployer unit composed of small and large firms may decide that the cost of being a small fish in a big pond is too high, and that he or she would rather protect his or her autonomy and remain independent. When a bargaining structure of a union embraces too many heterogeneous groups and it becomes unworkable, a union may decide either to restructure the existing framework or to develop new decision-making procedures to accommodate the conflicting pressures.

The Impact of Government

Bargaining structures do not operate in a vacuum; legislation, the courts, and government administrative agencies all influence the dimension of bargaining structures. The bargaining unit decisions of the NLRB undoubtedly shape and influence the characteristics and nature of the present bargaining structure, not only in the private sector but possibly in the public sector.

Power Tactics

Weber states that "each party will seek to devise a structure that will maximize its capacity for inflicting real or expected costs on the other party in the course of the bargaining process." Both unions and employers attempt to develop bargaining structures that would maximize their bargaining power. Sometimes lengthy strikes result from labor-management confrontations over dimensions of bargaining structures.

For multiplant employers engaged in the production of the same product in a number of plants, the optimal structure may consist of individual single-plant bargaining units. Such units may optimize the employer's bargaining power in negotiations. Thus, if a strike developed in any one plant, the other plants can continue production. Furthermore, some production can be transferred from striking to nonstriking facilities. Obviously, in such firms, a union would tactically desire multiplant bargaining for the same reason that the employer would strongly oppose such structures. In such situations, according to Weber, "the union inevitably will seek to broaden the negotiating unit to encompass all the production facilities."

In the case of multiplant vertically integrated production, where each plant is engaged in a different phase of the total production process, the employer may be inclined to centralize bargaining, whereas the union may object to such an arrangement. In such an operation, a strike in one plant could bring all the plants to a standstill; thus, the union would not need a multiplant bargaining unit in order to achieve its bargaining objectives.

Weber claims that tactical bargaining structure considerations "are not determinate in the evolution of bargaining but they may exercise an important influence in individual cases, especially in the early stages of the bargaining relationship."

Perry and Angle have expressed the view that bargaining unit structure can have organizational outcomes. In a 1981 article they evaluated the effects of different unit structure on "union affairs, labor-management relations, organizational performance, and employee attitudes." Their study was based on a sample of public mass transit organizations. The authors concluded that although structure of units "may have temporary or passing dysfunctional effects on organizational and individual outcomes," over time the parties adjust to structural limitations. Other authors also recognized that bargaining structure may affect bargaining outcomes. According to Mills, decentralized structures can increase strike activity. Weber states that bargaining structure has an input on economic leverage, on bargaining power, and on worker satisfaction. In a recent article, Hendricks and Kahn suggest that "some portion of the relationship often found between structural variables (such as firm size, concentration, labor intensity, and union rivalry) and bargaining outcomes (such as relative wage levels) may occur indirectly through the formation of different bargaining units." According to Weber the structure of collective bargaining can be viewed as the "vital element in a chain of interdependence linking together the aspirations and demands of the parties, the bargaining process and the external environment."[29]

THE CRAFT BARGAINING UNIT

The purpose of this section is to examine the status of craft employees within the context of the collective bargaining structure. In the *American Potash and Chemical Corporation* case, the NLRB defined a true craft unit as "a distinct and homogeneous group of skilled journeymen, craftsmen, working as such, together with their apprentices and/or helpers. To be a journeyman's craftsman an individual must have . . . a substantial period of apprenticeship or comparable training. . . . Furthermore such craftsmen must be primarily engaged in the performance of tasks requiring the exercise of their craft skills."[30]

Craft employees can be found in all sectors of the economy. They are employed as electricians, plumbers, toolmakers, stationary engineers, and in a variety of other trades. In some firms, they form their own units and bargain separately from the other employees. In other firms, they are included in large comprehensive units together with unskilled and semiskilled workers. The bargaining status of craft employees within a firm depends on the nature of the craft, type of industry, collective bargaining history in the industry, and, most important, on the policies and practices of the NLRB. If given the choice, most craft workers would probably opt for separate craft units, since such units would provide them with more bargaining power and status than they could obtain within a comprehensive industrial unit. A union representing a small unit of electricians can normally obtain better contract terms than an industrial union representing many different categories of employees. From the point of view of industrial unions, it is not desirable to permit craft workers separate representations. The bargaining power of an industrial union could erode significantly if it allowed some of the critical crafts to depart from the unit. In case of a strike, it is much easier to replace semiskilled than skilled workers. A strike by a small strategic craft union could easily close down a large operation and thus deprive the great majority of industrial workers of work. Thus, the right of self-determination for craft workers may in effect reduce some of the rights of the majority. The bargaining power of an industrial union tends to vary directly with the size of its constituency. Thus, it is in the interest of the industrial union to represent as large a constituency as possible, both in terms of absolute size and skills.

The industrial union is a political entity and its elected officials have to be responsive to the demands of the majority of union members. This majority usually consists of unskilled and semiskilled people. The industrial union, however, cannot entirely ignore the interest of the craft minority, since to do so could lead to wildcat strikes, petition to the NLRB for severance, and a general level of internal turmoil and dissatisfaction. Such developments would be detrimental to the industrial union, and to all members of the bargaining unit.

In some industrial unions, in order to protect the rights of craft workers within the industrial unit, the union grants them a limited right of separate ratification on issues which directly affect them.[31]

Power of the Craft Employees

Craft employees, even if submerged in comprehensive industrial units, are not necessarily without power. Their skill and higher income provide them with status and prestige within the comprehensive unit. This, in some instances, may help them influence the majority to support their interests.

The rights of crafts within an industrial unit may also be protected by an employer. In a tight labor market, to reduce turnover and attract skilled workers, management may act as a strong advocate of craft interests.

Another way for crafts to protect their position is to participate actively in the governance process of an industrial union, as by appointments to major committees and election to important union positions. The wildcat strike is still another approach utilized by dissatisfied craft employees, and may force the industrial union and the employer to become more responsive to the needs and objectives of craft employees.

Employers and the Appropriate Unit for Craft Employees

Employers do not hold a unified position about the most appropriate bargaining unit for craft employees. Where some employers prefer to bargain separately with their craft workers, the majority probably prefer to bargain with as few unions as possible.

There are a number of reasons why some firms may favor separate bargaining with their crafts. In some cases, having a craft submerged in a comprehensive unit could create industrial-relations and personnel problems for the employer. Also, this approach would appeal to the employer who subscribes to the divide-and-conquer strategy, who thinks that by depriving the industrial union of strategic crafts he can gain financially at the bargaining table. Management may be willing to pay craft employees more than they would be getting if they were a part of an industrial union, but the extra cost may be more than offset by the employer's lower total wage costs for the majority of semiskilled and unskilled workers.

Separate bargaining units for craft employees may, nevertheless, have drawbacks for the employer. A firm negotiating with a number of different unions becomes vulnerable to "whipsawing."[32] Bargaining with many unions increases administrative costs and makes it more difficult to plan reliable production and marketing schedules. Usually, continuity of production is more secure with fewer unions.

Another advantage of a comprehensive bargaining unit, from the point of view of the firm, is that the resolution of potential friction among the different groups of employees takes place within the confines of the unit. Since a work force of a comprehensive unit may consist of people with heterogeneous interests, most of their conflicting interests can be resolved internally rather than at the bargaining table. This may be more desirable not only from the point of view of the employer, but also from the point of view of public interest and industrial peace.

The NLRB and the Craft Bargaining Unit

Under the Wagner Act of 1935, the NLRB has been vested with the authority to certify craft bargaining units. The craft bargaining unit cases confronting the NLRB can be divided into two broad categories: (1) Initial certification cases of craft employees who were never represented in a collective bargaining relationship with a particular firm and (2) severance cases of craft employees who request the board to separate them from existing industrial units. In both instances, the NLRB has to decide whether the craft satisfies the NLRB criteria for certification. It is easier for a craft to gain separate certification rights when there is no successful history of collective bargaining within the context of a larger unit.

Certification by the NLRB is not the only route available to craft employees who desire to establish a bargaining relationship with their employer. A craft union representing a majority of craft employees may ask an employer for recognition without utilizing the NLRB apparatus. Some employers may accede voluntarily. However, the majority of firms would want to utilize the NLRB procedures and have the union officially certified as a bargaining agent.

The NLRB is willing to certify craft employees in separate bargaining units when some of the following conditions are met: the craft employees are unrepresented, they are engaged in traditional craftwork which is performed in a separate and distinct location apart from other employees, they have a separate community of interest and do not "interchange with other employees,"[33] and the union seeking recognition is a craft union traditionally representing the craft in question.

To understand the present bargaining framework of craft employees, it is necessary to examine the NLRB craft severance policy, which has changed several times since the formation of the board in 1935. The source of craft bargaining unit problems, confronted by the NLRB, has been the competition between industrial and craft unions over bargaining rights for craft workers. The outcome of this rivalry usually has to be decided by the NLRB. The Board can submerge a craft unit in a comprehensive industrial unit. The decisions of the board have implications for the survival of craft unions.

The first major craft certification decision by the NLRB was the *Globe Machine and Stamping Company* case of 1937. The *Globe* decision provided craft employees with the right of self-determination through an election. In essence, the board's Globe doctrine or Globe election allowed craft employees to decide by secret ballot whether to be included in a comprehensive industrial unit, before any bargaining unit was certified. The *Globe* case established the principle of self-determination for craft employees but was significantly modified by subsequent board decisions. The NLRB approves of Globe elections when a large proportion of craft workers desire a separate unit and when in the board's view the craft employees represent a "true" craft. This usually implies traditional crafts. The board objects to separate craft certifications when a separate craft unit may prove detrimental to labor relations and collective bargaining. Under the Globe doctrine, when a group of employees can either be certified as a separate unit or be part of a larger unit, the NLRB has the discretion to allow "the desires of the employees to be the determining factor." In such cases, the board conducts a separate election among the groups and the results of the election determine the appropriateness of unit or units. "If a 'Globe' election is directed the Board does not make the final determination of the unit until the employees have voted."[34]

Other important NLRB craft certification decisions were the *American Can Company* case in 1939; the *National Tube Company* case of 1948; the *American Potash and Chemical Corporation* case of 1959; and the *Mallinckrodt Chemical Works* case of 1966.

In the *American Can Company* case,[35] the board was petitioned by a craft union to carve a craft unit out of an existing comprehensive industrial unit. The unit had a stable history of bargaining on an industrial basis. The NLRB refused to grant the severance on the grounds that the act did not authorize the board to split an existing appropriate bargaining unit, "established by collective bargaining and embodied in a valid exclusive bargaining contract."[36] The American Can doctrine was a serious legal setback to craft unions.

In 1946 and 1947 craft unions campaigned hard to have a provision included in the amended Wagner Act that would exempt crafts from the American Can doctrine. Congress responded favorably by enacting Section 9(b)(2) of the National Labor Relations Act. This section states that "the Board shall not . . . decide that any craft unit is inappropriate for such purposes on the grounds that a different unit has been established by a prior Board determination unless a majority of the employees in the proposed craft unit vote against separate representation."

Section 9(b)(2) received its first NLRB test in the *National Tube Company* case.[37] The board's interpretation was not favorable to craft unions. The board decided that although under 9(b)(2) prior board determinations cannot be applied as the "sole ground" for refusal of craft severance, nevertheless, the board has the right to refuse to certify such units when other factors are present that would justify such decisions. The board refused the craft petition for a separate unit in this case, claiming that a highly integrated work force in the production processes, and a stable history of collective bargaining in the steel industry, make the existing comprehensive industrial unit more appropriate for that industry. This decision established what is known as the National Tube doctrine. In subsequent decisions, the NLRB extended the refusal to certify units on the grounds of integrated production processes to three other industries, wet milling,[38] lumber,[39] and aluminum.[40] The Fourth Circuit Court extended the National Tube doctrine to the plate glass industry.[41]

In 1954, in the *American Potash and Chemical Corporation* case,[42] the NLRB became more lenient toward craft certification. The board decided that craft workers who were employed outside National Tube industries should not be prevented from bargaining in separate craft units simply because the industry in which they are employed is highly integrated. The board stated that it will not extend the practice of denying craft severance on an industry-wide basis. The board decision, however, did not affect the status of national Tube doctrine industries. Under the *American Potash* interpretation of Section 9(b)(2) of the act, the board agreed to consider craft severance petitions only when the following criteria were met: the unit requested is a "true craft group" and the union is one "which traditionally represents that craft."

In 1966, in the *Mallinckrodt Chemical Works* case, the NLRB proclaimed a major policy shift regarding craft certification. Under the Mallinckrodt doctrine, the board decided no longer to differentiate between National Tube Industries and any other industry. Under the new policy, all craft severance cases were to be decided on a case-by-case basis, regardless of the industry in which they occurred. The following criteria would be applied by the board in such cases:

1. Whether or not the proposed unit consists of a distinct and homogeneous group of skilled journeymen craftsmen;
2. The history of collective bargaining of the employees sought;
3. The extent to which the employees in the proposed unit have established and maintained their separate identity during the period of inclusion in a broader unit;
4. The history and pattern of collective bargaining in the industry involved;
5. The degree of integration of the employer's production processes;
6. The qualifications of the union seeking to "carve out" a separate unit.[43]

The craft certification criteria that emerged in the *Mallinckrodt* case and their application did not improve the position or the future outlook for craft unions. Laurence J. Cohen, who reviewed the board's decision under the Mallinckrodt doctrine, states:

> The future for separate craft of departmental units seems dim in general and positively bleak where severance is attempted. For one thing, the very application of the doctrine to date will tend to inhibit the filing of new petitions for severance. And, when such petitions are filed, the history of the Mallinckrodt doctrine to date affords little hope that those petitions will be granted.[44]

John E. Abodeely states that

> The principles established by the Board in Mallinckrodt are to be commended. However, subsequent applications of those principles reveals that, in reality, the standards set forth in Mallinckrodt have been used not to reach a conclusion, but rather to support one.[45]

The board, confronted with the dilemma between the right of self-determination of craft employees and a potential threat to stability in industrial relations, is willing to trade off self-determination for industrial peace. The position of the board on this issue is very well summarized in the *Mallinckrodt* case. The board states that in making unit determination in severance cases the nature of the issue underlying such determination "is the need to balance the interest of the employer and the total employee complement in maintaining the industrial stability and resulting benefits of a historical plant-wide bargaining unit as against the interest of a portion of such complement in having an opportunity to break away from the historical unit by a vote for separate representation."[46]

In the *Mallinckrodt* case, the board suggested that the interests of craft employees should not always prevail. The board concluded that craft severance may break "unity of association" of other employees "whose collective strength is weakened by the success of the craft . . . in pressing its own special interests."

> Prior to the *Mallinckrodt* decision, Board craft severance decisions were inconsistent, depending more on the policy preferences of the Board majority than on any established analytic decision-making procedure. Mallinckrodt established a framework with which the Board could engage in a structured, yet flexible analysis allowing for a balance between employees' freedom of choice and the promotion of harmonious labor relations.
>
> To its discredit, the Board does not make use of the *Mallinckrodt* criteria in reaching its craft severance decisions. Rather, the Board has embraced prior bargaining history as indicative of stable and harmonious labor relations, the Board's preeminent priority.[47]

An empirical study by Dallas L. Jones[48] suggests that craft severance has relatively little impact on stable labor relations. Since the NLRB has been very cautious in certifying such units, it is difficult to predict whether a more liberal craft severance policy by the board would have had no adverse impact on stable labor relations. The board probably should continue to exercise caution in craft severance cases. The emergence of too many craft units could have an adverse effect on industrial peace. John E. Abodeely states that "should the Board adopt a policy of freely granting separate representation to craft employees, it may well be sowing the seeds of labor relations instability."[49]

A discussion of craft bargaining units would be incomplete without considering the impact of technological change.[50] New technology has simplified some production techniques, thus opening work previously performed by craft workers to semiskilled people. In some instances, sophisticated machinery has replaced certain craft categories, as in the printing industry. In still other situations, new technology has put new demands on craft employees, forcing them to upgrade the level of their technical competence and training. The industrial electrician who services automated and computerized equipment has to be better trained now than in the past. Some unions have responded to the technological challenge by merging with related craftsmen. Others have begun organizing semiskilled workers, thus increasing their bargaining and organizational strength.

Technology is not standing still and craft workers everywhere will be experiencing many new pressure for change in their traditional bargaining structures. The construction industry has been one of the major targets of change. Presently, the industry is organized and bargains on a craft, or multicraft, basis. The development of factory, prefabricated, and modular housing that can be built by semiskilled people may force construction crafts to adjust to the new conditions and form different structures for purposes of bargaining.

Technological change will confront the NLRB, with new challenges in the form of more application for separate units from new crafts and groups of technical workers. Chamberlain and Kuhn[51] state, "We may well see in the coming years more skilled and technical employees seeking narrow bargaining units and excluding other types of workers." If the past is a guide to the future, the NLRB will probably be very reluctant to sanction these new skilled workers as separate entities for collective bargaining—especially if some of them have been members of comprehensive bargaining units with a relatively stable history of collective bargaining.

THE MULTIEMPLOYER BARGAINING UNIT

When a number of employers join forces for purposes of collective bargaining, the unit structure is described as a multiemployer bargaining unit. The structure may consist of an association representing employers, or even a whole industry, or it may be composed of only a few employers who bargain as a group, or through an association. Sometimes agreements negotiated by a few large employers are signed without negotiations by smaller employers in the industry. Multiemployer bargaining may take place within many different geographical subdivisions. These may cover a metropolitan area, a region, or the whole country. Some of these arrangements may embrace the whole industry within a particular geographical area, others may cover only a portion of such an industry.

A review of 1980 agreements covering 1000 workers or more indicates that, in some industries, multiemployer bargaining covers a significant proportion of the organized labor force. In the transportation industry, 398,850 employees out of 469,550 were covered by multiemployer contracts; the statistics exclude railroads and airlines. In the food and kindred products industry, 130,350 out of 234,200 employees were in multiemployer units. In the apparel industry, 191,850 employees out of a total of 207,900 were in such units, and in construction, 1,190,950 out of 1,195,000 were covered by multiemployer bargaining (see Table 6.1) discussed earlier.[52]

Effects of Multiemployer Units on Employers and Unions

The advantages and disadvantages of multiemployer bargaining units have been covered in great detail in many publications.[53] In 1947 extended briefs and testimony were presented on this topic to congressional committees. The purpose of this section is to review briefly some of the effects of multiemployer bargaining on unions and management. Competitive pressures are the dominant force that encourage both unions and employers to enter into multiemployer or industry-wide bargaining relationships. In some industries, such as the apparel industry, both unions and employers may want to see uniformity of wages. Multiemployer bargaining could assist the parties to reach this objective.

Small employers in highly competitive and labor-intensive fields may find it easier to operate with uniformity of labor cost. The unionized employer subjected to intensive competition from the nonunionized sector may be highly supportive of multiemployer bargaining units, particularly if such units could affect the nonunionized employers who use substandard wages to undercut prices in the product market. Employers of such broader units would not have to be too concerned with some employers within the unit paying their workers less than the agreed-upon scale. Union supervision would assure compliance with contract terms. Otto Pollack states that there is "one common ground on which labor and at least parts of management can meet and cooperate: the area of limitation of competition."[54]

The multiemployer unit is particularly advantageous to both sides in industries composed of many small, financially weak employers. In such industries, there are bargainable issues such as health and pension plans, which may be difficult to negotiate and implement through single-employer bargaining. A small employer, apart from the fact that he may not have the professional personnel necessary for negotiation of complex fringe benefit programs, may also be concerned with the cost and competitive implications of introducing such programs. The fear of increased costs, to which the firm's competitors would not be subjected, would be a strong deterrent against the introduction of major benefit programs. Thus, in some industries, multiemployer bargaining undoubtedly overcomes a major stumbling block in negotiation of fringe benefit programs.

Multiemployer bargaining provides both management and unions with significant cost savings in negotiation of labor agreements. It is cheaper to negotiate one master multiemployer agreement than a number of single-employer agreements. There are, however, other considerations than costs, such as intraorganizational issues, that the parties take into account before opting for multiemployer units. Multiemployer bargaining may not only overlook the needs of various employee groups, but also ignore particular requirements of individual employers. In some cases, bargaining may become more intensive among the various employers within the extended group than between the employers' group and the union. Production costs and organizational structure of firms are not uniform. Thus, what may be readily acceptable to one employer may be considered as financially disastrous by another. The marginal firm in the multiemployer unit is more vulnerable under such an arrangement than it would have been had it bargained on its own. To arrive at multiemployer agreements is much more difficult than to arrive at single-employer contracts. The expanded size of the unit composed of many heterogeneous groups leads to intensive intraorganizational bargaining both on the union's and on the employer's side. At times, these intraorganizational pressures may lead to lengthy delays in negotiations and even to breakdown of bargaining. A uniform master contract covering the employees of a number of firms may overlook the requirements of its component units. The desires and needs of employees within a bargaining unit are not homogeneous. Here, as in other organizations, the larger the unit, the greater the diversity that has to be suppressed for purposes of uniformity. In some multiemployer units, to protect the aspirations of different groups of employees, master contracts cover only such items as wages and major fringe benefits. Other issues are negotiated on a local level.

Despite the various shortcomings, multiemployer bargaining is favored by many unions and employers. A congressional committee report states that the great majority of presentations by labor and management representatives claim that the "usefulness and strength" of multiemployer bargaining "outweigh its weaknesses."[55] Professor Rehmus claims that both employers and unions are supportive of multiemployer bargaining arrangements. He states that "in those industries where industry-wide or regionwide bargaining now exists . . . both labor and management (with extremely limited exceptions) support it strongly. They believe that it is necessary to preserve a rational system of industrial relations."[56]

Bargaining Power in the Multiemployer Bargaining Unit

Emergence of multiemployer bargaining units has a direct implication on the level of bargaining power retained by the parties. The possibility that one side may be able to strengthen or equalize its bargaining power through the formation of multi-employer units may set the necessary forces into motion toward the creation of such bargaining frameworks. This is not always a peaceful process; sometimes it is accompanied by confrontations, frictions, and work stoppages.

There are a number of reasons for employers forming multiemployer units: In some instances, employers are willing to give up bargaining power in order to lessen competition in the product market or to achieve industrial peace and greater stability in industrial relations. The need for employers to come up with countervailing power to strong unions may also be a catalyst for the formation of industry-wide multi-employer bargaining units. In highly competitive labor-intensive industries composed of many small employers with a high degree of unionization concentrated in a few unions, the only way for employers to have significant bargaining power is to form industry-wide bargaining units. In such industries, an individual employer may be at a disadvantage if he or she bargains independently. Strong unions may concentrate their initial bargaining against firms that are likely to be the most generous. Such contracts can then be used as a basis for pattern following by the rest of the industry. Strong unions may also use the whipsawing strategy, whereby each settlement is a floor rather than a ceiling for negotiations with the other employers in the industry. The existence of such conditions serves as a strong impetus for employers to try to improve their bargaining strength through the creation of multiemployer frameworks.

Some unions may be interested in multiemployer bargaining as a means of increasing their bargaining power. Henle states that "in setting its bargaining policy, a union tries to develop the type of bargaining structure within which it can exert the most influence on behalf of its membership. There is no single union policy dealing with the size of bargaining units nor is there any compulsion for a given national union to adopt a fixed policy that has to be applied under all circumstances."[57] The ability of a union to strike all employers within an industry would provide it with a significant amount of power at the bargaining table; the union would not have to concern itself with the possibility of an employer who is on strike being assisted by nonstriking firms, as was the case in some industries such as airlines.[58]

In some instances, the bargaining power of a union may decline under industry-wide bargaining. Supplying strike benefits to employees of a whole industry may strain significantly the financial resources of a union and thus lower its bargaining power. Also, if all employers are on strike, individual employers do not have to concern themselves with the danger of losing a share of their market to their nonstriking competitors. Cox et al. conclude that industry-wide bargaining may strengthen employers since "the industry as a whole can face strike threats which might be disastrous to a single employer through the loss of his market."[59] The bargaining power of unions under industry-wide bargaining may also be reduced by pressure of public opinion and threat of government interference. In some industries, however, if bargaining were conducted on a single-employer basis, the union would be the weaker partner. The waterfront and the Longshoremen's Union is a case in point. The bargaining position of the union improved significantly when collective bargaining moved from a single- to a multiemployer level. The broader structure improved coordination among the longshoremen; it became impossible for the employers "to play one port against the other."[60]

In some instances, it may be in the interests of the union to give up some of its power as a means of satisfying its other objectives. Improving the survival rate of firms in the industry, thus maintaining employment opportunities for union members, is a union goal for which it may be worthwhile to sacrifice some bargaining power in the short run. In the cutthroat, bankrupt-ridden garment industry of New York, the union welcomed multiemployer bargaining as a means of improving the financial health and lifespan of firms in the industry. The union was willing to sacrifice some of its short-run power for other considerations that could benefit the union and its members over the long run.

Although the bargaining power of unions engaged in multiemployer bargaining may decline for the reasons just outlined, some employers may also suffer loss of bargaining power resulting from multiemployer units. The small employer, as a member of a multiemployer unit containing some large firms, may have very little power to influence the outcome of negotiations. Also, large and financially strong firms bargaining separately may have more power than if they bargained jointly. This explains to some extent the refusal of the copper industry to bargain on a multiemployer basis.

The Pros and Cons of Multiemployer Bargaining from the Point of View of Public Interest

One of the consequences of multiemployer bargaining is the uniformity of contract terms that accompany such frameworks. There is opposition to such structures on the grounds that such standardization may be detrimental to the public interest. Some scholars claim that multiemployer bargaining could strengthen monopolistic forces in the economy and lessen competition. This in turn could lead to lower levels of output and higher prices, easier to pass on to the consumer. Professors Chamberlain and Kuhn point out that the uniformity of contract terms in such units "squeeze out marginal firms, discourage the entry of new small firms, and allow, if not encourage collusion between union and management leaders at the expense of the public."[61] Although the standardized contract may be applauded by both unions and management, it is not so warmly received by consumer advocates who fear that consumers pay for it through higher prices.

Another argument against industry-wide bargaining is the increased possibility of government control and interference. Under such bargaining frameworks, a strike could encourage government intervention. Increasing government presence in the labor relations arena may not necessarily be advantageous from the point of view of the public or of the bargaining parties: "Excessive private power must lead inevitably to excessive governmental power to control it."[62]

One major criticism of multiemployer bargaining is that it widens the extent of labor conflict. A report of a congressional General Subcommittee on Labor states that although its inquiry "should not be considered definitive on this subject, the information developed to date suggests the possibility that multiemployer association bargaining has a tendency to widen the area of the dispute."[63] The congressional committee's report was primarily concerned with association bargaining on an industry-wide scale. Many multiemployers bargaining units do not fall in this particular category. However, a strike in a multiemployer bargaining unit, regardless of whether the unit is national or local in scale, could have serious implications for the affected consumers if the unit is the primary supplier of a particular service or product.

Another criticism of multiemployer bargaining is that it reduces competition and increases monopolistic practices. Harold Stassen, former president of the University of Pennsylvania (inter alia), states that although industry-wide bargaining sets wage scales for the whole industry, this does not stop competition. The competition, rather than based on lowering wages, would be based on "developing increased productivity . . . more effective use of . . . modern machinery . . . better distribution and . . .better reaching of markets."[64] Professor Lester, who studied seven industries in which national and regional bargaining took place, made the following statement regarding monopolistic factors in these industries:

> From our study of wages under national and regional collective bargaining, we found that there were no evidences of more monopoly in the seven industries subject to national and regional bargaining than in industries and firms operating under company or individual plant bargaining.[65]

One of the major arguments directed against critics of multiemployer bargaining rests on the proposition that under expanded bargaining frameworks the frequency of strikes diminishes; and that labor relations in such units are more stable and mature. The participants are more sensitive and responsive to public opinion and government pressures. The level of expertise and sophistication of negotiators on both sides is considerably higher than in an industry consisting of many small firms bargaining individually.

Also under multiemployer bargaining, two types of strikes would not occur—the strike where the union tries to punish an erring employer and bring him into line with the other firms in the industry, and the strike where a firm is selected as a target for new union demands.

The arguments for and against multiemployer bargaining structures are frequently based on the premise that each multiemployer unit is a national unit, and that its bargaining results may have major repercussions throughout the economy. The fact is that many multiemployer bargaining units are not national in nature but negotiate on a city or regional basis. In the final analysis, the negotiations of every agreement in any type of bargaining unit have some economic consequences. Multiemployer bargaining with its heterogeneity of bargaining units cannot be selected as the only potential villain against the public interest. Multiemployer bargaining cannot be simply labeled as "bad" or "good." As discussed above, there are many costs and benefits to such units. However, their relative importance may vary significantly from case to case. Each situation would have to be evaluated on its own merits, and a value judgment made as to whether its benefits outweigh its costs. A blanket condemnation of such units is certainly not warranted, even though it may be argued that in some industries the public interest would benefit from single-employer bargaining.

Labor Law and the Multiemployer Unit

There are no specific multiemployer determination provisions or prescribed certification criteria in the National Labor Relations Act. The statute provides the NLRB with the necessary authority for certification of multiemployer bargaining units. The NLRB does not play as significant a role in establishing multiemployer units as it does in the area of single-employer units. In approving such units, the board primarily applies two criteria: "The existence of a controlling bargaining history, and the intent and conduct of the parties." The board determines intent when there is "joint participation in negotiations of several employers, and unit of action for arriving at identical contract terms for the participants." The board is willing to recognize "multi-employer units stemming from consensual arrangements." In its twenty-fifth annual report, the board states that "collective bargaining history is not a prerequisite to finding a multiemployer unit appropriate" for certification.[66]

Many existing multiemployer bargaining units probably never applied for NLRB certification. Those that do apply and obtain such certification usually have a history of bargaining on a multiemployer basis. One may ask why the parties of an existing multiemployer bargaining unit would bother petitioning the board for certification. The answer is that the board's action may be beneficial to both unions and management. A certified multiemployer unit protects unions from raids by rival unions. It is much easier to displace an incumbent union from a single-employer than from a certified multiemployer bargaining unit. The protection that the larger unit extends to an incumbent union may also be advantageous to an employer. Management may prefer to continue its relationship with an incumbent union rather than be forced to bargain with a new labor organization.

The life span of certified multiemployer bargaining units is not infinite. Either one of the parties can initiate board proceedings for withdrawal from such units. Abodeely et al. provide an excellent review of NLRB and court decisions on legal guidelines for withdrawal from multiemployer bargaining units.[67]

The Future of Multiemployer Bargaining

In a 1982 labor law text, Summers et al. state that "although three-fourths of all collective agreements are limited to workers of a single employer, more than 40% of all employees covered by labor contracts are in multiemployer units." The conduct of multiemployer bargaining varies considerably among industries. In the clothing industry, employer associations exercise a significant amount of bargaining authority over individual companies, as contrasted with trucking where a single contract is negotiated but the association has less control over their members. In the retail sector a standard agreement is signed for the industry but the contract may be modified by some employers. In the rubber industry, rather than negotiating on a multiemployer basis the companies engage in parallel and simultaneous bargaining, sometimes in the same hotel on different floors.[68]

Multiemployer bargaining units still represent a large number of workers covered by collective agreements. In recent years, however, some authors raised the possibility of a trend away from multiemployer bargaining. In a 1983 article Hoffman writes that in the trucking industry many firms rejected the Teamsters national trucking agreement. The trend seems to continue in 1985. Recently, more trucking firms served notice that they want out of the National Master Freight Agreement with the Teamsters, which expired March 31, 1985. They intend to negotiate individually with the union instead of as a group. Hoffman also states that between 1978 and 1980 400,000 employees were no longer covered by multiemployer contracts. Also there has been a significant increase in NLRB cases with regard to employers trying to withdraw from multiemployer units. Between 1971 and 1975 the board decided only 27 such cases; between 1976 and 1980 the NLRB issued decisions on 97 cases. According to *The New York Times* in 1982, 200 firms decided to bargain on their own rather than through their associations. In the steel industry because of intense economic pressures companies have been restructuring, modernizing, and closing down some operations. Some firms "are debating whether to scrap the multiemployer approach in the 1986 round of negotiations and bargain on the individual circumstances of each company."[69]

Bargaining units are not a static entity; they respond to a variety of internal and external forces. According to Kochan and Katz, in recent years concession bargaining, worker-participation experiments, pressures for higher productivity, for lower labor costs and for a change in work rules all contributed to a "return to more intensive negotiations at the plant level." These developments may be an early indication of increased potential pressures towards decentralization of bargaining. In the future the single-plant and the single-firm bargaining unit may occupy a more prominent position than it does today within the U.S. bargaining structure.[70]

COORDINATED AND COALITION BARGAINING

Introduction

The terms *coalition* and *coordinated bargaining* are subject to different interpretations. Some authors use the terms interchangeably and consider the processes almost identical, while others make a clear distinction. Hildebrand claims there is little difference between the two processes, stating that "the IUD [Industrial Union Department of the AFL−CIO] prefers the term 'coordinated bargaining' presumably to avoid adverse legal connotations though the difference between effective coordination and a coalition is negligible."[71] By contrast, both Wagner[72] and Schwarz[73] make a clear distinction.

Wagner defines *coalition bargaining* as the bargaining by two or more unions for a common master agreement covering all the employees within the coalition. Schwarz similarly states, "True coalition bargaining occurs when a common, 'mixed' negotiating committee of all interested unions jointly settles with management on a common contract with terms applicable to all units."

Wagner describes *coordinated bargaining* as situations "where two or more unions representing separate bargaining units negotiate jointly not for a common master agreement but for individual unit contracts containing similar terms." Schwarz gives a more descriptive definition, stating that coordination takes place when

> negotiating committees consist of representatives of all interested unions, but allow the authority to accept or reject a contract offer to remain with the representatives of the unit to be bargained for and sequentially settle on separate contracts often with common terms for each traditional bargaining unit.

Schwarz states that coordination may also take the form of a central policy committee directing a number of bargaining teams, but with each team signing a separate contract.

For purposes of this section, the terms *coalition* and *coordination* will be considered as interchangeable, without any implication that the cooperating unions do or do not sign a common agreement. For purposes of consistency and when there is no conflict with direct quotations, the term *coordination* rather than *coalition* is primarily applied in this section.

Coordination is a form of joint bargaining under which two or more local and/or international labor organizations participate. It was first conducted by craft unions as early as the 1880s,[74] and some still continues. However, not all joint bargaining is coordinated bargaining. According to Schwarz, the main targets of coalition bargaining, as contrasted with other joint bargaining, are large multiplant corporations. Chernish[75] states that coalition bargaining "is a new industrial relations development" which is to be distinguished from other forms of joint bargaining. Coordinated bargaining is usually orchestrated and directed by the Industrial Union Department (IUD) of the AFL−CIO. The traditional joint bargaining arrangements, such as multicraft bargaining, developed without the direct sponsorship of the IUD or the AFL or the CIO. Chernish further states that

> the most important differentiating feature of coalition bargaining as contrasted to other forms of joint bargaining is that the other efforts have come about as a result of voluntary agreement between the employer and the union. Coalition bargaining programs are designed to force an employer to bargain with a representative of the various participating locals on a joint basis.[76]

Why Do Unions Want Coordinated Bargaining?

As noted, the union target of coordinated bargaining is the large multiplant corporation; it is an attempt by unions to increase their bargaining power with large employers. For example, General Electric has scores of plants scattered across the nation, organized in varying locations and proportions mainly by the automobile, electrical, and machinists' unions, but also by a dozen or more smaller unions as well. Hildebrand states that "the coalition movement has come from a combination of union weakness in bargaining in some situations and a thrust for more power from some large aggressive labor organizations."[77] He claims that the three factors responsible for the development of coordinated bargaining are "competitive plants," "community of interest," and "union drive for power."

The characteristics of the "competitive plant" model are as follows: (1) The industry is not completely organized. (2) The negotiation framework of the organized employers is decentralized. (3) Unions bargain at the level of local plants. (4) There is a differential in wages and other contract terms, both within individual firms and within the industry. (5) The different plants of the same employer and employers in the industry compete in the same product market. (6) Individual employers produce similar products in a number of substitute plants; thus, they can transfer production from plant to plant; this provides them with a significant amount of bargaining power.

National unions suffer a lack of power when they compete. One way to improve their position and to achieve a greater uniformity of terms in an industry is to employ coordination. The Standard Oil of Ohio situation is an example of unions trying to apply coordinated bargaining to a competitive model consisting of substitute plants.[78] The competitive model was originally developed by John R. Commons in his classic *History of American Shoemakers, 1648–1895.*

The second reason for coordinated bargaining presented by Hildebrand is "community of interest." Unions and employees of multiplant firms may want uniformity, not only in wages, but also in such fringes as pensions and major medical plans. Standardization may be much more difficult to attain through decentralized bargaining, under which employers can slow down drives for uniformity by playing local unions against each other. For example, termination dates of local contracts may differ and give employers an edge in bargaining. Also, exchange of information among local unions may be lacking. Thus, coordinated bargaining may be a way for unions and their members to overcome their bargaining handicaps.

The third force proposed by Hildebrand as leading toward coordination is "union drive for power." A union can increase its power in many different ways. An obvious one is legislation that protects and encourages union activities. A second is growth, as through mergers, absorption of smaller unions, and organizing the unorganized. Strong leadership also enhances union power, and under coalition bargaining some unions assume the mantle of leadership. Their dominant role not only gives them more prestige within the labor movement but also provides them with more power in bargaining and a stronger base for future growth.

Conway and Ginsburg of the IUD[79] identified four reasons for unions to coordinate. First, such activity would enhance growth in organizing because it would provide a good index of union weaknesses and strengths. Second, coordination would force unions to use computers for bargaining and contract analysis. Third, greater cooperation among unions might significantly reduce jurisdictional conflict. Finally, coordinated bargaining communicates to employers that it is a "struggle on behalf of the entire labor movement, not just one particular segment of it."[80]

Large-scale union efforts toward coordinated bargaining began in the mid-sixties, when conditions seemed ripe. There was little unemployment and little excess capacity. When confronted with uniform demands from a coalition group, employers were at a disadvantage, since they could not readily shift production from the affected plants to other plants within their companies. Furthermore, the union movement had dynamic leaders like the late Walter Reuther, who was willing to fight for coordinated bargaining and was referred to as the "intellectual father of coalition bargaining." The sixties were also a period of major corporate changes that potentially strengthened managements relative to unions, and that unions wanted to counter. There were many mergers; it was the era of conglomerates and multinationals. Many large corporations also experienced rapid growth. In response to these developments, the AFL−CIO department established a coordinated bargaining program. Its purpose has been to provide coordination in negotiations for different unions that have a collective bargaining relationship with the same employer. The IUD establishes committees of representatives of unions that are interested in working together. The committees are responsible for development of "a program for cooperative and coordinated bargaining." According to Howard D. Samuel, President of the IUD department, the growth of conglomerates contributed to the development of coordinated bargaining.[81] Bok and Dunlop state,

> In an era of rapidly growing conglomerates it is understandable that the unions should be seriously concerned over the ability of companies to sustain a strike by continuing production in other plants not involved in the dispute and by maintaining profits through diversified operations in other divisions of the enterprise.[82]

Along with local labor relations offices, the large multiplant corporations have corporate headquarter labor relations departments that coordinate and centralize labor relations for the whole corporation. Coordinated bargaining is the unions' response to employer orchestration of labor relations throughout a corporation or even an industry.

A central force behind coordinated bargaining is the IUD of the AFL−CIO. When the potential for coordinated bargaining is discerned in a particular situation the IUD develops a detailed plan of action for the interested unions. An IUD pamphlet on coordination states that the IUD "at the request of the involved unions . . . helps organize and implement joint negotiations for any company or industry." Under such a program,

> all the involved unions get together, establish a procedure, compare notes, agree on common objectives, and plan bargaining strategy. When they cannot negotiate jointly, they exchange information either through having representatives of other unions sit on their bargaining teams as observers, or through frequent coordinating committee meetings or both.[83]

Employers' Opposition to Coordinated Bargaining

The main reason for employers' opposition to coordinated bargaining is potential loss of bargaining power[84]—the same reason that makes coordination attractive to unions. Why, asks Northrup, "should a company whose employees have chosen different unions to represent them open up the company to more encompassing strikes by agreeing to widen the bargaining basis"?[85]

In the well-known GE coordination case, the company released in its *Employee Relations News* a nine-point statement opposing coordinated bargaining. Two of these points are that

> the coalition stands as little more than an outright strike broadening and strike lengthening effort. . . . By trying to centralize negotiations that have been traditionally localized, the coalition inevitably would submerge the varying needs and concerns of employees in more than a hundred different General Electric businesses. This risks the now common danger of inviting local strikes even after national strikes are settled.[86]

A good summary of the rationale of corporate opposition to coordination is provided by Hildebrand.[87] Here are some of his points: The objective of unions is to negotiate, through coordination, master agreements or local agreements with identical termination dates. Such agreements would give unions the ability to strike simultaneously a multiplant company or even a total industry. Such strikes would be more costly to the employer and thus could strengthen unions in bargaining. Some employers think that the ultimate goal of coordination is centralization. This is a one-way street because it may be difficult for employers to move back to smaller bargaining structures from company-wide or industry-wide units. Eventually, coordination could also lead to three levels of bargaining: at the individual plant, at the company multiplant level, and at the industry level, providing unions with repeated opportunities to apply pressure and strike threats. This, in turn, could complicate negotiations and lead to costlier contracts for employers.

Multiplant companies that bargain locally sometimes benefit from interplant wage differentials that reflect differences in local labor markets. Coordination that aims at uniformity would make it more difficult to continue such plant differentials.

Employers also fear that coordinated large-scale bargaining will invite government intervention. Engle, an official of Union Carbide, stated that "there is no way for government to stay out." He further stated that

> coalition bargaining if it is allowed to develop as the IUD has blueprinted it will destroy true collective bargaining, will create a few all-powerful labor leaders, and would eventually substitute the corporate state for free enterprise.[88]

Not all employers oppose coordinated bargaining. Some multiemployer bargaining frameworks include coordinations among unions in an arrangement that both unions and employers approve as mutually beneficial. The multiemployer, multiunion bargaining framework may occur in industries composed of many small employers who find it easier to negotiate with a number of unions. However, employer consent to coordinated bargaining does not extend to most large multiplant employers, who "want no part of coalition bargaining, and will continue to fight it."[89]

SUMMARY

The major objective of coordination is uniformity of contract terms. Success, however, could carry a very high price. To reach internal agreement in a coalition composed of groups with many diversified interests could be extremely difficult. Hence, coalitions usually confine their activities to such major issues as wages, pensions, health plans, escalator clauses, and common contract expiration dates, leaving all other issues to local bargaining. But even on major issues like wages and pensions, great differences may prevail. A union local composed of young workers would probably be more interested in higher wages, as opposed to a group of middle-aged workers who would be more concerned with pension and health plans. Reconciling these conflicting interests within the coalition could be difficult indeed, and could lead to long delays and the breakdown of negotiations.

Greater centralization of labor relations functions by corporations and unions may be another consequence of coordinated bargaining. Under such centralization, local needs may be ignored by both sides as local union leaders and the plant-level labor relations managers lose some of their autonomy and become ineffective spokesmen for local needs. However, this result can to some extent be overcome through supplementary bargaining at the local level.

To conclude, thus far labor-management confrontations over the status of coalition and coordination bargaining have been fought on two fronts: the legal front, where both sides sought support from the NLRB and the courts, and the bargaining front, where bargaining power was brought to bear. It is too early to draw major conclusions as to winners and losers. Both sides have experienced significant gains and losses.[90] The major battles of the future will also be fought at the bargaining table, at the NLRB, and in the courts. There are some unanswered legal questions regarding the status of coordinated bargaining, as well as its impact on good-faith bargaining and the appropriateness of bargaining units. Eventually, these questions will presumably have to be answered by the Supreme Court.

NOTES

[1]Neil W. Chamberlain, "Determinants of Collective Bargaining Structures," in Arnold R. Weber (ed.), *The Structure of Collective Bargaining* (New York: Free Press of Glencoe, 1961), p. 6.

[2]John T. Dunlop and James J. Healy, *Collective Bargaining, Principles and Cases* (Homewood, Ill.: Irwin, 1955), p. 23.

[3]Edward Herman, *Determination of the Appropriate Bargaining Unit* (Ottawa, Canada: Department of Labour, 1966), p. 14.

[4]Weber, *op. cit.*, pp. 25–26.

[5]Archibald Cox, Derek Curtis Bok, and Robert A. Gorman, *Cases and Materials on Labor Law* (Mineola, N.Y.: Foundation Press, 1977), p. 295.

[6]Weber, *op. cit.*, p. 26.

[7]Subject to legislative restrictions under Section 9(b)(2) of the National Labor Relations Act regarding crafts, guards, and professional employees.

[8]*Ibid.*

[9]E. Robert Livernash, "Recent Developments in Bargaining Structure," in Weber, *op. cit.*, p. 52.

[10]*Characteristics of Major Collective Bargaining Agreements* (Washington, D.C.: Department of Labor, Bureau of Labor Statistics, 1981), p. 19.

[11]*Fifteenth Annual Report of the NLRB*, 1950 (Washington, D.C.: U.S. Government Printing Office, 1951), p. 39.

[12]*Ibid.*

[13]John T. Dunlop, *Collective Bargaining* (Chicago: Irwin, 1949), p. 27.

[14]Derek C. Bok, "Discussion," *Proceedings of the 19th Annual Winter Meeting of the Industrial Relations Research Association*, San Francisco, December 28–29, 1966, p. 104.

[15]Robert A. Gorman, *Basic Text on Labor Law, Unionization and Collective Bargaining* (St. Paul, Minn.: West, 1976), p. 67.

[16]John E. Abodeely, Randi C. Hammer, and Andrew L. Sandler, *The NLRB and the Appropriate Bargaining Unit*, rev. ed., (Industrial Research Unit, The Wharton School, University of Pennsylvania, 1981), pp. 11–83.

[17]*Labor Law Course*, 23rd ed. (Chicago: Commerce Clearing House, 1976), p. 1825.

[18]Fifteenth Annual Report of the NLRB, *op. cit.*, p. 39.

[19]Gorman, *op. cit.*, p. 69.

[20]Abodeely, *op. cit.*, p. 14.

[21]Cox et al., *op. cit.*, p. 295.

[22]Weber, *op. cit.*, p. 28.

[23]Harry Wellington and Ralph K. Winter, *The Unions and the Cities* (Washington, D.C.: The Brookings Institution, 1971), p. 98. *Source:* James L. Perry and Harold L. Angle, "Bargaining Unit Structure and Organizational Outcomes," *Industrial Relations*, 20, no. 1 (Winter 1981), pp. 47–59.

[24]*Save-On Drugs, Inc.*, 138 NLRB 1032 (1962). Source: E. Edward Herman and Gordon S. Skinner, *Labor Law* (New York: Random House, 1972), pp. 156–60.

[25]Jack Barbash, "Collective Bargaining: Contemporary American Experience—A Commentary," in *Collective Bargaining: Contemporary American Experience*, Gerald G. Somers, ed., Industrial Relations Research Association Series, 1980, p. 579; Douglas V. Brown and George P. Schultz, "Public Policy and the Structure of Collective Bargaining," in Weber, *op. cit.*, p. 314.

[26]Berton B. Subrin, "Conserving Energy at the Labor Board: The Case for Making Rules on Collective Bargaining Units," *Labor Law Journal* (February, 1981), pp. 105–113.

[27]Cox, et al. *op cit.*, p. 295. *Joy Silk Mills, Inc.* v. *NLRB* (D.C. Cir., 1950), 185 F. 2d 732. In Gorman, *op. cit.*, p. 105. 419 U.S. 817, 95 S. Ct. 429 (1974); see Gorman, *op. cit.*, p. 105.

[28]Arnold R. Weber, "Stability and Change in the Structure of Collective Bargaining, Challenges to Collective Bargaining," in Lloyd Ulman (ed.), *The American Assembly*, Columbia University (Englewood Cliffs, N.J.: Prentice-Hall, 1967), pp. 13–36.

[29]James L. Perry and Harold L. Angle, "Bargaining Unit Structure and Organizational Outcomes," *Industrial Relations*, 20 (Winter 1981), pp. 47–59; Weber, *The Structure of*

Collective Bargaining, op. cit., p. 3, pp. 181–195; Daniel Quinn Mills, *Labor-Management Relations* (New York: McGraw-Hill, 1978), p. 404, and Wallace E. Hendricks and Lawrence M. Kahn, "The Determinants of Bargaining Structure In U.S. Manufacturing Industries," *Industrial and Labor Relations Review*, 35, no. 2 (January 1982), 181–195; Arnold Weber, "Stability and Change in the Structure of Collective Bargaining," *op. cit.*, pp. 15–32.

[30]107 NLRB 1418 (1954).

[31]Interview with Nathan Headd, UAW Research Department, Detroit, Michigan.

[32]"Whipsawing"—union stratagem seeking to obtain benefits from a number or group of employers by applying pressure to one, the objective being to win favorable terms from the one employer and then use this as a pattern or perhaps a base to obtain the same or greater benefits from the other employers, under the same threat of pressure (including a strike) used against the first one. Source: Harold S. Roberts, *Roberts' Dictionary of Industrial Relations*, rev. ed. (Washington, D.C.: BNA, 1971), p. 581.

[33]St. Vincent's Hospital, 223 NLRB 98. Source: Forty-First Annual Report of the NLRB, 1976, pp. 56–57.

[34]NLRB 294 (1937). Labor Law Course, 24th ed. (Chicago: Commerce Clearing House, 1979), p. 1827.

[35]13 NLRB 1252 (1939).

[36]*Ibid.*

[37]76 NLRB 1199 (1948).

[38]*Corn Products Refining Company*, 80 NLRB 362 (1948).

[39]*Weyerhaeuser Timber Company*, 87 NLRB 1976 (1949).

[40]*Permanente Metals Company*, 89 NLRB 804 (1950).

[41]*NLRB* v. *Pittsburgh Plate Glass Company*, 270 F. 2d 167 (4th Cir., 1959).

[42]107 NLRB 1418 (1954).

[43]162 NLRB 387 (1966).

[44]Laurence J. Cohen, "Two Years Under *Mallinckrodt:* A Review of the Board's Latest Craft Unit Policy,'" *Labor Law Journal*, 20, no. 4 (April 1969), pp. 195–215.

[45]John E. Abodeely, *The NLRB and the Appropriate Bargaining Unit* (Wharton School, University of Pennsylvania, 1971), p. 110.

[46]162 NLRB 387 (1966).

[47]Abodeely et al., *op. cit.*, p. 110.

[48]Dallas L. Jones, "Self-Determination Versus Stability of Labor Relations," *Michigan Law Review*, Vol. 58, January 1960, pp. 313, 346.

[49]Abodeely, *op. cit.*, p. 111.

[50]*Ibid.*

[51]Neil W. Chamberlain and James W. Kuhn, *Collective Bargaining*, 2nd ed. (New York: McGraw-Hill, 1965), p. 250.

[52]*Characteristics of Major Collective Bargaining Agreements* (Washington, D.C.: Department of Labor, Bureau of Labor Statistics, 1981), p. 19.

[53]Neil W. Chamberlain, *Collective Bargaining* (New York: McGraw-Hill, 1951), chaps. 8 and 9; Chamberlain and Kuhn, *op. cit.*, chap. 10; see also Jesse Freidin, *The Taft Hartley Act and Multi-Employer Bargaining*, Industry Wide Collective Bargaining Series (Philadelphia: University of Pennsylvania Press, 1948). Clark Kerr and Lloyd H. Fisher, "Multiple Employer Bargaining: The San Francisco Experience," in R. A. Lester and J. Shister (eds.), *Insights into Labor Issues* (New York: Macmillan, 1948).

[54]Otto Pollack, *Social Implications of Multi-Employer Bargaining* (Philadelphia: University of Pennsylvania Press, 1948), p. 12.

[55]*Multi-Employer Association Bargaining and Its Impact on the Collective Bargaining Process*, Report of the General Subcommittee on Labor, Committee on Education and Labor, House of Representatives, December 1964 (Washington, D.C.: U.S. Government Printing Office, 1965), p. 1.

[56]Charles M. Rehmus, *Multi-Employer Bargaining*, Current History 48, August 1965, p. 92.

[57]Peter Henle, "Union Policy and Size of Bargaining Unit" in Weber, *op. cit.*, p. 111.

[58]James C. Hardman, "Cooperation in Collective Bargaining, the Airlines and Railroads Try Novel Approaches," in Max S. Wortman, Jr. (ed.), *Critical Issues in Labor*, Text and Readings (London: Collier Macmillan, 1969), p. 323.

[59]Cox et al., *op cit.*, p. 329.

[60]*Pacific Longshore Case*, 7 NLRB 1008 (1938). Source: Chamberlain, *op cit.*, p. 180.

[61]Chamberlain and Kuhn, *op cit.*, p. 245. See also David A. McCabe, "Problems of Industry Wide or Regional Trade Agreements," *American Economic Review*, Vol. 33, Supplement (1943), pp. 163–73; and John Van Sickle, "Industry-Wide Collective Bargaining and the Public Interest" in *Unions, Management, and the Public*, E. Wight Bakke and Clark Kerr (eds.), (New York: Harcourt, Brace and World, 1948), pp. 521–25.

[62]Chamberlain, *op cit.*, p. 203.

[63]*Multi-Employer Association Bargaining and Its Impact on the Collective Bargaining Process, op. cit.*, p. 30.

[64]Labor Relations Programs, Hearings on S. 55 and S.J. Res. 22, 80th Cong., 1st sess., Part 1, p. 577. Source: Chamberlain, *op. cit.*, p. 207.

[65]Richard A. Lester and Edward A. Robie, "Wages Under National and Regional Collective Bargaining," 1946, in Chamberlain, *op cit.*, pp. 207–208.

[66]Twenty-fifth Annual Report of the NLRB (Washington, D.C.: U.S. Government Printing Office, 1960), pp. 40–41, Thirty-first Annual Report of the NLRB, 1966 (Washington, D.C.: U.S. Government Printing Office, 1967), p. 89.

[67]Abodeely et al., *op. cit.*, pp. 224–240.

[68]Clyde W. Summers, Harry H. Wellington, Alan Hyde, *Cases and Materials on Labor Law*, 34, 2 (Mineola, N.Y.: The Foundation Press, Inc., 1982), pp. 649–652.

[69]Robert B. Hoffman, "The Trend Away from Multiemployer Bargaining," *Labor Law Journal* (February 1983), pp. 80–93. See also "Business Digest," *New York Times*, June 22, 1982, p. 1.

[70]Thomas A. Kochan and Harry C. Katz, "Collective Bargaining, Work Organization, and Worker Participation: The Return to Plant-Level Bargaining," *Labor Law Journal* (August, 1983), pp. 524–530.

[71]George H. Hildebrand, "Cloudy Future for Coalition Bargaining," in Richard L. Rowan (ed.), *Readings in Labor Economics and Labor Relations*, rev. ed. (New York: Irwin-Dorsey, 1972), pp. 300–317.

[72]Lynn E. Wagner, "Multi-Union Bargaining: A Legal Analysis," *Labor Law Journal*, 19, no. 12 (December 1968), p. 737.

[73]Phillip J. Schwarz, *Coalition Bargaining* (Ithaca, N.Y.: Cornell University Press, 1970), p. 2.

[74]*Ibid*.

[75]William N. Chernish, *Coalition Bargaining* (Philadelphia: University of Pennsylvania Press, 1969), p. 7.

[76]*Ibid*., 271.

[77]Hildebrand, *op. cit*., pp. 301, 304–305.

[78]*Ibid*., p. 303, see also Jack T. Conway and Woodrow L. Ginsburg, "The Extension of Collective Bargaining to New Fields". Industrial Relations Research Association, *Proceedings* of the Nineteenth Annual Winter Meeting, San Francisco, December 28–29, 1966, pp. 303–11.

[79]*Ibid*., Conway.

[80]*Ibid*., p. 304.

[81]*Coordinated Bargaining*, pamphlet issued by the IUD Department, AFL–CIO, Washington, D.C., p. 1.

[82]Derek C. Bok and John T. Dunlop, *Labor and the American Community* (New York: Simon and Schuster, 1970), p. 258.

[83]*Coordinated Bargaining, op. cit*., p. 14.

[84]Hildebrand, *op. cit*., p. 311.

[85]Herbert R. Northrup, "Boulwarism v. Coalitionism—The 1966 G.E. Negotiation," *Management of Personnel Quarterly*, 5, no. 2 (Summer 1966), p. 8.

[86]General Electric Company, *Employee Relations News*, No. 66–28, July 25, 1966, p. 1. Source: Chernish, *op. cit*., pp. 97–98.

[87]Hildebrand, *op. cit*., pp. 311–12.

[88]Earl L. Engle, "Coordinated Bargaining," *Labor Law Journal*, 19, no. 8 (August 1968), 522–23.

[89]Schwarz, *op. cit*., p. 23.

[90]David Lasser, "Coordinated Bargaining, a Union Point of View," *Labor Law Journal*, 19, no. 8 (August 1968), p. 512; and Chernish, *op. cit*., p. 130.

PREPARATION FOR BARGAINING

7

In this chapter, we begin our examination of the process of collective bargaining. All the practical aspects of negotiations are covered without special emphasis on those factors which determine the actual settlement. Those issues, and other topics of a more theoretical nature will be covered in a later chapter. We also reserve coverage of conflict and the resolution of impasses to a later chapter. Here we examine the actual behaviors of unions and managements as they prepare to negotiate a collective bargaining agreement.

The process of preparation for bargaining is influenced by such factors as the scope, size, and dimension of the bargaining unit, the organizational structure of the union and of the employer, and the nature of the relationship between labor and management. Preparations for bargaining in the small single-location, single-employer bargaining unit are not as complex as they would be in a large multiplant or multiemployer unit. Bargaining units can have a direct effect on the size and composition of bargaining teams, on the method of formulation and on the content of bargaining demands. Employer and union organizations can influence the nature and the degree of sophistication of bargaining preparations. A large union or a large employer with a large staff and a centralized approach to negotiation can spend considerably more time and effort on preparation than unions or employers which lack adequate resources. The structure of the institutional relationship between labor and management, as conceptualized by Benjamin M. Selekman et al.,[1] could also affect the preparation process. When the parties operate within the Selekman framework of "accommodation" or "cooperation," there could be some open communication in gathering data for bargaining and even some joint preparation. In a "conflict" or "containment" relationship, as defined by Selekman, where the parties hate or dislike each other intensely, preparation is primarily directed to reinforce "pre-determined and rigidly fixed positions . . . [and] help the negotiator . . . let the other party know the settlement point and how firmly it is held rather than convince the opposite party about the reasonableness of a given position."[2]

The character of the bargaining process, its outcomes, and its failures or successes can all be influenced by the quality of the preparation process. The purpose of this chapter is to review in some detail the steps that the parties can take in preparing for bargaining.

Preparation for bargaining is a complex process that demands the participation of many people who possess expertise in a variety of areas. Before bargaining can begin, union and management negotiating teams have to be appointed, supporting data have to be gathered, bargaining books, if they are to be used, have to be prepared, proposals have to be formulated, tactical moves must be initiated, and bargaining procedures agreed upon. We will now explore all these preparatory steps in some detail.

MANAGEMENT BARGAINING TEAM

Who sits at the bargaining table? What might not seem to be a particularly important question can have significant impact upon the bargaining process. Although there is no set formula to determine the number and types of people that should compose a management bargaining team, there are some studies that show the existing patterns.

A survey by the National Industrial Conference Board (NICB)[3] revealed that there is no such thing as a uniform management negotiating team in terms of size or composition. Although there are considerable variations in size, the most common range is from three to five members. According to the NICB, the following factors influence the composition of management teams: size of the firm, its bargaining structure, personality characteristics of the opposition, and bargaining skills of managers available to the firm. In large firms, the bargaining team is usually composed of experienced labor relations professionals. It may include a variety of experts from a vice president of industrial relations to fringe benefit specialists. In contrast, in smaller firms the bargaining team may contain people with limited experience in industrial relations. It may include the company's president, first-line supervisors, and finance and production people. In both large and small companies attorneys almost always participate in the bargaining process, sometimes as members of the bargaining team—more often, however, as advisors to negotiators and as drafters of contract terms. It has become more and more common over the recent years for outside attorneys or other consultants to provide bargaining services for the firm. This is particularly true of smaller firms, where the time and expense necessary to develop adequate internal expertise are excessive in relation to the benefits.

The bargaining structure directly affects the composition of the bargaining team. In the case of multiemployer bargaining, the team may include representatives appointed by the various employers within the bargaining unit. In some cases, bargaining in such units is delegated to an association which appoints its own team. In the case of single-employer, multilocation bargaining, the team may be composed of only head office staff, or it may include some local representation. In the case of multilocation employers who bargain separately for each location, the team may be confined to local management, or it may include a representative from the firm's head office. In single-employer, single-location bargaining, the team may consist of the top management of the company.

Some firms are engaged in dual bargaining. They negotiate separately a master contract and a local contract. Major issues such as wages and fringe benefits are negotiated at the corporate level by head office staff. Issues of local interest are resolved by local officials with assistance from the head office.

The composition, size, and selection of the management team in terms of expertise, personality, and level of militancy is influenced by the complexity of the contract to be negotiated and the nature of the opposition. In union-management relations, the history of the relationship plays a large role, and each party reacts to that history and the behavior of its opposition. Unfriendly or militant behavior on the part of the union or management may create the desire for the other party to choose team members who can respond in kind. Just as possible, cooperative behavior can cause both teams to take the more abrasive personalities away from the bargaining table.

The effectiveness of a bargaining team is not determined by its size but by its ability, knowledge, and experience. A team well versed in tactics, strategy, and timing would be in a better position to avoid impasses and strikes and would end up with a better agreement than a team composed of inexperienced people.

The bargaining process, the behavior and conduct of negotiators at the bargaining table, and the terms agreed upon all have an impact on the structure of the institutional relationship that evolves between the parties. Experienced negotiators will attempt to use the bargaining process as a means of building the type of relationship structure desired by the principals in their organizations.

The most important member of the bargaining team is its spokesperson. Such an individual is responsible for the major presentation of positions, communicating priorities, timing concessions, making threats and commitments, and deciding on the appropriate role of each team member. Spokespersons are like orchestra conductors, coordinating and timing the activities of the different individuals toward the achievement of a common objective. Perhaps crucial to the success of the negotiations is whether the spokesperson has the authority to settle the contract. While policies vary from firm to firm, Thomas Kochan has shown that ultimately the authority to conclude the agreement lies at the corporate level.[4]

UNION BARGAINING TEAMS AND COMMITTEES

Union bargaining teams, like management teams, come in various sizes. There are situations where a business agent alone represents membership in bargaining, and there are cases where the full bargaining team or committee may be up to a hundred people.[5] When a committee is that large, negotiations are usually delegated to a much smaller subcommittee. The larger group keeps in touch with the subcommittee, provides it with assistance, but does not participate directly in negotiations. However, the approval of the larger group becomes necessary before the contract can be finalized.

Union teams, like management teams, also require assistance from experts in various fields. The economist, the fringe benefits specialist, the actuary, and the attorney are all background participants in the bargaining process.

The bargaining structure and the size and dimensions of the bargaining unit have a direct impact on the size and composition of the union bargaining team. In national negotiations, the union team is usually large and is composed of officers of the national union, staff experts from the national, and some representatives from local unions. In local bargaining, the negotiating committee is relatively small. If the bargaining committee is elected by the local, it typically includes union officers, a business agent, and some shop stewards. In some instances, a representative of a national union may assist the local union either as an advisor or as a full-time member of the bargaining team. The representative of the national union helps locals formulate demands and assists them in the process of negotiations.[6] National unions are concerned with maintaining the uniformity of contract terms within industries that they represent. It is usually the responsibility of the national representative to prevent local concessions from falling below the minimum industry norm established by the national union. With the increased complexity of contract terms, the trend has been for national unions to assume a larger role in local negotiations.

The issue of size of the bargaining team is more significant for unions than for management. Whereas management in appointing a bargaining team is primarily interested in having an effective negotiating team, a union has also to consider the political implications of size and composition. The union as a democratic organization has to have enough people on the team so that an adequate feedback on the progress of negotiations can be provided to its membership. Also, the size of the team has to reflect political realities. Bargaining units are composed of heterogeneous groups of employees. In order to obtain contract ratification, it is important that these divergent interests be represented at the bargaining table.

PREPARATION OF BARGAINING DATA

The purpose of this section is to outline some of the data that can be helpful to both sides at the bargaining table. Careful preparation of proposals can reduce uncertainty, improve communication, and thus contribute to effective bargaining. Better preparation provides the parties with broader perspectives which, in turn, increase flexibility and can accelerate the negotiation process.

Knowledge of the opposition is an important ingredient in bargaining. Before bargaining starts, management may attempt to find out everything it can about the union: its financial strength, its organizational structure, any internal problems, the formal and informal power structure, bargaining experience of other employers with the union, and type of settlements arrived at elsewhere. Information on some of these subjects can be obtained informally through conversations with union leaders, discussions with labor relations officers of other firms who have dealt with a particular union, published Bureau of Labor Statistics survey data, union publications or newspapers, union contracts, and published reports from the Bureau of National Affairs. Under Title II, Section 201(B) of the Reporting and Disclosure Act of 1959 (Landrum—Griffin Act), every labor organization must file a financial report annually with the secretary of labor. These reports are in the public domain, and are a good source of financial information about unions.

Unions, like management, try to find out as much as possible about the weaknesses and strengths of their opponents. The following management data can be helpful to union negotiators: financial information on the company and the industry, annual reports, financial reports to stockholders, and reports filed with the Securities and Exchange Commission. Other useful sources are the U.S. Department of Commerce reports, trade journals, and industry association reports. The AFL—CIO in its publication *Lining Up the Facts*[7] advises union negotiators not only to examine company profits but to obtain information on sales, production, pricing policies, new technology, new products, investment plans, and trends of new orders. If a company is publicly owned and traded on one of the exchanges, information can also be obtained from such stock market services and publications as Moody's, Standard and Poor's, Value Line, *Commercial and Financial Chronicle, Wall Street Journal, Barron's, Forbes, Business Week*, and *Fortune*. Individual firms are also reviewed by some of the large brokerage houses such as Merrill Lynch et al., E.F. Hutton, and Bache Halsey et al.

TABLE 7.1. USEFUL BARGAINING DATA

Internal to the Firm	External to the Firm
(1) Number of workers in each job classification	(1) Comparative industry wage rates
(2) Compensation per worker	(2) Comparative occupational wage rates
(3) Minimum and maximum pay in each job classification	(3) Comparative fringe benefits
(4) Overtime pay per hour and number of annual overtime hours worked by job classification.	(4) Consumer price index
(5) Number of employees, by categories, who work on each shift[1]	(5) Patterns of relevant bargaining settlements
(6) Cost of shift differential premiums[1]	
(7) History of recent negotiations	
(8) Cost of fringe benefits	
(9) Cost-of-living increases	
(10) Vacation costs by years of service of employees	
(11) Demographic data on the bargaining unit members by sex, age, and seniority	
(12) Cost and duration of lunch breaks and rest periods	
(13) An outline of incentive, progresson, evaluation, training, safety, and promotion plans[1]	
(14) Grievance and arbitration awards	

[1]*If applicable.*

Knowledge of the opposition is not confined solely to an understanding of the economic strengths and weaknesses of the respective organization. Part of the preparation can be an investigation of the personalities, internal conflicts and pressures to which the other side is subject.

The AFL−CIO publication *Lining Up the Facts* advocates a thorough preparation for bargaining and states that "facts may not point to specific answers in bargaining. They can help narrow the difference, reduce the area of controversy, and indicate the general range of a reasonable settlement."

Both sides usually compile economic data for purposes of bargaining. Although the nature of the data varies, there is a basic statistical package that most negotiators find helpful. They try to assemble data on business conditions, the state of the economy, and terms of settlement in the region and in the industry in question. They also gather statistics on wages, fringe benefits, profitability, productivity, family budgets, and the consumer price index. Data internal and external to the firm is also very important to the process of bargaining, both for the purpose of effective negotiations and to accurately cost the agreement. See Table 7−1.

Before sitting down across the table, both sides have a fairly accurate picture of the cost of the existing bargaining package. In the case of a first contract, a breakdown of all the existing labor costs is prepared. It is much easier for an employer than for a union to gather such data. In some instances, however, employers may be willing or compelled by the NLRB to share such information with their unions. In preparing for bargaining, both parties attach importance to prevailing wage rates and fringe benefits outside the bargaining unit. They try to gather information on such data from recent labor contracts negotiated within their labor market, their industry, and the economy. Sometimes employers compile such material from wage and fringe benefit surveys. Under NLRB rulings, management may be compelled to share the results of such surveys with their unions. In a General Electric case, the company was directed to "furnish to the union correlated information concerning the respondent's area wage surveys and other information necessary to enable the union to bargain intelligently on rates of pay."[8]

The wage and fringe benefit survey can be a useful tool for formulating wage proposals and anticipating the moves of the opposition. Many employers conduct wage and fringe benefit surveys either by telephone or by mail. They usually seek information on base rate of pay of various job classifications and on fringe benefits. These surveys are commonly confined to the local area of the employer.

Local unions usually try to obtain wage and fringe benefit data from international unions, from the AFL−CIO, and from locally negotiated contracts. The Industrial Union Department of the AFL−CIO issues an annual comparative survey of major collective bargaining settlements and the March issue of the *Federationist* presents an overall view of wages and fringe benefits negotiated in the preceding year.[9]

There are many additional sources of wage surveys: the individual firm, employer and trade associations, Chambers of Commerce, the American Management Association, the Conference Board, private consulting firms, unions, the computer data bank of the AFL−CIO, and the U.S. Department of Labor, Bureau of Labor Statistics. The BLS is the cheapest and most acceptable source of survey results, wage and fringe benefit data, and other pertinent information for collective bargaining purposes.

The following BLS publications can be helpful to negotiators: *Current Wage Developments, Industry Wage Surveys, Area Wage Surveys, The National Survey of Professional, Administrative, Technical and Clerical Pay Employees, Union Wages and Hours, Employment and Earnings, Consumer Price Index, Wage Calendar, Productivity Indexes for Selected Industries, Digest of Selected Pension Plans,* and *Characteristics of Major Collective Bargaining Agreements.*

Current Wage Developments (CWD)[10] is a monthly publication of the BLS. It provides information on general wage and benefit changes in all collective bargaining contracts involving 1,000 or more production or nonsupervisory employees in manufacturing and selected nonmanufacturing industries. Although there is a lag of a few months between contract settlement date and the availability of the contract terms in a published form, the CWD is a useful guide on general trends of wage and benefit changes, frequently referred to by unions, management, and mediators. It is also used by federal government agencies. It should be pointed out, however, that the data do not reflect changes in employee earnings, they only provide information on changes in wage rates and benefits.

Other important sources of information for purposes of bargaining are occupational pay and supplementary benefits surveys published by the BLS. The BLS publishes three types of occupational wage surveys: industry wage surveys, area wage surveys, and a national survey of professional, administrative, technical, and clerical employees.

The industry wage surveys[11] supply statistical data for selected occupations as to range of rates and methods of wage payment. The surveys provide information regarding straight time, hourly earnings, weekly work schedules, shift operations and differentials, and miscellaneous fringe benefit practices. They also provide estimates of coverage of the industry by labor-management agreements. The surveys cover fifty manufacturing and twenty nonmanufacturing industries. Most of these are surveyed on a five-year cycle; some are on a three-year cycle. The shortcoming of these surveys is a time lag; by the time data are published they are outdated. There is no particular date during which specific reports are published. The bulletins are released as the surveys are completed.

The area wage survey,[12] published annually, employs the same concepts, definitions, and methodology as the industry wage survey. This survey, rather than analyzing occupations within individual industries, covers specific geographical areas. The survey supplies statistics for occupational categories common to a broad spectrum of industries within a particular area. The surveys provide statistics on seventy areas[13] in which the BLS conducts surveys of occupational earning and related benefits. In each area, occupational earning data are collected annually. Material on employer practices and supplementary wage benefits is gathered every third year. The purpose of the area wage survey is to review the level and movement of wages in a variety of labor markets. The survey examines the level and distribution of wages by occupation and the movement of wages by occupational category and skill level.

The annual survey of selected professional, administrative, technical, and clerical occupations in private industry provides salary information on a broad spectrum of industries throughout the United States, except Alaska and Hawaii.[14] The occupations studied cover a wide range of duties and responsibilities. Public and private employers use the results of this survey in examining their wage and salary scales. This survey provides information on average salaries, salary levels in metropolitan areas, differences by industry, and employment distribution by salary.

Employment and Earnings is another useful publication of the BLS. It is published monthly. It provides national, state, and area statistics on employment, unemployment, hours, earnings, and labor turnover rates. The data include hourly and weekly earnings from manufacturing and major nonmanufacturing industries with breakdowns by states and by major cities.[15] The data in this publication must be interpreted carefully. Earnings in industry "A" may be higher than in industry "B" not because particular occupations are paid more, but because of different ratios of skilled to unskilled people.

During inflationary periods, the most popular BLS publication around the bargaining table has been the *Consumer Price Index,* issued monthly to measure the prices of selected consumer goods and services. The Index provides national data as well as figures for major cities. Currently, many agreements contain cost-of-living allowance escalator clauses (COLA) which relate the wage level to living cost, as measured by the Index (see Chapter 13). In recent years there have been significant employer pressures on unions to give up their COLA clauses.

In 1978, the BLS introduced major changes in the structure of the *Consumer Price Index.* As of January 1978, the BLS began releasing two new consumer price indexes, one for "all urban consumers" and one for "urban wage earners and clerical workers." This change affected 8 million workers covered by union contracts containing wage escalator clauses tied to the *Consumer Price Index.*[16]

Productivity indexes for selected industries issued by the BLS are another useful source for negotiations. These indexes provide data on employment, employee hours, output per employee, and output per employee hour. In the 1983 edition, the BLS published indexes for 116 industries, some of which covered retail food stores, gasoline service stations, copper mining, coal mining, petroleum refining, steel, primary aluminum, air transportation, and telephone communications.[17]

Another BLS source is the 1425-series on various aspects of collective bargaining agreements. Each bulletin in this series covers in detail some topic of collective bargaining. Recent publications have included studies of *Union Security* (Bulletin 1425-21), *Plant Movement* (Bulletin 1425-20), and *Pay for Union Business* (Bulletin 1425-19).

VALUE OF ECONOMIC DATA

A word of caution is appropriate regarding the employment of economic data; too much stress on such material may involve the parties in long academic debates regarding value and applicability of data and methodology rather than in negotiations over the terms of the contract. Economic data, even if elaborately compiled and impressively presented, are not necessarily applicable or pertinent for every argument at the bargaining table. Some of the available government statistics are outdated, and presentation based on such data may be irrelevant Probably the most important function that the collection of data serves is that the parties are able to place the economic terms of the contract in a comparative framework. They are able to compare the wages and fringe benefits of the bargaining unit members to others in similar occupations, industries, and areas of the country.

Parties have a tendency to present biased statistical data and to leave out material that could contribute to a balanced picture. A deterrent to such an approach would be an agreement between the parties, at the beginning of negotiations, on sources of economic data to be utilized. Such an approach could provide an incentive for negotiators to use data selectively for purposes of specific arguments rather than applying it in a shotgun manner.

Negotiators should not rely on one-sided data or on weak and questionable statistics since such an approach could be counterproductive and lead to a loss of credibility, an important ingredient at the bargaining table. One author states that "being caught in an error means losing the initiative."[18] Apart from presenting arguments based on their own data, negotiators should also be prepared to respond to unfavorable material presented by the opposition.

Preparation of economic data for purposes of bargaining is a major task for both union and management. Negotiators differ on the importance of such material in negotiations. A good summary of the attitudes of union and company negotiators toward economic data can be found in Chamberlain and Kuhn, quoted below. Some union and employer representatives claim that economic data are useless at the bargaining table, that the only thing that counts is bargaining power. This view is not shared by the majority of negotiators. Some management negotiators consider economic data as a means of keeping union wage demands "within competitive limits." Some feel that "without factual information, the results may easily be less satisfactory to all."[19]

According to most negotiators, the bargaining status of economic data is not as prominent as it should be. This, however, is changing. In recent years, negotiators began referring to economic data with much greater frequency, and this trend is most likely to continue. Inflation, cost-of-living provisions, escalator clauses, supplementary unemployment benefits, guaranteed annual income programs, pensions and other fringe benefit plans all contribute to the significance of economic data in bargaining. Such data represent important constraints within which the parties must live.

Although today's negotiators are armed with considerably more economic data than their counterparts twenty or thirty years ago, the data, still used in a partisan manner, are seldom utilized by both sides "as the basis for arriving at agreement."[20] The parties spend an inordinate amount of time arguing over the relevancy, validity, and interpretation of supporting material. This preoccupation with data slows the bargaining process and imposes unnecessary obstacles to settlement.

Chamberlain and Kuhn suggest that the bargaining process is adversely affected if economic data are primarily used as ammunition for debate. Such an approach leads to reliance on one-sided material which may be valuable for scoring debating points, but its usefulness in obtaining bargaining concessions is highly questionable. Also, credibility of all material becomes suspect even if it is obtained from independent research sources.

Some negotiators claim that economic data can be beneficial to both sides, and can help build a better relationship between unions and management. A first step in this direction could be the involvement of the parties in joint research activities. The parties could develop a data bank of economic information which could be used by both sides.* Chamberlain and Kuhn suggest that parties establish "joint fact finding commissions, either permanent or ad hoc in nature; or joint employment of impartial third party investigators."[21] The availability of data that would be acceptable to both sides would help reduce conflict over data, but without eliminating it completely. Even the most legitimate data are subject to different interpretation and value judgment, each side trying to interpret such material on terms that will be most advantageous to its bargaining position. This idea might be most useful in the interpretation of the company's financial position. In the early 1980s, many firms were willing to open their financial records to the union in order to prove their weak financial condition. There is still disagreement over the interpretation of such records, however, and the assistance of outside parties might prove very useful in this context.

BARGAINING BOOKS

Over the years, labor agreements grew in complexity, size, and number of clauses. To be able to cope with the vast quantity of data, many negotiators keep a separate folder for each clause or section of the contract.[22] Such folders may contain all relevant information regarding these clauses or sections. The content of such folders is sometimes compiled into a comprehensive set of materials referred to as the "bargaining book." The complexity of some agreements necessitates the preparation of a separate book for each section of the agreement.

Some firms include in their B (bargaining) books detailed presentation outlines for their negotiators; however, few companies preprogram their negotiators to such an extent. As a guideline for negotiators, some B books contain a priority designation code for each clause of the contract.

B books can be structured in a number of different ways. The National Industrial Conference Board[23] provides several illustrations of how management negotiators organize them. A book prepared by management may contain only existing contract clauses and proposed changes, with reasons, but exclude any known or anticipated union demands. Sometimes management would want to retain existing wording of a particular clause while changing its interpretation. The new interpretation would be included in the book, and it would be a subject of discussion at the bargaining table. Some books are structured along anticipated or known union demands, and management's intended response with reasons. In some books, evaluation of contract clauses extends to comparisons with contract terms in other bargaining units. Some B books

---

*In the Canadian Federal Public Sector the Canadian Pay Research Bureau is required to provide the parties to bargaining with research findings on rates of pay, employee earnings, conditions of employment and related practices prevailing both inside and outside the public sector. The Director of the Bureau is expected to "consult regularly with employer representatives and certified bargaining agents to ensure that, as far as possible . . . their requirements are reflected in the Bureau's Programme." For example, see "Trends in Rates of Pay in the Public Service of Canada: An Update 1972 to 1977," Canada Pay Research Bureau, Public Service Staff Relations Board, 1980.

contain internal payroll data, demographic factors, and other relevant statistics generated within the organization. Such books may also encompass external, economic and statistical data, evaluation of earnings, cost of living, wage trends and fringe benefits development within the industry and the economy.

A study of management preparation for collective bargaining by Ryder et al.[24] states that B books of some large corporations may include the following material for each contract clause: (1) the wording and history of each clause as it has appeared in successive contracts, (2) evaluation of similarities and differences of the clause with other contracts in the industry, (3) internal inputs regarding the clause such as special problems, interpretations, correspondence, grievances, and their disposition, (4) legal status of the clause in terms of NLRB and court decisions, (5) suggested changes in determination of maximum and minimum positions, (6) outline of past union demands and arguments relevant to the clause and management's response with reasons, (7) statistical evidence and cost estimates, where applicable, and any other material upholding a particular bargaining position, (8) status of negotiations regarding each clause and enclosure of any drafts and arguments presented at the table.

B books are advantageous to negotiators before, during, and at the end of negotiations.[25] Before the start of negotiations, the B book helps negotiators focus on problem areas that may arise in negotiations. It also assists them in anticipating and responding to the moves of the opposition. The book can facilitate the conduct of negotiations in a more organized and orderly manner. The book, through its cross-reference system, can assist negotiators in obtaining pertinent information quickly.

According to a study by the Conference Board,[26] the books encourage concentration on one item at a time. Negotiators do not have to bring up too many items simultaneously for fear of forgetting them. A well-organized book protects negotiators and gives them a certain sense of security. They know that nothing will be overlooked, that each item will be discussed at the proper time if they follow the B book outline.

In some negotiations, a significant amount of time is devoted to arguments as to when a particular clause was amended or adopted, and B books that contain background on each clause can reduce debates over issues that are readily verifiable. B books can also help in decreasing impasses over troublesome or emotional issues. Problems can be put aside and resurrected when the chances for an agreement are improved. The books can help speed the bargaining process. Issues can be resolved faster if research is completed in advance and if there is no need for long postponements to gather data. Also, the presence of a data file on each clause brings the parties down from generalities to specifics.

The B book permits negotiators to review at any time the overall status of negotiations and progress made toward an agreement. This is facilitated by blank spaces in the B book in which negotiators can make notes on clauses over which an agreement has been reached.

Poorly prepared negotiators tend to be defensive. This in turn can lead to stalemates, accusations, confrontations, and emotionalism that impede bargaining. The B book can be a confidence builder for negotiators. It provides them with information and arguments for answering the opposition. This adds to their sense of security and self-assurance, a valuable ingredient at the bargaining table.

The book can lower the workload of the chief negotiator by making it possible to divide responsibility for different parts of the contract among members of the bargaining team. Also, in case someone departs from the team, it facilitates familiarizing the successor with the responsibilities of the position.

The B book can also be of value at the end of negotiations and during the life of the contract. It is much easier and faster to draft the final version of the contract if all the changes and agreed-upon clauses can be abstracted from one central source. There are also many questions and problems relating to the interpretation and administration of the contract raised during its life. The B book, if it includes summaries of intent and arguments, can provide valuable guidance and assistance in contract administration.

Although both sides may have at their disposal comprehensive B books, such books are not necessarily brought to the bargaining table. Negotiators usually like to approach the table with as few papers as possible. They may bring along a few folders covering clauses on the day's bargaining agenda, but not complete B books. Such books, if available, are usually kept out of sight. Many negotiators feel that their counterparts would view such material as a crutch, and this in turn could reduce their effectiveness at the table. When neutral territory like a hotel is selected as a site for negotiations, both parties may house the B books and their research and advisory staff in adjoining rooms. In case the books have to be consulted, a recess is called and the team moves to the next room.

Not everyone is impressed with the value of B books. Some firms claim that their negotiators are familiar enough with the contract and do not need such books. Some firms feel that the cost of preparation is higher than the benefits obtained. When books are brought to negotiations they create a formal atmosphere which may have an adverse effect on spontaneity and creativity, restricting the parties in finding new solutions to existing problems. Since it is more common for management to come equipped with bargaining books, union teams may feel threatened by a too-well-prepared opposition. Their insecurity may express itself in aggressive behavior that could lead to a breakdown of negotiations. One employer representative who was critical of B books stated that such books provide the union team with "the impression that all the company arguments are manufactured and are ersatz, and makes the presentation too formal when it should be casual."[27]

To conclude, a B book is a useful source of information; it should probably be prepared by both sides and be continuously updated. It should be kept away from the bargaining table and kept out of sight of the opposition. The negotiators should bring to the bargaining table only data necessary for the day's discussion. Recently, in many organizations the B book has been superseded by the personnel computer and the B disk.

In preparation for bargaining and as a guideline for formulation of bargaining proposals, unions and managements collect and review labor relations information, wages, and financial, statistical, and economic data. In addition, one of the best guides for preparation of bargaining proposals is the study of existing contracts. There are a number of useful sources of information available on the strength and weakness of the existing agreement. These are: (1) analysis of grievances and arbitration awards, (2) review of content of other agreements and exchange of information with other firms and unions, and (3) input from supervisors, employees, and stewards. In the following sections, these three sources are examined.

Grievances and Arbitration Awards

An examination of grievances and inside arbitration awards is an important phase of bargaining preparations. Grievances can be analyzed for problem areas related to text or ambiguity of contract language. Specifically, grievances can be analyzed as to content and causes. Grievances can reflect difficulties in contract administration and interpretation. A study of grievances enables management to develop contract modification proposals.

Grievances can be classified according to contract clauses under which they are filed. If a particular clause is responsible for too many grievances, management may try to have it modified. To obtain a quick reference to troublesome areas, management sometimes prepares a frequency distribution of grievances by contract provisions under which they occur. An evaluation of grievances does not have to be confined to contract provisions that are responsible for grievances. Such review can also extend to clauses that could, but have not, contributed to grievances, since trouble-free provisions may provide valuable lessons.

A study of in-house arbitration awards can provide useful guidelines for revisions of existing agreements. Unfavorable awards provide clues as to weaknesses and needs for modification of contract language. Furthermore, some understandings reached during arbitration proceedings can be incorporated into new contracts.

The analysis of grievances and arbitration awards can be further supplemented by an examination of contract violations, such as work stoppages, slowdowns, and activities that lead to disciplinary sanctions. Contract violations may be symptomatic of employee discontent with the contract.

Content of Other Contracts and Exchange of Information with Other Organizations

In preparing for negotiations, management pays considerable attention to union achievements in other contracts, not only in terms of wages and fringe benefits but also in the area of new types of benefits. Employers know that if a particular union of a major employer or industry achieves a breakthrough on a new benefit, there is a strong possibility that they will be confronted with similar demands in the near future. It is helpful for management to anticipate such demands, since proper evaluation and formulation of appropriate responses may require a few months of research and preparation.

Management monitors labor relations developments in other companies by reviewing labor contracts, as well as through interaction and exchange of information with officials of other firms. Communication among industrial relations managers can take the form of meetings and telephone conversations or it can take the format of a survey of employers in a particular region or industry. In some cases, the trade or industry association can act as a clearing house of labor relations data. Conventions and periodic meetings of labor relations people provide further opportunities for exchange of information. Likewise, unions share information from district to district within unions and among international unions. Pattern developments within industries or new approaches to sticky topics of bargaining are passed along in union conventions and through the facilitating efforts of the AFL−CIO and its divisions.

Input from Supervisors and Stewards

There are no perfect labor agreements, since none can incorporate answers to all possible problems that may arise in their administration. Since an agreement governs a relationship among people, there is an infinite number of permutations and combinations of problems that may appear during its lifetime. Santayana once said that those who do not learn from history are condemned to repeat it. This piece of wisdom also applies to formulation of contract proposals. If an existing contract has generated many operating problems, one way of reducing them is to find out which contract clauses are responsible and try to revise them.

Because first-line supervisors and stewards come most frequently in contact with the collective agreement, they can be a valuable source of information regarding its weaknesses and strengths. Their reactions and views can be helpful in formulating bargaining proposals. The National Industrial Conference Board cites four methods that can be employed in soliciting input from supervisors: the meeting, the questionnaire, the interview, and the contract booklet.[28] While unions tend to be much less formal in their approach to information gathering of this type, the regular stewards' meeting can serve this same function. Their knowledge of the operation of the contract tends to be exactly parallel to that of first-line supervision.

Under the meeting approach, supervisors meet in small groups with a discussion leader and examine critically each provision of the agreement. They inform the leader of clauses with which they have difficulties. A variation of this approach is for a number of small committees to meet and evaluate the content of the contract. These committees then report to a general meeting of all supervisors. The recommendations of all the committees are discussed, evaluated, modified, or ignored, or additional suggestions are made and finally adopted as recommendation for action to be forwarded to the appropriate officials. Still another variation of this approach is to monitor supervisors' reactions and views toward the current contract continuously. This is a preferable avenue of action since it reduces the possibility of arriving at recommendations in an atmosphere charged with emotion, such as frequently prevails before negotiations.

Some firms, rather than conducting meetings or as a supplement to meetings, use questionnaires as a means of getting supervisors' reactions to various parts of the contract. Such questionnaires would list various provisions of the contract and supervisors would be asked to approve, disapprove, or suggest modification of such clauses.[29]

Another variation on the questionnaire is for professional interviewers to interview supervisors. The advantage is that skilled interviewers can obtain information that can be more valuable than data obtained from questionnaires. The main drawback is cost.

Still another method for obtaining contract reactions from supervisors is a "bargaining booklet." When a new contract comes into effect, special copies are prepared for supervisors printed on one side of the page, with the other side reserved for comments. Supervisors are expected to enter in the booklet any problem related to any clause. The bargaining booklet information is collected and reviewed a few months before contract expiration, and it may be discussed during meetings of supervisors. Some companies use interviewers who follow through, in more depth, on the meanings of such entries. In some firms, all entries are tabulated, thus providing the committee charged with formulation of proposals with a valuable input on the troublesome parts of the contract.[30]

The self-esteem of lower-level supervision improves when they are asked to participate; it gives them the feeling of being part of management. Some firms also report that suggestions from supervisors are helpful in the areas of discipline, seniority, and wage payment, as well as in clarification and interpretation of contract language. Not every firm considers the input from its supervisors as useful for purposes of proposal formulation. Some managers feel that lower level supervisors are primarily concerned with the impact of the contract on their own operation and tend to ignore cost of implications. The supervisor is also viewed by some employers as too emotional to be helpful. Despite these criticisms, supervisors can make valuable contributions in formulating bargaining proposals.

To this point, we have focused on sources of information and methods of information collection that are useful to both parties to negotiations. Where a distinction was important, we have noted the different applicability to either the union or management. Once the parties have collected the preparatory data, their prenegotiation behaviors differ dramatically. Thus, we now shall examine first management formulation of proposals and second, union formulation of proposals.

There are certain similarities and differences in proposal preparation between unions and management. Both sides carefully review their current contract, searching for weaknesses and potential modifications. Changes in legislation may also necessitate amendments of existing contract terms. New legislation, such as ERISA in 1974, increases in social security taxes, changes in wage and hour rulings regarding overtime, higher minimum wage laws, and a variety of other legal developments may necessitate the amendment of an expiring contract.

Traditionally, unions have been on the offensive, whereas management has attempted to maintain the status quo. In recent years, management has become more aggressive, demanding contract changes not only as a negotiation tactic and as a trading currency but as a real effort to change existing contract terms.

One similarity in contract preparation between union and management involves their sources of information. Management seeks information from its foreman and its first-line supervisors; the union is briefed by its shop stewards and business agents. Here, however, the parallelism or similarity ends. A union, because it is a democratic organization with elected officers, has to devote more attention to internal responses than does the employer. The firm is essentially authoritarian, with top management ultimately deciding on the offer to be made to the union. This does not mean, however, that the high echelons within a large company can completely ignore internal reactions. Although top management possesses a high degree of authority, as a matter of good management it should not be arbitrary or dictatorial. To manage effectively, management must consider the many management pressure groups within a company, whose interests and personalities differ considerably and may need to be reconciled. Failure to do so could lead to internal conflict and adverse consequences.

FORMULATION OF MANAGEMENT PROPOSALS

A firm is a dynamic entity, and its methods of production, equipment, technology, labor-to-capital ratio, product mix, and organizational structure are in a constant state of change. These changes have to be taken into account when proposals are prepared.

When asked how far in advance they start preparing for a forthcoming negotiation, industrial relations officers usually state, "The day after the current agreement is signed."[31] Although this may be the case in some companies, in the majority of firms preparations start three to nine months before the start of negotiations. The average preparation period for large multiplant companies is nine months.[32] Smaller firms that employ professional negotiators spend three to four months in preparation for bargaining.

Management's preparation of proposals is a two-stage process. In the first stage, data are collected and analyzed. In the second stage, decisions are made as to the type of proposals to be presented at the bargaining table. The responsibility for the first stage of preparation usually rests with the industrial relations department, which is charged with drafting contract proposals. The text may be sent for review and comments to operating departments and works managers. Furthermore, the text is reviewed and if necessary modified by in-house or outside lawyers. The legal contribution is not always appreciated by negotiators since lawyers have a tendency to introduce too much technical jargon and legalism into bargaining. In some negotiations, opposing lawyers battle over language and technicalities rather than over substance. Extensive participation of lawyers in bargaining is not only costly, but may also be detrimental to the negotiating process.

Large multiplant corporations have an industrial relations department at the corporate, division, and local plant level; the distribution of responsibility among these departments depends on the organizational and bargaining structure of the corporation. In some firms, the major responsibility for bargaining preparation is vested with the top corporate level department; in others, the focus of activity may be at the divisional or plant level. Local autonomy would be more common in firms that negotiate separate agreements for each division or plant rather than having a master contract.

Management's decision-making mechanisms vary considerably among firms. Ryder et al.[33] state that in firms where one international union represents a large proportion of the company's blue-collar work force, corporate executives participate fully in the decision-making process. In firms organized on a divisional basis, where each division serves a different product market and union strength is confined to individual divisions, the decision-making authority is vested at the local level. In such situations, corporation officers and industrial relations experts provide guidelines and act as consultants to local management. In some firms, industrial relations departments are responsible for formulating proposals subject to approval from above. In other firms, various aspects of the contract are reviewed by different groups. These units collect and analyze data and prepare recommendations on contract proposals. Such groups may be composed of representatives from industrial relations, production, finance, and marketing.[34]

According to Ryder et al.,[35] industrial relations managers exert a major influence on "Management's Pre-bargaining Decisions," particularly in the area of noneconomic aspects of the contract, but their influence also extends to economic issues.

Within the corporate structure, the authority for the final decision usually rests with corporate officers, particularly the president. Although the chief operating officer has the final say, in some large firms contract decisions are made by subordinates. Boards of directors commonly stay out of labor relations, particularly in the prebargaining stage. In many firms, decisions regarding bargaining proposals are made by industrial relations officers or executive committees trusted by top management.[36]

Some contracts are negotiated by employer associations. The association negotiators usually possess complete discretion in the noneconomic area. They are also influential on decisions regarding economic issues, but the final word rests with their clients.

Opinions differ among industrial relations managers as to whether it is productive to formulate specific contract language in advance of negotiations. An objection is that it hardens the position of negotiators before issues are properly explored. Advance preparation can be partially counterproductive when creative solutions are needed.

In situations where in advance of negotiations management negotiators prepare written contract language, they prefer to wait for a general exploration of topics before presenting their written proposals to the other side. Some management negotiators offer written proposals only in response to union demands.

Another argument against preparation of written proposals in advance is the potential for leaks which can produce unnecessary accusations before the start of bargaining. There is also the fear that written proposals may generate a strong union counterattack.[37]

Although there are lengthy discussions among industrial relations experts regarding the value of written proposals, many firms nevertheless prepare written contract language in advance, as well as fallback positions in case their first choices are rejected.

Firms preparing written contract language find it useful for critical evaluation of the potential agreement. Some firms submit their version of the contract to the union in the early stages of bargaining, claiming that it provides a better focus for negotiations. Some negotiators favor an exchange of written proposals. Such an approach makes it easier to detect and concentrate on problem areas. Some employers also think that those unions that have a tendency to publicly distort employers' positions have more difficulty doing this when proposals are written.

FORMULATION OF UNION PROPOSALS

Unions require data from different sources in formulating bargaining demands. According to Odessa Komer, international vice president of the United Auto Workers (UAW), the UAW considers the following factors in formulating demands: level of economic activity, stage of the business cycle, economic forecasts for the economy, relationship between prices and wages, real earnings of workers, and unemployment levels within specific groups and within the economy. Although "the data are not the primary determinant of the demands" that a union makes, they do help the union to "find solutions to problems that arise in shaping demands at the bargaining table."[38]

Odessa Komer states that the UAW wants its negotiators to have all the financial and economic data that would be significant for negotiations. The necessary data are gathered from such sources as company reports to stockholders, and to the Securities and Exchange Commission, registration statements, prospectuses, industry statistics, and any materials providing information on sales, profits, financial resources, employment prospects, and industry trends.

One of the problems confronted by all users of data is that of availability and reliability. This is probably more of a problem for unions than for employers, because of the confidential nature of employer data. Odessa Komer states that the UAW has difficulty obtaining from employers productivity data as well as other data which would be relevant for bargaining. The problem of availability is particularly acute when it comes to negotiations of new programs or modification of old ones. Sometimes the necessary data have never been compiled or do not even exist.

Komer states that published corporate data could be of greater assistance to unions in negotiations if they contained information on the following subjects: profitability, labor costs, plant and corporate productivity and separate data for wages, salaries, and fringes, breakdowns between direct and indirect labor costs, data on hours worked and hours compensated, data on prices, sales, and distribution expenses, data on advertising costs and on research and development expenses, information on management compensation packages, clear separations between operating and nonoperating revenues and expenses, and more detail on specific product line breakdowns and geographic breakdowns.

Another problem confronting unions is that of reliability and consistency of accounting reports. According to Odessa Komer, the UAW encountered financial reports on benefit plans certified by CPA firms that "were not internally consistent." Furthermore, accounting procedures among firms are not standardized, which fact makes intercompany comparisons difficult. Firms do not use identical inventory valuation procedures or depreciation methods. Differences in accounting methodology can account for differences in reported profits rather than in "underlying profitability."

Komer also questions the reliability of employment and unemployment statistics published by the U.S. Department of Labor. There is a discrepancy between the two employment series, one based on household interviews, the other on a survey of establishment payrolls. These two series should be more compatible. Furthermore, the unions would like the BLS to report on plant closing and relocation. Another problem confronting unions regarding government data is timing; most data at release time are out of date.

Unions turn to many sources in formulating their demands. They consider economic conditions, their own accomplishments with other employers, and contracts negotiated by other unions within the region, the industry, and the economy. They study grievances, complaints, and arbitration awards for clues to problem areas under existing contracts. In order to determine rank-and-file priorities and expectations, they hold membership meetings, conduct employee surveys, and interview shop stewards, business agents, and active union members.

The process of formulation of demands differs among single- and multilocation and multiemployer bargaining units.[39] Some single-location units appoint committees charged with formulation of proposals. If the unit is affiliated with a national union, a representative of the national would usually be a member of such a committee. These committees, after arriving at a set of proposals, present these at a regular or special general membership meeting for discussion, amendments, rejection, or adoption. Proposals approved by the membership are presented as demands to the employer. Rank and file do not necessarily participate directly in the formulation of demands in every union local. In some instances, membership meetings are just formalities, and membership input is obtained informally and selectively. In such bargaining units, the demand formulation committee plays a crucial role in deciding on the type of demands to be presented to the employer.[40] In some local unions, formulation of demands is left to business agents, who consult each other as well as union officers and rank-and-file members. This approach is utilized in the construction industry.[41] The nature of this industry in terms of seasonality, major fluctuations in its labor force, and mobility of workers among job sites and employers makes the business agent a stable force in a mobile environment.

Formulation of demands is more complex in multilocation units. In multilocation units, the town meeting approach which may be appropriate in a single unit has been modified in favor of a representative government model. Under such a model, the bargaining proposal committee is composed of elected representatives of all the locals within the multilocation unit. The larger the multilocation unit, the more complex the process of delegation of authority. In some instances, locals elect representatives to regional committees, and these in turn make recommendations to a national committee that is responsible for formulating final proposals for submission to management.

Although the rank and file in multilocation units do not participate directly in the approval of final bargaining demands, the membership provides inputs in the initial stages. Usually, local committees formulate proposals subject to membership approval. The local demands are communicated upward to local delegates appointed to regional or national committees. These delegates are expected to defend and represent local interests.

The trend over the years has been to move the process of demand formulation from the local to the national. Whereas locals provide important inputs for demand preparations, national unions seem to be assuming a larger share of responsibility for final formulation. The ever increasing complexity of issues contributed to the shift. Even when negotiations are conducted locally the national still exerts a significant influence; it provides representation at the bargaining table, offers research and computer facilities, gives advice, sets minimum standards on specific issues, offers negotiation help, and in general exerts influence on the nature of major demands.

Two types of union demands appear at the bargaining table. First are the traditional demands for improvements of existing wages and fringe benefits and requests for concessions on noneconomic issues. Such demands include an attempt by unions to keep up with the achievements of other bargaining units. Second are the pioneering demands that unions present. These are proposals for concessions that were never granted before to the union or to any other union. An illustration is the

1955 United Auto Workers breakthrough on supplementary unemployment benefits at Ford Motor Company. Although bargaining may be intense on the first type of demands, the hardest task confronting negotiators is achieving a breakthrough on pioneering demands. It is much harder to convince management to grant concessions on provisions that do not appear in other contracts. No firm wants to be the first to give in on a new issue. Management's objections are not always motivated by financial considerations but may be related to image factors of management. No firm wants to give the impression that it caves in under union pressure. At times, a breakthrough on a new issue is achieved only after a work stoppage. In some instances the foundation for a new demand is built over a number of years and the theme is repeated in successive negotiations. When a new demand is introduced for the first time, both sides usually recognize that no agreement will be reached. However, such a gradual approach helps in lowering management's resistance and eventually may result in a generous dividend to the union. Hence, the more sophisticated unions engage in long-term planning in formulating and presenting innovative demands. They usually avoid building up high membership expectations and keep a low profile on such demands. This reduces face-saving problems on proposals that may be difficult to deliver on the first round.

STRATEGIC PREPARATIONS FOR BARGAINING

Preparations for bargaining by unions and employers are not confined to the collection of data and formulation of proposals. They also extend to strategic moves by both parties. According to Walton and McKersie,[42] the purpose of these strategies is to manipulate the "strike cost of party and opponent."

Major prenegotiation strategies that can be utilized by employers are inventory buildup, transfer of production to plants not affected by negotiations, mutual assistance agreements with other firms in the industry, and buildup of financial resources.

Inventory buildup cannot be employed in every industry, and not every firm that could benefit from it has the necessary financial resources to use it. It has been frequently applied in steel and coal but would be futile in the fashion or perishable goods industries. The size of the inventory buildup can communicate to the union the duration of a potential strike that an employer could tolerate.

Transfer of production is another prebargaining strategy used by employers. Its effectiveness depends upon its credibility. To threaten the union with a transfer of cement production from Ohio to Florida would obviously lack credibility since cement because of high transportation cost is usually produced relatively close to geographical markets. However, the presence of a geographically close cement plant with excess capacity would make such a threat plausible and effective. Thus, the potency of this strategy depends upon the capacity and location of alternate production sites that would not be directly affected by the outcome of negotiations. As a prenegotiation strategy, it is not necessary to transfer any production; it is usually sufficient for an employer to make the appropriate transfer arrangements and communicate them to the union.

An assistance pact with other firms in the same industry is still another strategy available to employers. It can take the form of financial or production aid. In the airline industry, prior to 1979, struck firms were eligible for financial help from other companies in the industry. In 1979, Congress in enacting the Air Deregulation Act outlawed the mutual aid pact in this industry. In the tire industry, a struck firm may have its output produced under its own label by a nonstriking firm. An article in the *AFL−CIO News* states that employer strike insurance pacts "must still be reckoned with in the publishing, printing and rubber industries.[43]

Still another strategy utilized by employers is building up financial resources before the start of negotiations. This can be accomplished in a number of ways. The firm may issue new stock or bonds, or it can announce an increased line of bank credit. The intent of such moves is to communicate to the opposition the ability to take a strike. The company, in effect, tells the union, "If you push us too far, we have the financial stamina to absorb the work stoppage."

The union also has an arsenal of strategies to weaken employer resistance. Accumulating a large strike fund, mutual assistance pacts, increasing workers' solidarity, strike votes, encouraging savings, securing other sources of income,[44] and buildup of grievances are bargaining strategies that can be utilized by unions.

A usual first step for unions is the buildup of large strike funds. Special membership assessments or mutual assistance pacts with other unions can help out the union treasury. Although the size of the strike fund may seem large in absolute dollars, in many instances there is only enough money in such funds to cover a few weeks of wages. Kuhn[45] states that, in the past, the strike fund of the UAW was equivalent to two and a half weeks of wages for General Motors employees. Another approach to building up the financial resources of a union is the Dubinsky approach.[46]

> Tradition has it that David Dubinsky sometimes opened a campaign to organize garment workers in a new area by depositing a substantial sum to the account of the union in a leading local bank. His well-founded assumption was that word of the deposit would reach the ears of the local garment manufacturer who would assume that the union was able to finance a long strike and [the manufacturer] would capitulate. Too late did they learn that the entire sum was borrowed on the express condition that it be returned intact after serving its psychological purpose.[47]

Before negotiations, unions build up rank-and-file support and worker solidarity. Membership meetings, letters to members, articles in the union press, and informal discussions all emphasize the significance of solidarity and warn of the danger of divisiveness and factionalism. Usually, the most impressive statement of union cohesiveness is the strike vote which a union may seek before the start of negotiations. A vote in which a high percentage of voters authorize strike action is interpreted as an expression of solidarity and confidence in the union. The outcome of such a vote is quickly communicated to management. In most such votes, the majority of union members provide the union with the necessary strike authorization not because they are willing to strike, but in order to strengthen the union's hand in bargaining.

To build up workers' ability to survive financially during a strike, unions urge workers to build up their savings accounts. Union newspapers and union officers plead with members to increase their rate of saving. Members are provided with guidelines on amounts to be put aside. In smaller communities, word of the success of such campaigns and of any increases in employee savings are quickly passed on by the local bankers to the affected employers.

In some communities, advance arrangements are made with local merchants, landlords, and financial institutions to assist the workers financially in case of a strike. This approach strengthens the union bargaining position and communicates to the opposition the willingness of the union to strike if a satisfactory settlement cannot be secured.

In some small communities with strong local and family ties, union officers try to find private sponsors who in case of a strike would provide support to striking employees. Under such sponsorship arrangements, families whose members work for nonstriking firms accept responsibility for helping out striking workers.

As an additional insurance against hardships during strikes and as a strategy move, unions try to develop other sources of income for their members. This can be accomplished by finding alternate employment opportunities or persuading legislators to provide strikers with better unemployment benefits.

Still another prenegotiation strategy which is popular with some unions is the buildup of grievances just before negotiations, to be used as a trading currency in bargaining.

All this preparation work by the union and the management is but the preliminary to the main event, the negotiation of the contract. To this point, each of the parties separately prepares itself to advance its case in bargaining with the opposition. In the chapter on the negotiations process, we shall pick up our description of the process as the parties meet at the bargaining table.

NOTES

[1] For various kinds of structures of institutional relationships, see B. M. Selekman, S. H. Fuller, Thomas Kennedy, and John M. Baitsell, *Problems in Labor Relations*, 3rd ed. (New York: McGraw-Hill, 1964), pp. 2–11.

[2] Meyer S. Ryder, Charles M. Rehmus, and Sanford Cohen, *Management Preparation for Collective Bargaining* (Homewood, Ill.: Dow Jones–Irwin, 1966), p. 8.

[3] *Preparing for Collective Bargaining*, Studies in Personnel Policy No. 172 (New York: National Industrial Conference Board, 1959), p. 26.

[4] Thomas A. Kochan, *Collective Bargaining and Industrial Relations* (Homewood, Ill.: Richard D. Irwin Inc., 1980), pp. 193–200.

[5] Bevars D. Mabry, *Labor Relations and Collective Bargaining* (New York: Ronald Press, 1966), p. 301.

[6] Neil W. Chamberlain and James W. Kuhn, *Collective Bargaining*, 2nd ed. (New York: McGraw-Hill, 1965), pp. 58–59.

[7] *Collective Bargaining: Lining Up the Facts*. An AFL–CIO pamphlet reprinted from March 1972, *AFL–CIO American Federationist*.

[8]*General Electric Co. & International Union of Machine Workers, AFL−CIO,* 192 NLRB 9 (July 14, 1971).

[9]*Collective Bargaining: Lining Up the Facts, op. cit.*

[10]*Major Programs Bureau of Labor Statistics* (Washington, D.C.: U.S. Department of Labor, Bureau of Labor Statistics, June 1983), Report 693, p. 2.

[11]*Ibid.,* pp. 16−17.

[12]*Ibid.,* pp. 15−16.

[13]For example, *Area Wage Survey,* Witchita, Kansas, April 1984, Bulletin 3025-11 (Washington, D.C.: U.S. Department of Labor, Bureau of Labor Statistics, April 1984).

[14]*National Survey of Professional, Administrative, Technical, and Clerical Pay,* March 1983, Bulletin 2181 (Washington, D.C.: U.S. Department of Labor, Bureau of Labor Statistics, 1983).

[15]*Employment and Earnings* (Washington, D.C.: U.S. Department of Labor, Bureau of Labor Statistics).

[16]*AFL−CIO News,* Saturday, January 7, 1978, p. 1.

[17]*Productivity Indexes for Selected Industries,* 1954−82, Bulletin 2189 (Washington, D.C.: U.S. Department of Labor, Bureau of Labor Statistics, 1983).

[18]James F. Honzik, "Assembling the Facts," in LeRoy Marceau (ed.), *Dealing with a Union* (New York: American Management Association, 1969), p. 65.

[19]Chamberlain and Kuhn, *op. cit.,* p. 75.

[20]*Ibid.*

[21]*Ibid.,* p. 78.

[22]Ryder et al., *op. cit.,* p. 62.

[23]*Preparing for Collective Bargaining, op. cit.,* pp. 35−39.

[24]Ryder et al., *op. cit.,* pp. 64, 65.

[25]James J. Bambrick, Jr., and Marie P. Dorbandt, "The Use of Bargaining Books in Negotiations," *Management Record,* 19, no. 4 (April 1957), 118−45.

[26]*Preparing for Collective Bargaining, op. cit.,* p. 36.

[27]*Ibid.,* p. 37.

[28]*Preparing for Collective Bargaining, op. cit.,* pp. 46−48.

[29]*Ibid.*

[30]*Ibid.*

[31]Ryder et al., *op. cit.,* p. 45.

[32]*Ibid.,* p. 48.

[33]*Ibid.,* p. 27.

[34]*Ibid.,* p. 25.

[35]*Ibid.,* p. 43.

[36]*Ibid.,* p. 44

[37]*Ibid.*, p. 55.

[38]Odessa Komer, international vice president, United Auto Workers, "The Role of Data in Collective Bargaining," *1978 Proceedings*, Sixth Annual Meeting, Society of Professionals in Dispute Resolution, October 29–November 1, 1978, pp. 118–24.

[39]Robert R. France, *Union Decisions in Collective Bargaining* (Princeton, N.J.: Princeton University, Industrial Relations Section, 1955), pp. 18–20.

[40]*Ibid.*, pp. 19–20.

[41]Mabry, *op. cit.*, p. 300.

[42]Richard E. Walton and Robert B. McKersie, *Behavioral Theory of Labor Negotiations* (New York: McGraw-Hill, 1965), pp. 75–82.

[43]*AFL–CIO News*, Washington, D.C., March 10, 1979.

[44]Walton and McKersie, *op. cit.*, pp. 79–81.

[45]Alfred Kuhn, *Labor Institutions and Economics*, rev. ed. (New York: Harcourt, Brace and World, 1967), p. 171.

[46]*Ibid.*, p. 171.

[47]*Ibid.*

COSTING
OF LABOR
CONTRACTS

8

Every clause in a contract, regardless of whether it applies to economic or noneconomic issues, can have cost implications. Some direct costs such as wages and fringe benefits are relatively easy to measure. Some indirect costs resulting from contract provisions governing such topics as seniority, layoffs, and grievance and arbitration procedures are more difficult to estimate. However, the most complex areas to measure are the interrelationships between changes in labor costs and such fields of corporate activities as capacity utilization, costing and pricing of output, labor productivity, product mix, capital and labor ratio, capital structure, profitability, financial management, and potential changes in behavior of workers, managers and union officials.

Contract clauses may impose both monetary and nonmonetary costs on the parties. Thus, if a particular contract provision has the potential for internal friction, the cost to the parties may be both financial and emotional.

It is relatively easy to compute the potential dollar cost of additional vacations. It is much harder to calculate the impact of such vacations on workers' behavior, equipment utilization, cost of recruitment and training, and the initial inefficiency accompanying additional workers who are hired to make up for the extra vacation. A new grievance procedure may have no easily detectable financial implications but if it were to generate more grievances, it would have an effect on loss of time by employees and management, on legal costs, and on productivity and equipment utilization. All these costs have to be considered when costing a contract.

Although the focus of this chapter is the costing of labor contracts and of labor costs directly affected by collective bargaining, employer's labor costs are not confined to those in collective agreements but also include Worker's Compensation and Unemployment Insurance, Old Age, Survivors Disability, and Health Insurance (OASDHI), and affirmative action plans.

The basic task of the present chapter is to consider the costing of labor contracts. Contract costing refers to the computations made by both unions and management in estimating the financial consequences of various bargaining proposals. Application of accurate contract costing methods can be important to both unions and employers. The present value formula and the discounted cash flow model that are reviewed in this chapter emphasize the significance of these concepts in bargaining. Estimates of potential costs can assist both parties in evaluating the impact of a settlement on employment, output, pricing, sales, product mix, and substitution of labor for capital. Costing procedures that consider these factors can benefit unions, management, and the bargaining process. The union, by increasing its level of sophistication in the application of costing procedures can formulate better contract demands as well as improve its ability to refute management's arguments. Better understanding of labor costs can help management defend its positions in bargaining and assist it in arriving at more advantageous contract offers. It can also improve its comprehension of the impact of such offers or demands on the total operation of its enterprise.

Costing enables both sides to compare the actual costs of different contract terms, and thus can help them arrive at a satisfactory settlement. Good costing procedures can provide both sides with a better understanding of financial costs, and can also assist them in comparing the levels of satisfaction or utilities that each set of proposals contains. Better understanding of these factors can facilitate negotiations and lead to more judicious use of power at the bargaining table. A comprehensive review of the relationship between power and utility is presented in the chapter on power and bargaining power.

There are a variety of methods of calculating the financial value of each contract package, some of which are discussed in this chapter. In some bargaining units, the parties rely on simple arithmetic in calculating the value of the package. In others, complex present value formulas and discounted cash flow models are utilized. Some large firms employ experts in costing who build elaborate models, not only trying to estimate direct costs associated with a particular contract but also trying to estimate its indirect effects.

A conversation that one of the authors of this book had with a contract costing manager for a very large corporation revealed that this particular firm has utilized a complex model for the costing of its contract. The costing model used by this firm took twenty years to develop. Although its detailed components are confidential, it was suggested to the author that the model was partly based on art and partly on science. The costing personnel of this particular firm undergo a lengthy apprenticeship period during which they are taught to develop a feel for the indirect implications of contract costs. In applying the model, this particular company has tried to isolate the financial impact of each demand from any other effect. Thus, if the firm would have to calculate the cost of an additional holiday, this would be done under *ceteris paribus*[1] conditions (other factors would be held constant). In computing the cost of the holiday, the firm would ignore such things as potential changes in output or schedules and any other development that might influence the cost of the additional holiday. This approach permits the company to compare the potential cost of each demand with its existing costs. When estimating the cost of an agreement, this company concentrates on exit costs. *Exit costs* are defined as the total estimated cost of the contract per hour of work at the end of the term of the newly negotiated contract.

It is beyond the scope of this chapter to discuss all areas of corporate activity that are financially influenced by the terms of the labor contract. An understanding of some of these interrelationships requires a background in such fields as economics, corporate finance, industrial management, marketing, engineering, and organizational behavior. This chapter confines itself to a discussion of the following topics: a review of methods applied by the Bureau of Labor Statistics for estimating cost of settlements from a macro and micro point of view, discussion of components that are included in the compensation package both in terms of wages and benefits, and data and methods used in computing the cost of individual settlements. Other topics discussed are critical review of current costing procedures, relationships between capital-to-labor ratio, applicability of the present value concept and of the discounted cash flow model to the costing of labor contracts, examination of the financial dimensions of management proposals, the concept of elasticity of demand, and computers and collective bargaining. In the two appendices to this chapter we have included material on steps for calculating contract costs.

THE BUREAU OF LABOR STATISTICS
ESTIMATES OF CONTRACT COSTS[2]

Policy makers, unions, employers, and economists require estimates of the cost of bargaining settlements. The major source of such information is the Bureau of Labor Statistics.* Prior to 1964, it was relatively easy for BLS statisticians to estimate the cost of labor settlements, since the only component in their calculations was the wage rate. In the sixties it became apparent that with the ever increasing proportion of labor costs going into fringe benefits a more comprehensive estimating approach would be required. In 1964 BLS commenced aggregating fringe benefit data from employers and estimating package contract costs covering the following items: wages, vacations, holidays, leave and cash payments, social insurance, health, welfare and pension

---

*In updating this section the authors gratefully acknowledge the assistance of Mr. Alvin Bauma Chief, Division of Developments in Labor-Management Relations, U.S. Department of Labor, Bureau Labor Statistics. Letter September 5, 1984.

funds, paid time for washups, and so on. The 1964 estimates covered a relatively small number of major agreements. Since 1966 this was extended to all agreements covering 5000 or more employees, excluding government workers. In addition, wage cost adjustments are measured for bargaining units of 1000 or more workers. In 1979, the series was extended to wage and benefit adjustments in state and local government contracts covering 5000 or more workers, and in 1984 to wage adjustments for state and local government contracts of 1000 or more. The BLS publishes its contract cost estimates in four publications: (1) *Current Wage Developments*—this is a monthly publication on employee compensation, incorporating changes in wages and benefits resulting from bargaining settlements and unilateral management decisions. The final detailed annual summary is published in the April issue of *Current Wage Developments*. (2) *Monthly Labor Review* in its January issue highlights important labor settlements for the preceding year. (3) Periodically, the BLS releases news bulletins on *Major Collective Bargaining Agreements.* The releases cover such topics as wage and benefit increases, wage rate adjustments, and escalator clauses. Data are issued for private industry for each calendar quarter and released four weeks after end of quarter; for state and local government they are issued semiannually, released in February and August. A summary of the news releases is published in its final form in *Current Wage Developments.* (4) Another BLS publication that provides information on anticipated union contract adjustments for the current calendar year is the *Bargaining Calendar.* The bulletin identifies major situations in which, during the year, agreements terminate, deferred wage increases become due, changes in the *Consumer Price Index* are reviewed, and contracts are reopened.

Estimating the cost of labor contracts by the BLS is essentially a four-step procedure.[3] First, data are secured on the cost of existing collective bargaining compensation packages. Second, the BLS estimates adjustments, increases, decreases, and freezes in increases in wages and benefits resulting from recent labor agreements. Third, the increases are related to existing expenditures. Fourth, the increases are calculated at an annual rate. All the calculations are made in cents per plant worker-hour. Plant hours encompass the total number of hours, including the overtime, that an employee spends at the place of employment.

There are many sources of data available to the BLS for estimating the cost of contracts. Some of the sources used are other bulletins published by the BLS. The BLS monthly survey of employment, payrolls, and hours provides information on hourly earnings. Supplementary sources for some of the above data for contract costing purposes are *Industry Wage Surveys,* labor contracts, annual corporate financial reports and workers' compensation rates. Whenever necessary, the data are further supplemented by other BLS surveys, secondary sources, and special inquiries. Although a significant amount of contract costing data is available to the BLS, there are some areas in which cost estimates have to be based on arbitrary assumptions rather than on solid evidence.

Some of the costing problems confronted by the BLS are also encountered by employers. Both the BLS and employers may have difficulties determining employee response to newly negotiated optional programs. New settlements may contain such optional programs as early retirement, voluntary health plans, and life insurance plans.

The total cost of such fringes is directly affected by employee participation rates, and these rates may be difficult to predict.

An important consideration in estimating the cost of optional fringe plans is the age, sex, length of service, and occupational characteristics of the work force. For example, if an attempt was made to estimate the cost impact of an early retirement option in two similar firms, one with a young labor force and the other with a work force primarily composed of older workers, eager to retire, the cost of the same options would be different for the two firms.

However, there are factors other than age that influence a worker's choice of early retirement. Possibilities of alternative employment, contract restrictions on such employment, the rate of inflation, and personal financial requirements can all have a bearing on whether an employee would exercise an early retirement option. In view of the many uncertainties accompanying such plans, the BLS assumes that the composition of the work force does not change over the life of the agreement; obviously, this is not always the case.

In cases of delayed settlements, some of which may have been accompanied by strikes, the BLS assumes that the contract duration is the period between the expiration dates of the old and the new agreements. The total contract cost for this period is then adjusted to an annual rate.

Not every agreement has a formal expiration date. Such open-ended contracts usually stipulate the date on which bargaining may commence and the date on which the newly negotiated terms may be implemented. The implementation date is considered by the BLS as the termination date of the previous contract. When an agreement is open-ended, without any dates given, the BLS treats such contracts either as of one-year duration or, where possible, it applies past bargaining patterns as a guideline for determining contract length.

Some contracts contain a reopening date. These are treated by the BLS as dates for new contract negotiations. The duration of such contracts is measured from the date an agreement is reached until the next contract reopener date. When a contract has a reopening provision without stipulating a specific date and it is reopened, the BLS allocates any increases in cost to the period starting with the effective date of the increases and terminating with the expiration date of the contract. The BLS does not compute cost. It estimates the adjustment in wages (or compensation) per work hour, expressed at an average annual rate. Except for open-ended contracts (which are assumed to run for one year or to the date of the last specified adjustment, whichever is later) factors mentioned are not relevant. For example, contract duration runs from effective date to first reopener; compensation packages cannot be unilaterally changed before the expiration of the contract and any bilateral change is considered a new settlement. The BLS estimates average adjustments negotiated at the time of settlement, and average changes implemented during the reference period as a result of settlements, deferred changes, or COLA. BLS does not provide cost estimates for individual settlements, although it publishes the terms of individual settlements.

To conclude, the government statistician does not have access to all the necessary data for accurate contract cost estimates. Also, the cost treatment of similar contract provisions may vary significantly among firms. The lack of uniformity makes it difficult for the BLS to provide accurate comparisons of contract cost estimates. These difficulties can have direct cost implications for individual firms. The BLS estimates are referred to by both unions and management, and errors in these estimates can affect the size of bargaining settlements.

Eventually, companies whose stock shares are available to the public may be required by regulatory agencies to provide uniform and comprehensive cost estimates of labor contracts. The accounting profession and the Securities and Exchange Commission may have to come up with standards that encompass areas presently covered by guesswork and hypothetical assumptions. Implementation of such standards could help increase the quality of BLS estimates of contract costs.

COMPONENTS OF THE COMPENSATION PACKAGE

In order to arrive at the total cost of an agreement, it is necessary to calculate the many different financial components that constitute labor costs. The total compensation package consists of direct pay and fringe benefits. The major part of the package is the direct paycheck disbursed to each employee. Direct pay may consist of hourly, daily, weekly, or monthly pay. It may also include incentive payments, commissions, mileage payments, automatic and merit increase progression plans, travel allowances, clothing, tool, and safety equipment allowances, various nonproduction bonuses, profitsharing plans, differentials for shift work, differentials for hazardous work and abnormal conditions, cost-of-living allowances, deferred wage increases, and overtime and premium pay.

According to a 1985 Report by the Bureau of National Affairs, fringe benefits in the United States equal 37 percent of pay for time worked.[4] In 1973, Levin estimated that between 25 percent and 33 percent of labor cost represented fringe benefits.[5] The U.S. Chamber of Commerce in its annual benefits survey shows that in 1959 benefits were 24.7 percent of payroll, they increased to 31.1 percent in 1969 and to 41.4 percent in 1980.[6] Although in recent decades the proportion of the U.S. compensation package paid out in fringes has been increasing, still in comparison with other industrialized nations, the United States is lagging behind. The Congressional Research Service (CRS), basing its finding on unpublished statistics from the Bureau of Labor Statistics, concludes that fringe benefits in Italy were 83 percent of compensation for actual time worked, in Japan, 75.5 percent, in Germany, 71 percent and in the United Kingdom, 38.3 percent. The CRS report points out, however, that caution must be exercised in evaluating such statistical data because of differences in valuation of fringe benefits among countries.[7]

There is no universal definition of fringe benefits. Generally, fringe benefits can be categorized into two broad groups: time-not-worked benefits and security and health benefits. The first category consists of compensations for time not worked during regular employment periods. The most common items under this heading include vacation, holidays, sick and funeral leaves, jury duty, appearances as court witnesses, military service, reporting pay, call-in and call-back pay, paid meal periods, rest periods, washup, cleanup, and clothes changing time, and time spent on union business. The second category of benefits includes life, medical, and accident insurance, workers' compensation insurance, sick leave pay, pensions, social security, unemployment insurance, guaranteed annual income, supplemental unemployment benefits, and severance pay allowances. Another approach to the classification of benefits is into the following five categories: (1) legally required payments (employer's share), for example, unemployment compensation, workers' compensation, and so on, (2) pension, insurance (employer's share), and so on, (3) paid rest periods such as lunch period and wash-up time, (4) payments for time not worked, such as vacations or holidays, (5) other items, such as profit-sharing plans, special bonuses, and education allowance.[8]

DATA UTILIZED FOR COSTING OF CONTRACTS

A study by Granof[9] reports that data used in costing of labor agreements can be divided into three major categories: demographic, accounting, and financial. Demographic data supply a breakdown and a statistical profile of the labor force in terms of such items as the age, sex, seniority, and marital status of workers. Accounting data provide payroll information on the work force regarding such specifics as direct pay, overtime, vacation, and holiday pay. Financial data furnish figures on projected revenues, output, product mix, and nonlabor costs.

According to Granof,[10] some firms rely primarily on demographic data in costing of contracts and do not consider financial and accounting information. Such firms try to negotiate the lowest "direct dollar or cents per hour cost" and disregard the impact of union demands on future profitability, which can be calculated from accounting and financial material. In such firms, general economic data and settlements by other companies, rather than financial and accounting inputs, are the important factors in costing of contracts.

Some firms utilize both demographic and accounting data in estimating contract costs but disregard financial data. Such companies are not only concerned with total labor costs based on demographic factors, but also consider the proportions of total cost disbursed for direct labor, for time-not-worked benefits, and for security and health benefits, including workers' compensation and social security taxes. Costs are also allocated to product lines, departments, and divisions. Such tabulations are based on historical accounting data. These calculations ignore financial inputs and thus by implication assume that product mix, level of output, relationship between overtime and straight time, and many other variables are not affected by the contract.

Granof[11] states that there are firms that utilize all three sets of data: demographic, accounting, and financial. However, the financial data are used more as a broad guideline of potential cost rather than as a detailed printout for a course of action. Company negotiators who rely on "financial data" are more sensitive to the effect of their activities on the profitability of their employers. They are more likely to structure the bargaining terms in such a way as to minimize the financial effects of settlements on their respective firms. As an example, if a firm's profit projections are more optimistic for the second rather than for the first year of a contract, they may try to delay the major portion of an increase to the second year. Availability of financial data may make it easier for a negotiator to sell a particular package, not only to opponents, but also to principals.

METHODS FOR COSTING CONTRACTS

According to Granof,[12] the four most common methods of calculating the cost of union demands are: (1) total annual cost of demands, (2) annual cost of demands per employee, (3) cost of total demands as a percent of payroll, and (4) cost of demands in cents per hour. The major advantages of these methods are simplicity, ease of computation, and ability to communicate bargaining results clearly to bargaining unit members.

Annual cost is calculated by totaling on an annualized basis all the union demands, in terms of wages and fringe benefits.

The annual cost of union demands per employee is calculated by dividing the total annual cost of the potential settlement by an average or actual size of the labor force. The labor force total can be computed in two ways. It may be based on the actual number of employees in the bargaining unit at the time the contract is negotiated, or it may be based on the average of the labor force for the year. The following illustration is a simplified calculation of annual increased labor costs per employee. Assuming a labor force of 100 workers, and cost of demands of $150,000, the average increased annual labor cost per employee would be $1500.

The cost of total annual demands, as a percent of payroll, is calculated by dividing the total cost of demands by the total payroll. Thus, if the total payroll is $1.5 million, and the demands amount to $150,000, then the result is 10 percent.

The cost of demands in cents per hour is arrived at by dividing the total demands by the total hours worked. Thus, if there are 100 employees working on the average 40 hours per week, 52 weeks per year, total hours worked are 208,000. If total demands are $150,000, then the cost of the demands in cents per hour would be

$$\frac{150,000}{208,000} = .72 \text{ or } 72\cancel{c}$$

Granof[13] reports that all the company negotiators that he interviewed for his costing of contracts study expressed the view that their primary objective in negotiations was "to minimize the cents-per-hour direct wage increase granted." The interviewees were also concerned with the actual cost of increases per productive hour. To calculate these costs, they multiplied agreed-upon cents-per-hour increases by an average number of hours for which each person was paid in the previous year. The sum of this calculation was then divided by an average number of productive hours "or an arbitrary number of annual hours such as 1,900 or 2,000"[14] per person. Calculations of productive hours for which workers are paid but during which they do not work exclude holidays, sick leave, and so on.

The following illustration converts the cost of direct cents-per-hour increases into the cost of these increases per productive hour. If the negotiated direct wage increase is 50 cents per hour, and in the previous year the company paid its workers for 240,000 hours, out of which only 200,000 were productive, then the actual increase per productive hour is 60 cents.

$$240,000 \times .50 = \$120,000$$

$$\$120,000 \div 2000,000 = .60 \text{ or } 60¢ \text{ per productive hour}$$

Cost-of-living allowances, overtime premiums, and shift differential provisions can be found in many contracts. Methods for calculating the cost of these wage-related provisions vary among firms. In the case of cost of living, some firms negotiate provisions that impose a ceiling on increases within the contract term. In estimating the future cost of such provisions, some firms assume that the ceiling will be reached. Others try to project the level of the cost-of-living index and estimate cost as being either the index or the ceiling, whichever is the lower of the two.[15] Thus, if the ceiling is 12 percent and projected increases in cost of living are 10 percent, the 10 percent figure will be used. Estimates of overtime premiums and shift differentials applied by some employers are based on historical data rather than on future projections. Many firms assume that the same number of premium hours that prevailed in the past will continue into the future.[16] Thus, if there were 1000 premium hours in the previous year, a firm negotiating a one-year contract would calculate the cost of premium pay on the basis of 1000 hours.

Procedures for Costing Fringe Benefits

As shown earlier, fringe benefits represent a significant proportion of labor costs. There is a variety of approaches for costing benefits. Stieglitz[17] suggests four computation methods: (1) annual cost of each benefit for all employees; (2) annual cost per employee; (3) benefit cost as a percent of payroll; (4) per-employee cost of benefits in dollars and cents per hour. The first approach is intended to provide the total projected annual expenditures for each proposed benefit. The second approach furnishes either an actual or an average annual cost of benefits per employee. Since some of these costs, such as group insurance expenditures, may be difficult to allocate to individual employees; some companies average out these costs over their entire work force. The average cost per employee is easier to calculate; it means dividing the total annual cost of benefits by the average size of the annual labor force. Thus, if total annual benefits are $550,000 and the average labor force is 100 employees, the average annual benefit expenditure per employee is $5500. The third approach, which computes benefit costs as a percent of payroll, is obtained by dividing the total annual cost of benefits by the annual payroll. Thus, if the total payroll is $1.5 million, and the total benefits are $450,000, then benefits represent 30 percent of payroll.

$$\frac{450,000}{1,500,000} = .30 \text{ or } 30\%$$

A company employing this approach is confronted with the problem of deciding what to include in the payroll total. Some items such as premium pay or bonuses are considered payroll by some employers, whereas others classify these as benefits. The percentage figure obtained would obviously vary depending on the definition applied to payroll. The percentage approach is not too helpful if negotiations extend to both wage and fringe benefit increases. The fourth approach is based on the hourly cost of benefits per worker.[18] According to Henderson,[19] this is the most frequently applied computation. One reason for its popularity is ease of calculation. Another factor is its public relations value. It is relatively simple and more meaningful to communicate value of benefits in cents per hour to bargaining unit members. This enables workers to compare value of benefits in relation to their hourly pay. The cost of benefits per hour is calculated by taking the total cost of benefits and dividing the total by the number of hours. Thus, if the total annual cost of benefits is \$450,000 and the total number of hours worked is 200,000, the cost of the benefits is \$2.25 per hour.

$$\frac{\$450,000}{200,000} = \$2.25$$

One of the difficulties with this approach is arriving at an appropriate number of hours worked. Some firms use the actual hours worked by its labor force, others use only productive hours,[20] excluding hours for which workers are paid but do not work. Still others[21] use arbitrary hourly figures based on the number of days per year during which the firm operates; this total is multiplied by number of hours per day times size of the bargaining unit.

Some areas of costing of fringe benefits such as pensions, life insurance, and various health plans are so complex that companies bring in outside experts to help them measure such costs.

Two expensive fringe benefits frequently referred to as pay for time not worked are vacations and holidays. Procedures for computing the costs of these benefits are discussed in the following paragraphs.

There a number of methods for calculating additional vacation hours, resulting from a negotiated settlement. Some firms arrive at extra vacation costs by multiplying the increase in vacation hours by base wage rates. Thus, if additional vacations amount to 4000 hours and the base rate is \$8.00 per hour, then the extra cost is \$32,000. Some companies base their calculations on the cost of making up time lost by extra vacations. Thus, if 4000 extra hours are allocated to vacations and the cost of making up the vacation time through holiday and overtime pay would cost an average of \$12 per hour, then the cost is not \$32,000 as presented in the previous example, but \$48,000. Increased vacations may have additional costs that are more difficult to measure, such as the cost of recruiting new employees to offset the additional vacation time. Also, initially new employees may be less efficient than the existing work force.

Firms employ a variety of procedures for calculating the cost of extra holidays.[22] The simplest approach is to multiply additional holiday hours by a base wage rate; thus, if additional holidays amount to 800 hours and the base wage is \$8.00 per hour, then the cost of holidays is \$6400. Another consideration applied to costing of holidays is to take into account not only the cost of extra holidays at regular rates, but also to consider premiums that may have to be paid to those employees who will be required to work during the holidays at premium rates; this may be necessary in firms on continuous operations. Thus, if there are 800 hours of additional holidays with the base rate of $8.00 per hour, and we assume that 400 of these hours will have to be made up at overtime rates of $12 per hour, then the cost of the additional holidays is $8000 rather than $6400, as calculated in the previous illustration. Increasing the number of holidays does not always result in a company's hiring extra workers. In some firms the additional holidays are offset by a loss of production, which may have an adverse effect on the firm's cost and profitability. Costs of additional holidays are also influenced by the number of employees who exercise the option to work during holidays at premium pay, assuming that a contract contains such an option.

Another approach to costing of labor contracts and of fringe benefits is the total-cost concept suggested by Walter A. Hazelton.[23] According to Hazelton, in the negotiation of most labor agreements there is a strong dependence "on comparison of average labor rates . . . to norms." These norms are based on local, industry, or national averages. As contrasted with wages, benefit comparisons are frequently "handled subjectively." Hazelton recommends that benefits, like wages, "should also be compared to norms," or be calculated as benefit costs per hour and be added to hourly labor rates—such total hourly costs could then be compared to industry norms. The major drawback toward the application of this concept is the scarcity of appropriate data. Although, according to Hazelton, there are a number of reports providing comparisons of aggregate benefits, "the reports available today are relatively useless." Eventually more firms, with some help from the accounting professions, may standardize the computation of benefit costs, and thus make the reported benefit comparisons and the Hazelton approach attractive for costing of fringe benefits.

Criticisms of Existing Methods of Costing Contracts

The existing methods of costing contracts are criticized by Granof,[24] who considers them inadequate. In his view, present approaches do not take into account the impact of increased contract costs on the firm as a total entity. The costing analysis employed is usually static rather than dynamic; it assumes that when labor costs go up, *ceteris paribus* (other things being equal) conditions prevail. Existing costing procedures are based on the assumption that the past will be repeated in the future. Also, current methods do not consider the value of money over time, a concept that will be discussed in some detail in a later part of this chapter.

The total costs of settlements are not always reflected in labor costs paid out to bargaining unit members. Increased contract costs may contribute to reduced profits because of the decline in output and sales. Granof illustrates this point with a hypothetical company that operates at capacity and agrees to provide its employees with two fifteen-minute rest periods per day. Typically, the cost of the rest period is computed by multiplying the number of workers times days worked, times rest period, times hourly wage. In reality, the cost to the firm could be higher. If we assume a hypothetical firm operating at capacity and not in a position to increase its labor force without additional investment, and unable to offset the rest period through higher productivity, then the extra rest period would be detrimental to the firm's output, sales, and profitability.

In multiproduct firms, the percentage of labor cost may vary among products. Some products require a large labor and a low capital input whereas, for others, the opposite is the case. Thus, the increased labor costs that accompany labor agreements could have considerably different cost implications for labor-intensive than for capital-intensive products. Although for purposes of bargaining it is important for firms to arrive at a detailed breakdown of cost on an individual product basis, this is not done by too many firms. Employers who are able to determine the cost impact of a labor contract for each item of their product line are in a better position to improve their performance in such decision areas as pricing, substitution of labor by capital, changes in product mix, discontinuation of unprofitable products, and introduction of new technology.

FINANCIAL DIMENSIONS OF
MANAGEMENT PROPOSALS

The financial dimensions of management bargaining offers are influenced by a variety of factors: labor contract terms prevailing in the industry, competitive conditions in other input and output markets, technical possibilities in the production of different outputs, and demand for output of the industry and of the firm. In markets where the firm has some control over output price, the ability of the firm to pass on higher cost to consumers in the form of higher prices can influence significantly the size of the firm's offer.[25] Although expected consumer responses to possible price changes can affect the final terms of a labor contract implicitly, these effects are usually not discussed explicitly during negotiation sessions. Management considers pricing to be a management prerogative to be kept out of bargaining. In the larger corporations even management's contract costing experts do not concern themselves with pricing, which is often delegated to departments outside the industrial relations field.

The impact of the decision-making mechanism on the size of bargaining offers, pricing policies, plant capacity, and levels of output varies significantly among firms. In smaller companies the manager or manager-owner may be wearing many different hats, including the responsibility for bargaining, the costing of the contract, and the costing and pricing of output. In large corporations these functions are scattered among different departments. Production and finance departments are responsible for computing the impact of various cost increases on cost of output; they also compute cost per unit of output at different hypothetical levels of output. On the product pricing side, marketing managers and economists try to answer the question of how consumers will respond to price increases. On the basis of data received from an army of experts, top management makes final decisions regarding optimum levels of output and pricing and on the appropriate size of the bargaining offer to be made to the union.

According to economic theory, the objective of the firm is to maximize equity return to stockholders, which can be conceptualized as long-run profit maximization.

Expected profits are maximized in the short run when the revenues expected from output and pricing decisions under existing markets are largest relative to the expected costs of producing that output with existing plants and factor markets. This is often expressed in terms of marginal (incremental) revenue and costs. Under existing market conditions of industry structure and plant capacity, firms will continue to expand output until the expected extra revenue is equal to the expected increase in costs, and no further. Firms maximizing profits successfully will behave as if they were equating marginal revenue and marginal cost,[26] even if they do not or cannot determine these magnitudes precisely.

Equity (long-run profits) maximization recognizes the price, output, and investment decisions that will generate expected revenue and cost streams in both the short run and the long run. The maximization of the difference between the present values of these expected streams of revenue and cost is equity or long-run profit maximization. Equity maximization involves decisions relative to plant capacity, plant location, technologies utilized, capital structure, product mix, research and development expenditures relative to new processes, and new products, as well as short-run pricing and output decisions.

The collective bargaining process is part of this short-run and long-run decision process. The size of the bargaining offer will reflect the assessments by management of many components as to the impact of that offer on short-run profitability and long-run equity position of the firm. The correct costing of contracts should reflect all these factors. Very seldom does the industrial relations expert have the perspective, the information, or the skills to make such determinations. It requires a combined knowledge of accounting, finance, marketing, economics, and production to cost a contract properly. The better the industrial relations specialist can communicate and interact with the specialists in these areas, the more involved they will be in the process of determining the management offer and produce a "costing" with credibility throughout the firm.

ELASTICITY OF DEMAND

Increased contract costs are often passed on to consumers as higher prices. The extent to which an individual firm can transfer such increased costs depends upon the elasticity of demand for its products, which reflects a number of factors. The first set of factors are those determining the market demand for the products. The elasticity of market demand depends upon consumer tastes and preferences for the product relative to substitute and complementary products, and the proportion of the consumer's budget spent on the product. These factors would determine the ability of all firms in the industry to transfer increased costs from an industry-wide settlement. This would be the relevant elasticity for most settlements in which identical costs are imposed on all firms in the industry.

In the individual bargaining situations, the ability to transfer increased costs to consumers would depend upon the elasticity of the firm's demand curve. The firm's demand curve depends upon the competitive relation among firms in the industry, reflecting whether the industry is competitive, monopolistic, monopolistic competitive, or oligopolistic.[27]

If the price of a product is increased relative to other products, the quantity sold of that product could decrease significantly or very little. The degree of responsiveness of quantity demanded by consumers to a price change differs within price ranges for the same product. This responsiveness is measured by the concept of price elasticity. Price elasticity is the ratio between the rate of change of quantity demanded and the rate of change of prices. In economic literature, elasticity of demand is classified into three categories: elastic, inelastic, and unit elastic.

Demand by consumers is considered elastic regarding price when the percentage change in quantity demanded is larger than the percentage change in price—for example, an increase in the relative price of housing by 10 percent causes quantity demanded to decrease by 20 percent. This indicates that the quantity demanded of this product is responsive to change in the relative price.

Consumer demand for a product is considered inelastic when the percentage change in quantity demanded is smaller than the percentage change in price. If the price of salt goes up by 10 percent but quantity demanded goes down by 1 percent, the demand for salt is considered inelastic; the quantity demanded is unresponsive to changes in the relative prices.

In the case of unitary elasticity, it is assumed that the percentage change in quantity demanded is identical to the percentage change in price—for example, the price of product Y increases by 10 percent, quantity demanded decreases by 10 percent.

Elasticity of demand can also be presented graphically. Figure 8–1 illustrates

FIGURE 8-1

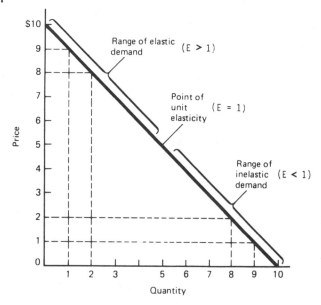

SOURCE: *Robert L. Heilbroner and Lester C. Thurow, The Economic Problem,* 4th ed. (Englewood Cliffs, N.J.: Prentice-Hall, 1975), p. 109.

elastic, inelastic, and unitary elasticity demand. Above $5.00 the demand curve is elastic; below $5.00 it is inelastic—for example, a fall in price from $9.00 to $8.00 results in demand increasing from 1 to 2 units, thus the price change results in proportionally larger change in quantity demanded. A fall in price from $2.00 to $1.00 increases demand from 8 to 9 units; in this case, the price change results in proportionally smaller change in quantity demanded.

The importance of the concept of elasticity can be illustrated by relating it to total revenue. Total revenue is price times quantity ($TR = P \times Q$). If 100,000 widgets are sold at $2.00 each, total revenue would be $200,000. If firms in the widget industry attempt to transfer costs of a labor settlement of 10 percent of total costs by increasing prices 10 percent (to $2.20), what will happen to total revenues? (1) If the demand for widgets is elastic, the percentage decrease in quantity would be greater than the percentage increase in price; therefore, total revenue would fall. Not only would the firms fail to recover their increased costs, their revenue would be less; for example, if we were to assume that at $2.20 only 80,000 widgets would be sold, total revenue would be $176,000. (2) If the demand for widgets is unitary, the percentage decrease in quantity would equal the percentage increase in price. The firms may not be able to recover their increased costs; for example, if we were to assume that at $2.20, 90,909 widgets would be sold, total revenue would remain at approximately $200,000. (3) If the demand is inelastic, the percentage decrease in quantity would be less than the percentage increase in price. Whether the increased revenue would equal the settlement would depend on how inelastic the demand; for example, if we were to assume that at $2.20, 98,000 widgets would be sold, total revenue would be $215,600, or $15,600 higher than before the price increase. It should be pointed out that the increased costs of a labor settlement would be affected by demand for widgets. A decline in demand may decrease the number of employees required; thus, the final cost effect of a labor settlement may be different than the 10 percent increase assumed above. The above conclusions may also be modified by dynamic factors in the economy such as productivity gains and increasing prices for substitute and complementary products coincidentally. A discussion of these factors is beyond the scope of this book.

As just shown, some feel for the elasticity of demand should be an important element at the bargaining table. Firms which plan to pass on increased contract costs to their customers but find themselves confronted with an elastic market demand could experience a decrease not only in revenues and profits but also in employment. It is important, therefore, for both the management and the union to be aware of elasticity of demand in setting strategy for the bargaining table. In some major corporations, economists with expertise in calculations of elasticity prepare estimates of the potential impact of higher prices on sales. Such professional help is often not available to the smaller company, which must then rely on the judgment of their marketing managers.

Although the concept of elasticity is unfamiliar to many practitioners in industrial relations, its impact on the results of the bargaining process are real. As illustrated above, the more elastic the firm's or the industry's demand, the more difficult it will be to pass increased costs on to consumers without adverse effects on profits and employment. This should be a factor to be considered by all parties in bargaining.

THE PRESENT VALUE CONCEPT

An important tool in the field of finance and economics is the concept of present value.[28]

Economists discuss marginal efficiency of capital as an investment determinant. Financial analysts have a variety of present worth valuation theories, and corporate financial officers utilize present value formulae in their investment decisions. All these approaches have a common denominator, which is the concept of the time value of money. The present value of $100 to be received one year from now is worth less than $100 to be received immediately. In other words, $100 is worth more today than the present value of $100 one year from now because a return can be earned on it during the year. One has to be aware of the distinction between the present value of future receipts, which is always smaller than the same amount of current receipts. Although the concept of the time value of money is applied to many business decisions, it is relatively dormant in the area of collective bargaining. Industrial relations literature does not have many references to it. The concept of amortization of contract costs is briefly discussed by Reder and by Cartter, and it is extensively covered by Granof.[29]

The present value concept is a useful tool for telling the parties the present value of future obligations assumed under an agreement. Its formula is:

$$PV = \frac{S}{(1 + i)^n} = S(1 + i)^{-n}$$

PV = The present value of a given obligation
S = The future value of the same obligation
i = The discount rate
n = The number of periods

Thus, if a hypothetical company, at the beginning of the third year of the contract, would consider giving its employees a one-time raise of $1 million, the present value of it, using present value tables[30] and applying a 10 percent discount rate,[31] would be $826,000 rather than $1 million if the raise were received now.

$$\$826{,}000 = \frac{1{,}000{,}000}{(1 + .10)^2} = 1{,}000{,}000\,(1 + .10)^{-2}$$

The basic formula can be modified to take into account a variety of contract terms. Under the above simplified version, it is assumed that the $1 million increase would be paid out in one lump sum at the beginning of the third year of the contract. Although merit[32] increases are sometimes distributed on this basis, it is more common to spread out increases over the life of the contract.

Another helpful formula provides the present value of equivalent dated series of equal expenditures, the first to be added at the beginning of a new contract; the formula reads:

$$PV = Ra_{\overline{n}|i} = R\,\frac{1 - (1+i)^{-n}}{i}$$

PV = The present value of a given obligation

i = The discount rate or interest per period

n = The number of interest or discount rate periods

$a_{\overline{n}|i}$ = These universally designated symbols read: a sub n at interest i. Values for the $a_{\overline{n}|i}$ formula are obtainable from standard present value annuity tables. Obviously, before values can be obtained, the appropriate discount rate (i) and capitalization period (n) has to be determined.

R = Total increases in contract cost over previous period to be disbursed at given intervals.

The following calculations show how the $Ra_{\overline{n}|i}$ formula can be applied to a hypothetical contract that would cost the employer $120,000 per year. The present value of such an expenditure would depend on the discount rate and on the time period over which the payment would be capitalized. Cartter states that unions are likely to have a significantly shorter time horizon than employers for capitalizing contract terms.[33]

The assumptions governing the application of the $Ra_{\overline{n}|i}$ formula to a hypothetical case are outlined next:

1. Assume a one-year contract.
2. All calculations are based on monthly totals.
3. Additional monthly expenditures or R for the new contracts are $10,000 ($120,000 annually).
4. Assume, for example, a monthly discount or interest rate (i) of ⅞ percent (10.5% annually).
5. Assume that we utilize Cartter's[34] model and capitalize expenditures over a ten-year period, or 120 monthly pay periods. Thus, n is 120. In reality, the additional contract cost expenditures continue into perpetuity.

The present value of the additional contract cost would be $741,097. This total is obtained in the following way:

$$PV = Ra_{\overline{n}|i} = \$10,000a_{\overline{n}|i} = \$10,000 \times 74.10975832 = 741,097.58$$

The 74.10975832 amount is obtained from a standard annuity table.

DISCOUNTED CASH FLOW MODEL

Labor contract costs have many implications for employers. As stated earlier, they may have an impact on price charged, on volume produced and sold, on product mix, and on capital-to-labor ratio. Granof[35] claims that most of the current contract costing procedures are inadequate because firms "base computations on historical, as opposed to projected, levels of operations." The past is relevant as an information base but not as a decision base. Firms stress contract costs and ignore the impact of costs on profits. Granof suggests that firms should cost contracts by utilizing the discounted cash flow model, referred to as the DCF model. The model is based on the time value of money, which is measured by present value formulas. At present, the model is used by employers for making investment decisions. In arriving at these decisions, management considers all future cash inflows and outflows that accompany investment expenditures and discounts these cash flows to their present value. Investments are made only if future results are expected to be profitable. The DCF model attempts to apply investment evaluation techniques to the costing of labor contracts. The model utilizes present value formulas for the costing of settlements but, rather than just applying these formulas to projected costs, it also applies them to projected receipts. In bargaining, settlement packages of various compositions are considered by the parties. In some instances, a union may feel indifferent about two management proposals, and either one may be equally acceptable. An application of the DCF model could reveal that one of the proposals is less expensive than the other. The model also looks beyond the direct cost of a labor contract. It examines the overall impact of a settlement on a firm. Under the model, all projected receipts and expenditures are discounted to their present value; and on this basis the most attractive bargaining package can be selected. Cash flows may differ among bargaining proposals; the model, through its present value approach, provides a common denominator enabling the parties to compare the cost of different options.

The model is not only important for management, it could also be useful to unions. It could highlight employment implications of various union proposals. One of the difficulties that unions would have in utilizing the model would be lack of the necessary financial data. Union contract analysts would have to employ intelligent guesswork in order to come up with the financial ingredients necessary for the structuring of a DCF model. The model could help unions anticipate management's reactions to their demands; it could also help them formulate better proposals.

Presently, the DCF concept is primarily used to evaluate capital projects rather than for the costing of labor contracts. A 1966 survey[36] indicated that relatively few of the companies surveyed applied DCF concepts for assessing capital expenditure plans. In 1971, a similar survey[37] showed that more than 50 percent of the respondents utilized discounting procedures. With the advent of computers, the world became more quantitatively oriented, and the number of firms applying sophisticated mathematical and statistical techniques to business problems began growing rapidly. If the trend is indicative, we will probably see increasing utilization of DCF concepts, particularly in large bargaining units. So far, the DCF model has not been too popular in the collective bargaining arena. According to Granof, the following reasons are responsible for its absence from the bargaining scene. First, the model stresses a single objective, the maximization of net present value of projected cash flow. In reality, a company may have numerous objectives, some of which may differ from the model. For some firms, it may be important to achieve a given annual earning per share, and this could be incompatible with results obtained under a DCF model. Second, the present value formula utilized in the model contains a discount rate that has to be determined arbitrarily. The most commonly used rate is the rate for the cost of capital.

However, that rate is difficult to define.[38] Third, the DCF model is based on projections of future cash flows; firms find it difficult to arrive at accurate long-term cash flow forecasts.[39] Furthermore, it should be pointed out that economic concessions in collective bargaining affect people and therefore cannot always be viewed as if they were simply competing alternative investment decisions. Despite the above limitations, the model has some potential for collective bargaining.

Recent college graduates entering the world of work are equipped with quantitative skills that their predecessors, even ten years ago, did not possess. This development plus major breakthroughs in computer technology increased the application of sophisticated costing techniques. Initially, these were confined to such fields as corporate finance and production. As the corporate staff becomes more familiar with quantitative tools, one can expect the utilization of these tools in all areas of corporate activities, including collective bargaining and the costing of labor contracts.

THE COMPUTER AND COLLECTIVE BARGAINING

The recent growth and popularity of the personal microcomputer has had a significant impact on costing of labor contracts. The major beneficiaries of this development have been smaller employers and unions. The importance of microcomputers for costing was recently illustrated to the authors of this book by our students. In 1985, for the first time, a few student teams participating in the collective bargaining simulation contained in this text decided, on their own initiative, to utilize microcomputers for costing calculations. They used the software package Lotus 1 2 3 to graph and compute alternative compensation packages. The exercise was highly successful.

Recent discussions with labor relations practitioners indicate that negotiators on both sides discovered the significance of the microcomputer—both the desk and the portable model—for purposes of bargaining and costing. A good software program can assist negotiators quickly to cost out different combinations of wage and fringe benefit packages. The availability of such information may be very significant in the last stages of bargaining, when the parties—in order to reach a settlement—may engage in intense trading of different items of the package. At such times, instantaneous access to cost estimates of alternatives could make a difference between an agreement or a strike. In recent years many companies have developed software programs tailored to their own needs. In the near future one can expect the appearance of many commercially developed sophisticated software packages that smaller employers and unions will be able to purchase at reasonable prices.

The importance of the microcomputer is being recognized both by unions and employers. In a recent article in the *AFL—CIO News*[40] a statement was made that "microcomputers, properly used, can be a source of bargaining power to union negotiating committees." This was acknowledged by twenty-five union research directors and negotiators who took part in a workshop at the George Meany Center for Labor Studies. The workshop covered such topics as the use of spread sheets and the use of data bases as a means of answering "what if" questions and providing contract analysis. The unionists were warned, however, not to ignore principles and not to become too absorbed with the numbers and computations.

In his management handbook, Loughran states that there is "an ever increasing use of computers for cost estimating purposes during labor contract negotiations."[41] Although he recognizes the value of computers for contract costing, he points out, however, that computers may have some drawbacks in negotiations. They may reduce the necessity of "mental gymnastics which can often help the negotiator to see a solution or tradeoff that might not occur to him if the calculations are done by computer."[42] Thus he warns the negotiator not to rely too much on the computer. Furthermore, he points out that security and confidentiality may be a problem and that there is always the possibility of unauthorized access to computer memory. Furthermore, generation of multiple copies of computer printouts increases the potential for a loss of costing confidentiality.

Some authors express the view that the computer can have a role in costing of contracts and can also help in reducing labor-management confrontations. Fraser and Hipel[43] suggest that parties with different objectives who are in a conflict situation can be assisted by means of an interactive microcomputer utilizing a conflict-analysis program.

As many labor relations practitioners seem to be gravitating toward the computer, it should be pointed out that computer technology was introduced into collective bargaining many years ago. One pioneer in this area was Jack Ellenbogen, who developed a computer model customized to the requirement of individual bargaining units. His model attempted to provide negotiators with three types of cost information: (1) total package costs of alternative proposals, (2) settlement cost details useful for "budgeting, product line planning, pricing, and profit estimates," and (3) cost of contract changes or additions. His model is discussed in some detail in the first edition of our text.[44]

One of the early works on the impact of computers on collective bargaining was published in 1969. In it, Dunlop expressed the view that "the computer has a comparative advantage and its advantages are greatest when you can get joint agreement in its use. . . . It is most likely to be useful in questions where large masses of data are relevant."[45] These observations are as applicable today as they were well before computer technology reached its current level of sophistication. To conclude, the impact of computers on collective bargaining was well summarized in a recent article in the *Personnel Journal*. The author, Deborah O. Cantrell, writes: "There were two new members present at the bargaining table during bargaining sessions with the union. Affectionately nicknamed 'Godzilla' and 'Frankenstein,' they have changed the process of collective bargaining."[46] The two were 256K microcomputers. Spreadsheet and wordprocessing software provided the parties with quick and precise cost analysis and redrafted contract language. Cantrell states that the personal computer made it possible "to communicate faster, analyze better, and more accurately predict the consequences of the entire collective bargaining process."

Unions are major beneficiaries of computer technology, not only in the area of cost computations and wordprocessing but also in availability of data on the employer. Unions can obtain immediate information on employers by dialing the Dow-Jones News Retrieval Services, and in some cases the Dialog Congressional, Record Abstracts, Geisco's Value Line Date Base, and Standard and Poor News Daily. Through these sources the union can receive information on such items as salaries paid to officers, 10K reports filed with the Securities and Exchange Commission, balance sheets and income statements, and any relevant congressional testimony. Both sides can also access the BLS data banks on employment, hours of work, and earnings for the United States. Such industry statistics are available on a national, state, and local level. Other data sources available to the parties through a computer are "Dialog's, BNA, On Line Labor Law Research, Lexus, and Mead Data Central's GOVDOC data banks."[47] In conclusion Cantrell states: "Technology may enhance the collective bargaining process, but a computer will never replace the cigar-chewing, table-thumping, red-eyed, human being–type negotiator. Why? Collective bargaining is a dynamic process, subject to the strong influence of personalities and politics. It is not a science; it is an art—specifically, the art of persuasion, practiced with high stakes—the lives and well-being of fellow employees. Collective bargaining is entered into to solve human problems. Its dimension can never be fully contained and analyzed in a computer. A computer can never make the judgment call at 3:30 A.M. that is the difference between a strike and a settlement. Only a seasoned negotiator has that sixth sense, gut-feel for the timing to make the final offer that both sides can live with. . . . A computer may help us negotiate smarter and even faster, but it is only a small part of the synergy of the collective bargaining process. We will always need the expertise of the human negotiators make it happen."[48]

COSTING SOURCES

This section provides a brief summary of some of the published material on costing that students are advised to consult.

Charles S. Loughran, *Negotiating A Labor Contract, A Management Handbook*. (The Bureau of National Affairs, Inc., Washington, D.C., 1984, Chapter 8, pp. 229–259). Chapter 8 of this book, entitled "Costing Contract Demands, Offers, and Settlements," although contained in a management handbook, can be quite helpful not only to management but also to union negotiators. The chapter addresses such topics as the role of the negotiator as a cost estimator, the use of specialists, and the use of computers. The chapter contains sections on the necessity of cost estimates, on costing of newly negotiated fringe benefits, and on the rollup concept. It evaluates the cents-per-hour issue as well as some key costing variables. The chapter offers illustrations and computations of specific contract changes. It also illustrates accumulation of all items into one overall total cost package. The author discusses the cost impact of a settlement beyond the bargaining unit. He also covers time weighting and present-value costing. In the last section he considers the issue of sharing cost estimates with the union. The author points out that unions are "legally entitled to actual labor cost data and other information within the control of the employer which is relevant to a mandatory subject of bargaining. Most cost data about existing wages and benefits fall into that category."

Wayne F. Cascio, *Costing Human Resources: The Financial Impact of Behavior in Organizations*. (Kent Publishing Co., a Division of Wadsworth, Inc., Boston, Mass. 1982). Cascio's book is a comprehensive source on the subject of costing human resources. It covers such areas as human resource accounting, costing employee-turnover rates, absenteeism, and attitudes. It views personnel programs from a return-on-investment perspective. It also estimates the costs and benefits of human resource development programs. Chapter 6 of this book, entitled "Labor Contract Costing," is particularly interesting for purposes of negotiating. In this chapter Cascio provides the reader with a method for computation of average compensation costs and the type of information necessary for such calculations. There is a section showing how to compute cost increases after the base compensation has been established. The author points out the importance of the rollup factor, or the effect of a wage increase on the increased cost of some existing fringe benefits. One of the sections illustrates the computation of hourly cost of compensation and shows how to separate hours worked from hours paid for. The final section of this chapter discusses the role of the computer in collective bargaining.

Donald L. Davis and Jack E. Steen, "DSS Analyzes Employee Information When it is Needed Most: During Contract Decisions." (*Personnel Journal*, November 1983, pp. 889–892). Although this article stresses the need for decision support system (DSS) for purposes of contract administration, the value of this approach could be extended to costing of contract costs as well as to preparation for bargaining. The article discusses a computer-based DSS system providing information on such topics as "lateness, absence, overtime assignment, grievance analysis, grievance response, and layoff and recall."

Robert E. Allen and Timothy J. Keaveny, "Costing Out a Wage and Benefit Package." (*Compensation Review*, Second Quarter 1983, Amacom, Periodicals Division of American Mangement Association, pp. 27–39). The authors provide a model for costing out a wage and benefit package. They point out that "labor costs represent the largest single cost of operations for most organizations. That is why everyone involved in setting compensation rates should be able to identify the cost of changes in wages and employee benefits." The authors point out that their model has some limitations. It assumes that history repeats itself; it emphasizes only the direct cost of a compensation package and ignores the time value of money.

SUMMARY

To conclude, both labor and management could benefit from more-open discussions of methods utilized for cost estimates of new proposals. Unions may find out that the actual cost of some of their demands is much higher than they anticipated, and this may induce them to revise demands or shift to less expensive options. By subjecting their cost estimates to review and criticism by unions, management may find out that their cost estimates are erroneous or inflated, and this may persuade them to come up with more generous offers. This, at times, could make a difference between a strike and a settlement.

Contract-costing procedures could be upgraded by relying more extensively on financial and economic concepts. Existing procedures use accounting methodology and are primarily based on the assumption that the future is a repetition of the past. Management sometimes ignores such important ideas as the time value of money. It considers as outlays only labor costs directly attributed to its employees. A firm, however, is a total entity; whatever happens in any subsystem can affect the total system. In reality, costs resulting from new settlements may be considerably higher than the actual totals paid out to labor in the form of higher wages and fringe benefits.

The costing of contracts poses major challenges to negotiators, who are not always familiar with finance, production, and pricing of output, all of which influence management's offer. In many firms, these decisions are heavily influenced by finance people who have no background in industrial relations. Greater familiarity with these areas by negotiators may give them more influence over the composition and magnitude of the bargaining package. For this to happen, however, labor relations experts would require better training in finance, accounting, and economics. As the level of costing expertise of management negotiators increases, unions will have to respond in kind. Union negotiators will also have to become better trained in quantitative skills. Union and management negotiators will have to acquire a sophistication and understanding of the quantitative tools presently applied by actuaries, accountants, economists, and financial experts. This is necessary in order to prevent these quantitatively but usually not labor-relations-oriented professionals from assuming a larger degree of influence over labor relations in the future.

For further material on costing, review Appendix A to Chapter 8, "Elementary Steps in Costing a Contract," and Appendix B to Chapter 8, "Calculating Compensation Costs." See table of contents for page numbers; both appendices are in the back of the book.

NOTES

[1]Economists concentrate their efforts on those issues which seem most significant, by assuming that other factors, except the ones on which they concentrate, are equal. As Marshall stated it, the economist "segregates those disturbing causes, whose wanderings happen to be inconvenient, . . . called ceteris paribus." Marshall also said, "The more the issue is thus narrowed, the more exactly can it be handled: but also the less closely does it correspond to real life." Source: Alfred Marshall, *Principles of Economics*, 8th ed. (London, 1959), p. 304. Although the *ceteris paribus* concept assumes that other things are equal, nevertheless it is a very useful analytical tool for purposes of model building and economic analysis; the reader is alerted to the fact that other things usually do not stay constant and that some changes may have significant cost implications.

[2]The source of material for this section is an article by Lily Mary David and Victor J. Sheifer, "Estimating the Cost of Collective Bargaining Settlements," *Monthly Labor Review*, 92, no. 5 (May 1969), 16–26.

[3]*Ibid.*, p. 17.

[4]*White Collar Report*, 57 (Washington D.C.: Bureau of National Affairs, Inc. (BNA), 1985) 61, 1–23.

[5]Noel Arnold Levin, *Negotiating Fringe Benefits* (New York: American Management Association, 1973), p. 1.

[6]*Employee Benefits 1980* (Washington, D.C.: Chamber of Commerce of the United States 1980), p. 27. *Source:* George T. Milkovich and Jerry M. Newman, *Compensation* (Plano, Texas: Business Publications, Inc., 1984), p. 364.

[7]*White Collar Report, op. cit.*, p. 61.

[8]Richard I. Henderson, *Compensation Management: Rewarding Performance*, 3rd ed. (Reston, Va.: Reston, 1979), pp. 309−339, see also Milkovich and Newman, *op. cit.*, p. 388.

[9]Michael H. Granof, *How to Cost Your Labor Contract* (Washington, D.C.: Bureau of National Affairs, 1973), pp. 20−21.

[10]*Ibid.*

[11]*Ibid.*

[12]*Ibid.*, pp. 5−6.

[13]*Ibid.*, p. 33.

[14]*Ibid.*, p. 34.

[15]*Ibid.*, p. 40.

[16]*Ibid.*, p. 42.

[17]Harold Stieglitz, *Computing the Cost of Fringe Benefits: Studies in Personnel Policy, No. 128* (New York: National Industrial Conference Board, 1952), p. 7. See also Henderson, *op. cit.*, pp. 343−44.

[18]Stieglitz, *op. cit.*, pp. 7, 10.

[19]Henderson, *op. cit.*, p. 345.

[20]Granof, *op. cit.*, p. 35.

[21]Henderson, *op. cit.*, p. 345.

[22]Granof, *op. cit.*, p. 50.

[23]Walter A. Hazelton, "How to Cost Labor Settlements," *Management Accounting* (May 1979), pp. 19−23.

[24]Granof, *op. cit.*, pp. 4, 7.

[25]Consumer responses to price changes are discussed in some detail in the next section under the heading of "Elasticity of Demand."

[26]For further discussion of this topic, see any introductory text in economics.

[27]Definition of these terms can be found in any introductory text in economics.

[28]The process of finding present value is termed "discounting."

[29]M.W. Reder, "The Theory of Union Wage Policy," *Review of Economics and Statistics*, 34 (1952), 38; Allan M. Cartter, *Theory of Wages and Employment* (Homewood, Ill: Irwin, 1959), p. 119; Granof, *op. cit.*, pp. 80−128.

[30]Financial tables are included in most mathematics of finance texts. See Paul M. Hummel and Charles L. Seebeck, Jr., *Mathematics of Finance*, 3rd ed. (New York: McGraw-Hill, 1971), pp. 251−361.

[31]"Discount rate" refers to the rate applied to calculation from future to present. The term "interest rate" is utilized for calculations from the present to the future. The discount rate used depends on prevailing money market conditions and interest rates. Granof, *op. cit.*, suggests that the discount rate used be the cost of capital rate (p. 110).

[32]Such one-time merit increases paid at the beginning of the second year of the 1979−81 contract were negotiated at the University of Cincinnati.

[33]Cartter, *op. cit.*, p. 119.

[34]*Ibid.*, p. 119.

[35]Granof, *op. cit.*, p. 127

[36]George A. Christy, *Capital Budgeting; Current Practices and Their Efficiency* (Eugene, Ore.: Bureau of Business and Economic Research, University of Oregon, 1966), p. 12. Source: Granof, *op. cit.*, p. 90.

[37]Thomas P. Klammer, "A Study of the Association of Capital Budgeting Techniques with Firm Performance and Firm Characteristics" (unpublished Ph.D. dissertation, University of Wisconsin, 1971), p. 77. Source: Granof, *op. cit.*, p. 90.

[38]Ezra Solomon, *The Theory of Financial Management* (New York: Columbia University Press, 1963). Source: Granof, *op. cit.*, p. 90.

[39]Alexander A. Robichek, Donald G. Ogilvie, and John D. C. Roach, "Capital Budgeting: A Pragmatic Approach," *Financial Executive*, Vol. 37, April 1969, pp. 26–39; and Eugene M. Lerner and Alfred Rappaport, "Limit DCF in Capital Budgeting," *Harvard Business Review*, 46 (September–October 1968), 133–39. Source: Granof, *op. cit.*, p. 90.

[40]*AFL–CIO News*, November 3, 1984, p. 6.

[41]Charles S. Loughran, *Negotiating a Labor Contract: A Management Handbook.* (Washington, D.C.: The Bureau of National Affairs, Inc., 1984), Chapter 8, p. 230.

[42]*Ibid.*

[43]Niall M. Fraser and Keith W. Hipel, "Computer Assistance in Labor-Management Negotiations" *Interfaces* 2, no. 2 (April 1981), 22–29, The Institute of Management Sciences.

[44]Jack Ellenbogen, Brochure by Ellenbogen Associates, also Tables for Costing Union-Management Settlements (Westport, Conn. 06880, 1975). See also E. Edward Herman and Alfred Kuhn, *Collective Bargaining and Labor Relations*, (Englewood Cliffs, N.J.: Prentice-Hall, 1981), pp. 259–265.

[45]The Computer in Dispute Settlement: A Panel and General Discussion. Panel Members: George W. Taylor, David L. Cole, and John T. Dunlop. *Source: The Impact of Computers on Collective Bargaining*, A.J. Siegel, ed. (Cambridge, Mass.: MIT Press 1969).

[46]Deborah O. Cantrell, Manager, Industrial Relations Dept., Gulf Oil Corp., Houston, Texas. *Personnel Journal* (September 1984), pp. 27–30.

[47]*Ibid.*

[48]*Ibid.*

THE NEGOTIATIONS PROCESS

In previous chapters, we have introduced the preparation for bargaining and the costing of the collective agreement. This chapter examines the bilateral process of negotiations, including basic strategies and concepts. While no two negotiations proceed in exactly the same manner, all have certain similarities, which can be covered in a comprehensive review such as this. We shall begin with the procedural aspects of negotiations and then move on to basic concepts and strategies.

BARGAINING PROCEDURE

Before bargaining over substance can begin, the parties must agree on a mutually acceptable bargaining procedure. The following can be classified as procedural issues:

1. Bargaining location
2. Agenda sequence
3. Authority to make firm commitments
4. Whose working draft to be used
5. Procedure during negotiations
   a. schedule
   b. caucuses
   c. record keeping

     d. confidentiality
     e. news releases
     f. tentative agreement on issues until full agreement is reached

One of the first such topics is the bargaining location. The usual alternatives are a neutral site versus employer facilities. The neutral site could be a hotel, the offices of the Federal Mediation and Conciliation Service, or any other public or private facility. The location, to some extent, depends on the level of negotiations. In multiplant or multiemployer bargaining, the parties usually select a neutral site. On the other hand, small single-plant employers frequently negotiate on their own premises. The National Industrial Conference Board[1] has reviewed the advantages and disadvantages of inside and outside bargaining locations. The inside locations have a number of advantages. First, they reduce the cost of bargaining. There are no rental costs for hotel rooms, no need to compensate people for travel expenses. Second, union democracy is fostered, since union negotiators tend to be more sensitive to the needs of their constituents if they are in close geographical proximity to them. Third, it is more convenient for management because materials and personnel are readily available.

There are, however, a number of drawbacks to on-site bargaining. First, if negotiators interact with the rank and file, there is a greater possibility of gossip and rumor. These can distort information and bring unnecessary pressures on negotiators. Second, the union team may feel patronized and resentful if bargaining takes place on employer premises. Whether this feeling is founded on fact or imagination is immaterial if it is detrimental to the bargaining process.

Bargaining away from employer premises also has drawbacks. First, issues tend to be magnified. Negotiators may feel that being away on an expense account requires larger concessions from the opposition. This attitude, at times, increases the significance of minor issues and results in extensive discussions over topics that should have been settled in a relatively short time. Second, being away from the workplace can lead to "less sober bargaining,"[2] being conducive to drinking at night and subsequent hangovers. Third, neutral site negotiations are frequently accompanied by marathon sessions conducted to the point of exhaustion and provide a bargaining advantage to the side with the greater physical stamina. In such an atmosphere, reaching an agreement dominates behavior and becomes an end unto itself. As a result, the final product may be less than adequate from the point of view of both sides. Fourth, since the parties are removed from the daily problems that exist under the current contract, they may push aside and ignore some of these difficulties. They would find it more difficult to do so if negotiations took place in closer proximity to their constituents. Finally, it is much harder to avoid the press on a neutral site. The negotiators are confronted with a dilemma. If they refuse comments to the media, they end up with bad press coverage. If they make comments to the media, they still may end up with bad press coverage. If they make a statement, it may be blown out of proportion or taken out of context, and thus may be detrimental. A comment to a reporter by one side forces a response from the opposition. This at times leads to collective bargaining in the news media rather than at the bargaining table.

Regardless of the site, there are a number of requirements of any facility. It must be free from disruption. The room must have chairs, tables, blackboard, chalk, paper, pencil, water, plenty of coffee, and sufficient illumination. It has to be accessible at all hours and should be close to food and refreshment facilities, and adjoining caucus rooms have to be available to both sides.

Bargaining Agenda

Another procedural issue to be resolved at the beginning of negotiations is the sequence of the bargaining agenda. The typical approach is for the parties to negotiate over minor issues first, the rationale being that it is difficult to resolve minor issues if they are left for later stages of negotiations. If major issues are agreed upon first, there is less incentive for the parties to settle anything else, since each side usually assumes that the opposite would not risk a strike over minor issues. The strike threat is not always necessary for the resolution of minor problems. In some instances, the parties may be willing to accommodate each other not because of threats but because they may want a better relationship. Typically, however, neither side is willing to rely on the good will of the opposition and therefore prefers to resolve minor issues early.

Authority To Make Firm Commitments

Under the NLRA, the parties are under an obligation to bargain in good faith; according to NLRB rulings, this means that negotiators must have the authority to make firm commitments on behalf of their principals. In spite of these legal requirements, the authority of negotiators varies considerably. Therefore, it is advisable to define the authority of both sides at the outset, thus reducing possibilities of misinterpretation later. One author states, "Negotiating frustrations can be spared if authority is clearly defined."[3]

Some union negotiators have full authority to conclude a final contract subject to membership ratification. Others require the approval of an executive committee before they can sign.

Some management negotiators are fully empowered to reach an agreement subject to almost automatic approval from top management. By contrast, in some firms negotiators have to clear each concession with their superiors.[4] The negotiators who have to check each move with their principals have the perfect out when cornered. However, such lack of authority makes it more difficult to extract concessions from the opposition and weakens bargaining effectiveness.

Working Drafts

In some bargaining situations, the parties exchange draft agreements. This presents a procedural question as to whether to negotiate from the union draft, the employer draft, or the existing agreement. Since management negotiators prefer working from their own drafts, because they think that it gives them a bargaining advantage, a procedural argument could develop over this issue. Usually, this issue is easily resolved, since unions are often willing to concede this point to their opposition.

Procedure During Negotiations

Certain procedural rules should be settled during the first bargaining session. The parties should establish a schedule and duration of negotiation sessions. Time of day or day of the week for sessions can have an impact on negotiations. Sessions that start in the afternoon are preferable to negotiations confined to evening hours, as negotiators may be too tired and irritable during the evening. At times, negotiations on weekends may be most effective.

In the early stages of bargaining, it is advisable to limit sessions to a few hours per day. When sessions get too long, tempers get short, fatigue sets in, the law of diminishing returns start operating, and the extra hours of negotiations can prove counterproductive. This does not suggest that long sessions are always detrimental. In the last stages of bargaining, marathon sessions may be necessary for concluding an agreement, particularly if both sides desire to reach a settlement by a certain deadline.

There can be a conflict of interest between the two sides over frequency of bargaining sessions. Sometimes management negotiators may find it advantageous to schedule a reduced number of meetings. Their purpose would be to provide less negotiation time to the union before contract expiration. As the contract deadline gets closer, the rank and file and union negotiators may become impatient. Such a development could strengthen management's bargaining position.

Another scheduling issue involves timeouts for caucuses. Typically, the parties agree to call caucuses as often as necessary.

Another procedural point that is usually resolved during the first session concerns the taking of minutes or record-keeping arrangements. A number of options are open to the parties. They may decide that each side keep its own records, they may employ a stenographer, they may install a recording machine, or they may dispense with record keeping altogether. Since the formality of record keeping can be detrimental to the bargaining process, the parties are probably better off without any stenographic assistance.

Another issue closely related to the keeping of records is the matter of confidentiality. In some cases, the parties agree to keep all proceedings confidential until an agreement is reached. This reduces the outside pressures on negotiators during bargaining. In other situations, there is a constant flow of news releases. This type of news media bargaining could have an adverse effect on the bargaining process.

There is a variety of views on the issue of confidentiality. Some suggest that the rank and file should be informed of developments at the bargaining table. The logic of this position is that the bargaining team enjoys more trust from its constituency if communications are always open. The other side of the coin is that too much openness is counterproductive to the bargaining process. When proceedings are out in the open, the parties are afraid to explore new ideas and flexibility suffers. Negotiations become an exercise in public relations and are directed to the audience rather than to the issues. Parties then tend to become more formal and commit themselves to specific positions. This at times can lead to impasses and to breakdowns of bargaining. Successful bargaining requires some confidentiality; if it is absent in formal sessions, it is sometimes replaced by off-the-record meetings between the representatives of unions and management. The final agreement, rather than being arrived at by the bargaining teams, may be hammered out in confidential meetings between the representatives of the two sides.

Another procedural point that has to be resolved by the parties concerns the status of articles on which agreement has been reached. Typically, the parties reach an understanding that each issue agreed upon is tentative and nonbinding until a complete agreement on all issues has been reached. This provides the parties with the flexibility to trade off agreed-upon items against outstanding issues.

Once bargaining has commenced, the ongoing negotiations tend to fall into patterns that are similar for most negotiations. For the purposes of our analysis, we shall refer to these as the *stages of negotiations*.

STAGES OF THE NEGOTIATIONS PROCESS

Most negotiations processes fall into four stages: the opening, the settling-in stage, the consolidation stage, and the finalization stage.[5] The stages are characterized by differences in the behaviors of the union and management representatives, in the level and intensity of the discussions that take place, and in the amount of actual bargaining (or trading) that takes place.

The opening stage is characterized by the first meeting or set of meetings between the union and management. Typically, the union first presents all its demands. Often press conferences are called for this opening of contract talks in important negotiations. Following the union presentation of demands, there typically is a recess, often for days or even weeks, as management formulates its initial proposals for presentation and its responses to the union demands. At the second meeting, management comes back with its own initial offers to the union proposals and its own demands. It should be noted that there is no hard and fast rule that the union first present its proposals, followed by management responses. This custom reflects the pattern that has developed in the United States. Generally, it has been the union which has desired to change the status quo and management which has defended it. There have been notable exceptions to this trend in recent years, however, with management being the party most desiring change in the collective agreement. At this point in bargaining the agenda (if not its order) for the negotiations and the limits of any potential collective bargaining solutions are already set by the parties. Each side has defined its own best outcome on each issue that is to be negotiated. It is considered somewhat of a faux pas in the negotiating arena to bring up completely new issues after this point in negotiation. Each party has had a chance to present any and all of its demands, and therefore to bring up another new issue at a later date is generally not considered acceptable.

The number of proposals that the union presents at the bargaining table can vary from a few to a few hundred. Frequently, the quantity of demands goes up with increases in the size and heterogeneity of the bargaining unit. This does not mean, however, that small and homogeneous units always confine themselves to a small list of demands.

There are essentially two basic approaches to the number of demands to be presented.[6] There are those who advocate a small number of serious demands and a screening out of all trivial proposals. This permits the union to concentrate on securing major concessions on all of its demands. By contrast, others object to such a screening and suggest that all noncontradictory membership demands be presented. This latter approach provides maximum membership input; it is democratic and politically attractive. Leaving out some demands can contribute to rank-and-file hostility against union leadership. It can be further claimed that it is unfair to solicit membership views and then ignore such inputs. The broad spectrum approach to demand presentation is not without its problems. Bargaining can be adversely affected by union officers abdicating their responsibility for final formulation in favor of the wishes of the rank and file. Too many demands can lead to confusion and erroneous signals to the opposition. Unnecessary impasses can result from the opposition attaching the wrong values to particular demands. In the final analysis, such an approach leaves it to management negotiators to eliminate many of the secondary demands. In negotiations, time is scarce, and too much spent on irrelevant issues leaves too little for important work. Finally, too many demands can make the union team look silly. A handbook prepared by the education department of the UAW[7] suggests that union leaders have a responsibility to decide what are the needs of their constituents as opposed to their wants. Members may give a low priority to improvements in pensions as contrasted to other economic proposals, even though such an improvement may be in their best long-run interest. The danger to union officials who consider needs rather than wishes is the possibility of being voted out of office. This also poses a basic philosophical question as to whether a union leader has the right to ignore membership wishes and make a parental value judgment as to what is in the best interests of the rank and file. The long-term needs of union members as perceived by the union officers may conflict with workers' short-term wants. Workers may be more interested in maximizing present wages than in obtaining better pensions twenty or thirty years in the future. This point was well demonstrated in the 1947 Ford/United Auto Workers negotiations, where membership opted for higher wages over better pension benefits. In view of such potential conflict, some unions before presenting to management internally controversial demands first attempt to educate and convince their members of the wisdom of their bargaining priorities.[8]

Responsible leadership implies more than just being a transmittal agent of membership demands. It means taking into account the long-term needs of the union and its members, though these needs may be in direct conflict with the immediate expectations of union members. Political realities and expediency can force union leaders to sacrifice statesmanship and long-term benefits for more immediate membership votes.

Negotiators are reluctant to submit too many proposals to the opposition, particularly if some are to be used for trading purposes. They feel that such action can lead to misinterpretation of signals. The union could underestimate the importance of some management proposals, and perhaps infer that all management proposals are tradeable. Although many negotiators frown on presenting a large number of trading proposals, in some firms it is almost a tradition for both sides to submit a long set of demands that are later traded off. But even in such situations, management is reluctant to present trivial proposals. Unions may have to include many initial demands because they originated with members or locals.

For example, although wage increases are a common denominator in all union demands, the formulation of the specifics of initial wage demands can be difficult. A publication of the UAW[9] suggests that, in formulating money demands, the union should ask for a "substantial raise" based on cost of living, employer's financial status, and productivity. Initial wage demands should be couched in general rather than in absolute terms, to provide flexibility. A demand that is explicit is usually too high. Such high demands require major retreats, which could weaken a union. Also, modern employers do not like the haggling approach which necessitates many modifications and under which they have to start very low and gradually increase their offer to a mutually acceptable level. The rationale behind a union's excessive wage demands is the assumption that the probability of generous concessions is greater when initial demands are high rather than close to final expectations. Also, this approach gives unions more room to maneuver. Management negotiators cannot afford to respond to an excessive union demand with a reasonable offer, because this could be interpreted by the union as a signal that its own demands are too low. The result of the initial excessive union demand is usually an unreasonably low management response. Bridging the gap may absorb a significant portion of negotiators' time and effort. As a consequence, there may be insufficient time to discuss other important aspects of the contract. There is also the danger that unreasonable proposals will not be taken seriously, and that they will reduce one's bargaining effectiveness.

In many cases, both sides react to each other's behavior and present many more demands than they expect to attain. Thus at the end of the opening stage of negotiations, many issues, which neither party has any realistic expectations of settling, may end up at the bargaining table.

The second stage of negotiations is the settling-in stage. As we said of the opening stage, the parties have defined the limits of what will be negotiated. The settling-in stage is characterized by a full discussion of each of the issues. Each party presents data to the opposition in support of its position. There is a general attempt by each side to find out what the other side really wants. This attempt to discover the others' priorities often involves a much fuller discussion of the issues and presentation of materials to back up those issues. For example, in an attempt to justify wage increases, unions go far beyond the simple presentation of the demand that occurred in the opening stage. Detailed analysis of industry wage trends, local wage trends, and national price trends might be presented, as well as any other supportive material. Likewise, management may make a presentation in order to define the limits of the increased costs that they can afford over the life of the proposed contract. They may present more-detailed data on labor cost structures, pricing structures, and competition within the industry, along with other supporting data. In the discussion of some issues at this point in time, third parties will be invited to the bargaining table to present data to be used in the negotiations. For example, in the area of pensions and health or life insurance, there is usually a third party carrier who will cover the policy for the collective bargaining agreement. Thus a representative from Blue Cross, Blue Shield, or a life insurance company will come in and provide detailed cost figures for the various proposals that the union and the management are making.

During the settling-in stage of negotiations, both sides will try to resolve issues on which agreement can easily be reached. Some issues merely require a full discussion of the problem behind the proposal before both sides discover mutual interests and solutions to the problem. Both sides will attempt to get the easy-to-solve issues out of the way and dispose of some of the other issues, which are exposed as blue-sky issues to be presented only for the purpose of trade-off. Thus, by the end of the settling-in-stage, only real issues are left on the bargaining table—issues over which there is a genuine disagreement. At this point, the parties can settle down to genuine negotiations.

The third stage of negotiations is a consolidation stage. All the basic arguments and supportive positions have been presented at the preceding stage, but perhaps a fuller elaboration or reiteration of position by each side is offered to the other side. At this time we can begin to observe movement on some issues as each side begins to offer concessions to the other side. Secondly, we begin to see trade-offs of small items, that is, items not near the top of each side's priority list. A discussion of the economic package usually begins in the consolidation stage. In nearly all negotiations, the wage and fringe benefit changes are naturally lumped together and referred to as the economic package. To management all aspects of the wage and fringe benefit package are direct costs. Thus, they are often indifferent between a pension improvement and an equal cost in wage improvement. Management is more generally concerned with the total labor cost change rather than its division, and they quite naturally prefer to discuss the wage and fringe changes as a whole. This translates directly into bargaining behavior for both sides in that they then tend to make all economic proposals and counterproposals as a package.

By the conclusion of the consolidation stage, most of the less-important items or the more easily settled issues are taken off the bargaining table either through agreement or one side or the other discarding them. Thus, at the end of the consolidation stage each side has a general feeling about the true priorities of the opposition.

The last stage of collective negotiation is the finalization stage. At this point in time, there are only a few items left on the bargaining table. They are all very important to both sides; otherwise they would have been dealt with or disposed of during the consolidation stage. Generally, at this stage, the parties know intuitively whether an impasse or a strike may occur. If a strike is imminent, both sides start serious preparation for such a development. For further discussion of this topic see Chapter 11. During the finalization stage, a mediator may be called in if necessary and desired in order to facilitate continued negotiations. Generally, the finalization stage is accompanied by a change from what we might call a more normal bargaining environment to one of crisis bargaining. Crisis bargaining is characterized as much as anything by the behavior of the parties. That is, they recognize that there is a fast-approaching time limit so they bargain much more intensely meeting on a daily basis and for longer periods of time.

In a later chapter, we will examine conflict and conflict resolution in more detail.

So we will leave further categorization and explanation of the bargaining process to that chapter. At this point we will turn to an examination of strategic and tactical considerations in collective bargaining.

BASIC NEGOTIATING CONCEPTS AND STRATEGIES

No two negotiations are the same, nor can two managements' or unions' strategies ever be exactly the same; however, there are some simple strategies that one might pursue and that are universal in nature. First, something that simply cannot be overestimated in importance is that every negotiating team should formulate a total plan of action. That is, there should be an overall goal to the negotiations. Each side must have some idea prior to negotiations where they intend to end up and how they intend to get there. Without a total plan, one may be successful on an individual topic but at the end of the negotiations find oneself dissatisfied with the totality of the contract. With a total plan and objectives that come from that plan clearly in mind, one can consider the effects of each small compromise on the achievement of one's overall goal.

Reed Richardson, in his book *Collective Bargaining by Objectives: A Positive Approach*,[10] advocates the adoption of a total system approach to collective bargaining which is parallel in notion to managing by objectives. Collective bargaining by objectives (CBO) is a straightforward step-by-step approach to preparation and negotiation, which results in the eventual preparation of a planning document for negotiations. This preparation requires the negotiator to define his or her objectives in negotiations and, for each individual item to be negotiated, develop an optimistic, realistic, and a pessimistic outcome. This allows a negotiator not only to be aware of goal attainment on individual topics but also to focus on the overall picture as well. While there are many other ways of approaching negotiations with a total plan, Richardson's approach can be very helpful to both sides.

In negotiations, each side must attempt to satisfy the needs of its own constituencies. For the union there are at least three distinct groups that are interested in the outcome of the negotiations. First, the union leadership has a political need. Elected union leaders are not always present at the bargaining table, but even if they are not, they are indirectly responsible for bargaining outcomes. The negotiating committee has been elected to represent the interests of workers in negotiations, and success or failure can mean the loss of position and prestige. Political needs will reflect themselves both in the type of issues presented and in the conduct of negotiations over these issues. The second group to which the union must pay attention is its membership. The membership has ratification rights in nearly all collective bargaining situations and thus exists as the final arbiter of the decision-making process. Thus union membership obviously must be satisfied. The third group about which the union needs to be concerned about is other unions and workers. While this group is the least important and is rarely present at the bargaining table, relationships among unions can still play a significant role. For example, in industries in which there is pattern bargaining among bargaining units and among unions, each union must uphold its end of the bargaining as it goes through negotiations.

On the management side, satisfying the needs of all the parties to the negotiation is important as well. Not only must management satisfy its internal requirements, but it also has responsibilities to stockholders and to the public as well.

Once an overall plan for negotiations has been formulated, behavior directed toward the attainment of those goals must be selected. While negotiating style is clearly an individual choice, there are generally accepted negotiating "truisms." Some negotiators fall into a pattern of hard bargaining, in which threats and personal animosity are a regular part of negotiations. Some experts counsel that a more prudent course of cooperative behavior be adopted, at the same time recognizing the difficulty of that proscription.

The American Arbitration Association's Education and Training Department has prepared a short set of basic negotiating concepts and strategies. They provide a reasonable set of guidelines to negotiator behavior, and among other things they advise:

BASIC NEGOTIATING CONCEPTS AND STRATEGIES[*]

Be prepared to trade. Negotiations usually involve a series of compromises. Follow the practice of most negotiators and begin above your objectives.

Don't compromise your objectives. Do not settle in the heat of negotiations for terms that you may later decide are unacceptable. Be prepared to lose the deal if you are not completely satisfied with the terms.

Sell. Successful negotiations are primarily the result of selling yourself and your objective to others. You get a raise because your boss is sold on you . . . you acquire a company because they are sold on you. You get your way through selling.

Don't oversell. Overselling—to accomplish short-term objectives—is one of the biggest temptations in negotiations. Whether you're trying to get a job, sell a product, negotiate a contract (wage or other), or convince a company to merge with you, any temporary successes in negotiations may be offset by subsequent failures—losing long term objectives.

Don't underestimate others. They are strong enough to be in the position of dealing with you.

Be calm. Maintaining your cool at all times confers an unquestionable advantage. Never lose your temper! (At least don't show it.)

Deal with strength. The successful negotiator deals most effectively after he or she has identified his or her strongest points and uses them strategically.

Keep the meeting on the track. Be alert for the person who continually digresses. Keep your objective in mind and the meeting on the subject.

Don't react too unfavorably to your own mistakes. Life is one huge negotiation, and if you are human, you will make mistakes. Try to keep them to a minimum.

Sleep on it. If you have any doubts about a proposal or particular terms, delay your decision until tomorrow. Do not yield to pressures for an immediate decision, which is usually unnecessary anyway.

Don't rush the other side. This may be one of the most important decisions of a person's career, and he or she needs time.

---

[*]This material is the property of the American Arbitration Association and may not be used or reproduced without the expressed permission of the AAA.

When the mission is accomplished—leave! This maneuver reduces the chance that some-one will change his or her mind or that you will continue to talk needlessly until you finally say the wrong thing.

The fewer the participants, the earlier the agreement. In all meetings, keep the number involved to a minimum—you will go home much sooner.

Make an early concession. Early in negotiations try to satisfy the other side on an area very important to them. They will usually reciprocate on areas important to you.

Don't wait to tell bad news. Most people hate surprises. If something unfavorable develops during negotiations, bring it up on a timely basis. If it has to be told, delaying only weakens your position.

Defer discussions of key issues. Allow enough time to elapse to enable everyone to learn all the facts and to evaluate fully the situation and the people involved. You may need to change your strategy or even your objectives, and it is best to know it before you have committed yourself.

Make promises with caution. It is easy, in the course of a series of meetings, to say you will do something, and it is just as easy later to find yourself unable to fulfill it.

Whenever possible, phrase questions for a positive answer. It is a good maneuver to get others in the habit of saying yes.

Be flexible. A minor compromise may pave the way to winning a major point later.

Make all terms specific. Never suggest a range of values—the other side will automatically assume that you agree to the least of them.

Each day means a new attempt. When negotiations take several meetings, do not be surprised if areas previously agreed upon are to be reopened or retraded. There has been time to sleep on it and people repeatedly change their minds.

Don't worry about the end result. If you concentrate on your plan and handle yourself well, the end result will see to itself.

Another set of tactical guidelines for productive bargaining is provided by Roger Fisher and William Ury.[11] They argue that negotiations are often frustrating and diminish the relationships between the parties because of the negotiator's dilemma.

> They see two ways to negotiate: soft or hard. The soft negotiator wants to avoid personal conflict and so makes concessions readily in order to reach agreement. He wants an amicable resolution; yet he often ends up exploited and feeling bitter. The hard negotiator sees any situation as a contest of wills in which the side that takes the more extreme positions and holds out longer fares better. He wants to win; yet he often ends up producing an equally hard response which exhausts him and his resources and harms his relationship with the other side. Other standard negotiating strategies fall between hard and soft, but each involves an attempted trade-off between getting what you want and getting along with people.[12]

Fisher and Ury argue that there is a third choice, that of principled negotiation. They suggest that negotiators should always look for areas of mutual gain and, where there are pure conflicts of interest, that decisions be made on the basis of objective standards. There is one obvious pitfall in the application of this technique to labor negotiations. Objective standards must first be accepted by both sides in order to be used. Standards for an issue such as wages may vary widely and thus present signifi-cant problems for the principled negotiator.

Legal Constraints on Bargaining Tactics

Although choices of bargaining tactics are a matter of almost unlimited options, there are important legal constraints on what unions and managements are able to do at the bargaining table. It was recognized at the time of passage of the NLRA that there must be a requirement to bargain once the union-management relationship is established by certification. The Wagner Act, as amended by the Taft–Hartley Act, contains legal standards in Sections 8(a)(5) and 8(b)(5) governing labor and management conduct at the bargaining table. Over the years, NLRB interpretation of these sections of the act has created strict guidelines about proper behavior at the bargaining table.

Both the union and management are required by the Taft–Hartley Act to meet at reasonable times to bargain in good faith over wages, hours, and other terms and conditions of employment. The act also requires both sides to agree to a written contract of agreement if either party requests. Neither union or management, however, is statutorily required to agree to any proposal nor to make a concession in bargaining. All of these provisions require the NLRB and the courts to interpret whether particular tactics are part of a good-faith effort to reach agreement. It has generally proven easier to define the absence of good-faith bargaining by upholding unfair labor practice charges against certain tactics. An absence of good-faith bargaining has been found to include:

1. An unwillingness to make counterproposals
2. Constantly changing positions in bargaining
3. The use of delaying tactics
4. Withdrawal of concessions after they have been made
5. Unilateral actions over topics of bargaining
6. Refusals to furnish necessary data for negotiations[13]

An interesting and widely publicized case of what constitutes good-faith bargaining is the General Electric Corporation's strategy of Boulwarism. In the 1950s and 1960s, G.E.'s bargaining strategy was twofold. It submitted to the union all the terms of the collective bargaining agreement under negotiation, and the company's negotiators would then refuse to alter their position unless the union could provide new information in support of a change. At the same time, the company publicized its positions to the employees, hoping to create employee pressure on the union to accept the new contract. The unions filed a series of unfair labor practice charges against General Electric, and eventually succeeded in convincing the NLRB and the courts that General Electric was not bargaining in good faith.[14] Thus, the sum total of actions, each of which could be individually legal, was construed as bad-faith bargaining.

To conclude, it is not easy to define good-faith bargaining. In practice, however, relatively few legal limitations are placed on unions and managements who have a sincere desire to reach agreement.

NOTES

[1]*Preparing for Collective Bargaining*, Studies in Personnel Policy No. 172 (New York: National Industrial Conference Board, 1959), p.20.

[2]*Ibid.*, p. 21.

[3]Arnold F. Campo, "Entering into Negotiations Dealing with the Union," in LeRoy Marceau (ed.), *Dealing with a Union* (New York: American Management Association, 1969), p. 65.

[4]Thomas A. Kochan, *Collective Bargaining and Industrial Relations* (Homewood, IL: Richard D. Irwin, Inc., 1980), pp. 193–4.

[5]Reed Richardson, *Collective Bargaining by Objectives*, 2nd ed. (Englewood Cliffs, N.J.: Prentice-Hall, 1985), pp. 166–7.

[6]Terrence F. Connors, *Problems in Local Union Collective Bargaining* (Detroit: United Auto Workers Education Department, 1975), p. 25.

[7]*Ibid.*, p. 26.

[8]Myron Roomkin, "Union Structure, Internal Control, and Strike Activity," *Industrial and Labor Relations Review* 29 (January 1976), 198–217.

[9]Connors, *op. cit.*, p.31.

[10]Richardson, *op. cit.*, pp. 108–112.

[11]Roger Fisher and William Ury, *Getting to Yes* (New York: Penguin Books, 1983).

[12]*Ibid.*, p. xii. from GETTING TO YES by Roger Fisher and William Ury. Copyright © 1981 by Roger Fisher and William Ury. Reprinted by permission of Houghton Mifflin Company.

[13]These and other case summaries of bad-faith bargaining listed in: Howard J. Anderson and John J. Kenny, *Primer of Labor Relations*, 22nd ed. (Washington, D.C.: BNA, 1983), pp. 50–55.

[14]*NLRB* v. *General Electric Company*, 418 F.2d 736 (1969).

BARGAINING THEORY AND BARGAINING POWER

This chapter is directed toward the theory of collective bargaining. We first discuss the nature of bargaining theory. We then present two applications of a more general bargaining theory model to labor-management relations: the behavioral theory of Walton and McKersie and the exchange theory of Alfred Kuhn. Before we review these two theories, we first examine the nature and terminology of bargaining theory.

BARGAINING THEORY

Bargaining theorists have tried to understand the process and predict the outcomes of negotiations between the parties. For example, when a consumer goes to a dealer to purchase an automobile, it is theoretically possible for any of a fairly wide range of prices to be the end point at which the seller and the buyer finally agree to conclude their exchange. After watching a number of consumers purchase autos, however, we may observe that the actual range of prices paid for the automobiles is fairly narrow. Nonetheless, differences do exist. Why is it that one consumer ends up paying a different price than another consumer? In our day-to-day lives, each of us regularly confronts bargaining situations like the automobile problem. As well, each of us engages in intuitive observations and in an understanding of the nature of the bargaining problem, at least as it is conceptualized in the purchase of an automobile. We know that some consumers and some automobile dealers are better bargainers than others.

Some automobiles are in shorter supply than are others. Some consumers live in cities in which there is a wide variety of choice of dealers for the same automobile. At a particular point in time, some consumers have a greater need for an automobile, just as at some points in time, some dealers have a greater need to sell automobiles. All these factors play a role in the prediction of the final price that is to be settled upon by the buyer and the seller of the automobile. Thus anyone attempting to develop a predictive model or a theory of what price is to be paid by the consumer would have to take into consideration the above-mentioned factors and probably many more. Bargaining theorists have attempted to move from this understanding of a specific problem into a more general framework, within which they attempt to describe the common elements of all bargaining, whether it be the purchase of an automobile or the terms of a labor-management contract.

Most bargaining theories make two basic assumptions about the parties to the bargain.[1] First, they assume that each side to the bargain has an incentive to deal with each other, in that each has something the other wants. In the case of our automobile dealer and buyer, both sides wish to conclude an agreement, since the buyer wishes to buy the car and the seller wants to sell it. A second presumption is that there is a disagreement over the level at which the exchange can take place. If there would be no disagreement over the price of the automobile, bargaining would not be necessary. It is only because the seller is trying to protect his or her interests by getting the highest price and the buyer is attempting to obtain the lowest price that bargaining can proceed. Thus bargaining theory rests on these two assumptions: that the parties must have an incentive to deal with one another and that there be a fundamental disagreement between the parties.

According to Bacharach and Lawler[2] bargaining theory models have other common elements. The first of these is the existence of bilateral monopoly. In a theoretical model, utilizing our automobile buyer and seller as an example, it would be as if there were only one automobile in the world and the person who owned that automobile wished to sell it. Likewise, there would be a single other person in the world who wanted to purchase that automobile. Thus, for the transaction to take place, these two parties would have to reach an agreement, and they would have no choice but to deal with one another. This element of bargaining theory is important in that it provides the parties with an incentive to bargain and to reach a settlement. In the real world, there are few manifestations of these assumptions; in labor-management relations, there are only close approximations.

A second element of bargaining theories is that negotiations may take place over such clearly defined issues as prices or wage rates. In our automobile problem, the *issue* may be the price of the automobile. This might be complicated further by the range of available options on the automobile, the delivery date, and other factors. In collective bargaining theories, the *issue* emphasized may be the wage rate, although we know that in the real world there are many other issues over which parties bargain. The general presumption of bargaining theorists is that in each negotiation there is a winner and a loser. Thus, the focus on wages is convenient for theoretical models but is rarely mirrored in its simplicity in real bargaining.

A third concept of bargaining theories is that there is a contract zone. The zone can have a positive or a negative range. The outer limits of the zone are determined by the bargaining parties. In our automobile problem there is a price at which the automobile consumer would rather walk than drive. Likewise, there is a price at which the seller would rather keep the automobile than sell it. The range of potential outcomes in the automobile problem may be limited by the dealer's cost and the buyer's perception of the cost of alternative forms of transportation. In general, the outer limits of the contract zone are points outside which the parties would prefer not to settle. Consider the issue of wages in labor-management negotiations: There is a wage at which management would make no profit and would have no incentive to remain in business and employ workers. On the other end of the scale, there is a wage at which workers would look for alternative employment rather than work at that wage. Within each contract zone the parties have opening offers, target positions, and resistance points. A resistance point indicates the minimum acceptable level on the spectrum of potential solutions on which the party would be willing to agree. Beyond that point the party would refuse to settle and thus be willing to accept the economic consequences of a breakdown of negotiations. Figure 10−1 details the two possible positions of resistance points in labor-management negotiations. In the case of a positive contract zone, Figure 10−1(a), the union and management resistance points are congruous; there is a range of possible settlements that the parties would prefer to a strike. A negative contract zone Figure 10−1(b) is said to exist whenever the resistance points are incongruent.

FIGURE 10.1*   CONTRACT ZONES FOR WAGES

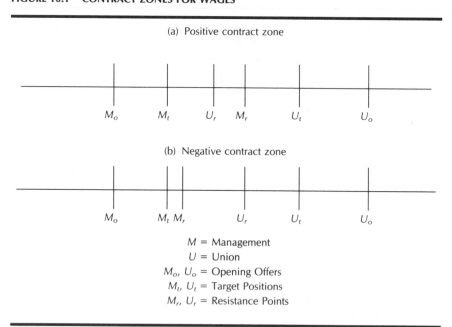

(a) Positive contract zone

M_o M_t U_r M_r U_t U_o

(b) Negative contract zone

M_o M_t M_r U_r U_t U_o

M = Management
U = Union
M_o, U_o = Opening Offers
M_t, U_t = Target Positions
M_r, U_r = Resistance Points

*See *Richard E. Walton and Robert B. McKersie*, A Behavioral Theory of Labor Negotiations, *(New York: McGraw-Hill, 1965) pp. 42−45.*

The fourth concept proposed by bargaining theorists is the convergence model. Under this approach the parties—through offers and counteroffers—move closer toward each other, gradually converging toward a point of potential agreement.

Some bargaining theories are based on the unrealistic assumption that there is a single determinant solution on which the bargainers can agree.[3] Some theories assume that there is only one logical outcome that will give each of the parties the best possible settlement. Students of labor-management relations and many theorists recognize that there is a range of possible bargaining solutions and that a determinant solution is not appropriate for a theory of the bargaining process. Some bargaining models assume that the parties have perfect information about the world around them and their opponents.[4] That is, that each bargainer has complete information about the needs, desires, and motivations of the other party. Again, most theorists recognize the weakness of such models.

Given this basic introduction to the elements contained in various bargaining models, we now examine in more detail two distinct theories of the collective bargaining process, the Walton and McKersie and the Kuhn models. The first theory to be discussed is the contribution made by Walton and McKersie.

A BEHAVIORAL THEORY OF LABOR NEGOTIATIONS: Walton and McKersie[5]

In their classic work, *A Behavioral Theory of Labor Negotiations*, Walton and McKersie advanced the proposition that the process of labor-management negotiations is not a single process. Rather it is comprised of four different subprocesses: The first subprocess is referred to as *distributive bargaining*, the second is *integrative bargaining*, the third is *attitudinal structuring*, and the fourth is *intraorganizational bargaining*. Each of these subprocesses, according to the Walton and McKersie framework, is distinguished by "its own function for the interacting parties, its own internal logics, and its own identifiable set of instrumental acts or tactics."[6] Under the distributive bargaining subprocess, the parties bargain over division of a particular pie under which the gain by one party is a direct loss to the opponent. In theoretical terms this approach can be described as a *fixed-sum game*. Negotiations over many issues can be described as distributive bargaining.

As contrasted with distributive bargaining, under the integrative bargaining subprocess both sides search for solutions that would increase the size of the pie. In game theory models, this approach is referred to as a *variable-sum game*. Under this subprocess the objectives of both parties need not necessarily be in conflict as the case is in distributive bargaining. An example of a problem that might be solved through integrative bargaining is the development of an employee-assistance program, which would help bargaining unit members with alcohol or drug problems. Such a program may help management improve productivity and provide help for union members.

The third subprocess introduced by Walton and McKersie is attitudinal structuring. Distributive and integrative bargaining refer to negotiations between unions and management. Attitudinal structuring represents a major departure from components contained in other bargaining theories. This subprocess of negotiations defines the quality and type of relationship between labor and management. Attitudinal structuring encompasses the efforts, intended and unintended, by the parties to shape their opponents' behavior. While Walton and McKersie acknowledge that attitudinal structuring can be influenced by such factors as the technical and economic context of the workplace, the social value system and the personalities of negotiators, they hypothesize that the negotiators' own behaviors can influence the attitudes and behaviors of their opponents.[7] The understanding of this subprocess is important because history and past behavior of negotiators can influence the success of current bargaining. The review of this subprocess suggests that a conflict-prone relationship may embody a set of attitudes which would make it difficult for the parties to move to a more cooperative relationship. In contrast to tactics used within distributive or integrative bargaining, in which the objective of a tactical move is to change the position of the other party on a particular issue, in this subprocess, the parties may engage in activities unrelated to specific bargaining issues. An example of such an activity would be the granting of concession as a means of gaining the trust of the opposition. The first two subprocesses of bargaining can be thought of as issue-oriented decision-making processes, while attitudinal structuring describes the atmosphere prevailing at the bargaining table and the tactics that the parties can employ in order to change that atmosphere.

The fourth subprocess that Walton and McKersie present is intraorganizational bargaining. It is the only one of the four subprocesses of bargaining that usually takes place away from the bargaining table. Intraorganizational bargaining refers to the internal negotiations taking place within each party. Walton and McKersie recognize that neither the union nor management represent a homogeneous constituency. On each side there are individuals with many conflicting views and interests. Each side must resolve some of these internal conflicts before it can reach a settlement with its opponents. On the management side of the bargaining table, intraorganizational bargaining takes place among various staff and departmental interests. On the union side the larger the bargaining unit, the greater the potential for internal conflict. Industrial units composed of different occupations, skills, age groups, and minorities provide union negotiators with ample opportunities for intraorganizational bargaining.

Walton and McKersie's theoretical and tactical framework of the four subprocesses of labor-management negotiations represents an important contribution to the literature of bargaining theories. First, they allow us to view collective negotiations not as a unidimensional contest of labor versus management, but rather as a complex process of distributive, integrative, and intraorganizational bargaining—as well as attitudinal structuring. Second, they suggest the existence of a strong link between bargaining behaviors, tactical decisions, and the goals of the parties to negotiations. In their view, by observing behaviors we can infer much about the goals of the parties. They claim that "the behaviors which we call distributive bargaining are indices for inferring goal conflict or perceived goal conflict."[8] Third, their framework suggests that any single action by a union or a management negotiator can contribute to a multiplicity of responses within the four subprocesses. For example, a threat made by a negotiator may further that negotiator's goal on a single issue in the distributive bargaining subprocess. At the same time, this action may affect the potential for future discussion of a problem in an integrative bargaining subprocess. The threat may make it difficult or even impossible to engage in integrative bargaining. Further, that same threat may have an adverse effect on the attitudinal structuring subprocess; thus it may have a negative effect on the existing and, perhaps, even future negotiations, Finally, that same threat may either satisfy or dissatisfy the constituency of the party making the threat, thus influencing the content of intraorganizational bargaining. Therefore, Walton and McKersie suggest that if union or management negotiators focus solely on a particular tactic within one subprocess, ignoring the linkages among the subprocesses, such action may lead to an unintended chain reaction, affecting adversely the other subprocesses. It is interesting to note the close parallel between this hypothesis and the overall plan of negotiations advanced by Reed Richardson in *Collective Bargaining by Objectives.*[9]

To conclude, Walton and McKersie provide us with an analytical framework for subdividing labor-management negotiations into the four subprocesses and thus give us a better understanding of the linkages among subprocesses and the tactics and behavior of negotiators. In the next section we discuss the theoretical contributions toward the concept of bargaining power made by Alfred Kuhn.

THE BASICS OF TRANSACTIONS—AND OF POWER, THE KUHN MODEL

Workers' loss of power in the transition from a feudal to an industrial society two centuries ago sparked the formation of unions, and the relative power of employers and unionized workers has been a central concern of their relationship ever since. The purpose of the following sections is to diagnose the nature of power, with some introductory notions about its care and feeding. The basic nature of power is much the same across many areas. Hence, in studying power in connection with union—management relations we will also be acquiring some understanding about important aspects of relations between nations, firms, husband and wife, or the president and the Congress.

A study of power is not the same as a study of negotiations. The first deals with the basic capacity to achieve desired results and the second with actual use of that capacity in a given situation—roughly the difference between a boxer's general strength and skill and his actually landing punches on an opponent in a given fight. Part of this section focuses directly on power only. In doing so it nevertheless identifies the kinds of components that are manipulated during the course of negotiations.

Before proceeding to the details of the present model, we note that it differs substantially from the bargaining models most widely introduced in connection with collective bargaining, such as those of Nash, Harsanyi, Pen, Zeuthen, and the like. Among the other models that deal most specifically with collective bargaining it more clearly resembles the approach of Walton and McKersie.[10] In other respects it more nearly parallels the approach to power found in connection with exchange theory in sociology, though with sharper definitions and analysis.

To proceed now to the model itself, several terms are needed for the analysis of power. Things people affirmatively want are *goods*. Goods can also be thought of as things a person will give something of value to get or receive. They could also be termed *positive goods*. By contrast, things people want to avoid or get rid of are *bads*. These are things one may give something of value to prevent or to have removed, and could also be termed *negative goods*. As we shall see, power is concerned with the kinds and quantities of goods and bads involved in interactions between parties.

Goods and bads have very broad meanings here. Goods include not only such marketable things normally dealt with by economists as bread, automobiles, or haircuts. They also include such relatively personal and nonmarketable things as praise, affection, sense of worth, or friendship. Bads are not marketable in the same sense as goods, since people will not give anything of value in exchange for them. The varieties of bads will be detailed later in connection with discussion of their uses.

A *transaction* is any interaction between parties in which goods or bads are exchanged. For certain purposes, a transaction may be defined more strictly as an interaction analyzed with respect to the values—goods or bads—involved.[11] Any set of negotiations in which a union and management establish the terms on which labor will be sold is a transaction. In the present approach, power and bargaining power are aspects of the analysis of transactions.* *Power* is the ability to get wanted goods from another party, and *bargaining power* is the ability to get them on good terms—that is, by giving relatively little in return. The meaning of these terms will be amplified later below.

In making a decision one weighs costs and benefits. If the benefits of a given course of action outweigh its costs it can rationally be accepted. If costs exceed benefits the action is rationally rejected. A transaction does not move us away from this basic condition of rational behavior. Instead, it moves us to a relationship in which each of two parties must make a decision, and in which the interaction will not be concluded unless the benefits equal or exceed the costs simultaneously for *both* parties. A transaction is thus seen to involve two *mutually contingent* decisions. Note that two mutually contingent decisions are *not the same* decision. In fact, the two decisions must be different or there can be no transaction. For example, in an exchange of my boa constrictor for your trailer hitch, I must decide whether to give up the boa and receive the hitch and you must decide whether to give up the hitch and receive the boa. One might say loosely that we both agree to the same thing, the exchange. But, more strictly, we can jointly agree on the exchange only if we separately decide that to me the hitch is worth more than the boa and to you the boa is worth more than the hitch. Only if the benefits equal or exceed the costs *to each of us separately* will the transaction be concluded. Hence, our analysis will focus on two separate but mutually contingent decisions.

Let us confine attention for the moment to transactions in goods, calling the two parties A and B and the two goods X and Y. A already possesses X and B already possesses Y. To A the benefit of the exchange is that A acquires Y. The cost is that A must give up X. Thus, A will decide to make the exchange if to him or her the value of Y (the benefit of the exchange) exceeds the value of X (the cost of the exchange). For the moment, we will ignore possible costs or benefits of the exchange process itself, as well

---

*This usage of "transaction" differs substantially from that used by Eric Berne and his followers.[12]

as some other items that we will return to later. A transaction cannot take place on the basis of *A*'s decision alone. *B* must also agree. This *B* will do if to him or her the value of *X* (the benefit of the exchange) exceeds the value of *Y* (the cost of the exchange). If to either party the cost and benefit are exactly equal, that party is indifferent as between completing and not completing the transaction. For simplicity, we will assume arbitrarily that all cases of indifference are resolved in favor of completing the exchange.

In short, *if* the benefits exceed the costs for *A and if* the benefits exceed the costs for *B*, *then and only then* will the exchange of *X* for *Y* take place. Thus, the exchange depends on four values: the value of *X* to *A*, the value of *Y* to *A*, the value of *X* to *B*, and the value of *Y* to *B*. We will call these four values, respectively, *AX*, *AY*, *BX*, and *BY*, and identify each more explicitly. For those who prefer it, *utility* may be substituted for *value* in any of these usages. Even more specifically, we may think of *subjective expected utility* if we wish to remind ourselves that all costs and benefits are ultimately subjective, and that actions are based on images and expectations rather than on reality, as such.

AX: The value of *X* to *A*. If *X* is a commodity, *AX* can also be described as *A*'s desire to keep *X*, or as his reluctance to give it up. If *X* is a service, *AX* is *A*'s desire not to perform it, or his reluctance to do so. "Desire not to perform" means such costs to *A* as the the time, effort, risk, frustration, money, materials, or adverse side effects, of performing the service. Adverse side effects could be particularly relevant when *X* is the giving of permission to *B*. In any case, *AX* is the cost to *A* of going through with the transaction.

AY: The value of *Y* to *A*. If *Y* is a commodity, *AY* is *A*'s desire to have it. If *Y* is a service, *AY* is *A*'s desire that *B* perform it. In either case, *AY* is the benefit to *A* of going through with the transaction.

BX: The value of *X* to *B*. With appropriate substitution of terms this is the parallel of *AY*.

BY: The value of *Y* to *B*. With appropriate substitution of terms this is the parallel of *AX*.

We can now express the relation more simply.

$$\text{If } AY \geq AX,$$
$$\text{and if } BX \geq BY,$$

then the exchange of *X* for *Y* will take place. Strictly speaking, a number of ancillary assumptions should be added, but we will mention only two. One is that neither party has any desires relative to the transaction other than those regarding *X* and *Y*. A second is that neither party through miscalculation terminates the negotiations by adamantly refusing terms that do, in fact, fall within the limits of acceptability to him. If those conditions prevail, we can thus say that *A* has the power to get *Y* while *B* also has the power to get *X*. Thus, in this approach, power is never a trait or characteristic of one party taken alone but is always the position of one party in a particular relation with some other party. Furthermore, the greater the amount by which *AY* exceeds *AX* and/or the greater the amount by which *BX* exceeds *BY*, (1) the greater is the likelihood that the transaction will actually go through and (2) the greater is the potential gain in utility to one or both parties. We will also say that the greater the likelihood that the transaction will take place, the greater is the power of *A* to get *Y* and the greater is the power of *B* to get *X*.

Thus, we see the core of power—that one party holds something valued by another party, which he or she can give or do if the other in return will give or do something wanted by the first party. More briefly, power resides in the ability to grant or withhold things wanted by others. We will see later why this statement also holds for power based on bads, like strikes, threats, or violence.

We said above that the greater the amount by which AY exceeds AX the greater is the likelihood that the transaction will take place, and hence the greater is A's power to get Y.* This means that A's power to get Y increases as AY increases, in parallel with the way his or her power to get a new corner cupboard that he or she would make increases with the intensity of his or her desire for it. A's power to get Y also increases as AX decreases, since the less reluctant A is to give us X, the more likely A is to do so and thus to get Y. That is, A is more likely to make the corner cupboard if A is more willing (less reluctant) to give the time and effort to make it. On B's side, we can make parallel statements about the way his or her power increases in proportion to the amount by which AX exceeds AY.

Another conclusion follows. If A's power to get Y rises, and if A gets Y by giving X to B, then B's power to get X also rises along with A's power to get Y. That is, in an exchange of goods A's power and B's power rise and fall together; one does not rise at the expense of the other. This aspect of power is recognized inadequately in the literature on power, though it is at least implicitly clear in economics, in Adam Smith's invisible hand. In this respect it differs sharply from bargaining power, to which we now turn.

Bargaining Power

Thus far we have dealt with transactions as if the goods involved were indivisible—a boa constrictor for a trailer hitch, a bowie knife for a hunting bow, a naval base for a treaty of friendship. We next discuss the *terms* of the exchange—the question of how much X will be given in return for how much Y. That is the question of *bargaining power*, which is the ability to get relatively much in return for relatively little—to get favorable terms in a transaction. We will illustrate with a transaction in which X is a divisible good, money; Y is an indivisible good, an automobile; A is a potential buyer; and B is the seller.

Each party must choose between two goods, the one to get and the one to give up. For convenience, we can join these two items for each party, and say that one party's *Effective Preference* is his or her net desire for the good held by the other. For A, this means A's desire for Y, or AY, minus A's desire to keep X, or AX.** If effective

---

*All statements of relationships of this sort are to be construed as assuming that other relevant factors remain unchanged—the traditional *ceteris paribus* assumption of economics.

**This could also be expressed as the desire for Y measured or expressed in units of X, or AY/AX. The reasons for preferring AY-AX to AY/AX are detailed in Kuhn. The more obvious reasons are that we typically think of a net gain from some action as the benefits *minus* the costs, not as benefits *divided by* costs. The former permits the net position to be a negative sum, or loss, as often happens in real life. By contrast, the "worst" position with the use of a fraction would be to approach zero. A further drawback of the fraction is that it wipes out any sense of absolute magnitudes, expressing the relationship of a battleship to a cruiser with a number of the same size as for the relationship of a match to a toothpick.[13]

preference is shortened hereinafter to EP, *A*'s desire for *Y* can be referred to as *A*'s EP for *Y*, or simply as *A*'s EP. An EP is a one-party equivalent of effective demand. This is desire backed by purchasing power, in which *A*'s desire for *Y* is the demand, or preference aspect, and the *X* offered in return is the purchasing power, or effective aspect. The explanation of *B*'s EP parallels that of *A*. We will illustrate bargaining power with the purchase of a used car because the price of cars is typically both negotiable and worth bargaining about.

You, *A*, are looking at a used Philander 6 automatic, and so on. Having examined its condition, your desire for the car (*AY*) and your desire not to part with your money (*AX*) are such that you would be willing to give as much as $2600. As shown in Figure 10−2, this means that your EP for the car extends to $2600, which may also be thought of as your *reservation price*, or the price above which you would rather keep your money than acquire the automobile. A reservation price is the most a buyer will give for an item or the least a seller will accept. Given the dealer's desire for money (*BX*) and his or her desire not to give up the car (*BY*), he or she would be willing to sell for as little as $2400. That is the reservation price, presumably reflecting the dealer's best assessment of what he or she thinks can be gotten from someone else. We will assume for the moment that you and the dealer are equally good negotiators. You eventually split the difference and settle for $2500, at *S*, as in Figure 10−2.

Let us now assume different conditions. Your EP extends instead to $3200 and the dealer's extends to $3000. After negotiations you settle for $3100, as in Figure 10−2(b). The terms are better for you in 10−2(a) ($2500) than in 10−2(b) ($3100). That is, you get a lower price in the first case than in the second: your bargaining power is better (greater). By contrast, the dealer would get better terms in the second case, which means that his bargaining power is greater in Figure 10−2(b) than in 10−2(a). Thus, unlike "plain" power, the bargaining power of the two parties moves in opposite directions. The dealer's goes up as your goes down, and vice versa. (We will never compare the bargaining power of the two parties directly, as by saying that *A* has more bargaining power than *B*, or vice versa.)

Let us examine some other situations. In Figure 10−2(c) we show your EP back in its original position at $2600. But the dealer's EP is now longer than in 10−2(a), extending to $2000 instead of to $2400. Still assuming that you are equally good negotiators and split the difference, what are the consequences? The settlement, *S* now occurs at $2300, compared to $2500 in Figure 10−2(a). By contrast, 10−2(d) shows the dealer's EP back to its original position of $2400 but shows your EP extended to $3000. Now the midpoint settlement has risen to $2700.

The main principles about bargaining power are now clear. Starting from any given position and with relative bargaining skills unchanged, either party's bargaining power rises with an increase in the other party's EP and decreases with an increase in his own EP. That is, the more intensely the other party wants what you have, the greater is your bargaining power, and the more intensely you want what he has, the less is your bargaining power. More formally, each party's bargaining power varies directly with the other party's EP and inversely with his own. These generalizations are equally true if one party is consistently more skilled at negotiations. The settlement terms, *S*, then fall consistently toward one end of the overlap rather than at the

FIGURE 10.2

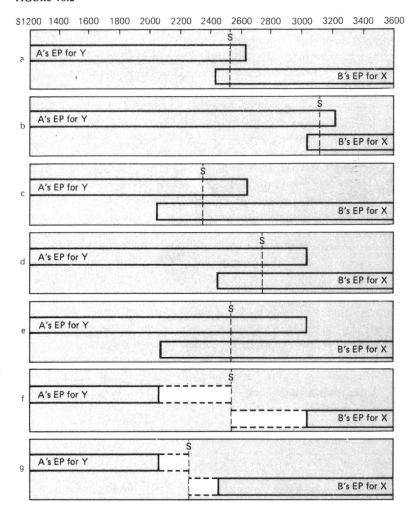

midpoint. But S moves with changing EPs in the same way as stated above, as you can readily test for yourself.

What happens if *both* EPs increase? If they increase by the same amount, no change in bargaining power results, as can be seen by comparing Figure 10−2(a) with 10−2(e). In the latter both EPs have increased by $400, but the midpoint remains unchanged at $2500. If the EPs change by different amounts, bargaining power shifts in favor of the party whose EP increases less, as you can readily test. Incidentally, one cannot relate power or bargaining power to the *length* of EPs, since the length depends on the wholly arbitrary point of origin in the diagram. It is relevant, of course, to note *which* EP changes most during negotiations, and whether either EP extends to some particular point, such as a set of terms proposed by a mediator.

We now shift to a transaction that will not necessarily go through. In Figure 10−2(f), your EP extends to $2000 while the dealer's extends to $3000. There is no overlap, and if the EPs stay that way no transaction is possible. We can call this gap between EPs a *negative overlap* of $1000.

In one sense, it seems pointless to talk of bargaining power when there are no terms on which you can get the car or the dealer can get your money. But let us compare Figure 10−2(f) with 10−2(g). In 10−2(g), your EP remains at $2000 while the dealer's increases to $2400. And, whereas the midpoint terms in 10−2(f) are $2500, in 10−2(g) they have dropped to $2200. Though this is of no use to either party if matters stop there, certainly *A*'s prospects look better in 10−2(g) than in 10−2(f). Thus, the previous generalization still holds: that *A*'s bargaining power is improved by an increase in *B*'s EP.

The same reasoning can be applied to (plain) power. For any given EP of *B* that does not overlap *A*'s, the longer *A*'s EP the closer *A* will be to overlapping *B*'s and getting the car. The longer *A*'s EP, the less distance *A* will have yet to go to get the car, or the less of a hurdle will remain to be overcome. If the EPs do overlap, then the greater *A*'s EP, the greater is *A*'s assurance that he will get the car, even if at a higher price. With this background we can now state the relation between power and bargaining power more simply. In transactions where terms are not already given (are negotiable) then, other things equal, the more you want something from someone else the more likely you are to get it but the more you will probably give for it. The more the other party wants what you have, the more likely you are to get what he has and the less you will probably have to give for it. In short, with respect to a given transaction, an increase in the other party's EP is all in your favor; an increase in your own EP is a mixed blessing. Parallel statements apply to *B*.

TACTICS AND STRATEGY

We have examined the effects of EPs, and of changes of EPs on power and bargaining power. We now shift from that general analysis to the question of how a party to a particular transaction can improve its position relative to that of the other party. Within the framework established above, two logically distinct questions arise, even if the means of utilizing them are often not clearly distinguished. Expressed from *A*'s point of view, the first question is: Assuming that the EPs of both *A* and *B* are given and are unlikely to change in consequence of negotiations, what can *A* do to achieve a settlement as near as possible to his own end of the existing overlap of EPs? We will use the term *tactics* to refer to such attempts to achieve the best possible settlement for oneself *within a given set of EPs*. We next remove the assumption about EPs being given. The second question, then, is: How can *A* seek to change one or both EPs in ways advantageous to himself? We will use the term *strategy* for any attempt by a party to alter the EPs themselves as a means of achieving a more satisfactory outcome. Although these definitions are somewhat more specific, they parallel the more general usage in which "strategy" refers to certain relatively long range or wide scope of action, while "tactics" typically accept the "strategic" situation as given and operate more narrowly within its limitations. The difference between tactics and strategies can be summarized in their present meaning by saying that the purpose of strategies is to influence the *position of the overlap* of EPs, whereas the purpose of tactics is to influence the location of the settlement *within a given overlap*. Given these clarifications, we can now define *negotiations* more precisely as the utilization of tactics and strategies to improve one's power or bargaining power in a transaction.

Let us note first some situations in which the EPs may be essentially immovable and tactics alone could be brought to bear. One example would be negotiations over the price of a car, in which the buyer's upper limit is firm because he or she can acquire an identical automobile for that amount just down the street. The dealer's EP is also firm at a price that has already been offered by another customer who is still eager to buy. Another example might occur if the negotiators are agents whose principals have set firm limits on the terms they will accept.

Strictly speaking, *tactics* deal with *beliefs* about the magnitudes of EPs, not with their actual magnitudes, and with attempts to manipulate those beliefs. The normal use of tactics is to try to learn the true length of the opponent's EP and then either to conceal one's own EP or to understate it as just meeting or barely overlapping the opponent's. The party who can successfully effectuate that tactic will achieve a settlement near his own end of the overlap and channel to himself nearly all of the jointly available gain of utility from the transaction. The most obvious use of strategy is to try to lengthen the opponent's EP while resisting any increase in one's own, or possibly shortening it. Given the complexities of human relationships, there is no limit to the ways in which tactics and strategies can be used. It is also possible that a move by a party designed to have one effect might also produce the other instead or in addition. For example, a union leader might say, "You know, the strike isn't really hurting our members very much!", intending the remark as a tactic to impress management that the union's EP for an early settlement *is* quite short. But the remark might cause management to think more carefully than it had done before about the real consequences of a long strike. Here we see a strategic effect of a move intended as a tactic. It is probable that the parties often do what they do with only an intuitive feel for its effect on the other party. And it is highly improbable that the parties consciously think of their actions as being tactical or strategic. That is the language of the textbook, not of the parties. Nevertheless, it is well for the student to know that there is a definite logical difference in nature and effect between tactics and strategy.

Hostility, Generosity, and Assorted Other Motives

Bargainers sometimes want to get what they can and do not care whether the other party is pleased or displeased. The desire to get as much and give as little as possible is a *selfish* stance. Not caring whether the other party is pleased or displeased, helped or hurt, is an *indifferent* state. The combination is selfish—indifferent, but for brevity we will call it simply *selfish*. Most union-management bargaining is selfish.

But bargainers are not always indifferent. Because of liking or sympathy they may want to help the other party or to hurt him out of anger or frustration. We will call the first attitude *generous* and the second *hostile*. Both can easily be accommodated in the above model. One's desire to help the other is represented by a generous extension of one's own EP, long if the generosity is large and short if it is small. Conversely, a desire to hurt the opponent contracts one's EP. Generosity or hostility could either reflect one's present feelings or be a means of influencing the opponent's feelings at some future time.

Other motives can similarly be accommodated, and we will cite just one. If *A* wants to leave the impression that *A* is a tough bargainer, *A* will seek better terms than his or her EP for *Y* alone might call for. This is logically the same as a greater reluctance to give up what *A* has. It shortens *A*'s EP, and thereby raises *A*'s bargaining power but decreases his or her power to get *Y*. A desire to appear "reasonable" would have the opposite effect. Other motives, like impatience to get the negotiations finished, can similarly be traced.

Bads as Strategies

We have defined *strategy* as the attempt to change EPs, usually by increasing the other party's desire for the good one has to offer. Sometimes, however, a party can alter an EP by imposing bads on the other party. Bads include criticism or insult, fear, pain, stench, destruction, frustration, insecurity, disease, noise, distraction, ugliness, or invasion of privacy. A bad can also lie in withdrawing or reducing the rate of providing a good, as in reducing a worker's pay, turning off a tenant's utilities, or calling a strike. Although pain and destruction are bads for almost everyone, what are goods or bads often depends on the persons and the situation.

A bad is almost necessarily a "service" rather than a commodity, as with inflicting pain, blowing up a truck, or calling a strike. It is not so much *things* that are bads, but the fact that, say, garbage has been dumped on your lawn, your tires have been slashed, or your income has been cut off. Bads play a large and apparently inescapable role in union-management relations for reasons spelled out below.

A Unique Property of Union-Management Relations

To have power or bargaining power, a party must be able to withhold something wanted by the other. When a union bargains with a management over, say, a wage increase, the thing wanted by the union is the increase, which management can withhold until the union can provide a sufficient inducement. The other half of the relationship, however, is unusual. The thing wanted by management is labor. But whereas the union bargains on behalf of workers, it does not *own* labor in the same sense that management owns money or the factory. In fact, during the life of a contract most employers operate under a management security clause something like:

> The right to hire, lay-off, discharge for cause, promote, or transfer employees is the exclusive prerogative of management, except as otherwise provided in this contract.

Although the contract may then say something about *who* is to be laid off, promoted, or transferred under certain circumstances, and provide for due notice, due process, or severance pay, under the typical contract the employer's unilateral right to increase or decrease his or her work force is unrestricted. Most contracts also outlaw strikes, slowdowns, or lockouts for the life of the contract. Even when the contract expires, the parties do not normally bargain over the quantity of labor, only over the rate of pay for whatever number of workers the employer chooses to hire and are willing to work.

In short, the union cannot get what it wants, like a wage increase, without first winning the agreement of the employer. But by the acts of hiring and operating from day to day, the employer continues to get the main thing he wants, labor, without even consulting the union, much less winning its agreement. Because the employer can withhold what the union wants but the union cannot withhold what the employer wants, the goods-based bargaining power in this basic relation lies heavily with the employer. As noted elsewhere herein, the power inherent to both sides would be more nearly comparable if a wage decrease rather than an increase were to be negotiated. So would it be if the management had to get the agreement of the union before it could increase or decrease the work force, change methods of production, or transfer employees to different work assignments. Thus, under conventional concepts of management rights, it is not merely unorganized employees who have little bargaining power with management, but also organized employees, until and unless they are prepared to strike.

There are, of course, exceptions, as when employees must be recruited through a union hiring hall, or the union effectively restricts the supply of workers. Some contracts specify the size of a work crew, though even those arrangements normally allow the employer to expand or contract the number of crews. In any case, these exceptions do not undercut the statement that employers generally can increase or decrease their work force without winning agreement from the union. True, a tight labor market raises the union's bargaining power. But it also raises the bargaining power of unorganized workers and hence can hardly be said to be the result of unionization. In short, a union cannot withhold labor in the same simple way that a car dealer withholds the car if you do not pay an acceptable price. The employer already "has" the labor. The only way the union can exert power, as contrasted to simple persuasion, is to be conspicuously unpleasant—to impose a bad on the employer in the form of a strike. As with any other bad, its purpose is to lengthen the employer's EP; hence, it constitutes a strategy.

Strategic bads involve two stages, imposition and relief. Whether one or both parties impose a bad on the other, they do not negotiate about imposing the bads. They negotiate about relieving them, and the bargaining about relief can come either before or after the bad is imposed. In a *stress transaction*, the bad is imposed first and the parties negotiate about relieving it. In a *threat transaction* the parties negotiate first, and the relief consists of not imposing the bad later if satisfactory terms are negotiated.

To provide power or bargaining power a bad must be relievable, the relief being the good, relatively speaking, that is bargained for. Kidnappers or hijackers, for example, destroy their power if they kill their hostages, as there then is no way they can undo or relieve the bad. The bad of a threat to burn a house actually lies in the promised good of *not* burning the house if the threatener's terms are met. This is the basis for the earlier statement that all power and bargaining power lie in the ability to provide goods, even if a bad must first be imposed to lower the satisfaction level from which something will look good. One must, of course, have the capacity to provide (produce) the bad, even as one can acquire power through goods only if he can produce the goods. To return to the main point, it is not unionization, as such, that provides bargaining power to workers; it is the ability through collective action to cut off the flow of labor to the employer—the ability to withhold—that provides the power. The sequence of events through which that power is made effective will be taken up in the next chapter, on negotiations.

Union-management relations typically involve both threat and stress. The threat comes first—"Agree to this or there will be a strike." As we shall see, the threat is nearly always present implicitly, even if no one ever mentions it. If the threat does not produce agreement, it is eventually converted into the stress of an actual strike. The threat stage involves the implied promise *not to apply the bad* if agreement is forthcoming. The stress stage involves the promise to *relieve the bad* if agreement is reached. The typical union-management relation is that of a threat that can later be converted into a stress. A strike can do this because it is relievable. By contrast, a threat to burn your house cannot be converted to stress because it is not relievable. Whereas a struck employer can be changed back to an unstruck employer, a burned house cannot be similarly changed back to an unburned one.

For convenience in introducing the concepts, we have separated stress and threats into relatively "pure" cases. Many real cases involve combinations or mixtures. For example, although strictly speaking the harm of a threat would come at some later point, to continue living under a threat is itself a form of stress, and may bring larger concessions than would be induced by the desire simply to avoid the eventual execution of the threat itself. In the reverse direction, a continuing stress often carries an implicit threat that the stress will be intensified if concessions are not forthcoming—as that an arm will be twisted harder or that a strike will be supplemented by boycott or violence. Such complications may make it difficult for an observer to know precisely what is going on in some real situation. But to the extent that one can know, the stress-threat analysis will help one to understand it.

THE IMPLEMENTS OF BARGAINING POWER IN COLLECTIVE BARGAINING

Violence

In light of the above general theory of power, let us look at some of the devices typically thought of as implements, or weapons, of unions and managements. First, the history of violence is long and checkered. Violence by employees against company property, customers' plants, or even company officials has occurred from time to time through the history of the labor movement, and is still fairly common in connection with strikes by such groups as miners and teamsters. As used against employers, violence tends to be counterproductive. We have seen that violence already executed holds no power or bargaining power. It can, of course, perform the tactical function of making the threat of subsequent violence more credible, but it is perhaps more likely to bring a hostile contraction of the employer's EP. If used by strikers against employees who continue to work, it may intimidate them into staying home, and thereby increase the pressure on the employer. Through most of our history prior to the 1930s, local police, private detectives, company guards, the army, or the national guard typically supported management, and often used coercive methods to break strikes and intimidate strikers. Harlan County, Kentucky, was by no means the only place where a union organizer stood a large chance of being shot or beaten. In many places, attempts to unionize were viewed as treason and were treated accordingly. Prior to the protections introduced by the Wagner Act, this violence against union members or organizers was often effective. Violence by labor is typically sporadic and done without union approval, because its usual effect is to turn the public and the police against the employees. Particularly during the thirties, there was evidence that employers sometimes secretly arranged to have their own properties damaged (slightly!) because of the adverse publicity the union would receive in consequence.

Employer Weapons

Employer "weapons" fall into two distinct categories. The first is to prevent or to eliminate the very existence of a union. The *blacklist* was a list of employees known to be active in or sympathetic toward unions. This would be circulated among employers, who would refrain from hiring any listed person. The *yellow-dog contract* was an agreement, which an employee was required to sign before receiving a job, that he or she would not join or support a union. A *company union* was an organization of employees financed and dominated by the employer, used to ward off "real" unionization. Sometimes highly effective, sometimes not, these practices are now outlawed. Nevertheless, there are claims that computerized blacklists are currently used in some places, with information about attendance at union meetings gathered with the help of local police and transmitted among communities through the police communications network.[14] More recently, some managements have sought to ward off unionization by treating their employees so well that they feel no need for a union. To be effective, this approach will probably need good methods of handling individual employee complaints and grievances. Another weapon increasingly employed by management is the use of professional "union-busting" labor relations consultants. A proliferation of specialists has sprung up to assist management in the creation of a "union-free environment." A wide variety of services is offered, ranging from seminars and training packages to on-site personalized consulting.

The second category of management weapons comprises those that try to increase the employer's bargaining power in negotiating with the union but without seeking to undermine or eliminate the union. Some companies have apparently automated farther than production costs alone would justify, so as to make themselves almost strike-proof. Some petroleum refineries and telephone exchanges, for example, can operate almost indefinitely without their unionized work force, even if certain repair, maintenance, and installation services must be postponed. Multiple plants doing the same thing (horizontal integration) make a company less vulnerable, as it can produce and ship from nonstruck plants if others are struck. Large textile companies have been most conspicuous examples, though some food processing, auto parts, and retailing are also involved. Diversification, or conglomerate structure, is a variation on the same theme. Even though the whole of a conglomerate's production of one product may be shut down, profits overall may be little affected because other subdivisions keep going. Multinational operation is a still more extended version of the same thing, although it may be hard to know, perhaps even by those who make the decisions, how much of the motivation behind it is to strengthen bargaining power with employees. Threats to close a plant and move its operations elsewhere, particularly to the South or Southwest, are sometimes pure bluff. But actual movements occur often enough to lend them credibility. Selling a plant to a larger and stronger employer occurs occasionally. Anticipatory inventory accumulation can help minimize a firm's costs during a strike. Strike insurance also strengthens management's hand, and has been used, among other places, by the airlines and by the Western (lettuce) Growers Association.[15] Of course, whenever a strike might be a means of inducing an employer to recognize the union (an organizing strike), any move which increases the management's bargaining power also raises its ability to prevent or eliminate unionization itself.

Boulwarism utilizes (among several other things) the adoption of an adamant stance by the employer at the outset, with the proclamation that the company will not budge no matter how long the union might strike—though this technique was declared, after some years, to be a refusal to "bargain in good faith" and thus a violation of the law.

A final question about "weapons" involves management's response to a strike. Some fully accept the mutual nature of the strike pressure, as detailed in Chapter 3. When a strike is called the company simply stops production until agreement is reached, in a behavior that is the core of the "accommodation"[16] approach. Others attempt to operate despite the strike, perhaps using wide publicity to urge strikers to return to work before a settlement has been reached with the union, or even hiring new employees. This behavior is know as the "power" approach.[17] It also typically appeals to employees over the heads of their leaders, seeking to drive a wedge between employees and union. Therein it contrasts with the accommodation approach, in which the employer deals only with the union itself, on the assumption that its officers are just as much the proper representatives of the employees as the executives are of the stockholders, and that they should not be bypassed. The power approach often leaves doubt as to whether the company is really trying to get rid of the union, rather than merely acting to increase the company's bargaining power.

Union Weapons

Union "weapons" also fall into two categories. The first is the effective primary strike, with all other weapons falling into a second category. In essence, *the* union weapon is to shut down the employer's operations—to stop production. This is the union's means of utilizing power, whether the objective is to win bargaining gains from the employer or to pressure him into dealing with the union. Except for what is already "in the pipelines," an effective strike stops the flow of income to the employer. However, if the employer continues to operate during the strike, using either regular employees or striker replacements, this primary strike is not fully effective. "Primary" here means that the employees who have a complaint act directly upon the employer from whom they want concessions. When the primary pressure is not effective, secondary pressures may be attempted. On the input side, these seek to enlist the cooperation of employers or unions who produce or deliver materials to the primary employer to stop doing so. For example, if the primary employer is a clothing manufacturer, a textile mill supplier might stop weaving or shipping cloth, or truckers might refuse to deliver it. On the output side, consumers might be asked to stop buying the struck clothing, retail stores might be asked to stop handling it, or (again) truckers might be asked to stop delivering it. These indirect actions are know as secondary boycotts, though some more strictly resemble strikes. We have already noted in Chapter 3 that most of these devices are illegal. It is important to note that secondary pressures only seek to do what the primary strike has failed to do—to stop the primary employer's operatons. If the primary strike is fully effective, secondary pressures are largely irrelevant.

Picketing is purely symbolic, or informational, if the employer shuts down when struck. No one is trying to go into the plant to work, so pickets are not needed to per-suade them to stay out. On the other hand, if the employer seeks to operate during the strike, the presence or absence of a convincing looking picket line may determine whether workers will stay out or go in. Thus, although it is the union that activates picketing or secondary pressures, it is mainly the employer's behavior that determines whether there will be any perceived need for them. The union's felt need for secondary pressures is likely to be greatest if the employer hopes to prevent or eliminate the union itself, rather than merely to resist bargaining concessions more readily.

Several variations of strikes are used at times. In a *slowdown*, employees stay on their jobs but work at a much-reduced pace, sometimes by the simple stratagem of meticulously following every detail of the employer's rules and regulations. Since the employees come to work and get paid, this is an effective strategy if they can get away with it, as it can hurt the employer considerably while costing the employees nothing. A "sick-in" is often used by professional or public employees, particularly if they are technically forbidden to strike. Here many employees call in as sick instead of coming to work. These and other variations are essentially partial strikes.

SUMMARY

The union is an agent of protest, not of management, a sort of permanent opposition party that never comes to power. Although it may have peripheral influence on the way these matters may affect employees, the union does not make, or even normally participate in, decisions about what the employer will produce, the techniques, plant location, expansion or contraction of plant, financing, distribution of profits, invest-ment, or diversification. In fact, the union is not even a factor supplier, in the sense that a utility supplies power, a textile plant supplies materials, or a bank supplies capital funds. It is merely the collective attorney, so to speak, for nonsupervisory employees. As such, the union has no means of exercising power on the employer (as contrasted to persuading the employer that something the union wants is also good for the employer), except by being dramatically unpleasant. This is done mainly by the strategic bad of stopping the flow of labor by means of a strike. Shutting down the plant is the means of exerting bargaining power. Only rarely is it designed to destroy the existence of the firm.

Whereas a company cannot operate without a management, it can operate without a union, and many managements would prefer it that way. Hence, management behaviors toward unions take two distinct forms. The one is to try to prevent or eliminate the existence of the union; the other is to raise management's bargaining power in dealing with the union, but without challenging its existence. In analyzing the devices used by employers, it is therefore crucial to understand whether they are directed against the existence of the union or merely against its bargaining power. Along similar lines, if someone is said to hold proemployer or antiunion attitudes, does this mean that he or she favors the elimination of the union, or merely that he or she wants the employer to be relatively stronger in bargaining?

NOTES

[1] Samuel B. Bacharach and Edward J. Lawler, *Bargaining: Power, Tactics, and Outcomes* (San Francisco, Calif.: Jossey-Bass, 1981), p. 4.

[2] *Ibid.*, pp. 4–6.

[3] *Ibid.*, p. 6.

[4] *Ibid.*, p. 6.

[5] Richard E. Walton and Robert B. McKersie, *A Behavioral Theory of Labor Negotiations* (New York: McGraw-Hill, 1965).

[6] *Ibid.*, p. 4.

[7] *Ibid.*, p. 5.

[8] *Ibid.*, p. 9.

[9] Reed Richardson, *Collective Bargaining by Objectives*, 2nd ed. (Englewood Cliffs, N.J.: Prentice-Hall, 1985).

[10] Walton and McKersie, *op. cit.*

[11] A. Kuhn, *The Logic of Social Systems, A Unified, Deductive, System-Based Approach to Social Science* (San Francisco: Jossey-Bass, 1974), p. 174.

[12] Eric Berne, *Transactional Analysis in Psychotherapy* (New York: Grove Press, 1961); *Games People Play: The Psychology of Human Relationships* (New York: Grove Press, 1964).

[13] Kuhn, *op. cit.*, p. 180.

[14] Ed McConville, "Dirty Tricks Down South, " *The Nation*, February 9, 1980, pp. 142–45.

[15] For the latter, see Richard Steven Street, "The Lettuce Strike Story," *The Nation*, January 19, 1980, p. 48.

[16] B. Selekman, S. Fuller, T. Kennedy, and J. Baitsell, *Problems in Labor Relations* (New York: McGraw-Hill, 1964). See also Chapter 3.

[17] *Ibid.*

THE APPLICATION OF THE BARGAINING THEORY MODEL

11

In the preceding chapter we spelled out a theory of transactions and of power and bargaining power therein. That theory is very general and applies equally to relationships among people within a family, a government, a school, an international crisis, a company, a union, or between a company and a union. As we noted, the model starts with a basic selfish stance, but it can easily be modified to accommodate generosity and hostility (liking and disliking) and the exchange of bads as well as goods. Negotiation, by contrast, is the process of actually carrying through a transaction under conditions where the terms are not fixed. By "fixed" in this sense, we mean that if the price of a beer at the bar is a dollar you buy or do not buy, but you do not negotiate over the price. The study of negotiation is thus the application of transactional theory to particular cases, in much the same sense that engineering is the application of physical sciences to particular problems. Like any other theory, it can be applied for two main purposes, the one to help understand the process and the other to help practitioners do it better. The present chapter will merge the two, on the comforting assumption that to improve understanding will also help to improve performance.

A fundamental difference between theory and practice is that the former can be relatively simple while the latter may be fantastically complicated. To follow the analogy of the preceding chapter, it is something like the difference between knowing the basic principles of boxing and knowing what to do second by second in an actual fight.

We will proceed as follows. We will start with a simple case, or model. This model will be defined by listing the factors that we will include in our analysis, and the more obvious ones we will exclude. To it we will apply the concepts and principles of power and bargaining power from the preceding chapter. As a first step, we will assume that the parties do not even contemplate the possibility of a strike. As a second step, we will examine the situation after a strike is under way, tracing the consequences of the strike upon negotiations. As a third step, we will reason backwards. Having noted the actual effect of a strike on negotiators, we will next try to trace the way negotiators will think and behave if they know that a strike is distinctly possible, but has not actually been called. Between steps two and three, we will relax several assumptions of the model one at a time to see the effects of various changes of circumstance.

THE SIMPLE MODEL

Statement of the Model

In the preceding chapter we described a general model of power and bargaining power, with only occasional references to the union-management relationship. In this chapter we construct a more specific model of the collective bargaining relationship, and then analyze it by applying to it the principles from the general model. We will assume throughout that the negotiation is over the renewal of an expiring contract, not over grievances or unfair labor practices. For the initial analysis we will adopt nine additional assumptions. These will then be relaxed one at a time to trace their consequences. These assumptions are as follows.

1. The negotiators have the necessary authorization to conclude and sign a contract, without referring it back to their principals for ratification.
2. The negotiators for both sides feel secure in their positions. They do not feel that their job tenure or income is significantly dependent on the outcome of their negotiations.
3. The negotiations are "wide open" and "for real," under conditions of substantial uncertainty about the outcome. They are not window dressing or a mock fight to amuse or impress observers. More specifically, the EPs* of either party may change significantly in response to pressures or persuasion from the other.
4. The union is recognized and secure, which status is known and accepted by both parties.
5. There is no concern that the company either will fail or be taken over by another company.
6. It is a single-employer, not a multiemployer, relationship, and the employer has no branches or divisions elsewhere that are represented in the negotiations.
7. The employer is private, not a branch of government.
8. The parties focus solely on the present contract. They give no thought to its possible tactical or strategic effect on subsequent negotiations of their own or on any present or future negotiations in any other bargaining unit. Among other things, they are not concerned with the way the images they present in the present negotiation may affect the response they will get in the future.
9. The parties do not contemplate arbitrating the terms of the new contract, though they do arbitrate grievances. Mediation either is not present or is not a factor in determining the outcome of their negotiations.

---

*Defined in the preceding chapter.

Incidentally, this list of things that are *not* involved in the initial model is a modest indication of the complications that *are* often involved.

We will further assume only two issues: The union wants a wage increase and the management wants a relaxation of seniority rules. On a straight cost basis, management would prefer no increase in wages. But management knows it must be able to hold and recruit employees and wants to avoid the possible withholding of effort that may follow if employees feel they are not receiving a reasonable wage. The union in a simple sense is willing to take as high a wage as it can get but is aware that the company must stay competitive and might have to be uncomfortably demanding of worker's effort if the wage is too high. As to seniority, the union would prefer to keep the present clauses, but the issue is not a burning one with its members. The management figures that looser seniority could reduce the wage bill by about 2 percent.

On the question of wages alone, management thinks a 5 percent raise would be about appropriate in light of labor and product market conditions and the recent rate of inflation, but would be willing to go to 7 as a gesture of good will. The union thinks that company productivity has risen much faster than the national average, and that there should be some increase in real earnings over and above an adjustment for inflation. The union is initially unwilling to settle for less than 15 percent. As shown in Figure 11-1(a), the initial actual EPs of management and union as extending to 7 and 15 percent, respectively. The parties start bargaining on wages alone for the moment.

There seems to be little doubt that each party's own EP is the same as what Walton and McKersie[1] call its *resistance point*. It represents that party's minimum acceptable terms, or the least it will accept. Walton and McKersie also use the concept of *target*, or the amount each side will shoot for. "The target of one is usually selected in a way that represents the best estimate about the other's resistance point"[2]—that is, one party's best estimate of the other's EP. The terms "target" and "resistance" are not used here "officially," but it is clear that our approaches differ only in the language involved. The particular approach used here appeared initially in Kuhn.[3]

NEGOTIATING

Using Tactics and Strategies

The parties obviously do not open by stating their true EPs. Management opens with an offer of 4 percent and the union demands 20, as shown in Figure 11-1(a). Each side knows that its opening proposal understates its own EP and confidently assumes that the same is true of the opponent. Hence, the opening proposals are not really credible. In plain English, each side is lying if it states that its opening proposal is the "most it will give." Whether at this or some subsequent point the core problem of tactics is to be able to retreat from a given position (i.e., acknowledge that you were lying about the true position of your EP), but nevertheless to remain maximally credible the next time you state a position. If by retreating you have revealed that you were lying the first time, why should the opponent not assume that you are lying this time, too?

FIGURE 11.1

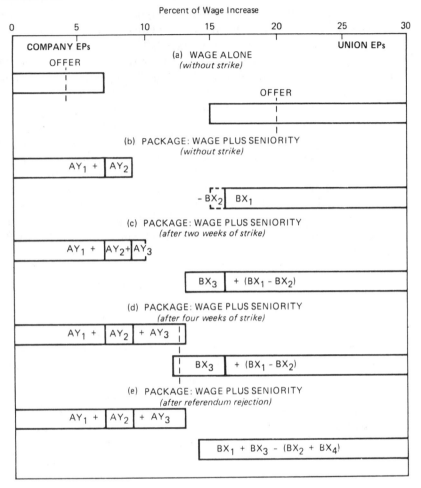

Since tactics interweave with strategy, let us shift to strategy for the moment, which usually is the attempt by one party to lengthen the EP of the other. The union may assemble data to show that the present wage not only has failed to keep pace with the cost of living but has also fallen behind both the industry and the labor market. If the data are convincing (which they might be under assumption 3), the employer may come to realize that it will take a larger wage than anticipated *to meet his or her own objectives.* Quite regardless of what the employer considers a good tactical move at the moment, the consequence may be an increase of his actual EP, say to 8 percent. On the other hand, the company might be able to gather data to show that it is already above its competitors, and that unless it slacks off in the rate of wage increases, jobs may be lost to the local union members in consequence. If these data are convincing, the union's EP may grow longer—that is, the union may be willing to accept a lower wage than before.

Now let us look at some possible interplay of tactics and strategy. Whether or not they are convincing strategies, the data may play a tactical role, known as the *new information* gambit. Management representatives could pretend to look thoughtfully at the union's data and then call a recess to talk among themselves. On returning they could say, "We were not really aware of how we stood relative to others. On the basis of this new information we are willing to offer you 6 percent." By pretending to learn something new, management could thus retreat without losing face—that is, without implicitly admitting that its prior statement of its position was false. The union might similarly use management's data to rationalize a graceful retreat.

But still further subtleties can surround the use of data. Suppose one side submits certain statistics in the belief, possibly correct, that the other party is not fully aware of certain relevant facts. If the statistics are to have their strategic effect of actually lengthening the other party's EP they must be "good." That is, under critical examination they must demonstrate what the party submitting them says they demonstrate. But therein lies a risk. You cannot expect your opponent to be influenced by the logic of data without implying that you yourself would be convinced by them. But after you have submitted data, suppose that the opponent can demonstrate that they are wrong, or that they mean something different than you said. Your position may then be weaker than if you had not submitted the data at all. In short, don't push statistics too hard unless you are sure they are solid, or you may get caught in their backlash.

Let us trace just one more stage of subtleties. To perform a bona fide strategic purpose, data must be "good," as stated. To cover a tactical retreat under the face-saving guise of "new information," it does not matter directly whether the data are good or weak. However, if (say) the union's figures are so obviously flawed that management could not reasonably have been convinced by them, it is then clear that for management to attribute a retreat to "new information" found in the union data is pure face-saving. And that leads to the next step—that if some move is very obviously a face-saving device it won't save much face. But even that is not the end of the line. If the union negotiator sees through the face-saving device, should the negotiator nevertheless pretend that he or she didn't, and accept the management's new position as a sincere change of heart? Although there may be exceptions, the general answer would be *yes*. The reason is that while you strengthen your own position by making it difficult for yourself to concede, you also strengthen it by making it easy for the opponent to concede. In simple behaviorist terms, reward the kind of concessions you want to encourage, don't punish them. These observations, of course, are all reciprocal.

With this perspective we can see that, except under extraordinary circumstances, total candor is simply not possible. One side cannot reveal its true EP at the outset. Nor can it frankly report whether the opponent's argument has or has not been convincing, or whether it does or does not see through the other side's tactics—though we will discuss later some conditions under which mutual frankness may develop.

What one communicates is crucial. In this respect, the stances one takes and the concessions one does or does not make may communicate far more than one's arguments. For example, once a party has stated a position there is a double edge to concession.[4] The first is the "appeasement" effect. Tactically, the concession may be taken as evidence of weakness, suggesting that the conceding party's EP is much longer than claimed. And, strategically, it may provide the opponent with a scent of smashing victory and bring a shortening of *his or her* EP. Either effect will tend to produce a hardening of the opponent's position and reduce the likelihood of counter-concessions. The opposite edge tends to soften the opponent. Tactically, it may suggest that the conceding party is strong and confident enough to be reasonable but will make no further concessions unless there first are some counterconcessions from the opponent. Strategically, any concession by one party comes closer to being acceptable to the other and may raise the latter's hope of an early settlement. Here either the tactical or the strategic effect will tend to induce a softening of the opponent's position and increase the likelihood of counterconcession, possibly bringing settlement. Nothing in the theory (i.e., no assumption in the present model) gives any clue as to which edge of concession will cut. Intimate knowledge of the personalities and the situation can be helpful. But even that is not infallible.

Commitment—as Tactic and Strategy

Suppose you say during negotiations, "This much will I concede, but no more." If your opponent feels absolutely sure that you won't concede any more, that is a fact of life that must be accommodated. By contrast, if your opponent believes that your brave words are pure tactical bluff, he will not make further concessions, at least not till some additional ones have been prodded out of you. Thus, there is great value in being credible when you take a firm stand. The question then is: How can you make your position credible when there are such obvious reasons for you to bluff? The answer is to demonstrate that you cannot afford to go back on your word. The way to do that is to make clear that there is some stake you will lose if you do *not* keep your word, and that you would lose more from forfeiting the stake than you would gain by breaking your word.[5] The act of putting yourself in a position to lose a stake is called *commitment*, and it is a crucial factor in many negotiations. Since a stake is a thing of value, its introduction into the bargaining relation affects the length of at least one EP and hence is a strategic ingredient. A clear illustration is a side bet. Suppose I am asking $110,000 for a house and you refuse to offer more more than $100,000. As I am trying to convince you that it is worth even more than I am asking, you show me an irrevocable bet (your stake) that you will pay $20,000 to some third party if you pay more more than $100,000. Since I know the house is not worth what it would cost you, including your stake, I am stuck. Either I must let you have the house for $100,000 or lose the sale. The cost of the commitment to you is that you have burned your bridges. If I later come down to $105,000 or you later would be willing to come up to $110,000, you no longer can get the house.

Union and management negotiators use stakes other than bets. The negotiator's own position could be a stake. "The union members (or top management) would throw me out on my ear if I give another inch," if credible, is one way to show that a negotiator cannot afford to make another concession. "I have gone on record that I will resign if I concede any more than this offer" may lend credibility to a stance, especially if accompanied by a confirming headline in the local paper. "The union members simply won't work for less than 15 percent" is no less credible, just because both sides know that the union negotiators deliberately worked them into believing they deserved that much and could surely get it if they are tough enough. (Needless to say, a union president's threat to resign if the company does not improve its offer would be ill advised if the company should happen to *want* a new union president! It could also lead to a company jibe during negotiations, like, "Hey, can we really count on that?" Commitment by the company could take the form of a well-publicized announcement that it will close the plant and move elsewhere rather than pay more than it has already offered.)

In an ongoing and repeated relationship, the credibility of credibility is perhaps the most persistent stake. Once having made a commitment, a negotiator will lose credibility if he or she backs down. Hence, a commitment may carry weight for no reason except that the opponent recognizes that the first party's credibility is at stake. The games played around commitment are mainly the following. The first is to avoid making a commitment until you are sure you are prepared to stick with it. A second and related one is to arrange a way to back out of the commitment—a way known to yourself, but not to the opponent. The third is to prevent the opponent from making a commitment, and the fourth is to find a way for him to get out of his commitment gracefully if he does make one.

Not making a commitment hardly needs illustration, though the temptation to "get tough" is not always easy to resist. One way to back down from a commitment is to have couched it in words that sounded firm but were actually flexible. "I won't budge till hell freezes over" could be followed eventually with, "I hear the fuel shortage has even reached down there!" Another way is to invoke some previously unsuspected third party: "My doctor just told me my blood pressure won't allow stringing these negotiations out any longer," "I heard the president's speech last night about inflation and I guess we all have to sacrifice a little," or "We just got a new report from accounting that shows things are a bit better than we thought." (These third-party retreats are also variations of the "new information" tactic.) One way to stall off the opponent's commitment is seemingly to stay flexible enough so that the opponent does not seem to need a commitment. Another way to avoid the opponent's commitment, which is also a way to make it seem reversible, is to ignore or downplay it, perhaps by rewording it. For example, if the opponent says, "I absolutely will not budge one more step!" one can reduce the seeming firmness of this commitment by responding, "I fully understand why you said you would not want to go beyond your present offer." One might also subtly refer to some third party who could be used by the opponent as a scapegoat to cover a retreat. Other devices will be seen below in the relationship between the negotiators and their principals.

We illustrated commitment earlier by a side bet in connection with the purchase of a house, showing that it could lead to the loss of the sale. Once one party has made an irrevocable commitment, the other party can hurt only himself if he makes a parallel but nonoverlapping countercommitment. As we will see shortly, however, the unique feature of a union-management negotiation is that the parties *must* agree eventually, and the transaction cannot fail. The consequence is that, even if one party seizes the initiative by making an irrevocable commitment, the other may be just cantankerous enough to respond with its own commitment. If so, one or both will eventually have to back down. The dilemma of commitment is that it is most effective if there is *no way out*—but it is risky indeed to leave no way out. Luck!

To the extent that commitment is a means of affecting the credibility of alleged EPs it is tactical. To the extent that it actually alters EPs it is strategic. The effects of commitment, as well as the devices that are appropriate to counter a commitment, differ as between the tactical and strategic elements, even if negotiators are not always aware of their precise intentions.

More than One Issue

Though initially we mentioned two issues, wages and seniority, we have thus far dealt only with wages. Let us now add seniority, continuing the assumption that to the company a loosening of the seniority clauses would save it 2 percent of labor cost. The union dislikes the proposed changes. While any translation of a nonmonetary provision into money value is conjectural, let us assume that the union would grant the loosening in return for an additional 1 percent in wages. Regarding the package of "wage plus loosened seniority," in Figure $11-1$(b) AY_2 represents the additional amount the company would give for the loosened seniority. The EP is extended because the package is worth more to management than is the wage settlement alone. By contrast, the union's EP is shortened by 1 percent (marked $-BX_2$) to 16, because the package is worth less to the union than was the wage alone. The gap between the EPs has narrowed by one point, since the management's EP has grown by two and the union's has shrunk by only one. But they still do not touch.

All the earlier statements about tactics and strategy still apply, with the further complication that the parties may now play back and forth between the two issues. Any number of additional issues can similarly be included in this system by simply extending or shortening each EP, depending on whether the item has positive or negative value to the party. The difficulties of actually keeping track of all the issues and their interrelations will probably rise much faster than the number of issues. But no new principles are needed to understand the logic of more-complex sets of issues.

Strike as Strategy

It is obviously possible that the EPs of the parties could have been different than we showed in the preceding section, that they could have overlapped, and a settlement could have been reached. But we left them with a gap between their EPs. Let us

FIGURE 11.1(b)

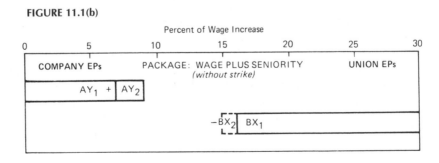

assume that they have continued to negotiate for a long time, and it is clear they will not agree. What next?

We now come to the crucial difference between the union-management relationship and most other purchase and sale relationships. If you go to an automobile dealer and fail to reach an agreement on price and trade-in, after a reasonable amount of discussion you leave. You do not make the purchase. The dealer does not make the sale. You part company, perhaps permanently. To move a little closer to the union-management relation, suppose a soft drink bottling plant has had a continuing contract with a sugar company to provide sweetener syrup over the past year. The contract has terminated, and the parties have negotiated about renewing it. But they cannot agree on price and delivery terms. So they stop doing business. The sugar company sells its syrup somewhere else, or perhaps simply sells less, and the bottling company buys its sweetener elsewhere. Here, too, the break may be permanent.

The unique feature of the union-management contract is that the parties *must agree,* even if they *don't agree.* True, there may be some circumstances when company and union can "take their business elsewhere." But they are the rare exception, which we need not deal with here. Any one contract is a particular bargain, subordinated to a longer run, underlying agreement that the parties will continue doing business with each other. In fact, they do not have to "agree" even on that. Once a union is recognized, the circumstances are such that they can hardly do otherwise. The question then is: How, in a free society, do we get parties who do not agree to agree? In terms of the present model: What can be done to extend one or both EPs till they overlap? Changing the EPs is a question in strategy, so the question is thus one of finding an effective strategy.

This is performed by the strike or (as we shall see in the next section) the perceived possibility of a strike. Like the bottler and the sugar company, after a failure to agree the union and management part company. And as might be expected in most other relationships, it is the seller stopping delivery, rather than the buyer refusing it, that constitutes the overt act of breaking the relation. The seller stops because he or she has not been promised a price that is acceptable.

But there the similarity ends. Whereas the break in an ordinary commercial relationship may be permanent, this one is viewed from the outset as temporary—not a termination of the relation, but a pause that will strategically push EPs until agreement is reached. The EPs grow because the strike has costs. These costs lengthen EPs in the same way that the employer's desire to remove the costs of a tight seniority clause lengthened his EP in the illustration above.

The strike was traditionally thought of as a union weapon. However sensible that view may be for certain stages of employer-employee relationships, in a disagreement over contract renewal in an established relationship it is at least a mutual weapon, and it is an open question whether it is useful to consider it a weapon at all. The costs it imposes on *both* parties are the inescapable consequence of a failure to agree. there is no a priori reason to assume that the strike is the *fault* of one party or the other, since either side could have avoided it by asking less or conceding more. The employer could, of course, initiate a lockout. But we have seen that it is normally the seller who stops delivery. We have also seen that management is in charge. It does what it likes, and automatically wins most disputes until and unless the union takes some protest action. Because of both inflation and rises in productivity, wage movements are typically upward. When a contract expires, wages tend to stay as they are until the union wins management's agreement to change them. If wage movements were typically downward, then it would be management that would have to win the union's agreement for a change, and lockouts would presumably be more common. But let us get on with the effects of strikes on EPs.

The Costs as Strikes Continue

Any attempt to recalibrate the cost of a continuing strike with a given amount of wage change is likely to be crude and conjectural. But, however inaccurately, people do—in fact, must—make such conversions. For the ensuing discussion, we do not assume that these estimates are necessarily accurate, but that they are the best the parties can do, and that they *do* serve as a basis for their behavior. We need not detail here whether the costs to management are those of lost sales, lost production, customer ill will, deterioration of raw materials or equipment, continuing fixed costs, or permanent loss of some customers. We also need not detail whether the costs to the union are those of lost income to employees, depleted union treasury, political battles within the union, loss of public sympathy, or something else. Again, we will simply assume that the decision makers for both sides can compare the costs of continuing the strike with the benefits of settling it, and can translate those costs and benefits into some equivalence with contract terms. The relevant costs of continuing a strike are, of course, always prospective, not historical, by which we mean the expected costs for some particular future period of the strike. Some typical kinds of costs are summarized in Table 11−1.

Let us now assume that a strike has been in effect for two weeks. The company has been able to make deliveries to its customers out of inventory, and expects to be able to continue to do so for another two weeks. The main anticipated financial burden for a strike lasting that long will be some overtime costs to rebuild inventory after the end of the strike. This is calculated to cost about 1 percent of the annual wage bill. As shown in Figure 11−1(c), that amount is represented by AY_3, which, when added to the company's EP, extends it to 10 percent.

The union members get no strike benefits from the international for the first

TABLE 11.1.

Strike Costs	
Labor's Costs	*Management's Costs*
1. Wages/union resources	1. Operating profits/market position
2. Institutional security	2. Status with constituents
3. Management goodwill	3. Labor goodwill
4. Public image	4. Public image

Table adapted from Information in Walton & McKersie, Behavioral Theory of Labor Negotiations, *pp. 31−32.*

FIGURE 11.1(c)

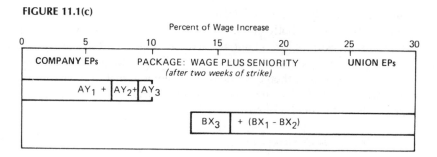

several weeks of the strike. Hence, the strike is shown as having been a significant financial burden on them. That amount is represented as BX_3 in Figure 11–1(c), and it extends the union EP to 13 percent. (To simplify visual representation, the negative effect of BX_3 is incorporated by reducing the length of the main portion of the EP bar.) The gap between the union and management EPs is still 3 percent, so no settlement occurs.

Two weeks later the company EP has grown considerably, because inventories are used up and customers are starting to shift to other suppliers. AY_3 is therefore enlarged, so that the entire company EP now extends to 13 percent, as shown in Figure 11–1(d). On the union side, AX_3 has grown by only one more point, mainly because the international union has started paying strike benefits. However, the EPs now overlap, and after some rounds of tactical maneuvering the parties agree on 12.5 percent.

Before going into a further complication, let us restate a central aspect of the above. The purpose of strategic moves it to lengthen the opponent's EP and possibly to shorten one's own. The portion of each party's EP that is directly related to the strike is a direct function of its own cost of continuing the strike. Hence, the frequent statement that the greater the cost one can impose on the opponent (lengthening EP), and the less the cost to oneself of imposing it (limiting one's own EP), the greater is one's bargaining power. The related tactic is to pretend one's EP is shorter than it actually is, which means to give the impression that one is not really hurting very much from the strike. It is the collective bargaining parallel of the boy saying, "Nah, it doesn't hurt" as

FIGURE 11.1(d)

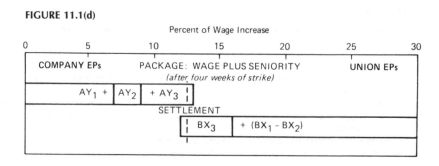

another tries to extract some goodies. If credible, it increases the opponent's estimate of how long he must endure and, with it, his willingness to settle.

Some Added Complications

As to a complication, in the preceding chapter we stated the relationship between power and bargaining power in negotiable transactions as: "The more you want something from someone else, the more likely you are to get it but the more you will probably pay for it." Once a strike is in effect, each party experiences a complex interplay among three pairs of ingredients. First, each party's EP is the resolution of its desires regarding the continuing costs of the strike. Second, each party's strength is affected by the continuing influence of the strike on both its own and the opponent's EP. And third, both the power and the bargaining power of each party change as the strike progresses. We cannot trace all the possible interrelationships here, but we can identify several. To illustrate the first item above, the more intensely the union wants the strike costs to end, the greater will be its EP and the less its bargaining power. However, the more the union wants the substantive contract gains, the more willing it will be to endure (not want to end) the continuing costs of the strike. The effect of this desire is to shorten the union's EP to end the strike and hence to increase its bargaining power. The model does not predict whether the lengthening or shortening effect will be greater. But both can be diagrammed in the model, as was done with BX_1 and BX_3 in (b), (c), and (d) of Figure 11−1.*

Regarding the relation between the first and second points above, the longer the union can hold out the more will management's EP be lengthened and the union's power *and* bargaining power be increased. The willingness and ability of the union to hold out is a straightforward matter of its plain power, in which the preference aspect of its EP is mainly its desire for the substantive gains and the effective aspect is mainly its financial resources for continuing the strike. To return to the original statement, the more the union wants the substantive gains, the more likely it is to get them because the more willing it will be to endure the strike costs till management gives in. The difference between "giving" stress (a bad) and giving goods in a transaction is that in the former the increased cost is that of implementing the stress, whereas in the latter it is a higher price paid to and received by the other party. Another way of saying it is that

---

*Note the possible contrary effects of intensity of desire, depending on the context. Taken as a straight transaction, without a strike, the union's intense desire (large BX) for a given item (X) to be received from management would lengthen the union's EP and make it willing to give more of other items (Ys) as concessions to management. That is, the greater BX, the greater is the cost the union would be willing to accept to acquire X. However, when a strategic bad has been imposed, in the form of a strike, this increased cost to the union does not take the form of larger concessions to management on other matters, which would be to management's advantage. Instead, this larger cost takes the form of the union's enduring a longer strike, which works to management's disadvantage. Thus an intense desire by the union can cut either way. It improves management's position in seeking to settle without a strike, but worsens management's position once a strike has been called. To keep the terms straight, this greater willingness/ability to endure a longer strike represents greater *plain* power. The concomitant worsening of "terms" is represented in the acceptance of larger total costs, in the form of concession costs plus strike costs. Like other aspects of power and bargaining power, this one is reciprocal.

with strategic bads one uses up some of his power as the cost of producing stress, which stress then provides both power and bargaining power. As with the other generalizations about power and bargaining power, the above apply reciprocally to management as well.[*]

We have now demonstrated the crucial role of the strike in union-management relations. It is not normally some unfortunate, aberrant event (though it is sometimes both) in the life of industrial relationships. It is the crucial strategic ingredient that lengthens one or both EPs far enough so that the parties who *must* agree eventually and with rare exception *will* agree. Those who contemplate outlawing strikes had better think carefully about what they would substitute for this force in a free society. The alternatives are not as easy as they might seem, as will be seen in the chapter on "Impasse: Resolution and Regulation."

RELAXING SOME ASSUMPTIONS

To diagnose the union-management relation step by step, we opened the chapter with a list of simplifying assumptions, which assumptions constituted the model we are analyzing. We have discussed above the core problems of negotiations, first without the possibility of a strike, and then with a strike, but all within the confines of the original model. In this section, we will relax those assumptions one at a time so as to see the consequences of different conditions. In doing so, we may or may not mention the strike, but the effect of most of the altered assumptions is much the same whether a strike is or is not in progress or contemplated.

Principal and Agent Relations: Assumption 1

Let us first relax assumption 1—that the negotiators had the necessary authority to conclude negotiations and sign a contract. Let us assume instead that the terms agreed upon by the negotiators must be submitted to the union membership for ratification. They turn down the 12.5 percent. But the vote does not specify what they *would* accept. After some inquiring, the union negotiators conclude that the members would probably accept 14 percent. Therefore, they return to post-referendum negotiations with an EP shown in Figure 11−1(e) as extending to that amount. The members' reluctance is designed BX_4 and is introduced as a negative quantity, shortening the union EP. Management's remains at thirteen. There is the additional possibility that a settlement agreed to by the management negotiator will be turned down at the top level, as when an agreement reached by the president of a university could later by turned down by the board. Rejection on the management side is far less frequent, however, since it is easier for negotiators to keep in touch with the small number of top decision makers on the employer side than with the large number of members on the

---

[*]Whether one offers goods or bads to another party as an inducement, he or she must be able to "produce" them. A major difference is that since bads are "services," they must be "produced" directly for or upon the other party to the transaction. By contrast, tangible goods can be produced, accumulated, or otherwise acquired quite without regard to the party, if any, with whom they will eventually be exchanged.[6]

FIGURE 11.1(e)

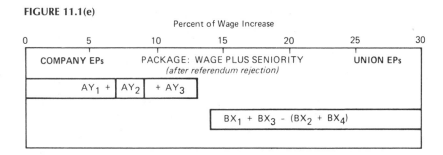

union side. Hence, management negotiators can more easily avoid agreeing to anything without advance assurance that it will be accepted.

There is no need to pursue the details thereafter. Management's EP may extend further as the costs of the strike continue to rise. Or it might shorten as they conclude from new information that a raise of 12.5 percent would wreck them competitively. Meanwhile, the union EP might start to grow again as the strike grinds on and members start facing foreclosed mortgages and repossessed TVs. Conversely, they may grow highly hostile toward the employer, swallow their losses, and shrink their collective EP. In any event, at some point a settlement ensues.

In addition to ratifications, the relation between agents and principals can also be used as tactics. One form is a relatively weak commitment, as in "I can't accept your proposal because I am positive my constituents would not accept it." The reverse is to use the relation as a means of backing out of a commitment, as, "I personally can't accept your proposal, and I feel sure my constituents won't either. But for whatever it may be worth I'll take it back and ask them." The negotiator could then return to his constituents with any of three main approaches. One is a simple question: "Are you willing to accept this?" A second is a *sub rosa* recommendation that they reject it if the negotiator feels a tough refusal will bring greater concessions from the opponent. The third is a recommendation to accept if he or she is convinced there will be no further concessions by the other side. The face-saving description when the negotiator returns from constituents to deal again with the opponent could be, "They sure surprised me. They accepted (rejected) even though I felt sure they would reject (accept)." This face-saving tactic can be used even if the constituents did exactly as the negotiator expected them to do—in fact, even if they precisely followed the advice of the negotiator.

Still another principal-agent relation can be used as a form of commitment and is easier for management than for the union, particularly if the top authority consists of only one or a few individuals. An instruction may be given to the negotiator, such as "Get the best settlement you can. But do not under any circumstances go above 15 percent or I'll fire you." The executive can then remain incommunicado on a fishing trip in the wilds of Canada till negotiations are finished. The main cost to him or her is—like that of any other irrevocable commitment—that no change of mind is possible even if changed conditions should warrant it. An additional cost is that the executive is also unavailable to handle dire emergency or sudden spectacular opportunity. Of course, there are ways to be inaccessible for some purposes but not for others, though to that extent the commitment is not wholly irrevocable.

Negotiators' Security: Assumption 2

Let us next relax assumption 2—that the negotiators for both sides are secure in their position. Substitute that a union election is coming up in several weeks. In it the union president will have to run against an insurgent who has raised considerable support for his assertion that the incumbent is soft on management and generally not aggressive and militant enough. The incumbent, a principal negotiator, is now under pressure to "really do something" for the members. The result will be a shortening of the union's EP. If the management likes the present union president and dislikes the challenger its EP will lengthen by the amount of that preference. If the management likes the challenger but not the incumbent its EP may shorten. The consequences of any of these changes upon the relative bargaining power of the parties can readily be traced.

Another way of conceptualizing this relationship is that there is a secondary transactional relationship going on between the union members, as principals, and the union negotiators, particularly the union president, as their agent. The main ingredients of this transaction are that the members give the officers votes, salary, and support of various sorts, and the officers give their services, including hard fighting over the terms of a contract, in return. Details of this relationship are spelled out under the heading of "intra-organizational bargaining."[7] Few repercussions of these relations will be included here.

Negotiations as Drama: Assumption 3

The need of the negotiators to look good in the eyes of their principals can be used in numberless ways as both tactics and strategy. This aspect can be discussed best if we simultaneously relax assumption number 3, that the negotiations are "for real," and assume instead that negotiations are to some significant extent a drama enacted for the benefit of the principals. In the extreme case, the negotiations are a tournament with rich trappings, all of which look very impressive as the audience alternately cheers, boos, groans, and perhaps bets. But it decides nothing, because both fighters already know how it will come out. They may know because the environment points to an outcome that is clearly visible to both. Or they may reach agreement early by subtle communications not perceived by the onlookers. Such a show is more likely to be staged for the benefit of the union audience than for management, mainly because of the more complex internal politics of the union organization and membership, notably its bottom-up structure that contrasts with the top-down structure of management.

Since a major function of the union is to get good things for its members from management, a union officer needs to look like a hard bargainer. There is no standard way to do this. Depending on the personality of the negotiator, it can range from name-calling and table-thumping to quiet and polite but dogged persistence. Since one is more likely to receive concessions if it is easy for the opponent to give them, management may get concessions more readily from the union negotiator if it accompanies its own concessions with some remark, possibly nasty-sounding, about the toughness and skill of the union negotiator. Further, if the union negotiator can make the management negotiators look tough and wily, he implicitly praises himself for having gotten anything at all from them. "You're a hard bargainer" and "Getting anything out of you is like getting blood from a turnip" are therefore much heard around the bargaining table. Though such remarks serve in part as tension-relieving banter, they can also be an indirect means of self-praise by praising the prowess of an opponent who has been met and matched. And all or most of this may be for the benefit of the audience, particularly on the union side. If praise of an opponent's wisdom, patience, skill, courage, or integrity should strengthen his position with his constituents, it could also free him to be more flexible.

When negotiations are mostly for show, so also may be the impressive charts, graphs, and diagrams that are introduced to "prove" the logic or justice of a position. If so, they are not instruments or strategy but simple gamesmanship. Under these circumstances, private conversations of the negotiators might include such exchanges as: "That industry survey I put up this morning had holes big enough to drive a truck through, and I really appreciate your not making a fool of me by pointing them out," or "Those price and profit figures I introduced were a perfect chance for you to save a big chunk of face. How come you didn't use them?"

Security of the Principals: Assumptions 4 and 5

Let us next relax assumption 4, that both parties are secure. Substitute first that the union is insecure and faces a decertification election in the near future. This condition will almost certainly affect the union's EP, though in which direction will depend on the circumstances. If the members have been thinking of the union as ineffective and weak in dealing with management, the effect may be to shorten the union EP. If management wants the union to be voted out its EP will shorten or lengthen, depending on which move seems most likely to turn the members against the union. On the other hand, if the company wants to build a secure and peaceable relation with the union, its EP will move in the direction that would solidify support for the union. These things, incidentally, illustrate why it is not possible to enforce literally the idea in the law that the employer should exert no power at all, as contrasted to persuasion, on the workers' choice of a bargaining agent.

We next relax assumption 5, that the company is financially secure. If, instead, the company faces imminent closing unless it can save money and become more competitive, and if the employees are as much in need of their jobs as many employees are, the union EP will lengthen considerably. In fact, it sometimes extends into the negative area of a wage decrease. See Chapter 18.

Multiemployer Bargaining: Assumption 6

Let us next relax the single-employer assumption, number 6, and substitute that the "employer" negotiator is the representative of a regional or industry-wide association of employers. Many things happen now, and we can mention only a few. First, disagreements within the employer side may be more difficult than those between the employer collectivity and the union. After all, the various employers are competitors, and some may be more interested in hurting their fellow members than in helping them. Second, a knowledgeable union negotiator may successfully exploit these differences. Third, the question arises whether the group should negotiate for uniform rates among them or merely for uniform rates of change, the latter leaving absolute differences intact. There is no one best answer, which depends on the circumstances and the parties. Fourth, and as the late George Taylor used to put it, the marginal firm becomes the darling of the employer association. Whether absolute levels of pay or rates of change are in contest, the firm that would most readily be bankrupted by a rise in wages is the one that limits the amount of increase for the whole industry. Whatever the basis of uniformity among the group, the most penurious employer has the shortest EP, which tends to become the EP for the whole group.[8] Hence, the union may want to make exceptions, so that the poorest employer does not limit the wage levels for the whole industry.

A coalition of unions bargaining with a single employer presents a sort of mirror image of the above. But the complexities are of a different sort that do not summarize easily, and we will not try to trace them here.

Public Employment: Assumption 7

Next let us relax assumption 7, that the employer is private, and substitute that the employer is a branch of government. There is an extended discussion of labor relations in the public sector in a later chapter, but one key ingredient should be mentioned here. We have observed the role of the strike in extending the EPs of one or both parties until they overlap and agreement is reached. In private employment the pressure is primarily economic, in the form of lost income to both parties. The unique feature of public employment is that while the employees lose income during the strike, the employer does not. Employer income comes from taxes, not from production and sale of goods. That income continues during a strike, while expenses in the form of wages and salaries go down dramatically. On strict economic terms, the employer is better off during a strike, and the pressure for settlement comes from citizens who are deprived of government services. That pressure may be particularly intense if police or firefighters are on strike, though it can also mount quickly when trash collection or snow removal is not done. That is, any pressure on the employer to settle is political, not economic. This situation more nearly resembles a strike in private employment in which the customers suffer more than the employer does, as is often the case in transportation and utility industries. In that respect, its underlying logic is much like that of public emergency strikes, as discussed in the impasse-resolution chapter.

Interrelated Negotiations: Effects over Time—Assumption 8

Assumption 8 was that the parties paid no attention to the possible tactical or strategic effect of their present negotiations on any other negotiation, whether by parties other than themselves or by themselves at some time in the future. Let us now relax that assumption and substitute first that in a present negotiation the parties may think about its effect on subsequent transactions between themselves.

Regarding tactics, their core is credibility. At least for the kinds of negotiations we are dealing with here, credibility is apt to be associated more closely with a person than with an organization. To take an obvious behavior, if a negotiator opens with grandiose demands and then later retreats great distances without even arguing very much, at the next contract expiration the other party will not take his opening demands seriously. Conversely, if a negotiator opens with a carefully planned position and retreats from it only for clear reason or under intense pressure, his opening demands will be given careful consideration the next time around. Hence, a negotiator must examine tactics, not only for their present effect but in light of their probable consequences over the years ahead. In fact, even one single outstandingly brilliant, stupid, considerate, or nasty behavior may affect the responses of others for decades.

To illustrate further, some negotiators feel uneasy if they do not logically justify every position they take. Others simply insist that they want what they want, and it is nobody else's business why they want it. The former tend to create some feeling of obligation in the opponent to justify *his* position, and a negotiator who is well prepared and logical may actually change the opponent's convictions. Here, too, a negotiator may need to think about the probable effect of his present behavior on subsequent negotiations. This fact then opens the next question. This is whether, having built one kind of reputation, one should play the expected role next time, or switch. For example, if you have built a reputation as a logical arguer, could a shift to stubborn inflexibility next time catch your opponent off guard? In short, is predictability a more effective instrument than unpredictability? There are no standard answers, which depend on great knowledge of detail in the particular situation—and even the wisest can be wrong. There is no reasonable doubt, however, that negotiators who develop high-level trust and understanding can cut through, perhaps avoid entirely, vast displays of window dressing and quickly get to the real core of the issues. Often, they can thereby speed agreement. Even if not, it can be immensely helpful if there can be an early identification of exactly what the points of agreement and disagreement are. Some negotiators who have repeatedly worked opposite each other report that they achieve subtle but reliable means of communicating, of which even they may not be consciously aware. Of crucial importance are signals that say, "Ignore this, it's just for effect" as contrasted to, "I'm serious about this one, so pay close attention." Readers interested in communication processes will recognize such signs as metacommunications, or communications about communications.

There are strategic as well as tactical relationships among successive bargains. If one side has won a very advantageous settlement in one year, it may relax and feel a duty to go a bit easy (display a longer EP) the next time. If the union accepted a substandard settlement one year because the company was in financial difficulties, it may expect reciprocal generosity by the company later when it is well heeled—and the company may feel obliged to respond. By the same token, if the union is confident that the company will be generous later when it has more money, the union will be more willing to accept a low settlement now. In short, not only do present behaviors affect expectations about the future, but expectations about the future affect present behaviors.

A settlement one year may affect certain economic realities of subsequent years, not merely expectations about them. For example, what the company agrees to pay now can affect its financial position, and hence its EP in bargaining, at the next contract negotiation. What the union settles for now can affect the financial position of its members, and hence *their* EPs, at the next negotiations.

Interrelated Negotiations: Effects over Space—Assumption 8 Continued

Continuing the relaxation of assumption 8, let us now move to interrelations among different negotiations that occur at more or less the same time but with different employers, whether they deal with either the same or a different union. Pattern setting is one such relation. Typically, the EPs of both parties are shorter if they are aware that they are pattern setters than if they are bargaining solely on their own behalf. For then any concession made by either union or management means a potential loss, not merely to the principals immediately involved, but to all other unions or managements, respectively, that follow the pattern. Knowledge that one will be a hero with the unions or managements elsewhere for putting up a successful fight may further shorten a negotiator's EP. So may a company's desire to stay within government wage-price guidelines, or a union's desire to display the power to break them. One of the interesting aspects of guidelines, or even of "controls," is that they may make any union that does *not* break them look ineffectual. (Union press releases can easily make *any* attempt at controls look like a management-government conspiracy against workers.)

A special pattern relation is that between different employers in the same competitive industry when they negotiate separately, particularly if wages are a high percentage of cost. In that case, the EP of any one employer may be shortened and that of its union lengthened, if it looks as if too high a wage may make the employer noncompetitive and lead to possible loss of jobs. Although wage data may be used with straightforward selfishness by both parties during such negotiations, both sides have some interest in a settlement that is in line with the rest of the industry. Fear of being out of line, of course, occurs with pattern followers, not with those who make the pattern. Whether in the same or different industries, pattern followers tend to have their EPs move at the outset of bargaining to roughly the position already set elsewhere. Since each party then knows to begin with approximately where the opponents' EP is, pattern-following bargaining is typically easier and quicker. Even a pattern follower, however, can have unique problems that drag out the negotiations. And some supposed pattern followers *may* hold out for something better (for the union or the management) than appears in the pattern. But the opponent's argument, "Others did it. Why can't you?", may be hard to answer convincingly. Other things equal, unions prefer to reach pattern-setting agreements with profitable and "flexible" employers while managements prefer the opposite.

There is no end to the number of possible tactical and strategic connections between one negotiation and another. Nor are the parties consciously aware of all these things normally, and they almost certainly do not categorize them in their own minds as tactics and strategies. Often, they may not discover the unintended consequences of their actions till it is too late. At the same time, there is much of what we have said here that the participants do sense intuitively, perhaps quite consciously, and they modify their behavior because of it. Furthermore, a good science of human behavior does not require that the actors understand the science, any more than a person's falling from a ladder requires that he understand gravity. There also is almost no end to the things we have not mentioned at all. Some of these are the role of the media, of self-image, or of political connections, the timing of a strike relative to public elections, the effect of a strike on national defense or international relations, sudden shifts in labor or product market conditions, and even the weather. You will have to fill in these details for yourself as well as that of agenda sequences in bargaining sessions.

BACKING AWAY FROM THE STRIKE

One might get the impression from the preceding discussion that most contract settlements come only as the result of a strike. The contrary is the case, with upward of 95 percent of all contract expirations being renegotiated without a strike. Why?

The first reason is that in some cases the EPs of the parties overlap without a strike or a strike threat—the first situation we examined. The second is more compelling. This is the mutual knowledge that if a settlement is not reached a strike will occur. Instead of waiting to feel the actual lengthening of EP that comes with a strike, the parties can imagine or compute its approximate magnitude, and then negotiate as if the EPs already *are* of that magnitude. As it is often put, the *strike becomes the criterion of the negotiated settlement*. All this is simple and effective in principle, and it works much of the time. But why does it sometimes fail? Again, the answers are those of tactics or strategies.

As to tactics, either party may underestimate its own EP and/or overestimate the opponent's, as those EPs would be during a strike. Hence, that party may reject the last offer that would avoid the strike. Either side may also make a tactical error in thinking that its own adamant stance will bring a last-minute capitulation by the other party and then fear excessive loss of face from its own last-moment concession.

In addition to errors of calculation, there may be other motives for a strike. A company may welcome a strike as a means of liquidating an overgrown inventory, and the union might welcome it to generate a sense of solidarity among a lackadaisical membership. What is more, the daily routine often gets boring, and a strike is exciting. It may also be expensive. But so are many other sources of excitement. And either side may fear that its ability to face a strike may decay from disuse.

Rather, regardless of issues or motives, the real pressure of a potential strike is often not felt very strongly until the strike deadline gets close. During the last hours the relation is much like a game of "chicken." Each side may fervently hope that a strike will not ensue, and is actually willing to concede enough to prevent it. But each hopes that if it sits tight the other will lose nerve first and concede. So both sides sometimes watch sadly as the pickets start to march, each wondering if it acted foolishly in holding out too long. sometimes the parties stop the clock just before midnight and furiously put together a settlement within the next few hours—but "before midnight."

As the strike deadline approaches another complication arises. Unless it seems clear that the parties will succeed in reaching agreement before the deadline, each must start making overt preparations for the strike. These preparations have both tactical and strategic effects. One such preparation is for the company to start building its inventory of finished goods, possibly by operating overtime. The tactical effect is to make credible the company's statements that it will take a strike rather than increase its offer. Its credibility is further enhanced if the required overtime involves higher unit costs. The strategic effect is to shorten management's EP once a strike starts, since its ability to sell out of inventory will decrease its costs from the strike. The union's building of a large strike fund has parallel tactical and strategic effects. Sometimes the employer must make substantial advance preparations for the strike, a notable case being the banking of furnaces in the steel industry. This is a costly operation, and must be done while the employees are still working. This act is also a form of commitment, the cost of banking the furnaces being the stake the employer has put up, which also constitutes a sunk cost regarding the strike. Having incurred part of the cost of the strike before it starts, the employer then finds the additional costs of the prospective strike reduced and his EP shortened.

There is also a two-edged psychological strategic effect of strike preparations. One edge is to sharpen awareness of the seriousness of the situation, lengthen EPs, and make the parties work harder for a settlement. The opposite edge arises from the fact that the precise purpose of a strike (including management's "taking" of a strike) is to make life unpleasant for the other party—to impose costs. As each party watches the other preparing to hurt him, tempers are apt to get shorter. The direct effect is to shorten EPs (see Chapter 10) and reduce the likelihood of settlement. As to which effect will dominate—it all depends!

This chapter's hard-headed attention to power and bargaining power is realistic. But ordinary human decency is not wholly absent. To cite just one example, on occasion either side could open negotiations with, "We may as well tell you at the outset that we simply can't afford a strike this year, though it looks as if you can. We hope you won't be too hard on us." In an established relation of mutual trust it may work. If it later turns out to be a tactical misrepresentation it could devastate the relation for years. And lest we leave a mistaken impression, let us note that though bargainers may remain skeptical of their opponents' statements during bargaining, they often develop the highest regard for each other's personal integrity in other matters.

WHAT ABOUT ARBITRATION— AND ASSUMPTION 9?

We have seen that the potential strike can serve as the criterion of a negotiated settlement and allow the parties to settle without a strike for what they think would have occurred if there had been a strike. This relation then leaves an intriguing question, which we can diagnose by relaxing assumption 9—that arbitration of the dispute is not contemplated. Why not have the parties agree in advance to binding arbitration if they fail to settle, and then let the potential arbitration serve as the criterion of the negotiated settlement? If it should fail, as the strike criterion sometimes does, then the dispute would get settled peaceably by arbitration, without the losses of a strike. Several factors preclude this relationship. The first relates to the nature of the decision. With or without a strike, a settlement reached by the parties is a *mutually accepted* decision. Even if one or both was reluctant to sign, each separately preferred the benefit of the settlement to the cost of not settling. By contrast, an arbitrator may hand down a decision that is simply not acceptable to one of the parties, possibly to both. Although arbitrators may be expected to be sensible, it nevertheless remains possible that in an extreme case an arbitrator's award could bankrupt the company or wreck the union. And once the parties have agreed to arbitrate, they lose this crucial control over the settlement. Few are willing to do it.

Second, whereas it is realistically possible to estimate the probable cost of a strike and thus estimate also the value of settling to avoid it, there is no way of predicting an arbitrator's award. Hence, the strike's logic of, "Settle for this now, since that's about what you're going to settle for eventually anyway," does not apply to a prospective arbitration.

Finally, the parties know that without arbitration they will eventually have to reach *some* agreement on every issue, even if the "agreement" is to drop the demand. Hence they tend to agree, at least tentatively, on numerous minor issues just to get them out of the way. With arbitration in prospect, they do not have to agree on anything. Some other complications of contract arbitration are dealt with elsewhere. These observations underscore even more strongly the role of the strike, or prospective strike, as the pressure that brings agreement between parties who otherwise would not agree, and the reasons why arbitration of contract terms (primary arbitration) is widely avoided by both unions and managements.

SUMMARY

It does not seem necessary to recapitulate the various discussions within this chapter. It seems worth noting, however, that the approach to power and bargaining power used in this volume enables us to couch the power and negotiating relations between union and management in a far tighter model than otherwise seems possible. The chapter opens with a simple, yet not hopelessly unrealistic, model. Once the principles are clarified in that simple situation, the various assumptions of the model are relaxed one at a time. Substitute assumptions are then inserted into the model, after which *their* consequences are traced. It is hoped that this technique has enabled the reader to get some grasp on the main complications that arise within collective bargaining while avoiding the "big, bloomin', buzzin' confusion" that arises from throwing all the complexities into the same pot simultaneously, so to speak. It is our hope that complexity *can* be dealt with in an orderly and comprehensible fashion. For those who wish to know in an introductory way how the present model compares or relates to other models, that topic is discussed in the note which immediately follows.

NOTES

[1]Richard E. Walton and Robert B. McKersie, *A Behavioral Theory of Labor Negotiations, An Analysis of a Social Interaction System* (New York: McGraw-Hill, 1965), p. 43.

[2]*Ibid.*

[3]Alfred Kuhn, *The Study of Society, A Unified Approach* (Homewood, Ill.: Irwin, and Dorsey Press, 1963), Chapter 17, based on Alfred Kuhn's *Labor: Institutions and Economics,* 1st ed. (New York: Holt, Rinehart and Winston, 1956), Chapter 7.

[4]Allan M. Cartter, *Theory of Wages and Employment* (Homewood, Ill.: Irwin, 1959), p. 122.

[5]Alfred Kuhn, *The Logic of Social Systems: A Unified, Deductive, System-Based Approach to Social Science* (San Francisco: Jossey-Bass, 1974), p. 193.

[6]*Ibid.,* p. 173f.

[7]Walton and McKersie, *op. cit.,* chaps. 8 and 9.

[8]Kuhn, *op. cit., Logic of Social Systems,* p. 218.

NOTE
TO CHAPTER 11:
A Comparison of Models

You are by now familiar with the general approach taken by the present model of power and bargaining power. If that model seems easy to comprehend and apply, and to provide a good understanding of the many details of negotiations and power as between unions and management, you may be willing to accept it. Otherwise, no amount of argument about the relative theoretical merits of the model will be likely to convey conviction. Several comparisons or contrasts may nevertheless be useful.

First, it can be easily demonstrated that the present model is logically compatible with the Chamberlain model.[1] The logical transformations required are to make some substitutions of terms (e.g., value of agreeing for cost of disagreeing) and to substitute a subtractive for a fractional relationship (e.g., $AY - AX$ instead of AY/AX). Since, according to Mabry, Chamberlain is basically similar to Pen[2] a further similarity is thus established. Mabry's own net-gain approach uses the formula:

$$P+_a + P-_a = NG_a$$

where P_a is pleasure, plus or minus A and NG is A's net gain. This is apparently a precise equivalent in different terminology of the present:

$$AY - AX = EP \text{ of } A$$

To move to a different point, the argument has already been made elsewhere[3] that a certain circularity is involved in those models that couch bargaining power as the ability of a party to get "one's own terms." The circularity is that one presumably does not even attempt to formulate one's "own terms" until one has first assessed bargaining power and what it will probably get. The present model avoids that circularity by couching bargaining power as a strength of push in one's favor rather than as a locus of achievement.

Game theoretic models, like those of Nash[4] and Harsanyi[5], require very restrictive assumptions that seem quite unrealistic for bargaining situations. The assumptions of game theory formulations may include, for example, those of rationality, maximization, knowledge of the opponent's utilities, substitutability of players, limited numbers of moves or stages, unchanging preferences, and continuous versus discontinuous functions. The present model requires only that each party at each stage of negotiations have some notion of the dividing line between what it will accept and what it will reject. A party need have no initial knowledge, or even vague guess, about the other's utility function. Although a party can presumably engage in smarter bargaining if it does know, it may conclude negotiations without ever knowing the opponent's true preferences. The present model allows for any number of changes in utilities during the course of negotiations, either autonomous or induced by the other party, with or without the expectation of "conflict." The eventual outcome in the present model can be positive, negative, or zero sum, depending on the relative magnitudes of the values gained from a settlement, if any, as compared to the costs to the parties of achieving the settlement, with or without a strike.

The present model assumes that the outcome of any given negotiation is in fact indeterminate. Hence, an indeterminate model more closely approximates the actual conditions of bargaining than does a determinate one. If the indeterminate model also provides understanding and explanation of why people behave as they do, and if it provides predictions of probable behaviors, given the perceptions and goals of the parties, but without presuming to anticipate what those goals and perceptions *are*, it should be considered a satisfactory model. Alternatives that do better on this score do not seem readily apparent.

To be more specific regarding determinacy, the reader should review the nine assumptions that constitute the model on which this chapter on negotiations is based. These are found near the beginning of this chapter. These assumptions were relaxed one at a time through the chapter and were replaced with substitute assumptions. Although the discussion in the chapter made no attempt to predict the precise consequences of any one assumption or change of assumption, it did try to identify the *kind* of change in behavior that would ensue. Any such change in behavior presumably having a potential for changing the outcome of negotiations. You can judge for yourself whether this analysis makes sense—that is, whether a difference in circumstance such as that stated in the assumptions and their subsequent relaxation would actually make a difference in the probable outcome. In fact, you need not agree with the *specifics* of the discussion but merely agree that *some* change in factors such as those listed are likely to produce *some* change in terms of settlement. The point of all this is that a model could not be *determinate* within this context unless it made very explicit assumptions, (1) about each of these nine points and possible others, and perhaps about two or more details within each, and (2) about the interrelations among the assumed conditions, since the conditions of the nine items probably do not change independently. Described in this light it seems quite impossible to describe any one model from which one could predict the specific outcome of negotiations. Given that even this model is a vast simplification of reality, it would seem that any model so simplified as to produce a determinate result must ignore so much of reality as hardly to be of any use in understanding the actual processes and consequences of negotiations. Hence our deliberate use of an indeterminate model.

Herbert Simon has proposed the substitution of a satisficing for a maximizing model of the firm in economics. In parallel, the present model of bargaining is essentially a satisficing one, as contrasted to the maximizing economic or game theory models. In it, the parties engage in a series of tactical and strategic moves. After some unspecified and unpredictable sequence of moves, they find some mutually acceptable solution—a satisficing condition. They accept it. Although Omniscience might know that some other settlement would provide a larger total utility, as, for example, in a Nash solution, the parties have no way of knowing where it is or how to get there. Moreover, they probably don't care. With bargaining as with managing a firm, "to optimize requires processes several orders of magnitude more complex than those required to satisfice."[6] Collective bargainers are often so relieved to reach *any* solution that they are in no mood to quibble whether it is theoretically optimal. To repeat, how could they know whether it is optimal?

In operationalizing the transactional model, it seems relatively easy to add to or subtract from an EP to reflect some modified or newly introduced cost or benefit, substantive or procedural. Once we know the direction and approximate magnitude of a change in an EP, it is then relatively easy in turn to discern its effect on the probable outcome. That seems far simpler theory than to recompute the boundaries of some utility surface, assuming that we already knew the previous utility surface. And, as contrasted to locating an optimum point on a utility surface, it similarly seems far easier for practicing bargainers to visualize expanding or contracting EPs. To expand this point, the transactional model can readily handle perpetual changes in the package of payoffs and of utilities that would make a near shambles of an approach through game theory, and at least a modest mess of an economic bargaining approach. Furthermore, any utilities associated with other models can readily be subsumed within the transactional approach, but the reverse is not possible.

NOTES

[1]Alfred Kuhn, "Bargaining Power in Transactions: A Basic Model of Interpersonal Relationships," *American Journal of Economics and Sociology*, January 1964, pp. 49−64.

[2]Bevars D. Mabry, *Labor Relations and Collective Bargaining* (New York: Ronald Press, 1966), p. 229.

[3]Alfred Kuhn, *The Study of Society, A Unified Approach* (Homewood, Ill.: Irwin, and Dorsey Press, 1963), p. 333; and Alfred Kuhn, *Labor: Institutions and Economics*, 2nd ed. (New York: Harcourt, Brace and World, 1967), p. 123.

[4]John F. Nash, "The Bargaining Problem," *Econometrica* 18 (1950), 155−62.

[5]John C. Harsanyi, "Approaches to the Bargaining Problem Before and After the Theory of Games," *Econometrica* 18 (1956), 144−57.

[6]James March and Herbert A. Simon, *Organizations* (New York: Wiley, 1968), p. 141.

IMPASSE: RESOLUTION AND REGULATION

We must first distinguish between bargaining over interests and bargaining over rights, which are essentially synonymous, respectively, with primary and secondary bargaining, or bargaining *over* the contract as contrasted to bargaining *under* the contract. To illustrate the difference, the people of a nation may have an *interest* in freedom of speech, in the sense that they want it and believe all human beings should have it. But until they get something like the First Amendment written into their constitution, or at least a law granting the rough equivalent, they have no *right* to freedom of speech. Employees in a company may have an *interest* in getting their wage rates raised, or in having a tighter seniority clause. Because of that *interest,* they may bargain hard over the subject. However, if and when a clause has been written into the contract granting a higher wage or tighter seniority, then and only then does an employee have a *right* to either one. Stated somewhat more legalistically, an *interest* is what you want; a *right* is what you have some enforceable way of getting. Generally, a right rests on some prior agreement or commitment. That commitment need not be in writing. But unless the parties are well known to each other and have a high level of trust in both their integrity and their memories, in contemporary society such agreements are generally put in writing, particularly if an organization, rather than an individual, is committed.

Primary (interest) bargaining, or bargaining over the contract, is the process of writing clauses into the contract. Because those clauses constitute the parallel of "law" between the parties, this process is also called the legislative aspect of the union-management relation. It is the process of establishing rights, normally for the union, the employees, and the employer. Secondary (rights) bargaining, or bargaining under the contract, corresponds to some combination of the executive and judicial processes. It is the process of seeing that the rights established by the contract are actually implemented—that they move from paper to reality.

Conflict, and the resolution of conflict, plays a major role in the establishment of these rights. Both unions and managements, in our system of private-sector industrial relations, are free, with some exceptions, to impose economic costs on their opponents through the strike and/or lockout. Clearly, it would be a more pleasant world if this were not the case, but in reality many times a strike is the only way for a union or management to obtain concessions from each other.

ON THE SOURCE OF BARGAINING IMPASSE: THE ORIGIN OF STRIKES

Impasse means that after some long period of negotiations, the parties show no signs of reaching agreement. But to deal sensibly with means of resolving impasse, we must first attend to its causes. A particularly difficult one occurs when at least one party does not *want* a settlement.

A management, for example, might want to break the union. Such a management might conclude that even a settlement quite unfavorable to the employees could nevertheless add credibility to the union presence. In that case, *no* concession from the union would be accepted by management. A management might also hope that protracted tension would split the union membership, undermine its leaders, or empty its treasury. In a quite different direction, management might want to help contain inflation, even though a noninflationary settlement would be wholly unacceptable to the union. There is also the possibility, particularly in a family-owned company, that the owners would rather go out of business than grant some demand that the union considers basic and actually do so despite certain legal constraints.

On the other side, the union might want to avoid settlement until a favorable pattern is set elsewhere. Or the union might use a protracted strike to embarrass the government or to publicize the union position on some government policy. Either side might use toughness now to "punish" the opponent for some past behavior, or to demonstrate for the next negotiations or to its own constituents that it is no "pushover." Impasse resolving techniques are not necessarily useless in such cases. But special considerations are involved when one or both parties wants *not* to settle.

John Dunlop has suggested that all strikes can be classified into four categories.[1] The first type of strike is one in which one of the parties wishes to change the established bargaining structure. The union may wish to combine several single-plant bargaining units into a multiplant structure covered by a single contract. Similarly, a firm might wish to get out of a multiemployer bargaining relationship to bargain one-on-one with the union. This type of conflict need not be confined to formal bargaining relationships. For example, in the early 1980s, strikes were observed in the steel, meatpacking, and airline industries, in which at least one of the issues was an employer's desire to break out of a cycle of industry pattern bargaining.

A second category of strike, according to Dunlop, is the strike to change relationships between negotiators and their constituents. As we have stated before, union members sometimes have much higher expectations for what is attainable at the bargaining table than does the union negotiating committee. The committee faces the management bargainers and their positions, which the union membership does not. Thus, situations can arise in which the only manner in which members expectations can be lowered is through the costs of a strike. Likewise, although less frequently, stockholders or top management sometimes have to be shown that the union is serious, and the only way their expectations can be altered is through a strike.

A third category of strikes are those called in order to change the position of a third party not present at the negotiating table. This kind of strike is most common in public-sector bargaining, although there are isolated cases of its occurrence in the private sector. Often in the public sector, the economic authority to settle collective bargaining is vested in the legislative branch of government whereas the procedural bargaining authority is vested in the executive branch. Thus, conflicts can occur in which a strike is not necessarily against management but rather against the budget-making power of the legislature.

The final category of strikes involves those that occur solely to alter the bargaining position of the union or management. As we have indicated in Chapters 10 and 11, there are cases of positive contract zones in which the parties cannot find their way to a settlement. In cases such as these a strike can sometimes exert sufficient pressures for a compromise. In the case of a negative contract zone, a strike may serve not only as a prod to communication and compromise, but may cause, through the imposition of real costs, a change in position of one or both of the parties.

Strike Activity in the United States

Table 12−1 presents data on strike activity in large (over 1000 workers) bargaining units from 1947 to 1984. Publication of other data series on all strikes, regardless of bargaining unit size, were discontinued in 1981 by the Bureau of Labor Statistics, but data in Table 12−1 are sufficient to illustrate several points about strikes in the United States.

There are many different methods of strike measurement and its impact upon the economy. Table 12−1 presents four different ways of looking at strike activity. Column 1 represents a counting of strike activity, the number of strikes that occur in a year. One can see that there is a cyclical nature to the data, with a generally downward trend, particularly from 1974 to 1984. A wide variety of interpretations can be inferred from the data. Year-to-year variations can be accounted for by differences in the number of negotiations. In general, there is also a downward trend in the number of bargaining units with more than 1000 workers; hence, there are lessened opportunities for strikes to occur. Other hypotheses related to variations in strike activity focus on changes in economic conditions and the political climate as providing favorable or unfavorable conditions for strike success by unions.

Column 2 represents the number of workers involved in strikes and gives us a

TABLE 12.1.   WORK STOPPAGES INVOLVING 1000 WORKERS OR MORE, 1947 to 1984

Year	Number of Stoppages Beginning in year	Workers Involved Beginning in year (in thousands)	Days Idle Number (in thousands)	Days Idle Percent of estimated working time
1947	270	1,629	25,720	—
1948	245	1,435	26,127	.22
1949	262	2,537	43,420	.38
1950	424	1,698	30,390	.26
1951	415	1,462	15,070	.12
1952	470	2,746	48,820	.38
1953	437	1,623	18,130	.14
1954	265	1,075	16,630	.13
1955	363	2,055	21,180	.16
1956	287	1,370	26,840	.20
1957	279	887	10,340	.07
1958	332	1,587	17,900	.13
1959	245	1,381	60,850	.43
1960	222	896	13,260	.09
1961	195	1,031	10,140	.07
1962	211	793	11,760	.08
1963	181	512	10,020	.07
1964	246	1,183	16,220	.11
1965	268	999	15,140	.10
1966	321	1,300	16,000	.10
1967	381	2,192	31,320	.18
1968	392	1,855	35,567	.20
1969	412	1,576	29,397	.16
1970	381	2,468	52,761	.29
1971	298	2,516	35,538	.19
1972	250	975	16,764	.09
1973	317	1,400	16,260	.08
1974	424	1,796	31,809	.16
1975	235	965	17,563	.09
1976	231	1,519	23,962	.12
1977	298	1,212	21,258	.10
1978	219	1,006	23,774	.11
1979	235	1,021	20,409	.09
1980	187	795	20,844	.09
1981	145	729	16,908	.07
1982	96	656	9,061	.04
1983	81	909	17,461	.08
1984	56	322	7,686	.02

SOURCE: *Monthly Labor Review* 108 (January 1985), 103.

better picture of year-to-year variation in strike activity. This data gives us a good example of the caution one must use in the interpretation of the data in Column 1. If one compares the years 1971 and 1974, one finds 1974 had many more strikes than the year 1971. But, many more workers were involved (720,000) in strikes in 1971. The measure contained in column 2 provides a weighting proportional to a strike's importance. That is, larger strikes involving more workers are weighted more heavily when one examines the total number of workers involved.

Column 3 provides a further refinement of the measurement in Column 2. This measure represents the number of potential working days lost to strikes. It corrects not only for the size of a strike in the number of workers involved but also for its duration. The concept embodied in this measurement is that a long, medium-sized strike can eventually cause just as much working time to be lost as a much larger, but shorter, strike.

Column 4 places the total amount of work time lost to strikes in another context by measuring it as a proportion of all potential work time. Those unfamiliar with industrial relations are often surprised at the relative smallness of these totals. To place these numbers in another context, the long-term average of time lost to workplace accidents is approximately 0.2%, or ten times the amount of time lost to strikes in 1984.[2]

Strike Patterns

Since we are concerned with the losses caused to our economy by strikes, industrial relations scholars have expended a significant amount of research effort towards an understanding of why and when strikes occur. These studies have been conducted at an economy-wide level, both within a single country and as intercountry comparisons. Typical of such intercountry comparisons is a study published by Everett M. Kassalow.[3] He shows that U.S. statistics on strike activity, in an international context, depend on which measure of such conflict is used. The United States consistently has larger and longer strikes than most other industrial countries but has fewer of them per 1000 workers.[4] If we used the measures presented in Table 12−1 to illustrate these conclusions, frequency (Column 1) would place the United States lower on international basis, whereas the number of workers involved (Column 3) and days lost (Column 4) would be higher. One must exercise caution in the interpretation of these comparisons because the purpose and uses of the strike and strike statistics vary widely among countries. In the United States, the strike is used almost exclusively for economic reasons, whereas in most Western European countries, the strike is used as a political weapon as well.

The understanding of strike trends within the United States has been related primarily to fluctuations in the business cycle (as represented by unemployment and inflation rates), the size of the organized labor movement, and prevailing political attitudes toward unionism.[5] While these aggregate studies are interesting and useful, they do little in providing an understanding of the motivations of individual parties at the bargaining table. For it is at this level that our efforts at limiting conflict within our society will be most successful, if we have a solid understanding of which parties are most likely to engage in conflict. Unfortunately, studies that analyzed bargaining unit data have not been consistent in their explanation of differences in propensity to strike.[6] Some patterns have been uncovered, however, and are illustrative of underlying patterns of conflict in our economy. It has been shown that the size of the bargaining unit is related to strike probability. Larger units are more likely to strike than are smaller units. Strikes are more likely to occur in workplaces located in supportive social and political climates, at least as measured by rates of unionization and the location of workplaces in southern and/or right-to-work states.[7] The history of a bargaining relationship plays a role as well. Unions and managements who have suffered a strike in previous bargaining rounds are much more likely to engage in strikes in future negotiations.[8]

We must conclude that research in this area has contributed relatively little to our understanding of why strikes occur. This may be indicative of the fact that strikes are idiosyncratic. That is, they occur where negotiations are beset by structural difficulties or by antagonistic negotiators. While we can be concerned about particularly strike-prone industries and direct our conflict reduction efforts toward those industries, as a society we have to consider an arsenal of weapons designed to reduce conflict. It is to that task that we now turn with a presentation of the variety of methods that are used to minimize and resolve impasse.

ON RESOLVING IMPASSE

The Parties Alone

In the general sense, impasse means that the parties have exhausted all efforts of their own to reach agreement. It may, therefore, sound contradictory to suggest the exploration of further possibilities by the parties themselves. But if the parties *think* they have reached impasse when actually they have not, some further explorations may be fruitful. In particular, a more candid acknowledgement of their real goals may reveal some alternatives that were not previously thought of.

To start with the improbable, if a party's real goal is to display its toughness it can hardly open an exploratory discussion with: "Our real goal is to impress you with how tough we are. Can you suggest any better ways to do this?"

Similarly, a management can hardly reveal that its real purpose is to get rid of the union and then expect the union's cooperation. By contrast, if a union openly admits in a post-impasse discussion that its real objective is to break some government policy, it is possible that management also has gripes about "government interference," and that together they could have greater impact by joining forces. Or perhaps joint discussion might reveal that severance pay could better achieve a kind of worker security that the union was seeking to implement through stricter seniority.

The Nonparticipative Observer

Sometimes it helps a discussion merely to have an outside observer present. Much as when husband and wife or parent and child discuss a disagreement, expressions of anger and departures from logic are tempered because their unproductiveness would be so obvious to a disinterested observer.

A third party can sometimes be tactically useful merely to get the parties to talk. For example, suppose negotiations have broken off with each saying, "We have nothing further to offer. If and when you are ready to make concessions, let us know." Following such a break, any move by either party to reopen negotiations might be construed by the other as a sign of weakness. Each side might nevertheless respond to a third-party inquiry by saying, "If the other side is willing to talk, we are too, provided it is clear that we did not initiate the new talks."

A somewhat more active third-party role is that of messenger. Diplomatic relations provide some parallels. A conspicuous one is the way the governments of Israel and Egypt for years would not talk directly. But they did convey messages (feelers) through the American government, or through such unofficial individuals as news correspondents. In the 1930s, many managements stated a willingness to talk to their own employees but not to "an organized union," typically referred to as "outside agitators." Although that particular relationship now occurs far less often, there are still occasions when there is felt to be less loss of face in talking through a third party. The messenger can be particularly useful when the responsible leaders are willing to talk, but their constituents cannot tolerate direct contact with the "hated enemy." Since the main reasons for not talking directly are those of appearances, the messenger function is mostly tactical.

The Active Mediator

We move now to full-fledged *mediation*, which is participation of a third party in the negotiation process, but with the final decision still resting with the principals. The mediator's role can be tactical, strategic, or both. Although tactics and strategy may be mixed or muddled in practice or in the minds of participants, the logic of the two is quite different. Hence, we will discuss them separately.

We have seen that the normal use of bargaining tactics requires one to try to learn the other side's resistance point while hiding one's own. Mediators can be very effective when they know both resistance points. For example, if the resistance points overlap (positive contract zone), the mediator's task is only to help the parties find a solution in that range. Thus, the mediator's job is one of assisting communications and perhaps offering alternatives.

To achieve this best, the mediator must have the almost absolute trust of both sides. Not only must they trust him to be discreet about what they say and avoid even subtle hints about it, each side must also trust him not to use such confidences to its disadvantage. To illustrate the many complications, let us assume that the mediator will propose terms of a settlement on the basis of the superior knowledge he gains from the parties, that the terms proposed lie somewhere close to the midpoint of the perceived overlap, and that the proposal has a high chance of being adopted. In these circumstances, a party may have as much to gain by understating its resistance point to the mediator as by understating it to the opponent. Hence, before either side will honestly state its true position to the mediator, it must also have confidence that he has enough sense to avoid being misled by the other party. Since a negotiator for either side can ruin his own reputation and hurt his constituents if confidence in a mediator is misplaced, experienced negotiators are likely to be wary. Hence, successful mediation on tactics is a tough assignment that deserves high praise. Good mediators are not expendable, and their reputations should not be sullied for light reason.

The strategic role of mediation is less demanding, though requiring skills of its own. It does not necessarily require high trust by the parties, as the mediator does not need confidential information from them to perform a strategic function of altering resistance points. The mediator may "just happen to mention" to the union the case of a firm that had to lay off 20 percent of its work force following a wage settlement that made it noncompetitive or mention to the employer the paint manufacturer that lost most of its customers because they switched suppliers during a long strike. True, the parties must trust that the mediator's tales are not invented for the occasion. But that involves a lesser confidence than does telling the mediator one's true resistance point. In any case, the mediator's hints of impending doom may be independently verifiable by the parties. Thus figuring how to "scare" the negotiators is perhaps more a matter of ingenuity than of trust.

The strategic function is not only easier than the tactical. It is also less risky. Second, although a mediator may call attention to a certain factor that will change a resistance point, it remains a voluntary act of the party. Hence, a mediator is "not to blame" in the same sense that he or she would be if he or she misjudged a position on the basis of confidential statements and then made misguided proposals based on that misjudgment. Third, in a pure strategic function, the mediator cannot violate a confidence, as he or she has received none.

To be most fully effective in all possible circumstances, a mediator presumably needs both sets of skills. In the long run, union and management will probably be best off if they respond to their own evaluations of situations, as viewed within the perspective that comes naturally to them, without possible short-run distortions of their values by a mediator in pursuit of a settlement. If so, a mediator will serve them best if he or she confines himself or herself to a tactical function if a positive contract zone exists and engages in strategic extensions of resistance points only when they do not. To say this, however, implies that in *any* case he or she must first engage in the tactical analysis, which is the more difficult.

There is sometimes a question about whether a mediator should "go public" with what he learns, in the hope of bringing public opinion to bear on the negotiations. Needless to say, unless this is done with the prior agreement of both parties, anyone's willingness to confide in him or her thereafter will be small indeed. If there is a prior expectation of such publicity, the situation merges with that of fact-finding, to which we now turn.

Fact-Finding

Fact-finding is sometimes resorted to in cases of impasse. *Fact-finding* is a variation of mediation in which an outsider (or panel of outsiders) assists in certain ways in achieving a settlement, but with the settlement itself still remaining entirely in the voluntary and mutual control of the parties. Its most frequent use is upon request of the parties or on imposition of public authority when the public welfare is involved. The typical report of fact-finders traces the history of the parties and of the particular dispute, identifies the issues, and states the positions of both parties on each issue, possibly summarizing the arguments with which they support their positions. Depending on their charge, the fact-finders may or may not recommend terms of settlement, and they may or may not report on all issues.

There are several possible objectives of the procedure. If tied to a mandatory postponement of a strike until fact-finding is completed, there is always the hope that a strike postponed may be a strike avoided. Second, if the "facts" are made public and reveal unreasonable demands, public opinion may encourage their withdrawal and raise the likelihood of settlement. Third, a conscientious job of fact-finding may bring to light some considerations that the parties had not thought of and that make it easier to settle.

Fact-finding with recommendations includes one additional tool. If the recommendations seem well done, they shift the burden of proof (or guilt) to the party that rejects them. Thus, each resistance point is lengthened to whatever extent the party feels some psychological or social cost of appearing responsible for continued impasse. That extension may be large or small, depending on the sensitivity of the parties and the ability of government or public to impose costs on the recalcitrant party.

Contract Arbitration

One sometimes hears the suggestion: "When parties cannot agree on something, they can take the disagreement to court and get a decision. Why not do the same with labor disputes?" Labor courts, or compulsory arbitration, is then conceived as an alternative to strikes that entail serious loss or disruption to nonparticipants. The suggestion misses the point. For courts *enforce* contracts, they do not *write* them. Courts can require parties to abide by the promises they have already made, but do not require the parties to *make* promises. The suggestion of labor courts is based on the fallacious assumption that courts decide matters of interest. In fact, they only decide matters of right, or of interest that is subsumed within some already established right. This does not mean that compulsory use of labor courts or labor arbitration *could not* be used in interest disputes. And it does not mean that the distinction between rights and interests is always as clear as this discussion may seem to imply. It merely means that the glib suggestion about adjudication of contract disputes makes an unwarranted assumption about the nature of the judicial function in general. And within that false assumption lie a host of difficulties.

Let us first look at some unusual circumstances where contract arbitration might be feasible. One would be a case in which the parties had gone through a long sequence of negotiations and possibly strike, mediation, and so on, had failed to reach agreement, and in which neither party had contemplated arbitration as a possible solution. If arbitration is then suggested "out of the blue," if it is reasonable to assume that an arbitrator would not award anything lying beyond the demands/offers already on the record, and if neither party feels it would be disastrous to be awarded what the other had already offered, arbitration might be a feasible solution. (Under these conditions, there is also a high probability that the parties would have reached a settlement on their own!)

But if the parties anticipate from early in negotiations that arbitration will be the last step their behavior will change from the outset. The urge to understate one's resistance point to the arbitrator is virtually the same as to understate it to the opponent. And whereas an arbitrator in a grievance dispute over rights may find that the "right answer" clearly falls on one side or the other, where there is no law or contract to constrain the arbitrator's judgment there is a strong tendency to "split the difference." Since any prearbitration concession by one party shifts the midpoint of the (negative) overlap in favor of the other party, and the "last offers" of the parties made before the arbitrator will probably be "split," an expectation of arbitration makes both parties unwilling to make preliminary concessions. There is also a feeling, not wholly unfounded, that if many minor issues come to the arbitrator he will tend to award approximately half to each party. Instead of settling minor issues, or "washing them out" of negotiations at an early stage, parties headed for interest arbitration tend to refuse to settle even issues on which their position and their interest is weak, in the hope that for every such issue the arbitrator denies them he will grant them another to compensate. For both reasons, the expectation of arbitration can weaken free bargaining.

Furthermore, once a new contract case is assigned to an arbitrator, both parties lose all control over the outcome. And whereas in grievance arbitration the nature of each case limits the amount of damage that can be done by an arbitrator's decision, and a decision may be appealed to the courts if an arbitrator exceeds his or her jurisdiction, there are no comparable limits to the power of an arbitrator in contract arbitration. Though it may be hoped that he or she would not abuse it, the arbitrator has the power to bankrupt the company or disrupt the union. For all these reasons, unions and managements in the United States persistently avoid contract arbitration and adamantly oppose its imposition by law. It is sometimes suggested that parties could place upper and lower limits on an arbitrator's award, and thereby make arbitration more acceptable. But by the time the parties could agree on those limits, they could probably also agree on a settlement. Besides, contract negotiations often involve issues for which "limits" in that sense have no clear meaning, as in a dispute between plant-wide and departmental seniority.

One factor somewhat softens the preceding conclusions. In contract arbitration, the decision is sometimes made by majority vote of a tripartite board rather than by one or more neutral arbitrators. Having their own representatives helping to formulate the final judgment, the parties remain informed of progress and of the direction of the neutral arbitrator's sentiment. The process of negotiation actually continues into the arbitration decision, and a representative of one party may make concessions at that stage in the hope of swinging the neutral arbitrator(s) in his direction. Neutral arbitrators may also do some negotiating, since they must elicit a signature from either the union or the management member(s) of the board before the decision is final. If they care to use it, neutral arbitrators have unusually persuasive mediative powers, since the parties know they have the reserve power to make the final decision. Despite these mitigating conditions, interest arbitration still delegates more power to outsiders than the parties are usually willing to allow.

A major exception to this attitude occurred in the transit industry for some fifty years starting about 1890. During that period, more than 600 wage arbitrations were conducted in the industry.[9] The distinguishing features that made such behavior feasible were fairly clear. Starting well before automobiles were numerous, the dominant union in the industry concluded that strikes would be very unpopular and would tend to push public sentiment toward management's side. Early in its history, the union therefore adopted a constitutional provision that no local could strike until it had first offered to arbitrate and had been refused by management. Because the industry was an essential utility and a regulated monopoly in most areas, transit managements generally found little difficulty recovering increased wages through higher fares. Hence, managements felt it safe to arbitrate. Besides, with the union enforcing its constitutional provision rather strictly, it was management that would have to bear the onus if a strike followed its refusal to arbitrate. Changed circumstances in the economics of the industry and in its industrial relations have markedly diminished the use of contract arbitration in recent decades.

An ingenious invention of recent years is *final offer arbitration*. As the name implies, an arbitrator is given authority to make a final and binding award to settle the disagreement. But the arbitrator's discretion is limited to choosing either the union's or the company's final offer. The expectation is that each party will be motivated to make concessions, in the fear that if it holds out for unreasonable terms the arbitrator will sensibly adopt the offer of the other party.

Final offer arbitration has been used with what might be described as somewhat better than modest success in major league baseball (as applied to individual salary negotiations), as well as in many states for some public-sector negotiations. Aside from baseball, the applications are predominantly for public employees, and especially for those in public safety jobs (police and firemen). As might be anticipated, the success of the process depends much on the parties and the circumstances. The main questions about the procedure are (1) whether each party's last offer must be accepted or rejected as a total package, as contrasted to allowing the arbitrator separately to award what is deemed best on each issue, and (2) whether the parties should be permitted to continue to modify their "final offers" until the arbitrator has made his award, or is close to making it, as contrasted to binding each party to the offer it made at some relatively early stage.[10] Nelson cites some additional usages, including one by university professors, and notes possible weaknesses of the process in pattern-setting situations.[11] All in all, however, most experts have concluded that arbitration with all its problems has been a useful substitute for the strike in public sector collective bargaining. The private sector, except for the cases noted earlier, has refrained from using it as a process of impasse resolution.

THE PUBLIC INTEREST IN IMPASSE

If PDQ TV Repair on East 72nd Street is struck for six months, the president, the governor, and the mayor will not lose sleep over it. The only parties affected are the management and the employees of the firm, some customers whose TVs go unrepaired, and perhaps some creditors of employees or management. But if a strike of truckers, steelworkers, or firefighters cause grocery shelves to go bare, factories to shut down, or houses to burn, the concern is intense. The general logic of strikes is that they put pressure on the parties until concessions settle the strike. But sometimes the pressure on others is much greater than on the parties to the dispute. Impasse then ceases to be a matter of merely private concern and induces government bodies to act. The problem is that of public emergency strikes, and to prevent them or soften their impact is a matter of serious concern.

The first level of government action is a standing obligation on the parties to *all* collective contracts subject to Taft−Hartley, whether or not failures to settle them are likely to create a public emergency. Section 8(d) of the Labor-Management Relations Act requires a sixty day written notice to the other party by either party which intends to terminate a contract when it expires. It must also offer to meet and confer about negotiating a new contract. The Federal Mediation and Conciliation Service (FMCS) must also be notified within thirty days of the notice to the other party. The contract must then remain in force for another thirty days after *that* notice—that is, till the expiration date of the contract. In this manner, the service is forewarned of a possible approaching dispute that might involve the public welfare—though it is unlikely that any major contract termination would fail to attract advance notice in the media or by the Department of Labor. It also seems unlikely that the notice of the parties to each other tell them anything they did not already know.

More broadly, the FMCS assists in some way in the settlement of twenty to twenty-five thousand cases in a typical recent year.[12] Within the past decade, there has been a steady increase in the service's work in the public sector, including assistance with settling disputes in instances of local police and firefighters and in cases of civilian employees of the armed forces. Public-sector cases now account for almost 10 percent of the FMCS caseload.[13]

Whether some strike causes an "emergency" is a matter of both intensity and scope. As to intensity, a strike in a single small hospital is an emergency if only a few lives are endangered or in a fire department if a single dwelling burns for lack of firefighters. By contrast, if 50 million people cannot work for several days for lack of coal, steel, transportation, or power, the loss is not intense at the same level, since few lives will be significantly changed in consequence. But the overall effect may be considered an emergency because the total loss runs to billions of dollars and public indignation is high. For many years, it was felt that strikes in private employment were tolerable but that strikes by public employees were not. But in recent decades the severity of impact is more the center of focus, when it is realized that public-park maintenance employees might strike for weeks with little consequence whereas private employees of utility, power, or transportation facilities might create an emergency within hours. Moreover, the inconvenience to the public from a transit strike is the same whether the lines are privately or publicly owned, and much the same is true for trash collection. The key question in emergency strikes, then, is: How can we get agreement in cases where the pressure on those who are not parties to the dispute becomes unacceptable before it induces settlement by the parties themselves?

There is little problem about identifying possible alternative ways to handle the situation. The question is, Will they work? The most obvious alternative is to prohibit strikes in public emergency situations and substitute an arbitrated settlement. A modified version is to postpone strikes in the hope that a settlement will be reached in the meantime. Enforced mediation might help. Changing the payoffs to the parties by fine, imprisonment, cancellation of government contracts, adverse publicity, tax incentives, or other means might also help. So could softening the effects of the strike (making it nonemergency), as by having the parties meet the real emergency needs of the public while nevertheless continuing the pressure on each other. For example, power or fuel could be supplied to hospitals while being cut off elsewhere, or critical military supplies could be hauled while the trucks were otherwise stopped. In transit, the "no-strike strike" has been used occasionally. Buses and trains continue to run but no wages are paid and no fares are collected. However, the riding public tend to "tip" the operators the equivalent of a fare, in which case the operators get much enlarged incomes. Meanwhile, the employer receives no income, while continuing to pay the costs of fuel and upkeep. Thus, the pressure on the parties is hardly equal, and managements object.

Can Strikes Be Prohibited?

Let us look at the other alternatives. To prohibit strikes is easy to say but not to do. The basic logic of the situation is intractable, particularly in private employment. Assuming that the old contract has expired, to prohibit a strike is to require employees to work against their will, at a wage they have not agreed to, for the profit of their private employer. Employers as well as workers may be wary of a precedent in which government requires a seller to deliver something of value for a price he considers unacceptable. Even wage and price controls, for example, specify a price per unit but do not require the seller to deliver. The problem of enforcement is even more difficult. The law could state that employers may discharge any striker who fails to come to work. But employers are already free to get rid of "economic strikers" if they can find permanent replacements. In any case, the problem is to get workers *into* the plant, not out of it, and if penalties are placed on strikers they may individually and collectively say "we quit." They are then no longer "strikers," and neither the government nor the employer has any claim on their services unless we accept something close to slavery. Even without anyone's quitting, penalities on a union or its offices may induce *them* to call off the strike. But the tradition of "no contract, no work," is strong in some industries. Hence, an order from the union to go back to work may simply be ignored by the workers. A final difficulty is that, even after the parties agree on all substantive issues, the union *must* insist as a condition of terminating the strike that all strikers be reinstated with full seniority (assuming that they have violated no law except that against striking). A union that did not insist on this condition would effectually sign its own death warrant. These conditions are not entirely the same for government employees as for private ones (see the public sector chapter), but even there the waiving of penalties against illegal strikers is likely to be crucial to final settlement. This statement of underlying logic is also a reasonably accurate summary of actual experience in numerous cases, both public and private, over many decades.

This is not to say that attempts to prohibit strikes will always be ineffective. Some employees and unions are not as militant or self-confident as others, and some may face internal or external weaknesses that prevent them from ignoring a legal prohibition. Nevertheless, it seems unwise to incorporate into public policy an assumption that a prohibition of strikes can be enforced, except in unusual circumstances. And as the late

George Taylor used to put it, the government should avoid revealing itself to be impotent. All that can be accomplished by an unenforceable prohibition is confusion, frustration, and anger on all sides.

We have noted earlier that although the strike is typically thought of as a union weapon, it is actually mutual. It is not only a union pressure on management, but also a management pressure on the union and employees. Hence, to prohibit strikes not only deprives the union of a weapon. It also prohibits management from forcing some sobering second thoughts on the union, as by making it face the consequences to themselves of a possible strike. Given the role of the strike as criterion of the negotiated settlement, it is hardly an exaggeration to say that to prohibit strikes (if it could be done successfully) would be to destroy the parties' main motive for concession, and hence to destroy bargaining itself. As the experiences of Australia and New Zealand since about 1900 demonstrate, to prohibit strikes *and* to substitute compulsory arbitration ends by increasing the number of strikes and by making government the chief determinant of wages. Forkosch and Levinson both give recent confirmation to this longstanding conclusion.[14]

Since the parties to a collective bargaining agreement, unlike those of most commercial agreements, *must* eventually agree on a new contract, if strikes are to be prohibited some alternative means of writing the new contract must therefore be provided. Whatever the name assigned to it, that alternative is compulsory arbitration in one or another of its variants, and its difficulties have already been outlined above. For such reasons compulsory arbitration, or even voluntary arbitration except in rare circumstances, does not appear as a workable means of impasse resolution in interest cases, in the private sector. Except during World War II, when the War Labor Board made binding decisions, we have not had compulsory arbitration imposed by the federal government in the United States. Even that was semivoluntary in a broad sense, since representatives of organized labor and of management had agreed that there should be no strikes or lockouts for the duration, and that both sides would voluntarily accept decisions of the War Labor Board. And even that arrangement, coupled with the fact that any strike at all seemed unpatriotically to impede the war effort, by no means eliminated strikes, though it clearly reduced them.

Compulsory Waiting Period

Compulsory postponement of strikes, in the hope of achieving a settlement during the waiting period, is partly similar to and partly different from a flat prohibition. The similarity is that even a temporary prohibition is no more enforceable than a permanent one if the employees are firmly resolved to strike. The difference is that the resolve of the parties to strike immediately is likely to be weakened since the parties themselves retain full control of the ultimate outcome, and can still put their differences to a test of economic strength after the waiting period if they so desire. The main difficulties are two. One is that circumstances may change during the waiting period in ways that substantially shift bargaining power. If so, the side disadvantaged by the shift quite sensibly sees the mandated postponement as unfair. Which way power would shift depends on the circumstances, and postponement presumably contains no inherent bias in itself. True, the employer might strengthen his position by accumulating inventory during the waiting period, but even that is of little advantage unless he had failed to do so before the contract expired.

A compulsory waiting period in emergency situations, despite the problems just described, is the course our society has taken. Sections 206 through 210 of the Taft—Hartley Act incorporate provisions for the handling of national emergency labor disputes. Action under the law is initiated by the president, when "a threatened or actual strike or lockout affecting an entire industry or a substantial part thereof . . . will, if permitted to occur or to continue, imperil the national health or safety." Note that public inconvenience and economic loss are not mentioned. Nor is intensity of the loss, or even of health and safety, if the dispute is local in scope. The law provides no further criteria, which are by no means self-explanatory. For example, is a near-total shutdown of basic steel an emergency, or threatened emergency, at the moment a strike starts? Or does it become an emergency only after inventories are depleted? What are the "national health or safety," and when are they "imperiled"?

These matters must be decided as each case arises. When the president thinks an actual or potential strike merits attention he appoints a board of inquiry, to report back at a predetermined time, with a statement of the facts but without recommendation. If the president then thinks the action justified, he asks the attorney general to petition a district court to enjoin the strike or lockout. Under Section 209 of the law, it is "the duty of the parties . . . to make every effort to adjust and settle their differences." The Federal Mediation and Conciliation Service is to assist the parties, but neither party is obligated to accept the recommendations. After sixty days the board is to reconvene, reporting the current status of negotiations and the positions of the parties to the president. The employer's last offer is also to be reported, and within fifteen days a secret ballot on that offer is to be taken by the NLRB among the affected employees. The union's last offer is not similarly reported, and no poll on it is taken among the affected employers (if there are multiple ones). After the results of the ballot are reported the injunction is discharged, and the status of the dispute is reported to the Congress, along with possible recommendations to the Congress, by the board of inquiry. In total, the injunction may run for no more than eighty days.

EVALUATION OF TAFT—HARTLEY IMPASSE
MACHINERY—AND OTHER IMPASSE LEGISLATION

The simplest and safest comment on the Taft—Hartley procedure is that the employee ballot on the employer's "last offer" is useless. In all cases but one, the last offer was soundly rejected. In that fifteenth case the election was totally boycotted—and no votes were cast.[15] The reasons are clear. First, for employees to accept an offer their negotiating team has turned down would undercut and discredit the team. Second, to reject the offer on the ballot does not preclude their accepting it before or possibly after the injunction is lifted. And third, since the employer can be presumed to understand the above reasons why this offer will be rejected there is good reason for employees to believe that the employer's "last" offer is not really the employer's "final and best" offer.

In other respects, the record of the law is mixed. Of the thirty-four times the act was invoked from 1948 to 1981, injunctions were issued in all but five. Of the twenty-nine cases in which injunctions were issued, fifteen were settled before the injunction expired, and in all fifteen a strike had been under way before issuance of the injunction. In six cases, all involving longshoring, a settlement was not reached during the injunction and a strike followed its termination. In one of those cases involving the West Coast docks, the Congress enacted special legislation after resumption of the strike. The overall history of this provision of the law leaves an impression that it was mainly a post–World War II phenomenon. The act was invoked (by the calling of a board of inquiry) ten times by President Truman, seven by Eisenhower, six by Kennedy, five by Johnson, five by Nixon, and once by Carter.[16] The one case under President Carter involved the extraordinarily long 110-day strike in coal. There a temporary restraining order was issued. As anticipated, the miners did not return to work. When a full injunction was sought, the court denied it on the ground that the national health or safety was not involved.

A full evaluation of the emergency provisions would require information that is essentially not knowable, such as how long a given strike would have lasted if no injunction had been issued, or whether the likelihood of the initial strike was increased or decreased because the parties expected government intervention. Since the presumed purpose of the legislation is to achieve a settlement during the injunction period, in this particular respect it succeeded in fifteen of twenty-six cases. In at least four additional cases, settlement was reached after the injunction expired and without resumption of the strike.

Several biases in the procedure may be noted. One is that injunction is traditionally conceived as directed against the union, plant seizure being the parallel "weapon" against employers. The law is one-sided in providing for injunctions against strikes but not seizure in case of lockout. Actually, the bias lies at a different level. Namely, adamant employers normally force strikes, they do not initiate lockouts. Thus, as a practical matter, only unions can be guilty of violating the law, and hence be subject to penalty for contempt. Whether these biases "in principle" have disadvantaged the union in the terms of the eventual settlements is probably not knowable, though in at least one instance in 1948 the United Mine Workers and its president, John L. Lewis, did have to pay fines of $.7 million and $10,000, respectively.

The second piece of federal legislation dealing with resolving impasse is the Railway Labor Act, applied to the railroads in 1926 and extended to the airlines in 1936. Long hailed as a model labor law, the Railway Labor Act is based on compulsory mediation and fact-finding with recommendations in interest disputes. The law worked well until about 1940, with the parties generally accepting the recommendations of the National Mediation Board established by the law. During World War II, however, any strike by the railroads almost instantly became a national emergency, and pressure to get it settled was intense. It was shortly discovered that if recommendations of the board were "appealed" to the president or to a strike (which would shortly bring presidential intervention), the union could generally get more than it could from the board. The law has not worked well ever since. It certainly has not avoided strikes in the airlines, a recent one closing down United Airlines in 1979 for 55 days. A decade-old dispute over railroad work rules, never successfully settled by the board, was referred to compulsory arbitration by the Congress in 1963.

Some states, notably Pennsylvania and New Jersey, have at one time provided machinery for resolving impasse in public utilities, about a half dozen providing compulsory arbitration. The results, overall, have been desultory. The laws are often ignored, in part because many utilities are so highly automated that supervisors can operate the facilities for weeks or months in case of strike. Managements have successfully appealed some decisions to the courts, and unions have "appealed" some of them to strike. At the same time, some utilities and their unions have submitted their differences to voluntary arbitration under their own control. As with the transit industry, mentioned earlier, the risks from arbitration are relatively low in utilities because of the monopoly nature of the industry and the relatively inelastic demand. Some cities have arrangements for impasse settlements involving crucial local employees. The machinery in New York City, long administered by Theodore Kheel, was certainly the most notable, though such local arrangements are generally unused or ineffective.

Regarding impasse settlement in the public sector, and as noted in the chapter on the public sector, employees of the federal government are often covered by both civil service and union contract. Except for two major exceptions, the prohibition of strikes by federal employees has been honored. In 1970, postal workers went on strike at some locations in the United States and in 1981 a nationwide strike of air traffic controllers resulted in the firings of 13,000 PATCO members. By contrast, the widespread flat prohibitions of strikes by state and local government employees, often on potential pain of severe penalty, are widely violated. To avoid violating the law too blatantly, such categories as police and firefighters often stage a "sick-in," calling in sick instead of calling their action a strike. Injunctions against strikes obtained under such laws are sometimes honored and sometimes not. But for reasons stated above, penalties are rarely applied.

The application of Ohio's Ferguson Act, until it was replaced in 1984, illustrated one common attitude. In the event of a strike the employing agency, such as a city government, simply did not activate the procedures specified by the law. The law then remained "not invoked," and the effect was much the same as if the law did not exist.

If any one thing might be considered a reasonably standard observation about impasse settlement machinery, it is that once the parties become familiar with it they can use it to prosecute, postpone, or settle their dispute, depending on their inclination. Almost any reasonable machinery will probably work fairly well if the parties feel generally obligated to subordinate their own interests to the public good. However, the temper of the recent past apparently considers it legitimate to push one's own special interest, while leaving it to others to protect *theirs*. All things considered, perhaps it is surprising that we have so few emergencies, not that we have so many. Perhaps, too, the recent difficulties in the professional and public sectors represent the growing pains of new unionization where paternalism and collegiality recently prevailed. If so, the years ahead may be less stormy.

NOTES

[1]John T. Dunlop, "The Function of the Strike," in *Frontiers of Collective Bargaining*, John T. Dunlop and Neil W. Chamberlain, eds. (New York: Harper and Row, 1967), pp. 103–120.

[2]Bureau of Labor Statistics, U.S. Department of Labor, *Handbook of Labor Statistics 1978*, Bulletin 2000, p. 554.

[3]Everett M. Kassaslow, "Industrial Conflict and Concensus in the U.S. and Western Europe," in *Labor Relations in Advanced Industrial Societies*, Benjamin Martin and Everett M. Kassalow, eds. (Washington, D.C.: Carnegie Endowment for International Peace, 1980), pp. 45–60.

[4]*Ibid.*, pp. 46–48.

[5]Bruce E. Kaufman, "The Determinants of Strikes in the United States, 1900–1977," *Industrial and Labor Relations Review* 35 (July 1982), 473–490.

[6]Martin J. Mauro, "Strikes as a Result of Imperfect Information," *Industrial and Labor Relations Review* 35 (July 1982), 522–538.

[7]Robert N. Stern, "Intermetropolitan Patterns of Strike Frequency," *Industrial and Labor Relations Review* 29 (January 1976), 218–35.

[8]Thomas A. Kochan, *Collective Bargaining and Industrial Relations* (Homewood, IL: Richard D. Irwin, Inc., 1980), p. 269.

[9]Alfred Kuhn, *Arbitration in Transit, An Evaluation of Wage Criteria* (Philadelphia: University of Pennsylvania Press, 1952).

[10]For an excellent discussion of this topic see Peter Feuille, "Final Offer Arbitration and Negotiating Incentives," *Arbitration Journal* (September 1977), pp. 203–20.

[11]Nels E. Nelson, "Final-Offer Arbitration: Some Problems," *Arbitration Journal* (March 1975).

[12]Federal Mediation and Conciliation Service, Thirty-fourth Annual Report, Fiscal Year 1981, p. 5.

[13]*Ibid.*, p. 13.

[14]M. D. Forkosch, "Compulsion in Collective Bargaining and Arbitration: A Comparison of American and Australian Industrial Law," *University of Toledo Law Review* (Winter 1976), pp. 457–99; David Levinson, "The New Zealand Waterfront Industry Tribunal," *Arbitration Journal* 25, no. 4 (1970), 201–68.

[15]Further detail on the last-offer ballots under Taft–Hartley can be found in Benjamin J. Taylor and Fred Witney, *Labor Relations Law*, 4th ed. (Englewood Cliffs, N.J.: Prentice-Hall, 1983), p. 566.

[16]*Ibid.*, pp. 568–9.

WAGES AND SECONDARY EFFECTS OF COLLECTIVE BARGAINING

In a text on collective bargaining there is no need to go into the details of wage determination in a manner appropriate to a course in economics, or even labor economics. At the same time, collective bargainers *do* make decisions about wages. Those decisions are not thought through in a vacuum but within a context of economic and institutional forces that may bear on their actions in many ways. The consequences of a given wage settlement will also be affected by those forces. Hence it can be helpful to the parties, and sometimes immensely so, if they have some general concepts of the economic forces that constrain their behaviors. Like the angry child who breaks a window with his or her fist, one can be badly injured if those constraints are not understood. The same kinds of knowledge may also assist in deciding what kinds of wage data to assemble for negotiations and in defending those data against attack.

We can place the forces that have an impact on wage bargaining into two broad categories: (1) those forces *external* to the firm, summarized here as the product and labor market context; and (2) those forces *internal* to the firm, such as productivity and the structure of internal labor markets (i.e., paths of promotion within and between occupations). We begin this chapter with a discussion of these forces and their impact upon wages and wage negotiations.

THE ROLE OF PRODUCTIVITY

The broadest and most pervasive constraint on wage settlements is the basic economic proposition about the relationship between real wages and production. Although the analogy should not be carried too far, it is a useful reminder in starting a discussion of wages to look at the Robinson Crusoe economy. One cannot have more goods than are produced. For one living alone, the amount produced will depend upon the person and the environment. The person must provide effort and skill, and the environment must provide some resources to be worked on. If nature is generous, the person may be able to live with no more skill or effort than is required to pick fruits, nuts, and berries or to pick up and open clams. If nature is stingy, as in desert sagebrush or arctic tundras, the effort and skills required just to stay alive may be considerable.

In an economy that consists of many thousands or millions of people, the basics remain. The average amount of real income per person will depend on the skill, effort, and capital provided by people taken in conjunction with the available resources provided by nature. The average real income per person cannot be more than the total produced divided by the number of people. But when many people are involved, the question of distribution is added—who gets how much of the total? Not surprisingly, managements usually emphasize increases in productivity as the means to increased income, and unions emphasize increasing labor's share, even if neither totally rejects the logic of the other.

Productivity seems the only sensible explanation of broad differences in real incomes over time and place. Why are real incomes about five times as high as they were a century ago? Why are real wages so much higher in advanced industrial nations than in undeveloped and underdeveloped ones? The sensible answer is that people have more when they produce more. At root, real income *is* what is produced. We cannot eat food that isn't grown, drive automobiles that are not produced, or watch movies (or even news programs) that were not made. Production is inescapably basic.

Interestingly, when productivity of workers goes up, the power of both workers and management tends to rise, other things being equal. The underlying reason is that a rise in productivity is a positive sum game. The power of management goes up because the firm can turn out more product at less cost. The power of labor goes up because a more productive worker is also more valuable to management, and hence can bargain a higher wage, even if the reason for the rise in worker productivity is solely an investment by management.

For those interested in the details, the wage is related to the *marginal* product of labor, the "product" being measured by the amount of net revenue added to an employer by the addition of a given worker. That refinement helps explain some of the details of wage differentials outlined in the pages that follow, as traced by Kuhn.[1] But we need not reproduce that reasoning here. Perhaps the best quick summary is that market forces of supply and demand are pervasive and powerful, and in general and on the average tend to be the dominant forces acting on wages. But they are broad first approximation thrusts, not precise determinants, and they leave much leeway for other forces to operate. They are something like a bulldozer pushing a pile of gravel. They determine the general location of the pile, but not its precise contours or the location of particular stones. We will now examine some of the wage-determining forces that seem relevant to unions and managements when they are negotiating specific contracts.

One aspect of wage theory has rather direct practical interest in many situations. According to basic marginal productivity theory the demand curve for labor by an employer slopes downward. This means that an employer would "buy" more employees at a low wage than at a high wage. Cartter[2] describes a "wage preference path" of unions and employers. This is the preferred response of each to a possible change in real wage. The employer would always prefer to stay on his demand curve, which is the marginal productivity of labor, increasing the size of the work force if the wage were to go down and decreasing the work force if the wage were to go up. Those moves maximize the return to the employer. By contrast, the union wage preference path is to take an available increase mainly in the form of higher wages, and any necessary decrease mainly in the form of reduced employment. These moves "maximize the return" to the union as an institution, whether or not they are in the best interests of the employees. That is, the union takes credit for the increase in wages if they go up while any blame for layoffs necessitated by the increase is assigned to the "profit-hungry" employer. Both sides are spared this choice while a firm is growing. In such firms, negotiated wage changes may have an impact on the level of employment only in the form of a slower (or zero) rate of employment growth. That is, if a union is able to secure wage changes, it may spur management to purchase capital rather than hire more workers.

In the post–World War II era, with a steadily growing U.S. economy, unions usually refused to accept any responsibility for adverse employment effects due to rising wages. In the past few years, however, a growing number of unions have recognized the existence and importance of the wage-employment trade-off within a firm. The 1979 and 1982 rounds of bargaining in the automobile industry are illustrative of this development. The domestic recession and a growing share of imported autos sold in the United States had created a crisis in the industry. By the late 1970s, Chrysler, and then later Ford Motor Co. and General Motors, negotiated reductions in labor costs with the UAW in return for employment guarantees by management. Both sides retreated from positions they had held for decades: the union insisting that employment reductions were not their fault and management insisting that the union should have no role in the determination of employment levels. One can only surmise that this type of wage-employment bargaining will become a more prominent feature of U.S. collective bargaining in the future.

Viewed overall, although unions and managements may differ about the relation between wages and productivity, in the final analysis productivity affects the general level of real wages. A recent subject of research by economists is the question of whether union workers, in comparison to similar sets of nonunion workers, are more or less productive within the same industry. For most of the industries that have been studied, it has been found that unionized workers were more productive.[3] In many of the cases that were studied, the difference in productivity at least partially offset the higher wages that unionized employers were required to pay. While more research needs to be done in this area, this has proven to be a very interesting sidelight on the role of productivity in wage bargaining. We now turn to some of the other forces which determine the details of wage levels under particular circumstances.

PRODUCT MARKET COMPETITION (INTERINDUSTRY DIFFERENTIALS)

When we become more specific than the overall average productivity of workers, the most conspicuous determinant of wages is the state of competition in the product market, with competitive industries being generally low paid and noncompetitive ones high paid. One of the authors performed the following experiment, which was convincing evidence. Some 500 industries or industry divisions were arranged in order of employee earnings in 1964, as reported in the Bureau of Labor Statistics, *Employment and Earnings Statistics for the United States 1909−64*, Bulletin 1312−2. Without exception, every one of the fifty lowest-paying industries is characterized by small capital, ease of entrance, and a large number of firms. Typical examples are saw mills, small retail stores, work clothing, furniture, leather products, toys, textiles, cigars, and processed seafood. By contrast, with very few exceptions, the fifty highest-paying industries display high capital requirements, difficulty of entrance, and relatively small numbers of firms. Typical examples are radio and telephone communication, flat glass, steel, petroleum refining, tires, motor vehicles, utilities, steam turbines, primary metals, and soap and detergents. Conspicuous high-paying but competitive exceptions, like contract construction and commercial printing, require high levels of skill and show strong unionization. For the most part, the industries that pay middle levels of wages also occupy a more nearly middle position on the competitive scale. Reynolds and Taft[4] reached a similar conclusion on the basis of a worldwide survey, and numerous other studies tend to confirm the crucial role of product market competition. One of the disconcerting consequences is that one may find a janitor in an oligopolistic industry receiving as much pay as a tool-and-die maker in a competitive firm nearby.

Whereas the order of industries might be different in earlier or subsequent years, the general rule of thumb would hold that the less competitive the industry, the higher the wage level. Incidentally, this is also true of profits generally. Thus, although it is not likely that management will fail to remind its own members as well as the union negotiators that failure to remain competitive in the sale of the company's product can be disastrous to both sides. However valid the observation may be in general, it nevertheless does not itself identify what level of wages is competitive.

Another source of interindustry wage differential is that of bargaining structure, an aspect within the control of the parties. It has been shown that the more concentrated (the larger) the scope of the bargaining unit, the higher the resultant wage levels.[5] Thus, company-wide bargaining is associated with higher levels of wages than plant-by-plant bargaining. Even in comparing two noncompetitive industries, the industry with the more centralized bargaining structure will tend to have the higher wages of the two.

OCCUPATIONAL DIFFERENTIALS

When a general level of wages is being negotiated in a company it may be necessary to take into consideration the occupational mix within the bargaining unit. Sometimes the wage structure is also under negotiation, in which case differences in pay for different occupations may become the center of focus. Failure to get the occupational differentials properly aligned within a firm may do much to disrupt morale for the employer and cause internal political disputes within the union. Such failure may also make it difficult to recruit and hold certain types of employees.

Occupational differentials are those associated with the type of work a person does. In recent years the *Dictionary of Occupational Titles* has listed some 22,000 different occupations, and obviously we can speak only generally about broad classes of jobs. In a broad way, level of skill is the second major determinant of level of pay, skill being measured mainly by the length of time it takes to become proficient in the job. Differences in pay for different skills are most readily observed within a given plant or industry. Although market forces are slow moving and imprecise in their effects, the main differences are predictable and pervasive. Within any one firm or shop there is a stubborn persistence in the way tool-and-die makers earn more than carpenters, who earn more than oilers, who earn more than material handlers, who earn more than janitors—no matter what the city or the year. In construction, electricians get more than painters; in laundries, pressers get more than extractors; in foundries, coremen get more than chippers; and in garages, body workers get more than mechanics.

Although this ordering of wage levels within a firm remains consistent over time, in many cases the political pressures within unions cause the relative difference to decrease over time. That is, in most bargaining in which a mixture of occupations are represented, the lower-skilled workers will outnumber those at the top skill levels. They will seek wage increases structured in such a way that gradually the absolute amount of the skill differential will be narrowed. It is a simple mathematical exercise to note that a wage increase in cents per hour will lower the percentage difference between two wages, whereas a percentage increase will maintain the difference. Thus, even the way in which a wage increase is granted may have significant internal considerations to the union.

Whether one compares different points in economic development or degree of industrialization, different sections of the United States, or different parts of the world, including both East and West, a persistent pattern emerges. Namely, the differences in pay between skilled and unskilled work are greater in the less industrialized areas. That is, a high level of industrialization is accompanied by a narrower range of occupational differentials. However, a rapid *rate* of industrialization seems to enlarge the differentials.[6]

Sometimes there is little overlap of skills across industries. For example, the textile industry employs spinners, weavers, doffers, carders, and loom fixers, while metal working employs machinists, lathe hands, milling machine operators, and molders. The difficult question then arises whether the differences in pay between textiles and metal working are attributable to the industries or to the occupations. There is no easy way to tell.

Occupational differentials are also influenced in the short run by the demand for and supply of people qualified to perform the occupation. Unionized workers in occupations facing a decline in aggregate demand are less likely to be able to successfully push for higher wages. Industrial and occupational demand trends have recently worked to the disadvantage of union members. Much of the employment growth in the United States over the past twenty years has been in the service industries and their related occupations, a lightly unionized sector of the economy. Future trends are expected to remain on a similar course (see Table 13–1).

TABLE 13.1. EMPLOYMENT GROWTH: 1982–1995

Occupations with:	
Highest projected growth rate (%)	*Highest projected absolute growth*
Computer service technician	Building custodian
Legal assistant	Cashier
Computer systems analyst	Secretary
Computer programmer	General office clerk
Computer operator	Sales clerk
Office machine repairer	Registered nurse
Physical therapy assistant	Waiter and waitress
Electrical engineer	Elementary school teacher
Civil engineering technician	Truckdriver
Peripheral EDP equipment operator	Nursing aide and orderly
Medical insurance clerk	Technical sales representative
Electrical and electronics technician	Accountant and auditor
Occupational therapist	Automotive mechanic
Surveyor helper	Blue-collar supervisor
Banking and insurance credit clerk	Kitchen helper
Physical therapist	Guard and doorkeeper
Employment interviewer	Food preparation worker
Mechanical engineer	Store manager
Mechanical engineering technician	Carpenter
Plastics machine operator	Electrical and electronics technician

SOURCE: *Occupational Outlook Quarterly*, U.S. Department of Labor, Bureau of Labor Statistics, 28, no. 1 (Spring, 1984), 29.

GEOGRAPHIC DIFFERENTIALS

Geographic differentials take two main forms—regional and rural-urban. The standard patterns are reasonably clear. Urban wages are higher than rural. The pattern is more or less worldwide and has persisted over long periods. The regional pattern is more complex. Briefly put, in the United States, the farther north and the farther west one goes, the higher will be the wage for a particular occupation or industry, except for that large central area encompassing mainly the Great Plains. Somewhat the same pattern is found in Europe as well, with wages in northern Europe being generally higher than those in southern Europe. Both in the United States and elsewhere, the pattern is associated broadly with that of industrialization, in that the northern areas were industrialized sooner and more completely than the southern ones. In "northern" we of course include the temperature zones, not the lands of the Eskimos and the Laplanders—though the developed sections of Alaska fall within the north-and-west pattern of the United States.

Awareness of geographic differentials may be necessary to determine whether wages in certain other areas are comparable to those being negotiated, and to determine what differentials, if any, are appropriate within a company that operates in widely separated geographic locations.

INTERFIRM AND INTRAFIRM DIFFERENTIALS

Some firms as a matter of policy decide that they want to pay average, above average, or below average wages for the types of employees they hire, depending on their views of the effects of wages on their ability to recruit employees as contrasted to their ability to save money. Sometimes there are clear, rational reasons for such preferences. Sometimes the preferences arise out of intuitions, prejudices, or unique experiences of the managers. Among the rational reasons are the kinds of cross-market connections faced by a particular employer. For example, a firm that needs to shift employees frequently from one plant to another in different geographic locations may find it advantageous to have wage levels about the same in all plants. Such uniformity avoids both complicated readjustments every time a person is moved and inequities between those who have been in a given plant for a long time and those recently transferred in. As a different situation, some firms are forced into their policy by collective bargaining. General Motors employs workers in many labor markets throughout the nation. It needs to pay wages high enough to attract competent employees in the high-wage areas. But there is no way it could achieve equality for all its installations without bringing up all the other installations, which are the vast majority, to match the high ones. Not only is this expensive, but it also puts the wages of auto employees out of line with other wages in some labor markets. The union, needless to say, prefers to equalize all wages upward to equal the high ones. But it lacks the necessary bargaining power. Even if it had the power, the union might nevertheless avoid embarrassing other unions by creating large wage discrepancies in low wage areas. The result is that General Motors is a very high-wage employer in some labor markets.

Intrafirm differentials are a different matter and can require much detailed attention in collective bargaining. "Wage structure" is another name for such differentials, which are the occupational differentials as they appear inside a given plant or company. In most firms, until approximately World War II, these wage structures "just grew." There was a great deal of individual bargaining, with each person receiving the most that could be bargained from each particular supervisor or office manager.

Not uncommon was the practice of supervision to leave each employee with the impression that his or her wage was higher than that of others doing similar work, and that the wage should be kept secret or otherwise it would have to be reduced. Often there was no wage scale at all, if by wage scale we mean a set of named jobs and job grades with a rate or range of rates attached to each. A classic case occurred when the War Labor Board asked United States Steel Corporation for a copy of its wage scale during World War II and, after a long delay, received several large cartons of papers from the company. It took the company and the Steelworkers together about three years to work out a simplified and rational wage structure from this mass of data.

Many small- to medium-sized firms still operate their wage rates on a catch-as-catch-can basis. However, if they are unionized, it becomes very difficult to negotiate on wages unless the assortment of rates is codified into some reasonably simple system. Most "well-managed" firms nowadays consciously decide their wage structures in comprehensive fashion by a job evaluation program. These programs analyze jobs with respect to their skill, responsibility, effort, working conditions, and possible other criteria, assigning "points" to each trait. Then they award higher rates of pay to the jobs with the larger number of points. The union may or may not participate directly in the job evaluation program or retain the right to challenge its conclusions. "Key" jobs, which are those widely found in other firms and industries, are the "hooks" on which are "hung" all those jobs that are relatively unique to the firm. In this fashion, the wages inside any given firm can be kept in line with the influences of supply and demand in the broader labor market outside. Job evaluation plans are most likely to be used in firms organized by industrial unions, which have a wide variety of occupations within their membership. Craft unions, which have only one or a few occupations within a given union, will usually negotiate directly about each rate of pay. In terms of market relatedness, *all* the jobs covered by a craft union resemble the *key* jobs in an industrial setting. Smaller industrial firms may not bother with formal job evaluation programs, but may negotiate directly with the union on all rates.

Intrafirm differentials can be affected by union politics a well as by the market. Those categories of employees who have the largest voting blocs inside the union will tend to get their wages raised relative to those with fewer votes. In most situations, the lowest-skill and lowest-paid jobs tend to outnumber those with higher pay and skill. The stage is thus set for conflicts between management and the union. The union may want the largest increases to go to the lowest-paid members, because they cast the most votes in the union. The management may want the largest increases to go to the highest-paid members, because they have the scarce skills that are hard to recruit and without which the employer can be most seriously injured.

THE MIXTURE OF EFFECTS

We have seen a variety of different axes around which wage rates tend to revolve. Almost any combination may come to the fore in any negotiation. That is, the negotiators might at some point have to give conscious consideration to the firm *and* the industry *and* the occupations *and* the geographic region *and* the union, not to mention the personalities of the chief figures on each side and any intraorganizational competition they may be facing at the moment. A given negotiation reflects a nexus of forces tugging in different directions, whose relative importance will shift from place to place and from time to time in the same place.

THE CRITERIA OF WAGE DETERMINATION

In the preceding sections we dealt with various forces affecting wages. These tend to operate whether or not the parties are conscious of them. In this section, we shift focus to the kinds of standards of wage determination the parties consciously apply to wages. These standards are most specifically stated in those relatively rare cases in which wage rates are arbitrated. Nevertheless, they may be espoused in negotiations that are not arbitrated. For purposes of the present discussion, we will not try to settle the thorny question of whether the criteria argued in negotiations do or do not materially influence the outcome, which is really a question of whether bargaining power dominates "evidence" in determining the outcome of bargaining.

Wage Criteria

Wage comparisons regularly appear in negotiations or arbitrations of wages. Their essence is to show the wages or changes in wages that prevail in allegedly "comparable" other locations. As may be predicted, unions find the greatest "comparability" in other spots where wages have risen the most, whereas managements find the areas of lower increases "more comparable." There is no simple answer as to which comparisons are "objectively" the best. Since labor is a factor of production, it might be argued that surveys of the labor market should provide the most economically rational comparisons. But we have already seen that product market competition is also a potent wage determinant, so that comparisons with wages elsewhere within the industry may carry weight. There is also no a priori best answer as to whether wage *levels* or *rates of change* are the appropriate thing to copy—and, again, each party will reliably propose the comparison that favors itself. Needless to say, wage comparisons are used far more extensively in pattern-following than in pattern-setting negotiations. All in all, the most compelling comparisons are the wages paid by tough product market competitors in highly competitive industries.

In one sense, wage comparisons are the essence of a market system. But there is a real problem if they are to be taken seriously—namely, the difficulty of getting reliable data. Firms differ in the numbers of employees in different job categories. They define and describe jobs differently, have different overtime provisions and fringe benefits, and vary as between base rates and incentive pay. For such reasons, to say that "Company X pays 7 percent more than Company Y" may be a vastly misleading comparison. Wage comparisons may therefore have more value as rhetoric than as logic.

Ability to pay is at the same time highly relevant and wholly irrelevant. It is irrelevant in the strict economic sense that all firms are expected to pay the same price for power and materials, whether they are well heeled or on the brink of bankruptcy. "So why shouldn't they pay the same for labor?" goes the argument about irrelevancy. On the other hand, the criterion *is* relevant, for the simple pragmatic reason that in our highly imperfect labor markets a given amount of wage increase can be bargained more easily from an employer with plenty of money than from one with little. When a union is really convinced that an employer is in serious financial difficulty, it often will make concessions, generally with the expectation that its consideration will be reciprocated later when the employer is in better shape.

Wage controls or guidelines have drifted in and out over recent decades. They are too complex to discuss in a short space, but a brief note on them may be in order. A wage is a price applied to an exchange of labor service for money. If any control is to be effective over an extended period, it must specify the content of both flows—not only the amount of money, but also the amount and type of labor given in exchange for the money. For example, if market conditions are such that both labor and management want to raise wages while the government proclaims that they may not rise, then by tacit joint agreement everyone's labor grade might be raised but not the actual content of his job. Everyone's pay will then rise to match his new title, even though ostensibly no wage rate has risen. Price controls can behave similarly, by downgrading the product while leaving the price unchanged. Except under an emergency severe enough for most people to feel a moral obligation to comply, the task of enforcing wage or price controls is overwhelming.

Productivity was the theme with which we opened this chapter, noting its role as a broad, underlying determinant of real wages, and Kuhn has traced some of the logical steps by which changes in productivity may be translated into changes in market rate of wages.[7] When, where, how, or why changes in productivity will actually be accepted by the parties to a negotiation as relevant to their wage settlement is not at all clear. It may be argued, for example, that if there is a definite rise in output per hour of work within a given plant, then the real wage should rise accordingly. However, the parties may disagree whether the result should be the same if the increase in productivity resulted from greater skill and effort by employees as if it resulted from increased investment in improved equipment by the company. It may also be argued that a given employer should pay the market rate, without regard to the relative level of productivity in the plant, in which case differences in productivity would presumably be reflected in profit levels rather than wage levels.

There is little doubt that over long periods, such as a century or more, overall average increases in real wages closely parallel increases in average productivity. In fact, for several decades after World War II it was widely felt that all wages should be geared to rise automatically by about 2.5 percent per year, the rate which represented the long-run average rise in labor productivity for many years. The best-known actual implementation of that proposal occurred in General Motors's contract with the Auto Workers, starting with the five-year contract signed in 1950.

The *living wage* criterion has been argued from time to time, but has apparently had little effect. It is essentially an argument about how much employees *ought* to be paid, usually alleged to be about 20 percent more than they are actually receiving. In that respect it differs from such relatively objective measures as prices and wage rates paid elsewhere and really only reflects continued desires to increase living standards when no other justification is available.

The Cost-of-Living Adjustment (COLA)

Of all the factors that are consciously argued in negotiations or interest arbitrations, changes in the value of money are most widely considered, normally as reflected in changes in the cost of living.

Once upon a time in our history, prices and wages sometimes went up and sometimes went down. The early twenties and early thirties, for example, were periods of sharp decline. There have also been extended periods of relative stability. Unfortunately, perhaps, these seem to be conditions we are not likely to face in the years just ahead.

Despite exceptions, it has not been generally contested that a wage must be measured ultimately by its purchasing power. It is the real wage, not the money wage, that counts. The concomitant presumption is that if the value of money declines through inflation, the real value of the wage ought to be maintained by an offsetting upward adjustment of the money wage. To discuss the means of doing this, let us think first of a contract which provided for percentage increases in wages promptly and precisely geared to increases in the monthly Consumer Price Index (CPI), known for many years earlier as the Cost of Living Index. To some, this might seem a sensible and more or less universal way of handling the problem. But things are not that simple.

A distinct minority of American workers are covered by some form of wage indexation.[8] That proportion is currently decreasing and is expected to do so in the near future. Nearly all those covered by cost-of-living arrangements are unionized workers, and of those most are in large bargaining units such as the Autoworkers, Communications Workers, and Teamsters. In the early 1980s the inflation rate decreased significantly and the demand for cost-of-living clauses dropped as well. Were higher inflation to appear again, however, the question of wage indexation is sure to be a serious topic and for that reason we shall devote some space to the issue.

There are many objections to wage adjustments that use the CPI as a measure of loss of purchasing power. To start with, the CPI is always somewhat behind time, so that adjustments to it always involve some lag. This lag is aggravated by the fact that adjusting wages to the index every month would be too costly in bookkeeping effort. Hence quarterly, semiannual, or annual adjustments are the normal practice. Second, there can be disagreement whether the national or some local city index should be used. As might be predicted, relatively small local firms use the latter, while large unions with widely dispersed locals use the former. Third, because of the internal political bias noted earlier, unions typically prefer uniform cents-per-hour adjustments, which provide relatively more in the lower wage brackets than would a flat percentage increase. These adjustments have for some years been calculated at 1 cent per hour of raise for about every .3 points rise in the index, which amount is less than enough to compensate for the rise in prices—though the Rubber Workers negotiated a substitution of .26 in mid-1979. It was expected that the change might well be copied by others. Fourth, most contracts incorporate ceilings, which range from 1 to 6 percent maximum COLA per year. Fifth, there is a distinct possibility that the CPI overstates the actual increase in the cost of living, as by giving undue weight to the price of housing and mortgages, and thereby actually helps *cause* inflation. Some other minor difficulties exist.[9] There is also a more stubborn background question as to whether we inescapably face a decline in average real incomes, because per-hour productivity has been declining during some recent periods and because the real terms of international trade have shifted markedly in favor of foreign suppliers of various imports.

Although COLA clauses increased in number throughout the 1970s and COLAs provided an increasing fraction of the actual amount of money wages, even in the inflationary times of the late 1970s, they provided little more than half of the amount of money required to offset inflation. A high point in percentage change in the CPI occurred in 1979. During that year, the inflation rate was estimated at 13.4 percent. Yet even fairly liberal COLAs provided only a 6.7 percent wage increase to offset that inflation.[10] The high point for COLAs, according to Audrey Freedman and William Fulmer of the Conference Board, was reached in 1976, when 35 percent of production workers in manufacturing were covered by COLA clauses.[11] According to their analysis, COLAs have covered fewer and fewer workers since that time. Also, many union concessions in the early 1980s revolved around suspension, or even revocation, of COLA clauses and the wage increases they produced.

Other, still murkier problems lurk in the background. COLA agreements were orginally conceived as compensating for an inflationary rise that had already occurred. But a common current practice is considered by some to cause inflation, not merely to respond to it after the fact. A large fraction of American workers are now covered by labor contracts that run for two or three years, and a few run longer. Typically, in recent years, the contract specified an amount of increase for the first year that was geared to cover the inflation that had already occurred. The contract then also specified an additional increase for each of its remaining years to cover the *anticipated increase* in prices during those late years. Those increased wages will, of course, constitute increased money costs of production during those years and hence will produce higher prices. Thus, to the extent that such contracts become widespread, they constitute self-fulfilling prophecies—they *cause* the price rise that they predicted. But since they are by no means the only inflationary pressure in contemporary society, the total actual inflation may turn out to be greater than the predicted inflation. The result next time around is to anticipate an even higher rate of increase in the years ahead and to write *that* higher rate of increase into the contract and into the economy, and so on.

UNION-NONUNION DIFFERENTIALS

Employers or employees who face the prospect of going union are often concerned about the consequences of unionization on wages, and there is also a widespread citizen interest as well. What *is* the effect of unionization on wages?

To many it seems obvious beyond question that unions raise wages for their members, while others may respond that it is as obvious as that the world is flat. There are by now enough studies of union impact, or lack of it, on wages, so that it would take a large volume merely to summarize them.[12] In some studies, union-nonunion differentials seem to show up clearly. In others, they seem elusive. Studies are clouded by the obvious difficulty that the industries and regions that paid the highest wages before widespread unionization have subsequently become the most strongly unionized. When studies are experimentally controlled for those biases, they are still not consistent. Some show a clear union influence and some do not, and in one particular situation, that of the steel industry shortly after World War II, a case can be made that unionization held wages down.[13] Recent research in this area, as summarized by Richard Freeman and James Medoff reaches the conclusion that,

> The common-sense view that there is a union wage effect is correct. Quantitative studies show the general magnitude of that effect to vary among people, markets, and time periods.[14]

Their studies show differences among individuals can be as much as 30 percent, with the greatest union wage advantages accruing to less-educated, minority, and younger workers.[15]

Differences among markets depend upon the competitiveness of the market and the extent of union organization within the industry. The extent of organization can overwhelm the competitiveness aspect within a market in some cases. It is also probably reasonable to conclude that wages in trucking, coal mining, and construction are higher than they would be without unionization.[16] Being rather easy to enter, these are three industries which on the basis of product market competition would tend to be low paid. It nevertheless seems doubtful, indeed, that unions have raised the share of total national income going to wages while reducing the share going to rents, interest, and profits—though factors like wars and boom-recession cycles have affected the relative shares markedly. As a rough guess—and that may be the best we can do—Rees suggests that perhaps a third of unions have raised their members' wages by 15 or 20 percent, another third by perhaps 5 to 10 percent, and the remaining third not at all.[17] The effect can vary over time as well. At some periods in time, nonunion workers' wages rise faster than union workers', and vice-versa. Thus the union wage differential will rise and then lower over time. Daniel Mitchell has suggested that concession bargaining can largely be explained as a result of a too-high union-nonunion wage differential.[18] The union-nonunion differential rose swiftly during the late 1970s and then due to the concessions of the early 1980s, it was corrected to a lower, more stable level.

Whether unions influence wages in general is perhaps a question of more interest to the academic than to the union or management negotiator. Whatever the answer to that question, it does not change the immediate interest of the particular employer or employee in a negotiation currently under way. What may be relevant at this point is the environmental connections that influence the parties. The employer is in competition with other firms in the same industry, possibly in related industries that produce substitute products and perhaps with imports. The union negotiator may be in competition with a rival within the same union, with other unions, or perhaps, in a certain sense, with a political figure who is trying to influence wages or other legislation about unions. A union that deals with employers in the same industry throughout the whole nation will have a different perspective than one that deals on only a local or regional basis. The representative of truck drivers for a department store may have different views, depending on whether the drivers are organized into the Teamsters Union or the Retail Clerks. Sophisticated bargainers on each side will try to know what kinds of standards of comparison dominate the thinking of the opponent.

Some studies suggest a possible causal relation opposite from that customarily discussed. Namely, high wages may "cause" more unionism, rather than the reverse.[19] Another study shows both a direct and an indirect effect of unionism. The direct effect is some increase in wages. The higher wage induces employers to use more capital-intensive methods. These methods require more highly skilled employees, who receive higher wages.[20] This sort of conclusion, of course, raises an interesting question of definition. If an effect of unionization is to substitute more skilled for less skilled employees, at wages already prevailing for the former, has unionism "raised" wages?

CURRENT DEVELOPMENTS IN WAGE BARGAINING

The negotiation of wages changed considerably in the early 1980s. It has been shown conclusively that wage changes negotiated by unions and managements were consistently higher than those granted to nonunion workers throughout the 1970s.[21] Table 13−2 shows the most recent results of collective bargaining outcomes in the private sector of the U.S. economy. As can easily be seen, the first part of this decade has been one of wage restraint on the part of negotiators. This has been due in large part to the labor cost reduction pressures which have fallen largely on unionized workers. These pressures have resulted in a lessening of the wage gap between union and nonunion workers in the U.S. economy as well as a narrowing of the gap between U.S. and foreign workers. It is difficult to predict whether this is a significant alteration of our

TABLE 13.2. PERCENTAGE CHANGES IN WAGE RATES FOR SETTLEMENTS COVERING MORE THAN 1000 WORKERS

	1979	1980	1981	1982	1983	1984[1]
Overall change	7.4	9.5	10.1	3.8	2.6	2.6
Percent of Settlements with:						
No wage change	—[2]	0	3	43	22	20
Decrease	—	0	4	2	15	7
Increase	—	100	93	56	63	73

[1]*First six months.*
[2]*Data for 1979 not available.*

SOURCE: U.S. Department of Labor, Bureau of Labor Statistics, *Major Collective Bargaining Settlements in the Private Sector* (1980 and 1981).

U.S. Department of Labor, Bureau of Labor Statistics, *Major Collective Bargaining Settlements in Private Industry* (1982, 1983, first 6 months, 1984).

wage structure or merely a temporary correction. At any rate, the remainder of this decade will provide an interesting clue as to the permanence of this trend.

The Impact of the Union-Nonunion Wage Differential

In 1960, Sumner Slichter of Harvard University, along with his colleagues James Healy and Robert Livernash, published *The Impact of Collective Bargaining on Management.*[22] This book presented the results of a three-year study of U.S. collective bargaining. Their study was directed at an understanding of the impact of collective bargaining beyond the bargaining table. Implicit in their analysis was the hypothesis that not only did unions increase the wages and reduce the hours of their members, but that the bargaining of those workplace changes has further and more long-ranging effects on workers and managers. This hypothesis has been further refined and tested in recent years. Thomas Kochan detailed a wide ranging set of "secondary" effects of collective bargaining in his research compendium on collective bargaining.[23] Freeman and Medoff's book *What Do Unions Do?* contains entire chapters devoted to the effects of collective bargaining on workers, managers, and the economy as a whole. What links all these efforts is the fact that they look at the ways in which workers and management respond to the higher wages that unionized workers receive. They all start from the proposition that if labor becomes more expensive to management, management will have to make certain adjustments to remain competitive. Similarly, if a worker earns significantly more in a union job than in comparable nonunion positions, that worker will make certain adjustments in his or her economic behavior. Kochan calls the managerial adjustments that are made to collectively bargained terms and conditions of employment the second stage of his sequential model of union effects.[24] He states that "The central question here is: How does management cope with, or adjust to, the increases in labor costs that are likely to occur as a result of collective bargaining and how does it recoup the potential productivity losses that are associated with union-negotiated improvements in such areas as wages, benefits, and working conditions?"[25]

Freeman and Medoff suggest that managers pursue two different adjustment courses when faced with negotiated wage changes.[26] First, they might respond through the avenues predicted by neoclassical economic theory. Economic theory suggests that managers would readjust their behavior in response to an increase in labor costs in several different ways. They might change the scale of output and employment in response to increased costs. Changes in labor costs could require a shift to greater or lesser production in order to maximize productivity. Management could also increase the price of the product, dependent upon the nature of the product market, by passing increased costs on through to the consumers. Finally, they might substitute capital for labor in their production process by increasing the rate of technological change.

The second adjustment course pursued by management is to change its managerial policies, practices, and structure in order to more efficiently use its labor force. These changes were first evaluated by Slichter, Healy, and Livernash and were expanded upon by a newly developed body of research in the 1980s.[27] All these adjustments might occur in various combinations and would create a new set of constraints for unions and workers.

THE IMPACT OF UNIONS ON THE WORKER

Unionized workers, when faced with the outcomes negotiated at the bargaining table, have altered their labor market behavior according to a wide variety of studies. Within this section of the chapter we examine some of these behaviors and try to link them to the collective bargaining outcome that produces that behavior.

One major difference between union and nonunion workers is that unionized workers voluntarily quit their jobs less frequently.[28] Freeman and Medoff have suggested that this behavior could result from two different mechanisms. First, unionized workers might be less willing than nonunion workers voluntarily to leave their jobs simply because their wages are higher and they thus have fewer attractive job alternatives. An alternative explanation, which Freeman and Medoff suggest, is that unionized workers quit less because of their participation in their union. Union workers channel their dissatisfaction through the collective bargaining system rather than by leaving their job. Both of these suggested mechanisms may explain the lower quitting rate of union workers. The question is: Which dominates? Before we turn to that answer, however, let us look at the impact of unionism on voluntary turnover. In their book, Freeman and Medoff review a wide variety of studies which looked at the quitting behavior of union and nonunion workers during the decade of the 1970s. These studies surveyed thousands of workers included in several large national samples of labor force characteristics. First of all, they found that the difference in quitting behavior between union and nonunion workers is large and consistent. Union workers quit an average of between 15 and 65 percent less than comparable nonunion workers according to seven surveys, which they report in their chapter on the exit-voice trade-off.[29] Additionally, even for workers paid exactly the same wage, these quit-rate differentials are still as large. They also examined the impact of hypothetically raising the wages of nonunion workers. That is, what would happen if we look at comparable groups of workers and examined the turnover propensity of higher-paid nonunion workers versus lower-paid nonunion workers. The difference in that situation is only the fact that they are paid more and Freeman and Medoff are able to estimate the impact of higher pay on quitting behavior and compare it with the impact of unionism. They find that a substantial wage increase of 20 percent would reduce voluntary turnover on the magnitude of 5 to 10 percent, while unionism reduces it by 15 to 35 percent. We can thus accept their conclusion that unionism reduces quitting behavior over and above that which is caused by an increase in wage rates. To return to our initial point then, we can conclude that collective bargaining reduces turnover in both of the ways hypothesized by Freeman and Medoff.

This reduction in turnover has other impacts on the work force. First, because of that reduced turnover, the average union worker, at any point in time, will have been on the job longer than the average nonunion worker. Second, the average union worker will be an older person than will be the average nonunion worker. This older and more firm-attached work force has important implications for management. On the positive side, we know that every time a new worker has to be hired and trained, costs are incurred. Thus, to managements for whom these costs are high, reduced turnover can be viewed as a benefit. On the other hand, one can see that this effect makes it more difficult for management to reduce their work force voluntarily. Attrition would be slower, and because of layoff provisions related to seniority, management could end up with an even older work force that is less likely to quit. Let us now turn to the question of reduction of work force. It is in this area also that we find a large union-nonunion difference in the behavior of workers within firms.

Though unionized workers are much less likely to quit, all studies that have examined the question of temporary separation (layoff) from the job have concluded that unionized workers are much more likely to experience such temporary separation.[30] This kind of involuntary separation is within the control of management under the collective bargaining agreement, although there are generally strict rules about who is to be laid off. One study of layoffs, although confined to an examination of manufacturing industries, showed that unionized workers are subject to a two to three times greater likelihood of being laid off in any one month than are comparable nonunion workers within the same industries. It was hypothesized that this was due to the fact that unionized employers, unlike nonunion employers, could not reduce wages or hours and thus were left with the layoff as the means to adjust for temporary business downturns. Therefore, the sum total of turnover behavior is a two-edged sword for unionized workers. On the one hand, they are more stable employees and respond to collective bargaining by not quitting their jobs, remaining with their firms longer and thus, over time, becoming an older, more-experienced work force. On the other hand, however, they are subject to relatively high (at least as compared with the nonunion sector) levels of temporary instability on the job through the much greater use of the layoff mechanism.

Collective bargaining of wages results in a complex quilt of direct and indirect effects on workers and managers. We are far from a complete understanding of all these effects, and it certainly will be an area requiring much more research.

NOTES

[1]Alfred Kuhn, *Labor: Institutions and Economics*, rev. ed. (New York: Harcourt, Brace and World, 1967), Chapters 17–19.

[2]Allen M. Cartter, *Theory of Wages and Employment* (Homewood, IL: Irwin, 1959), pp. 91ff.

[3]Richard B. Freeman and James L. Medoff, *What Do Unions Do?* (New York: Basic Books, 1984), Table 11–1, p. 166.

[4]Lloyd Reynolds and Cynthia Taft, *The Evolution of Wage Structure* (New Haven: Yale University Press, 1956).

[5]Wallace Hendricks, "Labor Market Structure and Union Wage Levels," *Economic Inquiry*, 13 (September 1975), 401–16.

[6]Clark Kerr, "Wage Relationships—The Comparative Impact of Market and Power Forces," in John T. Dunlop, ed., *The Theory of Wage Determination* (New York: St. Martin's Press, 1957).

[7]Kuhn, *op. cit.*, pp. 292ff.

[8]Victor J. Sheifer, "Cost-of-Living Adjustment: Keeping Up with Inflation?" *Monthly Labor Review* (June 1979), pp. 14—17.

[9]*Ibid.*, p. 16.

[10]Mark S. Sniderman, "Inflation and Cost-of-Living Adjustment Clauses," *Economic Commentary*, March 24, 1980 (Cleveland: Federal Reserve Bank of Cleveland, 1980).

[11]Audrey Freedman and William E. Fulmer, "Last Rites for Pattern Bargaining," *Harvard Business Review* (March—April 1982), pp. 30—48.

[12]H. Gregg Lewis, *Unionism and Relative Wages in the United States* (Chicago: University of Chicago Press, 1963). This volume provides an early summary of these studies.

[13]Albert Rees, "Wage Determination in the Steel Industry," *American Economic Review* (June 1951), pp. 389—404.

[14]Freeman and Medoff, *op. cit.*, p. 59.

[15]*Ibid.*, p. 49.

[16]Frank C. Pierson, "Industry and National Wage Levels Under Big Unionism," *1961 Proceedings*, Industrial Relations Research Association, pp. 260—274.

[17]Albert Rees, *Wage Inflation* (New York: National Industrial Conference Board, 1957), pp. 27f; Paul A. Samuelson, *Economics*, 11th ed. (New York: McGraw-Hill, 1980), pp. 552—553.

[18]Daniel J. B. Mitchell, "Recent Union Contract Concessions," *Brookings Papers on Economic Activity*, 1 (1982), 166—167.

[19]Orley Ashenfelter and George Johnson, "Unionism, Relative Wages and Labor Quality in U.S. Manufacturing Industries," *International Economic Review*, 13, no. 3 (October 1972), 488—507.

[20]Lawrence M. Kahn, "Unionism and Relative Wages: Direct and Indirect Effects," *Industrial and Labor Relations Review* (June 1979), pp. 520—532.

[21]Mitchell, *op. cit.*, p. 166.

[22]Sumner H. Slichter, James J. Healy and E. Robert Livernash, *The Impact of Collective Bargaining On Management* (Washington, D.C.: The Brookings Institution, 1960).

[23]Thomas A. Kochan, *Collective Bargaining and Industrial Relations* (Homewood, Ill.: Richard D. Irwin, Inc., 1980).

[24]*Ibid.*, pp. 332—335.

[25]*Ibid.*

[26]Freeman and Medoff, *op. cit.*, p. 164.

[27]For example, see Kim Clark, "The Impact of Unionization on Productivity: A Case Study," *Industrial and Labor Relations Review*, 34 (July, 1980), 451—468.

[28]Freeman and Medoff, *op. cit.*, p. 96.

[29]*Ibid.*

[30]James L. Medoff, "Layoffs and Alternatives Under Trade Unions in United States Manufacturing," *American Economic Review* 69 (June 1979), 380—395.

EMPLOYEE BENEFITS

14

A historical review of negotiated fringe benefit plans indicates a significant growth and liberalization of the following major benefits over the last few decades: wage employment guarantees, supplementary unemployment benefits, severance pay, pensions, health plans, vacations and holidays.

The purpose of this chapter is to discuss these fringes and their importance in labor settlements, with particular attention to statistical, historical, and legislative developments. The characteristics and profiles of the most prevalent plans as they appear in major labor agreements are also discussed.

The list of fringes available to many workers is considerably longer than the one covered in this chapter. Not every fringe benefit to which an employee is entitled is necessarily incorporated into a labor contract. Some fringes have a long history preceding unionization and collective bargaining. Many contracts have "maintenance of practices" provisions, which cover practices and policies that precede unionization. In both the private and public sector, numerous fringes have evolved over time; they are not explicitly stated in the labor agreement but are expected by employees and provided by management. A review of published arbitration decisions reveals instances of disagreement between labor and management over some of these silent and traditional fringe benefits.

Other fringe benefits not explicitly covered by agreements are those that are legally mandated. Employers' contributions to social security, workers' compensation, and unemployment insurance are examples.

All the fringes discussed in this chapter can be labeled economic benefits. The potential cost of each can be calculated, but these are not always accurate and sometimes major miscalculations develop. Interestingly, costs are usually not audited by management against original estimates. To avoid embarrassment and career repercussions, management people responsible for original cost estimates of fringe benefits are not interested to discover at the expiration of a contract that their original estimates may have been wrong.

Whereas some fringes lend themselves to costing procedures, there are others to which it is difficult or impossible to attach a financial tag, particularly in the short run. Flextime, grievance procedures, and seniority provisions in such areas as layoffs, promotions, and transfers could be considered fringes for which it is hard to provide estimates of economic cost to the employer or economic benefit to the employees, even though both might be substantial.

Charts 14-1 and 14-2 provide an overview of the extent and characteristics of eleven private-sector employee-benefit plans financed either fully or partly by employers. The source of these charts, as indicated, is a 1984 study of employee benefits in medium and large firms, released by the U.S. Department of Labor in June of 1985. Chart 1 shows the percent of full-time employees receiving paid time off for vacations, holidays, rest time, sick leave, personal leave, and lunch period. Chart 2 indicates the percent of full-time employees entitled to health insurance, life insurance, pensions, sickness and accident insurance, and long-term disability insurance.

CHART 14.1. PAID TIME OFF: PERCENT OF FULL-TIME EMPLOYEES COVERED, MEDIUM AND LARGE FIRMS, 1984

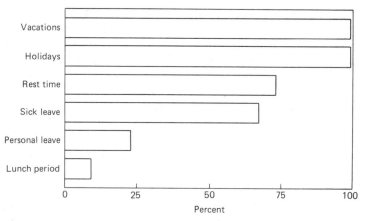

SOURCE: *Employee Benefits in Medium and Large Firms, 1984,* U.S. Department of Labor, Bureau of Labor Statistics, June 1985 (Bulletin 2237), p. 2.

WAGE EMPLOYMENT GUARANTEES

The purpose of Wage Employment Guarantees (WEG) is to insure employees a specified minimum amount of work or compensation for a predetermined period of time. The existing guarantees range from one week to a year or more.[1]

CHART 14.2.   INSURANCE AND PENSION PLANS: PERCENT OF FULL-TIME EMPLOYEES COVERED, MEDIUM AND LARGE FIRMS, 1984

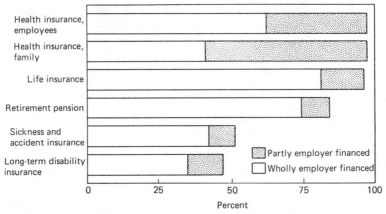

SOURCE: *Employee Benefits in Medium and Large Firms, 1984*, U.S. Department of Labor, Bureau of Labor Statistics, June 1985 (Bulletin 2237), p. 2.

WEGs have a long history in the United States. The first negotiated plans emerged in the wallpaper, brewery, textile, and printing industries during the 1890s. In 1894, the National Association of Machine Printers and Color Mixers and the National Wallpaper Company negotiated an agreement guaranteeing eleven months of employment. This was extended to twelve months in 1896. During the same period, in Philadelphia and in New York, the National Union of the United Brewery Workmen of the United States negotiated a contract restricting layoffs of regular employees to a limited number of days during the slow season of the year.[2]

At the beginning of the twentieth century, some small firms reached oral agreements to provide certain employees with year-round work. The BLS reports that in 1905 a retail men's furnishing store guaranteed regular employees fifty-two weeks of work per year, and that in 1912 a coffee-roasting employer started paying production workers full pay during the slack season.[3]

Despite these examples of guaranteed wage plans, the total number of employees covered by such plans was relatively small prior to World War II. A 1940 *Monthly Labor Review* reports that only "a fracton of 1 percent of the 7000 union agreements on file with the Bureau of Labor Statistics" contained a reference to wage guarantees.[4]

The Bureau of National Affairs (BNA) maintains a file of over 5000 agreements out of which a 400-contract sample is selected for survey purposes.[5] According to the BNA sample survey, income maintenance provisions were found in 38 percent of contracts in 1966, and by 1983 this total had increased to 51 percent.[6] The BNA classifies income maintenance into three major categories: work or pay guarantees, severance pay provisions, and SUB plans. The latter two categories are discussed in subsequent sections; in this section we will evaluate only work or pay guarantees. Under some contracts, such guarantees are offered on a weekly, monthly, or annual basis. In some instances employment guarantees are provided for the duration of an agreement; some contracts go even further and furnish lifetime guarantees. When weekly guarantees are offered they range from fifteen to forty hours per week. Some contracts, rather than specifying hours, specify minimum weekly pay or a certain number of shifts per week. When guarantees are provided on a monthly basis they are computed on number of hours of work or on monthly pay or as a percentage of average monthly pay. Most guarantees are confined to regular employees. Some contracts stipulate a minimum amount of service for eligibility. Some employers reserve the right to cancel guarantees in case of strikes, unexcused absences, and lack of orders. Guarantees are more prevalent in nonmanfacturing (21 percent) than in manufacturing (5 percent).[7] Weekly guarantees can be found in food, retail services, and transportation industries; monthly guarantees, in construction and machinery; annual guarantees, in the maritime and utility industries; and lifetime guarantees, in the printing industry.[8]

The following actual contract clauses illustrate various types of guarantee provisions:

> Level of guarantee: All White Time Card employees (regular full-time employees with one year's seniority) shall be covered by a forty (40) hour guarantee, except for White Time Card employees in continuous twenty-four (24) hour machine operations which restrict hours of work, shall continue to be covered under thirty-seven and one-half (37½) hour guarantee. (Spiegel Inc. and Teamsters; exp. 2/83)[9]

> Monthly Guarantee: The Employer agrees to guarantee to each employee recruited and transported to the jobsite, work at the rate of 173 compensable hours of work per month at the basic rate of pay, provided that the agreed term of employment covers more than the minimum of thirty (30) days and the employee is ready, willing, and physically able to work. . . . (Associated General Contractors of America, Inc., Alaska Chapter *and* Teamsters; exp. 6/85)[10]

> Conditions of Guarantee: . . . such guarantee (forty hours of work during regular workweek and thirty-two hours of work during a holiday workweek) may be suspended, without notice, in the event of an act of God, or other circumstances beyond the control of the Employer. (FedMart Stores, Inc. and Retail Clerks; exp. 7/81)[11]

To conclude, the basic ingredients of most WEG plans are duration, eligibility, and waiver. Duration varies from one week to over a year, with the majority of plans confined to weekly guarantees. Eligibility usually extends to all regular full-time employees, and the plans start as of the date of hiring. Most plans contain waiver clauses permitting employers to suspend guarantees under some circumstances.[12]

SUPPLEMENTARY UNEMPLOYMENT BENEFITS

The supplementary unemployment benefits (SUB) plans are an outgrowth of some WEG plans. The objective of SUB plans is to provide weekly supplements to state unemployment insurance payments to laid-off employees. Most plans start paying benefits after the first week of layoffs.[13] To qualify, however, workers must have at least one year of service. To ease the economic hardship of unemployment some plans also provide such benefits as moving allowances, severance pay, and payments of health insurance.[14] Employees are not entitled to SUB payments if they are on strike or are suspended or discharged for cause.

There was strong opposition to the early SUB guaranteed annual wage plans from many firms and employer associations, with the Chamber of Commerce leading an aggressive campaign against such plans. In 1954, one Chamber publication warned that such plans would "put the bonus on idleness, discourage job seeking and raid . . . state unemployment compensation systems."[15] A review of three decades of operation of SUB plans suggests that the dangers listed by the Chamber did not materialize.

Financing

All SUB plans are financed by employers. Plans can be funded in one of the following ways: individual account fund, single-employer pooled fund, multi-employer pooled fund, and unfunded plans.[16] Under an individual account fund, the employer's contribution would be deposited to the accounts of individual employees, with benefit payments directly debited against such accounts. At terminaton, an employee would be entitled to any balance left in the account. Under a single-employer pooled fund, employer contributions would go to the common fund for all employees. Under such a plan, an employee is not entitled to any residual or vesting. A multiemployer pooled fund operates on the same principal as a single-employer fund except that more than one firm makes contributions to the fund. As contrasted with these plans, the unfunded plan does not require a company to set up a reserve for future SUB obligations. The firm is expected to make payments out of operating funds.

The first SUB plan was negotiated by the United Automobile Workers and the Ford Motor Company in 1955.[17] Within a short time, the other auto makers and a significant number of major unionized companies and industries followed Ford's lead and agreed to SUB plans. Since 1955, a number of important developments affected SUB plans. The older plans were significantly revised and liberalized since the implementation of the original Ford plan. Also, the composition of employees and industries covered by SUB plans changed. SUB plans were also adopted by many small and medium-sized firms.

SUB plans can be found in the following industries: transportation equipment, primary metals, machinery, electrical machinery, fabricated metals and rubber, stone-clay and glass, fuel, mining, construction, furniture, maritime and retail.[18] The following major unions have been successful in negotiating SUB plans: United Auto Workers, The International Association of Machinists, The United Rubber Workers, The International Union of Electrical Workers, The Seafarer's International Union, and the United Food and Commercial Workers Union.[19]

SEVERANCE PAY

The purpose of severance pay (SP) plans is to cushion the loss of jobs when a firm permanently dismisses employees for reasons other than cause. Permanent layoffs can be due to technological changes, to closing down of inefficient operations, to geographic transfers of operations, and to a variety of other factors. The BLS defines severance pay as "a monetary allowance graduated by length of service to displaced employees, generally upon permanent termination of employment with no chance of recall, but often upon indefinite layoff with recall rights."[20] The monetary allowance is referred to by a variety of names: It is termed severance pay, termination pay, dismissal allowance, separation benefit, and permanent layoff allowance.

Under almost all SP plans, an employee is entitled to an allowance if the separation is involuntary.[21] In many agreements, involuntary permanent separation was defined as one resulting from "plant closing, transfer of operations, physical disability and the like."[22] Under almost all contracts, in order to be entitled to severance pay, workers must have some minimum length of service, usually six months to a year.[23] Length of service is not only important for establishing eligibility but also for determining the amount of benefits. Under almost all contracts, the size of the severance allowance is directly related to seniority. Some plans provide a fixed amount of benefit per unit of service. This is frequently expressed as one week of pay for each year of service. Under some plans, proportionately larger payments go to low-seniority employees, and the allowance is increased at a decreasing rate. Thus a worker may be eligible for four weeks of pay for three to five years of service, and this could go up to seven weeks for seven to ten years of service.[24] Some plans increase allowances to senior employees at an increasing rate; thus, if a worker with five years of seniority is entitled to 5.2 weeks of pay, a worker with twenty-five years is eligible for 31.8 weeks of pay.[25] Under some plans, a ceiling is imposed on the amount a worker can receive; thus seniority beyond a certain number of years does not increase the amount of severance pay.

According to a labor contract survey conducted by the Bureau of National Affairs (BNA), 39 percent of the agreements surveyed contained an SP provision. Out of these, 45 percent were in manufacturing and 28 percent in nonmanufacturing.[26] The contracts reviewed represented sixteen manufacturing and nine nonmanufacturing industries. BNA reports that more contracts contained SP provisions in their 1983 survey (47 percent than in their 1979 survey (39 percent).[27] These were SP provisions for employees terminated in case of permanent shutdowns. This increase is not surprising; adverse economic conditions and many plant shutdowns in recent years made such provisions extremely important for unions and their members.

Severance pay is usually determined according to seniority and level of pay. Most plans contain a graduated schedule of compensation; the longer employees have been in service, the higher their benefits. Some plans provide a defined number of weekly pay or a flat weekly amount for each year of service. Duration of weekly severance pay has a very broad range. It could be anywhere from ten to 104 weeks; fifty-two weeks is the most frequent contract provision. Years of service is one of the limitations applied to SP plans. To be eligible employees must satisfy minimum service conditions, these range from one month to fifteen years. The most prevalent requirement is one year of service.[28] Under some contracts, employees who are eligible for pensions or reject other work are refused compensation. In almost all cases the cost of

SP is financed by the employer. However, the BNA reports that under one contract, employees are also required to contribute to the plan.[29]

There are major differences in availability of SP plans among industries. According to the BNA, such plans are contained in every contract surveyed in the communication industry. They are common in "chemicals, food, leather, machinery, paper, petroleum, printing and rubber." They are very rare in construction, furniture, and textiles and are not found in apparel and lumber.[30]

To conclude, in view of all the recent plant closing and industrial restructuring taking place in the United States, unions will continue to stress the importance of income-maintenance plans. This will include demands for new provisions or improvements of existing plans in such areas as severance pay, supplemental unemployment benefits, and guarantees of work or pay.

PRIVATE PENSION PLANS

The BLS defines a private pension as "a plan established unilaterally by an employer or a union or jointly by both that provides a cash income for life to qualified workers upon retirement."[31]

The first private pension plan in the United States was started by the American Express Company in 1875. By 1916, 117 pension plans were in operation, by 1930, 720 plans existed, and by 1951 there were 14,000 plans in effect covering 9.6 million employees.[32] According to a 1983 BLS Bulletin 84 percent of employees of medium and large firms were covered by private pension plans, with the employer usually covering the entire cost of the retirement program.[33] A 1983 BNA survey of contracts states that almost all contracts in their sample made some reference to pension plans. In 1929 U.S. pensions represented .2 percent of wages and salaries; by 1963, this total went up to 2.4 percent, and by 1983 it was 3.6 percent.[34]

The major impetus for growth of negotiated pension plans has been the landmark Supreme Court case *Inland Steel Company* v. *NLRB* (1949).[35] The case made pension and employee welfare plans a mandatory subject of collective bargaining.

Characteristics of Pension Plans

Pension plans can be classified as qualified and nonqualified. A qualified plan is one that under the rules and regulations of the Internal Revenue Code permits a firm to treat pension contributions as a deductible business expense. Such contributions are not considered current income to employees. Thus, a qualified plan has tax advantages both for the firm and for the employee. A nonqualified plan would not be eligible to treat pension contributions as deductible expenses.

The eligibility rules of most pension plans specify the categories of employees to be covered, the necessary age for early and compulsory retirement, and the minimum period of employment that qualifies participants for vesting rights. Vesting rights are earned pension rights that cannot be canceled. Retirement benefits are usually not extended to temporary casual and part-time employees and under many plans to workers under twenty-five.

The typical plan incorporates vesting provisions which entitle an employee who leaves the firm before retirement to some pension benefits. The Employee Retirement Income Security Act of 1974 (ERISA) mandates vesting of all private pension plans. According to a recent BLS study, most retirement plans require ten years of service before benefits are fully guaranteed. Some plans exclude years of service before age twenty-two in computing vesting eligibility. Some plans provide for graduated vesting, which under ERISA calls for 25 percent vesting with five years of service; the percentage is gradually increased with each year of service. Fifteen years is the maximum requirement for this type of vesting.[36]

The 1978 Amendments to the Age Discrimination in Employment Act (ADEA) increased the allowable age for mandatory retirement, for most employees, from sixty-five to seventy.[37] A 1983 BLS study reports that 42 percent of all pension plan participants in medium and large firms were covered by plans that stipulated age sixty-five as the earliest age for retirement with full benefits. Most of such plans had no service requirements. Plans providing retirement at earlier age usually had length-of-service provisions. In their recent book, Miner and Miner state that because of legislative changes, "compulsory retirement at a fixed age now has been shifted for most employees from sixty-five to seventy. . . .The norm of retirement at age sixty-five or perhaps before seems to be still with us, in spite of changes in the law."[38]

Pension Funding Plans

There are four[39] approaches to funding pension programs: current expenditure method, trusteed programs, insured programs, and profit-sharing plans.

Current expenditure plans rely on a general cash fund to pay benefits to retired employees. The health and welfare fund between the United Mine Workers and the bituminous and anthracite coal industry can be described as a current expenditure or pay-as-you-go plan.[40] The plan is financed by employer payments based on coal mined.

Some of the plans financed under the current expenditure approach have ignored actuarial standards for protecting employee retirement interests, thus leaving these plans with inadequate resources. The 1974 Pension Reform Act has attempted to remedy some of these inequities.

Trusteed pension plans are administered by banks, trusts, or employers. A firm can and sometimes does act as its own trust or insurance company. Under such plans, actuaries determine the amount that has to be contributed into the fund each year to keep it solvent. Actuarial calculations take into account the age of employees, mortality rates, labor turnover rates, and anticipated return on investment.

Insured plans are administered by insurance companies, which collect all premiums and assume administrative responsibilities and future liabilities for pension payments. One shortcoming is that their administrative cost is considerably higher than that of trusteed plans.

Profit-sharing pension plans are financed from employer profits. Since profits vary from year to year, contributions are not consistent. In years that a firm loses money, no contributions are made. In some reasonably profitable companies, the plans have been successful and the companies were able to make consistent contributions to their pension funds.[41] The problem which such plans is that employees must accept some of the business risks affecting profitability. Although the profitability of a firm may be favorably influenced by productivity of its employees, in many instances profitability depends on factors beyond the control of the firm's labor force. Thus diligence of the work force does not always lead to higher pensions.

Pension plans financed jointly by employers and employees are referred to as *contributory*, as opposed to *noncontributory* plans just discussed. The 1983 BNA study of contracts states that 92 percent of the plans reviewed were noncontributory; in the remaining 8 percent, costs are shared in various proportions between employers and employees.[42]

A point of friction at the bargaining table concerns pension premiums for time not worked. Employers attempt to confine the base for pension premiums to straight working hours, excluding holidays and overtime. Management also tries to establish a minimum number of monthly hours of work before a contribution is to be made on behalf of an employee. Employers are unwilling to make pension contributions for laid-off or sick employees. Unions, on the other hand, demand that some pension contributions be made for regular workers, even if they are not on the active payroll. In some settlements, a compromise is reached under which a company agrees to contribute a certain sum for a specified period of time for sick and laid-off employees.[43]

The Legal Framework

Pension funds are subject to various state and federal statutes and regulations, some of which are: the Labor Management Relations Act of 1947; the Welfare and Pension Plans Disclosure Act of 1958; the Employee Retirement Income Security Act of 1974; registration provisions of the Securities Exchange Act of 1934; and tax, estate, and inheritance provisions of various state and federal laws.

Under Section 302(C) of the Labor Management Relations Act of 1947, pension trust funds in which unions participate as administrators must have equal representation from employers and neutral persons agreed upon by both sides. Although there are many different models for administration of pension funds, the most prevalent ones are either joint labor and management plans or those under the complete control of employers.[44]

The performance of private pension funds over the years has been far from satisfactory. Some plans provide excellent coverage for their participants, whereas others because of questionable past practices force their retiring members onto welfare rolls. In the past many plans have been insufficiently funded, funds were poorly invested, and vesting rights were inadequate. A 1973 congressional investigation disclosed that out of the 35 million employees covered by private plans, one-third to one-half would never receive benefits.[45]

In order to reduce abuses and provide better protection, Congress in 1974 enacted the Pension Reform Law (ERISA). Although ERISA does not compel employers to establish pension plans, it prescribes strict standards for existing and newly implemented plans. The law sets minimum funding requirements and investment standards, mandates actuarial audits, and stipulates standards of conduct and accountability for administrators.[46] The act also grants employees portability rights by permitting them to transfer vested benefits among pension plans.

ERISA has been criticized by many employers because of its many complex and demanding reporting requirements. Within three years of enactment of ERISA (between 1974 and 1977), approximately 18,000 private pension plans were discontinued.[47] Some authors claim that the burdensome requirements of ERISA were responsible for this development; others state that many of these plans would have been terminated regardless of ERISA. Although the act has many critics, some employees benefited greatly from its provisions.[48] Despite various ERISA safeguards, some plans could still fail. To protect employees and insure benefits, the act established the Pension Benefit Guarantee Corporation (PBGC), which is supported by premiums from employers. In case of failure of a pension fund, PBGC assumes responsibility for some vested benefits. When Braniff International Pension plans were terminated, PBGC took over at a cost of $37 million. There were other pension funds that PBGC had to bail out; as a result, at times, the PBGC funds themselves are underfunded. When this occurs, Congress mandates larger employer contributions to the funds.[49]

Private pension programs are supervised by two departments of the federal government: The Internal Revenue Service and Office of Pension and Welfare Benefits Programs of the Department of Labor. Employers must satisfy the Internal Revenue Code provisions in order to claim pensions as a business expense.[50]

During the last few years the Federal Government has been legislatively active in the pension area. Under the Economic Recovery Tax Act of 1981 (ERTA), employees could augment their pension plan by a tax-deductible contribution of up to $2000. Employer pension and profit-sharing plans were eligible for such contributions, as were IRA plans.[51] The Tax Equity and Fiscal Responsibility Act of 1982 (TEFRA), enacted by Congress in August of 1982, contains a new set of standards that pension funds must satisfy to be eligible for favorable tax treatment. The act also significantly reduced maximum benefits and contributions for IRS-qualified pension plans. The TEFRA versions affected higher-paid employees.[52] The Retirement Equity Act of 1984 (REA) equalized the treatment of women and men regarding retirement benefits.[53]

In a recent article on pension plans, Facciani, who has served as president of the American Society of Pension Actuaries, expressed the view "that Congress and the administration are planning a major frontal offensive on the favorable tax advantages afforded private retirement plans. . . . The national legislative and administrative front is reflecting an increasingly hostile attitude toward employer sponsored fringe benefit plans."[54] All these developments are related to the budget process, tax-simplification proposals, and budgeting deficits. In a 1985 article, Georgine, of the National Coordinating Committee for Multiemployer Plans, states that in the near future "Congress, with input from the Administration will decide whether to tax employee benefits." According to Georgine, "there are powerful forces pressing to do so by repealing, or at least curtailing, the historical tax-favored treatment of employee benefits,"[55] All these developments may have significant implications for future collective bargaining. Adverse tax treatment of fringe benefits and pensions may force unions and union members to rearrange their demand and bargaining priorities in future negotiations.

Inflation and Variable Annuity Plans

The purpose of pension plans is to provide retired workers with a standard of living that would not be too far removed from their preretirement income. Whereas the social security system is expected to provide a subsistence level of income, private plans are expected to give workers more than that. Unfortunately, private pension plans, because of inflation, find it difficult to preserve a retiree's standard of living. Indexing of pension benefits to inflation is one possible but very costly response to this particular problem. To protect pensioners from the erosion of purchasing power, some plans give participants an option to subscribe to a variable rather than to a fixed annuity plan. Under such plans, contributions are invested in stocks rather than in bonds, and benefits are based on performance of the stock market. In some countries, return on bonds is tied to a cost-of-living index. If such securities ever become available in the United States, they would be an ideal vehicle for investment of pension funds.

Replacement Rates under Pension Plans

Charts 14-3 and 14-4, based on a 1984 U.S. Department of Labor study, provide graphical information on pension replacement rates offered to employees in various earning brackets. *Replacement rate* is a measure of a retiree's final-year earnings that are replaced by retirement income. Chart 14-3 covers replacement rates for private pension plans as well as for combined private pension and social security payments. The average benefit is based on thirty years of service. The range of earnings for workers' final years is from $15,000 to $40,000. Chart 14-4 provides information on

CHART 14.3.   REPLACEMENT RATES UNDER PENSION PLANS INCLUDING AND EXCLUDING SOCIAL SECURITY PAYMENTS: AVERAGE BENEFITS BASED ON 30 YEARS OF SERVICE, MEDIUM AND LARGE FIRMS, 1984

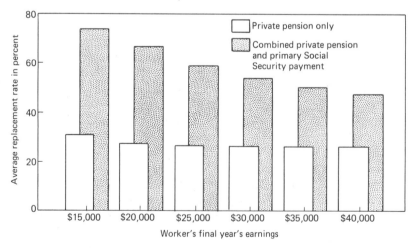

SOURCE: *Employee Benefits in Medium and Large Firms, 1984*, U.S. Department of Labor, Bureau of Labor Statistics, June 1985 (Bulletin 2237), p. 13.

**CHART 14.4.   REPLACEMENT RATES UNDER PRIVATE PENSION PLANS: AVERAGE
BENEFITS BASED ON 30 YEARS OF SERVICE BY TYPE OF PENSION FORMULA,
MEDIUM AND LARGE FIRMS, 1984**

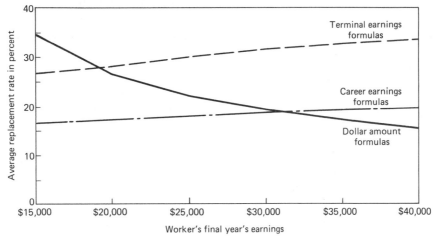

SOURCE: *Employee Benefits in Medium and Large Firms, 1984,* U.S. Department of Labor, Bureau of Labor Statistics,
June 1985 (Bulletin 2237), p. 13.

replacement rates based on terminal earnings, career earnings, and dollar-amount
formulas. Earnings formulas are computed on the basis of the worker's annual income
per year of service. Terminal earnings formulas are based on employees earnings in the
final years of employment. Career earnings formulas are computed on the basis of
average of career earnings. Plans that are based on dollar-amount formulas pay
employees a specified dollar amount for each year of service. Table 14–1 provides
statistical data on private pension plans according to methods applied for determining
retirement payments. Table 14–2 shows average pension replacement rates based on
final annual earnings as well as years of service.

Negotiation of Pension Funds

Negotiation of pension benefits is difficult because of the many legal requirements that such plans must satisfy, because of the complexity of the subject matter
which brings to the bargaining table lawyers, actuaries, accountants, and financial
analysts, and because of the internal pressures generated on union negotiators within
the bargaining unit. The amount of money over which parties bargain is limited. Any
improvements in pension benefits can be accomplished only at the expense of other
economic items within the bargaining package.

How much of a settlement should be channeled toward pensions creates problems for management and unions. Both sides may feel that the benefits of present and
future retirees are inadequate; increasing these benefits, however, may not always be a
viable alternative. From an employer's point of view, a trade-off of wages for higher
pensions could prove costly in terms of an increased turnover rate and greater difficulty
in recruiting qualified personnel. For a union, giving up some wage increases for

TABLE 14.1.   PRIVATE PENSION PLANS:[1] PERCENT OF FULL-TIME PARTICIPANTS BY METHOD OF DETERMINING RETIREMENT PAYMENTS, MEDIUM AND LARGE FIRMS, 1984

Basis of payment[2]	All participants	Professional and administrative participants	Technical and clerical participants	Production participants
Total	100	100	100	100
Terminal earnings formula	54	70	71	36
No alternative formula	24	31	39	12
Terminal earnings alternative	8	12	10	5
Career earnings alternative	3	4	4	2
Dollar amount alternative[3]	19	23	17	17
Percent of contributions alternative	(4)	1	(4)	(4)
Career earnings formula	14	22	15	10
No alternative formula	8	12	9	5
Career earnings alternative	1	1	1	1
Dollar amount alternative[3]	6	8	6	4
Dollar amount formula[3]	28	4	10	50
No alternative formula	27	4	10	48
Dollar amount alternative[3]	1	—	(4)	2
Percent of contributions alternative	(4)	(4)	(4)	(4)
Percent of contributions formula	2	1	(4)	3
No alternative formula	1	(4)	(4)	3
Percent of contributions alternative	(4)	(4)	(4)	(4)
Money purchase	2	4	3	1

[1]*Excludes supplemental pension plans.*

[2]*Alternative formulas are generally designed to provide a minimum benefit for employees with short service or low earnings.*

[3]*Includes formulas based on dollar amounts for each year of service and schedules of benefits that vary by length of service.*

[4]*Less than .5 percent.*

NOTE: *Because of rounding, sums of individual items may not equal totals. Dash indicates no employees in this category.*

SOURCE: *Employee Benefits in Medium and Large Firms, 1984,* U.S. Department of Labor, Bureau of Labor Statistics, June 1985 (Bulletin 2237), p. 43.

improved retirement benefits could produce a strong backlash against union leadership from younger workers. Union negotiators are subjected to conflicting internal pressures when negotiating pension benefits. Some union members are interested in maximizing current incomes, whereas others are concerned with security after retirement. One well-known, although unusual, case where a union was confronted with such a dilemma was the 1947 contract negotiations at Ford Motor Company. In this case, the negotiators resorted to an ingenious solution to their problem by letting membership decide on the trade-off between pensions and wages. When the 1947 contract was concluded, membership was presented with two alternative proposals for ratification. One proposal contained a pension plan plus a 7 cents per hour general wage increase. The alternative was a 15-cent increase without a pension plan. The membership opted for the no-pension proposal by voting 51,832 to 16,720 for the larger wage increase.[56]

TABLE 14.2. PRIVATE PENSION PLANS: AVERAGE REPLACEMENT RATES FOR SPECIFIED FINAL EARNINGS AND YEARS OF SERVICE MEDIUM AND LARGE FIRMS, 1984

Final annual earnings	Years of service						
	10	15	20	25	30	35	40
	Private pension only						
All participants							
$15,000	11.0	16.1	21.0	26.0	30.8	35.0	38.9
$20,000	9.9	14.4	18.8	23.2	27.4	31.0	34.3
$25,000	9.7	14.2	18.4	22.7	26.6	30.0	33.0
$30,000	9.7	14.2	18.5	22.6	26.5	29.7	32.6
$35,000	9.7	14.3	18.6	22.7	26.5	29.6	32.3
$40,000	9.8	14.4	18.7	22.8	26.6	29.6	32.3
Professional and administrative							
$15,000	10.6	15.5	20.3	25.0	29.4	33.3	36.6
$20,000	10.2	14.8	19.3	23.6	27.7	31.2	34.3
$25,000	10.5	15.2	19.7	24.0	28.1	31.5	34.5
$30,000	10.8	15.7	20.4	24.8	28.9	32.3	35.1
$35,000	11.0	16.2	21.0	25.6	29.7	33.0	35.8
$40,000	11.3	16.6	21.6	26.3	30.4	33.8	36.5
Technical and clerical							
$15,000	10.5	15.4	20.1	24.6	29.0	32.8	36.1
$20,000	10.1	14.8	19.4	23.8	27.9	31.4	34.4
$25,000	10.5	15.3	20.0	24.5	28.6	32.1	35.0
$30,000	10.8	15.9	20.8	25.4	29.5	32.9	35.8
$35,000	11.1	16.5	21.4	26.1	30.3	33.7	36.5
$40,000	11.4	16.9	22.0	26.8	31.0	34.4	37.2
Production							
$15,000	11.4	16.7	22.0	27.3	32.5	37.1	41.5
$20,000	9.6	14.0	18.3	22.6	26.9	30.7	34.2
$25,000	8.9	13.0	16.9	21.0	24.8	28.1	31.2
$30,000	8.5	12.4	16.2	20.0	23.6	26.6	29.4
$35,000	8.2	12.1	15.8	19.3	22.8	25.6	28.2
$40,000	8.1	11.8	15.4	18.9	22.2	24.9	27.4
	Combined private pension and primary social security benefit						
All participants							
$15,000	53.9	59.0	64.0	69.0	73.8	78.0	81.8
$20,000	49.0	53.5	58.0	62.3	66.5	70.1	73.4
$25,000	42.4	46.8	51.1	55.3	59.3	62.7	65.7
$30,000	37.5	42.0	46.3	52.6	54.3	57.5	60.4
$35,000	33.8	38.4	42.7	46.8	50.6	53.7	56.4
$40,000	30.9	35.5	39.8	43.9	47.7	50.7	53.3
Professional and administrative							
$15,000	53.6	58.5	63.3	67.9	72.3	76.2	79.6
$20,000	49.3	53.9	58.4	62.7	66.8	70.3	73.4
$25,000	43.2	47.9	52.4	56.7	60.8	64.2	67.2
$30,000	38.6	43.5	48.2	52.6	56.7	60.1	62.9
$35,000	35.2	40.3	45.1	49.7	53.8	57.1	59.9
$40,000	32.4	37.7	42.7	47.3	51.5	54.9	57.6

TABLE 14.2. *(Continued)*

Technical and clerical						
$15,000	53.4	58.3	63.0	67.6	72.0	75.8	79.0
$20,000	49.3	54.0	58.5	63.0	67.0	70.5	73.5
$25,000	43.2	48.0	52.7	57.2	61.3	64.8	67.7
$30,000	38.6	43.7	48.6	53.2	57.3	60.7	63.6
$35,000	35.2	40.6	45.5	50.2	54.4	57.8	60.6
$40,000	32.5	38.0	43.1	47.8	52.1	55.5	58.3

SOURCE: *Employee Benefits in Medium and Large Firms, 1984*, U.S. Department of Labor, Bureau of Labor Statistics, June 1985 (Bulletin 2237), p. 49.

In his elaborate study of fringe benefits, Freeman reports that unions have had a significant positive effect on the amount spent on employee fringes, particularly on pensions.[57] Alpert also concludes that unions have had an important positive impact on employee pension benefits.[58] In a recent article, Fosu finds that a union can exert "a strong positive impact on the likelihood that a pension plan is offered in an employee group." He concludes, however, "that unionism does not raise pension expenditures among established plans." Furthermore, he states that his research "does not support the standard assumption that union choice would lead to a larger benefit level than nonunion choice."[59] He recognizes, however, that union threats to organize may induce comparable nonunion employers to augment pensions to union levels. In view of this, the Fosu study provides inconclusive evidence on the impact of unions on the size of pension plans in unionized companies.

The Future of Private Pension Plans

To conclude, the future of private pension plans is cloudy. The burdensome requirements of ERISA, high social security taxes, increasing importance of IRAs, and tax reform legislation all may have adverse effects on private pension plans. These forces, however, will not lead to the extinction of such plans, the survival of which will be assured by union pressures at the bargaining table and in legislative chambers.

HEALTH CARE PLANS

In many firms, unions have been an important force in establishing comprehensive health plans. The unions also have had an impact on nonunionized employees who have been the beneficiaries of union accomplishments. To meet competitive pressures for qualified people and to deter potential unionization, many companies established health plans. Motives of employers who voluntarily provide health care coverage vary from genuine concern for the welfare of workers to competitive forces. The principles of modern personnel management suggest that firms establish adequate medical coverage since employees provided with such benefits are more productive. Health benefits are tax-deductible expenses to the firm. Thus, part of the cost comes from potential tax liabilities. The health insurance industry, with its highly effective marketing techniques, has probably been a factor in the rapid growth of health insurance programs during the last few decades.

The 1983 BNA survey of labor contracts indicates that over 80 percent of the reviewed agreements contained coverage for sickness, accident, and hospitalization benefits. Only 60 percent of the plans, however, provided maternity care, major medical insurance, dental care, accidental death and dismemberment benefits. A BNA comparison of vision care and prescription drug benefits between the results of the 1975 and 1983 studies shows a significant increase in such plans. In 1975 prescription drug insurance was incorporated in only 16 percent of sample plans; this total increased to 29 percent by 1983. In 1975 optical care was included only in 3 percent of sample agreements; this total increased to 31 percent by 1983.[60]

Chart 14-5 provides graphical data on trends in wholly employer-financed health insurance plans both in terms of employee and family coverage between 1980 and 1984. Chart 14-6 supplies a breakdown of the coverage by health insurance plans of the following types of medical care: dental care, extended-care facility, alcoholism treatment, drug abuse treatment, home health care, second surgical opinion, and hearing care. Chart 14-7 shows trends in deductible amounts of major medical plans between the years 1979 and 1984. Table 14−3 provides statistical information on the percent of full-time participants by providers (funding medium) for selected types of coverage. Table 14−4 shows categories of medical care offered to various classifications of employees.

Types of Plans

A wide variety of health and hospital plans is in existence at present. Most plans

CHART 14.5.   TRENDS IN WHOLLY EMPLOYER-FINANCED HEALTH INSURANCE: PERCENT OF FULL-TIME EMPLOYEES COVERED, MEDIUM AND LARGE FIRMS, 1980−84

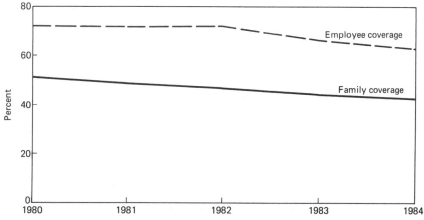

SOURCE: *Employee Benefits in Medium and Large Firms, 1984*, U.S. Department of Labor, Bureau of Labor Statistics, June 1985 (Bulletin 2237), p. 9.

**CHART 14.6. COVERAGE FOR SELECTED TYPES OF MEDICAL CARE: PERCENT OF FULL-TIME
PARTICIPANTS IN HEALTH INSURANCE PLANS, MEDIUM AND
LARGE FIRMS, 1983–84**

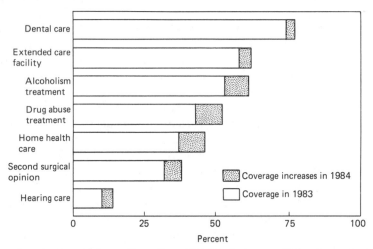

SOURCE: *Employee Benefits in Medium and Large Firms, 1984*, U.S. Department of Labor, Bureau of Labor Statistics,
June 1985 (Bulletin 2237), p. 8.

**CHART 14.7. TRENDS IN SELECTED DEDUCTIBLE AMOUNTS: PERCENT OF FULL-TIME
PARTICIPANTS IN MAJOR MEDICAL PLANS, MEDIUM AND LARGE FIRMS, 1979–84**

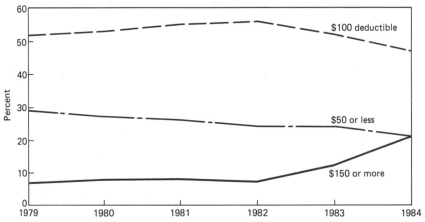

SOURCE: *Employee Benefits in Medium and Large Firms, 1984*, U.S. Department of Labor, Bureau of Labor Statistics,
June 1985 (Bulletin 2237), p. 7.

fall into four distinct categories: "insured, sevice benefit, group practice prepayment,
and self-insured."[61]

The insured plan[62] consists of a contract between an employer and an insurance
company. In return for premium payments, the insurance carrier agrees to compensate employees for hospital and medical expenses. The reimbursement varies accord-

ing to the terms of the contract. The better plans have low deductibles and include in their coverage not only physicians' fees and hospitalization, but also drugs and dental and psychiatric care. The main advantage of the insured plan is the flexibility of coverage, which allows the parties to design a specific program. The scope of such plans is limited only by the premiums paid to the carriers. The insured plan permits the multilocation employer, who operates in different geographic regions, to provide a standard coverage for all employees. Its main shortcoming is higher cost.

Service benefit plans are usually provided by nonprofit organizations. The best known are Blue Cross/Blue Shield plans. Blue Cross refers to hospital insurance plans sponsored by the American Hospital Association. The plans are operated on the regional or state level, each plan having local autonomy. Nationwide coordination is provided by the Blue Cross Commission. To provide an integrated package of health services, the Blue Cross coverage is supplemented by the Blue Shield plan, which covers physicians' fees. The main advantage of such plans is premium costs that are lower than those paid for insured plans. The lower premiums are the result of the nonprofit nature of these plans and lower hospital rates available to plan participants. On the negative side, the plans are unable to provide uniform coverage for multilocation employers. Also, the plans do not provide a full insurance package that would include disability and life insurance coverage.[63]

Another approach to health care is the group practice prepayment plan or a Health Maintenance Organization plan (HMO).[64] Some of these plans have a long history; the Kaiser Foundation Plan in California[65] provides total health and hospital coverage at a fixed monthly fee.

An HMO plan involves a private nonprofit organization, which provides services through an affiliation of hospitals, clinics, and medical personnel. The plans provide a broad spectrum of health care services, supplied through clinics staffed by physicians who are either salaried or under contract to provide services on a demand basis.

In 1973, Congress enacted the Health Maintenance Organization Act. This statute has provided an impetus toward the formation and growth of HMO plans. According to the statute, if a community has an established and qualified HMO plan, employers who provide other medical coverage must give their employees the option of choosing between the HMO and the existing medical plan. If the cost of the HMO is higher than that of the alternative plan, the difference has to be paid by the employees.[66] HMO plans have many advantages: they provide comprehensive medical care to participants, stress preventive medicine, and are cheaper than alternative equivalent plans. One drawback of the HMO is the limited list from which participants can choose physicians and hospitals.

Another type of health coverage is the self-insured program.[67] Under such a plan, the employer acts as administrator and assumes full liability for all medical claims. Some self-insured employers, in order to reduce their exposure, share risks with insurance carriers. The rationale for a self-insured plan is reduced cost. These plans can also have some internal public relations value to the firm. Generous benefits that are promptly and directly paid to employees can enhance the image of the company in the eyes of its workers. One of the drawbacks of such plans is that lenient administration could prove costly to employers. Another shortcoming is that unions and

TABLE 14.3. HEALTH INSURANCE: PERCENT OF FULL-TIME PARTICIPANTS BY FUNDING MEDIUM FOR SELECTED TYPES OF COVERAGE, MEDIUM AND LARGE FIRMS, 1984

Funding medium	All participants					Technical and clerical				
	Basic hospital[1]	Basic surgical[1]	Basic medical[1]	Major medical[2]	Dental	Basic hospital[1]	Basic surgical[1]	Basic medical[1]	Major medical[2]	Dental
Total	100	100	100	100	100	100	100	100	100	100
Provided coverage	71	71	50	91	77	67	67	43	93	75
Blue Cross-Blue Shield	25	17	16	13	4	25	15	14	14	4
Commercial carrier	23	27	16	44	43	21	25	13	45	41
Independent health plans	24	27	18	34	29	22	26	15	33	29
Labor/management[3]	19	22	13	33	27	16	20	9	33	28
Health Maintenance Organizations[4]	5	5	5	[5]	2	6	6	6	[5]	2
Other[6]	—	[5]	[5]	—	[5]	—	[5]	[5]	—	[5]
Combined	[5]	[5]	[5]	[5]	[5]	[5]	[5]	[5]	[5]	[5]
Not provided coverage	29	29	50	9	23	33	33	57	7	25

Funding medium	Professional and administrative					Production				
	Basic hospital[1]	Basic surgical[1]	Basic medical[1]	Major medical[2]	Dental	Basic hospital[1]	Basic surgical[1]	Basic medical[1]	Major medical[2]	Dental
Total	100	100	100	100	100	100	100	100	100	100
Provided coverage	68	67	42	93	79	75	75	58	89	76
Blue Cross-Blue Shield	24	13	12	12	4	26	19	19	13	5
Commercial carrier	22	28	15	48	45	24	28	18	41	42
Independent health plans	22	26	14	33	30	26	28	21	34	29
Labor/management[3]	16	20	8	32	27	22	25	18	34	27
Health Maintenance Organizations[4]	6	6	6	[5]	2	4	4	4	[5]	2
Other[6]	—	[5]	[5]	—	[5]	—	[5]	[5]	—	1
Combined	[5]	[5]	[5]	[5]	[5]	[5]	[5]	[5]	[5]	[5]
Not provided coverage	32	33	58	7	21	25	25	42	11	24

[1] A plan provision was classified as a basic benefit when it covered the initial expenses incurred for a specific medical service. Under these provisions, a plan paid covered expenses in one of several ways: 1) In full with no limitation; 2) in full for a specified period of time, or until a dollar limit was reached; and 3) a cash scheduled allowance benefit that provided up to a dollar amount for a service performed by a hospital or physician. For a specific category of care, a plan may require the participant to pay a lump sum amount each disability or year (deductible) or a nominal charge each visit or procedure (copayment) before reimbursement begins or services are rendered.

[2] Major medical benefits cover many categories of expenses, some of which are not covered under basic benefits, and others for which basic coverage limits have been exhausted. These benefits are characterized by deductible and coinsurance provisions that are applied across categories of care.

[3] Includes plans that are financed by general revenues of a company on a pay-as-you-go basis, plans financed through contributions to a trust fund established to pay benefits, and plans operating their own facilities if at least partially financed by employer contributions. Includes plans that are administered by a commercial carrier through Administrative Services Only-Minimum Premium Plan (ASO-MPP) contracts and plans in which a commercial carrier provides protection only against extraordinary claims.

[4] Includes federally qualified (those meeting standards of the Health Maintenance Organization Act of 1973, as amended) and other HMOs delivering comprehensive health care on a prepayment rather than fee-for-service basis. All HMOs are included here regardless of sponsorship, e.g., Blue Cross-Blue Shield or a commercial insurance carrier.

[5] Less than 0.5 percent.

[6] Includes independent prepaid plans providing health benefits less comprehensive than those of an HMO. Dental benefits plans sponsored by local dental societies are also in this category.

NOTE: Because of rounding, sums of individual items may not equal totals. Dash indicates no employees in this category.

SOURCE: Employee Benefits in Medium and Large Firms, 1984, U.S. Department of Labor, Bureau of Labor Statistics, June 1985 (Bulletin 2237), p. 40.

TABLE 14.4. HEALTH INSURANCE: PERCENT OF FULL-TIME PARTICIPANTS BY COVERAGE FOR SELECTED CATEGORIES OF MEDICAL CARE, MEDIUM AND LARGE FIRMS, 1984

Category of medical care	Total	Care provided				Care not provided
		All	By basic benefits only	By Major medical only	By basic benefits and major medical	
All participants						
Hospital room and board	100	100	17	28	54	(3)
Hospitalization—miscellaneous services	100	100	16	29	54	(3)
Outpatient care[4]	100	100	12	27	60	(3)
Extended care facility[5]	100	62	24	28	11	38
Home health care[5]	100	46	22	16	9	54
Surgical	100	100	32	29	39	(3)
Physician visits—in hospital	100	100	12	49	38	(3)
Physician visits—office	100	96	6	83	7	4
Diagnostic X-ray and laboratory[6]	100	100	25	42	33	(3)
Prescription drugs—nonhospital	100	98	14	81	3	2
Private-duty nursing	100	96	6	89	1	4
Mental health care	100	99	10	28	61	1
Dental	100	77	72	5	—	23
Vision	100	30	26	4	(3)	70

TABLE 14.4. (Continued)

Category of medical care	Total	Care provided				Care not provided
		All	By basic benefits only[1]	By Major medical only[2]	By basic benefits and major medical	
Professional and administrative						
Hospital room and board	100	100	16	32	52	(³)
Hospitalization—miscellaneous services	100	100	15	33	51	(³)
Outpatient care[4]	100	100	9	30	61	(³)
Extended care facility[5]	100	66	22	31	13	34
Home health care[5]	100	48	20	18	10	52
Surgical	100	100	31	33	36	(³)
Physician visits—in hospital	100	100	11	58	32	(³)
Physician visits—office	100	99	7	88	4	1
Diagnostic X-ray and laboratory[6]	100	100	23	49	28	(³)
Prescription drugs—nonhospital	100	98	12	82	4	2
Private-duty nursing	100	99	7	91	1	1
Mental health care	100	100	8	31	60	(³)
Dental	100	79	74	5	—	21
Vision	100	26	21	5	(³)	74
Technical and clerical						
Hospital room and board	100	100	16	32	51	(³)
Hospitalization—miscellaneous services	100	100	14	33	52	(³)
Outpatient care[4]	100	100	10	31	59	(³)
Extended care facility[5]	100	63	18	31	13	37
Home health care[5]	100	47	18	18	11	53
Surgical	100	100	32	33	35	(³)
Physician visits—in hospital	100	100	11	56	32	(³)
Physician visits—office	100	99	7	87	5	1
Diagnostic X-ray and laboratory[6]	100	100	23	48	29	(³)
Prescription drugs—nonhospital	100	97	11	84	3	3
Private-duty nursing	100	99	7	89	2	1
Mental health care	100	99	8	32	60	1
Dental	100	75	70	5	—	25
Vision	100	26	21	5	(³)	74

TABLE 14.4. (Continued)

Category of medical care	Total	Care provided				Care not provided
		All	By basic benefits only	By Major medical only	By basic benefits and major medical	
Production						
Hospital room and board	100	100	18	25	57	(3)
Hospitalization—miscellaneous services	100	100	18	25	57	(3)
Outpatient care[4]	100	100	16	24	60	(3)
Extended care facility[5]	100	60	27	24	9	40
Home health care[5]	100	44	24	13	7	56
Surgical	100	100	32	25	43	(3)
Physician visits—in hospital	100	100	14	42	44	(3)
Physician visits—office	100	94	5	79	9	6
Diagnostic X-ray and laboratory[6]	100	100	27	36	37	(3)
Prescription drugs—nonhospital	100	98	17	79	2	2
Private-duty nursing	100	93	5	87	1	7
Mental health care	100	99	13	25	62	1
Dental	100	76	71	5	—	24
Vision	100	33	30	3	(3)	67

[1]A provision was classified as a basic benefit when it related to the initial expenses incurred for a specific medical service. Under these provisions, a plan paid covered expenses in one of several ways: (1) In full with no limitation; (2) in full for a specified period of time, or until a dollar limit was reached; or (3) a cash scheduled allowance benefit that provided up to a dollar amount for a service performed by a hospital or physician. For a specific category of care, a plan may require the participant to pay a specific amount each disability or year (deductible) or a nominal charge each visit or procedure (copayment) before reimbursement begins or services are rendered.

[2]Major medical benefits cover many categories of expenses, some of which are not covered under basic benefits, and others for which basic coverage limits have been exhausted. These benefits are characterized by deductible and coinsurance provisions that are applied across categories of care.

[3]Less than 0.5 percent.

[4]Coverage for any of the following services charged by the outpatient department of the hospital: Treatment for accidental injury or emergency sickness; surgical procedures; rehabilitative or physical therapy; and treatment for chronic illness (radiation therapy, etc.).

[5]Some plans provide this care only to a patient who was previously hospitalized and is recovering without need of the extensive care provided by a general hospital.

[6]Charges incurred in the outpatient department of a hospital and outside of the hospital.

NOTE: Because of rounding, sums of individual items may not equal totals. Dash indicates no employees in this category.

SOURCE: Employee Benefits in Medium and Large Firms, 1984, U.S. Department of Labor, Bureau of Labor Statistics, June 1985 (Bulletin 2237), pp. 30–31.

employees may question the ability of such self-insured programs to provide full benefits during periods of economic slow-downs.

Employers, Unions, and Health Care Costs

Collective bargaining and unions play an important role in the provision of health care services. Unions have been able to negotiate the establishment and expansion of many health care plans. With the escalating cost of medical services, health care has become a significant component of the total compensation package. Rossiter and Taylor report that: "Both the total health insurance premium per eligible employee and the dollar amount and percentage paid by the employer were found to be higher for employees in firms with a union."[68] Skyrocketing medical costs present labor negotiators with a major challenge: finding a method of curtailing these costs. An article in Business Week states that "no issue has given labor negotiators more trouble in recent years than health benefits—and who pays for them".[69] Employers are attempting to control medical premium costs by trying to restrict benefits. Obviously, unions are resisting such moves. Both parties, however, are very concerned with runaway medical costs.

Some employers and unions are currently exploring alternative approaches to health care plans. At General Motors, the UAW and the company devised three options for workers. Their health care plan may not only keep medical costs constant but may possibly lead to some cost reductions. One option is an HMO plan. The second option is the establishment of a medical group of preferred providers that supply services at a discount. The third option is a modified traditional plan, which requires preauthorization for certain types of treatment. According to studies by the Health Data Institute, a consulting firm, such options could cut health costs by 10%. The UAW–GM approach to health care insurance will most likely be emulated by many employers and unions in the future.[70]

Another approach to the problem of rising health care costs is through the establishment of community health care coalitions. The recent emergence of such coalitions in many communities reflects the concerns expressed in many quarters over the escalating medical costs. Usually such coalitions include businesses, hospitals, physicians, labor unions, and Blue Cross/Blue Shield, as well as other insurance carriers.[71]

According to Jeff Goldsmith, a health policy consultant to Ernst & Whinney, a large accounting firm, "The U.S. Health-Care system is in the throes of a revolution. . . . Power so carefully accumulated for almost five decades is shifting from those who provide care to those who pay for it."[72]

Costs are not the only problem facing health care plans. Another challenge to fringe benefits, including medical benefits, may be coming from the government. The tax-exempt status of many fringe benefits is being challenged in Washington. The U.S. Treasury and various tax reformers would like to eliminate tax exemption of many existing fringe benefits, including health care insurance. One recent estimate is that the taxes on health insurance premiums paid by employers could contribute $34.4

billion of additional revenue to the federal treasury.[73] The opposition to the taxing of fringe benefits is very intense, and only time will tell whether it is strong enough to stop our tax reformers from taxing health care plans.

VACATIONS

Paid vacations are a relatively recent phenomenon. In the 1920s, only some salaried employees received paid vacations. In 1925, only 18 percent of firms provided paid vacations to production workers.[74] Prior to 1940, paid vacations were unusual for hourly workers in the private sector. When employees were eligible for vacations, these were confined to one week and were taken without compensaton.[75] In 1940, only about 25 percent of all employees covered by labor contracts were entitled to a vacation allowance. By 1943, this total has increased to 60 percent.[76]

The World War II National War Labor Board was responsible for the significant increase in paid vacations. The board approved of a standard plan of one week's vacation after one year of service and two weeks after five years.[77] By 1952, nine out of ten organized workers were covered by paid vacation provisions.[78]

According to the BNA sample survey of labor agreements, 91 percent of all agreements contain vacation provisions, and the total goes up to 98 percent without the construction industry.[79] Over the years, the amount of vacation time has increased significantly, as shown in Table 14−5. In 1957, only 15 percent of contracts provided four weeks of vacation, and none of the contracts allowed five or more weeks. By 1983, 83 percent of contracts provided four weeks, 58 percent provided five weeks, and 20 percent provided six weeks of vacations.

Table 14−6 shows the relationship between length of service and vacation entitlements. The BNA survey indicates that in 71 percent of the total sample of contracts, 33 percent of employees were provided with one week of vacation for less than one year of employment; in 67 percent of the contracts, they had to complete one year of service in order to satisfy the eligibility requirements. Six weeks of vacation were provided only in 20 percent of the contracts;[80] out of these, to be eligible, 37 percent needed 25 years of service and 40 percent required 30 years. The balance is broken down into different yearly requirements as shown in Table 14−6.

According to the BLS,[81] paid vacation plans can be grouped under four major headings:

1. Graduated plans
2. Funded plans
3. Ratio-to-work plans
4. Uniform plans

Graduated vacation plans increase vacation benefits with years of service.[82] There are many variations of this plan. The trend in graduated vacation plans has been to lengthen maximum vacation periods and lower years of service. In 1957, most

TABLE 14.5.   TREND IN AMOUNT OF VACATION PER YEAR

(Frequency Expressed as Percentage of Contracts)

	1957	1961	1966	1971	1975	1979	1983
Three weeks	71	78	84	86	85	86	87
Four weeks	15	32	50	73	76	79	83
Five weeks	—	—	2	22	42	53	58
Six weeks	—	—	—	5	10	16	20

SOURCE: *Basic Patterns in Union Contracts*, 10th ed. (The Bureau of National Affairs, Inc., 1983), p. 89.

TABLE 14.6.   VACATION SERVICE REQUIREMENTS

(Frequency Expressed as Percentage of Contracts
Granting Specified Amounts of Vacation*)

| | Amount of Vacation | | | | | |
Service requirement:	1 week	2 weeks	3 weeks	4 weeks	5 weeks	6 weeks
Less than 1 year	33	8	1	—	—	—
1 year	67	26	4	—	—	—
2 years	—	31	1	—	—	—
3-4 years	—	29	3	1	—	—
5 years	—	7	24	2	—	—
6-9 years	—	—	32	2	—	1
10 years	—	—	27	13	1	—
11-14 years	—	—	3	13	—	2
15 years	—	—	4	32	4	—
16-19 years	—	—	—	13	8	1
20 years	—	—	—	21	35	2
21-24 years	—	—	—	—	8	5
25 years	—	—	—	1	37	37
26-29 years	—	—	—	—	2	7
30 years	—	—	—	—	3	40
31-34 years	—	—	—	—	—	1
35 years	—	—	—	—	—	2

Because of rounding sums may not total 100.
SOURCE: *Basic Patterns in Union Contracts*, 10th ed. (The Bureau of National Affairs, Inc., 1983), p. 89.

agreements required that an employee complete fifteen years of service before eligibility for a third week of vacation.[83] In 1983, according to a BNA survey,[84] 87 percent of agreements provide for three weeks of vacation. Out of these, 9 percent mandate less than five years of employment, 24 percent stipulate five years, 32 percent require six to nine years and 27 percent require ten years of service; see Table 14–6.

Funded vacation plans are found in multiemployer contracts. They are popular in the apparel and construction industries. The seasonal nature of the industries, continual shift of workers among employers, and irregular employment patterns necessitate this particular approach to paid vacations. Under these plans, employers make contributions into a central fund from which vacation allowances are dispersed to employees.[85] Many are multipurpose plans that also provide such benefits as life insurance, hospitalization, pensions, and medical care.

The ratio-to-work plans correlate time worked to vacation allowances.[86] In some contracts, a worker is entitled to a vacation credit for each shift worked. Most ratio-to-work plans are concentrated in four industries: apparel, printing and publishing, transportation equipment, and transportation.[87]

Uniform vacation plans ignore length of service. All employees with a minimum of one year of service receive the same vacation allowance. The following provision from the contract of Metropolitan Lithographers Association, Inc. and Typographical Union (ITU) illustrates this type of a plan: "Each employee who shall have worked for the employer for one year without any absence immediately prior to each May 1st shall receive, therefore, four weeks vacation with pay."[88]

Many administrative questions have to be considered in negotiating a vacation plan, regardless of type. Each plan has to consider the following issues:[89]

1. Minimum work requirement in hours, days, weeks, or months in the preceding year that an employee must accumulate to qualify for a vacation (70 percent of agreements studied by the BLS incorporated this factor in their vacation provisions).

2. Qualifying date or specific point in time at which an employee has to satisfy minimum service requirements in order to be entitled to a vacation (according to the BLS, 95 percent of contracts specify a qualifying date).

3. Base for computing vacation pay (under most contracts, employees receive the same pay during vacation that they might have received had they continued working).

4. Pay in lieu of vacation (most agreements studied by the BLS have not addressed this issue; some agreements specifically allow employees to receive pay in lieu of vacation; a few have specific prohibitions against employees working elsewhere).

5. Vacation scheduling (some contracts permit vacation scheduling throughout the year; others limit it to a contractually specified period).

6. Split or long consecutive vacations (40 percent of contracts reviewed by the BLS refer to nonconsecutive vacation; in many of these contracts such vacation required mutual consent between the firm and the employee).

7. Accumulation of vacations (very few contracts allow accumulation of vacations from year to year; some contracts specifically prohibit such an accumulation).

8. Holidays during vacation periods (most contracts compensate employees for holidays occurring during vacations; compensation is usually in the form of extra pay rather than time off).

9. Retirement and termination (in 25 percent of contracts studied by the BLS, an employee at time of retirement is entitled to vacation earned; most contracts compensate employees for vacation up to the time of termination regardless of the cause for the separation).

10. Vacations for part-time employees (very few agreements allow vacation compensation for part-time employees; those contracts that do, prorate such pay).

Table 14–7 was compiled by the U.S. Department of Labor. It provides a detailed outline of paid-vacation policies for selected periods of service.

TABLE 14.7.   PAID VACATIONS: PERCENT OF FULL-TIME EMPLOYEES BY AMOUNT OF PAID VACATION PROVIDED AT SELECTED PERIODS OF SERVICE, MEDIUM AND LARGE FIRMS, 1984

Vacation policy	All employees	Professional and administrative employees	Technical and clerical employees	Production employees
Total	100	100	100	100
In plans providing paid vacations ...	99	99	100	99
At 6 months of service:[1]				
Under 5 days	7	4	5	10
5 days	39	49	48	30
Over 5 and under 10 days	10	14	15	5
10 days	4	7	6	2
Over 10 and under 15 days	(²)	(²)	(²)	—
15 days	(²)	1	(²)	—
Over 15 days	(²)	1	—	(²)
At 1 year of service:				
Under 5 days	(²)	(²)	(²)	(²)
5 days	30	7	13	51
Over 5 and under 10 days	1	(²)	(²)	2
10 days	62	79	83	43
Over 10 and under 15 days	2	3	3	1
15 days	3	8	1	1
Over 15 days	1	2	(²)	(²)
At 3 years of service:				
Under 5 days	(²)	(²)	(²)	(²)
5 days	4	1	1	6
Over 5 and under 10 days	1	—	(²)	1
10 days	80	76	87	79
Over 10 and under 15 days	8	7	6	10
15 days	5	12	5	2
Over 15 and under 20 days	(²)	1	(²)	(²)
20 days	1	2	(²)	(²)
Over 20 days	(²)	1	(²)	(²)
At 5 years of service:				
Under 5 days	(²)	(²)	(²)	(²)
5 days	1	(²)	1	1
Over 5 and under 10 days	(²)	—	(²)	(²)
10 days	47	32	39	59
Over 10 and under 15 days	7	7	6	7
15 days	42	54	51	31
Over 15 and under 20 days	1	2	1	(²)
20 days	1	3	1	(²)
Over 20 days	(²)	1	(²)	(²)
At 10 years of service:				
5 days	1	(²)	(²)	1
Over 5 and under 10 days	(²)	—	(²)	(²)

TABLE 14.7. *(Continued)*

Vacation policy	All employees	Professional and administrative employees	Technical and clerical employees	Production employees
10 days	6	3	3	10
Over 10 and under 15 days	1	(^{2})	1	1
15 days	68	64	74	66
Over 15 and under 20 days	7	6	4	9
20 days	15	25	17	10
Over 20 days	1	2	1	1
At 15 years of service:				
5 days	1	(^{2})	(^{2})	1
Over 5 and under 10 days	(^{2})	—	(^{2})	(^{2})
10 days	3	1	2	5
Over 10 and under 15 days	(^{2})	(^{2})	(^{2})	(^{2})
15 days	28	20	23	34
Over 15 and under 20 days	3	3	3	3
20 days	60	69	68	52
Over 20 and under 25 days	2	2	1	2
25 days	2	2	2	1
Over 25 days	1	1	1	1
At 20 years of service:				
Under 10 days	(^{2})	(^{2})	(^{2})	1
10 days	3	1	1	5
Over 10 and under 15 days	(^{2})	(^{2})	(^{2})	(^{2})
15 days	9	6	7	13
Over 15 and under 20 days	1	1	(^{2})	1
20 days	56	60	66	49
Over 20 and under 25 days	3	4	3	3
25 days	25	26	21	26
Over 25 and under 30 days	1	1	1	1
30 days	(^{2})	(^{2})	(^{2})	(^{2})
Over 30 days	(^{2})	(^{2})	(^{2})	1
At 25 years of service:				
Under 10 days	(^{2})	(^{2})	(^{2})	1
10 days	3	1	1	5
Over 10 and under 15 days	(^{2})	(^{2})	(^{2})	(^{2})
15 days	8	6	6	10
Over 15 and under 20 days	(^{2})	1	(^{2})	(^{2})
20 days	30	34	35	26
Over 20 and under 25 days	2	3	3	2
25 days	48	48	48	47
Over 25 and under 30 days	1	1	1	1
30 days	5	5	4	5
Over 30 days	1	1	1	1
At 30 years of service:[3]				
Under 10 days	(^{2})	(^{2})	(^{2})	1
10 days	3	1	1	5
Over 10 and under 15 days	(^{2})	(^{2})	(^{2})	(^{2})

TABLE 14.7. *(Continued)*

Vacation policy	All employees	Professional and administrative employees	Technical and clerical employees	Production employees
15 days	8	6	6	10
Over 15 and under 20 days	(²)	(²)	(²)	(²)
20 days	29	33	34	24
Over 20 and under 25 days	1	1	1	1
25 days	43	42	45	43
Over 25 and under 30 days	1	1	1	1
30 days	10	12	9	10
Over 30 days	3	2	2	3

¹Excludes situations where employees are credited with vacation days during the first 6 months of service but, as a matter of establishment policy, must wait beyond 6 months before taking those days off.

²Less than 0.5 percent

³Provisions were virtually the same after longer years of service.

NOTE: *Data include anniversary year bonus days and exclude extended vacations. Dash indicates no employees in this category.*

SOURCE: *Employee Benefits in Medium and Large Firms, 1984,* U.S. Department of Labor, Bureau of Labor Statistics, June 1985 (Bulletin 2237), p. 20.

HOLIDAYS

Paid holidays for nonoffice employees emerged during World War II and have gained an almost universal acceptance since. Before and during the early years of World War II, holidays granted to hourly workers, as contrasted with holidays for administrative and clerical personnel, were usually without pay.[90] According to the BLS as late as 1943, contracts in manufacturing, construction, and mining did not provide for paid holidays.[91] The situation changed significantly as the result of a ruling by the National War Labor Board and following the issue of Executive Order 9240. To stimulate more production during World War II, the order required the payment of time and one-half for work performed during six holidays. The NWLB permitted the granting of six paid holidays, if such payments reflected "the prevailing practice in the industry or the area."[92] This was an important ruling, since wage increases were strictly regulated by the NWLB, and payment for holidays was an economic fringe that was in compliance with the board's guidelines. After World War II, many employers recognized six paid holidays as a standard fringe benefit to be included in labor contracts. According to the BLS, by 1953 the acceptance of paid holidays "had almost reached its present degree of prominence among large organized employers."[93]

The 1983 BNA sample survey of contracts indicates that 99 percent of contracts contain holiday provisions. Out of these 89 percent are observed without a sacrifice of pay. Since World War II, unions have been successful in increasing the number of paid holidays in labor agreements. Whereas in 1957 only 4 percent of contracts provided for ten or more holidays per year, by 1966 the number increased to 7 percent, by 1979, to

59 percent, and by 1983, the number went up to 72 percent.[94] See Table 14–8.

Table 14–9 provides data on the number of paid holidays to different categories of workers, such as professional, administrative, technical, clerical, and production employees.

TABLE 14.8.   TREND IN NUMBER OF HOLIDAYS

(Frequency Expressed as Percentage of Contracts)

	1957	1961	1966	1971	1975	1979	1983
None specified	1	1	1	1	1	2	2
Fewer than 7	36	22	16	11	6	4	3
7, 7½	43	47	39	15	10	8	5
8, 8½	12	23	31	25	12	11	8
9, 9½	4	5	7	27	29	17	11
10, 10½	4	5[1]	7[1]	16	20	27	23
11, 11½	—	—	—	4	12	15	20
12, 12½	—	—	—	3[2]	10[2]	11	13
13 or more	—	—	—	—	—	6	16

[1]*10 or more.*

[2]*12 or more.*

SOURCE: *Basic Patterns in Union Contracts*, 10th ed. (The Bureau of National Affairs, Inc., 1983), p. 19.

TABLE 14.9.   PAID HOLIDAYS: PERCENT OF FULL-TIME EMPLOYEES BY NUMBER OF PAID HOLIDAYS PROVIDED EACH YEAR, MEDIUM AND LARGE FIRMS, 1984

Number of days	All employees	Professional and administrative employees	Technical and clerical employees	Production employees
Total	100	100	100	100
Provided paid holidays	99	99	100	98
Under 6 days	3	1	1	4
6 days	4	3	6	4
6 days plus 1 or 2 half days	(¹)	(¹)	(¹)	(¹)
7 days	6	5	6	7
7 days plus 1 half day	(¹)	(¹)	(¹)	(¹)
8 days	7	7	7	6
8 days plus 1 or more half days	1	1	2	(¹)
9 days	12	13	16	10
9 days plus 1 or 2 half days	1	2	2	(¹)
10 days	26	26	25	27
10 days plus 1 or more half days	1	1	1	1
11 days	17	19	17	16
11 days plus 1 or 2 half days	1	1	1	(¹)
12 days	11	9	9	13
12 days plus 2 half days	(¹)	(¹)	(¹)	—
13 days	6	8	5	6

TABLE 14.9. *(Continued)*

13 days plus 1 half day	(^{1})	(^{1})	(^{1})	(^{1})
14 days	1	1	1	2
More than 14 days	(^{1})	(^{1})	(^{1})	(^{1})
Number of days not available	(^{1})	(^{1})	(^{1})	(^{1})
Not provided paid holidays	1	1	(^{1})	2

^{1}*Less than .5 percent.*

NOTE: *Because of rounding, sums of individual items may not equal totals. Dash indicates no employees in this category.*

SOURCE: *Employee Benefits in Medium and Large Firms, 1984,* U.S. Department of Labor, Bureau of Labor Statistics, June 1985 (Bulletin 2237), p. 19.

In 98 percent of agreements, the most commonly observed holidays are Thanksgiving, Labor Day, and Christmas. The next most common paid holidays are Independence Day and New Year's Day (97 percent), Memorial Day (95 percent), the day after Thanksgiving (56 percent), Good Friday, including a half day (52 percent), and Christmas Eve (51 percent)[95] Since 1958, the concept of a floating holiday was incorporated in some agreements. This provides employees with an option of having two consecutive paid holidays or long weekends. Under some agreements, the date for the floating holiday is subject to agreement and consultation between the employer and the union.

The recent trend seems to be toward grouping of holidays[96] in order to provide longer weekends or two sequential days off with pay. The federal government was a pioneer in this area. As of 1971, federal agencies by statute have to observe certain holidays on Mondays,[97] thus increasing the number of three-day weekends.

SUMMARY

The threat of permanent layoffs resulting from changing economic conditions, technological change, foreign competition, and geographic shifts and relocation of industry will increase union demands for more and better wage employment guarantees, supplemental and unemployment benefits, and severance pay allowances. In the 1980s, job security has been, and will continue to be, one of the top union priority issues at the bargaining table.

In the future, private pension plans will probably decline in importance. The burdensome requirements of ERISA may deter employers who currently do not offer pension plans from starting such plans. Some firms with pension plans may decide to drop them. The popularity of individual retirement accounts (IRA) could be another factor leading to the decreased importance of company-sponsored private pension plans. Under IRA, an employee can establish, with a wide variety of financial institutions, an individualized pension program. The contributions to such plans are deductible from taxable income. Still another factor that may affect existing private pension programs is the legal extension of the mandatory retirement age to seventy.

In the health benefit area, we can also expect changes in the next few years. Rapidly escalating medical costs have forced both employers and unions to explore alternatives to existing health care plans. This is one area in which during the late 1980s we will probably witness a significant amount of cooperation between labor and management. Both sides realize that joint effort will be necessary in order to slow down skyrocketing medical expenses. One approach may be a greater stress on expansion of HMO plans, which may alter the method of delivery and financing of existing health care programs.

The fringe benefit needs of bargaining unit members are not homogeneous. Some employees may be interested in good pension plans, particularly if they are middle-aged or older. Others may be concerned with maximizing current income—particularly those who do not plan to stay with an employer very long. The fringe benefit needs of younger workers are different from those of older workers, and the needs of single workers are different from those who are married or those who have dependent children at home. The variety of pressures that these different groups exert on their bargaining agents are usually reconciled and compromised within the context of bargaining and the labor agreement. In recent years, the process of accommodation of these heterogeneous interest groups has taken a different format. Some employers and unions, rather than finding an accepted middle ground for the various pressure groups, have adopted a cafeteria approach to benefits.

Under the cafeteria plan a firm provides to its employees basic benefits in such areas as pensions, medical care, life insurance, and vacations. Beyond the basic benefits, employees are allocated credits for the purchase of additional benefits according to their particular needs. Thus, one employee may use the credits to purchase medical and dental insurance, whereas someone else may apply the credit for a longer vacation.

One of the major issues affecting the outlook for cafeteria plans is the Internal Revenue Code—both in terms of interpretation of the code and the anticipated reforms of the tax law. In a 1982 article Cockrum writes that "Employee Benefit cafeteria plans have had an 'on-again-off-again' life during the past decade. Its checkered history has been largely due to concern regarding the cost benefit in employer/employee relations and the federal income tax treatment of cafeteria plan benefits to employees."[98]

In order to reduce medical costs, some cafeteria plans offer employees the option to put aside a portion of their wages tax-free for payment of medical or dental expenses. Some companies offer "Zebras" in Zero Balance Reimbursement Accounts, under which employers compensate employees for medical cost by deducting such expenses from paychecks, thus reducing taxable income. The purpose of such plans is to reduce health care costs. In 1984 the IRS announced that such plans do not qualify for tax-exempt status. Employers are upset by this announcement. Charles Rogers, Chairman of the Employers' Council on Flexible Compensations, asked Congress to declare a two-year moratorium on the IRS rules affecting flexible plans and not to tax income from Zebra plans.[99] Cafeteria plans have many attractions; however, before employers and unions will move more aggressively in this direction, Congress will have to address and resolve the tax issues in favor of employees.

American life styles underwent major changes in recent years. Divorce statistics, the number of unmarried living together, the growing number of women in the work force, and the increasing number of couples who postpone or pass up on parenthood all reflect the changes that have been taking place in the traditional life style. These changes have significant implications for fringe benefit policies. In a recent article, the following comment was made: "The work force is characterized by a greater variety of family and behavior patterns than before. As a result, a personnel chief planning a benefits package must consider, for instance, an employee's obligations not only to a spouse and at-home children but possibly to a former spouse, children living else-where, or a live-in partner who is not a marriage partner."[100]

The changing life styles may require more future choices in fringe benefits. When both a husband and a wife work, health insurance policies may have to be adjusted to eliminate duplication. The employee who may want to forgo a particular fringe benefit may want the money saved by his or her employer contributed to a different benefit. Some employers assess everybody for benefits that are only useful for a particular category of employee. All employees may be asked to pay for survivorship plans, even though some of them may not have any dependents or potential beneficiar-ies of such plans.

The changes taking place in our society and the growing sophistication of employees may necessitate major changes in future fringe benefit policies. The cafete-ria plan could be a possible response to the changing needs of employees in the decade of the eighties.

NOTES

[1]*Supplemental Unemployment Benefit Plans and Wage Employment Guarantees, June 1965*, Bulletin 1425-3 (Washington, D.C.: U.S. Department of Labor, Bureau of Labor Statis-tics), p.1.

[2]*Guaranteed Wage Plans in the United States: A Report on the Extent and Nature of Guaranteed Plans and the Experience of Selected Companies*, Bulletin 925 (Washington, D.C.: U.S. Department of Labor, Bureau of Labor Statistics, 1947), p.3.

[3]*Ibid.*

[4]*Monthly Labor Review*, August 1940, pp. 283—89.

[5]*Basic Patterns in Union Contracts*, 10th ed. (The Bureau of National Affairs, 1983), p. V.

[6]*Ibid.*, p. 35.

[7]*Ibid.*

[8]*Ibid.*

[9]*Collective Bargaining Negotiations and Contracts*, Bureau of National Affairs (BNA) no. 919, 8-21-80, pp. 41—44; no. 1000, 9-29-83, pp. 39—44; no. 1026, 9-27-84, pp. 35—36.

[10]*Ibid.*

[11]*Ibid.*

[12]*Ibid.*

[13]BLS Bulletin 1425-3, *op. cit.*, p. 4.

[14]*Ibid.*

[15]*Jobs? or Jobless Pay? The Real Issue Behind the New Guaranteed Wage Proposals* (Washington, D.C.: Chamber of Commerce of the United States, 1954), p.3.

[16]BLS Bulletin 1425-3, *op. cit.*, pp. 5–6.

[17]*Ibid.*, p. 1.

[18]*Basic Patterns in Union Contracts, op. cit.*, pp. 38–41.

[19]*Ibid.*

[20]*Characteristics of Major Collective Bargaining Agreements Covering a Thousand Workers or More,* July 1, 1976, Bulletin 2013 (Washington, D.C.: U.S. Department of Labor, Bureau of Labor Statistics, 1979), p. 79.

[21]*Major Collective Bargaining Agreements: Severance Pay and Layoff Benefit Plans,* Bulletin 1425-2 (Washington, D.C.: U.S. Department of Labor, Bureau of Labor Statistics, 1965).

[22]*Ibid.*, p. 17.

[23]*Ibid.*, p. 30.

[24]*Ibid.*, pp. 39–41.

[25]*Ibid.*, p. 44.

[26]*Basic Patterns in Union Contracts, op. cit.*, pp. 36–38.

[27]*Ibid.*

[28]*Ibid.*

[29]*Ibid.*

[30]*Ibid.*

[31]*Characteristics of the Private Pension Structure* (Washington, D.C.: U.S. Department of Labor, Bureau of Labor Statistics), *Monthly Labor Review* (July 1964), p. 774.

[32]*Pensions in the United States,* study prepared for the Joint Committee on the Economic Report by the National Planning Association (Washington, D.C.: U.S. Government Printing Office, 1952), 82nd Cong., 2nd sess. p. 11; and Max S. Wortman, Jr., and C. Wilson Randle, *Collective Bargaining Principles and Practices,* 2nd ed. (Boston: Houghton Mifflin, 1966), p. 411.

[33]*Employee Benefits in Medium and Large Firms, 1982.* (U.S. Department of Labor, Bureau of Labor Statistics, August 1983), Bulletin 2176, p. 10.

[34]BNA *Basic Patterns in Union Contracts, op. cit.*, p. 69; *Employee Benefits 1983,* (Washington, D.C.: United States Chamber of Commerce, 1983), pp. 30–31. The Source of some of the statistical data is the United States Department of Commerce.

[35]*Inland Steel Company* v. *NLRB,* 170 F. 2d247 (7th Cir., 1948), cert. denied 336 U.S. 960 (1949).

[36]BLS, Bulletin 2176, *op. cit.*, pp. 12–13, p. 44.

[37]Philip L. Rones, "The Retirement Decision: A Question of Opportunity?" *Monthly Labor Review* (November 1980), pp. 14–17.

[38]BLS Bulletin 2176, *op. cit.*, p. 10. See also John B. Miner and Mary Green Miner, *Personnel and Industrial Relations,* 4th ed. (New York: Macmillan Publishing Co., 1985), p. 596.

[39]Herbert G. Zollitsch and Adolph Langsner, *Wage and Salary Administration*, 2nd ed. (Cincinnati: Southwestern, 1970), p. 655.

[40]Negotiated Pension Plans, text of 30 agreements with editorial summary (Washington, D.C.: Bureau of National Affairs, December 1949), pp. 46–55.

[41]James P. Roscow, "Profit Sharing Without Profit?" *Pension World*, 11, no. 3 (March 1975), 9–10, 59; and Zollitsch and Langsner, *op. cit.*, p. 657.

[42]*Basic Patterns in Union Contracts, op. cit.*, p. 72.

[43]Noel Arnold Levin, *Negotiating Fringe Benefits* (New York: Amacom, division of American Management Association, 1973), p. 7.

[44]*Ibid.*, p. 5.

[45]Jacob K. Javits, "The Scandal of Our Pension Plans: What's Wrong and What Can We Do About It?" *Family Weekly*, November 11, 1973, cited in Herbert J. Chruden and Arthur W. Sherman, Jr., *Personnel Management*, 5th ed. (Cincinnati: Southwestern, 1976), p. 500. See also Paul Pigors and Charles A. Myers, *Personnel Administration*, 8th ed. (New York: McGraw-Hill, 1977), p. 386.

[46]ERISA, sec. 203.

[47]P.S. Greenlaw and W.D. Biggs, *Modern Personnel Management* (Philadelphia: Saunders, 1979), p. 513. *Source:* Randall S. Schuler, *Personnel and Human Resource Management*, 2nd ed., (St. Paul, Minn.: West, 1984), pp. 364–365, 379.

[48]Schuler, *op. cit.*, pp. 364–365.

[49]Braniff, *Business Week*, September 6, 1982, p. 40; on International Harvester, see *Wall Street Journal*, December 7, 1982, p. 35. *Source:* Schuler, *op. cit.*, p. 364, 379.

[50]Richard I. Henderson, *Compensation Management: Rewarding Performance* (Reston, Vg.: Reston, 1985), pp. 75, 442.

[51]Schuler, *op. cit.*, p. 365.

[52]Gene Carter, *Private Pensions: 1982 Legislation.* "Social Security Bulletin," August 1983, p. 3. See also Schuler, *op. cit.*, p. 365.

[53]*NCCMP Update*, National Coordinating Committee for Multiemployer Plans, January 1985, p. 9.

[54]Gerald D. Facciani, "Perspectives on National Pension Policy," *Journal of Pension Planning and Compliance* (February 1984), pp. 5–11.

[55]NCCMP Update, *op. cit.*, p. 1.

[56]Benjamin M. Selekman, Stephen H. Fuller, Thomas Kennedy, and John M. Baitsell, *Problems in Labor Relations*, 3rd ed. (New York: McGraw-Hill, 1964) p. 496.

[57]Richard B. Freeman, "The Effect of Unionism on Fringe Benefits," *Industrial and Labor Relations Review*, 34 (July 1981), 489–509. *Source:* Fosu, Augustin Kwasi, "Impact of Unionism on Pension Fringes," *Industrial Relations*, 22, no. 3 (Fall 1983), 419–425.

[58]William T. Alpert, "Unions and Private Wage Supplements," *Journal of Labor Research* (Spring 1982), pp. 179–199. *Source:* FOSU, *Ibid.*

[59]*Ibid.*

[60]*BNA Basic Patterns in Union Contracts, op. cit.*, pp. 42–51.

[61]William T. Ryan, "Hospital, Surgical and Medical Coverages," in Arthur J. Deric (ed.), *The Total Approach to Employee Benefits* (New York: American Management Association, 1967, p. 65.

[62]*Ibid.*, pp. 65–67.

[63]*Ibid.*, p. 68.

[64]Mitchell Meyer and Harland Fox, *Profile of Employee Benefits*, Report No. 645 (New York: Conference Board, 1974), p. 24.

[65]Ryan, *op. cit.*, p. 68.

[66]A. Blostin, and W. Marclay, "HMOS and Other Health Plans: Coverage and Employee Premiums," *Monthly Labor Review*, 106, no. 6 (1983), 23–33, *Source:* Miner, *op. cit.*, pp. 592–609.

[67]Ryan, *op. cit.*, p. 70.

[68]Louis F. Rossiter and Amy K. Taylor, "Union Effects on the Provision of Health Insurance," *Industrial Relations*, 21, no. 2 (Spring 1982), 167–177.

[69]*Business Week*, September 10, 1984, pp. 45–46.

[70]*Ibid.*

[71]"Health Care Coalitions Gain Nationwide Popularity But Need Cohesiveness, Trust, To Work Properly," *Employee Benefit Plan Review* (March 1984), pp. 42–46.

[72]*The Wall Street Journal*, March 18, 1985, p. 33.

[73]*Newsweek*, February 25, 1985, pp. 70–71.

[74]Zollitsch and Langsner, *op. cit.*, p. 664. See also *Monthly Labor Review* (March 1963), p. 290.

[75]G.H. Moore and E.J.N. Hedges, "Trends in Labor and Leisure," *Monthly Labor Review* (February 1971), pp. 3–11; Dale S. Beach, *The Management of People at Work*, 5th ed. (New York: Macmillan Publishing Co., 1985), p. 567.

[76]BLS Bulletin 1425-9, "Paid Vacation and Holiday Provisions," p. 1. See also "Vacation and Holiday Provisions in Union Agreements," *Monthly Labor Review*, May 1943, p. 924.

[77]*Ibid.*, p. 1. See also *Termination Report of the National Labor Board, Vol. 1* (Washington, D.C.: U.S. Government Printing Office, 1948), p. 338.

[78]BLS Bulletin 1425-9, *op. cit.*, p. 5; see also *Labor Management Contract Provisions, 1952*, Bulletin 1142 (Washington, D.C.: U.S. Department of Labor, Bureau of Labor Statistics, 1952), p. 1.

[79]*Basic Patterns in Union Contracts, op. cit.*, p. 89.

[80]*Ibid.*, p. 93.

[81]BLS Bulletin, 2013, *op. cit.*, p. 56.

[82]For sample contract provisions of graduated vacation plans, see BLS Bulletin 1425-9, *op. cit.*, pp. 5–12.

[83]*Ibid.*, p. 11.

[84]*Basic Patterns in Union Contracts, op. cit.*, p. 93.

[85]For sample contract provisions, see BLS Bulletin 1425-9, *op. cit.*, pp. 13–19.

[86]For sample contract clauses, see BLS Bulletin 1425-9, *op. cit.*, pp. 18—22.

[87]BLS Bulletin 2013, *op. cit.*, p. 58.

[88]BLS Bulletin 1425-9, *op. cit.*, pp. 22, 140.

[89]*Ibid.*, pp. 23, 26—29, 32—42.

[90]Moore and Hedges, *op. cit.*, pp. 4 and 5; see also Beach, *op. cit.*, p. 567.

[91]BLS Bulletin 1425-9, *op. cit.*, pp. 1—2.

[92]*Ibid.*, p. 2.

[93]*Ibid.*, p. 58.

[94]*Basic Patterns in Union Contracts*, *op. cit.*, p. 19.

[95]*Ibid.*, p. 21.

[96]*The Office* (January 1971), pp. 110—11; Miner and Miner, *op. cit.*, p. 587.

[97]BLS Bulletin 1425-9, *op. cit.*, p. 60.

[98]Robert B. Cockrum, "Has the time come for employee cafeteria plans?" *Personnel Administrator* (July 1982), p. 66.

[99]*The Cincinnati Enquirer*, April 3, 1984, p. C-12.

[100]*Business Week*, February 11, 1980, p. 111.

MANAGEMENT AND UNION SECURITY

15

We have distinguished earlier between problems of advantage and problems of survival. Things dealt with thus far deal mainly with advantage—the attempts of each party to enhance its own welfare by gaining concessions from the other while minimizing the concessions it must give in return. In this chapter, we focus on the fact that when managements and unions bargain they must also consider survival. A union cannot achieve advantages for its members unless it continues to exist, and in a conflict between the two it will almost necessarily choose survival over advantage. Management's survival in collective bargaining refers to its ability to remain master in its own house and to retain managerial authority, without which it ceases to be management. In the event of conflict management, too, will choose survival. Since the mere continuance of an organization's existence is of little consequence if it cannot perform its basic functions, the *security* of union or management means the condition in which survival of its ability to function is assured.

For this analysis, we will talk as if survival and advantage can be separated into relatively "pure" specimens. This does not mean that they are separable in fact, or that unions and managements isolate them in their own minds. However, there is a distinct difference in logic between the two questions, and we can understand each better if we separate them for purposes of discussion.

PART I: MANAGEMENT SECURITY

THE NATURE AND STATUS OF THE PROBLEM

When a firm buys typewriters or electricity, the sellers (if paid) do not care if the electricity is wasted or the typewriters are abused. Nor do the typewriters and electricity complain. But when an employee sells his or her time, ability, and effort, he or she goes with them. The employee cares how they are used, and part of the job of a union is to see that the conditions of use are satisfactory to the employee. The employee's continued presence gives almost *any* management action potential influence on the employee and leads in turn to the employee's potential desire to influence almost any management action. This is an important element in the management security problem.

Management security refers to the freedom of management to make managerial decisions—that is, to perform the function of management—without interference from the union. Management's freedom to make decisions about employees is stated in the following management security clause, which was also cited in Chapter 10.

> The right to hire, lay off, discharge for cause, promote, or transfer employees is the exclusive prerogative of management, except as otherwise provided in this contract.

But the very purpose of a union is to "interfere" with management's decisions and to bring them more into accord with the desires of the employees. Hence, if unions are to function at all, they necessarily interfere in some degree with management's freedom, by introducing the exceptions referred to in the above clause. The real problem is to find out what constitute "managerial" decisions, why and whether management should make them, and how much freedom management should have in doing so. The problem is crucial, for on its outcome depend much of the nature of the union-management relationship and some important characteristics of the private enterprise system.

The problem is illustrated in hiring a housekeeper or a full-time babysitter. The employer will discuss with the applicant such things as wages, duties, and days off. If the discussion is satisfactory, an agreement will be reached, specifying conditions that are mutually acceptable and that may not be changed except by mutual consent. The wages, hours, duties, and conditions of work are said to be *bargainable issues*. They fall within the scope of bargaining and are subject to joint determination.

But if the housekeeper were to suggest that the employer discuss the color of the living room walls and that they reach an agreement about color in the same way they did about wages, the housekeeper would probably be informed that this was none of his or her business. The employer does not necessarily have to disapprove of the housekeeper's choice of color or the housekeeper's objection to magenta walls, but the employer denies the housekeeper's right to be consulted. The employer asserts that the color of the walls falls outside the scope of bargaining. Employers consider it their exclusive prerogative to determine the color by unilateral decision. The housekeeper, in turn, would normally assert that it was his or her exclusive prerogative to decide unilaterally how he or she would spend a day off or whether to send part of his or her wages to a widowed sister.

The hiring of a housekeeper illustrates three kinds of decisions found in employer-employee relationships. Some seem to belong exclusively to the employer, some belong exclusively to the employee (or union), and some involve joint determination. As unions have grown in power, they have steadily increased the number of questions subject to joint determination, narrowing the areas of unilateral decision by management. Hence, the problem is also said to involve the *scope* of collective bargaining. Management often asserts that many decisions are prerogatives that belong to management by the inherent right of the owners to manage their property as they see fit. Hence, the problem is also known as the *management prerogative issue*; it is illustrated graphically in Figure 15-1. The late twentieth century finds unions typically trying to expand the scope of bargaining, managements trying to contain it, without an agreement on permanent boundary lines. Because of disagreement on this basic issue, the Labor-Management Conference called by President Truman in November 1945 to build peaceful and constructive labor relations was abandoned in midpassage with little significant result. The positions argued there still illustrate the problem.

The management representatives at this conference felt that the following management decisions should not be subject to collective bargaining: product or service to be produced; location of plants, including opening new ones and closing old ones, although employee representatives might be consulted; plant layout and selection of equipment; methods of manufacture and distribution; materials (unless health or safety was involved); financial policies and procedures; prices; organizational structure and the selection of management personnel; job duties; size of work force; work assignments, production standards; scheduling of operations and number of shifts; maintenance of discipline; customer relations; and safety and health where legal liability of employers was involved.[1] The union representatives agreed that "the function and responsibilities of management must be preserved if business and industry is to be efficient, progressive, and provide more good jobs."[2] But they refused to agree that any one function belonged unqualifiedly to management at all times and places. Management, in turn, saw in the union refusal an intention to "expand into the field of

FIGURE 15.1

DECISION MAKING IN EMPLOYER-EMPLOYEE RELATIONSHIP

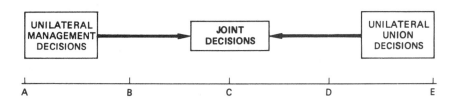

management." The spokesmen for business added that "the only possible end of such a philosophy would be joint management of enterprise."[3]

FREEDOM AND THE PROBLEM OF PREROGATIVES

Several kinds of logic are conventionally asserted in justification of management security—of management "rights." The most obvious is that management is the agent for the owners. Since ownership can hardly be defined without reference to the right of control, the accompanying conclusion is that management has the right to control the organization as it likes because it has been delegated the legal rights of ownership. In its strongest form, this argument means that at the outset management has *all* rights of control. In signing a contract with a union, management voluntarily agrees to share some of the decisions that are inherently its own. Nevertheless, it follows that management automatically retains as *residual rights* any and all decisions not explicitly shared with the union. The argument of *trusteeship* follows the same logic, merely shifting the emphasis slightly by noting that management acts as trustee for the owners.

The following pages do not gainsay any part of that approach. Their main point is rather that a sensible understanding of the topic can be derived from the logic of the relationship. More specifically, there are two sets of ownership. The equity holders own the plant, and are represented by management as their agent. The employees own their persons and their labor and are represented by the union as *their* agent. The union has no inherent right to say what is to be done with the plant, and the management has no inherent right to say what is to be done with people or their labor. Stated in another way, and viewed within the context of the union-management relationship, workers have an initial right to do as they like with their persons and their labor, and management has an initial right to do as it likes with its plant. Since production requires both, each must give up some of its unilateral control over what it owns as a condition for acquiring access to the other. Short of slavery, at one extreme, and complete worker ownership of the plant, at the other, there is presumably no way that either side would cede complete control of its own contribution to the other side. Thus, who gives up how much control over its own contribution is a matter to be determined by a bargain struck between the two sides, the outcome of which is determined by the bargaining power of the parties and the underlying logic of the situation. We have already examined bargaining power factors in previous chapters. The present chapter suggests that there is also a basic logic to this aspect of the relationship, which logic to a large extent is independent of bargaining power factors.

More specifically, there apparently is little, if anything, that can be classified unequivocally as the sole prerogative of either side for all times and situations, so long as employers are free to select who shall work for them and employees are free to choose whether they will work for a particular employer. Take some hypothetical examples. An employer may refuse to hire an applicant for a logical reason, such as the applicant's lack of experience. But if an employer so chooses and so long as he or she does not violate affirmative action guidelines, the Labor Management Relations Act, or any other law, the employer can also refuse employment for a seemingly irrelevant reason, such as the applicant's dislike for spinach. Similarly, workers may refuse to work for a logical reason, such as dissatisfaction with the wage rate, or for an illogical one, such as the fact that the company president has red hair. Many frustrated employers have been known to complain: This is my plant. Why can't I run it the way I like? To which the employees answer: You have complete freedom to run your plant any way you like—as long as you run it yourself. But if you want employees to help you run it, you can have them only on terms that are acceptable to them as well as to you.[4]

In a free economy, it is pointless for either side to claim inherent rights to bargain or not to bargain about any particular subject. Each party can insist that the other bargain about most subjects. There are, however, legal limitations imposed by the NLRB and the courts regarding nonmandatory or permissive subjects over which the parties do not have to negotiate and a refusal to bargain is not considered a violation of the law. Examples of such nonmandatory subjects would be interest arbitration clauses, performance bonds, internal union affairs, and benefits of retired employees.

Apart of legal constrains, in any one union-management relation, some line does necessarily exist at any given moment separating those things that fall within the scope of bargaining from those that fall outside. The location of that line may be vague or precise, contested or uncontested, written or unwritten. The pages below will examine some forces that help determine where that line will lie.

THE UNILATERAL CONTROL OF STRATEGY

If bargaining is to have any meaning, each party must control its own strategy and leadership in dealing with the other. Entirely on its own, the union must formulate its demands, decide when or whether to strike, select its bargaining representatives, accept or reject the company's offer, and so on. Similarly, management cannot share with the union decisions about how much it will offer, who is to sit on its negotiating committee, whether it will force a strike rather than concede, and the like. Some legal aspects of such independence in bargaining have been discussed in earlier chapters.

In years past some employers have actually participated in planning union strategy by engaging labor spies, who occasionally became influential officers in unions. Such practices are now illegal, as is the "company union," which tended to have the same effect. Some occasional managements have also attempted to negotiate into the union contract certain procedural matters internal to the union, such as providing more "democracy" or locating and scheduling elections so that all eligible union voters could get to the polls. Some managements have also tried to work with certain factions within a union to help defeat an "undesirable" union officer. Although one can easily imagine situations where such management activity might make the union more responsive to the wishes of its members, the risks of converting the union into a spokesman for management are manifest.

Despite infrequent union representation on some corporate boards of directors, it is very difficult for unions to infiltrate top management in this particular way. By other methods, however, unions have sometimes tried to influence management's bargaining strategy, as when John L. Lewis once temporarily refused to negotiate with the coal operators unless they would withdraw their bargaining representative and substitute one more acceptable to Lewis. Such actions are usually interpreted by the National Labor Relations Board as bad-faith bargaining and constitute an unfair labor practice. Obviously, unless each side unilaterally controls its own strategy and selects its own bargaining representatives, bargaining ceases to have any meaning. One party's right hand would be bargaining with its left while the other party looked on.

INTEREST AND THE MAKING OF DECISIONS

The Nature and Types of Interest

Beyond the necessity that each party control its own bargaining strategy, it is difficult to find any kind of decision that falls neatly into the realm of either joint or unilateral determination. We can, however, discern some factors that would seem to determine how hard a party will fight either to get participation in a decision or to keep the other party from participating. The two most conspicuous criteria for allocating decision-making powers seem to be interest and ability.

By the *interest criterion*, we mean simply the degree to which a party is affected by a decision. A party strongly affected by a given decision will have a strong interest and presumably be willing to fight hard to influence it. A party totally unaffected by a decision, either by immediate or subsequent consequences (including its precedent setting qualities), will not stand to suffer by sharing that decision with the other party. In addition, if that decision originally was made by the other party, the first will not gain by fighting to share it. It is basically immaterial whether the interest is immediate, such as one's profit or salary, or indirect, such as one's ability to exercise the authority on which the profit or salary depends.

A parallel situation exists between two sets of investors in the corporation. Because bondholders receive a fixed return (short of near bankruptcy), they are willing to invest without exercising control over the company's operations, and, in fact, they have none. Because stockholders, on the other hand, are directly influenced by the profitability or unprofitability of the company, they have the vote. At the point of bankruptcy or near bankruptcy, bondholders' interests are affected; at that point they normally are, in fact, considered—as in court proceedings in bankruptcy cases.

Applying the Interest Criterion

To illustrate, management normally has a high degree of interest in having its machines properly cared for, whereas most employees do not care whether the machines last one year or twenty. It normally seems reasonable for management to decide unilaterally whether to maintain the machines in good shape or to spend the money instead on replacing them more frequently. But if the machine happens to be a large, high-speed grinding wheel that may fly apart and kill the operator, the employee has a more intense interest in its condition than does management. It might then be reasonable, not only for union and management to determine maintenance policy jointly, but even to allow the employee to refuse to operate the machine unless it is properly maintained.

The same principle operates in other areas. Management normally determines which machines will be used in processing, say, a diesel crankshaft through a machine shop. If a batch of crankshafts is followed by a batch of compressor pistons, the employees may have to be reassigned to different machines. Management has a high interest in the efficient use of the workers and equipment. If each person in the shop is an all-round machinist and if the pay is the same on all machines, the employees have only a slight interest in who is assigned to which job. Under these circumstances, the job assignments could logically be decided unilaterally by management. But if the rates of pay are different on different machines, or if transfer may involve loss of seniority, the employee has a definite interest in the assignments. The effect of job transfers on wage rates and seniority may then logically become a matter for joint determination.

The opposite situation exists with ushers in theaters. Measured in terms of dollar income to the theater, there is little difference in the "productivity" of different ushers, and all are normally paid the same rates. Hence, the ushers could decide among themselves who should usher for which shows, as by giving the senior ushers first choice. The employees could presumably write almost any kind of seniority clause they chose without seriously affecting management's interests.

Theater managements could, of course, insist on their right to make job assignments. But this would do little to protect their interests and would interfere with those of the ushers. In the machine shop the union could similarly insist on the right not to be "pushed around," even though all jobs paid the same and no seniority rights were involved. To do so, however, would contribute little to the interest of the machinists and would seriously interfere with that of management. The attempt to settle such problems on the basis of "prerogatives" or "inherent rights" holds the prospect of extended futile disagreement. An approach based on interests can bring a settlement that is both logical and realistic. Though not without cries of alarm from those who believe such questions must be settled "on principle," wide segments of American industry seem to be operating along the "realistic" lines just described.

ABILITY AND THE MAKING OF DECISIONS

The Nature of the Ability Criterion

The *ability criterion* is that either party will tend to insist on participation in a decision in proportion to his ability in the subject matter involved—assuming that he also has an interest. It is not necessary to raise the question of whether representatives of union or management are better or wiser people but simply to note that we live in a world of specialization. One's interest in one's own health is presumably greater than a doctor's interest in it. But in making decisions, the patient's stronger interest will give way to the physician's superior ability. The same kind of reasoning applies to some management decisions. Policies regarding prices, advertising, methods of production, financing, sources of materials, internal organization, and so forth can be made and coordinated intelligently only by someone familiar with all aspects of the firm's operations. Normally, only top officials possess this kind of information.

Modifications of the Ability Criterion.   There is thus a presumption that employees or unions should not participate in top management decisions, since they are not in a position to make those decisions wisely. This generalization is adhered to rather strictly in many union-management relationships but is subject to two reservations. First, the engineer's ideal plan is often modified by nonengineers because the ideal method is too costly, is unattractive, or impinges seriously on the environment. Patients often deviate from the doctor's advice because of costs, whims, or convenience. In short, even if the manager has definitely superior knowledge in management matters, it does not follow that his or her judgment should not be modified for nonmanagerial reasons.

Second, in some industries union leaders have considerable competence in management problems. For example, in the clothing industry some union leaders have at one time owned and operated their own firms, and some union officers probably have as much "know-how" as many clothing executives. The unions do, in fact, participate more deeply in management decisions in this industry than in most others. For example, the unions in both men's and women's clothing maintain their own management engineering departments to give technical advice and assistance to managements, and both have made loans to employers. In brief, ability does not necessarily lie entirely with management.

Analysis versus Practice.   The reader should be aware that the interest and ability criteria represent the outside analyst's view, not that of the parties. Their approach is apt to be catch-as-catch-can, with full exploitation of bargaining power. Unions sometimes seem to fight to participate in decisions that affect them little or regarding which they have little competence. And managements sometimes seem to defend to the last ditch their "right" to make undiluted decisions in areas where bargaining would not hurt them. Which attitude a management will take will depend much on its general attitude toward unions, toward some broader ideological problems, and toward "principle for principle's sake" as contrasted to "realistic adaptation to reality."

THE RATIONAL ALLOCATION OF PREROGATIVES

Decision Making in a Worker-Owned Plant

The Development of a Management.   A simple way to discover that the need for strong management security is based on something more than abstract "rights of ownership" is to assume that the employees purchase a controlling share of stock in the corporation they work for. The board of directors will then be selected by the employees, and if there are such things as inherent rights, the employees will possess all of them. This new board of directors will shortly discover that, as top management, it desires certain conditions that conflict directly with the immediate wishes of the employees who elected them. For example, the manager's desire to keep prices low enough to meet competition and sell the firm's product may run directly counter to the employee's desire to raise wages. The new managers might study the market conditions and report them to the workers, who could then balance their desire for higher wages against their desire to stay in business and set the price accordingly.

Sound price policies, however, depend not only on wages and market conditions but on costs of materials, location of customers, rates of depreciation, and many other factors, including some highly discretionary aspects of cost accounting. Workers might eventually recognize their inability to vote intelligently on such complex decisions and then logically give the board unilateral control over prices, subject only to the ultimate threat of loss of office. In due time similar arrangements would be made for maintenance policy, the borrowing of money, and the negotiation of leases; and eventually the board might be assigned simply the broad responsibility for keeping the firm in sound condition.

The board would have to insist, in turn, that if it is given the responsibility for keeping the firm solvent, it must also have the authority to make the decisions that affect solvency. In brief, officers elected by the employees would shortly be found behaving like management, for the simple reason that they *are* management. Their desire for freedom to make certain decisions grows from their interest in the job they do, not from the nature of the group they represent. Soon their experience would also give them a superior ability over the rank and file.[5]

The Development of a Protest Function.   At the same time, some interesting discoveries would be made by the rank-and-file workers. They too could find their interest as owners conflicting with their interest as workers. For example, a worker's health may fail, producing a marked decline in productivity. As an owner, he wants inefficient producers weeded out. But as a worker he wants desperately to keep the job and, if possible, the previous rate of pay. Since wage income is probably many times dividend income, his worker interest greatly outweighs his owner interest. In this and many other situations the employer takes a worker point of view, and in due time he may try to get the managers to give overriding consideration to employee welfare. But the managers cannot do this without abdicating their responsibility for all the other factors that affect solvency.

The workers would also discover—as all democracies do—that to elect leaders is no guarantee that they will not be arbitrary, careless, or inclined to play favorites. Governments, therefore, establish a judicial system through which citizens may redress unfair or discriminatory acts by their elected government. So too in the worker-owned plant, in the promotion, transfer, discipline, and replacement of individuals, there would almost certainly arise charges of favoritism and stupidity against the supervisors. If so, some channel could be established through which to handle the protest function against management without having to throw out the managers. This organized method of protest might not take the form of a union, but it could easily do so.

It seems significant that ordinary citizens get redress against their government through the judicial branch of the government. But those who are also employees of the government have joined unions in fairly large numbers to protect their employee interest against the employer they helped elect. Similarly, many employees of unions are also organized and bargain collectively with the union that employs them. The officers of unions at first showed no greater enthusiasm for this development than did "capitalist" managements, but under pressure they have now accepted it.

The esssential point is that in this respect there are two functions within the organization. One is that of managing, and the other is that of protesting against the management in the name of those managed. The need for management arises out of the nature of organization and the need to have someone who will assume the responsibility for keeping income equal to or greater than expenses. The need for the protest function arises because managers, being human, are less than perfect in dealing with their subordinates and because the welfare of the employees is not and cannot be the sole, or even the primary, concern of the managers.

In short, management must necessarily think of labor as a factor of production, and therefore as a cost. The job of the union is to think of labor as human beings and to insist that they be treated as such. To some extent the two views coincide, since persons who are treated well also produce better. But there are many ways in which human beings like to be treated well above and beyond those that bring a return to management. Even the most enlightened management will presumably not venture into these areas on its own initiative. This distinction exists equally whether the managers are appointed by private capitalists, by the workers, or by a socialist state.

SECURE VS. INSECURE MANAGEMENTS

The Condition of Security.   Despite the apparent impossibility of drawing a sharp line to delineate the scope of bargaining in general terms, there is a line in each plant at any given moment, and there is a considerable uniformity as to its location throughout American industry, particularly among large firms. The following is an example of a "management clause" taken from the 1982 contract between the United Auto Workers and the Ford Motor Company:

> The Company retains the sole right to manage its business, including the rights to decide the number and location of plants, the machine and tool equipment, the products to be manufactured, the method of manufacturing, the schedules of production, the processes of manufacturing or assembling, together with all designing, engineering, and the control of raw materials, semi-manufactured and finished parts which may be incorporated into the products manufactured; to maintain order and efficiency in its plants and operations; to hire, lay off, assign, transfer and promote employees, and to determine the starting and quitting time and number of hours to be worked; subject only to such regulations and restrictions governing the exercise of these rights as are expressly provided in this agreement.[6]

If management achieves, regularly reviews, and vigorously enforces a strong management clause by techniques to be described below, the executives should be able to sleep soundly at night, comforted by the thought that if the enterprise goes bankrupt it was their fault, not the union's. Elsewhere in the contract are clauses covering wages, hours, pensions, seniority, holidays, and other items of interest to the employees. Many of these cost the company money and can therefore have an adverse effect on its balance sheet. But the same thing can be said of raw materials, energy, and rent, for which the firm may also pay high prices despite strenuous bargaining. The price it pays for labor (including fringes) is merely one of many items in the firm's economic environment. The important fact is that under a strong management clause, rigorously guarded and enforced, the executives are free to study that environment and decide how best to live with it, and then carry out those decisions without interference from the union. That is the core of management security.

A Bad Case of Insecurity.   Probably every reader of this material has heard a description of some firm that apparently had no management security. As these cases are usually related:

> A union came into the plant and "took over." The "union wouldn't let the company fire anybody" for incompetence, insubordination, or any other reason. It told the company who was to be promoted and who was to be laid off. It told the managers whether new machines could be installed and had a superintendent replaced by one more satisfactory to the union. The union leaders "strut" or "swagger" around the plant "as if they owned it."

Although personal bitterness adds color to such stories, there are probably scores, perhaps hundreds, of plants where conditions like those just described have actually prevailed. Even though most are comparatively small plants, the problem is by no means unimportant. It is apt to arise when a particular type of aggressive labor leader faces a management that is weak or inept in dealing with the union.

Can Management Defend Its Security?   In such a plant certainly the manager is not managing, and he may in desperation raise his arms and cry, "But what can I do?"

Considering the frequency of the complaint and the apparent helplessness of the persons who make it, the answer is amazingly simple and is revealed by asking another question: What would the same management do if the union demanded a wage of $500 an hour?

There is no reason to believe that the union would not ask for $500 if it thought the company would give it—which it certainly would not. But if the company can refuse a particular wage concession to the union, by the same token and by the same method, it can also refuse any other concession. If it allows union officials to "run the plant" at will but does not similarly grant them any particular wage that happens to suit their fancy, management is indicating very clearly that it values its wage scale more highly than it values its freedom to manage. A company need only defend its freedom to manage with the same tenacity that it defends its wage scale, and it will remain master in its own house.

On occasion, some firms, of course, may be bankrupted in the fight for their rights. But so might they be if they do not regain control, and it is an open question whether such firms and their managers would not be better off to close down rather than to operate under such perpetual harassment. Union leaders have often lost their jobs, their homes, and sometimes their lives to defend the cause of unionism. If managers do not believe strongly enough in their freedom to manage to take some real risks occasionally, they may lose that freedom. Those risks are apparently one of the prices of a free enterprise system, and if management is not willing to take them, then management security is presumably not as important as business enterprisers claim. Though reality is more complicated than this abstracted illustration, the main point is nevertheless clear.

The Salients of Defense.   In practice, the defense of management security hinges on two crucial points. Can management prevent wildcat strikes? Can management prevent insubordination? Each, in turn, arises at two successive levels. Can management get the necessary clauses into the contract? Can it then adequately enforce these clauses? Ultimately, however, the answers all depend on bargaining power.

Regarding wildcat strikes, it is clear that if employees can freely walk out and shut down the plant any time something displeases them, management is not in charge. Management's first step is, therefore, to get a no-strike clause into the contract. In its simplest form, such a clause reads: "During the life of this contract the parties agree that there shall be no strikes or lockouts." As we will see in a later chapter, to be workable such a clause must be accompanied by a grievance procedure to handle disagreements that arise during the life of the contract.

But how does management get the union to agree to such a clause? We note first that managements already have such clauses in the vast majority of contracts with American unions. The process of achieving them was essentially that described above in connection with the $500 hourly wage. Management made clear that the union could strike as long as it liked; the company simply would not settle without a no-strike clause. Actually, few present-day unions deny the propriety of no-strike provisions, and probably fewer did in the past than some managements believed.

The following contract provisions illustrate prohibitions on union or employee participation in strikes. They also stipulate penalties for violation of such pledges. The penalties range from discharge of employees, to cancellation of agreements and to judicial enforcement of no-strike clauses:

Employees who are subject to discharge.

Neither the Union nor employees will authorize, assist, support, permit or cause, or take part in any picketing of or interruption of the Company's operations, and any employee taking part in, or assisting or supporting such picketing or interruption of such operations shall be subject to discharge. (International Harvesters *and* Teamsters; exp. 6/83).[7]

Company has option of cancelling agreement.

. . . the Union agrees that it will not engage in, initiate, authorize, sanction, ratify or support any strike, slowdown, stay-in, or other curtailment or restriction of production or interference with the work in or about the Company's plant or premises during the life of this agreement . . . In case a strike or stoppage of production shall occur, the Company has the option of cancelling this agreement at any time between the tenth (10th) day after the strike occurs and the day of its settlement . . . (Hayes—Albion Corporation. Albion Malleable Div. *and* Auto Workers; exp. 4/83).[8]

Company may seek judicial enforcement of no-strike provision.

The Company shall have the right to seek judicial specific enforcement of the no-stike agreement herein contained . . . (Lone Star Steel Company *and* Steelworkers; exp. 10/83).[9]

To turn now to the second salient of defending management security, establishing discipline and avoiding insubordination also seem to depend heavily on management's clear understanding of what it needs and its determination to get it. The problem is not as difficult as might be anticipated and falls in line with the earlier analysis of the interest criterion.

Suppose a supervisor wants to discipline an employee for alleged violation of rules, but the employee claims he is innocent. If innocent, the union must try to get the discipline withdrawn, or the union will be judged worthless. At the same time, management has nothing to gain and much to lose if it nevertheless insists on an inherent right to discipline an innocent person. If the employee, however, is obviously guilty, then management must fight hard to sustain the discipline or it will lose control of the plant. The union, on the other hand, has little to gain by fighting fair discipline. Most workers, in fact, feel uneasy when discipline is lax and are unwilling to support a strike designed to prevent proper discipline. The significant interest of both sides is met by discipline that is tight but fair.

This problem has often been complicated in practice when persons have been disciplined for prounion activity rather than for violating rules. The predictable response is a prompt walkout, since the union feels that its very existence is jeopardized. The equally obvious prescription, now widely accepted, is that management agree not to discipline for union activity. The situation can be nasty if the company disciplines a union leader for violating rules but the workers believe he was "picked on" for union activity. This problem normally disappears once the employees gain confidence that the employer has no desire to "bust" the union. Until that time (or if the employer really *does* want to get rid of the union), the situation is delicate and often unpleasant.

The problem is most difficult for the small employer who faces a large union, such as a small trucking company dealing with the Teamsters. Here there may be simply no way of protecting management security short of bankruptcy. The only recourse may be to increase the company's bargaining power, as through collective action by employers.

BACKGROUND FACTORS IN
MANAGEMENT SECURITY

Above and beyond the actions discussed above are several background factors that bolster management security and put it in a different context from union security, which is the subject of the second part of this chapter.

Institutional Security.   As an institution in our society, management has a high degree of security. However much management may be liked or disliked in individual cases, few doubt that there must be a management. Whereas a plant can operate indefinitely without a union, we have noted that even if the union were to own the plant the essential function of management would remain. In this respect management has a type of security that can never be matched, probably not even approached, by unions.

Security and Internal Discipline.   A second factor aiding the security of management is its high degree of internal discipline. By controlling the selection, placement, promotion, and firing of employees, including those within the management level itself, top executives can assure themselves of solidarity within their organization. For example, since such action would normally bring prompt firing, employers rarely have to fear capitulation to the union during negotiations because of a split within their own ranks. Under multiemployer bargaining, however, divisions may occur within the employer ranks, and often do.

The Basic Goals of Unions.   A third factor of importance to management security is that most American unions do not want to participate in some of the so-called management decisions, although this may be changing, see union representation on corporate boards, latter section of this chapter. The union's essential function is that of protest. But it cannot strategically protest against decisions that it has itself made or accepted. In the question of wages, for example, the union leader stands on firm ground if he or she returns from negotiations and reports, "I fought hard for an increase. But they're a stubborn bunch and won't budge an inch." But the same leader may well lose the next election if he tells the members: "The boss and I decided you'll have to go along for another year at the old rates." The general union preference is to fight for all they can get and to let management worry about paying for it.

In the United States, at least, the danger to management is not so much that unions consciously desire to invade the area of management decisions, since most union leaders prefer to avoid the responsibility. It is rather that unions desire to participate in particular decisions that affect their members and that, through a series of such incursions, they eventually develop a total amount of participation greater than they themselves might have wanted.

There are also some labor leaders who think the union should participate directly in management at the top level, possibly along the lines of codetermination in Germany, or as is done in many plants in Israel and Yugoslavia. The appointment of Douglas Fraser to the board of Chrysler in 1980 has brought new attention to the idea.

Some managements are not averse to the idea—for somewhat the same reasons that some managements favor profit sharing with employees—on the assumption that the logic of management will subvert that of the union, not the reverse.

The indications are that the future will bring considerable diversity of approach. Some managements will refuse to discuss certain issues "on principle." Other managements will experiment with joint approaches to a wide variety of problems. To judge from the present situation, it may be guessed that most of the companies that experiment will do so only on the basis of a strong management security clause.

With the full consent of many managements, many unions are now participating in decisions to a degree that management would have considered unthinkable only a decade ago. Whether the union constitutes a "free personnel department" in these areas or a "grave threat to management" is perhaps less a question of fact than of the particular set of attitudes through which a management looks at the union. Whatever else the future may hold, change is apparently one assured component.

A "Basic Patterns" study of 400 contracts by the Bureau of National Affairs found management rights provisions in 76 percent of the contracts surveyed. Table 15−1 indicates the frequency with which different management prerogative subjects are covered in contracts containing such provisions. It is interesting to note the significant differences in managerial prerogative in various areas. Whereas in 79 percent of the contracts with a management-rights clause, the direction of the work was a managerial prerogative, instituting technological change as a managerial prerogative was only allowed in 17 percent of the clauses and plant closing or relocation was allowed in 11 percent of such provisions.[10]

Some contracts place definite restrictions on managerial prerogatives. Eighty eight percent of the sample contracts surveyed by the BNA limit managerial authority. As shown on table 15−2 some contracts contain a general statement limiting managerial rights, others set restrictions in such areas as subcontracting, performance of work by supervisors, technological changes and plant shutdown or relocation.[11]

TABLE 15.1. MANAGEMENT RIGHTS PROVISIONS

(Frequency Expressed As Percentage of Management Rights Statements)

	All Industries	Manufacturing	Nonmanufacturing
Direct work force	79	81	77
Manage business	71	75	65
Control production	38	48	19
Frame company rules	28	26	32
Determine employees' duties	25	22	30
Close or relocate plant	11	12	9
Change technology	17	18	14

SOURCE: Bureau of National Affairs, *Collective Bargaining Negotiations and Contracts*, 1983, p. 109.

TABLE 15.2.   RESTRICTIONS ON MANAGEMENT RIGHTS

(Frequency Expressed as Percentage of Contracts)

	All Industries	Manufacturing	Nonmanufacturing
General statement	52	55	47
Subcontracting	50	45	58
Supervisory performance of work	54	69	32
Technological changes	21	20	21
Plant shutdown or relocation	18	21	12

SOURCE: Bureau of National Affairs, *Collective Bargaining Negotiations and Contracts*, 1983, p. 111.

MANAGEMENT SECURITY

Union Representation on Corporate Boards

Traditionally, labor unions and employers in the United States have objected to union presence on corporate board of directors. Both sides have preferred instead to utilize the adversarial process of negotiations. Some authors suggest that the reason for union objections to board representations stems from their apprehension that such participation may decrease the importance of collective bargaining and reduce their independence.[12] Despite these concerns in 1973, the first union gained representation on the board of directors of the Providence and Worcester Railroad. Only twenty workers were affected by this pioneering official union entry into the corporate boardroom.[13] In 1980, in a precedent-setting side agreement with the UAW, Chrysler Corporation appointed UAW president D. A. Fraser to the board of directors of the corporation. This was a unique nomination for a major U.S. union leader. Boards have very broad powers in establishing corporate policies in all areas of activity, including labor relations. Being on the board may confront a union leader with a conflict of interest between his responsibilities to the corporation and toward the union. The Fraser appointment was not well received by other firms in the auto industry. Executives of Ford Motor Company were apprehensive of the new development. The Chairman of General Motors, T. A. Murphy, criticized the Fraser appointment. He felt that it "creates a fundamental conflict of interests that could upset future labor negotiations in the auto industry." In his view, it did not make any sense for the number-one auto maker to have to bargain its labor costs with the director of one of its competitors. He felt that the new approach threatened "the long-established adversary relationships" under which the industry negotiates its contracts. In the final analysis, management may consider the Fraser appointment a success if it has no effect on corporate policy. Mr. Fraser's staff associates at UAW's Solidarity House were also questioning his new role. Some of them felt that the union can be most effective and best serve the interest of its membership through its "traditional adversary relationship between labor and management and that it has no business mixing in board room affairs." Other union leaders have been lukewarm or opposed to the Fraser appointment. Lane Kirkland of the AFL—CIO adopted a wait-and-see attitude. George Poulin, vice-president of the International Association of Machinists, expressed opposition to the concept.[14] In 1976, a few years before the Fraser appointment, Thomas Donahue of the AFL—CIO stated that "we do not seek to be a partner in management . . . to be, most likely, the junior partner in success and the senior partner in failure . . . we guard our independence fiercely."[15] In the past, Lane Kirkland of the AFL—CIO expressed the view that the American worker "is smart enough to know . . . that salvation lies—not in the reshuffling of chairs in the board room or the executive suite—but in the growing strength and bargaining power of his autonomous organization."[16]

In recent years some union leaders have become more receptive to the concept of board room representation.[17] There are a number of reasons for the change in attitudes: large permanent layoffs of union members in a number of industries, particularly steel, auto and rubber; decreasing union membership as a percentage of the work force, automation, increased antiunion activities by management and more sophisticated antiunion personnel policies, increasing management resistance to union demands, and growth of management bargaining power relative to union power. The growth of European-owned industry in the United States could also encourage the importation of *codetermination* or representation by workers on boards of directors, into this country, since union members on the boards of directors of European companies may favor codetermination for the U.S. subsidiaries. Also, many U.S. firms have European branches that operate under codetermination.

Europe has been providing workers with representation on board of directors for many years. The system is referred to as *codetermination*. The U.S. union approach to the board room differs considerably from the European system. The class consciousness of the European worker and the class by birth of European management creates a gap that codetermination attempts to bridge through legislation. In the United States, unions and managements are more democratic than their European counterparts. They are nonideological and pragmatic. Business unionism advocated by Samuel Gompers, one of the founders of the American labor movement, took deep roots in the United States. United States unions prefer to bargain with private employers rather than "government bureaucrats."[18] The great majority of U.S. union leaders and their members feel that more can be achieved at the bargaining table than through codetermination. Their answer to codetermination is the collective bargaining process. European codetermination is largely the result of legislative and political effort. The UAW breakthrough at Chrysler was achieved through collective bargaining. Labor movements in Western Europe have traditionally relied on political and legislative methods to resolve issues affecting the workplace; there has also been a close cooperation between European unions and political parties. As a result of this cooperation, European unions find it easier, within the context of a parliamentary democracy, to achieve certain benefits in the legislative chambers, benefits that U.S. unions would attempt to obtain at the bargaining table. Codetermination is a legally mandated way of life in most Western European countries.

United States business fears codetermination. Comments in the U.S. business community of German, Dutch, and Scandinavian firms subjected to demanding regulations under codetermination laws, which are detrimental to management and productivity, has not endeared the concept to U.S. management. The attitude of U.S. management toward codetermination is very well summarized in the following statement by the Trilateral Commission:

> Management is firmly convinced, whether in a unionized situation or not, that employee directors would not add to the efficiency of the board. In this view employees are not qualified to serve as directors. If they were, they would be promoted to management posts. Most U.S. managers believe, even where unions are not recognized, that the appointment of employees to the board would undermine the unity of the board.[19]

Although the Trilateral Commission questioned the appropriateness of having union representation on corporate boards, recently a number of corporations followed the Providence and Worcester Railroad and Chrysler examples and accepted union representation on their boards of directors.[20] Usually, these appointments were made in conjunction with union concessions in wages and benefits.

Not every union effort to gain a seat in the board room has been successful. At the 1972 annual meeting of the United Airline Company, the pilots strived for a board seat; they received only 5% of the vote. The United Rubber Workers tried unsuccessfully to join the General Tire and Rubber Company Board in 1973. The Teamsters sought two union seats to the Anheuser–Bush board in 1976, and during the same year, the International Federation of Professional and Technical Engineers attempted to obtain a seat on the board of the American Telephone and Telegraph. These two attempts also met with failure.[21]

The issue of labor unions in the board room has some ramifications in terms of antitrust legislation. Section 8 of the Clayton Act prohibits interlocking directorates. Legal journals have been exploring the applicability and the implications of this provision for unions, particularly where the same union would try to occupy seats on boards of competing firms. Douglas claims that "the Clayton Act demands neither a blanket exemption for labor unions from Section 8 coverage nor a blanket prohibition against union members serving as board representatives."[22] He argues, however, that the Clayton Act's ban on interlocking directorates would apply to unions.[23] Other issues raised regarding the legality of the presence of unions in the board room are related to a number of sections of federal labor law. Hamer examines the legal position of the parties under Section 8(a)(2) of the Labor Management Relations Act and under Section 501(a) of the Labor Management Reporting and Disclosure Act. He concludes that union representation on board of directors is not in violation of federal labor law.[24]

Overview of Some Legal and Practical Aspects

Where employees are represented by a union, the Taft–Hartley Act requires an employer to bargain with respect to "wages, hours, and other terms and conditions of employment." Since the highest possible degree of management security is to have no union at all and to bargain about nothing, the law mandatorily expands the scope of bargaining and reduces the area of unilateral management control. That is, to the degree that the law requires management to bargain at all, it reduces management security. The precise boundary line between what management will and will not be required to bargain about is determined by the National Labor Relations Board and the courts.

The law gives a sort of negative protection to management security in that it does not require bargaining over issues other than those explicitly stated by the NLRB and the courts. Although the wording of the law can hardly be stretched to require bargaining over such things as pricing policy, products to be manufactured, or methods of finance, many managements feel the interpretations have already been much too broad.

Many managements would like to have the law define the bargainable area specifically, in the form of either a short list of bargainable issues or a long list of nonbargainable ones. How much good this would do management is problematic. First, a legal obligation to bargain is explicitly not an obligation to concede. Its presence may simply change the wording from, "I refuse to discuss a pension" to "I refuse (after due bargaining) to grant a pension."

It is easy enough to pass a law that says, for example, that wages are bargainable and methods of production are not. But what happens to the nonbargainability of methods of production if the union proposes to substitute a change in methods for a wage increase—a not unknown situation? Despite some marginal cases, if it is in the employer's interest to bargain about methods, he will probably do so, whether the law requires it or not. And if it is sufficiently in an employer's interest to reject the union proposals about methods, he will probably do so, even if the law requires bargaining about them. (If the employer really needs the housekeeper and the housekeeper is nauseated by magenta walls, the employer may *have* to bargain over the color of walls.)

In short, it may be suspected that in the larger picture it is the interests of the parties, rather than some abstract concept of inherent rights, that will determine what will be bargained about and what will not. The term "interest" in this context includes bargaining power factors. If so, the main impact of the law on the scope of bargaining will depend more on its overall effect on bargaining power than on its explicit provisions about bargainable issues. Both the union and market forces are relevant to bargaining power.

PART II

UNION SECURITY

The Meaning of Union Security

Union security has a number of meanings. It refers to the continued existence of the union as an organization. It means the continued existence of the union as a bargaining agent for each bargaining unit that it represents. Union security can also be defined as the union's freedom to perform the function of collectively representing employees without interference from management or other sources. The last definition parallels that of management security in that both are defined in terms of freedom to function. One difference should be noted. Dealing with the union is only one of management's many functions, and for all practical purposes only those interferences with the management function that come from the union are significant to the union-management relation. By contrast, the function of collectively representing employees is so overwhelmingly important in the union's life that the union normally goes promptly out of existence if this function ceases. Hence, any clear threat to the union's continued status as bargaining agent, whether from management or from other sources, is directly relevant to the union-management relation. Thus, the words "or from other sources" appear in the definition of union, but not management, security.

Whether a protest function is necessary or desirable in the enterprise and whether the union is its appropriate instrument will not be debated here. Within the organized sector, the union is currently so thoroughly established in this function that we will accept this fact as given for the present chapter. The major questions that arise are: How much and what kind of security are necessary for the union to function properly? How is it achieved? Does it interfere with management security? Does it interfere with the workers' interest, public interest, or bargaining power? What standards, if any, should a union be required to meet before being accorded a secure position?

SOME THREATS TO UNION SECURITY

Before discussing whether a union should be made secure and by what methods, it is necessary to note the forces that threaten its security and how serious they are.

The Nonessentiality of Unions and the Likelihood of Management Opposition

One of the basic threats to the security of a union is so obvious that it is sometimes overlooked. Although an enterprise cannot operate without a management, it can operate without a union. The steel industry without a union is a tenable concept, and in fact prevailed for some fifty years. But the United Steelworkers without the steel industry is an absurdity. However logical and desirable the protest function and the union may be, they are dispensable. The members may question from time to time whether they really need a union. And many managements feel they can perform the function of looking after the human needs of their employees even better than the union does. Although the union-management relationship is often likened to a marriage, it is often a marriage from which one partner would prefer divorce. The underlying position of the union is essentially defensive. Drucker likens it to an opposition party that never comes into power.[25] This subordinate position is the starting point of the problem of union security and partially explains many characteristics of union behavior.

In many places management dislike takes active forms and keeps the union's existence in perpetual jeopardy. Although the law says they shall not do so, numerous managements nevertheless succeed in systematically weeding union members or leaders out of the plant. In many places, particularly in the South and Southwest, it would be naive to assume that an employee is really free to join a union. This lack of freedom, too, is a threat to the union's security.

Absence of Recognition

If management refuses to recognize and bargain with a union, the union's security is threatened directly and indirectly—directly because it cannot function, and indirectly because it will then lose support and die. Absence of recognition is a serious threat to the security of a union.

For many years one of the most difficult tasks facing unions was to get employers to recognize and deal with them. Since the Wagner Act of 1935, the employer is required to deal with a union if it represents a majority of the employees. Hence the union automatically achieves recognition if it keeps enough members. The main problem of union security in everyday life is to get and hold members, and the ensuing discussion will treat it in that light.

Loss of Membership and Income—The Basic Problem

The outsider may wonder why a problem of membership exists.

> If employees want union representation, they will join the union and get it. If not, they will stay out and do without representation. And if only a minority wants union conditions, it should certainly not be able to force them on the majority.

Unfortunately the problem is not so simple, and unions face a fundamental difficulty. According to both the law and common sense, a contract between union and employer must apply equally to all persons in the area covered by the contract, whether they belong to the union or not. Therefore, when a union bargains with management, it is negotiating just as much for the nonunion employees as for the union members. It is illegal to do otherwise, because the employer is prohibited by law from discriminating between union and nonunion. Even without the law, one can imagine the problems that would arise if an employer tried to favor either group. Furthermore, such differentials are also outlawed by defining a majority union legally as the "exclusive representative" within its bargaining unit. A union's ability to organize workers and collect dues is complicated further by right-to-work laws, discussed in more detail in Chapter 3.

"Exclusive representation" also applies in a personal sense. By a 1953 ruling of the NLRB, which is still binding, the union, as exclusive bargaining agent, must process the grievance of any individual employee against the employer, including arbitration if necessary, even if the employee is not a member of the union and pays no dues.[26] According to the ruling, the union will be deprived of representation rights if it bills the nonmember for its costs on his behalf. It is doubtful whether most persons would like the kind of representation they would probably get under these circumstances. But the meaning of exclusive representation and of the union's obligation is clear.

Thus the union faces a difficult problem. The employee gets the same representation, at least the same contract terms, whether he belongs to the union or not. But he pays for it only if he joins. If a person desires the benefits a union can win it makes sense from a purely economic point of view to work in a unionized plant without joining the union. The number of employees who place a high value on their voting privilege in the union is not high enough to alter this situation very much. The law furthers this discrepancy by designating the union as the exclusive representative of the employees whether they join it or not. Theoretically, a group of employees could vote unanimously to be represented by a union without any of them joining or paying dues.

This problem is clearly reflected in the typical union appeals that membership be kept up and dues paid. Appeals for "solidarity," "participation," and "being a good union member," as well as the virulent denunciation of the "free rider," all parallel the means a tax collector would have to use if payment of bills could not be enforced. When the nonessentiality of membership by any one individual is added to the nonessentiality of the union itself, it is little wonder that heads of unions tend to be "jumpy" about threats to the security of the union and its income.

The problem is aggravated still further because the same logic also applies at the level of the strike. After a strike is settled, the strikebreakers who continued to earn full wages during the strike get the same benefits as those who honored the picket line and lost their wages.

It is sometimes suggested that if only the union were to do a better job the employees would readily join and pay dues. Perhaps so. But the result must depend on social or moral pressures, not economic logic, as the following situation illustrates:

> You put a $5 package of goods on the table. The rules are that I get the package whether I pay for it or not, but you ask me to pay. I don't pay. You complain and ask that the rules be changed to require me to pay.
> I answer, "The way to get people to pay is to do more for them. Put a $10 package on the table instead."
> "And change the rules to require payment?"
> "No. Same rules."

Loss of Membership: Additional Factors

Employees may avoid the union for reasons other than a desire to "ride free." Some object to unions in principle. Others think the dues are too high or are misused, and some feel the pinch of even reasonable dues. Inertia counts others out. Some see no positive value in unions or think them mainly negative and objectionable. Others fear that joining may displease the boss. In addition, factional differences may bring membership below the majority point and put the union out of existence.

Anything less than full membership means a proportionate loss of dues. Studies suggest that between 6 and 15 percent of the employees will stay out, if they can, in companies where the union is well established in a stable work force, and the percentage may be much higher where there is a high labor turnover and a less clearly established union. To a large national union, the difference between the voluntary level of membership and full membership may be significant.[27]

If membership is barely above the majority level and if the employer might call for a decertification election, some dropouts may put the union's very existence in jeopardy. It may also be threatened by raiding by another union. This threat has been reduced considerably by the no-raiding and jurisdiction settlement techniques of the AFL–CIO. But it has not been entirely eliminated, particularly if the threat comes from an "independent," such as the Teamsters or District 50.

Because a continuous membership is necessary for the union's security and because there are so many reasons why membership may be avoided, unions have come to view compulsory membership as the chief device for achieving security. In fact, it is not uncommon to find the terms "union security" and "compulsory membership" used interchangeably.

SECURITY—A PREREQUISITE OF SATISFACTORY UNION PERFORMANCE

Granted that there are many threats to the security of a union and that they cause it great concern, this fact does not in itself justify relieving the union of the task of holding itself together. Nor does it justify forcing people into the union who may wish to stay out. Why, then, the great emphasis on and widespread use of compulsory membership?

The Union Function, Union Responsibility, and Union Security

The function of unions has already been delineated as that of representing and bargaining collectively for employees. In American unions, the leaders normally carry the responsibility for planning and executing bargaining strategy. The successful execution of bargaining strategy often requires the concerted action of the entire worker group. The whole success of a strike, for example, may be jeopardized if the union lacks the disciplinary power to get all the workers out of the plant during a strike or to prevent some from returning before the strike ends. We have already noted the temptation to disregard the strike call, in that anyone who works during the strike receives the same benefits as those who stayed out but suffers none of the losses. Union leaders without disciplinary powers lack the authority to effectuate the strategy for which they are responsible. Management faces no such problem; any lower executive who openly sided with the union during a strike would promptly be fired.

For the union, the discrepancy between authority and responsibility can be substantial in the area of contract enforcement. The contract that the union signs with management covers the entire bargaining unit, members and nonmembers. The union is the agent responsible for seeing that its side of the contract is upheld, and can be sued for breach of contract. One of the obligations most frequently undertaken by the union is to prevent strikes, slowdowns, or sitdowns. In the factory, it may be relatively easy for the employer to discipline infractions. But in looser employer-employee relations, as in building construction, stevedoring, or small trucking, where a few stray pickets may snarl a whole large operation, the union may be the only organization capable of disciplining the offender. If the union is to be able to carry out its contractual obligations, either to protect its treasury or to fulfill its pledge to the employer, it may need the power to discipline those who break the contract.

Whether disciplinary power is needed for the orderly execution of bargaining tactics or the faithful observance of the contract, the ultimate discipline in all organizations except government is expulsion. But as long as union membership is voluntary, expulsion from union membership is an ineffectual disciplinary action. The expelled individual remains in the bargaining unit and continues to be represented by the union and to receive its benefits. Only expulsion from the bargaining unit—that is, discharge from the job—will have a disciplinary effect. Effective discipline, therefore, requires either (1) that union membership be a condition of employment or (2) that the union be able to discipline nonmembers as well as members. Since the second alternative has never been seriously suggested, only the first will be discussed here. Compulsory membership is the device that makes the union's authority commensurate with its responsibility—a situation traditionally considered a prerequisite of sound organization.

Union Security and Sound Industrial Relations

The meaning of "sound industrial relations" is vague and need not be detailed here. In general, however, the term implies that in protecting the interests of their constituents both union and management behave with restraint and intelligence, recognize the rights of others, and realize that what is good for the opponent is not necessarily bad for themselves.

To state the conclusion before the evidence is presented, it seems safe to say that sound relations between union and management are impossible unless *both* management and union possess a rather high degree of security. Almost every responsible study ever made of the subject supports this conclusion.[28] The reasons are not hard to find.

It has already been observed that survival must take priority over interests, as is illustrated by the quip "Take my life, I need my money." Threats to survival often arouse intense emotions and push logic into the background. One who is drowning may grab his rescuer around the neck, though in calmer circumstances he would know better. Just as management, if it feels its freedom to manage will thereby be infringed, may resist a simple proposal that greatly benefits the employees and costs management little, so will unions reject the most sensible proposal from management if they feel it will reduce membership, loyalty, or solidarity. Wisdom and moderation are not characteristic of persons or organizations whose life is in jeopardy.

Insecurity puts the union leaders under constant pressure to "sell" the union. Now, while "selling" oneself or one's product is normally considered commendable in a market economy, a notable difference between the union (as an agent of protest) and the company (as an agent of production) may be overlooked.

> One marvels at the masochism of the employer who objects to union security and proclaims: "Let the union sell itself." He is implicitly recommending that the union improve its product. Now the "product" the union sells is concessions from the employer, and a "better" product is bigger concessions. Freely translated, "Let the union sell itself" means "Come on. Beat me till I give you bigger concessions."

Not only will the employer have to pay for the union's advertising in the form of a frequently renewed display of shiny big concessions. Selling also involves making the prospective customer dissatisfied with what he has, which for the insecure union means perpetual criticism of management. A common technique for showing one's prowess is to exaggerate the fearfulness of the opponent, which produces similar results. The insecure union, like the insecure individual, often tends to be permanently aggressive and belligerent. This tendency involves seeking unreasonable concessions as well as reasonable ones. It means inventing grievances and pressing every grievance, whether right or wrong. It means calling management nasty names and imputing improper motives to it. Whatever else such activities may do, they do not make for pleasant or sound relations between a company and its union.

MANAGEMENT AND UNION SECURITY

It is often assumed that employers universally and automatically oppose union security. Actually, many employers see distinct advantages in a secure union—assuming there already *is* a union. This attitude is more marked in large firms and among those who have dealt longest with unions.

For one thing, if all employees belong to the union, disciplinary action can be viewed on its merits, not as possible antiunion discrimination. Since we noted in the preceeding chapter that management security is closely linked to the ability to maintain discipline, in this respect security for the union may make it easier for management to defend *its* security. Second, it is destructive of morale to have resentment, distrust, and argument between union members and nonmembers; mandatory membership removes this friction. Third, if membership actually drops below a majority, the union may disappear, only to put on a new organizing campaign to get back in. Such on-again-off-again relations can be extremely disruptive. Fourth, a union leader free from the worry of holding members has more time to work with management on difficult problems. The leader is also freer to consider solutions on their merits, not on their effects on membership. Fifth, union security removes any suspicion that management will look with disfavor on employees who join the union. Otherwise the more responsible employees may stay out and leave the union to the "hotheads." These are some of the reasons one study found that 39 percent of the managements surveyed agreed that "labor's demand for the union shop is a legitimate right for them."[29]

An important reservation expressed by managements was that compulsory membership makes the union too strong. This reaction is most evident on the part of the employer who has some hope that he or she may prevent or eliminate the union. To such an employer, the signing of a union security clause means that the union is there to stay and its position is obviously much "stronger." But if by "strength" we mean bargaining power, then it is not at all clear that a secure union is able to get larger concessions than an insecure one.

Many employers oppose union security on the principle that they do not want to be party to a contract that requires employees to join a union against their will. Furthermore, some pursue this position *in principle*, despite their belief that union security *in practice* is of net benefit to themselves. However, to many who have seen the way in which thousands of employers in the past have systematically destroyed workers' freedom *to join* unions, their present high moral concern over workers' freedom *not to join* is subject to skepticism. Some workers suggest that they would rather not have their rights defended at all than to have them defended by employers.

Another important question to management is: Does union security come at the expense of management security? The answer seems to depend on the stage at which the question is asked. As was made clear in the preceeding chapter, the highest possible degree of management security is the complete absence of a union. Since the mere presence of *any* union brings a sharp reduction in management security, obviously a *secure* union represents a much smaller degree of management security than *no* union. Thus, management that hopes to avoid or eliminate unionization correctly senses a sharp conflict between union security and management security.

Once management accepts that the union will be with it indefinitely the alternatives change. It is then no longer a question of secure union versus no union, but of secure union versus insecure union, both equally real and permanent. At this point, there is no apparent reason why formal union security will necessarily reduce management security. In fact, the secure union may be more willing to sign a strong management security clause than will an insecure one. If the union is under less pressure to "sell itself," it can more safely relax and let management be management.

THE FORMS OF UNION SECURITY

Of the many ways to establish union security, most involve some form of compulsory membership. There has been much argument about which method is "best," most of it about as fruitless as arguing whether a saw or a plane is a better tool for a carpenter. Each is a device for doing a certain job under certain conditions.

The Closed Shop

A *closed shop*, which is illegal, is one in which each employee must be a union member before being hired. Often the union serves as the employment office through a hiring hall. In clothing, printing, construction and longshoring jobs, for example, an employer who wants employees may simply call the union, which sends him or her the number requested from a rotating list. If preferred, the union will send extras so that the employer has a choice.

A closed shop is workable only where one or a limited number of clearly defined skills are involved and where preselection, such as apprenticeship or experience, assures that everyone on the list is qualified. Strictly speaking, a closed shop limits the employer's discretion, since he cannot hire anyone who is not already a member of the union. Whether or not the employer suffers thereby will depend on whether the union is able to provide an adequate supply of competent workers. If all competent crafts workers are already members of the union (as is the case with the printing or building trades in some cities) a formal closed shop adds no restriction not already created by comprehensive unionization.

In jobs where people typically work for only a short period for each of a succession of different employers, there could be no union security—indeed, perhaps no collective bargaining—except under the closed shop. As was widely predicted, the closed shop has continued virtually intact among longshoremen, building crafts, and one-night-stand musicians, despite the prohibitions in the Taft−Hartley Act and the laws of many states. The prohibition is probably unenforceable in such jobs short of eliminating collective bargaining itself.

The Union Shop, Agency Shop, and Maintenance of Membership

The Labor Management Relations Act of 1947 (LMRA) allows the following types of union security provisions, some of which, however, may be disallowed by state law under Section 14(b) of the LMRA: union shop, modified union shop, maintenance of membership, and agency shop. The U.S. Department of Labor in a 1982 study provides the following definition of each of these union security provisions:

> *Union shop:* Nonunion workers may be hired, but they must join the union on or about 30 days (after 7 days in construction) and remain members as a condition of employment.
> *Modified union shop:* Workers who were not union members when the agreement became effective or who were hired before a specified date are exempted from compulsory membership. All new hires are required to join the union as a condition of employment.
> *Agency shop:* No employee is required to become or remain a union member, but nonmembers must pay union dues or equivalent service fees to the union.
> *Maintenance of membership:* No employee is required to join the union, but those who are or become members must remain members during the term of the agreement.[30]

The union shop requires membership in the union after hiring but not before. It places no restriction on the employer's freedom to hire. The restriction is on the employee instead, who must usually join the union within thirty days, the minimum period allowed by the Taft−Hartley Act except for the seven-day provision in construction. This is the only type of compulsory membership feasible in mass production industry, with its numerous types and levels of jobs and with relatively permanent employment. The employer in mass production industry would hardly tolerate the hiring restrictions of a closed shop. Furthermore, the closed shop could wreck the union if it had to decide which of its members to send out for each of dozens of different kinds of jobs. The closed shop is no more applicable to mass production industry than the union shop with a thirty-day period is to longshoring.

Several varieties of *modified union shop* have also appeared. The most common provision requires union membership of all workers, except those who were not members of the union before the effective date of the agreement. The provision requires new employees to join and members to maintain their membership.

An *agency shop* requires all employees in the bargaining unit to pay dues to the union but not to become members. Its practical effect is nearly identical to a union shop, since most people who pay the dues feel they may as well get voting rights as well. Nevertheless it preserves an option for those who are for some reason distressed by membership as such.

Maintenance of membership provides a lesser degree of union security than does the union shop but is applicable under the same general conditions. It does not require anyone to join the union who does not want to. But it does require anyone who is a member as of some specified date to remain a member and pay dues for some specified period, usually the duration of the contract. There is usually an escape period of from fifteen to thirty days at the end of each contract period, during which any member may resign and thereafter remain out of the union.

Maintenance of membership is the ingenious device given wide vogue during World War II by the War Labor Board, when it was the final arbiter of labor disputes. The board felt strongly that the government should not require any person to join a union as a condition of getting a job. Therefore, although it would *allow* a closed or union shop if the parties agreed to it, the board would not *order* one. At the same time, the board recognized that in its absence there would have been a steady increase in the number of union shops. Thus the board felt it improper either to order a union shop or to deny it. The maintenance of membership compromise made it possible for a union to have an assured membership at a known level for a definite period. But it did not require anyone to join against his will or even to retain membership indefinitely.

If turnover is high or contracts are of short duration, the security provided by maintenance of membership is distinctly limited. Members who leave may be replaced by persons who do not join, thus jeopardizing both the union's income and its majority status.

In 1982 the Department of Labor, Bureau of Labor Statistics, studied 1327 major collective bargaining agreements, which covered about 6 million workers. Union security provisions were incorporated in 1100 (83 percent) of these contracts, 787 had union shop provisions, 52 had modified union shop, 87 had agency shop, 46 had maintenance of membership, and 128 had a combination of union security provisions or other arrangements.[31]

Miscellaneous Forms of Union Security, and Its Extent

In a *preferential shop*, the employer gives preference in hiring to union members. In practice, it may work like the closed shop, since the latter normally allows the employer to recruit nonunion employees when the supply of union ones is exhausted. Its usefulness lies in the same kinds of situations to which the closed shop is applicable, particularly skilled crafts.

The *checkoff* of union dues from a worker's paycheck is partly a security and partly a bookkeeping device. It protects the union against loss of dues and possible loss of members through inadvertence or recalcitrance. It is a supplement to other devices, not important in its own right.

Another security device is *superseniority*, which gives union officers and stewards top seniority in their jobs for the purposes of layoff, regardless of how long they have held their jobs. Otherwise, a union's ability to function might be seriously impaired if key leaders held low seniority in departments hard hit by layoffs. And absence of seniority might tempt some employers to arrange their layoffs with an eye toward weakening the union.

Although not primarily devices for union security, several additional things contribute to it. Some unions have funds for retired or disabled members. Since continued membership is required of recipients, such funds provide an incentive to stick with the union. Recreational and educational activities engender loyalty in the union, and therefore add to its security. Union health and welfare funds, such as those in mining and the clothing trades may benefit the employers as well as the union, since they are an incentive for workers to remain in the industry as well as in the union.

Several other terms describe the absence of security rather than its presence. The *open shop*, strictly defined, is open on equal terms to members and nonmembers. If members are less than a majority, no collective bargaining occurs and no contract is signed; the shop remains *nonunion*. If a majority want the union, it becomes a unionized shop, with the union as bargaining agent. During their earlier days, unions were often recognized as bargaining agents for their members only. Under the Wagner and Taft–Hartley acts, this method has been replaced by exclusive representation which does itself provide a union some security. It provides motivation to join for those persons who do not want to be considered "free riders." It also provides substantial protection from raiding by competing unions, in that there is almost no reason for a member of the bargaining unit to join another union unless it is expected to succeed in actually taking representation rights away from the incumbent union.

THE BASIC CONTROVERSY IN UNION SECURITY

The basic conflict over union security is now clear. On the one hand, union security seems to be a requisite condition for sound industrial relations. On the other, compulsory membership curtails the individual's freedom of choice. The choice between a particular type of freedom and a workable system of industrial relations is a value judgment, and hence cannot be decided by rational analysis alone. As it is often argued, the choice seems to be between two incompatible principles: (1) that no person should be required to join or pay dues to any private organization as a condition of holding his job, and (2) that any person who is in fact represented by a union and who lives under the contract it negotiates should contribute to its support. Disconcertingly, it is logically possible to believe in *both* principles, taken separately.

There would be no problem of course, if everyone, or nearly everyone, joined voluntarily. This has long been the situation through much of British industry, where compulsory membership was neither prohibited nor needed. In many crafts and industries, workers simply took it for granted that they would join, and the nonunion worker was so loathsome that no one would work next to him or her. Union security provisions have nevertheless been introduced in recent decades, with about 40 percent of British workers being in the closed shops in the early sixties.[32] Differences in terminology, however, make it difficult to translate the British experience into American categories. Formal security has also been less important in Britain, since the employers there accept unionization as normal and long ago stopped fighting the existence of unions. However, as of mid-1980 the aggressive Conservative government of Margaret Thatcher in Great Britain was pushing to require an 80 percent employee vote in favor before a new closed shop could be established, along with periodic review and a possible vote requirement for closed shops existing prior to the change in regulation. At the time about 5.2 million British workers were covered by closed shops.[33] In Belgium, where membership constitutes a large proportion of the work force and the feeling against the "free rider" is strong, many employers pay their employees a bonus for belonging to the union.[34] Union security without compulsory membership also prevailed for many years in the railway unions in the United States and in some skilled crafts, where the apprentice automatically joined the union during training. The American developments have been in the direction of the concept that membership is required as a condition of industrial citizenship.

Compulsory Membership, Union Democracy, and Individual Rights

If union membership is compulsory a serious problem can arise. In unions not characterized by high-level democracy, individual rights may be infringed on in two ways. As to the first, in the past, some unions restricted their membership by admitting only friends or relatives of present members, and others placed numerical restrictions on membership. If membership is both *required* and *unavailable*, the applicant is denied the right to work in the job being sought. Because of legal developments during the last few decades this is no longer a problem in unionized organizations. Whatever other controversy exists about compulsory membership, there is much agreement that if membership is *required*, it must also be *available* to any qualified applicant. That is, whatever one might think about either a closed shop or a closed union taken separately, a combination of the two would be unacceptable to most Americans.

As to the second possible infringement of individual rights, if a union is undemocratically operated, the closed or union shop might free the worker from the arbitrary control of the employer only to bring him under the arbitrary control of the union. If unions are to be allowed to require membership, it would seem reasonable to require them in turn to provide guarantees of members' rights and freedom from arbitrary discipline within the union. We now have legislation designed to protect such rights, mainly in the form of LMRDA, but cannot reach clear conclusions about its effectiveness.

Most legislation about union security since World War II has moved in the direction of prohibiting compulsory membership. This, of course, prevents the abuse of the union's disciplinary power by abolishing it. For example, the Taft–Hartley Act is so written that a union shop contract cannot, in fact, compel membership; it can merely require the payment of dues. It should be noted in this connection that there is no necessary conflict between democracy and disciplinary power. For although democracy implies the right to participate in formulating rules, it does not include the right to violate them. Absence of discipline is anarchy, not democracy. The way our legislation has handled this thorny problem of the relationship between compulsory membership, union democracy, and union responsibility shows more evidence of political jockeying than of logical rationality.

Worker Reaction to Union Security

Under the original Taft – Hartley Act, workers had an opportunity to express their feelings on the union shop in numerous secret-ballot elections supervised by the National Labor Relations Board, usually conducted in the plant during working time. All employees in the bargaining unit, whether union members or not, were eligible to vote. Out of 89,000 such elections held before this provision was repealed in 1951, almost 87,000, or 97 percent, were decided in favor of the union shop. Out of a total of 10.5 million votes cast in these elections, 9.17 million, or 92.5 percent, favored the union shop. At the same time some 15 percent did not vote. Whether they should be counted as indifferent or opposed is problematic. Their *effect* was clearly the same as a negative vote, however, since a majority of those *eligible* to vote was required for approval. It is therefore possible to conclude that as few as about 77 percent (92.5 minus 15 not voting) actually favored the union shop—a much less impressive figure. Furthermore, the percentages were showing a downward trend by the time the union shop polls were eliminated in 1951 by revision of the law.[35]

The provision for such votes was written into the law at the request of employers who believed that the union shop was being foisted on unwilling workers by ambitious leaders, and that workers would overwhelmingly vote against compulsory membership if given the chance. The elections weakened this argument, as clauses for mandatory membership then increased more rapidly than ever before. The results seem to support the general historical conclusion that if the union leaders recommend one course of action while management prefers another, the employees will normally support the union leadership—though recent decades may reflect a weakening of this behavior.

Workers may not like compulsory membership. But they like a divided union even less. During the five years of modified union shop at General Motors, only one-tenth of 1 percent of the new workers elected to drop out of the union after their year of compulsory membership. Considering the issue not worth fighting over, the company granted the full union shop in 1955. The move was followed shortly by most of the industry.

ANTIUNION ACTIVITIES

In 1935, over fifty years ago, the United States Congress enacted the Wagner Act, which in Section 1 states that it is the declared policy of the United States to encourage "the practice and procedure of collective bargaining." Despite this legislation and a long history of collective bargaining in the United States, many employers still do their utmost to keep unions out. The attitude of employers toward unions can be illustrated by the following statement from a popular textbook on personnel and industrial relations:

> There seems little question that the preferred approach to organizational maintenance insofar as labor relations are concerned has been to keep the unions out if at all possible, and personnel managers have devoted, and still are devoting, considerable effort toward just this end.[36]

In 1977 Lane Kirkland, (then the secretary treasurer) the president of the AFL−CIO, expressed the view that unions are the target of a large-scale propaganda offensive conducted by management, whose familiar refrain is that "labor is a narrow special interest group; that union bosses are dictators; that union members are their tools; that American workers are overpaid; that American unions have priced themselves out of the market."[37]

According to the AFL−CIO, "Union busting is a growth industry. It has attracted some 1500 practitioners," who identify themselves as management consultants.[38] The number of consultants has been growing rapidly. Existing consulting firms are enlarging their staffs, some universities present seminars on prevention of unionization—thus offering some respectability to such activities—and some law firms that in the past accepted the concept of unionization for their clients "are today keeping up with the competition usually by retaining at least a few lawyers who are hardcore union fighters."[39] Management consultants who specialize in defeating unions include lawyers, employer and trade associations, psychologists, detectives, and nonprofit antiunion organizations. Some of these experts have degrees in labor relations, psychology, and other social sciences.[40]

There are a number of reasons for the increase in antiunion activities by employers and for the recent popularity of antiunion experts. First, a significant proportion of union organizing activity has been taking place in the antiunion South. Thus, the increase in antiunion drives is a direct response to an increase in organizational campaigns by unions in that part of the country. Second, organizational activity is usually conducted by large and strong unions; employers fear that such unions may force them to provide large wage concessions. Therefore, they try to prevent unionization. Third, today the antiunion methods applied by antiunion specialists are considerably more sophisticated and legal and thus more attractive to employers than the lockouts and the violence of the 1930s.[41] According to unions, they are confronted with a new breed of "union busters" or consultants who apply "psychological and legal dirty tricks" and thus create "an atmosphere of fear in the workplace." These consultants advocate that management adopt "a love-thy-worker gospel" as a means of preventing unionization.[42]

Some of the antiunion consultants offer seminars under such headings as "Strategies for Preserving Nonunion Status" and "The Process of Decertification." They coach employers in antiunion tactics. They sell training manuals on how to defeat unions in NLRB elections and provide management with strategies and preventive programs for keeping unions out. One firm, Advance Management Research, Inc. (AMR), provides in-company training programs on "How to Make Unions Unnecessary." AMR employs labor attorneys and industrial psychologists who coach employers in antiunion techniques.[43]

Antiunion labor attorneys help employers operate within the law, while at the same time making it very difficult for unions to gain recognition. They advise firms to announce strict no-solicitation rules before the start of a unionization campaign, they suggest the establishment of multiple entries to make it more difficult for organizers to distribute leaflets, they advise employers on how to benefit from legally permissible electioneering tactics, and they utilize NLRB election postponement procedures in order to time elections in favor of employers. Since delay is usually viewed as an employer's weapon, the legal strategies are usually aimed toward delays. Among the delaying approaches suggested by antiunion experts are the following: refusal to agree to a consent election, contesting the NLRB's jurisdiction by refusal to stipulate the impact of the business on interstate commerce, gaining additional time by refusing to stipulate that the organizing union is a "labor organization," and disagreeing over the appropriateness of the bargaining unit and over the eligibility status of particular employees within the unit.[44]

Some antiunion employers engage the services of industrial phychologists and other social scientists who in the antiunion activities apply such concepts as "positive reinforcement, organizational and individual effectiveness, employee value-systems, negative feedback, problem-solving orientations, and performance through motivation." According to Payne, some psychologists attempt to train workers "through a system of positive and negative reinforcement, so that they will feel no need for a union." The psychologists analyze the underlying value system of employees and their emotional and economic needs. They make recommendations to employers on how these needs can be satisfied to "cause workers to identify themselves with management rather than with a union."[45]

Some consultants advise management on hiring procedures that can help filter out potential union sympathizers with activists. Some advise employers to hire as many women as possible. Woodruff Imberman, a Chicago consultant, suggests to his clients that "it's obviously legal to scare the bejesus out of your female employees with threats of strikes, violence and picket lines." Imberman also suggests that employers hire only as many blacks as legally required, "because blacks are more prone to unionize." Some consultants employ survey instruments which help separate pro-union and antiunion workers. Following such separation, the prounion employees are assigned to duties that reduce or eliminate their interaction with their fellow employees.[46]

In some cases, managements in their new antiunion drives go as far as hiring undercover agents to break up organizing drives by unions. In recent testimony before a house labor subcommittee, an undercover agent testified about his antiunion work at Anja Engineering Corporation of Monrovia, California. He said, "Anybody we overheard talking pro-union, we would write their names down . . . and if their names appeared on more than one agent's report, we would find ways to set them up, get them fired, or arrested by Monrovia police."[47]

In Salisbury, North Carolina, during an organizational campaign by the Teamsters, employees received a recorded dramatization of a strike conducted by Teamsters twenty-five years ago. The record included sounds of gunshots, screams, and breaking of glass. Furthermore, the actors who portrayed union supporters spoke in "the argot of a black ghetto." This frightened the predominantly white work force. The union lost this election, 1272 to 883.[48]

In recent years social, industrial, and organizational psychology and the sociology of complex organization have all been applied to the area of personnel management. The work of the antiunion industrial psychologist has been facilitated by the acceptance and application of behavior sciences in the area of personnel administration.

Decertification Elections and the Union Shop Deauthorization Poll

Another antiunion weapon is the decertification election. Section 9(c)(1)(A) of the Taft–Hartley Act provides a procedure for decertifying a labor union. An NLRB certification of a labor organization to represent all employees in the bargaining unit for the purpose of collective bargaining is valid only for one year. After the year is up, employees within the unit can request a decertification election; a union defeat in such an election results in decertification of the union as a bargaining agent.

In the last few years there has been an increase in research activity in the area of union decertification. Statistically, decertification elections account for only about 10 percent of the total number of NLRB representation elections held; however, the percentage of such elections has been increasing over time. Also the frequency of union losses has been going up. Despite these developments some authors claim that the number of decertification losses are presently statistically insignificant and of minor consequence for the U.S. labor movement. This could change and the decertification route could gain importance as an antiunion tool of the future.[49]

Another potential antiunion weapon is the union shop deauthorization poll. Under the Taft–Hartley Act, Section 9(c)(1), employees can petition the NLRB to conduct a union shop deauthorization poll. A winning vote for deauthorization gives the employees the right to remove the union shop provision from the labor contract. Although the number of polls held and employees affected by such polls is still very small, the number of petitions for such polls increased significantly over the past twenty-five years.[50]

SUMMARY

Union and management security share an important trait. If either is approached as a question of principle or inherent right, debate on it can be endless. But if either is approached as a technique for achieving satisfactory performance of an organization function, rational criteria can be applied and mutually acceptable conclusions reached. Which approach is "proper" is, of course, a value judgement. The actual developments are nevertheless clear: Both management security and union security have in fact been established in the majority of areas now subject to collective bargaining. This situation could have resulted from mutual acceptance of mutual security on a problem-solving basis. It could also have resulted from each side's victory for its own version of the principle of its own security. Although the espousers of principle are more visible to the public, they have probably not had the actual major influence. Though in the minority, the number of areas in which insecurity still prevails on both sides remains significantly large.

NOTES

[1]The President's National Labor—Management Conference, November 5—30, 1945 (Washington, D.C.: U.S. Department of Labor, 1946), p. 58.

[2]*Ibid.*, p. 61.

[3]*Ibid.*, p. 56.

[4]A case that illustrates this situation in classic simplicity is related in Douglas McGregor, *The Human Side of Enterprise* (New York: McGraw-Hill, 1960), p. 23. See also Neil W. Chamberlain and James W. Kuhn, *Collective Bargaining*, 2nd ed. (New York: McGraw-Hill, 1965), p. 89.

[5]This conclusion may need to be softened somewhat if the entire work force is well educated. See, for example, the discussion of the kibbutz in Arnold S. Tannenbaum et al., *Hierarchy in Organizations* (San Francisco: Jossey-Bass, 1974).

[6]Agreement between the UAW and the Ford Motor Co., February 13, 1982, pp. 15—16.

[7]*Collective Bargaining Negotiations and Contracts, Strikes, and Lockouts* (Washington, D.C.: Bureau of National Affairs, 1982), No. 956—957, pp. 75, 78.

[8]*Ibid.*

[9]*Ibid.*

[10]*Collective Bargaining Negotiations and Contracts, Basic Patterns: Management and Union Rights* (Washington, D.C.: 1983), Bureau of National Affairs, pp. 65:1—65:3, 109—111, No. 991.

[11]*Ibid.*

[12]Brian Hamer, "Serving Two Masters: Union Representations on Corporate Board of Directors," *Columbia Law Review*, 81 (April 1981), 639.

[13]*Wall Street Journal*, February 16, 1973, p. 5, Source: *Columbia Law Review, op. cit.*, p. 640; D.M. Douglas, "Labor Unions in the Boardroom: An Anti Trust Dilemma," *The Yale Law Journal*, 92 (1982), 106.

[14]*Cincinnati Enquirer*, October 27, 1979, p. B7; *Newsweek*, November 5, 1979, p. 82; *Wall Street Journal*, November 8, 1979, p. 22.

[15]Ted Mills, "Europe's Industrial Democracy: An American Response," *Harvard Business Review* (November-December 1978), pp. 143—52.

[16]James N. Ellenberger, "The Realities of Co-Determination," *AFL-CIO American Federationist* (October 1977), pp. 10—15.

[17]Informal conversation by one of the authors with Mr. D.M. Fraser, at the monthly dinner meeting of the Greater Cincinnati Chapter of the Industrial Relations Research Association, Winter, 1984. See also Hamer, *op. cit.*, pp. 639—640.

[18]Ellenberger, *op. cit.*

[19]Benjamin C. Roberts, Hideaki Okamoto, and George C. Lodge, *Collective Bargaining and Employee Participation in Western Europe, North America and Japan,* Report of the Trilateral Task Force on Industrial Relations with the Trilateral Commission, 1979, p. 67.

[20]Pan American World Airways, *Wall Street Journal,* May 13, 1982. *Source: The Yale Law Journal, op. cit.,* p. 106.

[21]*Wall Street Journal,* April 28, 1972, p. 34; December 13, 1971, p. 25; *New York Times,* March 27, 1973, p. 5; Lassus, "What the Teamsters Really Wanted," *Beverage World* (June 1976), p. 34. *Sources: The Yale Law Journal, op. cit.,* p. 106, *Columbia Law Review, op, cit.,* p. 640.

[22]*The Yale Law Journal, op. cit.,* p. 106.

[23]*Ibid.,* p. 127.

[24]*Columbia Law Review, op. cit.,* pp. 639–61.

[25]Peter F. Drucker, *The New Society* (New York: Harper, 1950), p. 113.

[26]See 32 *Labor Relations Reference Manual* (Washington, D.C.: Bureau of National Affairs, 1954), pp. 1010ff., 1232, for the case of Hughes Tool Company and the Independent Metal Workers' Union. The case arose in Texas, which also prohibits the union shop.

[27]James W. Kuhn, "Right-to-Work Laws—Symbol or Substance?", *Industrial and Labor Relations Review* (July 1961), p. 589. See also Keith Lumsden and Craig Petersen, "The Effect of Right-to-Work Laws on Unionization in the United States," *Journal of Political Economy* (October 1975), pp. 1237–48. See also Ronald Miller, "Compulsory Union Membership in the United States," *British Journal of Industrial Relations* (July 1976), 188. See also Janet C. Hunt and Rudolph A. White, *The Effects of Right-to-Work Legislation on Union Outcomes: Additional Evidence,* pp. 47–63. *Journal of Labor Research,* 4, no. 1 (Winter 1983).

[28]See, for example, Committee on the Causes of Industrial Peace, *Fundamentals of Labor Peace, A Final Report* (Washington, D.C.: National Planning Association, 1953), pp. 61, 75ff., and *passim.* On p. 76 it is pointed out that it is considered important to good relations, for example, that management actually encourage workers to join and support the organization that represents them. The attitude also appears in the stark simplicity of a notice to employees put on the bulletin board by the London General Omnibus Garage in 1927. After pointing out that no one was under obligation to join the union, the notice continued: "The Company finds it mutually convenient to have some organization to represent the staff collectively on their behalf." See Jean Tripp McKelvey, "The Closed Shop Controversy in Post War Britain," *Industrial and Labor Relations Review* (July 1954), p. 554. See also E. Wight Bakke, *Mutual Survival, The Goal of Unions and Management,* 2nd ed. (Hamden, Conn.: Archon Books, 1966); Miller, *op. cit.,* p. 190; Lee Dyer, D.B. Lipsky, and T.A. Kochan, "Union Attitudes Toward Management Cooperation," *Industrial Relations,* 16, no. 2 (May 1977), 169–70.

[29]Mark Thompson and Larry Moore, "Managerial Attitudes Toward Industrial Relations, A U.S.-Canadian Comparision," *Relations Industrielles,* 30, M-3 (1975), 335–37.

[30]*Major Collective Bargaining Agreements: Union Security and Dues Checkoff Provisions,* U.S. Department of Labor, Bureau of Labor Statistics, Bulletin 1425–21 (May 1982), p. 5.

[31]*Ibid.*

[32]Robert Taylor, *Fifth Estate Britain's Unions in the Seventies* (London: Routledge & Kegal Paul, 1978), p. 19; Everett M. Kassalow, "Will West European Unions Embrace the Union Shop?" *Monthly Labor Review* (July 1979), p. 35. See also W.E.J. McCarthy, *The Closed Shop in Britain* (Oxford: Blackwell, 1964), p. 53.

[33]*Financial Times* (London), July 21, 1980.

[34]Roger Blandain, *Public Employee Unionism in Belgium* (Detroit: Institute of Labor and Industrial Relations, University of Michigan-Wayne State University, 1971), p. 8. See also *Monthly Labor Review* (August 1964), p. 929.

[35]Compiled from the annual reports of the NLRB by Sidney C. Sufrin and Robert C. Sedgwick, *Labor Law* (New York: Crowell, 1954), p. 273; Kuhn, *op. cit.*, p. 590.

[36]John B. Miner and Mary Green Miner, *Personnel and Industrial Relations*, 3rd ed. (New York: Macmillan, 1977), p. 479.

[37]Lane Kirkland, "The Renewed Assault on Labor," *AFL—CIO American Federationist*, 84 (July 1977), p. 1.

[38]"Stopping the Modern Union Buster," *AFL—CIO News*, January 15, 1983, p. 2.

[39]*Forbes*, June 25, 1979, pp. 29—30.

[40]"Management Consultants," *AFL—CIO News*, December 4, 1982, p. 2. Statement of George Meany, *quoted in* Payne, "The Consultants Who Coach the Violators," *AFL—CIO Federationist*, September 1977. *Pressures in Today's Workplace: Oversight Hearings Before the House Subcommittee on Labor-Management Relations*, 96th Cong., 1st Sess. 410 (1979) (statement of Robert A. Georgine, President, Building and Construction Trades Department, AFL—CIO). "Union-Busting and the Law: From Benign Neglect to Malignant Growth," study prepared by Jules Bernstein of the Washington, D.C. law firm of Connerton & Bernstein, 1980. John Sheridan Associates, Inc., "Preventive Labor Relations," presented to National Retail Merchants Association, January 17, 1979.

[41]*Newsweek*, January 28, 1980, pp. 67—68.

[42]*Forbes, op. cit.*, p.29.

[43]Phyllis Payne, "The Consultant Who Coached the Violators," *AFL—CIO American Federationist* (September 1977), pp. 23—24.

[44]*Ibid*.

[45]*Ibid*.

[46]*Forbes, op. cit.*, p. 30; *Wall Street Journal*, November 19, 1979, pp. 1, 26; *Newsweek, op cit.*, p. 67.

[47]*Newsweek, op cit.*, p. 67.

[48]*Ibid.*, p. 68.

[49]Dennis Ahlburg and James Dworkin, "The Influence of Macroeconomic Variables on the Probability of Union Decertification," *Journal of Labor Research* (Winter 1984), pp. 13—28; John C. Anderson, Gloria Busman, and Charles A. O'Reilly, III, "What Factors Influence the Outcome of Decertification Elections?" *Monthly Labor Review*, 102, no. 11 (November 1979), p. 32; John Anderson, Charles O'Reilly, and Gloria Busman, "Union Decertification in the U.S.: 1947—1977," *Industrial Relations, 19 (Winter 1980), 100—107*; John Anderson, Gloria Busman, and Charles O'Reilly, "The Decertification Process: Evidence from California," *Industrial Relations*, 21 (Spring 1982), 178—195; I. Chafetz and C.R.P. Fraser, "Union Decertification: An Exploratory Analysis," *Industrial Relations*, 18 (Winter 1979), 59—69; Alfred DiMaria, *The Process of Deunionization* (New York: Executive Enterprises Publications, 1982); James Dworkin and Marian Extejt, "Recent Trends in Union Decertification/Deauthorization Elections," *Proceedings* of the Thirty-Second Annual Meeting of the IRRA (Madison, Wis., 1980),

pp. 226–234; Ralph Elliott, and Banjamin Hawkins, "Do Union Organizing Activities Affect Decertification?" *Journal of Labor Research*, 3 (Spring 1982), 153–161; William E. Fulmer, "Decertification: Is the Current Trend a Threat to Collective Bargaining?" *California Management Review* (Fall 1981), pp. 14–22; William E. Fulmer and Tamara A. Gilman, "Why do Workers Vote for Union Decertification?" *Personnel* (March-April 1981), pp. 28–35; Joseph Krislov, "Decertification Elections Increase But Remain No Major Burden to Unions," *Monthly Labor Review* (November 1979), p. 30; John J. Lawler and Greg Hundley, "Determinants of Certification and Decertification Activity," *Industrial Relations*, 22, no. 3 (Fall 1983), 335–347; Marcus Sandver and Herbert C. Heneman III, "Union Growth Through the Election Process," *Industrial Relations*, 20 (Winter 1981), 109–111; Ronald Seeber and William Cooke, "The Decline in Union Success in NLRB Representation Elections," *Industrial Relations*, 22 (Winter 1983), 34–44.

[50]James B. Dworkin and Marion Extejt, "The Union-Shop Deauthorization Poll: A New Look After 20 Years," *Monthly Labor Review* (November 1979), pp. 36–40.

CONTRACT ADMINISTRATION

16

In previous chapters we have discussed the history of organized labor, the legal and institutional aspects of the relation between unions and managements, bargaining and preparation for bargaining, and the wages and fringe benefits provided to workers in collective contracts. To this point, we have not looked at the day-to-day impact of collective bargaining on workers or supervisors, nor have we focused on the relations between unions and managements in the period between negotiation of new agreements. In this chapter, we shall focus upon that aspect of industrial relations. Given that rules of conduct are negotiated in collective bargaining, how are those rules translated into the daily behavior of employer and employee? If there are disputes over the interpretation or application of those rules, how are the disputes to be resolved? It is these questions and others that we will address in this chapter.

PLANT GOVERNMENT AND CONTRACT ADMINISTRATION

The Nature and Meaning of Plant Government

A principal function of management is to direct the work force. The welfare of its employees is not the primary concern of management. Management's chief objective is to remain solvent and make a profit, and employees are only one of many means to that end. Viewed as a government of the plant, management does not and cannot govern primarily in the interests of "the governed." The presence of a union, however, prevents management from disregarding the interests of its "subjects" and governing solely in the interests of the rulers.[1] Except in very small firms, members of management are also employees in the broad sense. However, for the purposes of this section, as for most of the book, "employees" means those at nonsupervisory levels who are eligible for protection under the National Labor Relations Act and are members of the bargaining unit. Nevertheless, it remains true that in many organizational and psychological ways some of the members of management, and particularly those at the lower levels, identify more closely with the employees' way of thinking than with management's. That identification is particularly strong in the many firms in which any increases in pay or benefits negotiated by the union representing the rank-and-file employees are extended more or less automatically to lower and middle levels of supervision. Supervisors may also be quite jealous of the kinds of job protections available to union members that are not available to themselves.

As viewed by employees, management is a dictatorship, in the sense that power comes from above and employees cannot replace the managers. But many people feel it pointless to live in a political democracy if the conditions of their work life—in which they spend the largest chunk of their adult waking hours—are dictatorial and deny freedom and dignity. Enlightened policies by management, a counterforce in the form of a union, or both, can keep management from destroying important human values in the plant. If some plants are run by authoritarian methods while others are not, the worker can, of course, leave the former for the latter. But workers generally do not feel that this market pressure is any more effective in forcing enlightened policies on management than it is in achieving satisfactory wages, since it depends on individual bargaining power. It is the purpose of this chapter to describe how a functioning union-management relationship can protect these human values and to inquire whether management alone can do the same.

The Concept of Industrial Jurisprudence.   Sumner Slichter first applied the term *industrial jurisprudence* to a functioning plant government. Its underlying idea is similar to that of public government in a democracy in that it is "a government of laws, not of men." Under the laws, each person's rights and duties are known or determinable. No one may be required to do what the rules do not require. Nor may one do what the rules forbid, especially if the act adversely affects the rights of others. In particular, in the plant an employee may be punished only for proved violations of known rules or standards, not at the discretion of a supervisor. Such conditions of "law" can exist without a union, and where managements have established them the urge of employees to unionize is usually low. The mere presence of a union does not guarantee that industrial jurisprudence will prevail. But the particular brand of plant government to be described below is widespread under unions. It will normally be one of the first things a new union seeks to attain, and will permanently remain one of the most important.

Some managers believe that industrial jurisprudence destroys management security. It is true, of course, that rules restrict both sides who have to obey them, just as public law limits the discretion of administrators and police as well as of citizens. But whether management security is curtailed by industrial jurisprudence depends on the particular rules that are written and the kinds of procedures that carry them out, and these must be examined in the individual case. It may be noted in passing that many plants have a better system of industrial jurisprudence for ordinary employees than for members of management. Executives, from foreman to president, often have little protection against arbitrary treatment.

In the broadest sense, industrial jurisprudence includes both primary and secondary bargaining, since the legislative function of contract making is quite as important as contract effectuation. But "jurisprudence" refers more specifically to interpreting the law and applying it to particular cases, and it is in that sense that the term will be used here.

Contract Administration. The initiative in contract administration lies with management. We have already seen that a contract consists mainly of things that management commits itself to do for employees, and of rules that limit management's freedom with respect to employees. Beyond a no-strike clause, it involves little or no commitment by union or workers. As seen earlier, the unique feature of the union-management contract is that the union does not supply labor. The employer receives what he wants from the relationship, not through agreement from the union but through the contracts of employment in which each individual agrees to accept and perform instructions from a supervisor under pain of discipline or discharge. For the most part, if management abides by the contract, it is thereby administered and requires no further action. This is an important background aspect of industrial jurisprudence and must be noted, although it requires no further elaboration. The aspect that requires attention arises when an employee or union feels that the employer has *not* followed the contract, and institutes action to bring him into line. Management can use similar action to bring the union into line within those limited areas that involve commitments by the union.

The Process of Continuous Negotiation. The entire concept of plant governance and contract administration can also be thought of as one in which unions and managements continue to negotiate during the life of the agreement. That is, the same behaviors of exploration of issues, proposals, and counterproposals can be observed. Sometimes the parties agree in principle in formal negotiations and leave the negotiation of the details of implementation for later. Other times, conditions might change so radically during the life of an agreement that modifications in the application of the contract language are necessary. Finally, the period between negotiations can serve to identify important topics for the next round of bargaining. Sometimes the parties will discover that the language they wrote at the negotiating table continuously produces grievances. This can create a desire to alter that particular part of the agreement. All in all, plant governance plays as significant a role in industrial relations as the more formal negotiation of agreements.

THE JUDICIAL PROCESS IN PLANT GOVERNMENT

The judicial aspect of plant government is embodied in its grievance procedure, the method by which the parties resolve disputes. Some method of resolving disputes between labor and management is contained in nearly all collective bargaining agreements.[2] Far and away the most common type of grievance procedure is one similar to that described in the following paragraphs.

1983–1985 Agreement Between Cornell University and Cornell Service and Maintenance Unit, United Automobile, Aerospace, and Agricultural Implement Workers of America, Local 2300

Article XI
Grievance Procedure and Arbitration

1. "Grievance" within the meaning of the Agreement shall be defined as any matter involving the interpretation or application of this Agreement which alleges a violation of the rights of an employee or the Union under the terms of this Agreement. . . .

13. All grievances shall be processed and settled in conformity with the following procedure:

   Step 1. All grievances must first be discussed by the employee with his/her immediate supervisor with or without a Steward present. The supervisor shall respond to the employee and the steward when involved, as soon as possible, but no later than three (3) working days from the date the grievance was discussed.

   Step 2. If the immediate supervisor's oral answer does not resolve the grievance and the employee chooses to pursue the matter further, it shall be reduced to writing setting forth the facts upon which the grievance is based, the section(s) of the Agreement pursuant to which the employee's rights are alleged to have been violated, and the remedy or correction sought, and within five (5) consecutive working days from receipt of the oral answer be appealed to the department head or designated representative. The department head or designee shall within five (5) consecutive working days from the date the grievance is appealed meet and discuss the grievance with the employee and a specified Union representative. Should the Union representative request it, the department head will grant the representative up to one-half hour at the start of the meeting to confer privately with the employee. A writen answer to the grievance shall be provided to the employee and the specified Union representative within five (5) working days after the date of the Step 2 meeting.

Step 3. If the grievance is not resolved in Step 2, the specified Union representative may appeal the grievance in writing within five (5) consecutive working days of receipt of the Step 2 answer. Within twenty (20) working days from the date the grievance was appealed to Step 3, a meeting shall be scheduled between the Director of Employee Relations or a designee and three (3) persons the Director of Employee Relations determines may assist in the resolution of the grievance, and a designated International Representative, a specified Union representative, and the aggrieved employee. The Director of Employee Relations shall provide the International Representative and the unit chairperson with a written answer on the appeal within ten (10) working days of the meeting.

Step 4. If the grievance remains unresolved after the Step 3 answer from the Director of Employee Relations, the designated International Representative may appeal the grievance to arbitration by submitting an official written notice to the Director of Employee Relations within ten (10) working days from receipt of the Step 3 answer.

Arbitration. The selection of an arbitrator and arbitration proceedings shall be conducted under the then current Labor Arbitration Rules of the American Arbitration Association. The jurisdictional authority of the arbitrator is defined and limited to the determination as to whether there have been violations of the provision or provisions of the Agreement as set forth in the written grievance; the arbitrator shall have no power to add to, subtract from, or modify any of the terms of this Agreement. The decision of the arbitrator shall be based exclusively on evidence presented at the arbitration hearings and shall be final and binding on all involved parties.

Where the decision of the arbitrator includes an award for back pay, back wages shall be limited to the amount of wages that the employee otherwise would have earned less any unemployment compensation.

The parties shall bear their own expenses and share in the arbitrator's fee and expenses equally. Each party shall be responsible for the expenses of its witnesses and representatives, except as provided in Section 5 of this Article. Either party may be represented by counsel.

Except as otherwise provided for in this Agreement, the University may temporarily fill any position pending the resolution of the grievance.

While the number of steps, the scope of the procedure, and the power of the arbitrator can all vary, the basic elements of the procedure remain fairly constant under most contracts.

The Grievance Procedure in Action.　Few grievance procedures are identical, yet their essentials are highly similar. We will describe our represenative grievance procedure in action.

A typical grievance might be an employee's complaint that he has been improperly disciplined. Since discipline is explained elsewhere in the contract, this complaint is within the definition of grievance contained in our representative contract. As the first step, the employee and/or the shop steward[3] will take the matter to the employee's supervisor. The supervisor occupies a difficult dual role in many grievance procedures, for he may be the defendant as well as the judge in this first step. The task requires discretion, wisdom, and self-control, and the training of supervisors has greatly increased in importance since the advent of unions. If the supervisor satisfactorily adjusts it, the grievance is closed. The settlement, of course, may not violate the contract—an important reason why unions insist that a shop steward be present at the discussions and why managements want their supervisors to be thoroughly conversant with the contract. Under the Taft–Hartley Act, an employee has the right to present his own case, but the shop steward has the right to be present.

If the supervisor's decision is not acceptable, the grievance is put in writing. As the second step, the grievance will go to the departmental head and a higher union official, such as the chief steward. Minutes of the meeting, perhaps initialed by both sides, may become part of the permanent record. If the petition is denied, it must be done so in writing and the grievance may go to the third step, which is the grievance committee, consisting of representatives of both sides. As at the previous level, no settlement may violate or alter the contract. Because the committee meets regularly— perhaps once a week—it gains experience and can often settle problems that prove difficult at the lower levels. Here, for the first time, the supervised and supervisor do not stand in the relationship of plaintiff and judge.

If a mutually satisfactory solution cannot be found, the fourth step is taken, involving a request for arbitration by the union. Regardless of the number of prior steps, the last is usually final and binding arbitration. The case may be decided by a single ad hoc arbitrator (an arbitrator selected to hear only a single case or group of cases), by a tripartite board (a board consisting of union, management, and impartial members), by a permanent umpire (an arbitrator hired for a definite term to handle all cases that arise during that period), or by some other person or group. In most states, arbitrators' decisions are enforceable in court. Despite occasional exceptions, it is the sense of industrial jurisprudence that no decision may add to, modify, or subtract from the contract. This concept is specifically referred to in our representative procedure. Thus, grievance arbitration interprets the contract or applies it to particular cases. To accomplish this, the arbitrator may have to determine questions of fact or principle about the behavior of employee, employer, or union. While we do not claim that all grievance procedures work like this one, the Cornell–UAW process provides the reader with a brief example of a grievance procedure in action. We shall examine in more depth the important parts of the grievance procedure.

The Scope of Grievance Procedures

As in all other areas of contract negotiations, unions and managements are free to fashion any grievance procedure that will suit their needs. Thus, it is up to them to decide what issues should be resolved by use of the grievance procedure, and most procedures begin with a definition of a grievance. While there is no standard definition of the meaning of *grievance*, most unions and managements choose to limit the definition in some way. Our sample grievance procedure defines the process to be applicable only to "the interpretation or application of this Agreement." Thus a worker complaint about any right given him or her under the agreement is a grievance.

The grievance procedure is used mainly by labor against management and only rarely by management against labor. This fact does not reflect bias in the system but merely the fact that management is in charge. If management is dissatisfied with an individual, it does not file a grievance; it fires, disciplines, transfers, or retrains him. The grievance machinery is a channel of protest. Hence, it is used mainly by the agency of protest, not by the source of authority.

Although the union promises little in the contract, its few obligations may be subject to grievance proceedings by the employer. Strikes authorized by a union in violation of a no-strike clause have been arbitrated, and some penalties have been levied on unions. Complaints that union business is being done on company time, that shop stewards are abusing their freedom to investigate cases, or that the union is misusing plant bulletin boards would be appropriate actions for grievance proceedings by management—although some cases could also be handled by disciplining the individuals involved. Grievance proceedings against the union would normally be initiated at the third step.

While no studies exist to document the most common grievance issues, arbitrators have found that only a few types of cases tend to occur frequently. Discipline cases account for, by some estimates, a quarter of all arbitrations.[4] Other issues that frequently reach arbitration are matters of seniority rights and application, subcontracting, scheduling (particulary of overtime), job classifications, and work methods. We can presume that this set of issues also represent items most commonly grieved as well.

Levels of the Grievance Procedure

All grievance procedures have more than one step. The first step nearly always involves the employee, the supervisor, and a union representative. Successive steps involve increasingly higher levels of authority on both sides. These levels of the procedure can be triggered into action either by management denials of the grievance at lower steps or in some cases simply by inaction by management. For example, in the procedure cited earlier, the supervisor must respond to the employee within three working days. If the supervisor's response is unsatisfactory to the grievant, a written grievance must be presented within five working days. The responsibility for action and a time in which to perform the action are clearly specified at each step. Thus, successive responsibility for a decision and action passes back and forth between union and management. In a multistep procedure in which both sides sequentially use the maximum allotted to them, a significant period of time can elapse. It is not uncommon for two or three months to pass before an unresolved grievance reaches the arbitration step of the procedure. The consequence of inaction at each level is usually quite different for the union and management. If the union fails to comply with any of the time limits at each step, the grievance is usually forfeited without a management waiver. Management failure to observe time limits usually is equated with grievance denial at that level and the grievance is pushed to the next higher step.

These successive levels of the grievance procedure and the time limits between them serve many functions. First, the time limitations require each party to process grievances quickly and efficiently. Enough time must be given at each level for a thorough review of the grievance. Second, the successively higher levels necessarily involve individuals with more experience and authority on both sides. The ability to settle sticky cases may rest only with higher levels of management and unions. Third, the levels of the grievance procedure serve as a filter in which at each step less worthy grievances are settled. Sometimes the fact that higher levels of authority are involved means that both the union and the management representatives are able to look at a case more objectively and see the issues outside the more personal steward-supervisor context.

METHOD OF FINAL RESOLUTION—ARBITRATION

By all accounts, the vast majority of grievances are settled at the early steps of the procedure. When the parties are unable to resolve their differences, they may end up in arbitration. Nearly all union-management grievance procedures contain an arbitration clause. There is an important relationship among the no-strike clause, the grievance procedure, and arbitration. It is improbable that a union and management could last the whole term of a contract without some unresolved dispute. During the life of a contract, it is unsatisfactory either to permit each unresolved issue to proceed to a strike or to permit the accumulation of many unresolved disputes, whose effect on morale and production might be worse than a strike. Hence, a no-strike clause is not feasible unless accompanied by a workable grievance procedure. The grievance procedure in turn is meaningless unless it is accompanied by a no-strike clause, for otherwise its decisions can be "appealed" to the strike. In the event of deadlock, a workable grievance mechanism must provide a definite settlement. Final and binding arbitration performs this function, and appears in the large majority of labor contracts in the United States.

Arbitrator Selection

The first task facing the parties wishing to arbitrate a grievance is the selection of the arbitrator. While there are many means by which this might be done, most unions and managements use one of two services for this purpose: The Federal Mediation and Conciliation Service or the American Arbitration Association. These two organizations maintain panels of qualified arbitrators. They are the source of most arbitrators in the country. Upon request of the parties, a list of arbitrators is sent to them so they might select one. Each side is allowed to strike names from the list in order to find a mutually acceptable arbitrator. A union or management might not want a specific arbitrator because of past experiences and thus they may strike his or her name from the list. Over a career, arbitrators acquire reputations based on their expertise in certain industries or on specific contractual matters. Also, managements and unions may cross off an arbitrator's name from the list because they believe he or she is hard (or soft) on a particular matter. This entire process results in the selection of arbitrators satisfactory to both parties.

Some employers and unions, especially those with a sizable and continuing demand for arbitration services, have found it beneficial to name a permanent arbitrator rather than to choose a new one for every case. The advantage in naming either one individual or a small rotating group as permanent arbitrators is their availability and experience. A permanent arbitrator is able to develop a better understanding of the nature of the work and of the collective bargaining agreement. A permanent arbitrator should be able to give priority to that relationship and the parties will thus be rewarded with prompt scheduling and quicker resolution of their grievances. Most unions and managements, however, find the permanent system unworkable either because of a small or unpredictable caseload.

The Arbitration Process

Once the arbitrator is chosen, the parties and the arbitrator set a date for the hearing to take place. In many instances, the parties will send prehearing statements of their cases to the arbitrator so that agreed-upon facts might be stipulated at the hearing. Both parties prepare to present their cases at this point. If the parties have done a reasonably conscientious job at the lower steps of the grievance procedure, the nature of the relevant arguments and evidence should be reasonably clear by the time the case gets to arbitration, though exceptions, sadly, are numerous. Although arbitration of grievances is typically less formal than are courtroom procedures, the logic of case preparation is not much different. The evidence and the arguments must be marshalled in logical and systematic form. If facts are in dispute, careful thought must be given in advance as to which documents or witnesses will be able to demonstrate the important points. Thought must also be given to questions that will elicit the facts from witnesses without seeming to "lead" or "coach" them, and the ways to counter possible adverse testimony that may come from one's own witnesses on cross-examination. Even if one side prefers relatively informal proceedings, it must know how to counter or avoid formal objections raised by the other party to certain testimony or documents. Management will normally provide such documentation as records of payroll, seniority, absences, and vacations, since neither the union nor the employee will be likely to have such records. Management, of course, will presumably not provide documents helpful to the union's case unless specifically asked for them, with reasonable advance notice.

Arbitration hearings often reflect the kind of a relationship that exists within the plant. In some companies, arbitration is formal and legalistic. Witnesses are sworn, rules of evidence apply as in courts, direct and cross examinations of witnesses follow the customary pattern, a stenographic record is kept, and formal briefs are often prepared. Such arbitration tends to attract, require, and be dominated by lawyers.

Others prefer informal arbitration. Witnesses may be questioned informally whenever their testimony seems relevant, and they are not sworn. Written notes are confined to those the arbitrator takes. Except for obvious filibustering, any reasonable material is admitted, with the understanding that the arbitrator will separate the relevant from the irrelevant when he or she makes a decision. To "get off the chest" whatever is bothering an employee is considered more important than strict rules of evidence. Informality of this sort is possible where the decision is made by the judge rather than a jury. Some parties want the arbitrator to interpret the contract strictly and apply it rigorously. In contrast is the "problem-solving" approach. Although its adherents would not openly flout a clear contract clause, they prefer a workable decision to one that is formally correct. Usually, the formality tends to increase with the size of the groups and the importance of the issue. Generally, though, the arbitration process is notable in its willingness to hear all sides of the story.

Following the hearing, the arbitrator is charged with rendering an award. Prior to the decision, the parties sometimes prepare posthearing briefs for the arbitrator. These briefs serve similar functions to the prehearing statements in that each party presents its own version of the case. The arbitrator's award, given in writing to the parties, is final and binding unless the parties have made other contractual arrangements.

The Common Law in Industrial Jurisprudence.   As case after case is processed in the company, the accumulated decisions can constitute a common law, establishing precedents for the detailed provisions that cannot be spelled out in contract. Two distinct attitudes have arisen toward such common law.

Those who oppose it want each grievance processed on its own merits as a unique event, without regard to preceding cases. When cases go to arbitration, they do not introduce other cases as precedents. They select arbitrators on an ad hoc basis so that a fresh viewpoint is brought to each case. They are interested in the substance of the decision rather than the reasons for it, and may discourage the writing of supporting opinions by the arbitrators.

Others desire maximum continuity. They note, follow, and possibly codify precedents. They prefer a permanent umpire who handles all cases during his tenure of office, and they give great weight to his opinions. Some carry the use of precedent beyond the single bargaining unit and, in the extreme case, feel that the whole of American experience should be welded into a single code of industrial practice. They make their own cases publicly available through reporting services, and in turn examine other cases for precedents.

ARBITRATION AND EXTERNAL LAW

There are two places in which the arbitration process has intersected with federal law: in the case of choice of forum and in the enforcement of arbitration awards.

Deferral to Arbitration.   In 1955, the NLRB decided that in those few cases where an unfair labor practice and a grievance might be filed over the same issue, it would in general defer to the arbitrator's decision.[5] The arbitration proceeding had to be fair, the parties had to agree to be bound by the award and the arbitration decision had to be consistent with the purposes and policies of the National Labor Relations Act. While this deferral to arbitration has been narrowed over time, in general it has been the continuous policy of the NLRB.[6]

There are some important exceptions to this deferral rule. If an employee charges his or her employer with racial discrimination and arbitrates the charge, the employee may also seek relief on the same claim under Title VII of the Civil Rights Act of 1964.[7] Also, in Fair Labor Standards Act cases (i.e., overtime payments), it has been held that employees need not wait for an arbitration decision before suing in federal court.[8]

Arbitration Enforcement

The courts have held that Section 301 of the Taft−Hartley Act gives them the power to enforce employer-union agreements to arbitrate disputes.[9] In general, the courts have declared that they will additionally enforce arbitration awards and will not rule on questions of contract interpretation.[10] Thus, the federal courts have removed themselves from the business of deciding whether an arbitrator's decision was correct. An agreement to arbitrate a dispute is thus a very serious matter since it is very difficult to mount a legal challenge to an arbitrator's decision. There are a number of important recent court and NLRB decisions interpreting the legal status of arbitration. References to these are provided and summarized in a recent article by Theodore J. St. Antoine.[11]

Duty of Fair Representation

In exchange for exclusive recognition, an accompanying duty is placed upon unions: They must represent all employees in the bargaining unit equally and fairly,[12] whether or not these employees are dues-paying members. This duty means that if an employee feels that the union has not represented him or her fairly, the employee may sue the union and the employer for breach of the collective bargaining agreement. To put this in the form of an example, think of an employee who is unfairly dismissed by an employer. If the employee's union then decides not to process the grievance for reasons unrelated to the merit of the grievance, the employee may then commence legal action as noted.

Unions thus have a responsibility to process each grievance individually, based solely upon the merits of the grievance in question. Court cases have accumulated over the years that more specifically lay out the scope of that duty,[13] and the interested reader should refer to them. Basically, unions are not allowed to trade a positive settlement of one meritorious grievance for the dismissal of another, and they are required to use objectivity toward all individuals in the processing of grievances.

In recent years, some concern has been exhibited by advocates and arbitrators over the functioning of the grievance-arbitration system. This concern has come from two related problems. It has been suggested that arbitration has become such a costly and time-consuming process that justice is not being fully served in the way originally intended by the arbitration process. In a recent article by Peter Seitz, the noted arbitrator, the position is advocated that "justice delayed is justice denied."[14] He then goes on to chide both advocates and arbitrators for their roles in needlessly delaying the procedure.

Experiments in alternatives to the standard grievance-arbitration model have been recently tried by some parties, with the major motivation being to reduce the time from grievance to eventual resolution and to reduce the cost of the procedure. Expedited arbitration procedures are one such experiment. In some of these expedited procedures, grievance steps are bypassed and the arbitration hearing is made to be speedy and informal. In some cases, the use of expedited arbitration provides impressive improvement in the reduction of costs and delay.[15] Another experiment that is being tried with less frequency is the addition of a mediation step at the end of the grievance process but prior to arbitration. This approach has been shown in at least one case to reduce the number of grievances that need to be arbitrated.[16] Both these alternatives suggest that improvement in the reduction of costs and delays in arbitration is possible. While neither system is widely used as an alternative to the regular procedures, the problems inherent in our grievance-arbitration system are clearly recognized and attempts are being made to minimize them.

INDUSTRIAL JURISPRUDENCE AS A POSITIVE CONTRIBUTION OF UNIONS

Despite its interference with management's freedom, a functioning grievance procedure may be a constructive addition to the human relations equipment of modern industry, even as seen by management. Several observations may be made in this regard.

Is Absence of Grievances a Good Sign?   Business people are sometimes heard to remark:

> Before the union came in our people were contented. We practically never had any gripes. Now the union keeps stirring them up. We have a steady stream going to the grievance committee, and lots of them have to be arbitrated.

In evaluating a grievance system, it is important not to equate absence of complaints with worker satisfaction. Grievances may be lacking because there are no complaints— the optimum condition of morale. But they may also be absent because workers are afraid to file them or assume they are fruitless—perhaps the worst condition of morale. Hence, an increase in grievances may mean that dissatisfaction is being "manufactured." Or it may mean that discontent is being relieved and its causes corrected.

Grievance Procedure and Channels of Communication.   A perpetual difficulty facing the top-level executive is to get an honest view of "things at the bottom." He may go through the shop from time to time. But somehow word gets around that the "big boss" is coming, and he or she does not witness routine performance. Casual conversation with shop workers reveals little, for many workers "freeze" when talking to executives or feel that criticisms might get back to the supervisor and cause trouble. Reports that go up through channels tend to be overly favorable, since they deal with things for which the writer of the report is responsible. Well-run firms have methods of opening the channels of communication. But there is constant danger of clogging, and no method is completely reliable.

A union grievance procedure changes things. Now the lowliest worker can carry his or her complaint to the fourth or fifth step, and the union has direct access to top management. Lower management cannot keep grievances from going to advanced stages by granting all requests, for therein lies a shortcut to chaos. Through grievances, executives can learn many details of day-to-day operations, for in the hearing almost any detail may come forth. With such information, top management can administer more intelligently, and under such scrutiny lower levels are kept more alert.

Grievance Procedure Without a Union.   A grievance procedure in which employees have full confidence is difficult to create without a union. Most grievances allege that management has acted improperly, which means that in a grievance mechanism sponsored by management the same party is both judge and defendant—not only in the lower step, but also in the crucial final step.

If a nonunion company desires to handle grievances effectively, it can establish unilaterally the five steps already described. Some plants have a grievance committee at the third step, consisting of company representatives and representatives elected by the employees. An atmosphere is created in which no one need hesitate to speak one's piece. There may even be someone to serve as attorney for the grievant.

Nevertheless, several real weaknesses may exist that revolve around the employee's lack of bargaining power in the event of a showdown. First, if the "attorneys" are paid by the company, they are subject ultimately to the company's control (on the assumption that the one who pays the piper calls the tune). If the employees decide to collect contributions to cover this cost, they control the attorneys—but they also have an incipient union. Second, although management may exercise great restraint and gracefully accept unpalatable recommendations from the grievance committee, it is still managerial self-discipline rather than employee bargaining power that brings fair treatment. So long as grievances deal with issues for which there is a clear, logical answer or with economic issues of modest proportions, this technique may produce about the same results as a union-management system. But when issues involve such matters as management prerogatives or large amounts of money, they tend to be resolved uniformly in favor of management. Even if the grievance is not momentous, the grievant rarely has the last-ditch protection of binding arbitration if he is dissatisfied with the management decision. Apparently, only a handful of nonunion companies have any arrangements for arbitration, and those that do rarely use it. The arrangement is of doubtful value, since the grievant has to pay all the costs of the arbitration instead of having them paid by the union. Even short of arbitration, formal grievance procedures in nonunion plants gets relatively little use; employees prefer informal chats in the personnel office. Even this channel may be inhibited if people fear to incur the foreman's suspicion. (Foremen, like corporals, do not like to be bypassed.)

In brief, in the typical nonunion plant, the employee with a grievance will probably face some frustrating hazards. And however generous the management, the grievant without a union is a subject petitioning for redress, not a citizen demanding justice. This situation may please many managements; but it is not necessarily in their own best interests.

SUMMARY

Historically speaking, industrial jurisprudence is largely a union contribution. Unions brought it on directly by insisting upon it. They also indirectly aided its advent, since many firms improved their employee relations in the hope of staving off unionization. Although the move toward scientific management would probably have been applied eventually to employee relations and would greatly have changed the careless and arbitrary treatment of employees in many firms, we have seen that a really satisfactory system of industrial jurisprudence is difficult for management to operate unilaterally.

At its rosy best, industrial jurisprudence is more than a set of techniques. It is a philosophy of industrial life. Without it, plant government is essentially a dictatorship, however kind and reasonable it may be. Often referred to as industrial democracy, industrial jurisprudence brings to the worker in the economic sphere what Magna Carta and the Declaration of Independence brought in the political arena. It puts a Bill of Rights into the industrial plant, complete with due process, the equivalent of trial by jury, and increased freedom of speech. It insists that industry, like government, be run for the benefit of human beings, not human beings for the benefit of industry. This means that human beings are more important than the production of material goods and that when productive efficiency conflicts with important human values, the latter shall be given weight. It permits the worker to deal with his boss as an approximate equal in bargaining power and human dignity.

At its worst, the machinery that is supposed to produce industrial jurisprudence can be worse than an arbitrary management. It can disrupt production. Union representatives can be stupid, careless, or play favorites, so that processing a grievance through the union system can be more frustrating than even a second-rate management system or none at all—and the worker must pay for the union system.

Two areas of due process are currently "in the wind," but have not received significant attention to date. Both are extension of free speech concepts to the industrial scene, and have potential repercussions well beyond it. The first concerns the status of the "whistle-blower." If an employee discovers that someone higher up in his or her organization is knowingly violating the law or hiding hazards, may the employee be disciplined for calling the violation to the attention of others inside or outside the company who might rectify it? Second, may an employee be disciplined for political activity wholly unrelated to the job? An example of the former was a salesperson "fired by U.S. Steel Corporation because he had called his superiors' attention to dangerous defects in a pipe he was required to sell; the pipe was later withdrawn from the market, but the salesperson was out of a job."[17] An example of the second was "an employee of the American Telephone and Telegraph Company, who was fired two weeks after attending a May Day demonstration in 1976."[18] Also on the latter point, two major oil companies require prospective employees to sign noncommunist affidavits. On both points, the courts have thus far held that the grounds for discharge from private employment do not justify intervention by the courts.[19] Regardless of the position of the courts on these matters, there is nothing to prevent unions from seeking to negotiate contractual protection of its members for either political or whistle-blowing activities.[20]

On balance, it seems that most union-management grievance procedures work, not perfectly, but not particularly better or worse than most other human institutions. Nevertheless, arbitration displays a somewhat disconcerting minority of cases that never should have reached arbitration. Some weak cases go to arbitration because the aggrieved employees and their buddies come to the union meeting and vote to arbitrate the case on a what-can-we-lose basis while the members not directly affected by the case, but who pay the bills, stay home. As the cost of arbitrations rise, some managements put pressure on the union treasury by arbitrating unnecessarily while passing their own costs on to the consumer. Along with industrial jurisprudence, nevertheless, goes the increased status that comes to ordinary employees, not from "asking" for fair treatment, but from holding an enforceable demand for it. Although it is less tangible and more difficult for the average worker to evalute and talk about than wages or vacations, industrial democracy is certainly an important result of collective bargaining. In the long run, it may prove its most important result.

NOTES

[1]The general line of reasoning here is that of Peter F. Drucker in his *New Society* (New York: Harper, 1949), Chapter 10.

[2]U.S. Bureau of Labor Statistics, *Characteristics of Major Collective Bargaining Agreements* (Washington, D.C.: GPO, 1981), Bulletin 2095.

[3]The shop steward is an appointed or elected representative of the union within a shop, division, or department of a company. He is normally a regular employee of the company but is allowed time away from his work to handle grievances. Time thus spent may be paid for by the company, by the union, or by the two jointly, depending on their particular arrangements.

[4]Harold W. Davey, Mario F. Bognanno, and David L. Estenson, *Contemporary Collective Bargaining*, 4th ed. (Englewood Cliffs, N.J.: Prentice-Hall, 1982), p. 186.

[5]*Spielberg Manufacturing Co.*, 112 NLRB 1080, 36 LRRM 1152 (1955).

[6]*Collyer Insulated Wire*, 192 NLRB 837, 77 LRRM 1931 (1971).

[7]*Alexander* v. *Gardner-Denver Co.*, 415 U.S. 36, 7 FEP Cases 81 (1974).

[8]*Barrentine* v. *Arkansas-Best Freight System*, 450 U.S. 728, 24 WH Cases 1284 (1981).

[9]*Textile Workers* v. *Lincoln Mills*, 353 U.S. 448, 40 LRRM 2113 (1957).

[10]*Steelworkers* v. *Warrior & Gulf Navigation Co.*, 363 U.S. 574, 46 LRRM 2416 (1960).

[11]Theodore J. St. Antoine, "Arbitration and the Law," in *Arbitration in Practice*, Arnold M. Zack, ed. (Ithaca, N.Y.: ILR Press, 1984), pp. 9–22.

[12]*Steele* v. *Louisville and Nashville R.R.*, 323 U.S. 192 (1944).

[13]See, for example, *Vaca* v. *Sipes*, 386 U.S. 171 (1967); and *Hines* v. *Anchor Motor Freight, Inc.*, 424 U.S. 554 (1976).

[14]Peter Seitz, "Delay: The Asp in the Bosom of Arbitration," *The Arbitration Journal* 36 (September 1981), 29–35.

[15]Marcus H. Sandver, Harry R. Blaine, and Mark N. Woyar, "Time and Cost Savings through Expedited Arbitration Procedures," *The Arbitration Journal* 36 (December 1981), 11–21.

[16]Steven B. Goldberg and Jeanne M. Brett, "An Experiment in the Mediation of Grievances, *Monthly Labor Review* 106 (March 1983), 23–29.

[17]Max Gordon, "Can Business Fire at Will?" *The Nation*, July 14–21, 1979, pp. 43f.

[18]*Ibid*.

[19]*Ibid*.

[20]"Curtailing the Freedom to Fire," *Business Week*, March 19, 1984, pp. 29–33.

COLLECTIVE BARGAINING IN THE PUBLIC SECTOR

17

Public-sector labor relations in the United States have developed on a track that is, at the same time, very similar and very different in comparison to the private sector. This chapter explores those similarities, differences, and complexities present in the U.S. system of public-sector collective bargaining. For a more complete treatment of this subject or of any specific topic contained in this chapter, a list of further reading is included at the conclusion of this chapter.

TRENDS IN PUBLIC-SECTOR EMPLOYMENT AND THE GROWTH OF COLLECTIVE BARGAINING

There has been considerable growth in public-sector employment in recent years. In 1946, the public sector employed 5.6 million persons (13 percent of all nonfarm employees); by 1980, the number had nearly tripled to 16.2 million (17.4 percent of the nonagricultural payroll).[1] The largest increases have occurred at the state and local level, as indicated by the comparative data shown in Table 17–1 for the post–World War II era. There has been a slight decrease in 1984, see Table 17-1.

Natural growth in the population and the consequent need for services partially explain the employment growth. This growth was magnified by changes in the age composition. The population over 65 and under 25, those with the largest service needs, grew at a faster rate. A second force in government employment growth

TABLE 17.1.   GOVERNMENT EMPLOYMENT

Year	Total Government Employment	Percent Increase	Federal Civilian Employment	Percent Increase	State and Local Government Employment	Percent Increase
1945	5,944,000	—	2,808,000	—	3,137,000	—
1950	6,026,000	1.4	1,928,000	−31.3	4,098,000	30.6
1955	6,914,000	14.7	2,187,000	13.4	4,727,000	15.3
1960	8,353,000	20.8	2,270,000	3.8	6,083,000	28.7
1965	10,074,000	20.6	2,378,000	4.8	7,696,000	26.5
1970	12,554,000	24.6	2,731,000	14.8	9,823,000	27.6
1975	14,686,000	17.0	2,748,000	0.6	11,937,000	21.5
1980	16,241,000	10.6	2,866,000	4.2	13,375,000	12.0
1984	15,969,000	−1.7	2,783,000	−2.8	13,185,000	−1.4

SOURCE: *Monthly Labor Review*, 108, no. 4 (April 1985), Table 9, p. 73.

involved an expanding desire for government to perform a wider range of functions in the U.S. society. The sum of these forces was the growth in employment shown in the figures in Table 17–1. As can be seen in the table, public sector employment growth has occurred at a rather high rate since the end of World War II. This rate of growth has been tempered only in the early 1980s by a changing view of the role of government. Most of the growth during the era represented in the table has occurred at the state and local level.

The growth in overall employment has been accompanied, if not exceeded, by a concomitant growth in union membership in the public sector. Some of the reasons for this growth are explained later in this chapter. Let us now briefly examine the historical background of the emergence and expansion of public sector unionism at the various levels of government.

Unionism among federal employees dates back to the early 1800s when crafts-men employed in navy shipyards joined unions already representing private-sector employees. Later in the nineteenth century, unionism emerged in the Government Printing Office and among letter carriers in the Post Office Department. The early federal unions functioned primarily as fraternal, social, craft, or benevolent organizat-ions.[2] After about 1880, however, such unions became increasingly involved in lobbying activities and in petitioning members of Congress to consider the demands of their membership. The lobbying activity, which was to become the hallmark of public employee unionism, was fostered by passage of the Pendleton Act in 1883. This act granted Congress the right to regulate wages, hours, working conditions, and other terms of employment for public employees. Increased lobbying efforts by federal unions were met by a series of "gag orders" issued by President Roosevelt (1902) and by President Taft (1909). These orders forbade federal employees, under threat of job dismissal, to seek an increase in pay or to influence legislation on their behalf except through their department heads.[3] In 1912, the Lloyd–LaFollette Act was passed in response to protests of these restrictive and constitutionally questionable gag orders. The act granted federal employees the right to petition Congress and postal employees the right to belong to employee organizations seeking to improve their working conditions. This latter set of rights stipulated that organizations not assist their members in strikes against the government. With the formation of the National Federation of Federal Employees in 1917 and of the American Federation of Government Employees in 1932,[4] the legislation prohibiting strikes was extended to other organizations of federal employees.

The Wagner Act (1935) specifically excluded the federal government from its definition of employer, thus denying federal employees the protection afforded by Section 7 and related provisions. The Taft–Hartley "amendments" (1947) continued this exclusion. Additionally, Section 305 of this act prescribed a mandatory loss of job and civil service status for federal employees who participated in a strike. The 1950s witnessed major clashes between union leaders and the federal government, particularly between the postal union and the Eisenhower administration. During this decade, the Rhodes–Johnston bill was repeatedly and unsuccessfully introduced into Congress. It called for union recognition, consultation, binding arbitraton, and grievance procedures.[5]

In 1961 President Kennedy appointed the Goldberg–Macy task force, whose main recommendations were incorporated into Executive Order 10988, issued in 1962 and described later in this chapter. This order has been hailed by union leaders as the Magna Carta for federal employee unionism. Labor relations in the federal sector came under statutory law with the passage of the Civil Service Reform Act of 1978, Title VII-Federal Service Labor-Management Relations.

Unionization of public employees at the state and local levels has a long history. Philadelphia, for instance, has had labor agreements containing provisions for union security and exclusive recognition since 1939. In fact, since 1957, it has recognized the American Federation of State, County and Municipal Employees (AFSCME) as exclusive bargaining agent for all nonuniformed workers. In Cincinnati, employee organizations have enjoyed de facto recognition since 1951. In New York City, Mayor Robert Wagner issued an executive order in 1958 declaring it policy to promote practices and procedures of collective bargaining for city employees by their majority representatives.[6]

Other than in these isolated instances, however, collective bargaining was not widely utilized until the 1960s. Public-employee legislation passed by state and local governments accelerated noticeably following the 1962 issuance of Executive Order 10988, with most state legislation having been enacted since 1965 and much of it patterned on the private sector model. Thus, by 1984, forty-one states and the District of Columbia had collective bargaining statutes covering all or some categories of public employees. In effect, there are currently only a few states without any legislative or executive authorization for public-sector bargaining.[7]

Let us now examine the extent of organization at the federal, state, and local levels of government. Table 17–2 presents the membership in unions and in bargaining organizations, defined as employee associations as well as traditional types of (trade) unions, by level of government from 1956 to 1978 and 1968 to 1978, respectively.[8]

Table 17–3[9] indicates the percentage of employees in exclusive units and covered by agreement as a percent of total employment in the federal sector. Wage

TABLE 17.2.   PERCENTAGE OF GOVERNMENT EMPLOYEES ORGANIZED
(Employment and members in thousands)

Year	Total Government			Federal Government			State and Local Government		
	Employment	Members[1]	Percent Organized	Employment	Members[1]	Percent Organized	Employment	Members[1]	Percent Organized

Panel A: Membership in Unions

Year	Employment	Members[1]	Percent Organized	Employment	Members[1]	Percent Organized	Employment	Members[1]	Percent Organized
1956	7,278	915	12.6	2,209	—	—	5,069	—	—
1960	8,353	1,070	12.8	2,270	—	—	6,083	—	—
1964	9,596	1,453	15.1	2,348	897	38.2	7,248	556	7.7
1966	10,784	1,717	15.9	2,564	1,073	41.8	8,220	644	7.8
1968	11,839	2,155	18.2	2,737	1,351	49.4	9,102	804	8.8
1970	12,554	2,318	18.5	2,731	1,370	50.1	9,823	947	9.6
1972	13,334	2,460	18.4	2,684	1,355	50.5	10,649	1,105	10.4
1974	14,170	2,920	20.6	2,724	1,391	51.1	11,446	1,529	13.4
1976	14,871	3,015	20.3	2,733	1,300	47.6	12,138	1,711	14.1
1978[3]	15,672	3,625	23.1	2,753	1,383	50.2	12,919	2,243	17.4
1980	—	—	—	—	—	—	—	—	—
1984	—	—	—	—	—	—	—	—	—

Panel B: Membership in Bargaining Organizations[2]

Year	Employment	Members[1]	Percent Organized	Employment	Members[1]	Percent Organized	Employment	Members[1]	Percent Organized
1968	11,839	3,857	32.6	2,737	1,391	50.8	9,109	2,466	27.1
1970	12,554	4,080	32.5	2,731	1,412	51.7	9,823	2,668	27.1
1972	13,334	4,520	33.9	2,684	1,383	51.5	10,649	3,137	29.4
1974	14,170	5,345	37.7	2,724	1,433	52.6	11,446	3,911	34.2
1976	14,871	5,852	39.4	2,733	1,334	48.7	12,138	4,518	37.2
1978[3]	15,672	6,094	38.9	2,753	1,420	51.6	12,919	4,674	36.2
1980[4]	16,056	5,764	35.9	—	—	—	—	—	—
1984[4]	15,748	5,661	35.9	—	—	—	—	—	—

SOURCE: Reprinted by permission from *Public-Sector Bargaining*, edited by Aaron, Grodin and Stern, IRRA Series, copyright © 1979 by the Bureau of National Affairs, Inc., Washington, D.C. 20037.

[1] Membership includes members outside the United States.

[2] Bargaining organizations include unions and bargaining associations, as those terms are defined in the text. The equivalent BLS terms are unions and employee associations.

[3] 1978 data are from *Directory of National Unions and Employee Associations, 1979*, Table 16, p. 67 and *Monthly Labor Review*, May, 1981, Table 8, p. 77.

[4] 1980 and 1984 data for overall membership are from Larry T. Adams, "Changing Employment Patterns of Organized Workers," *Monthly Labor Review*, Vol. 108, No. 2, February 1985, Table 1, p. 26.

TABLE 17.3.   EMPLOYEES IN EXCLUSIVE UNITS* AND COVERED BY AGREEMENT AS A PERCENT OF THE TOTAL EMPLOYMENT 1972–1977

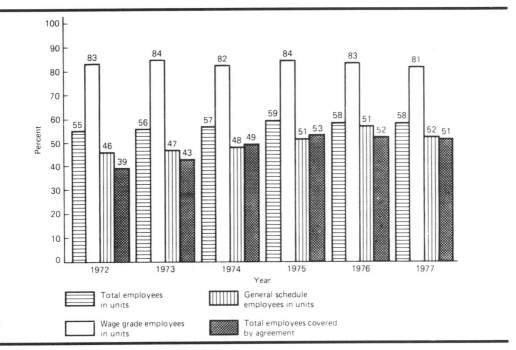

**Exclusive Unit—The grouping of employees within an agency, activity, or installation for purposes of exclusive recognition and representation.*

SOURCE: U.S. Civil Service Commission, *Union Recognition in the Federal Government—November,* 1977 (Washington, D.C.: U.S. Government Printing Office, 1977).

grade or system employees are defined as trades, labor, and other employees paid on a prevailing wage rate basis. General-schedule employees are white-collar employees, including those designated as professionals.

FACTORS INFLUENCING THE GROWTH OF PUBLIC SECTOR COLLECTIVE BARGAINING

As public-sector employment has rapidly expanded, so has the growth of public sector unions, particularly since the early sixties. Major reasons include:[10]

1. Removal of restrictive legislation by means of executive orders and legislation at the federal level and collective bargaining statutes enacted by forty states.
2. Awareness of a disadvantageous economic shift between private and public employees.
3. Acceptance of the institution of trade unionism by public sector employees much as it has been accepted by their private sector counterparts for several decades.
4. Effectiveness of confrontation tactics, with many of labor relations' direct pressure tactics modeled on those utilized by the civil rights movement in the early to mid-sixties.

5. Breakdown in and loss of respect for many forms of authority.

6. Indifference of public agency officials to job-related complaints or grievances which, in turn, led to employee frustration and increasing receptiveness to union organizing attempts.

For educational and health care employees, there have been additional factors influencing the growth of collective bargaining. The post–World War II baby boom generation contributed to a major increase in elementary and secondary school enrollments. This, in turn, created a substantial demand for public school teachers, many of whom differed from their predecessors because of their relative youth and because many were male. Combined with the emerging favorable legal climate and general restiveness among public white-collar employees, these factors have resulted in dramatic increases in unionization among public school teachers. Unionization among college and university professional educational employees has progressed more slowly and for somewhat different reasons. The main factors responsible for these developments have been and are expected to continue to be economic benefits and job security, particularly since declining enrollments and budgetary constraints are becoming commonplace in academia. In the health care field, there has been an explosive increase in demand for medical services, largely as a result of the legislation that created Medicare and Medicaid, together with an older population needing such services. The resultant increase in health care job opportunities has not gone unnoticed by the labor movement. The health care industry had long been known for its poor working conditions (low wages, long hours, inadequate vacation and holiday allocations, etc.). Thus, certain national and international unions—including the Retail, Wholesale, and Department Store Union; Local 1199, Drug and Hospital Employees Union; Service Employees International Union; International Brotherhood of Teamsters; and the American Federation of State, County, and Municipal Employees—have been active organizing employees of health care institutions.[11]

THE MAJOR UNIONS IN THE PUBLIC SECTOR

This section describes certain characteristics of major public sector unions by level of government and government structure and function starting at the national level.

Unions of Federal Employees

Two of the oldest trade unions are the National Association of Letter Carriers (NALC) and the American Postal Workers Union (APWU). Postal unions have traditionally been among the most experienced and effective congressional lobbyists. Despite such success, however, postal union leaders sought to replace what they considered "collective begging" by collective bargaining. In 1970 the postal workers, led by its New York City unit, which lacked exclusive recognition at the national level under the bargaining structure created by the Executive Orders, engaged in a successful, though illegal, strike. They demanded improved economic benefits and a bargaining structure similar to the private sector's. As a result, the 1970 Postal

Reorganization Act was passed, enabling represented workers to avail themselves of traditional NLRB remedies. The scope of bargaining for postal worker union members now includes wages, hours, and conditions of employment, with the exception of pensions (which remain under congressional jurisdiction) and certain other personnel actions (still controlled by civil service regulations). The act prohibits compulsory union membership and the right to strike, substituting for the latter the right to take "interest" disputes to arbitration. Postal unions are expected to continue to place primary emphasis upon achieving most of their goals through bargaining rather than through congressional action.

According to James L. Stern, when the first Executive Order was issued in 1962,

> unions of federal employees—with the exceptions of the long-established International Association of Machinists (IAM) and the AFL—CIO Metal Trades Council (MTC) units in shipyards and other industrial-type establishments—were underfinanced, understaffed, and relatively inactive.[12]

As of 1980, the major unions in the federal government and their approximate membership were:

> American Federaton of Government Employees (AFGE), AFL—CIO: 255,000 members
> National Treasury Employees Union (NTEU), independent: 53,000 members
> National Federation of Federal Employees (NFFE), independent: 40,000 members[13]

According to the BNA, these three unions represent about 70 percent of the organized federal employees. Many other unions, most of them with a primary membership base outside the federal government, hold recognition rights to federal employees. As of 1976, over eighty unions represented federal employees.[14]

The American Federation of Government Employees is the largest union representing federal employees. It continues to face a "free rider" problem, evidenced by a large gap between actual membership and representation, which has been only partially explainable by the Civil Service Reform Act's prohibition of the compulsory payment of union dues. The union leadership is expected to continue to strive to remove union security restrictions in order to increase its own membership.

The National Federation of Federal Employees began in 1917 as a union of federal government employees. In 1962, NFFE condemned the Executive Order and even instituted litigation, though unsuccessfully, challenging its constitutionality. Two years later, after a change in top leadership, the union reversed its position on this issue. A traditionally conservative union, NFFE is now considering consolidation of bargaining units and other changes that depart from its conservative principles.

The National Treasury Employees Union originated in 1938 as a union of professionals in the Internal Revenue Service. It now consists primarily of Treasury Department employees, though some members are employed by other federal agencies. The transition during the past decade from a group of rather specialized, middle-level professionals to an agency-wide, industrial-type union with a considerable representation of clerical workers has not always been smooth. However, the NTEU has emerged as a stronger union, as evidenced by consolidating local into agency-wide collective bargaining agreements. It also gained national recognition rights for all IRS employees and is expected to grow further in strength during the eighties.

State and Local Unions

We now turn to unions at the state and local levels. The dominant noneducation union is the American Federation of State, County, and Municipal Employees (AFSCME), AFL–CIO. Between 1964 and 1977, AFSCME membership more than tripled, to about 750,000. In 1978, approximately 250,000 members of the New York State Civil Service Association joined AFSCME, making it not only a million-member union but also one of the largest AFL–CIO affiliates. Unlike most other unions, AFSCME has continued to grow in the late 1970s and early 1980s, with its membership reaching a high of 1.1 million in 1980.[15]

Other major state and local unions are: the American Nurses Association (ANA), which represents private sector nurses covered by Taft-Hartley and nurses employed by state, county, and city governments; the International Association of Fire Fighters (IAFF), AFL–CIO, which represents most firefighters; and the International Conference of Police Associations (ICPA), which is the largest police organization, followed by the Fraternal Order of Police (FOP). There are also three major unions that represent local transit employees, including bus drivers, the Amalgamated Transit Union (ATU), the Transport Workers Union (TWU), and the United Transportation Union (UTU).

Additionally, many unions with their origins in the private sector have attracted a significant public-employee membership. Unions such as the International Brotherhood of Teamsters (IBT) and the Service Employees International Union (SEIU) have a sizable number of public employees within their ranks.

National Educational Unions

There are three major unions in education: (1) the National Education Association (NEA), (2) the American Federation of Teachers (AFT), and (3) the American Association of University Professors (AAUP). Unlike the situation in the federal sector, membership in the educational unions exceeds the extent of collective bargaining coverage, since many AAUP chapters still do not engage in collective bargaining.

The NEA is an independent union whose 1977 membership approximated 1.7 million. It originally functioned as a professional organization. Since 1962, however, it has become somewhat similar in its bargaining approach to the AFT. The NEA still differs from the AFT in that it opposes affiliation with the AFL–CIO, allows school administrators a say in its affairs in certain states, and remains comparatively conservative in its policies toward collective bargaining. The AFT is an AFL–CIO affiliate with approximately 550,000 members. It represents teachers in many major cities, including New York, Philadelphia, Detroit, Boston, Pittsburgh, Cleveland, Cincinnati, Minneapolis, Denver, and Baltimore. Like the NEA, the AFT (during the 1977 convention) decided to organize groups other than teachers. These two teacher unions remain very competitive despite several discussions of merger.

The AAUP is an independent organization, with about 66,000 active members. Long an advocate of faculty governance, the AAUP abandoned its opposition to collective bargaining by deciding in 1972 to engage in this process. According to James L. Stern, of the 60,000 members in 1977, 15,000 elected the AAUP as a bargaining agent. They are in forty-four bargaining units represented either by the AAUP alone or by the AAUP together with either the AFT or the NEA. There is, however, still considerable rivalry between the traditionally professional AAUP, most of whose bargaining units are at four-year colleges, and the two other unions, which are stronger at two-year institutions.

THE SOVEREIGNTY DOCTRINE

The sovereignty doctrine asserts that a governmental source of law/power exists that is final and definitive. The sovereignty doctrine is a broader concept than is the management rights concept in the private sector. According to Moskow, Loewenberg, and Koziaria, the theoretical application of the sovereignty doctrine permits only unilateral action by the government employer to establish the terms and conditions of employment. Thus, any system of collective bargaining whereby such terms are determined jointly is incompatible with the doctrine.[16] The federal executive orders and law and the state statutes, discussed in the next two sections, have been careful to preserve the sovereignty doctrine. Specificaly, Section 12 of Executive Order 11838 and sections 7106(a) and (b) of the Civil Service Reform Act delineate management's rights in unilateral decision making. Additionally, federal employee representatives cannot negotiate wages, fringe benefits, and hours, subjects normally within the scope of bargaining in the private sector, because they are covered by statute and by regulations of the U.S. Civil Service Commission.

The sovereignty doctrine also contributes to another feature of collective bargaining in the public sector, namely, the impropriety of the strike. Thus, the federal and most state and local governments deny the right to strike. The rationale for preventing strikes in the public sector is based not only on the sovereignty doctrine but also on the essentiality of government services. Governments have traditionally not distinguished between the essentiality or nonessentiality of their services when denying strike rights. In recent years, however, some state and local governments have differentiated between strikes in terms of the essentiality of services, and a few states now permit some of their employees the right to strike. The right to strike is discussed in more detail in a latter part of this chapter.

EXECUTIVE ORDERS AND FEDERAL LEGISLATION

In 1961, the President's Task Force on Employee-Management Relations in the Federal Service issued a report whose recommendations formed the basis for Executive Order 10988, signed by President Kennedy in January 1962. The development and implementation of this order undoubtedly provided the biggest single impetus to the growth of unionization in the federal sector. It was followed by President Nixon's Executive Order 11491, effective January 1, 1970, which contained several important revisions and improvements, and by Executive Orders 11616 (effective November 1971), 11636 (effective December 1971), and 11838 (effective May 1975).

Among the main provisions of E.O. 10988 were

1. Federal employees were granted the right to form, join, and assist an employee organization or to refrain from such activity.
2. Three types of union recognition were established—informal, formal, and exclusive—based upon extent of employee membership within an appropriate unit.
3. The scope of bargaining was restricted by law and established regulations, by the management rights clause, and by specific exemption from negotiations of certain other subject areas.
4. Primary responsibility for the implementation of the order was placed in each federal agency.

President Nixon issued E.O. 11491 on October 29, 1969. The major purposes of the new executive order were to strengthen then existing labor-management relations in the federal government, to eliminate confusing policies and procedures, and to standardize yet others. E.O. 11491 provided for only one type of recognition for employee organizations—exclusive recognition. It authorized a Federal Labor Relations Council (FLRC) to resolve major policy disputes by negotiations, as well as a Federal Service Impasse Panel, in an attempt to strengthen some of the weaknesses of the earlier executive order.

In September 1971, President Nixon issued Executive Order 11616. It expanded Executive Order 11491 by requiring grievance procedures in all new contracts. Additionally, it strengthened the jurisdiction of the assistant secretary of labor in public sector unfair labor practice cases. In May 1975, President Ford issued Executive Order 11838. It stipulated that all agency regulations were negotiable unless the agency could show a "compelling need" not to negotiate; that any proposed changes in personnel policies were mandatory bargaining subjects, even when a contract was already in effect; and that the scope of grievance procedures was expanded to include not only terms of the negotiated agreements, but also interpretations and applications of agency regulations.

An important development in the federal sector was the passage of Title VII-Federal Service Labor-Management Relations, as part of the Civil Service Reform Act of 1978, effective January 1979. Together with President Carter's Reorganization Plan No. 2 of 1978, effective January 1, 1979, establishing a statutory administrative agency, the Federal Labor Relations Authority (FLRA), this law governs labor-management relations in the federal government. The law recognizes that collective bargaining in the federal sector is in the public interest and affords statutory protection of bargaining rights while attempting to insure certain employee obligations to the public. Coverage of the law extends to most federal executive branch employees, with some exemptions, including persons involved in national security functions and any person who participates in an illegal strike. The administration of the law differs somewhat from that under the executive orders and is described later in this chapter. Many of the substantive areas of the law are essentially the same as in the past. Those areas which have been expanded in scope, such as unfair labor practices, will be discussed herein.

According to an issue of the *FLRA Newsletter,* the case filings for early 1979 increased dramatically from those filed under the executive order program in 1978. Unfair labor practice complaints and negotiability appeals exceeded all of the Authority's projections; the number of such cases filed in the first five months of 1979 surpassed the total number of such cases filed throughout 1978. The comparative figures follow:

	1978	Jan–May 1979
Unfair labor practice	1024	1046
Representation	545	283
Negotiability appeals	49	81
Arbitration award appeals	51	22

This brief example illustrates the flurry of activity which followed the passage of the Civil Service Reform Act. Both parties sought to clarify the limits of the legislation, and this activity has continued, particularly in the area of interpretation of negotiability.[17]

The Postal Reorganization Act of 1970 was a direct response to the first national strike of federal employees. The act removed the Postal Service from the coverage of E.O. 11491 (and subsequent executive orders) and conferred upon postal workers virtually all of the collective bargaining rights, with the exception of the right to strike, enjoyed by employees in the private sector. The act conferred upon the NLRB the responsibility of determining appropriate bargaining units, supervising elections, and hearing unfair labor practice cases of postal employees. Salaries of postal workers are now set by collective bargaining between the U.S. Postal Service and four unions holding national exclusive recognition: the National Association of Letter Carriers, the American Postal Workers Union, the Rural Letter Carriers Association, and the Laborer's International Union.

Because the Federal Reserve System had been excluded from both the Taft–Hartley Act and the Executive Order, its Board of Governors issued, in May 1969, a "Policy on Unionization and Collective Bargaining for the Federal Reserve Banks."[18] It recognized the right of certain types of employees to join or refrain from joining labor organizations. It established procedures for bargaining unit determination, elections, and recognition. It provided for grievances and set forth a rather familiar list of unfair labor practices. The policy is administered by the Federal Reserve System Labor Relations Panel.

STATE AND LOCAL LEGISLATION

The legal status of state and local labor relations has undergone a major transformation during the past two decades. By 1980, thirty-eight states had passed legislation that obligates the respective state and local governments to allow their (public) employees to join unions and to recognize bona fide labor organizations.[19] Prior to the early 1960s, less than a handful of states had such legislation.

"There is a . . . lack of any common pattern in current State legislation dealing with public employee bargaining. No model system has emerged. A haphazard mixture of statutes, local executive orders, resolutions, ordinances, court decisions, and civil service statutes and procedures has developed in the States. . . . Thus, the states are clearly involved in developing a wide variety of models for public sector labor relations.[20]

Nevertheless, all statutes provide for exclusive recognition with one slight modification in New York State. In most states, an administrative agency is empowered to certify organizations and to conduct representation elections when necessary. At the local level, many governments voluntarily recognize unions, even when they are not statutorily required to do so. Most states currently have criteria for bargaining unit determination. As in the private sector, the designated administrative agency must, prior to the conduct of a representation election, decide which groups of employees will be represented by the organization and who is thus eligible to vote. Reference to union security clauses is notably absent but not explicitly prohibited by most state laws. The scope of bargaining differs among and within state and local governments. Grievance procedures also vary considerably, yet many states have kept intact procedures established by civil service commissions. Neither unfair labor practices nor impasse procedures are uniformly specified.

In sum, the variety of state legislation on each of the aforementioned subjects is so broad that only the barest of trends can be identified.

ADMINISTRATIVE AGENCIES AND FUNCTIONS

Federal Sector

Under Executive Order 10988, issued in 1962, final decision-making authority remained in the hands of the agency head. Under Executive Order 11491, issued in 1969, three new components were created to centralize decision making formerly exercised by individual agencies. These included (1) the Federal Labor Relations Council to administer the order, (2) the Federal Service Impasses Panel to assist the parties in resolving negotiating impasses, and (3) the assistant secretary of labor for labor-management relations to determine many issues formerly decided by the agency head.[21] Additionally, the Federal Mediation and Conciliation Service was granted the role of mediating negotiations and disputes for federal employees.

The FLRC consisted of the chairman of the Civil Service Commission, the secretary of labor, and the director of the Office of Management and Budget. The council administered and interpreted the order, decided major policy issues, prescribed regulations, and made recommendations to the President. It also considered appeals made by the assistant secretary of labor for labor-management relations on questions of representation and unfair labor practices and reviewed disputes regarding the negotiability of items as well as exceptions to arbitration awards.

The Federal Service Impasse Panel (FSIP), an agency within the FLRC, was authorized to consider negotiation impasses that still existed after third-party mediation had failed. It did not deal with an item at impasse if management had declared it nonnegotiable. It had the authority to order union and management to resume negotiations. If requested by both parties, voluntary fact-finding with public recommendations could be authorized. If agreement were reached on the method of selecting an arbitrator and of sharing his cost, the panel could authorize binding arbitration. Moreover, the panel could unilaterally authorize fact-finding and issue recommendations based on the facts, or it could even settle the case itself and issue a binding decision. As of 1980 the FSIP had exercised this last option only twice.

Under the Executive Order, the assistant secretary of labor for labor-management relations had authority to decide questions regarding composition of the bargaining unit; to supervise and certify representation elections; to decide whether labor organizations were eligible for national consultation rights; and to handle unfair labor practice charges and violations of the Standards of Conduct for unions. The secretary could not, however, become involved in such disputes if they were specifically covered by grievance or appeal procedures. Decisions made by the secretary could be appealed to the FLRC when they involved major policy issues or when they were apparently arbitrary and capricious. The assistant secretary, or persons designated by him, supervised all elections for certification which, as in the private sector, are conducted by secret ballot. Appropriateness of bargaining units and elections, recognition, and certification are discussed elsewhere in this chapter.

Since January 1979, when Title VII of the Civil Service Reform Act of 1978 and Reorganization Plan No. 2 of 1978, discussed earlier, became effective, there has been considerable change in the administration of public sector labor relations law for federal employees. The 1978 statute places central authority to oversee labor-management relations in federal agencies in the FLRA. It consists of three members appointed by the President who, unlike their predecessors at the FLRC, may not hold other employment or office. The general counsel of the FLRA, also a presidential appointee, is empowered to investigate alleged unfair labor practices and to file and prosecute complaints.

The basic function of the FLRA is to provide leadership in establishing policies for the administration of the statute. The structure of the FLRA is modeled largely on that of the National Labor Relations Board. Among the new and expanded responsibilities of the FLRA are:

1. The General Counsel is authorized to file and prosecute unfair labor practice cases. (Under the executive order program, charging parties, usually individuals, were required to prosecute their own cases.).
2. The FLRA is authorized to "conduct," not merely "supervise," elections in representation cases.
3. New unfair labor practices, described later in this chapter, are proscribed for both agencies and labor organizations.
4. The FLRA is empowered to determine the criteria for granting government-wide consultation rights and to resolve disputes as to entitlement.

5. The FLRA can seek enforcement of its decisions and orders in the U.S. Circuit Court of Appeals.

6. When an unfair labor practice complaint is issued, the FLRA may petition any U.S. district court for appropriate relief, including a temporary restraining order.

7. Subpoena power is issued for the first time; the FLRA may seek enforcement of subpoenas before the federal courts.

8. The FLRA may delegate decisional authority to regional directors and administrative law judges. (Under the orders, this authority had been vested in the assistant secretary.)

9. A union may negotiate the voluntary deduction of membership dues when it can demonstrate a membership of at least ten (10) percent of the employees in an appropriate bargaining unit.

10. The FLRA may seek judicial enforcement of the assistant secretary's decisions regarding the standards of conduct for labor organizations of federal employees.

11. The FLRA's jurisdiction has been extended to cover two agencies of the Congress, namely, the Library of Congress and the Government Printing Office.*

The responsibilities of the Federal Service Impasses Panel remain essentially the same under the act as under the executive order. The assistant secretary of labor for labor-management relations now has a relatively minor role, however. He or she administers the public sector's internal standards of union conduct and the private sector's similar standards under the Landrum–Griffin Act.

State and Local Level

Most of the forty states that have statutes or executive orders providing legal frameworks for collective bargaining have a designated agency to administer the agreements. There is considerable variety among and within states, however. In large government units, such as a complex school district, a major city, or an entire state, size and complexity dictate that management have a specified process for administering the agreement. On the other hand, in small cities or school districts, informal interpersonal relations may be adequate. States with designated agencies empower them to establish bargaining units, in keeping with established unit determination criteria, and to hear unfair labor practices stipulated in their statutes and usually similar to those in the private sector. Some states have a two-tiered administrative structure, with one agency for state and the other for local government matters. Connecticut, in fact, has three statutes and four administrative agencies for public sector bargaining. There is one agency each for state and for municipal employees. There are two additional agencies for teachers, one dealing with representation matters and the other for processing unfair or prohibited labor practices. Minnesota has a mediation agency and a public employee relations board, the latter handling appeals from the mediation agency, as well as elections and unfair labor practices.[22]

According to a 1974–75 study of eight state governments by Ralph Jones, there is usually "close coordination" between the central labor relations office and the line departments in transmitting information on new contract terms and case data.[23]

Federal Labor Relations Authority Fact Sheet, mimeo, 1979.

Grievances are generally handled by individual departments during the first two or three steps. Then, at the step before arbitration and at the arbitration or court stage, a central office unit usually assumes principal responsibility for settling the dispute. Large cities or counties engaged in collective bargaining face many problems in administering their agreements that are similar to those faced by states. Collective bargaining at the municipal level, however, tends to be more formal and more adversarial, and administrative agencies tend to respond accordingly.

DETERMINATION OF THE APPROPRIATE BARGAINING UNIT: FEDERAL AND STATE LEVELS

Bargaining unit determination in the public sector at the federal level closely resembles the private sector method (see also our bargaining unit chapter). The Executive Order established and Title VII of Civil Service Reform Act of 1978 has continued to apply a test to determine whether an appropriate unit exists by deciding whether the employees have a "clear and identifiable community of interest." The law authorizes the establishment of a unit on a plant or installation, craft, functional, or any other basis that insures community of interest among the employees. Some of the criteria used to determine whether a "clear and identifiable community of interest" exists are: common skills, similar working conditions, common supervision, common work site, and identical duties. Additionally, the statute requires that an appropriate unit must also promote effective dealings with the agency involved. The extent to which a particular union has been successful in organizing employees may *not* be used to determine the bounds of an appropriate unit. Rules pertaining to supervisors and professionals resemble those in the private sector.

When a federal agency and the union are unable to reach agreement on an appropriate bargaining unit, the dispute is referred to the FLRA. A review of decisions made at this level under the Executive Order indicates that large units were generally found more acceptable than small ones.

The determination of an appropriate bargaining unit for purposes of collective bargaining is probably no less crucial in terms of outcomes at the state and local levels than at the federal level. Interestingly enough, most state statutes have been much more specific in prescribing criteria for bargaining unit determination than has legislation in the private sector.[24]

In those states where "community of interest" is the sole or primary criterion of unit determination, the result is usually "a proliferation of relatively narrow units organized along lines of particular occupational distinctions or organizational components of the employer."[25] According to the Advisory Committee on Intergovernmental Relations (ACIR), there are four broad ways to define "community of interest:"

1. Similar wages, hours, working rules, and conditions of employment
2. Maintaining a negotiating pattern based on common history
3. Maintaining the craft or professional line and status
4. Representation rights, which involve the inclusion or exclusion of supervisors or nonprofessionals (this refers to organizations such as police or fire departments)[26]

Community of interest has been referred to as an empty vessel into which other criteria (for establishing the appropriateness of a bargaining unit) are poured.[27] Public managers generally seek to avoid proliferation of bargaining units and favor large units because small units increase total bargaining time, increase the difficulty of achieving uniform application of wages and benefits, and increase the potential for interunion rivalry. Unions frequently favor whatever unit size will provide them with representation rights and enhance their bargaining power.

The question of bargaining unit proliferation reached major proportions in the 1970s. In Massachusetts, for example, a 1975 decision consolidated many state employee bargaining units into ten (five professional; five nonprofessional) statewide units. The Massachusetts Labor Relations Commission specifically weighed the choice between ". . . the chaos of fragmentation and, on the other, the rigidity and unwieldness of 'monolithism.' "[28] Other states have chosen to mandate bargaining units legislatively, rather than face the unit proliferation that comes from the accumulation of separate recognition and unit decisions.

Another public-sector bargaining unit issue concerns inclusion of supervisors in the same units as their subordinates. Although some authors[29] argue that when supervisors are organized, they should be in a separate organization, Gilroy and Russo[30] advocate the opposite. They believe that supervisors should be in the same unit with employees to moderate demands and create less militant organizations. As in the private sector, professionals in the public sector are excluded from bargaining units containing nonprofessional employees unless they vote to the contrary.

The public-sector bargaining structure is complex and highly fragmented. Its development may be attributed to rigid legislative certification guidelines that have encouraged the emergence of fragmented bargaining structures, composed of many small units, and to the inability of many administrative agencies to modify existing bargaining frameworks. One of the major arguments favoring small bargaining units is the right of employees to self-determination. Yet protecting this right, as in the private sector, can create problems (see our bargaining unit chapter). The existence of many small bargaining units can lead to interunion rivalry because of efforts to represent competing interests. Labor relations in the public as well as in the private sector are affected by the dimensions of bargaining units. In the public sector, particularly at the local level, civil service commissions and related agencies have often fragmented the personnel responsibility without substantial benefits to either management or labor. Inappropriate bargaining units may have an adverse effect on labor relations by complicating classification systems, increasing wage inequities, and weakening the bargaining process and contract administration.

ELECTIONS, RECOGNITION, AND CERTIFICATION AT THE FEDERAL AND STATE LEVELS

The rights of federal employees to organize and to choose their representatives are set forth in sections 7111, 7112, and 7116(e) of Title VII of the Civil Service Reform Act of 1978. Originally, under Executive Order 10988, three categories of recognition were available, namely, informal, formal, and exclusive. Exclusive representation rights required a 60 percent showing of employee support. Then, under Executive Order 11491 (1970), only exclusive recognition was continued, requiring that a simple majority of eligible employees select the union through secret-ballot elections.

Under the current law, consent elections may be held to determine the exclusive representative of a bargaining unit. The FLRA will, however, investigate whether a question of representation exists if anyone alleges that 30 percent of a bargaining unit believe their exclusive representative no longer represents the majority of the unit or, where there is no exclusive representative, that 30 percent wish to be exclusively represented for the purposes of collective bargaining. Following a hearing, the FLRA will schedule an election. Any union that can show that it is the unit's exclusive representative or that it has at least 10 percent support may be placed on the ballot. As under Taft–Hartley procedures, employees may vote for the choice of no representation. If no union receives a majority vote, a runoff election is held. The union receiving a majority vote is then certified by the FLRA as the exclusive representative.

At the state and local level, there are procedures for election certification and recognition both in the absence and in the presence of legislation. In the absence of statutory guidelines, the parties resolve these issues among themselves. Generally, the union and the public employer will agree (sometimes after lengthly negotiations) on the appropriate unit, which may be based entirely on the extent of organization. Recognition is often granted informally. If granted formally, however, it may be by school board resolutions, municipal ordinances, or various other legislative or quasi-legislative measures. Some parties simply follow the recognition procedures of the NLRB.

Under public sector legislation, many states have established agencies to implement recognition procedures, including unit determination, elections, and certification. According to Wellington and Winter, most agency procedures are derived from the NLRB. As support for a particular decision, certain state boards have cited NLRB rulings and federal labor case law.[31] Most states require a 30 percent showing of interest (as evidenced by authorization cards, dues deduction cards, or notarized membership lists). As in the federal and private sectors, the winner must receive a majority of the valid ballots cast. Most statutes allow the certified bargaining agent a period of unchallenged representation, frequently tied to the budget submission date of the employer.[32]

UNFAIR LABOR PRACTICES

Under Title VII of the Civil Service Reform Act of 1978, practices that were prohibited under the Executive order are retained as prohibitions, but several additions have been made. Under Section 19(a) of the old order, management could not interfere with, restrain, or coerce an employee in the exercise of his or her rights; encourage or discourage membership in labor organizations; sponsor, control, or otherwise assist a labor organization; discipline or otherwise discriminate against an employee for filing a complaint or giving testimony under the order; refuse to accord appropriate recognition to a union qualified for same; or refuse to consult, confer, or negotiate with a labor organization as required by the order. Under Section 19(b), labor organizations were prohibited from coercing, disciplining, fining, or taking other economic sanctions against a member as punishment for or to hinder his or her work performance or productivity; condoning strike or prohibited picketing activity by failing to take affirmative action to prevent or stop it; discriminating in membership because of race, color, creed, sex, age, or national origin; or refusing to consult, confer, or negotiate with an agency as required by the order. Under Section 19(d), both management and unions were to file unresolved complaints with the assistant secretary of labor.

Under Title VII, agency and union unfair labor practices generally parallel unfair practices under the Taft–Hartley Act. Additionally, it is an unfair labor practice for an agency (1) to refuse to consult or negotiate in good faith with a union or (2) to enforce a new regulation that conflicts with an already existing collective bargaining agreement. Unions commit unfair labor practices if they refuse to cooperate in impasse procedures or if they engage in a slowdown, strike, or other than informational picketing against an agency.

Under the new law, an issue can be raised both under a grievance procedure and as an unfair labor practice charge. Under the executive order, however, an individual had no choice but to select one procedure or the other.

Employer (agency) free speech, other than threats or promises or comments made under coercive conditions, is protected activity during a representational election, as it is in the private sector.

When an unfair labor practice complaint is issued, the FLRA may petition any federal district court for relief, including a temporary restraining order. Under the Executive Order, no such judicial relief had been possible.

THE PROCESS OF COLLECTIVE BARGAINING
IN THE PUBLIC SECTOR

The process of bargaining in the public sector has been analyzed recently by Professor Daniel J.B. Mitchell, who contends that it is more difficult to model the process theoretically than its private sector counterpart.[33] The goals of employers are frequently difficult to understand since "they represent a conglomeration of interest pressures even more complex than those that reside in a union."[34] John F. Burton has discussed the tendency for budgetary authority in the public sector to be fragmented, particularly between the legislative and executive branches.[35] Such fragmentation complicates the collective bargaining process, since it may be unclear who has the final managerial authority. To represent the management side, Burton believes, however, that the authority over budgetary commitments on wages is gradually shifted toward the executive branch by collective bargaining. Thomas A. Kochan[36] has recently found that decentralized, multilateral bargaining authority plays into the hands of unions, which may obtain from one level of government what they had been denied at another.

Milton Derber also finds public sector bargaining not totally unlike that in the private sector.[37] Specifically, he believes that, like their private sector counterparts, public sector unions show a tendency to ignore detailed financial information provided by the employer to which management is quite sensitive in formulating wage proposals. Instead, the unions rely on employer resistance to excessive wage demands as a means of protecting opportunities for employment.

THE SCOPE OF BARGAINING IN THE PUBLIC SECTOR

The range of subjects negotiated between public employee unions and government managers varies considerably among jurisdictions. Frequently, there is a threefold division made between topics determined by legislative bodies, those left exclusively to civil service regulations and public managers, and those within the scope of bargaining. At the federal level, negotiations are narrowly confined to personnel policies and practices, while wages, fringe benefits, and other major conditions of employment are excluded. At the state and local levels, the range of bargainable items is generally much broader, yet it is difficult to find much uniformity among jurisdictions.

The scope of bargaining in the private sector was clarified in the 1958 Supreme Court decision, *NLRB* v. *Wooster Division of the Borg-Warner Corp.*, affirming earlier approaches of the board and the courts.[38] Subjects of bargaining were classified as mandatory (subjects over which labor and management *must* bargain), permissive (subjects over which labor and management *may* bargain), and illegal or prohibited (subjects over which labor and management *cannot* bargain). A general discussion of scope of bargaining appears in our chapter on management security. In the public sector, there is frequent debate over the appropriateness of utilizing the *Borg–Warner* analysis, especially in the permissive category. On the question of classifying a subject as mandatory, one author states that,

> The main public sector justification for excluding a legal topic from the mandated bargaining process is that the demand involves a significant public policy question which should not be determined in the isolation of the bargaining process in which other vital public interests are not directly represented. If a topic is "too significant" to be classified as a mandatory subject of bargaining, does it make any sense to say it may be bargained about if labor and management agree?[39]

Certain major characteristics are notably different in the private and public sectors and some are notably similar. First, the differences:

1. The common law doctrine of sovereignty suggests "that the private sector industrial relations model is per se inappropriate for the public sector" since bilateral decision making is thwarted by the employer's sovereignty.
2. The vital public interest which may be present in public sector bargaining is generally absent in private sector bargaining.
3. The extent of both regulation and protection is far greater for public than for private sector employees.
4. "Market constraints and employer mobility" which may moderate union demands in the private sector are usually absent in the public sector.

5. "Unions and public employees are able to influence the outcome of political elections that determine the composition of the public management which will be on the other side of the bargaining table. . . . There is little counterpart to these political activities in the private sector."[40]

The foregoing distinctions between the public and private sectors are usually advanced by those arguing that the appropriate scope of bargaining in the public sector should be significantly narrower than in the private sector. On the other hand, there are several increasingly well recognized ways in which traditional distinctions are becoming blurred. First, concepts of sovereignty and illegal delegation are no longer serious general impediments to defining the scope of bargaining in the public sector in private sector terms. Thus, the new style sovereignty–illegal delegation argument resembles the concept of inherent management rights developed in the private sector and articulated by the Supreme Court in the *Fibreboard* decision.[41] Second, in the areas of strikes and interest arbitration, the distinctions between the actual practices in the two sectors are narrowing, with a resulting effect on the appropriate scope of bargaining in each. Third, fiscal constraints throughout the economy, particularly when layoffs are involved, suggest the need for a coordinated public policy and a reexamination of bargaining scope doctrines in both sectors. Fourth, each sector must comply with a continuing number of federal and state laws and regulations which bring to the bargaining process external pressures that are directly related to the scope of such bargaining. Finally, as public sector bargaining matures and as key scope disputes are settled by litigation, the current prominence of scope issues may decrease to the level existing in the private sector.[42]

Executive Order 11491, the 1978 labor law, and the Postal Reorganization Act defined the scope of bargaining for federal employees. Sections 11(a) and 11(b) of the Executive Order stated that the scope of bargaining was limited by applicable laws and regulations, including personnel policies published by the Civil Service Commission in the *Federal Personnel Manual* (FPM), and by agency personnel policies. Section 12(b) further limited the scope by excluding from negotiations an expansive list of management rights. Under Title VII of the Civil Service Reform Act of 1978, the scope of bargaining is constrained in a fashion similar to that under the Executive Order. The duty to bargain does not extend to the following facets of an agency's operations: mission, budget, organization, number of employees, and internal security practices. Management's right to hire, assign, direct, lay off, retain, or take disciplinary action against employees is also not subject to negotiation. According to Section 7106(b) of the act, however, an agency, at its option, may bargain with a union on the numbers, types, and grades of employees or positions assigned to any organizational subdivision or work project. It may also agree to bargain on the technology, methods, and means of performing work; the procedures to be used in exercising management's authority; and arrangements made for employees adversely affected by the exercise of such authority. Wages and fringe benefits are currently controlled by Congress and the President, with actual pay scale determinations governed by the Federal Pay Comparability Act.

Under the Postal Reorganization Act, the scope of bargaining is considerably wider than for other federal sector units, since it is governed by relevant provisions of the Taft–Hartley Act to the extent that such are consistent with other provisions of the

Reorganization Act. Representatives of postal workers, unlike those who represent federal agency employees, can negotiate "wages, hours and other terms and conditions of employment," except those expressly reserved to management.

On the state and local levels, a rather different situation exists concerning the scope of bargaining. Most states that have enacted some form of bargaining legislation prescribe a management obligation to bargain over wages, hours, and other terms and conditions of employment. Regarding schoolteachers, some states have enacted legislation authorizing negotiations by this group under separate statutes containing a broad list of permissible subjects, including class size, course content, and even textbook selection. Despite this apparent flexibility, there *are* limitations of the scope of bargaining at the state and local levels. Section 8(d) of the Taft–Hartley Act is incorporated in some laws. In addition, state courts and public employee relations boards have relied on the mandatory—permissive—illegal distinction made by the Supreme Court in the landmark *Borg–Warner* case. There is an important distinction, however, between the private and the public sector's handling of attempts to draw the line between mandatory and permissive subjects. In the former sector, the controversies are handled on an ad hoc basis by the NLRB and the courts, while in the latter there is much more emphasis on statutory distinctions.

UNION SECURITY

A comprehensive discussion of union security and its various forms is provided in our Chapter 15. Union security clauses which would require union membership as a condition of employment in the federal sector were prohibited under E.O. 11491, as amended, and under the Postal Reorganization Act. Title VII of the Civil Service Reform Act of 1978 continues this prohibition. The most widespread and least controversial forms of union security in the public sector are dues checkoff and exclusivity. The dues checkoff is an agreement between a union and an employer to deduct union dues from employee wages. Most public sector statutes and agreements stipulate that the dues checkoff must be individually authorized, and that it must be revocable either after one year or at the end of the contract. Another common form of union security is exclusivity. Under such an arrangement, an employee organization is given the right to represent and bargain for all the employees in the bargaining unit, nonunion as well as union. Most public sector statutes provide for exclusive bargaining rights. They also provide for the right of individual employees to present their grievances or opinions regardless of whether they belong to a union, often allowing the exclusive bargaining agent to be present at the hearing and/or to be notified of it.

The agency shop, which is discussed in some detail in our chapter on union security, and the fair-share arrangements are more prevalent in the public sector than the union shop. Most public sector statutes do not state whether an agency shop is allowed, and there have been conflicting court decisions in recent years as to whether the right to refrain from joining a union prohibits the agency shop. Legislation authorizing agency shop agreements does, however, exist in many states.

Another form of union security in the public sector is the fair-share provision.

This variation of the agency shop requires nonmembers to pay the union a prorated share of bargaining costs as a condition of employment. The fee is calculated to compensate the union for negotiating a contract and processing grievances. Thus, the nonunion member pays only for direct services of the union, not for activities such as political campaigning or lobbying.

In the public sector there is considerable controversy regarding union security, which requires actual union membership or the payment of money to a union as a condition of an employee's continued employment. Opponents of such requirements contend that they violate (1) certain merit principles prevalent in much of the public sector, (2) an individual's freedom of speech and association as protected by the Constitution's First and Fourteenth amendments, (3) a person's right to work, and (4) teacher tenure laws. Another criticism of union security arrangements centers on the complacency that may result on the part of a financially secure union. In response to such criticism, some argue that democratic processes within the union itself will prevent inefficient representation. A secure union with a solid financial base can contribute to stable labor relations and to industrial peace. In recent years this has been recognized by many state and local government officials, who no longer resist as strongly as in the past union pressure for a greater degree of security.

THE RIGHT TO STRIKE

Federal employees were prohibited from striking by the Executive Order; this prohibition has been continued with stronger sanctions under Title VII of the Civil Service Reform Act of 1978. Most states prohibit the right to strike either by statute or by court decisions. Despite these legal obstacles, strikes in government have not been uncommon, nor are they a recent phenomenon. Nearly a century ago, strikes occurred in navy shipyards and in the Government Printing Office. The famous Boston police strike of 1919 brought Governor Calvin Coolidge to national attention with his assertion that there was no right to strike against the public safety by anybody, anywhere, anytime.[43]

Strikes among public employees, particularly at the state and local levels, have become increasingly frequent during the 1958 to 1979 period. The 1970 postal strike was followed by a strike of FAA air traffic controllers. The vast majority of public sector work stoppages, however, occur on the local level, with teachers participating more frequently in strike activity than any other single occupational group. As indicated by Table 17–4, there was a particularly sharp rise in strike activity in 1968, somewhat of a leveling off in 1974, followed by a decline in 1976 and an increase from 1977 to 1979.

The most recent year for which strike data were published is a fairly typical one. Education strikes in 1979 were responsible for over half of the total (314 out of 593). Among other functional divisions, law enforcement and corrections experienced the largest number of strikes in 1979 (52). Strike issues in the public sector are not very different from those in the private sector. General wage changes were the major issue in over two-thirds of the strikes in 1979. Some states have proven to be particularly

TABLE 17.4. WORK STOPPAGES BY LEVEL OF GOVERNMENT, 1958–79

(Workers involved and days idle in thousands)

Year	Total			Federal Government			State Government			Local Government		
	Number of Stoppages	Workers Involved	Days Idle During Year	Number of Stoppages	Workers Involved	Days Idle During Year	Number of Stoppages	Workers Involved	Days Idle During Year	Number of Stoppages	Workers Involved	Days Idle During Year
1958	15	1.7	7.5	—	—	—	1	( )[1]	( )[1]	14	1.7	7.4
1959	25	2.0	10.5	—	—	—	4	.4	1.6	21	1.6	8.8
1960	36	28.6	58.4	—	—	—	3	1.0	1.2	33	27.6	57.2
1961	28	6.6	15.3	5	4.2	33.8	—	—	—	28	6.6	15.3
1962	28	31.1	79.1	—	—	—	2	1.7	2.3	21	25.3	43.1
1963	29	4.8	15.4	—	—	—	2	.3	2.2	27	4.6	63.3
1964	41	22.7	70.8	—	—	—	4	.3	3.2	37	22.5	67.7
1965	42	11.9	146.0	—	—	—	—	—	1.3	42	11.9	145.0
1966	142	105.0	455.0	—	—	—	9	3.1	6.0	133	102.0	449.0
1967	181	132.0	1250.0	—	—	—	12	4.7	16.3	169	127.0	1230.0
1968	254	201.8	2545.2	3	1.7	9.6	16	9.3	42.8	235	190.9	2492.8
1969	411	160.0	745.7	2	.6	1.1	37	20.5	152.4	372	139.0	592.2
1970	412	333.5	2023.2	3	155.8	648.3	23	8.8	44.6	386	168.9	1330.5
1971	329	152.6	901.4	2	1.0	8.1	23	14.5	81.8	304	137.1	811.6
1972	375	142.1	1257.3	—	—	—	40	27.4	273.7	335	114.7	983.5
1973	387	196.4	2303.9	1	.5	4.6	29	12.3	133.0	357	183.7	2166.3
1974	384	160.7	1404.2	2	.5	1.4	34	24.7	86.4	348	135.4	1316.3
1975	478	318.5	2204.4	1	( )[1]	( )[1]	32	66.6	300.5	446	252.0	1903.9
1976	378	180.7	1690.7	—	—	—	25	33.8	148.2	352	146.8	1542.6
1977	413	170.2	1765.7	2	.4	.5	44	33.7	181.9	367	136.2	1583.3
1978	481	193.7	1706.7	1	4.8	27.8	45	17.9	180.2	435	171.0	1498.9
1979	593	254.1	2982.5	—	—	—	57	48.6	515.5	536	205.5	2467.1

[1]Fewer than 100.

SOURCE: *Work Stoppages in Government, 1979* Report 629 (Washington, D.C.: U.S. Department of Labor, Bureau of Labor Statistics, 1980).

strike-prone over time. California, Illinois, Michigan, Ohio, and Pennsylvania all had more than fifty strikes in 1979.[44] These five states alone accounted for well over half of all public strikes that occurred in 1979. Significantly, when new public-sector labor legislation was adopted in 1984 in Ohio and Illinois, both provisions allowed some public employees the right to strike.

At the federal level, both Executive Order 10988 and Executive Order 11491 excluded from their protection any employee organization that engaged in or assisted in a strike.[45] The 1978 statute continues this exclusion. At the state level, prior to 1967, public sector strikes were prohibited *ab initio* in all fifty states. In that year, Vermont became the first state to enact legislation permitting limited strike rights for public employees. By 1985, ten states were granting public employees some protection to engage in strikes.

Prohibition of public sector strikes has proved ineffective. Despite stringent potential penalties, many public employees *have* struck in recent years, as there is scant evidence of any reversal of this trend. In fact, "Data on public employee strikes indicate that a large majority of these strikes have taken place in the presence of laws barring their use. Public employees strike when they feel it is necessary, preventive laws often notwithstanding."[46] There are many arguments for and against legalizing public sector strikes. We will discuss some of these. Advocates of "legislatively legitimizing" public employee strikes believe that more attention could be given to substantive matters concerning the parties if the strike issue were eliminated, at least in terms of its legality. They reason that the whole strike issue is detrimental to good labor relations and that it detracts from a positive labor relations atmosphere. Second, proponents of strike legislation claim that legitimate group conflict can have a positive or cathartic effect. Clark Kerr believes that even if strikes do not occur, the threat of strikes or lockouts facilitates the resolution of conflict at the bargaining table.[47] Credibility of threats requires occasional strikes, and public employees are sometimes prepared to strike regardless of the legal status of their actions. Third, proponents insist that strikes serve as the ultimate test of a union's strength as a bargaining representative. In this light, a potential strike can be used as a bargaining strategy more than as a real weapon. Still another argument for strike legalization centers on achieving comparability with private sector employees engaged in the same or similar function (e.g., transit, health care, teaching, etc.) who already have the legal right to strike.

Opponents of the right to strike for public employees base their arguments on private-sector analogies. Public-sector management is at a distinct disadvantage because it lacks private-sector constraints governed by profit, competition, and input and output markets. Strike critics argue that economic objectives should be settled at the bargaining table and political objectives in the politcal arena. Additionally, granting strike rights would lead to a further erosion of government authority. Opponents also argue that to legalize public employee strikes would contribute significantly to increased taxes and inflation. Furthermore, they contend that such strikes are detrimental to public welfare and safety, and harm third parties who have no influence on the outcome. Finally, strike opponents argue that to allow strikes only for nonessential public employees would be unjust and inequitable, thus bolstering their contention that strikes should be prohibited for all public-sector employees.

Many states, in substitution for the strike, have adopted some form of impasse-resolution procedure binding upon both of the parties. It is thought that the right of arbitration will be an equalizing force at the bargaining table and reduce the necessity for public-sector conflict. For a more elaborate discussion of such procedures, see Chapter 12, Impasse: Resolution and Regulation.

THE FUTURE OF COLLECTIVE BARGAINING IN THE PUBLIC SECTOR

The rapid growth of public sector unionization during the sixties and seventies "has brought to light the inexperience of both public officials and public employees in grappling with the problems of negotiating a contract, establishing a grievance procedure, and defining the new employer-employee relationship. . . . Collective bargaining has introduced some of the features of an adverarial relationship into a setting which heretofore had been . . . characterized as paternalistic or collegial."[48] Many labor relations authorities claim that the seemingly higher level of tension present in the public as compared with the private sector may be traced to the inexperience of both parties and the difficulties in adjusting to new relationships with each other.

Let us now speculate on the future of collective bargaining in the public sector in terms of trends in the federal service, anticipated management posture, scope of negotiations, worker militancy, new dispute resolution mechanisms, and new or amended labor legislation.

Benjamin Aaron, in an analysis published in 1979, has described the anticipated growth of unionism in the public sector as follows:

> In the short term . . . there is at least the possibility of a rather anomalous development: continuing, steady, if not spectacular growth in the total membership of all public-sector bargaining organizations, accompanied by a diminution in the membership of some, together with an overall decline in bargaining effectiveness in the context of an unfavorable economic and political environment. . . . Much depends upon factors over which public employees have little or no control, including the general state of the economy, the rate of growth in public employment, and shifts in political power at both federal and state levels.[49]

Aaron foresees certain trends in the federal service, the postal service, and education. He quotes former Secretary of Labor and Director of the Federal Mediation and Conciliation Service W.L. Usery, who contends that there is little true collective bargaining "because there is so little that can be bargained for" in the federal sector:

> Congress preempts the economic issues. . . . Many of the primary noneconomic issues—seniority, job transfers, discipline, promotion, the agency shop, and the union shop, are nonnegotiable—because of a combination of law, regulation, management rights, and thousands of pages in the Federal Personnel Manual.[50]

Despite this fact, the 1981 air traffic controllers dispute with the federal government was over some of those economic issues. The subsequent strike and President Reagan's firing of the strikers set the tone for a tougher management position in the 1980s. This can be witnessed in the postal workers' unwillingness to strike in the 1984 negotiations, despite a significant history of union militance.

In the educational arena, continued rivalry between the American Federation of Teachers and the National Education Association is expected to contribute to organizational gains by both.

On the management side, government managers are expected to become more assertive and thus provide an effective countervailing force against the political and economic power of unions. We may see an attempt on the part of local management groups to form multiemployer bargaining units to match similar developments among strong government unions.

The current decade should witness concerted efforts by established federal-sector labor organizations to broaden the scope of negotiations so as to participate in determination of such matters as the hiring and firing of employees, supplementary benefits, criteria for promotion and transfer, standards of professional conduct, and salary grades. According to Charles S. Bunker, "It is not reasonable to assume that federal employees will be granted the legal right to strike, that Congress will give up its constitutional authority to determine wages and related matters, or that the civil service commission regulations on matters of personnel policy will be drastically changed in the immediate future."[51]

On the state and local front, the right to strike will be the most intensely sought legislative goal of unions. Strike activity is expected to continue, regardless of whether or not the strike is eventually legalized. One can only guess as to whether the frequency and intensity of public strikes will continue to increase. Recent indications point to a lessening of these tensions for the balance of the 1980s.

Daniel J.B. Mitchell's analysis of the impact of collective bargaining on worker compensation in the public sector[52] is relevant for the coming decades. Mitchell suggests that the "prevailing-wage provision" (which ties negotiated increases in government earnings to those existent in the local or area private sector) will probably be repealed in many instances in an attempt to tighten local budgets.

Regarding worker militancy, E. Wight Bakke predicted increased militancy during the seventies in a paper presented in May 1970.[53] Certain of the reasons for such activity are no longer relevant; yet others loom as important factors for the eighties and beyond. Among the latter are (1) nearly one-quarter of the states have yet to enact legislation granting public sector unions the right to organize and bargain collectively; (2) even where the right to bargain is recognized, many public managers have yet to recognize those rights and engage in good faith bargaining; (3) there is still considerable jurisdictional conflict between the so-called professional associations and the traditional trade unions; (4) direct action and coercive mass pressure have increasingly become more acceptable, even for upper-middle-class individuals; and (5) presuming that the use of the strike weapon will not be uniformly legalized during the eighties, it will nevertheless be used, along with other forms of reduction or withdrawal of services.

The eighties will likely witness certain changes in dispute resolution mechanisms in the public sector. There will continue to be no single national formula for dealing with "emergency disputes" such as exists in the private sector. The changes will be primarily in the area of increased experimentation with new methods of impasse resolution. According to Benjamin Aaron:

> As of mid-1978, the ratio of states that have opted for compulsory arbitration of public-sector impasses to those that grant a limited right to strike is a little more than two to one. There does not seem to be much likelihood either that this ratio will change significantly in the near future, or that compulsory arbitration will be abandoned in favor of combinations of mediation and fact-finding that do not necessarily result in some resolution of the dispute.[54]

On the legislative front, it is doubtful that there will soon be a federal preemptive labor law for state and local public employees comparable to the private sector's Taft—Hartley.

NOTES

[1]*Handbook of Labor Statistics*, BLS Bulletin 2070, December 1980, Table 72.

[2]Richard J. Murphy, "The Federal Experience in Employee Relations," in Richard J. Murphy and Morris Sackman (eds.), *The Crisis in Public Employee Relations in the Decade of the Seventies* (Washington, D.C.: Bureau of National Affairs, 1970), p. 1; and Russell Smith, Harry Edwards, and Theodore Clark, *Labor Relations Law in the Public Sector* (New York: Bobbs-Merrill, 1974), p. 1.

[3]Murphy, *op. cit.*, pp. 1—2.

[4]*Ibid.*

[5]*Ibid.*

[6]Advisory Commission on Intergovernmental Relations, *Labor—Management Policies for State and Local Government* (Washington, D.C.: U.S. Government Printing Office, 1969), p. 11; and Richard J. Murphy, "The State and Local Experience in Employee Relations," in Murphy and Sackman, *op. cit.*, p. 15.

[7]Joan Weitzman, "Current Trends in Public Sector Labor Relations Legislation," *Journal of Collective Negotiations in the Public Sector*, Vol. 5, No. 3, 1976, p. 233 and *Summary of Public Sector Labor Relations Policies: Statutes, Attorney Generals' Opinions and Selected Court Decisions* (Washington, D.C.: U.S. Department of Labor, Labor-Management Services Administration, 1979), p. v. In addition, both Ohio and Illinois adopted public sector bargaining legislation in 1984.

[8]*Directory of National Unions and Employee Associations, 1979*, BLS Bulletin 2079, September 1980, Table 16, p. 67; and *Monthly Labor Review*, 104, no. 5 (April 1981) Table 8, p. 77.

[9]U.S. Civil Service Commission, *Union Recognition in the Federal Government— November 1977* (Washington, D.C.: U.S. Government Printing Office, 1977).

[10]Charles S. Bunker, *Collective Bargaining: Non-Profit Sector* (Columbus, Ohio: Grid, 1973), pp. 11—13.

[11]*Ibid.*, pp. 13—14.

[12]James L. Stern, "Unionism in the Public Sector," in Benjamin Aaron, Jospeh R. Grodin, and James L. Stern (eds.), *Public Sector Bargaining* (Washington, D.C.: Bureau of National Affairs, 1979), p. 54.

[13]Courtney D. Gifford, ed., *Directory of U.S. Labor Organizations, 1982-83 Edition* (Washington, D.C.: Bureau of National Affairs, 1982), Table 23, pp. 70–71.

[14]Stern, *op. cit.*, p. 55.

[15]Gifford, *op. cit.*, p. 70.

[16]Michael Moskow, J. Joseph Loewenberg, and Edward Clifford Koziaria, *Collective Bargaining in Public Employment* (New York: Random House, 1970), p. 17.

[17]Henry H. Robinson, *Negotiability in the Federal Sector,* (Ithaca, N.Y.: ILR Press, 1981), pp. 9–10.

[18]Federal Reserve Press Release, "Policy on Unionization and Collective Bargaining for the Federal Reserve Banks," May 9, 1969.

[19]*Summary of Public Sector Labor Relations Policies: Statutes, Attorney Generals' Opinions and Selected Court Decisions, op. cit.*

[20]Russell A. Smith, Harry T. Edwards, and R. Theodore Clark, Jr., *Labor Relations in the Public Sector* (Indianapolis: Bobbs-Merrill, 1974), p. 73.

[21]AFL–CIO Manual for Federal Employees, *Government Employee Relations Report*, 61, no. 451 (January 10, 1977), p. 51.

[22]*Summary of Public Sector Labor Relations Policies: Statutes, Attorney Generals' Opinions and Selected Court Decisions, op. cit.*, pp. 1–63.

[23]Ralph T. Jones, "Public Management's Internal Organizational Response to the Demands of Collective Bargaining," draft final report prepared by Contract Research Corp., Belmont, Mass, for Labor-Management Services Administration, U.S. Department of Labor, undated, p. 27, cited in Milton Derber, "Management Organization for Collective Bargaining in the Public Sector," in Aaron et al., *op. cit.*, p. 108.

[24]Summary of Public Sector Labor Relations Policies, *op. cit.*

[25]Government Employee Relations Report, "Statewide Bargaining Units in State Governments," *Labor Management Relations Survey* (Washington, D.C.: Bureau of National Affairs, 1977), Vol. 61, pp. 41–42.

[26]Advisory Commission on Intergovernmental Relations, *Labor–Management Policies for State and Local Government* (Washington, D.C.: Government Printing Office, 1969).

[27]A. Balfour, "Appropriate Bargaining Units for State Employment," *State Government*, Autumn 1976, pp. 212–17, cited in John Rehfuss, "The Public Sector Bargaining Unit— Thoughts Raised by the Literature and the Illinois Experience," *Journal of Collective Negotiations*, 7, no. 1 (1978), pp. 46–49.

[28]Hugh D. Jascourt, ed., *Government Labor Relations: Trends and Information for the Future* (Oak Park, Ill: Moore Publishing Co., 1979), pp. 74–75.

[29]Public Sector Unit Determination, Administrative Procedures and Case Law (Washington, D.C.: U.S. Department of Labor, Labor-Management Services Administration, 1979), p. 7.

[30]T. Gilroy and A. Russo, *Bargaining Unit Issues: Problems, Criteria, Tactics* (Chicago: International Personnel Management Association, 1973), p. 33.

[31]Harry H. Wellington and Ralph K. Winter, Jr., *The Unions and the Cities* (Washington, D.C.: Brookings Institution, 1971), p. 87.

[32]*Ibid.*, pp. 87–88.

[33]Daniel J.B. Mitchell, "The Impact of Collective Bargaining on Compensation in the Public Sector," in Aaron, Grodin, and Stern, *op. cit.*, p. 142.

[34]*Ibid.*

[35]John F. Burton, Jr., "Local Government Bargaining and Management Structure," *Industrial Relations*, 2, no. 2 (May 1972), 124.

[36]Thomas A. Kochan, "A Theory of Multilateral Bargaining in City Governments," *Industrial and Labor Relations Review*, 27, no. 4 (July 1974), 526.

[37]Milton Derber, "Management Organization for Collective Bargaining in the Public Sector," in Aaron et al., *op. cit.*, pp. 80–117.

[38]*NLRB* v. *Wooster Division of the Borg-Warner Corp.*, 356 U.S. 342 (1958).

[39]June Miller Weisberger, "The Appropriate Scope of Bargaining in the Public Sector: The Continuing Controversy and the Wisconsin Experience," *Wisconsin Law Review*, no. 3 (1977), pp. 688–89.

[40]*Ibid.*, pp. 694–98.

[41]379 U.S. 203 (1964).

[42]Weisberger, *op. cit.*, pp. 707–709.

[43]Richard J. Murphy, "Public Employee Strikes," in Murphy and Sackman, *op. cit.*, p. 71.

[44]*Work Stoppages in Government, 1979*, BLS Report 629, March 1981, Table 10, p. 16.

[45]Murphy, *op. cit.*, pp. 71–72.

[46]Paul D. Staudohar, "The Grievance Arbitration and No-Strike Model in Public Employment," *Arbitration Journal*, Vol. 31, June 1976, p. 117.

[47]E. Wight Bakke, Clark Kerr, and Charles W. Anrod (eds.), *Unions, Management and the Public* (Chicago, Harcourt, Brace and World, 1967), p. 270.

[48]Charles Redenius, "Public Employees: A Survey of Some Critical Problems on the Frontier of Collective Bargaining," *Labor Law Journal*, 27, no. 9 (September 1976), 591.

[49]Benjamin Aaron, "Future of Collective Bargaining in the Public Sector," in Aaron, Grodin, and Stern, *op. cit.*, pp. 293–94.

[50]W.J. Usery, Jr., speaking at the Collective Bargaining Symposium for Labor Relations Executives, Warrenton, Va., July 8, 1974, cited in Aaron, Grodin, and Stern, *op. cit.*, p. 295.

[51]Bunker, *op. cit.*, p. 233.

[52]Mitchell, *op. cit.*, pp. 118–49.

[53]E. Wight Bakke, "Reflections on the Future of Bargaining in the Public Sector," *Monthly Labor Review*, 93, no. 7 (July 1970), 21–25.

[54]Aaron, Grodin, and Stern, *op. cit.*, p. 306.

CONCESSIONS AND THE FUTURE OF COLLECTIVE BARGAINING

18

The collective bargaining that has taken place in recent years between unions and managements in the United States represents a very profound change in our system of industrial relations. Unions, beginning in the late 1970s, found themselves reeling under the dual shock of significant membership losses to plant closings and layoffs and the demand for negotiated concessions from employers. We will attempt to assess the significance of this period. In this chapter we survey the concession bargaining era and look toward the future of industrial relations and unionism in the United States. We first examine the causes of concession bargaining. Second, we look at the extent of concessions and the form that they have taken. Third, we discuss the long-term impact of concessions on collective bargaining. Fourth, we review the divergence of trends of behavior in U.S. collective bargaining. Finally, we look at the future of collective bargaining.

From the end of World War II until the late 1970s, the United States economy generally enjoyed a long upward trend of strong economic growth, marred only by short recessions. Unions, through bargaining, were able to make substantial improvements in the standards of living of their members. The major question in any particular negotiation was not the direction of the change in wages and working conditions but only how much change would occur. During this period, there were relatively few instances of unions and managements engaging in concession bargaining.

Daniel Mitchell has noted at least two earlier periods of concession bargaining, in 1930–31 and in the post-Korean War recession.[1] In both cases, unions agreed to concessions in order financially to shore up firms and/or industries until business returned to a more prosperous level. Also, in the mid-1970s, concession bargaining was utilized by various unions and local governments in an attempt to assist cities to survive short-term financial crises.[2] Concession bargaining to save jobs was also of note in the early 1970s. Peter Henle found that older plants within profitable firms were often made more competitive by the downward adjustment of wages and working conditions through what he called "reverse" collective bargaining.[3] The most recent period of concession bargaining is unique in that the phenomenon has been so widespread and has so often involved some of the largest and most powerful unions and companies in the United States.

THE CAUSES OF CONCESSION BARGAINING

There have been many different factors responsible for each case of concessions. They include economic, political, social and local features. Most of the forces described below gained importance throughout the 1970s and were intensified during the recession of 1979–80 and the second, more severe, recession of 1981. We discuss import and domestic competition, decline in union strength, and the rise of management aggressiveness and the impact of these forces on concession bargaining.

Import Competition

One economic force that contributed to a concessions environment was the increased penetration of imported goods into domestic markets formerly dominated by U.S. producers. While the absolute numbers were not always large,[4] the rate of increase of imported goods sold in some sectors of the economy had a significant adverse effect upon the financial well-being of some companies. One need look at only two cases to understand the labor-cost pressures resulting from imports.

In the auto-producing sector, domestic companies enjoyed a virtual monopoly of the U.S. marketplace until the early 1970s. Imported automobiles were a quirk in consumer tastes and did not represent a significant share of the market. Two developments in the 1970s changed this picture. First, the oil crises of 1973 and 1979 drove gasoline prices to historically high levels and created demand pressures for more fuel-efficient automobiles. Second, aggressive marketing practices by Japanese auto producers provided fuel-efficient high-quality cars demanded by American consumers. Domestic producers were not prepared to compete effectively with the Japanese. They offered the wrong mix of autos to the American public, and the subsequent shift in consumer tastes toward foreign cars significantly reduced demand for domestic cars. Figures from the UAW document the intensifying competitive pressures in the late 1970s and the early 1980s.[5] The domestically produced share of autos sold in this country was 82.1 percent as late as 1978. By 1982, that proportion had declined to

72.1 percent, with the difference made up by increased sales of Japanese cars; the European share of the market also declined during that four-year period. If the overall market had grown during these years, perhaps the declining market share could have been better tolerated by the U.S. companies. Complicating the picture, however, was a one-third decline in the overall number of cars sold in the United States.

One of the largest components of the price of automobiles is labor cost, estimated for the auto industry to be about one-fourth of all costs.[6] Thus, one way for the auto companies to seek relief from foreign competition was to obtain concessions from the UAW. While no exactly comparable data exists, it has been estimated that U.S. labor costs were about double those of the Japanese. The first company fully to feel the effects of these trends was the Chrysler Corporation, which in 1979 found itself on the verge of bankruptcy. Through a complicated series of tripartite negotiations between Chrysler, the UAW, and the federal government, a series of loan guarantees were made by the government. These guarantees were conditioned upon, among other things, wage and benefit concessions by the UAW. In 1982 Ford and General Motors also sought concessions from the UAW, both citing increasing foreign competition and the much higher U.S. labor costs as reasons.[7] Similar trends in imports occurred in the domestic steel and rubber industries, and in both of those industries concessions were sought and gained by the companies to place themselves in a better competitive position vis-á-vis importers.

Because of the well-publicized problems in auto, steel, and rubber, one should not assume that competition from imported goods was an issue confronting only heavily unionized companies and industries. Parallel problems also emerged in industries with a relatively low level of unionization. The clothing industry, for example, is unionized in the same proportion as the U.S. economy (20 percent), but it still faced similar import pressures as the auto industry. According to a report of the *AFL−CIO*[8] in 1970, 90 percent of the clothing sold in the United States was domestically produced; by early 1983, this dropped to less than 50 percent. Import competition in this industry has not produced the visible concession atmosphere prevailing in other industries, because the industry is not highly unionized and the wages paid leave little room for concessions. In many instances, rather than seek concessions, employers sped up the movement of capital for clothing production to low-wage (relative to the United States) countries such as Taiwan.

Domestic Competition

There were industries in which wage and benefit differentials between the union and nonunion producers were large by the late 1970s. Some authors argued that in a prosperous economic environment, unionized and nonunionized firms can compete in the same market because union workers are more productive.[9] In declining markets, however, the compensation differential works to the competitive disadvantage of the unionized firms within the industry; as a result, unionized companies seek concessions from their labor unions in order to improve their competitive position.

The nonunion sector within some industries has been strengthened by technological change and deregulation. The technological innovations that have occurred in some industries provided a competitive advantage, allowing productivity of nonunion workers to grow faster than that of union workers. Probably the most extreme example of this economic pressure on the union sector within an industry was the situation in meatpacking. Long a stronghold of a few large firms, new production techniques began to emerge in the industry in the early 1960s. The technological innovations made by the Iowa Beef Company contributed to a fundamental change within the industry, first in the beef packing side and then more recently in the packaging of pork products. The company was new to the industry and was able to build state-of-the-art production facilities. The firm was able to process meat at considerably lower costs than its competitors, who generally worked with much older equipment. Not only was there a capital advantage but a direct wage advantage as well, for Iowa Beef pursued an aggressive strategy toward its workers and unions. It attempted to remain nonunion wherever possible, and where its workers did unionize, the company pursued aggressive negotiating strategies, often resulting in long and bitter strikes. The result of this strategy was an advantage in labor costs for Iowa Beef over its competitors of about 30 to 40 percent by the late 1970s.[10] Iowa Beef, as well as other new entrants into the industry, exerted strong competitive pressures on the older, unionized sector of the industry. This competition resulted in concession bargaining in every unionized firm in the industry. This was necessary in order to alleviate part of the production cost differential between union and nonunion firms: Some firms neared the point of bankruptcy,[11] and one (Rath) was sold to its own employees.[12]

Another factor that contributed to a competitive disadvantage of unionized workers was deregulation of such industries as airlines and over-the-road trucking. Prior to deregulation, both of these industries were subjected to strict regulations by the federal government, which protected markets from competition, both through rate structures and by limiting competition. In the late 1970s, both industries were deregulated.[13] This made it easier for new firms to enter these markets and compete for the available business. In the air travel industry, this led to the emergence of new nonunionized firms paying wages lower than the prevailing union scale. This forced unionized airlines to seek concessions from their employees in order to stay solvent and retain a share of the market formerly protected by regulation. Similar patterns developed in the interstate transportation of goods by trucks. Deregulation attracted into the trucking industry nonunion firms, with significantly lower labor costs and operating at a significant price advantage over unionized firms. This compelled unionized employers to seek concessions from their unions.

The Decline in Union Strength and the Rise of Management Aggressiveness

Unions were not as successful in the organization of new members during the decade of the 1970s as they had been in prior years.[14] This contributed to a decline in union strength and bargaining power. A good summary of the decline in union bargaining power on an industry-by-industry basis can be found in an article by Charles Craypo.[15] A weakened labor movement was not in a position to resist concession pressures. These pressures were intensified as a result of a severe downturn in economic activity. The first industries to be affected by a recession were those sensitive to consumer spending and higher interest rates: autos, housing, and their suppliers. Then, as the economic downturn accelerated, its effects began to filter back into other areas of the economy. In nearly all the early concession cases, the bargaining was precipitated by actual or threatened plant closings, extensive layoffs, or financial crises. Later, some firms sought concessions not because of serious financial strains but rather they saw it as an opportunity for lowering labor costs. It was reported in a 1983 survey that many managers sought concessions because they felt that the time was right.[16] A *Business Week* survey in January 1982 revealed that there were many firms who planned to seek concessions at the bargaining table even though no severe economic crisis existed or was expected in the near future.[17] The combination of union weakness and management aggressiveness led to concessions in some firms and industries.

In summary, the forces that produced concession bargaining were (the recession) reduced union strength, technological change, import competition, and political decisions (deregulation). All contributed to an atmosphere where concessions were pursued by employers in order to lower costs and to maintain a competitive position. In the next section we discuss the extent of concession bargaining.

THE EXTENT OF CONCESSION BARGAINING

Examination of Bureau of Labor Statistics data on wage settlements from 1981 to 1984 reveal that very few collective bargaining agreements settled during that time period resulted in wage or benefit reductions.[18] Virtually all the bargaining characterized as concession bargaining involved only freezes in compensation or deferral of previously negotiated increases. First-year wage settlements in 1982 (perhaps the height of the concessions era) show that only 2 percent of the large agreements (those covering 1000 or more workers) resulted in a wage decrease. Forty-two percent resulted in no wage change in the first year, and the remaining 56 percent resulted in some first year wage increases.

During the concession era, important contract changes often came not in the wage and benefit area, but in the form of relaxation of work rules and job classifications. A concession bargaining situation can be defined as one that results in any give-back of importance.[19] Concessions can consist of wage cuts, wage freezes of previously negotiated increases, benefit reductions, work-rule changes that result in increased management flexibility, and other language amendments.

There have been very few actual surveys of the extent of concession bargaining, since it is difficult to compile a list from the thirty to forty thousand contracts that are negotiated in the United States every year. Daniel Mitchell, in a Brookings Institution study, attempted to identify major concession agreements and their contents but was unable to estimate the depth of the trend over the years 1979 through 1981.[20] Peter Capelli and Robert McKersie, through the analysis of Bureau of National Affairs' data, were able to make an estimate of the proportion of union workers by two-digit Standard Industrial Classification (SIC) sector who have been affected by concessions agreements as of 1982.[21] Their analysis revealed that from 30 to 50 percent of all unionized workers in eight sectors had granted concessions to their employers in the following industries: apparel, rubber, leather, metal, machinery, transportation equipment, air transportation, and trucking.[22]

To summarize, by the end of 1984, a substantial portion of the unionized private-sector work force agreed to some form of give-backs to their employers. Early indications point to the fact that the concessions outside the sphere of compensation are permanent, at least for the foreseeable future. By all accounts, a substantial change in the U.S. system of industrial relations has occurred during the period of concessions. Let us now turn to what we see as the more significant implications of that change.

The Significant Implications of Concession Bargaining

While some observers of the collective bargaining process may disagree about the lasting significance of the concessions era, many suggest that there have been changes that will affect collective bargaining for the rest of the century.

Concession bargaining has demonstrated that negotiated wages and salaries can go down as well as up, and although this was a major surprise to some, it is not the only topic of significance in compensation bargaining. Settlements of large collective bargaining agreements remained very moderate well into the economic recovery of 1983–1984, suggesting that even though the economic environment for bargaining is better, unions are unlikely to achieve the growth of wages and benefits that had become routine in earlier years.

Of greater significance than changes in wage levels are the changes in methods of wage payment. Traditionally, collectively bargained wages were determined for the life of a labor agreement, with some contracts providing additional cost-of-living protection. At least four distinct variances from this system emerged during the concession era, and all appear to have acquired enough popularity in labor-management negotiations to represent a significant change. First, there has been a major movement toward two-tier wage structures. Theoretically, under such system management may be able gradually to replace higher-paid workers with lower-paid workers through attrition. Two wage structures are negotiated with current workers "red-circled" into the higher categories. These structures have been popular with management negotiators and accepted by union negotiators because they offer management the prospect of gradually lowered wages and do not hurt the current union membership. Some of these plans have only lower starting wages for new employees, with gradual wage increases over time toward the top of the scale, but some exclude gradual equalization. Despite their recent popularity these plans contain the potential for conflict. At some point in the future, when a significant portion of union membership in a bargaining unit is being paid a lower wage rate than their co-workers who have more seniority, pressure within the unit to equalize wages may intensify. The higher tier might then serve only as initial bargaining position for a higher, single wage rate for all the members of the bargaining unit.

Another set of issues revolves around management efforts to keep total hourly labor costs at low levels. This is being accomplished in two ways. One is the payment of one-time bonuses during the life of the agreement. For example in the second and third years of the 1984 GM – UAW agreement, bonuses of an average of $725, rather than the traditional percentage increase, were paid to the bargaining unit members.[23] This approach has the advantage of keeping low roll-up costs of such items as overtime, holidays, and vacations. It also makes the cost of a future percentage wage increases lower. Still another way of reducing fixed labor costs is through profit sharing, a share-the-risk form of wage payment in which workers receive a lump sum payment once the firm achieves profit in excess of a minimum rate of return.

A recent trend in wage bargaining is a lessened emphasis on cost-of-living clauses. The trend toward COLA clauses in collective bargaining agreements peaked when inflation did in the late 1970s.[24] At present, when COLA clauses would constitute a less expensive part of the compensation package, managements have been successful in removing them from many contracts.

A second major set of substantive changes that is likely to have long-term impact is the way in which job security is addressed in collective bargaining agreements. The former "standard" in U.S. collective bargaining was significantly influenced by the jurisdictional history of craft and trade unions. Unions traditionally attempted to place into contracts a set of rules designed to keep demand for their members high. In effect, these work rules allocated work and protected ownership rights among unions. Even within single industrial unions, complicated allocation schemes for the division of work among occupational groups were developed. In combination with seniority systems, these rules safeguarded the interest of unions and union members during periods of economic growth. During economic slowdowns, such as those that took place in the late 1970s and early 1980s, these rules severely limited managerial flexibility and contributed to inefficient allocation of resources. Moreover, unions found that the contract could not protect the entire bargaining unit. Thus when concessions were sought, management was not only trying to reduce labor costs but also to eliminate restricting work rules.

In one case the United Steel Workers negotiated a contract which provided for superclasses of occupations under which management can assign such superclass workers to various types of work within the bargaining unit. The Teamsters have agreed to reduce the rigid differentiation between over-the-road and city drivers so that all classes of truck drivers can be employed on the basis of available work. Historical protections of particular occupations or crafts was traded by many unions for other forms of overall job security. These have reflected attempts by unions to protect security of the entire bargaining unit.

New methods of job security have taken many forms, and we here list only a few. All have a single feature in common, and that is the tradeoff of occupational protection for some security of the entire unit. Unions and managements have negotiated a wide variety of short-term employment guarantees. Among the most prevalent types of guarantees have been moratoriums or longer advance notices on plant closings, layoff through attrition provisions, and specified minimum employment levels. All of such provisions give the whole unit a greater degree of security than it had in the past but at times at the expense of the already laid-off workers.

Other forms of unit protection have been provisions that make it more costly for management rapidly to reduce employment levels. Again, the auto industry can prove instructive. In the 1982 round of bargaining, Ford and the UAW attempted unsuccessfully to embody a concept of lifetime employment in their contract, an effort likely to be repeated in the future. The General Motors and UAW agreements embody a similar concept in spirit through the guaranteed income stream (1982) and the retraining fund for laid-off workers (1984).

The scope of collective bargaining is still another area of significant change. Whereas on the one hand, the NLRB has slightly narrowed what is to be considered a mandatory topic of bargaining,[25] unions and managements have been expanding their notion of what is proper for discussion and inclusion in a collective agreement. Some firms have relaxed their strong resistance to release of confidential financial and product information and have agreed to share it with their unions. Some managements provided unions with information as a means to prove the case for concessions, but in other situations the information sharing has continued into the realm of product development and even future employment plans. This could have significant implications for industrial relations in that it brings the union as an active participant into an area once exclusively reserved for management.

Union members and officials have been appointed to boards of directors, a myriad of cooperative plans have been established at all levels of bargaining relationships, and quality-of-work-life plans have taken root in a wide-ranging set of agreements. All of these developments represent unfamiliar territory for U.S. labor management relations, and none have been in place long enough to be judged as successful or as a permanent element of union management relationship.[26]

There are also differences in strike activity that have emerged during the concessions era. All the available data on both the public and the private sector indicate a lessened number of strikes. Although the Department of Labor has curtailed its data collection and publication, available indices indicate a drop in strikes involving more than 1000 workers. Preliminary data for 1984 reveal fifty-six such strikes, less than one-sixth of the total for 1974.[27] It is not entirely clear why this decline in conflict has occurred, although in the past the level of unemployment has been negatively correlated with the level of strike activity. Also, it seems that workers have been more reluctant to strike their employers because of job uncertainty. Whatever the reason, concession bargaining apparently has not led to more conflict.

The framework of collective bargaining has undergone a change during the concession era. The trend appears to point toward decentralization of bargaining structures as contrasted with centralization developments prevailing during the period 1945 through 1980. In his 1980 collective bargaining book, Thomas Kochan gives sixteen industry examples of centralized structures.[28] These sixteen industries represented a large proportion of the unionized workforce in the United States. By 1985, in five years, over half of those industries had moved toward a more decentralized framework. This occurred in a number of ways: the fragmentation of strong industry patterns (autos), the negotiation of local concessions that significantly altered the more centralized agreements (steel), the fragmentation of multiemployer and multicraft bargaining (construction), and the breakup of a regulated monopoly (telephones). Given that a centralized bargaining structure has statistically been associated with greater wage gains for unions,[29] the implications of this procedural change may imply more moderate wage settlements in the future. There is also another change taking place: More bargaining seems to be based upon firm and local labor market conditions rather than on national wage trends.

Another collective bargaining change discussed earlier is the shift of management toward the offensive. Until the concession era, managements usually attempted to defend the status quo of existing collective agreements. Recently, management became the initiator of change, forcing the union into a defensive position. This role reversal has altered the items over which the parties negotiate. This change may complicate the bargaining process and make it more difficult to attain settlements in the future.

COOPERATION OR CONFLICT

During the past few years, two distinct management approaches toward collective bargaining emerged in the United States. On the one hand, there have been firms facing the possibility of financial disaster who together with their unions negotiated packages of concessions as a means of saving the company. On the other hand, some companies in financial difficulties choose to use whatever means possible, including bankruptcy, to minimize their bargaining obligations and the role of their unions. Which trend is dominant? Are we headed into a new era of heightened conflict in U.S. industrial relations? Or one of greater cooperation between unions and management?

Thomas Kochan, in his work on strategic choice, has noted these trends as two of the "anomalies of industrial relations . . . ."[30] He and his coauthors suggest that we are in a transition period in industrial relations practice in the United States and it may be only in the latter part of this century before stable, accepted roles emerge for unions and managements. This notion challenges that of earlier scholars, who suggested that stability in the roles of unions and managements would emerge from a mature industrial relations system.[31] In the next two paragraphs we briefly look at examples of both ends of the spectrum of management behavior, at conflict and at cooperation.

In 1983, The Wilson Foods Corporation, facing huge economic losses and burdened with a union contract that the company claimed put it at a substantial disadvantage vis-á-vis its competitors, took a drastic step. In April of 1983 the firm filed for reorganization under the bankruptcy code and at the same time unilaterally changed contract terms with the United Food and Commercial Workers (UFCW).[32] In a letter to all bargaining unit employees, the chief executive officer of the firm announced the terms of a new collective bargaining agreement. A subsequent strike by the UFCW failed to change substantially the terms of the unilaterally imposed agreement, and eventually the workers returned to their jobs. The bankruptcy tactic, although new, is reminiscent of an earlier era of union-management relations in which each side used whatever weapons it had in its arsenal in an effort to subdue the other side. The Greyhound corporation sought concessions from the Amalgamated Transit Union, and when the union refused, the *Wall Street Journal* reported, ". . . Greyhound pushed through most of the labor concessions it wanted by means of an old-fashioned strikebreaking campaign. The bus company hired replacements for

12,000 striking drivers and resumed limited operations—with the protection of wire fences and armed guards."[33]

At the other end of the spectrum, Xerox Corporation and the Amalgamated Clothing and Textile Workers have formed joint union-management teams searching for ways of cutting production costs.[34] Quality-of-work-life programs and other plant-floor employee-involvement approaches have been implemented in many workplaces, some of which were negotiated and incorporated in contracts. Some firms have negotiated provisions providing for union representation on corporate boards of directors.[35]

It is far too early to tell which of the above management approaches to labor-management relations will prevail. At this point in time it is difficult to predict if either will establish a pattern of behavior that becomes the new norm in industrial relations. A major survey of management by the Conference Board reveals that most companies are pursuing a middle ground.[36] The major findings of the report suggest the competition destabilized collective bargaining in the early 1980s and has resulted in a more innovative and experimental climate of employee relations. The results of the survey of managers led the authors to conclude that a return to the wage patterns of the 1970s is unlikely.[37] To summarize, all available evidence suggests that collective bargaining is in a period of major transition in the United States.

THE NEW INDUSTRIAL RELATIONS AND THE FUTURE

In his 1982 presidential address to the Industrial Relations Research Association, Milton Derber focused on the question, "Are We in a New Stage?"[38] He discussed the arguments of the supporters of the "rerun theory," who argue that we have seen this all before. That is, the decline of the labor movement, concession bargaining, cooperative ventures between unions and management, the dominance of antiunionism have all occurred at least once in this century prior to the recent turbulence in industrial relations. Therefore, the advocates of the rerun theory suggest that we are merely at a different point in a continually evolving cycle of industrial relations behavior. Derber's response to this view is as follows:

> These strategic factors lead me to the belief that although many of the changes resemble past events, the magnitude of the changes . . . justifies the conclusion that we are, indeed, in a new stage.[39]

What will this new stage bring to our system of industrial relations? Some suggest that unionism and collective bargaining have outlived their usefulness. We disagree with this statement. In our view, the U.S. Labor unions and the collective bargaining process will retain their central role in our economic system. No industrial democracy can exist for long without an independent labor movement. Even though our collective bargaining system has recently been in turmoil, we can anticipate its adaptation to problems as yet unforeseen. As Derber puts it,

. . . the ability of unionism to rebound from setback and the resurgent capacity of the collective bargaining system have been quite remarkable features of the past century.[40]

NOTES

[1]Daniel J.B. Mitchell, "Recent Union Contract Concessions," *Brookings Papers on Economic Activity*, 1(1982), 172–175.

[2]For an example, see Joan P. Weitzman, "The Effect of Economic Restraints on Public-Sector Collective Bargaining: The Lessons of New York City," *Employee Relations Law Journal* 2 (Winter, 1977).

[3]Peter Henle, "Reverse Collective Bargaining? A Look at Some Union Concession Situations," *Industrial and Labor Relations Review* 26 (April, 1973).

[4]For example, with all of the attendant publicity associated with the decline of the United States steel industry, the fact is often overlooked that domestic producers still account for roughly 80% of the steel sold in the U.S.

[5]Summary Statement of Douglas A. Fraser before the Senate Committee on S. 2300, Fair Practices in Automotive Products Act, December 16, 1982.

[6]Mitchell, *op. cit.*, p. 184.

[7]Lydia Chavez, "G.M. Sets Closing of 4 Parts Plants," *New York Times*, February 26, 1982, p. D1.

[8]A report by the International Ladies' Garment Workers' Union states that forty-one percent of all apparel is now imported, as compared to two percent in 1960. Cited in *Solidarity* (May 16–31, 1983), p. 8.

[9]Charles Brown and James Medoff, "Trade Unions in the Production Process," *Journal of Political Economy* 86 (June, 1978).

[10]"The Slaughter of Meatpacking Wages," *Business Week*, June 27, 1983, pp. 70–71.

[11]The Wilson Foods Corp. unilaterally reduced wages by 40 percent and filed for bankruptcy on April 22, 1983.

[12]In June, 1980, the Rath employees began the systematic purchase of their company through stock purchase. The firm has since declared bankruptcy.

[13]Air transportation was deregulated in 1979 and the interstate trucking industry in 1980.

[14]Ronald L. Seeber and William N. Cooke, "The Decline in Union Success in NLRB Representation Elections," *Industrial Relations* 22 (Winter, 1983).

[15]Charles Craypo, "The Decline in Union Bargaining Power," in *New Directions in Labor Economics and Industrial Relations*, Michael Carter and William Leahy, eds. (South Bend, Ind.: Notre Dame Press, 1981).

[16]D. Quinn Mills, "When Employees Make Concessions," *Harvard Business Review*, 61 (May-June, 1983).

[17]Peter Capelli and Robert B. McKersie, "Labor and the Crisis in Collective Bargaining," in *Challenges and Choices Facing American Labor*, Thomas A. Kochan, ed. (Cambridge, Mass.: MIT Press, 1985).

[18]*Major Collective Bargaining Settlements in Private Industry, 1981–4*, USDOL, BLS.

[19]For example, Mitchell defines a concession as any of the following cases, ". . . wage cuts, wage freezes, premature renegotiation of existing contracts . . . , an easing of work-rule restrictions . . . other notable breaks from past practice," Mitchell, "Recent Union Contract Concessions," p. 168.

[20]Mitchell, *op. cit.*, pp. 168–169.

[21]Capelli and McKersie, *op.cit.*, p. 229.

[22]*Ibid.*, p. 230.

[23]*Business Week*, October 8, 1984, pp. 160–162.

[24]Audrey Freedman and William E. Fulmer, "Last Rites for Pattern Bargaining," *Harvard Business Review* (March-April 1982), pp. 30–48.

[25]*Milwaukee Spring Division*, 268 NLRB 601 (1984).

[26]For a good summary of a set of QWL experiences, see Thomas A. Kochan, Harry Katz, and Nancy Mower, *Worker Participation and American Unions: Threat or Opportunity* (Kalamazoo, Mich.: W.E. Upjohn Institute, 1984).

[27]*Monthly Labor Review*, 108 (January 1985), p. 103.

[28]Thomas A. Kochan, *Collective Bargaining and Industrial Relations* (Homewood, Ill.: Richard D. Irwin, 1980), p. 94.

[29]*Ibid.*, pp. 310–313.

[30]Thomas A. Kochan, Robert B. McKersie, and Peter Capelli, "Strategic Choice and Industrial Relations Theory and Practice," *Industrial and Labor Relations Review*, to appear, pp. 3–4.

[31]John T. Dunlop, *Industrial Relations Systems* (Carbondale, Ill.: Southern Illinois University Press, 1971).

[32]"Wilson's Back-Door Bid to Cut Labor Costs," *Business Week*, May 9, 1983, p. 32.

[33]Ralph E. Winter, "Even Profitable Firms Press Workers to Take Permanent Pay Cuts," *Wall Street Journal*, March 6, 1984, p. 5.

[34]John Hoerr, "Now Unions are Helping to Run the Business," *Business Week*, December 24, 1984, pp. 69–70.

[35]"Labor's Voice on Corporate Boards: Good or Bad?" *Business Week*, May 7, 1984, pp, 151–3.

[36]Audrey Freedman, *The New Look in Wage Policy and Employee Relations*, Conference Board Report No. 865, 1985.

[37]*Ibid.*, p. 33.

[38]Milton Derber, "Are We in a New Stage," *Proceedings of the Thirty-Fifth Annual Meeting*, Industrial Relations Research Association, December 28–30, 1982, pp. 1–9.

[39]*Ibid.*, p. 6.

[40]*Ibid.*, p. 3.

APPENDIX A
TO CHAPTER 8*

ELEMENTARY STEPS IN COSTING A CONTRACT

Perhaps no other issue in collective bargaining more easily defies precision and yet looms larger in the minds of negotiators than cost of the economic package. A review of the literature on the subject leads quickly to the conclusion that there are as many approaches to costing the package as there are companies and unions that consider the question. Yet the need for both labor and management to determine, with considerable accuracy, the financial consequences of labor contract proposals is of critical importance to the success of the collective bargaining process. Labor costs are among the largest costs incurred by most corporations and the cost of labor depends not only on the overall size of the compensation package, but upon its component parts as well. For labor unions, negotiating benefits for its members represents one of its major functions. Unions are, therefore, keenly interested in obtaining the best settlement possible.

The job of evaluating the cost of contract proposals is no easy one. Every item in the agreement—the fringe benefit package, changes in work schedules and job classifications, seniority rules and other contract changes—must be examined to determine the actual cost to the company and the benefit to the union membership. An understanding of these factors is essential to negotiators to enable them to trade one item of a proposal or counter proposal for another.

This understanding is as crucial to the effective mediator as it is to the negotiators. The mediator who understands the importance of being able to accurately cost out a proposal and who can aid the parties in developing the figures enhances his or her ability to develop alternatives that can mean the difference between a settlement or a strike.

The material for this collection of examples was originally gathered by Edward F. O'Brien, Regional Director, Region 4, of the Federal Mediation and Conciliation Service. The purpose of this data is to aid members of the Service in better understanding the methods by which the parties may compute costs. It is also intended to be a guide for the career development of new mediators and to provide resource material for those who are familiar with costing practices.

Although the Office of Technical Services would encourage mediators to utilize this costing information, at the outset, it should be emphasized that the material is only a guide and that it in no way purports to be the best approach or an approach advocated by the Service.

The methods of costing presented in this [Appendix] are intended to indicate how

---

*The material for this appendix was prepared by Edward F. O'Brien, Regional Director, Region 4, and by the Division of Research, Planning and Development, Office of Technical Services, Federal Mediation and Conciliation Service.

the cost of one aspect of the total package may influence other aspects of the contract and how such costing can be accomplished.

In the final analysis, however, the mediator must use his or her professional judgment as to its appropriate application in contract negotiations.

Wages

Wage rates and wage increases vary greatly by industry, occupation, and union status. Wage rates and wage rate changes are published monthly by the Bureau of Labor Statistics.** Shown below are a few simple methods for calculating wage increases.

There are at least two basic methods by which to calculate the direct cents per hour cost of a wage increase.

Method 1. If a wage increase of $.45 per hour is granted, the cost is then $.45. If the increase is not a flat across the board increase, but rather an average increase of $.45, then the increases are weighted.

100 workers with increases of $.40
80 workers with increases of $.45
50 workers with increases of $.50

$$
\begin{array}{rl}
100 \times \$.40 = \$\ 40 \\
80 \times .45 = 36 \\
\underline{50} \times .50 = \underline{\ \ 25} \\
230 \qquad \$101
\end{array}
\qquad
\frac{101}{230} = \$.44
$$

1. Hourly cost per employee = $.44
2. Total annual cost = $210,496

   Average hourly increase × number of hours paid × number of employees
   .44 × 2,080 × 230 = $210,496
3. Annual cost per employee = $915.20

$$
\frac{\text{Annual total cost}}{\text{Number of employees}} \qquad \frac{\$210,496}{230} = \$915.20
$$

Method 2. This method takes into account hours paid for but not worked. The total increase in wages is divided by either the total projected or total estimated number of productive hours to be worked. Assume a standard number of paid hours, 2080, for the workers in this above example:

$$
\begin{array}{l}
100 \times 2080 \times \$.40 = \$\ 83,200 \\
80 \times 2080 \times .45 = 74,880 \\
50 \times 2080 \times .50 = 52,000 \\
\text{Total increase in wages} = \$210,080
\end{array}
$$

**Two Bureau of Labor Statistics publications that contain such information are *Monthly Labor Review* and *Employment and Earnings*.

This is then divided by the total numbers of projected productive hours. (Assume each employee works 2000 hours per year.)

Total number of productive hours = number of employees × number of productive hours for each worker.

$$230 \times 2000 = 460,000$$

$$\frac{\text{Average cost}}{\text{Productive hours}} \quad \frac{\$210,080}{460,000} = \$.46 \text{ per hour}$$

(*Note:* If productive hours had been determined to be 1900, the increase would have been $.48.) Generally, the previous year's average number of productive hours per employee is used.)

Method 3.   In order to determine the average hourly cost of a wage increase of a multiyear contract, calculate the increase by the number of years or months each increase will be in effect and divide by the total number of years or months of the contract.

A three-year contract provides for the following increases. (This calculation utilizes 2080 hours per year, as does Method 1.)

$$\begin{aligned}
\text{December 1, 1983} &= \$ \ .50 \text{ per hour} \\
\text{December 1, 1984} &= \quad .45 \text{ per hour} \\
\text{December 1, 1985} &= \quad \underline{.40} \text{ per hour} \\
&\quad \ \ \$1.35
\end{aligned}$$

TABLE 1

In Years			In Months		
$ Per Hour		Years in Effect	$ Per Hour		Months in Effect
.50	×	3 = $1.50	.50	×	36 = $18.00
.45	×	2 = .90	.45	×	24 = 10.80
.40	×	1 = .40	.40	×	12 = 4.80
		$2.80			$33.60

$\dfrac{\$2.80}{3}$ years = $.93 per hour $\dfrac{\$33.60}{36}$ months = $.93 per hour

Method 4.   An alternative method for calculating the average hourly cost of the wage increase over the life of the contract is to sum the total wage increase over the period in which it is in effect and then divide this sum by the total time period of the contract.

For example:

TABLE 2

	$ Per Hour		Months in Effect
First 12 months	$ .50	×	12 = $ 6.00
Second 12 months $.50 + $.45	.95	×	12 = 11.40
Third 12 months $.50 + $.45 + $.40	1.35	×	12 = 26.20
			$33.60

$$\frac{\$33.60}{36 \text{ months}} = \$.93 \text{ per hour}$$

(Note: This method assumes 2080 hours per year, as does Method 1.)

The technique of computing increases by the number of months for which an increase is to remain in effect is particularly useful when the company is attempting to stay within certain cost limitations and the union is influenced by the total package increase as opposed to the actual money in hand. For example, a $1.50 total wage increase over three years of $.25 at six-month intervals may be more acceptable than one which is front loaded but does not yield as high a wage increase over the same period than a $.50–$.50–$.20 package. In fact, the first package may even become an acceptable compromise if the company is willing to increase the wage rate over the period by the $1.50 amount but is unable or unwilling to front load the package in, say, a $.50–$.50–$.50 fashion.

This approach has often been used in instances where the parties desire to create or expand a differential between different bargaining units. The parties can stay within the same average cost for all bargaining units and end up with varying wage rates. By applying this method in certain situations, such as delaying a second or third year increase for a month or two, it is often possible to persuade the parties to apply the savings to a fringe demand costing one or two cents per hour.

Method 5. This method determines the average yearly wage increase over the term of the contract and is frequently used by the parties to describe a wage settlement. The same three-year contract and increases given in Method 3 applies to this example.

TABLE 3

In Years			In Months		
$ *Per Hour*		*Years in Effect*	$ *Per Hour*		*Years in Effect*
.50	×	3 = $1.50	.50	×	36 = $18.00
.45	×	2 = .90	.45	×	24 = 10.80
.40	×	1 = .40	.40	×	12 = 4.80
		$2.80			$33.60

$$\frac{\$2.80}{6 \text{ years}} = \$.47 \text{ per hour} \qquad \frac{\$33.60}{72 \text{ months}} = \$.47 \text{ per hour}$$

Table 9 gives the cost of .005¢ to 50¢ hourly increases over periods ranging from one day to three years and is particularly useful in demonstrating long-term costs of hourly increases to the parties.

Reduction In Hours

About 70 per cent of all major collective bargaining agreements provide for a forty-hour scheduled work week. Another 8 percent of such agreements specifically schedule work weeks of less than forty hours. Over the years, the work week has declined and a demand for a reduction in the work week is not uncommon.

A reduction in the work week with no loss in weekly pay represents an increased hourly pay. If the work week were to be cut from forty hours to thirty-five hours, the increase in hourly wages needed to provide the same pay received for forty hours would be approximately 14 percent.

For a specific example in dollar-and-cents terms: if hourly wages average $5.00, weekly pay for forty hours is $200, then a reduction in hours to thirty-five would require an hourly increase of 71¢ to maintain the weekly wage of $200, a 14.2 percent hourly wage increase. If the hours reduction in this example were only to thirty-seven and a half hours, the hourly increase needed to maintain the weekly wage of $200 would be 33¢, a 6.6 percent hourly wage increase.

Cost-of-Living Clauses

Estimates of the number of employees covered under cost-of-living adjustment (COLA) clauses vary greatly—from 5 million to a possible 10 million—including employees not under collective bargaining contracts. Basically, the COLA is a means of maintaining the existing ratio between the Consumer Price Index (CPI) and average hourly earnings. Such agreements had traditionally been popular during periods of rapid inflation. Regardless of the basic differences in COLA language found in collective bargaining contracts, each COLA provision contains the same basic elements. These elements are: (1) The Selection of the actual index to be used. Most agreements use the Consumer Price Index published by the Bureau of Labor Statistics or some variation of it. (2) Selection of the base year upon which changes in the COLA are to be measured. (3) Agreement on the length of time that shall elapse between wage-adjustment periods. (4) Agreement on whether the adjustment shall be incorporated into the actual wage rate or shall be paid apart from basic wages. (5) Agreement as to whether upward wage adjustments will be unlimited or capped during the duration of the agreement. (6) Adoption of a formula to determine the amount of the wage adjustment to be made.

In estimating the total costs of an escalator clause, the anticipated rise in inflation or the CPI for the contract duration must also be projected. (*Note:* Most experts have repeatedly failed to accurately predict yearly inflationary rates so that the costing of a COLA clause is at best a rough approximation.)

In the following costing example, the length of time between COLA adjustments is quarterly, the adjustment is unlimited or uncapped, the wage adjustment formula is a $.01 hourly wage increase for each .3 point quarterly rise in the CPI, the length of the agreement is fifteen months and the CPI is expected to increase by a 10 percent yearly rate with quarterly increases as listed below. The estimated cost to the employer of such a COLA agreement would be calculated as follows:

TABLE 4

	CPI Level	Point Change	Quarterly Cents Per Hour Increase
Base period	155.4	—	—
End of 1st quarter	157.8	2.4	$ .08
End of 2nd quarter	160.6	2.8	.093
End of 3rd quarter	163.1	2.5	.083
End of 4th quarter	165.5	2.4	.08
Total		10.1	.336

The first quarterly COLA adjustment would take place three months after the effective contract date and would be in effect for twelve months since the example uses an agreement of fifteen months' duration. The second increase would be six months after the start of the contract and would be in effect for nine months, or three-fourths of a year. The third increase would be in effect for six months, or one-half year, and the fourth would be in effect for three months or one-fourth of a year.

The estimated cost of each of the four quarterly increases is equal to:

Hourly increase × number of hours paid × number of employees.

TABLE 5

Cost of Each Quarterly Adjustment			
First quarterly adjustment	$.08 × (2080) × 230	=	$ 38,272
Second quarterly adjustment	.093 × ¾ (2080) × 230	=	33,368
Third quarterly adjustment	.083 × ½ (2080) × 230	=	19,854
Fourth quarterly adjustment	.08 × ¼ (2080) × 230	=	9,568
Estimated total cost of COLA adjustments		=	$101,062

If the contract were for twelve months and the CPI were assumed to rise in the same manner as the above example, the quarterly adjustments over this contract period would be calculated as follows:

TABLE 6

Cost of Each Quarterly Adjustment			
First quarterly adjustment	$.08 × ¾ (2080) × 230	=	$28,704
Second quarterly adjustment	.093 × ½ (2080) × 230	=	22,246
Third quarterly adjustment	.083 × ¼ (2080) × 230	=	9,927
Estimated total cost of COLA adjustments		=	$60,877

(*Note:* The first quarterly increase would be in effect for nine months, or three-fourths of a year, the second for six months, and the third for three months. The fourth quarterly increase would not go into effect until the end of the year and does not appear as a cost in these calculations.)

Some contracts provide for a limit or cap on the amount to be paid under COLA. Such a cap may be $.10 or $.20 during a year or over the life of a contract. Other contracts state that the cost of living would have to exceed a certain predetermined percentage before any adjustment would be made.

Fringe Benefits

According to a study by the Conference Board, a private research firm, a large number of U.S. companies have liberalized their employee benefits, which now account for $.327 of every payroll dollar. Ten years ago, benefits represented $.256 of every dollar. The study reported two major trends: (1) companies increasingly are paying the full cost of employee benefits, and (2) more and more firms are providing the same benefits to all employees, rather than differentiating between blue and white collar workers. Because fringes are becoming more important to the bargaining process, a few examples on costing such benefit increases may be helpful.

Holidays

According to the Bureau of National Affairs (BNA), in union contracts covering 5000 or more workers, paid holidays were provided in 99 percent of the agreements. The median number of paid holidays was 10 in manufacturing contracts and eight in nonmanufacturing contracts.

The determinants in costing an additional holiday are the number of workers affected, the average rate, and the number of hours of holiday pay, which is usually eight.

Examples are shown next.

1. Total annual cost

   Number of workers (230) × average hourly rate, assume ($5.00 × number of paid holiday hours, assume (8).

$$230 \times \$5.00 \times 8 = \$9200$$
   Total annual cost is $9200

2. Hourly cost per employee per year

$$\frac{(\text{Annual cost} = \$9200)}{\text{Average hours paid per year (2080)} \times \text{number of workers (230)}}$$

$$\frac{\$\,9200}{478,400} = \$.019 \text{ per hour cost}$$

3. Annual cost per employee

$$\frac{\text{Annual cost (\$9200)}}{\text{Number of workers (230)}} = \$40$$

Overtime Premiums

Ninety percent of all major contracts provide for daily overtime rates and sixty five percent provide for weekly overtime rates. Generally, in manufacturing contracts, time and one-half is specified for work after the normal work day and/or work week. Double or triple time is generally paid for work during normal leisure periods, such as Saturdays, Sundays, and holidays. In costing any increase in overtime, Saturday, Sunday, or holiday work, it is standard to assume that the number of hours paid at premium rates will be the same as in prior years. Once the number of hours paid at premium rate is determined, the cost is calculated by multiplying the change in rates by the number of hours.

If, for example, the company paid time and one-half for all work on Saturday and this was increased to double time for Saturday work and the number of Saturday hours worked the previous year was 38,800, the increase would be calculated as follows. Also, assume the wage rate is $5.00 per hour and a work force of 230 employees.

Current Cost of Overtime Payments

1. Total annual cost

$$\text{Wage rate} \times 1\tfrac{1}{2} \times \left(\begin{array}{c}\text{number of hours worked on}\\ \text{Saturday in the previous year}\end{array}\right) =$$
$$\$5.00 \times 1\tfrac{1}{2} \times 38{,}800 = \$291{,}000$$

2. Hourly cost per employee per year

$$\frac{\text{Total cost}}{\text{Total number of hours paid} \times \text{number of employees}} =$$
$$\frac{291{,}000}{2080 \times 230} = \$.61$$

3. Annual cost per employee

$$\frac{\text{Total Cost}}{\text{Number of employees}} = \frac{291{,}000}{230} = \$1{,}265$$

Anticipated Cost of Overtime Payments

1. Total annual cost

$$\text{Wage rate} \times 2 \times \text{number of Saturday hours worked} = \$5.00 \times 2$$
$$\times 38{,}800 = \$388{,}000$$

2. Hourly cost per employee per year

$$\frac{\text{Total cost}}{\text{Total number of hours paid} \times \text{number of employees}} =$$
$$\frac{\$388{,}000}{2080 \times 230} = \$.81$$

3.   Annual cost per employee

$$\frac{\text{Total cost}}{\text{Number of employees}} = \frac{\$388,000}{230} = \$1687$$

Increased Cost of Anticipated Overtime Payments

1.   Increased total costs

$$\$388,000 - 291,000 = \$97,000$$

2.   Increased hourly cost

$$\$.81 - .61 = \$.20$$

3.   Increased annual cost per employee

$$\$1,687 - 1,265 = \$422$$

Shift Differentials

Premiums are frequently paid for shifts either as flat cents per hour or percent calculation of the average straight time hourly rate. Work performed in the third shift is generally paid at a higher rate.

Calculation of Shift Differentials

Shift 1—no premiums for 100 workers
Shift 2—$.20 per hour for 65 workers
Shift 3—$.40 per hour for 65 workers

1.   Total annual cost

$$65 \text{ workers} \times 2080 \text{ hours} \times \$.20 = \$27,040$$
$$65 \text{ workers} \times 2080 \text{ hours} \times \$.40 = \underline{\$54,080}$$
$$\text{Total annual cost is } \$81,120$$

2.   Hourly cost per employee per year

$$\frac{\$81,120}{230 \times 2080} = \$.17$$

3.   Annual cost per employee

$$\frac{\$81,120}{230} = \$352.70$$

Vacation Pay

Vacation policy varies by industry and company. [See chapter 14]. More leisure time is frequently a demand, and in order to calculate an additional week of paid vacation, it is helpful to know the present vacation eligibility, the average hourly rate of each group of workers in each eligibility classifications, and the hours of vacation.

Present Vacation Eligibility

15 workers—less than 1 year—no vacation
50 workers—   1 year—40 hours
100 workers—   1–2 years—80 hours
65 workers—   3–10 years—120 hours

TABLE 7

1. Total Annual Cost

Workers		Average Hourly Rate		Vacation Hours		Current Annual cost
50	×	$4.50	×	40	=	$ 9,000
100	×	5.00	×	80	=	40,000
65	×	5.50	×	120	=	42,900
				Total annual cost		$91,900

2. Average hourly cost per employee per year

$$\frac{\text{Annual cost (\$91,900)}}{\text{Hours paid per year (2080)} \times \text{number of workers (230)}} = \$.193$$

3. Annual cost per employee

$$\frac{\$91,900}{230} = \$399.57$$

Example 1.   Additional cost of providing additional week or 40 hours after 15 years.

$$
\begin{array}{rll}
15 \times \$4.00 \times & \text{no vacation eligibility} \\
50 \times \ \ 4.50 \times & \ \ 40 = \$ \ 9,000 \\
100 \times \ \ 5.00 \times & \ \ 80 = \ \ 40,000 \\
40 \times \ \ 5.50 \times & 120 = \ \ 26,400 \\
25 \times \ \ 5.50 \times & 160 = \underline{\ \ 22,000} \\
& \ \ \ \ \ \ \ \ \ \$97,400
\end{array}
$$

1. *New* total annual cost— $97,400
   Old total annual cost—−91,900
   Additional annual cost $5,500

2. Additional hourly cost
   (2080 hours × 230 employees) $\dfrac{\$5,500}{478,400} = \$.012$

3. Annual cost per employee

$$\frac{\$5,500}{230} = \$23.91$$

Example 2.   Providing 1 week after 6 months.

$$
\begin{array}{rll}
5 \times \$4.00 \times & \text{no vacation eligibility} \\
10 \times \ \ 4.25 \times & 40 = \$ \ 1,750 \\
50 \times \ \ 4.50 \times & 40 = \ \ \ 9,000 \\
100 \times \ \ 5.00 \times & 80 = \ \ 40,000 \\
65 \times \ \ 5.50 \times & 120 = \underline{\ \ 42,900} \\
& \ \ \ \ \ \ \ \ \$93,650
\end{array}
$$

1. *New* total annual cost— $93,650
   Old total annual cost—−91,900
   Additional annual cost $ 1,750

2. Additional hourly cost

$$\frac{\$1,750}{478,400} = \$.0037$$

Supplemental Unemployment Benefits and Severance Pay

Unlike most other benefits, supplemental unemployment benefits (SUB), or some form of unemployment pay, have not been widely negotiated. About 30 percent of all workers covered by major collective bargaining agreements are covered by a SUB provision or wage protection plan. About the same number are covered by severance pay plans. Generally, SUB funding is based on a specified time for which benefits will be paid and at a certain percent of current pay. Length of service benefit variations and dependent allowances are also built into the costing. Severance plans, on the other hand, generally provide a flat week's pay for service benefit, which may vary by length of service, such as ten weeks pay for five years service.

Rest Periods

In order to calculate the cost of including two ten-minute rest periods, which may or may not be written into a contract, the basic formula includes the number of workers × average hourly rate × annual number of rest hours.

1. Total annual cost—$99,670.50

$$230 \times \$5.00 \times 86.67^* = \$99,670.50$$

2. Cost in cents per hour—$\dfrac{\$99,670.50}{2080 \times 230} = \$.21$

3. Per year cost per employee—$\dfrac{\$99,670.50}{230} = \$433.35$

Other Pay for Time not Worked Benefits

A number of fringe benefits fall into this pay for time-not-worked category, in addition to holidays, vacations, and rest periods. Paid sick leave (aside from sickness and accident benefits provided under health insurance coverage), funeral leave, jury duty, military duty leave, paid meal periods, and wash-up, clean-up time. Sick leave benefits, for example, are provided by about one-third of all major contracts and cover the same percentage of workers.

Sick benefits and provisions vary greatly and may be based on length of service, for example, one day after one year, two days after two years and so forth, to a

---

*The two rest periods a day represent 100 minutes a week and 5200 minutes per year or 86.67 hours per years. (20 minutes × 5 work days × 52 weeks) =

$$\frac{5,200}{60} \text{ minutes} = 86.67$$

maximum of twelve days. Other contracts might provide a flat number of days for all employees after a certain period of service. Benefits not used during the year may be either lost, accumulated, or paid for. If, for example, the parties agree to give all employees three days of sick leave per year, the total annual cost would be:

1. Total annual cost

$$230 \times (\$5.00 \text{ per hour} \times 24 \text{ hours}) = \$27,600$$

2. Hourly cost per employee per year

$$\frac{\$27,600}{478,400} = \$.06 \text{ per-hour cost}$$

3. Annual cost per employee

$$\frac{\$27,600}{230} = \$120 \text{ per employee}$$

Pension

Increased benefits and improvements in pension plans are generally costed by actuarial firms. It should be noted, however, that new protections and guarantees for workers covered under private pension plans are provided in the Employee Retirement Income Security Act of 1974.

Insurance

Sickness and accident, hospitalization and life insurance plans, either establishing new plans or improving benefits, is best left to the actuarial experts.

Spillover

One element in costing a contract that may be discussed is the effect that wage and benefit changes have on nonbargaining-unit employees or other represented workers. For example, pension and/or health and welfare increases or improvements may have to be extended to other employees in separate units or not represented if the company has only one plan. Similarly, an additional holiday closing would affect the entire work force.

If historical wage differentials exist between bargaining-unit and nonbargaining-unit employees, a wage increase in one may affect the other's rates.

Roll-Up

The terms "roll-up," "impact," "creep," or "add-on" are commonly used, . . . to describe the costs which must be added to the . . . wage-and-benefit package in order to accurately reflect the ultimate labor cost for a given contract term.

Some parties talk about a 10 cent-per-hour wage increase, plus an additional holiday at 1 cent, as an 11-cent package. However, at some point in negotiations or afterwards, the total cost of that change in wages and benefits must be calculated. The following are typical factors which may automatically increase when the hourly wage rate is increased:

Overtime
Weekend and holiday premium pay
Vacations
Holidays
Sick leave
Life insurance
Sickness and accident benefits (in some cases)
Pensions (in some cases)

Simply stated, roll-up is a factor (total cost of old wages divided by total cost of old fringes) used to calculate the new fringe benefits based on the new contract. A simple example is provided below for illustration. In this example, the company employs 230 people who receive an average wage rate of $5.00 per hour and fringe benefits of $1.50 per hour. The total worker-man hours paid to the 230 was 478,400 (230 × 2080). The wage increase to be granted is 44 cents per hour and new fringes will equal 67 cents.

Shown below are two measurements of roll-up. Wage roll-up computes the increased costs of current benefits as a result of the wage increase. Package roll-up is a further refinement and costs out the newly negotiated fringes at the higher wage rate. Since the proposed new fringes were costed at the old rate, it is appropriate to calculate the new cost.

1. Wage-increase-only roll-up:
    (a) Determine for the prior year the total cost of fringes that vary with changes in the wage rate. For example, $1.50 multiplied by hours paid, 478,400, equals $717,600.
    (b) Determine the prior year's total direct wages. Average hourly earnings multiplied by hours paid. $5.00 × 478,400 equals $2,392,000.
    (c) Divide total fringe costs by wages to get the roll-up percentage.

    $$\frac{\$717,600}{2,392,000} = 30\%$$

    (d) Multiply the proposed direct hourly wage increase by this percentage roll-up figure to get indirect labor costs increase. $210,496 × .30 = $63,149. This represents the increase in the cost of fringe benefits attributable to the increase in the wage rate or the wage roll-up.
2. Package roll-up: Steps (a)(b)(c)
    (d) Divide the total cost of proposed fringe improvements[*] by the total direct wages for the prior year to determine the percent fringe roll-up.

___

[*]Since COLA is a flat cents-per-hour amount, it does not vary with fluctuations in wages. It is not subject to roll-up.

$$\$.67 \times 478{,}400 = 320{,}528$$

$$\frac{\$320{,}528}{2{,}392{,}000} = 13.4\%$$

(e)   Multiply the cost of the wage increase, \$210,496, by 13.4% = \$28,206. This represents the increase in cost of proposed benefits attributable to the increase in the base wage rate or the package roll-up.

Note: In making quick comparisons, the roll-up percentages may be applied to the cents per hour wage or fringe costs, as contrasted with the calculations in dollar costs.

$$\frac{\$5.00}{1.50} \text{ per hour} = 30\%$$

TABLE 8

Benefits Negotiated	Total Annual Cost Increase	Hourly Cost Increase Per Employee	Annual Cost Increase Per Employee
1. One additional holiday	9,200	.02	40
2. Double pay for Saturday or sixth day of week	97,000	.20	422
3. Shift differential	81,120	.17	353
4. Inclusion of two ten-minute rest periods	99,670	.21	433
5. Three days of sick leave per worker	27,600	.06	120
6. Additional vacation week after fifteen years	5,500	.01	24
Subtotal of proposed fringe improvements	\$320,090	\$ .67	\$1392
7. Wage increase (taken from method 1)	\$210,496	\$ .44	\$ 915
8. Roll-up (a) Cost of existing benefits as a result of wage gain	\$ 63,149	\$ .13	\$ 275
(b) Increase in proposed benefits as a result of new wage rate	28,206	.06	130
9. Cost of living estimates	60,877	.13	265
10. Pension and insurance cost charges		unknown	
11. **Grand Total**	\$682,818	\$1.43	\$2977

First-Year Cost Of Package

A number of hypothetical benefit changes have been presented, and—in order to determine the package costs—all negotiated items should be listed. The costs shown represent only one year of increased costs and if the contract is for a two- or three-year duration, this should be calculated. Similarly, not all benefits may become effective the same year and this would be taken into consideration in costing the package.

TABLE 9. COST CHART IN DOLLARS

Lump Sum Amounts for Periods Indicated

Cents Per Hour	3 Years 6240 Hours	2½ Years 5200 Hours	2 Years 4160 Hours	1½ Years 3120 Hours	1 Year 2080 Hours	½ Year 1040 Hours	1 Month 173.33 Hours	1 Week 40 Hours	1 Day 8 Hours
.005	$ 31.20	$ 26.00	$ 20.80	$ 15.60	$ 10.40	$ 5.20	$ .87	$ .20	$ .04
.01	62.40	52.00	41.60	31.20	20.80	10.40	1.73	.40	.08
.02	124.80	104.00	83.20	62.40	41.60	20.80	3.47	.80	.16
.03	187.20	156.00	124.80	93.60	62.40	31.20	5.20	1.20	.24
.04	249.60	203.00	166.30	124.80	83.20	41.60	6.93	1.60	.32
.05	312.00	260.00	208.00	156.00	104.00	52.00	8.67	2.00	.40
.06	374.40	312.00	249.60	187.20	124.80	62.40	10.40	2.40	.48
.07	436.80	364.00	291.20	218.40	145.60	72.80	12.13	2.80	.56
.08	499.20	416.00	332.80	249.60	166.40	83.20	13.87	3.20	.64
.09	561.60	468.00	374.40	280.80	187.20	93.60	15.60	3.60	.72
.10	624.00	520.00	416.00	312.00	208.80	104.00	17.33	4.00	.80
.11	685.40	572.00	457.60	343.20	228.80	114.40	19.07	4.40	.88
.12	748.80	624.00	499.20	374.40	249.60	124.80	20.80	4.80	.96
.13	811.20	676.00	540.80	405.60	270.40	135.20	22.53	5.20	1.04
.14	873.60	728.00	582.40	436.80	291.20	145.60	24.27	5.60	1.12
.15	936.00	780.00	624.00	468.00	312.00	156.00	26.00	6.00	1.20
.16	$ 998.40	$ 832.00	$ 665.60	$ 499.20	$ 332.80	$166.40	$27.73	$ 6.40	$1.28
.17	1060.80	834.00	707.20	530.40	353.60	176.80	29.47	6.80	1.36
.18	1123.20	936.00	748.80	561.60	374.40	187.20	31.20	7.20	1.44
.19	1185.60	988.00	790.40	592.80	395.20	197.60	32.93	7.60	1.52
.20	1248.00	1040.00	832.00	624.00	416.00	208.00	34.67	8.00	1.60
.21	1310.40	1092.00	873.60	655.20	436.80	218.40	36.40	8.40	1.68
.22	1372.80	1144.00	915.20	686.40	457.60	228.80	38.13	8.80	1.76
.23	1435.20	1196.00	956.80	717.60	478.40	239.20	39.87	9.20	1.84
.24	1497.60	1248.00	998.40	748.80	499.20	249.60	41.60	9.60	1.92
.25	1560.00	1300.00	1040.00	780.00	520.00	260.00	43.33	10.00	2.00
.26	1622.40	1352.00	1061.60	811.20	540.80	270.40	45.07	10.40	2.08
.27	1684.80	1404.00	1123.20	842.40	561.60	280.80	46.80	10.80	2.16
.28	1747.20	1456.00	1164.80	873.60	582.40	291.20	48.53	11.20	2.24
.29	1809.60	1508.00	1206.40	904.80	603.20	301.60	50.27	11.60	2.32
.30	1872.00	1560.00	1248.00	936.00	624.00	312.00	52.00	12.00	2.40
.31	$1934.40	$1612.00	$1289.60	$ 967.20	$644.80	$322.40	$53.73	$12.40	$2.48
.32	1996.80	1664.00	1331.20	988.40	665.60	332.80	55.47	12.80	2.56
.33	2059.20	1716.00	1372.80	1029.60	686.40	343.20	57.20	13.20	2.64
.34	2121.60	1768.00	1414.40	1060.80	707.20	353.60	58.93	13.60	2.72
.35	2184.00	1820.00	1456.00	1092.00	728.00	364.00	60.67	14.00	2.80
.36	2246.40	1872.00	1497.60	1123.20	748.80	374.40	62.40	14.40	2.88
.37	2308.80	1924.00	1539.20	1154.40	769.60	384.80	64.13	14.80	2.96
.38	2371.20	1976.00	1580.80	1185.60	790.40	395.20	65.87	15.20	3.04
.39	2433.60	2028.00	1622.40	1216.80	811.20	405.60	67.60	15.60	3.12
.40	2496.00	2080.00	1664.00	1248.00	832.00	416.00	69.33	16.00	3.20
.41	2558.40	2132.00	1705.60	1279.20	852.80	426.40	71.07	16.40	3.28
.42	2620.80	2184.00	1747.20	1310.40	873.60	436.80	72.80	16.80	3.36
.43	2683.20	2236.00	1788.80	1341.60	894.40	447.20	74.53	17.20	3.44
.44	2745.60	2288.00	1830.40	1372.80	915.20	457.60	76.27	17.60	3.52
.45	2808.00	2340.00	1872.00	1404.00	936.00	468.00	78.00	18.00	3.60
.46	$2870.00	$2392.00	$1913.60	$1435.20	$956.80	$478.40	$79.73	$18.40	$3.68
.47	2932.80	2444.00	1955.20	1466.40	977.60	488.80	81.47	18.80	3.76
.48	2995.20	2496.00	1996.80	1497.60	998.40	499.20	83.20	19.20	3.84
.49	3057.60	2548.00	2038.40	1528.80	1019.20	509.60	84.93	19.60	3.92
.50	3120.00	2600.00	2080.00	1560.00	1040.00	520.00	86.67	20.00	4.00

APPENDIX B
TO CHAPTER 8:
CALCULATING
COMPENSATION
COSTS*

Compensation consists of both salaries and/or wages and fringe benefits. It encompasses all forms of wage payments (including, for example, bonuses, commissions, and incentive payments) as well as the cost to the employer of all types of fringes.[1] Obviously, the higher-paid, senior employees in the bargaining unit tend to enjoy higher compensation, while the compensation of those at the opposite end of the salary and seniority spectrums tends to be lower.

For bargaining purposes, the most relevant statistic is the unit's average compensation or, more specifically, its *weighted* average compensation. The weighted average compensation (hereafter "average compensation" or, simply, "compensation") is merely an expression of how much it costs the employer, on the average, for each person on the payroll. It is this figure which presumably will be increased through negotiations.[2]

Although precision in computing these compensation costs depends very much on detailed data usually available only in the employer's payroll records, it is possible

---

*SOURCE: *The Use of Economic data in Collective Bargaining*, U.S. Department of Labor, Labor Management Services Administ., by Marvin Friedman et. al., Washington, D.C., 1978

[1]Technically, employee compensation may also include the cost of legally-required employer payments for programs such as social security, unemployment compensation, and worker's compensation. These items are disregarded in this analysis.

[2]It is also referred to as the "base" compensation—that is, the compensation figure against which the cost of any settlement will be measured in order to determine the value of the settlement.

to develop some reasonably accurate approximations even without such detailed information.

Indeed, the ability to do so may be quite important in making judgments as to whether a settlement proposal is or is not satisfactory. Moreover, an awareness of the concepts and techniques that are involved in these computations can prove invaluable in carrying on the bargaining dialogue or in dealing with a third-party neutral.

These computations, it must be remembered, are not performed simply to engage in a mathematical exercise. The reason for seeking out this type of information is its usefulness at the bargaining table.

The value of salaries and fringe benefits must be known so that the value of any bargaining offer or settlement can be judged. Logically, therefore, the base compensation costs as of the point in time of negotiations — or, more accurately, immediately prior to the receipt of any increase — must be known.

The information that is needed in most cases in order to compute compensation costs is (a) the salary scales and benefit programs, (b) the distribution of the employees in the unit according to pay steps, shifts, and length of service, and (c) for purposes of some medical care programs, the employees' coverage status. If this information is in hand, just about all but one item of compensation can be readily computed.

The sole exception is the cost of the overtime premium. Overtime is apt to vary widely from week-to-week or month-to-month. Consequently, the data for any one pay period are an inadequate gauge where overtime is concerned. Simply by chance, it may cost the employer more one week than the next. It is common practice, therefore, to cost-out the overtime premium by averaging the cost of that benefit over the prior 12 months.

So far as the other elements of compensation are concerned, however, it is not necessary to study a full year's experience. With salaries, vacations, holidays, etc., the costs can be based on a snapshot taken at a fixed point in time on the basis of the provisions in the current collective bargaining agreement and the current distribution of the employees in the bargaining unit. That snapshot of compensation costs should be made as of the time the parties are at the bargaining table.

The purpose of this section is to provide guidance on how to perform those computations, as well as the computations to determine the cost—the value—of an *increase* in compensation. The development of such compensation information gives the parties a basis for weighing the value of any particular wage and fringe benefit package.

Before the value or cost impact of any increase in compensation—whether in salaries, fringes or both—can be gauged, the first step is to develop the base, or existing, compensation figure. A pay increase of $500 per employee, for example, means something different for a bargaining unit whose existing salary and fringe benefit cost per employee amount to $20,000 per year than for a unit whose compensation is $10,000. In the latter case, it represents an increase of 5 percent, but on a base of $20,000 it amounts to only 2½ percent. Thus, the base compensation figure is essential in determining the percentage value of any increase in compensation.

In order to demonstrate the computation methods for arriving at the base compensation figure, a Sample Bargaining Unit has been constructed and certain levels of employment, salaries, fringe benefits, and hours of work have been assumed:

TABLE 1. SAMPLE BARGAINING UNIT

(a) Employment and Salaries

Classification	Number of Firefighters	Salary
Probationary		
Step 1	5	$10,100
Step 2	10	11,100
Private	65	12,100
Lieutenant	15	13,500
Captain	5	14,500
	100	

(b) Longevity Payments

Longevity Step	Number of Firefighters	Longevity Pay
Step 1	20 Privates	$ 500
Step 2	10 Privates	1,000
Step 2	15 Lieutenants	1,000
Step 2	5 Captains	1,000

(c) Hours of Work

The scheduled hours consist of one 24-hour shift every three days (one on; two off), or an average of 56 hours per week and a total of 2,912 hours per year.

(d) Overtime Premium

All overtime hours are paid at the rate of time-and-one-half. The sample bargaining unit is assumed to have worked a total of 5,000 overtime hours during the preceding year.

(e) Shift Differential

The shift differential is 10 percent for all hours between 4 p.m. and 8 a.m. However, 10 members of the unit work exclusively on the day shift, from 8 a.m. to 4 p.m.

(f) Vacations

15 employees—(probationers) 5 shifts
35 employees—(privates) 10 shifts
50 employees—(all others) 15 shifts

(g) Holidays

Each firefighter is entitled to 10 paid holidays, and receives 8 hours pay for each holiday.

(h) Clothing Allowance

$150 per employee per year.

(i) Hospitalization

Type of Coverage	Number of Firefighters	Employer's Monthly Payment
Single Coverage	15	$20.00
Family Coverage	85	47.00

(j) Pensions

The employer contributes an amount equal to six percent of the payroll (including basic salaries, longevity, overtime and shift differentials).

1. Computing Base Compensation

On the basis of the foregoing information on employment, salaries and benefits, we are now in a position to compute, for the Sample Bargaining Unit, its average base compensation—in essence, the cost of compensation for the average employee.

TABLE 2(a)

(a) Average Straight-time Salary

(1) Classification	(2) Number of fire-fighters	(3) Salary	(4) Weighted Salaries (2) × (3)
Probationary			
Step 1	5	$10,100	$ 50,500
Step 2	10	11,100	111,000
Private	65	12,100	786,500
Lieutenant	15	13,500	202,500
Captain	5	14,500	72,500
	100		$1,223,000

Average Annual Basic Salary =

$1,223,000 ÷ 100; or $12,230 per year

TABLE 2(b)

(b) Longevity Pay

(1) Longevity Step	(2) Number of Fire-fighters	(3) Longevity Pay	(4) Total Longevity Pay (2) × (3)
Step 1	20	$ 500	$10,000
Step 2	30	1,000	30,000
			$40,000

Average Annual Longevity Pay =

$40,000 ÷ 100;* or $400 per year

*Since the unit is trying to determine its average base compensation—that is, all the salary and fringe benefit items its members receive collectively—the total cost of longevity pay must be averaged over the entire unit of 100.

The combined average salary cost and average longevity cost amount to $12,630 per year. On an hourly basis, this comes to $4.337 ($12,630 ÷ 2,912 hours). This hourly rate is needed to compute the cost of some fringe benefits.

TABLE 2(c)

(c)   Average Cost of Overtime

Overtime work for the Sample Bargaining Unit is assumed to be paid for at the rate of time-and-one-half. This means that part of the total overtime costs is an amount paid for at straight-time rates and part is a premium payment.

	(1) Annual Cost	(2) Number of Firefighters	(3) Average Annual Cost (1) ÷ (2)
Straight-time cost ($4.337 × 5,000 overtime hours)	$21,685.00	100	$216.85
Half-time premium cost (½ × $21,685.00)	10,842.50	100	108.43
Total Overtime Cost	$32,527.50		$325.28

It can be seen from these overtime-cost calculations that the half-time premium is worth $108.43 per year on the average, while the straight-time portion is worth $216.85. This means, of course, that total pay at straight-time rates amounts to $12,846.85 ($12,630 plus $216.85) per firefighter.

TABLE 2(d)

(d)   Average Cost of Shift Differential

The Sample Bargaining Unit receives a shift differential of 10 percent for all hours worked between 4 p.m. and 8 a.m. But 10 members of the unit who work in headquarters are assumed to work hours that are not subject to the differential. This leaves 90 employees who receive the differential.

Since the differential is paid for hours worked between 4 p.m. and 8 a.m., it is applicable to only two-thirds of the normal 24-hour shift. It, therefore, only costs the employer two-thirds of 10 percent for each 24 hours. That is the reason for column (5) in the following calculation. Each employee receives the differential for only two-thirds of his or her 24-hour tour.

(1) Classification	(2) No. on Shift Pay	(3) Salary	(4) 10% of Col. (3)	(5) .667 of Col. (4)	(6) Total Cost (2) × (5)
Probationary					
Step 1	5	$10,100	$1,010	$ 674	$ 3,370
Step 2	10	11,100	1,110	740	7,400
Private					
Longevity-0	35	12,100	1,210	807	28,245
Longevity-1	17	12,600*	1,260	840	14,280
Longevity-2	7	13,100*	1,320	880	6,160
Lieutenant	12	14,500*	1,450	967	11,604
Captain	4	15,500*	1,550	1,034	4,136
	90				$75,195

Average Annual Cost of Shift Differential = $75,195 ÷ 100;** or $751.95 per year

Basic salary plus longevity pay.

**Since the unit is trying to determine its average base compensation—that is, all the salary and fringe benefit items its members receive collectively—the total cost of the shift differential must be averaged over the entire unit of 100.*

TABLE 2(e)

(e) Average Cost of Vacations

Vacation costs for the unit are influenced by (a) the amount of vacations received by the employees with differing lengths of service, and (b) the pay scales of those employees.

(1) Classification	(2) Number of Firefighters	(3) Hourly Rate*	(4) Hours of Vacation**	(5) Total Vacation Hours (2) × (4)	(6) Total Vacation Costs (3) × (5)
Probationary					
Step 1	5	$3.468	120	600	$ 2,080.80
Step 2	10	3.812	120	1,200	2,574.40
Private					
Longevity-0	35	4.155	240	8,400	34,902.00
Longevity-1	20	4.327	360	7,200	31,154.40
Longevity-2	10	4.499	360	3,600	16,196.40
Lieutenant	15	4.979	360	5,400	26,886.60
Captain	5	5.323	360	1,800	9,581.40
	100				$125,376.00

Average Annual Vacation Cost = $125,376 ÷ 100; or $1,253.76 per year

Derived from annual salaries (including longevity pay), divided by 2,912 hours (56 hours × 52 weeks). The 10 firefighters who do not receive shift differential would be on a regular 40-hour week and would, therefore, have a different hourly rate and vacation entitlement. The impact on cost, however, would be minimal. It has, therefore, been disregarded in this computation.
**Since each firefighter works a 24-hour shift, the hours of vacation are arrived at by multiplying the number of work shifts of vacation entitlement by 24 hours. For example, the figure of 120 hours is obtained by multiplying 5 shifts of vacation × 24 hours (one work shift).*

TABLE 2(f)

(f) Average Cost of Paid Holidays

Unlike vacations, the number of holidays received by an employee is not typically tied to length of service. Where the level of benefits is uniform, as it is with paid holidays, the calculation to determine its average cost is less complex.

In the Sample Bargaining Unit, it is assumed that each firefighter receives 8 hours of pay for each of his 10 paid holidays, or a total of 80 hours of holiday pay:

(1) Average Annual Cost of Paid Holidays = $346.96 (80 hours × $4.337 average straight-time hourly rate), or

(2) Total Annual Cost of Paid Holiday hours per year = 8,000 (80 hours × 100 employees)

Total annual cost of paid holidays = $34,696.00 (the unit's average straight-time hourly rate of $4.337 × 8,000 hours)

Average annual cost of paid holidays = $346.96 (34,696.00 ÷ 100 employees)

TABLE 2(g)

(g) Average Cost of Hospitalization				
(1)	(2)	(3) Yearly Premium Cost to Employer	(4) Total Cost to Employer (2) × (3)	
Type of Coverage	Number of Fire- fighters			
Single	15	$240	$ 3,600	
Family	85	564	47,940	
	100		$51,540	

Average Annual Cost of Hospitalization =
$51,540 ÷ 100; or $515.40 per year

(h)   Other Fringe Benefits

(1) Pensions cost the employer six percent of payroll. The payroll amounts to $1,370,723 (salary cost—$1,223,000; longevity cost—$40,000; overtime cost—$32,528; and shift differential cost—$75,195). Six percent of this total is $82,243 which, when divided by 100, yields $822.43 as the aveage cost of pensions per firefighter, per year.

(2) The yearly cost of the clothing allowance is $150 per firefighter.

As the recapitulation below indicates, total compensation—salary plus fringes—for each firefighter averages $16,795.78 per year.

Once having determined the base compensation costs, it is now possible to compute the value—or cost —of any increase in the items of compensation. The methods used to make these computations are essentially the same as those used to compute the base compensation data.

Before proceeding to that exercise, however, a general observation about the computation of base compensation should be made. Since the purpose is to produce an average *total* cost per employee—whether by the hour or by the year—it follows that the objective must be to capture and include in the computation, for each of item of compensation, the full amount of the employer's expense. This is why accurately maintained payroll records are desirable.

TABLE 3. AVERAGE ANNUAL BASE COMPENSATION FOR THE SAMPLE BARGAINING UNIT

(a)	Straight-time earnings		$12,846.85
	Basic salary	$12,230.00	
	Longevity pay	400.00	
	Overtime	216.85[*]	
(b)	Fringe benefits		$ 3,948.93
	Overtime premium	$ 108.43	
	Shift differential	751.95	
	Vacations	1,253.76	
	Holidays	346.96	
	Hospitalization	515.40	
	Clothing allowance	150.00	
	Pension	822.43	
(c)	Total		$16,795.78

[*]*This is only the straight-time portion of overtime pay.
The premium portion appears with the fringe benefits.*

Among other things, such records can help to resolve what might otherwise be protracted debates over approaches to the costing-out process on certain complicated benefit programs.

One such item that comes to mind is paid sick leave. Many paid sick leave programs permit the employee to accumulate unused sick leave. Suppose, for example, the employees are allowed five paid sick leave days each year, with the opportunity to "bank" the unused days and, upon separation or retirement, to receive pay for one-half of the days in the "bank."

With such a program, it is likely that not all of the employees in the unit would use all five days each year. It would be incorrect, however, to cost out sick leave on the basis of the days actually taken each year since, at some subsequent point, there would be partial reimbursement for the unused days. Further complicating matters is the fact that the employee's rate of pay at the time the reimbursement takes place will very likely be higher than it is when the unused days are put in the "bank." Obviously, there is no way of knowing what that future rate of pay will be, so there is no way to determine now how much those "banked" days will be worth at the time of reimbursement.

One way to cost out the unit's paid sick leave in any year may be simply to charge everyone with five days. Needless to say, this may misstate the true cost and may generate controversy and debate.

Such disputes may be avoided if the actual total dollar cost of the sick leave program for the year can be derived. To do this, however, it would be necessary to have the dollar costs for each piece—that is, in our example, the cost of the days used in the year plus the cost of the reimbursements made in the year—in order to produce a total annual cost. That total, divided by the number of employees in the unit or by the number of hours worked by the unit during the year, would then yield the cost per employee or per hour for this particular benefit.

In a case such as the sick leave program cited above, the availability of dollar amounts reflecting total annual costs would, as mentioned earlier, help to forestall controversy over the procedure to be used for costing out the benefit. And this approach would be consistent with the basic concept that is involved in costing out the other elements of employee compensation. That approach, as was also mentioned earlier, seeks to capture and include in the computation the full amount of the employer's expense for each item of compensation.

2. Computing the Cost of Increases in Items of Compensation

In order to demonstrate how to cost-out any increases in compensation, it will be assumed that the Sample Bargaining Unit negotiates a settlement consisting of the following package:

　　—An increase of 5 percent in basic salaries;

　　—Two additional shifts of vacation for all those at the second step of longevity;

　　—An improvement in the benefits provided by the hospitalization program, which will cost the employer an additional $4.00 per month for family coverage and $2.50 for single coverage.

The cost of this settlement—that is, the amount of the increase in compensation that it represents—would be computed in the manner presented below, starting first with the cost-impact of the salary increase. As will be noted, the objective of the computation is to find the *average* cost of the increase—that is, the cost per firefighter, per year.

(a) Increase in Cost of Salaries. The increase in average annual basic salary (0.05 × $12,230) is $611.50. The cost of longevity pay does not increase. This is because longevity increments for the unit are fixed dollar amounts. If these payments were based on a percentage of salary—that is, if they were linked to the pay scales—then the cost of the longevity payments would also have risen by 5 percent. However, as a fixed dollar amount, these payments remain unaffected by the increase in basic salaries.

As a result, the increase in the unit's total average salary ($12,230 in basic salary plus $400 in longevity) is, in reality, not 5 percent, but only 4.8 percent ($611.50 ÷ $12,630).

This difference is important because of the way in which pay increases impact on the cost of fringe benefits. This is commonly referred to as the "roll up". As salaries increase, so does the cost to the employer of such fringes as vacations, holidays, overtime premiums, etc. This increase in cost comes about even though the benefits are not improved.

Some fringes, however, are not subject to the roll up. This is the case with respect to those fringe benefits that are not linked to pay rates. Examples of this type of fringe benefit include shift differentials that are stated in cents-per-hour (in contrast to a percentage of salary), a flat dollar amount for clothing allowance, and most group insurance programs.

(b) Cost Impact of the "Roll up". The increase in average straight-time pay (basic salary plus longevity pay) of the Sample Bargaining Unit was shown to be 4.8 percent. This means that the average cost of every benefit linked to salary will likewise increase by 4.8 percent. In our example, therefore, the average cost of compensation will go up by $611.50 per year in salaries, *plus* however much this adds to the costs of the fringe benefits as a result of the roll up.

But there is more. For our example, it is also to be assumed that the Sample Bargaining Unit will gain a vacation improvement—two additional shifts at the second step of longevity—and an improved hospitalization program.

The employer's contribution for the hospitalization program of the Sample Bargaining Unit is a fixed dollar amount and is, therefore, not subject to any roll up. Thus, we need in this instance be concerned only with the costing-out of the improvement in that benefit.

This is not the case with the vacations. Here the cost-increase is double-barreled—the cost of the improvement *and* the cost of the roll up.

None of the other fringe benefits of the Sample Bargaining Unit will be improved. Consequently, so far as they are concerned, we need only compute the increases in cost due to the roll up. The fringes which fit this category are overtime premiums, holidays, sick leave, shift differentials, and pensions.

TABLE 4

(1) Fringe Benefit	(2) Base Average Annual Cost	(3) Roll up Factor	(4) Increased Cost (2) × (3)
Overtime			
Straight-time	$216.85	0.048	$ 10.41
Premium	108.43	0.048	5.20
Shift differential	751.95	0.048	36.09
Holidays	346.96	0.048	16.65
Pensions	822.43	0.048	39.48
			$107.83

As is indicated in Table 4, column (3)—the added cost due to the roll up—is obtained by multiplying the base (pre-settlement) cost by 0.048. Obviously, if shift differentials and/or pensions were based on a set dollar (or cents) amount (instead of a percentage of salary), there would be no roll up cost associated with them. The only increase in cost that would result in such a situation would be associated with an improvement in the benefit item.

Having performed this computation, we can now begin to see the impact of the roll up factor. As a result of the increase in pay, the four fringe benefit items will together cost the employer an additional $107.83 per firefighter, per year.

(c) Increase in Cost of Vacations. As noted earlier, the vacation improvement of two shifts—48 hours (2 shifts × 24 hours)—is to be limited to those whose length of service is equal to the time required to achieve the second step of longevity in the salary structure. Thus, it will be received by 30 members of the unit—10 privates, 15 lieutenants, and 5 captains.[3]

The first step in the computation is to determine the cost of the *new* benefit under the *existing* (old) salaries—that is, before the 4.8 percent pay increase:

---

[3]In costing out an improvement in vacations, the computation should cover the cost impact in the first year *only*. There is no need to be concerned with the impact in subsequent years when, supposedly, more and more employees become eligible for the improved benefit. For computational purposes, it must be assumed that the average length of service in the unit remains constant. This constancy is caused by normal personnel flows. As the more senior staff leave because of retirement or death, the staff is replenished by new hires without any accumulated seniority. Thus, for this type of computation, it must be presumed that the proportion of the workforce which benefits from the improved vacation will be constant year after year.

It should be noted that an improvement in vacations (or any other form of paid leave) that is offset by corresponding reductions in on-duty manning does not represent any increase in cost to the employer.

TABLE 5

(1) Number of Firefighters	(2) Hours of Increased Vacation	(3) Total Hours (1) × (2)	(4) Existing Hourly Rates	(5) Cost of Improvement (3) × (4)
10 Privates	48	480	$4.499	$2,159.52
15 Lieutenants	48	720	4.979	3,584.88
5 Captains	48	240	5.323	1,277.52
				$7,021.92

The calculation thus far reflects only the additional cost of the vacation improvement based on the salaries existing *prior* to the 4.8 percent pay raise. In other words, if there had been no pay increase, the vacation improvement would result in an added cost of $7,021.92. But there was a pay increase. As a result, the base year vacation costs—including now the added cost of the improvement—must be rolled up by the 4.8 percent factor. Every hour of vacation—the old and the new—will cost 4.8 percent more as a result of the pay increase:

TABLE 6

(1) Classification	(2) Existing Vacation Costs	(3) Increase in Cost*	(4) Adjusted Base Costs (2) + (3)	5) Roll up Factor	(6) Increased Cost from Roll up (4) × (5)
Probationary					
Step 1	$ 2,080.80	—	$ 2,080.80	0.048	$ 99.88
Step 2	4,574.40	—	4,574.40	0.048	219.57
Private					
Longevity-0	34,902.00	—	34,902.00	0.048	1,675.30
Longevity-1	31.154.40	—	31,154.40	0.048	1,495.41
Longevity-2	16.196.40	$2,159.52	18,355.92	0.048	881.08
Lieutenant	26,886.60	3,584.88	30,471.48	0.048	1,462.63
Captain	9,581.40	1,277.52	10,858.92	0.048	521.23
	$125,376.00	$7,021.92	$132,397.92	0.048	$6,355.10

*From data in preceding table.

By adding the two "new" pieces of cost—$7,021.92, which is the cost of the improvement, and $6,355.10, which is the cost due to the impact of the wage increase—we obtain the total increase in the cost of vacations. It amounts to $13,377.02. In order to figure the *average* cost, this total must be divided by the number of firefighters in the Sample Bargaining Unit. The increase in the average cost of vacations, therefore, is—

$$\$13,377 \div 100, \text{ or } \$133.\overset{.}{7}7$$

Had the vacation improvement been granted across-the-board, to everyone in the unit, the calculation would have been different—and considerably easier. If the entire unit were to receive an additional 48 hours of vacation, the total additional hours would then be 4,800 (48 hours x 100 employees). These hours would then be multiplied by the unit's old average straight-time rate ($4.337), in order to arrive at the cost of the additional vacation improvement which, in this case, would have come to $20,817.60 (4,800 hours x $4.337). And, in that case, the total cost of vacations— that is, the across-the-board improvement, plus the impact of the 4.8 percent salary increase— would have been computed as follows:

TABLE 7

(a) Roll up of old vacation costs ($125,376 × 0.048)	= $ 6,018.05
(b) Cost of vacation improvement	= $20,817.60
(c) Roll up cost of improvement ($20,817.60 × 0.048)	= $ 999.24

These pieces total to $27,834.89. When spread over the entire Sample Bargaining Unit, the increase in the average cost of vacations would have been $278.35 per year ($27,834.89 ÷ 100 employees).

This latter method of calculation does not apply only to vacations. It applies to any situation where a salary-related fringe benefit is to be improved equally for every member of the unit. An additional paid holiday would be another good example.

(d) Increase in Cost of Hospitalization.   In this example, it has been assumed that the Sample Bargaining Unit has negotiated as part of its new package an improvement in its hospitalization plan. As with most hospitalization programs, the one covering this unit is not linked to salaries.

This improvement, it is assumed, will cost the employer an additional $4.00 per month ($48 per year) for family coverage, and $2.50 per month ($30 per year) for single coverage. Thus, based on this and previous information about the breakdown of employees receiving each type of coverage, the calculation of the increase in hospitalization costs is as follows:

TABLE 8

(1) Type of Coverage	(2) Number Covered	(3) Annual Cost of Improvement	(4) Total New Cost (2) × (3)
Single	15	$30	$ 450
Family	85	48	4,080
			$4,530

The unit's average hospitalization cost will be increased by $45.30 per year ($4,530 ÷ 100 employees).

3. The Total Increase in the Average Cost of Compensation

At this point, the increase in the costs of all the items of compensation which will change because of the Sample Bargaining Unit's newly-negotiated package have been calculated. All that is left is to combine these individual pieces in order to arrive at the total increase in the unit's average cost of compensation. This is done in the tabulation which appears below.

As the recapitulation shows, the average increase in salary costs amounts to $621.91 per year, while the average increase in the cost of the fringe benefits (including *new* benefit costs, as well as *roll up* costs) comes to $276.49, for a total increase in average annual compensation of $898.40 per firefighter, per *year*. That is the total annual cost of the settlement per firefighter.

TABLE 9. INCREASE IN AVERAGE ANNUAL COST OF COMPENSATION FOR SAMPLE BARGAINING UNIT

(a)	Straight-time earnings		$621.91
	Basic salary	$611.50	
	Longevity pay	—	
	Overtime (straight-time portion)	10.41	
(b)	Fringe benefits		$276.49
	Overtime premium	$ 5.20	
	Shift differential	36.09	
	Vacations	133.77	
	Holidays	16.65	
	Hospitalization	45.30	
	Clothing allowance	—	
	Pensions	39.48	
(c)	Total Increase in Average Annual Cost of Annual Compensation		$898.40

There remains one final computation that is really the most significant— the *percent* increase that all of these figures represent. The unit's average base compensation per year was $16,796. The total dollar increase amounts to $898. The percent increase, therefore, is 5.3 percent ($898 ÷ $16,796), and that is the amount by which the unit's package increased the employer's average yearly cost per firefighter.

4. Computing the Hourly Cost of Compensation

The increase in the cost of compensation per *hour* will be the same. The approach to the computation, however, is different than that which was used in connection with the cost per year. In the case of the hourly computation, the goal is to obtain the cost per hour of *work*. This requires that a distinction be drawn between hours worked and hours paid for. The difference between the two is leave time.

In the Sample Bargaining Unit, for example, the employee receives an annual salary which covers 2,912 regularly scheduled hours (56 hours per week, times 52). In addition, he works an average of 50 hours of overtime per year. The sum of these two—regularly scheduled hours and overtime hours, or 2,962—are the total hours paid for.

But they do not represent hours worked, because some of those hours are paid leave time. The Sample Bargaining Unit, for example, receives paid leave time in the form of vacations and holidays. The number of hours actually worked by each employee is 2,600 (2,962 hours paid for, minus 362 hours[4] of paid leave).

The paid leave hours are, in a sense, bonuses—hours paid for, above and beyond hours worked. Thus, in order to obtain the hourly cost represented by these "bonuses" —that is, the hours of paid leave—the annual dollar cost of these benefits is divided by the annual hours *worked*.

It is the same as if we were trying to compute the per-hour cost of a year-end bonus. The dollar amount of that bonus would simply be divided by the total number of hours worked during the year.

So it is with *all* fringe benefits, not only paid leave. In exchange for those benefits the employer receives hours of work (the straight-time hours and the overtime hours). Consequently, the hourly cost of any fringe benefit will be obtained by dividing the annual cost of the benefit by the annual number of hours *worked*. In some instances that cost is converted into money that ends up in the employee's pocket, as it does in the case of fringe benefits like shift differentials, overtime premiums and clothing allowances. In other instances—such as hospitalization and pensions—the employee is provided with benefits in the form of insurance programs. And in the case of paid leave time—holidays,[5] vacations, sick leave, etc.—the return to the employee is in terms of fewer hours of work.

The average annual costs of the fringe benefits of the Sample Bargaining Unit were developed earlier in this chapter in connection with the computations of the unit's average annual base compensation. They appear in column (2) of Table 10.

---

[4]Each firefighter receives 80 hours in paid holidays per year. The average number of hours of vacation per year was derived as follows:

15 firefighters × 120 hours (five 24-hour shifts)	= 1,800 hours
35 firefighters × 240 hours (ten 24-hour shifts)	= 8,400 hours
50 firefighters × 360 hours (fifteen 24-hour shifts)	= 18,000 hours
	28,200 hours

This averages out to 282 hours of vacation per firefighter (28,200 ÷ 100) which, together with 80 holiday hours, totals 362 paid leave hours).

[5]Typically, of course, firefighters do not receive time off, but are paid an extra day's pay for working a holiday.

In order to convert the costs of those fringe benefits into an average hourly amount, they are divided by 2,600—the average hours worked during the year by each employee in the unit. As can be seen, the hourly cost of all fringe benefits amounts to $1.518.

TABLE 10

(1) Fringe Benefit	(2) Average Annual Cost	(3) Average Hours Worked	(4) Average Hourly Cost (2) ÷ (3)
Overtime Premium*	$ 108.43	2,600	$0.042
Shift Differential	751.95	2,600	0.289
Vacations	1,253.76	2,600	0.482
Holidays	346.96	2,600	0.133
Hospitalization	515.40	2,600	0.198
Clothing Allowance	150.00	2,600	0.058
Pensions	822.43	2,600	0.316
	$3,948.93		$1.518

Includes only the premium portion of the pay for overtime work.

In addition to the fringe benefit costs, compensation includes the basic pay. For our Sample Bargaining Unit this is $12,630 per year (average salary plus average cost of longevity payments). On a straight-time hourly basis, this comes to $4.337 ($12,630 ÷ 2,912 hours). Even with the straight-time portion for the year's overtime included ($216.85), the average straight-time hourly rate of pay will, of course, still remain at $4.337 ($12,846.45 ÷ 2,962 hours).

A recapitulation of these salary and fringe benefit cost data produces both the average *annual* base compensation figure for the Sample Bargaining Unit and the average *hourly* figure:

TABLE 11

	Hourly	Yearly
Earnings at Straight-time	$12,846.85 ÷ 2,962 =	$4.337
Fringe Benefits	3,948.93 ÷ 2,600 =	$1.519
Total Compensation	$16,795.78	$5.856

As indicated, on an annual basis, the average compensation cost comes to $16,795.78, a figure that was also presented earlier in this chapter. And on an hourly basis, the average compensation of the unit amounts to $5.856.

Essentially the same process is followed if the *increase* in compensation is to be measured on an hourly (instead of an annual) basis.

The five percent pay increase received by the Sample Bargaining Unit would be worth 21 cents ($12,230 × 0.05 = $611.50; $611.50 ÷ 2,912 = $0.21). The annual increase in the unit's fringe benefit costs per firefighter— $276.49 for all items combined—works out to 10.6 cents per hour ($276.49 ÷ 2600 hours).

Together, these represent a gain in average compensation of 31.6 cents per hour, or 5.4 percent ($0.316 ÷ $5.856). This is one-tenth of a percentage point off from the amount of increase (5.3 percent) reflected by the annual data—a difference due simply to the rounding of decimals during the computation process.

BARGAINING SIMULATION: COLLECTIVE BARGAINING IN PRIVATE INDUSTRY*

CONTENTS

SUPPLEMENTARY APPENDICES

*The earlier version of this simulation was developed by E. Edward Herman and Douglas M. Yeager.

INTRODUCTION

This simulation permits you to "go to the bargaining table" in a key contract negotiation between a large company and the union representing a segment of its production employees. Every effort has been made to simulate an actual bargaining situation. However, the Company and Union presented here are fictitious.

The simulation starts in the midst of negotiations. A number of items have been tentatively agreed to and the parties now confine their negotiations to the remaining open issues:

Wages
Cost-of-living adjustment
Holidays
Vacations
Union security
Management rights
Contracting out
Severance pay
Medical insurance

As you and your colleagues face off on the above issues, you will set strategy, develop demands or offers, conduct negotiations, and, it is to be hoped, conclude those negotiations. You will assume the role of a particular participant and feel some of his or her pressures and frustrations—some across the table and some in the caucus room. The purpose of this simulation is to acquaint you with tactics, strategies, procedures, attitudes, ideas, pressures, and issues emerging in the bargaining process. You will learn to work with other participants as a bargaining team. You will acquire negotiation experience under "real world" constraints in terms of budget, time pressures, actual agreement provisions, and current labor statistics from the Bureau of Labor Statistics.

The Company bargaining committee will consist of the Industrial Relations Manager, the Plant Manager, and the Plant Controller. The Union's committee will include the International Representative, the President of the Local, and the Local's Benefits Specialist.

Your group is expected to negotiate and reach a settlement. To attain this objective you must study your goals and that of the opposition. You should anticipate demands and offers that will be made by your opponents and you should be prepared to respond to these. Develop tactics and strategy that will help you attain your objectives.

One of the objectives of this simulation is for the Union team to reach a better settlement than any other union group participating in this simulation. The objective for the management team is to reach a better agreement than that by any other company team.

Team scoring in this simulation will reflect how well you achieve the objectives given your bargaining committee by Union or Company officials. Post-game self-evaluation is also included to measure how effectively you carried out your particular role assignment and what you learned about the process of negotiations during the course of simulation.

SIMULATION INSTRUCTIONS

1. Consultation or fraternization with the opposition or with other teams is prohibited during the course of the simulation.
2. If the parties do not reach an agreement at the contract deadline set by the instructor, a strike will take place. The contract deadline cannot be extended by mutual agreement of the parties.
3. Negotiators are not permitted to attend negotiations of other teams.
4. Although all team members will participate in negotiations of all issues, each team will also select a spokesperson who will be responsible for particular subjects. Each team member will be given an opportunity to represent the team in bargaining over specific topics.
5. In order to reach an agreement and provide a realistic negotiation environment, each team can compromise positions, trade issues, drop demands, and offer counterproposals.
6. During the first negotiation session, each labor-management group will reach agreement on the following procedural issues:
    a. Duration of negotiation session and of each caucus; both of these issues can be renegotiated later by the parties.
    b. Agenda sequence of the first session and how agenda sequence will be determined in future sessions.
    c. Status of each issue on which agreement has been reached. (Can issues agreed upon be renegotiated before the final contract is reached?)
7. You may caucus as often as necessary
8. You should notify opposition who is going to be the spokesperson for your team.
9. You may use pocket calculators may be helpful in costing out the contract.
10. Review the suggested sequence for this simulation.
11. Forms IV−VIII are to be utilized as a guide in costing out your negotiation positions on wages, cost-of-living, and fringe benefits.
12. To determine the current wage at EDP, consult the latest available issue of *Employment and Earnings.**
13. For sources of library material consult this text's bibliography.
14. At conclusion of bargaining give Forms II−X and Appendices B−E and the content of your bargaining file to your instructor. The file should include all your notes, statistical data, agreed-upon and proposed contract language, evaluation forms, your library research, and other relevant data, including notes of phone inquiries.

---

*A monthly periodical featuring detailed employment, hours, earnings, and labor turnover by industry, area, occupation, and so on. U.S. Department of Labor, Bureau of Labor Statistics.

PERFORMANCE EVALUATION

Your team and individual performance in this simulation will be evaluated according to the following criteria:

Team Performance

1. Team's compliance with confidential guidelines.
2. The evaluation of your team by your opposition.
3. Your team's bargaining preparations.
4. Your team's bargaining performance as well as team's application of various tactics and strategies during negotiations as observed by your instructor.
5. The content of your bargaining file submitted to your instructor at the end of the simulation, as per item 14 of your instructions.
6. The achievement of projected contract terms as stated by your team on Form I. Before your team starts to negotiate this form is to be submitted to your instructor; this is to take place immediately after the conclusion of the first caucus.
7. The final results achieved by your team on contract language changes.
8. The final results achieved by your team on cost of wages and fringe benefits.

Individual Performance

1. The confidential evaluation by each of your teammates of your individual contribution and performance.
2. The confidential evaluation by each of your opponents of your individual contribution and performance.
3. Your individual bargaining preparation.
4. Your contribution to the team's bargaining file submitted to your instructor at the end of the simulation.
5. Your individual performance in negotiations as observed by your instructor.

SUGGESTED SEQUENCE

	Instructor	Participant	Suggested Time Increments
Read Players Manual	X	X	Outside preparation
Assign roles	X		Thirty minutes
Review instructions and suggested sequence	X		
Announce year in which negotiations take place	X		

Continuation—Suggested Sequence

	Instructor	Participant	Suggested Time Increments
Read Players Manual	X	X	Outside preparation
Conduct library research, consult sources listed in section entitled "Bureau of Labor Statistics Data"	X	X	Outside preparation
Distribute company and union packets to the respective teams	X		
Hold separate caucuses to establish initial demands or offers and team strategy		X	Decide jointly with your opponents, length of the first caucus
Submit Form I to instructor		X	
Commence bargaining: 1. Establish procedure 2. Present positions 3. Caucus to analyze opponents' demands or offers 4. Caucus as necessary 5. Establish strike deadline		X	Length of simulation is approximately three to nine hours (depending upon strike deadline established by the instructor)

BACKGROUND OF THE COMPANY

EDP, Inc. manufactures, markets, and services a line of business equipment. Founded in 1920 by a mechanical engineer, Robert Jefferson, the Company now employs about 6000 people throughout the United States. Of these, slightly over 1000 are in the bargaining unit at the Company's largest and oldest plant located in the Midwest. The midwest plant in which the bargaining is taking place manufactures some essential components for other plants of the company. These components, however, can be purchased, with some delays, from outside suppliers. This plant also produces business equipment sold to retail outlets. Because of limited capacity, even during periods of slow business activity, this plant has usually operated on two shifts.

Although the Company has experienced steady growth since its founding, the mix of employees has undergone a significant change in recent years. The production force is no longer such a dominant part of the overall operation. This change occurred as the Company moved from its traditional line of mechanical products into the era of electronics. Direct labor content in the product dropped significantly as manufacturing became increasingly an assembly operation of components and subassemblies purchased from other companies. Low-skill assembly jobs replaced the high-skill jobs of earlier years such as toolmaking, machining, modelmaking, and so on. As the proportion of factory employees fell, dramatic expansion occurred in the number of professional employees, especially in the area of programming and systems development. None of these professionals have chosen to align themselves with a union.

The conversion from mechanical to electronic products has also brought a new and intense level of competition to the market EDP, Inc. serves. Whereas the Company formerly enjoyed a virtual monopoly and the comfortable profit margins of that position, today's situation is quite different. Many electronic companies have emerged as major competitors, margins are small, product cycles are short, and EDP is competing hard to stay in many of the markets it once tended to dominate.

The competitive situation and the change in production skills required have impacted significantly on the relative position of EDP's factory employees against the community. In earlier years, wage rates were as good as or better than any in the area, regardless of industry. Today, they are competitive with the electrical industry generally and well below the leaders in high-paying industries. EDP's average rate is also lower in the community because of the large number of low-skill assembly jobs which have replaced the high-skill jobs formerly characterizing its operation.

BACKGROUND OF THE UNION

The Union has represented the production and maintenance (P&M) employees at EDP's midwestern plant for over twenty-five years. Labor relations during this period can be described as generally cooperative, as evidenced by more than two decades of strike-free settlements and by wage and fringe packages which for years matched or led the community.

Since the conversion to electronics, however, EDP's wages and fringe benefits have begun to fall behind certain other employers in the community, and the last negotiations resulted in the first strike by the Union since it was certified at EDP a quarter of a century before.

During the last ten years, the Union has faced representation challenges from two larger international unions. Three NLRB-conducted elections have resulted in victories for the incumbent Union, but with each succeeding election, the Union's winning margin has narrowed. This year a bare majority kept the Union in power, and the significance of this vote was not lost upon the officers as they prepared to enter into contract negotiations with the Company. Out of the 1000 employees in the bargaining unit, 550 are union members.

The problem facing the Union is one of obtaining a sufficiently impressive settlement to counteract the dissidents but to do so without further eroding EDP's competitive position in the business equipment industry. The Union officers are, by and large, a responsible group and are anxious to avoid a strike if at all possible. They are convinced, however, that the threat of a strike is very real. In fact, they have a fairly precise cents-per-hour figure in mind as to what it will take to secure ratification and prevent a strike. Although they want the Company to succeed in the marketplace just as the management wants it to succeed, the Union officers must be properly sensitive to the demands of the membership and extract the kind of improvements which will insure ratification.

Prior to the start of contract negotiations, the Union officers worked closely with the membership on initial demands to be submitted to the Company. They promised a program of regular and detailed progress reports on the bargaining via the Union newspaper and bulletin board announcements. They privately worried, however, as to how they could release enough information to neutralize the dissidents without releasing "too much" and thereby reducing their flexibility at the bargaining table.

FINANCIAL INFORMATION

As a publicly held corporation, EDP, Inc. is required by law to disclose financial information. The primary device utilized for this purpose is the Company's annual report. Copies go to each shareholder, the media, employees, investment firms, business libraries, financial institutions, and individuals and organizations requesting copies.

Veteran analysts are little influenced by the glossy paper, the four-color printing, and the slick photography. They turn immediately to the data on earnings and financial position. The key tables are the Income Statement and the Balance Sheet. Each is reproduced here. Also included are a highlights table and a ten-year review of operating revenue, and net income.

The Income Statement shows what happened over the twelve-month period, while the Balance Sheet is a snapshot, so to speak, of the Company's financial condition at year end. Both must be analyzed to determine the Company's financial position.

Special attention should be given to net income. This is, after all, what business is all about. It is not enough, however, just to look at the dollar figure or the "bottom line," as it is often called. One must also consider what the profit is as a percent of sales.

Performance indicators for other companies in EDP's industry and related industries can be obtained from the *Fortune* 500 listings for the appropriate year. Major competitive companies include Burroughs, Control Data, Honeywell Information Systems, IBM, NCR, and Sperry Univac.

Depending upon the depth of analysis desired, various ratios can be developed from financial statement data. Dun & Bradstreet, for example, publishes annually more than a dozen different ratios on more than seventy manufacturing industry groups.*

TABLE I. EDP, INC.

Highlights of Last Year's Operations

Operating Revenue	$171,026,385
Net Income	6,322,259 (see Table II)
Expenditures for Property	
Plant, and Equipment	24,272,937
Depreciation	14,122,742
Taxes	11,304,745
Cash Dividend	1,908,856
Net Income per Share	$3.96
Dividends per Share	$1.20

---

*"The Ratios of Manufacturing," *Dun's Review*, November issue each year.

TABLE I. *(Continued)*

Year-End Data	
Total Assets	$180,815,862 (see Table III)
Working Capital	64,286,855
Long-Term Debt	47,987,280
Stockholders' Equity	34,137,308
Common Shares Outstanding	1,596,614
Number of Stockholders	4,665

TABLE II.   EDP, INC.
         LAST YEAR'S INCOME STATEMENT

Income	
Income from Sales, Services & Rentals	$171,026,385
Other income	3,395,885
	174,422,270

Costs and Expenses	
Manufacturing	79,553,505
Selling, general & administrative	58,408,598
Research & Development	6,005,647
Depreciation	14,122,676
Interest	3,371,505
Minority Interest	462,580
Taxes	6,175,500
	168,100,011
Net Income for the Year	$6,322,259

TABLE III.   EDP, INC.
         LAST YEAR'S BALANCE SHEET

Assets	
Current Assets	
Cash	$4,699,381
Marketable Securities	8,532,762
Receivables	45,307,927
Inventories	59,926,404
Prepaid Expenses	1,967,651
	120,434,125
Property, Plant & Equipment	59,208,323
Other Assets	1,173,414
Total Assets	$180,815,862

(continued)

TABLE III. *(Continued)*

Liabilities & Stockholders' Equity	
Current Liabilities	
Notes Payable	$15,356,112
Payables & Accruals	20,142,670
Accrued Taxes	7,103,006
Current Installments on Long-Term Debt	392,391
Dividends Payable	478,654
Customer Deposits & Service Prepayments	12,674,437
	56,147,270
Long-Term Debt	47,987,280
Lease Purchase Obligation	322,200
International Employees' Pension & Indemnity Reserves	2,996,918
International Operations Reserve	1,374,363
Minority Interests	1,896,925
Stockholders' Equity	34,137,308
Earnings Retained for Use in the Business	35,953,598
	$180,815,862

TABLE IV. EDP, INC.
      TEN-YEAR REVIEW

Year	Operating Revenue	Net Income
Last Year	$171,026,385	$6,322,259
2 Years Ago	155,963,595	5,774,898
3 Years Ago	131,895,971	5,266,359
4 Years Ago	119,173,367	4,683,714
5 Years Ago	106,071,820	4,012,643
6 Years Ago	100,959,759	4,169,447
7 Years Ago	92,880,236	5,387,542
8 Years Ago	81,950,138	4,270,403
9 Years Ago	75,012,456	3,938,716
10 Years Ago	70,480,534	2,968,536

BUREAU OF LABOR STATISTICS
AND THE BUREAU OF NATIONAL AFFAIRS DATA

Each negotiating team should familiarize itself with recent economic developments and the latest results of major negotiations. The simulation participants should consult the most recent issues of the following publications:

Employment and Earnings.   A monthly periodical featuring detailed employment, hours, earnings, and labor turnover by industry, area, occupation, and so on. U.S. Department of Labor, Bureau of Labor Statistics (BLS).

CPI Detailed Report.   A monthly periodical featuring detailed data and charts on the consumer price index. U.S. Department of Labor, BLS.

Monthly Labor Review (MLR).   One section of the *MLR* provides current principal statistical labor series data collected and calculated by the BLS. The tables present information on hours and earnings by industry, consumer price indexes, productivity, and labor-management data. U.S. Department of Labor, BLS.

Press Releases.   The BLS statistical series are made available to the news media through press releases. Many of these releases are also available to the public upon request. Press releases regarding latest "Major Collective Bargaining Settlements" can be very useful for this simulation. U.S. Department of Labor, BLS.

Area Wage Surveys.   These are cross-industry studies conducted annually by the BLS. Each survey covers a standard metropolitan statistical area. U.S. Department of Labor, BLS.

Basic Patterns in Union Contracts.   Consult the latest edition of Collective Bargaining Negotiations and Contracts, Bureau of National Affairs.

Handbook of Labor Statistics.   This publication provides in one volume the major series available from the BLS. U.S. Department of Labor, BLS.

Current Wage Developments.   A monthly report on employee compensation, including wage and benefit changes resulting from collective bargaining settlements and unilateral management decisions; statistical summaries; and special reports on wage trends. U.S. Department of Labor, BLS.

Major Collective Bargaining Agreements, the 1425 series.   This series of studies prepared by the U.S. Department of Labor, BLS, is designed to survey in depth the entire scope of collective bargaining agreement provisions. The following list provides titles of bulletins in the 1425 series:

Bulletin number	Title

Major Collective Bargaining Agreements:

1425-1	Grievance procedures
1425-2	Severance pay and layoff benefit plans
1425-3	Supplemental unemployment benefit plans and wage-employment guarantees
1425-4	Deferred wage increase and escalator clauses
1425-5	Management rights and union management cooperation
1425-6	Arbitration procedures
1425-7	Training and retraining provisions
1425-8	Subcontracting
1425-9	Paid vacation and holiday provisions
1425-10	Plant movement, transfer, and relocation allowances
1425-11	Seniority in promotion and transfer provisions
1425-12	Administration of negotiated pension, health, and insurance plans
1425-13	Layoff, recall, and worksharing procedures
1425-14	Administration of seniority
1425-15	Hours, overtime, and weekend work
1426-16	Safety and health provisions
1425-17	Wage administration provisions
1425-18	Wage-incentive, production-standard, and time-study provisions
1425-19	Employer pay and leave for union business
1426-20	Plant movement, interplant transfer, and relocation allowances
1426-21	Union security and dues checkoff

EDP, INC., PRESENT CONTRACT ARTICLES
AND TERMS

Union Security

Membership in the Union is not compulsory. Employees have the right to join or not join, maintain or drop their membership in the Union as they see fit. Neither party shall exert any pressure on or discriminate against any employee as regards such matters. The union is the exclusive bargaining agent and representative of all employees, both union and non-union, in the bargaining unit.

However, all employees covered by this agreement shall, as a condition of employment, pay to the Union, the employees' exclusive bargaining agent and representative, an amount of money equal to that paid by other employees in the bargaining unit who are members of the Union, which shall be limited to an amount of money equal to the Union's periodic dues and the initiation fees uniformly required as a condition of acquiring or retaining membership. Payments shall start thirty days following the date of employment.

Management Rights

Section 1.   The management of the business and the direction of its working forces, including the right to hire, retire, transfer, change assignments, promote, suspend, discharge, discipline, and to relieve employees for lack of work or other legitimate reasons, and to maintain discipline and efficiency of all employees, to establish work schedules and to make changes therein essential to the efficient operation of the plant and to be the judge of the physical fitness of employees are the exclusive rights of the Company.

Provided however, that in the exercise of such rights the Company shall observe the provisions of this agreement.

Any employee who feels he or she has been discriminated against because of any Company action in this respect has recourse to the grievance procedure set forth in this agreement.

Section 2.   Further, the Company shall be the exclusive judge of all matters pertaining to the products to be manufactured, the location of plants or operations, production schedules, and the methods, processes, and means of manufacture and materials to be used, including the right to introduce new and improved methods or facilities.

Section 3.   The Union agrees that the rights of Management as set forth in Section 2 of this article are not subject to the grievance procedure.

Contracting Out

The Company can contract out work that does not constitute regular bargaining unit work. Such contracting out of work shall be for either economic reasons or for the purpose of expediting necessary work. The Company shall inform the president of the

Union of any such work before any contracts are signed with outside contractors. The Company will provide the Union with an opportunity to offer an alternate means of performing the work, but the Company is not obligated to accept any alternate plan. The Union will also receive, upon request, a cost breakdown of all the terms of all the contracts performed by outside contractors.

Severance Pay

If the company should permanently close the entire plant, or a portion thereof, then any employee whose continuous service shall not have been broken prior to the date of closing and whose job is discontinued, shall receive severance pay according to the following schedule:

Completed Years of Continuous Service as of Date of Closing	Amount of Severance Pay
1 or more but less than 5 years of service	2 weeks
5 or more but less than 10 years of service	4 weeks
10 or more but less than 15 years of service	6 weeks
15 or more but less than 20 years of service	8 weeks
20 or more but less than 25 years of service	10 weeks
Over 25 years of service	12 weeks

Hours of Work

The regular daily or weekly schedule of hours of work shall not exceed eight hours per day or forty hours per week. The employee's daily starting and quitting times, the time and length of the meal period, and the work week shall be scheduled by the Company.

For hours scheduled by the Company in excess of the regular schedule, the employee shall be compensated at overtime rates.

Fringe Benefits

Approximate Percentage of Total Hourly Wage and Fringe Benefit Costs (THWF)[1] Spent on Each Fringe Benefit[2]	
1. Holidays	3% of THWF
2. Vacations	5% of THWF
3. Other Fringe Benefits:	25.33% of THWF
Medical Insurance	
Pension	
Government Payments	
Miscellaneous Insurance	
	33.33%

[1]*THWF is total base compensation (wages and fringes) for EDP, Inc. Wages are 67 percent of THWF and fringes are 33 percent.*
[2]*Contract articles for each fringe benefit listed on this table are presented below.*

Holidays—Approximate Cost 3 Percent of THWF.

Within the term of this agreement in each calendar year, the company will pay an employee for eight (8) holidays not worked if they occur during the employee's regular work week. To be eligible for holiday pay an employee must have been employed at least thirty (30) days prior to any holiday noted below:

New Year's Day
Memorial Day
July 4
Labor Day
Thanksgiving
Christmas shutdown (2 days)
Martin Luther King Day

Employees required to work on Sunday or recognized holidays will be compensated at the rate of double time for each such hour worked.

Vacations—Approximate Cost 5 Percent of THWF.

Vacations with pay will be granted in each calendar year to hourly rated employees as follows:

Years of Continuous Service	Vacation
1 or more but less than 5 years of service	1 week
5 or more but less than 10 years of service	2 weeks
10 or more but less than 20 years of service	3 weeks
20 or more but less than 25 years of service	4 weeks
Over 25 years of service	5 weeks

Eligibility for vacation shall begin after the completion of twelve (12) months of continuous service following appointment.

Length of service of employees in the bargaining unit:

Less than 5 years of service*	300
5 or more but less than 10 years of service	350
10 or more but less than 15 years of service	100
15 or more but less than 20 years of service	100
20 or more but less than 25 years of service	50
Over 25 years of service	100
	1,000

*SOURCE: *Employment and Earnings,* Table heading: "Establishment Data Hours and Earnings . . . Gross hours and earnings of production or nonsupervisory workers . . . " Subheading: "Machinery, Except Electrical, Office, and Computing Machines."

Medical Insurance—Approximate Cost 6% of THWF

Hospital coverage pays:

"reasonable and customary" charges up to semiprivate room rate. Maximum 365 days of hospitalization

Surgical coverage pays:

"reasonable and customary" charges

Major Medical pays:

80% of charges not compensated under other parts of medical insurance coverage. There is a $250 deductible.

The company shall assume full cost of medical insurance. All employees, and their immediate families, who have completed ninety days of continuous service with the company shall be eligible for medical insurance.

Pension—Approximate Cost 6% of THWF

Full benefits at 62
Five-year vesting
Early retirement at 55 with actuarial reduction
Benefit: 1% of annual earnings (averaged over last 5 years of employment) multiplied by years of service
*100 Employees less than one year
  50 Employees one or more, but less than three years
 150 Employees three or more, but less than five years
 300 Employees less than 5 years

The present pension plan as described in full in a separate document is hereby made part of this agreement.

Government Payments—Approximate Cost 9% of THWF

covers:

Worker's compensation
Unemployment compensation
Social Security

Miscellaneous Insurance—Approximate Cost 4% of THWF

covers:

Group Life Insurance
Accidental Death and Dismemberment Insurance
Accident and Sickness Benefits

All employees who have completed ninety (90) days of continuous service with the Company shall be eligible for the above coverage.

The Company shall assume the full cost of the above coverage.

DURATION OF AGREEMENT:

This agreement shall remain in full force and effect commencing on the 1st day of the month of _____ 19_____, and terminating on the last day of the month of _____ 19_____ (2 years later). This Agreement shall automatically renew itself from year to year thereafter unless notice is given in writing by either the Union or the Company to the other party not less than sixty (60) days prior to the expiration date of this Agreement or any anniversary date thereafter, of its desire to modify, amend, or terminate this Agreement.

COST OF LIVING ADJUSTMENT

Present Contract has no cost-of-living adjustments clause.

CURRENT WAGES AND BENEFITS EDP, INC.

To determine the current wages and benefits at EDP, Inc., each team or the instructor will consult the latest available issue of *Employment and Earnings** and determine the average hourly earnings for the office and computing industry. This amount will be the average hourly earning under the existing contract. For purposes of this simulation assume that all the employees in EDP's bargaining unit are paid the same wage.

Assume that EDP's average hourly earnings is a median** for the industry. Assume that the dispersion of earnings in the industry is such that the highest paid workers in the industry earn 20 percent above EDP's rates and the lowest paid workers earn 20 percent below EDP's rates.

Fringe benefits are assumed to be average for EDP's industry. This means they constitute one-third of the total payroll cost. To calculate the total hourly payroll cost for EDP, Inc., simply multiply EDP's average hourly wage rate by 150 percent. To

---

*SOURCE: *Employment and Earnings*, Table heading: "Establishment Data Hours and Earnings . . . Gross hours and earnings of production or nonsupervisory workers . . . " Subheading: "Machinery, Except Electrical, Office, and Computing Machines."

**The median may be defined as the middle measure or middle item in a series in which all measures have been arranged in the order of their size.

compute the total hourly fringe benefit cost multiply the total hourly payroll cost by 33 percent. For example: (a) if the average hourly wage is \$4.40, then the total hourly payroll cost is \$6.60 (\$4.40 × 150%); (b) fringes represent approximately one-third of \$6.60 or \$2.18 per hour (\$6.60 × 33%), or 50% of \$4.40 = \$2.20.

To compute the total annual payroll cost of the existing contract multiply the number of hours worked per year (2080) times the number of employees in the bargaining unit (1000) times the total hourly payroll cost, which consists of wages and fringe benefits (hourly wage rate times 150%).

Individual fringe benefits can be calculated by referring to the worksheet for the percentage represented by each. Vacations, in this example, would be 33 cents per hour (5% × \$6.60); holidays would be about 20 cents per hour (3% × \$6.60), and so on. Consider in your negotiations the rollup effect.*

LABOR NEGOTIATIONS BEGIN AT EDP, INC.
JOINT PRESS RELEASE

Labor negotiators for EDP, Inc. and the Union representing its production employees opened contract negotiations today.

The Company's bargaining team is comprised of the Industrial Relations Manager, who serves as chairperson, the Plant Manager, and the Plant Controller.

Representing the Union are three veteran negotiators: the International Representative, the President of the Union Local, and the Union's Group Benefits Specialist.

Bargaining sessions will be held in a downtown hotel. Representatives were also quoted as being willing to meet as frequently as necessary to reach a peaceful settlement by the expiration date of the current contract.

Note: The commencement of bargaining between representatives of EDP, Inc. and the Union began with this short press release.

PRELIMINARY AREAS OF AGREEMENT

The pace and intensity of negotiations have been gradually building. The early get-acquainted meetings of the first several weeks soon moved into more frequent, more intense working sessions in which the parties tackled a number of tough questions. Tentative agreement was slowly reached on many items, including pensions, medical insurance, and miscellaneous insurance.

With final** agreement reached on many issues, *including a two-year contract*, both parties seemed to experience a psychological lift, and they prepared for the bargaining over wages and benefits with a vigor not seen at the negotiating table for

---

*The rollup effect measures the impact of wage increases on costs of some wage-related fringe benefits.

**In actual negotiations, it is customary that no agreement on any one issue is final until total agreement has been negotiated.

some weeks. A final, no-strike settlement was anticipated, but the more experienced negotiators knew that this momentum could be easily lost in the delicate process of maintaining a balance between arm's-length, hard bargaining on purely economic issues, on the one hand, and good-faith efforts to solve mutual problems, on the other. Good examples of each had been experienced, however, and the negotiators turned to the final economic issues with guarded optimism.

At the close of the last bargaining session, the Company representatives and the Union representatives agreed to finalize their respective positions and present them at the next meeting. They agreed not to negotiate over improvements of holidays and vacations for the first year of the contract. They enumerated the following items to be bargained over in future sessions:

Wages
Cost-of-living adjustment
Holidays
Vacations
Union security
Management rights
Contracting out
Severance pay
Medical insurance

INSTRUCTIONS FOR WORKSHEET "A"

1. Compute the hourly cost of each benefit.
2. Compute the total hourly wage and fringe benefit costs (THWF)
3. Compute total annual cost of wages and fringes under the present contract.

   Total annual cost can be calculated by multiplying total hourly compensation by 2080 hours by 1000 employees.
   Each 1 cent per hour equals $20,800 cost (or value) per year (1¢ × 2080 hours × 1000 employees = $20,800)

WORKSHEET A
WAGES AND BENEFITS

List all team members:

Current Average Hourly
Wage at EDP
$CAHW^3$ = Current
Average Hourly Wage
$ _____ /hour

$CAHW \underline{\hspace{2cm}} \times 150\% = THWF$
$CAHW$ = Current Average hourly wage
$THWF$ = Total Hourly Wage and Fringe Benefit
Costs or Total Hourly Payroll Costs.

$THWF \underline{\hspace{2cm}} - CAHW \underline{\hspace{2cm}} = \underline{\hspace{2cm}}$ [2]

	A. Percentage of total base compensation spent on each fringe benefit		B. Total Hourly Payroll Cost (THWF or CAHW × 150%)[1]		C. Dollar cost, per hour, of various fringe benefits[1]
	A	×	B	=	C
Holidays	3%	×	$ _____ /hr	=	$ _____
Vacations	5%	×	$ _____ /hr	=	$ _____
Other fringe benefits: Medical insurance Pension Government payments Miscellaneous insurance _____	25.33%	×	$ _____ /hr	=	$ _____
TOTAL	33.33%	×	$ _____ /hr	TOTAL	$ _____

The sum of this column equals 33.33% of the total hourly payroll cost.

Total Annual Cost (Wages and Fringes under Current Contract) = THWF $ _____ / _____ × 2080 hours ×

1000 workers = $ _____

[1] See previous section, "Current Wages and Benefits, EDP, Inc.": for example, if total hourly payroll cost is $6.60 ($4.40 × 150%) then holiday cost is $6.60 × 3% or approximately 20 cents.

[2] Hourly cost of fringe benefits.

[3] The current hourly wage rate at EDP is the average hourly earnings for office and computing machines nonsupervisory workers, published in the latest available issue of Employment and Earnings (E&E), see E&E table heading: "Establishment Data Hours and Earnings . . . Gross hours and earnings of production and nonsupervisory workers . . ." Subheading: "Machinery, Except Electrical, Office and Computing Machines." U.S. Department of Labor, Bureau of Labor Statistics. The current hourly wage at EDP represents approximately 67% of the total payroll dollar.

APPENDIX A
Role Profiles

You are expected to assume one of the role profiles of the negotiators outlined below. In effect what they have already done, you have done. What takes place next is up to you.

UNION

International Representative

This role involves the broadest responsibility on the Union team. On the one hand, you are responsible to the International Headquarters for carrying out its objectives, relating the settlement to others the Union has negotiated and will be negotiating with other companies, protecting its resources from an unnecessary strike, and preserving its influence on the Local involved in these negotiations. On the other hand, you must relate to the others on the bargaining team and through them to the membership of the Local. You must know and understand their priorities and respond to them if you can.

You must provide the proper balance between wages and benefits because many in the unit (and even at the bargaining table) will disagree vehemently on this split. Differences among your negotiators will require your utmost skill to bring about sufficient consensus to ultimately get the committee to recommend a tentative package to the membership for ratification.

You must constantly appear sufficiently aggressive to satisfy the more militant members of the Union without unduly antagonizing the Industrial Relations Manager.

Local President

This role involves a more specialized interest than that of the International Representative. You are elected by the membership of the Local and must necessarily satisfy that constituency. In cases where the interests of the Local and the International Headquarters are in conflict, your loyalty is to the Local. You want a settlement that will satisfy the membership and if you cannot obtain it, a long strike is acceptable. In that case, as you see it, your Local deserves strike benefits from the International even if the Fund is low. You feel your members have paid their dues for many years and have that support coming to them if they need it. Nonetheless, you are seldom belligerent at the bargaining table and are glad to have the International Rep play the "heavy." You must preserve a decent working relationship with the Industrial Relations Manager, with whom you will be dealing almost daily during the term of the new agreement.

Benefits Specialist

This role is the most highly specialized role on the Union bargaining team. You are the individual who catches the flack from the members when their hospitalization doesn't cover a particular bill or when they sit down to calculate their potential retirement benefits. No one complains to you because the wages aren't high enough or because the seniority system is not satisfactory; they only complain to you about benefits.

Your day-to-day contact is with the members, and you seldom deal with the Industrial Relations Manager, only infrequently with the Local President, and almost never with the International Rep. Your allegiance is clear.

COMPANY

Industrial Relations Manager

This role involves broadest responsibility to the Company and to the employees. On the one hand, you must see to it that the settlement is satisfactory to management in all functional areas and at both the plant and corporate levels. On the other hand, the settlement must be perceived as equitable by a majority of employees if it is to be ratified.

You must insure proper balance between wages and benefits. You must be sensitive to differences among your own negotiators and reconcile those differences. You also must be sensitive to differences among negotiators on the Union side and not allow them to derail the overall objective of reaching a settlement.

You will be dealing with the Union almost daily during the contract term and thus must behave in such a way as to maintain your credibility and retain the respect of the Union representatives.

You accept the Union's role as agent for the employees but bargain as hard as you can to achieve the Company's objectives.

Plant Manager

This role involves a more specialized interest to be served than the Industrial Relations Manager's. You are primarily concerned with obtaining a settlement which provides you with maximum flexibility to manage the plant at lowest possible cost.

You will have little dealings with the Union during the contract term and therefore are not too concerned about your relationship with the union representatives. In fact, you are generally resentful of the Union's involvement in what you consider to be management prerogatives.

You are easily frustrated by the bargaining process and are anxious to conclude negotiations and get back to what you like to do best—manage the plant.

Plant Controller

This role is the most highly specialized role on the management bargaining team. Financial considerations are primary; everything else is secondary.

You handle all costing calculations during negotiations and bring economic data to bear on as many issues as possible.

You see the bargaining process primarily as an economic struggle between two powerful antagonists and are often oblivious to the nuances of the interpersonal and intergroup dynamics which are of such great concern to the Industrial Relations Manager.

APPENDIX B

Evaluating Group Behavior and Effectiveness

To be completed by each participant

Group_____

Your Name_____

Role_____

1. How effectively do you think your group functioned in this simulation?

   ☐ very effectively
   ☐ effectively
   ☐ not very effectively
   ☐ ineffectively

   Why?

2. What contributed most toward the effectiveness of your group?

3. What most inhibited the effectiveness of your group?

4. How would you evaluate your overall contribution to the effectiveness of your group?

   ☐ substantial
   ☐ above average
   ☐ average
   ☐ below average

5. How could you have made a greater contribution?

6. How effectively did you carry out your assigned role:

   (a) during the process when your group was establishing its initial demands/offer?

   ☐ very effectively
   ☐ effectively
   ☐ not very effectively
   ☐ ineffectively

   Why?

   (b) during the process of negotiations?

   ☐ very effectively
   ☐ effectively
   ☐ not very effectively
   ☐ ineffectively

   Why?

   (c) during the process of concluding a settlement?

   ☐ very effectively
   ☐ effectively
   ☐ not very effectively
   ☐ ineffectively

   Why?

7. How satisfied were you with the final outcome?

   ☐ very satisfied
   ☐ satisfied
   ☐ not very satisfied
   ☐ dissatisfied

   Why?

APPENDIX C

Evaluating the Process of Negotiations:
Rate Your Group

To be completed by each participant
Group_____
Your Name_____
Role_____

Rate your group as it functioned during the three major elements of negotiations. Mark the line, in each case, at the point which you feel best describes the group.

I. Process of Establishing the Initial Demands/Offer

Cooperativeness within the group.

5	4	3	2	1
high degree	above avg.	avg.	below avg.	low degree

Tolerance of individual roles and views.

5	4	3	2	1
high degree	above avg.	avg.	below avg.	low degree

General agreement on strategy.

5	4	3	2	1
high degree	above avg.	avg.	below avg.	low degree

General agreement on demands/offer.

5	4	3	2	1
high degree	above avg.	avg.	below avg.	low degree

General willingness to accept leadership.

5	4	3	2	1
high degree	above avg.	avg.	below avg.	low degree

II. Process of Negotiations

Outside preparation by individuals comprising the group.

5	4	3	2	1
high degree	above avg.	avg.	below avg.	low degree

Persuasiveness in presenting position.

5	4	3	2	1
high degree	above avg.	avg.	below avg.	low degree

Effectiveness of counterarguments to opposition arguments.

5	4	3	2	1
high degree	above avg.	avg.	below avg.	low degree

Grasp of the issues.

5	4	3	2	1
high degree	above avg.	avg.	below avg.	low degree

Group's utilization of original strategy.

5	4	3	2	1
high degree	above avg.	avg.	below avg.	low degree

Group's ability to adapt strategy to changing situation.

5	4	3	2	1
high degree	above avg.	avg.	below avg.	low degree

Group's internal cohesiveness.

5	4	3	2	1
high degree	above avg.	avg.	below avg.	low degree

Group's willingness to accept leadership.

5	4	3	2	1
high degree	above avg.	avg.	below avg.	low degree

Group's inclination to compromise individual roles to advance the total group.

5	4	3	2	1
high degree	above avg.	avg.	below avg.	low degree

III. Process of Concluding Negotiations

Final willingness of group to compromise individual goals for group goals.

5	4	3	2	1
high degree	above avg.	avg.	below avg.	low degree

Final willingness of group to compromise group goals to obtain a settlement.

5	4	3	2	1
high degree	above avg.	avg.	below avg.	low degree

Group's agreement on terms of the settlement.

5	4	3	2	1
high degree	above avg.	avg.	below avg.	low degree

Group's satisfaction with final settlement.

5	4	3	2	1
high degree	above avg.	avg.	below avg.	low degree

General satisfaction of individuals with final settlement.

5	4	3	2	1
high degree	above avg.	avg.	below avg.	low degree

APPENDIX D
Evaluating Opponent's Group Behavior and Effectiveness

To be completed by each participant
Group_____
Your Name_____
Role_____

1. How effectively do you think your opponent's group functioned in this simulation?

   ☐ very effectively
   ☐ effectively
   ☐ not very effectively
   ☐ ineffectively

   Why?

2. In your view what contributed most toward the effectiveness of your opponent's group?

3. In your view what most inhibited the effectiveness of your opponent's group?

APPENDIX E

Evaluating the Process of Negotiations: Rate Your Opponent's Group

To be completed by each participant

Group_____

Your Name_____

Role_____

Rate your opponent's group as it functioned during negotiations. Mark the line, in each case, at the point which you feel best describes the group.

I. Process of Negotiations

Cooperativeness within the group.

5	4	3	2	1
high degree	above avg.	avg.	below avg.	low degree

Tolerance of individual roles and views.

5	4	3	2	1
high degree	above avg.	avg.	below avg.	low degree

Persuasiveness in presenting position.

5	4	3	2	1
high degree	above avg.	avg.	below avg.	low degree

Effectiveness of counterarguments to your group's arguments.

5 high degree	4 above avg.	3 avg.	2 below avg.	1 low degree

Grasp of the issues.

5 high degree	4 above avg.	3 avg.	2 below avg.	1 low degree

Group's ability to adapt strategy to changing situations.

5 high degree	4 above avg.	3 avg.	2 below avg.	1 low degree

Group's internal cohesiveness.

5 high degree	4 above avg.	3 avg.	2 below avg.	1 low degree

Group's willingness to accept leadership.

5 high degree	4 above avg.	3 avg.	2 below avg.	1 low degree

Group's inclination to compromise individual roles to advance the total group.

5 high degree	4 above avg.	3 avg.	2 below avg.	1 low degree

Group's agreement on terms of the settlement.

5 high degree	4 above avg.	3 avg.	2 below avg.	1 low degree

FORM I (Confidential) Initial Demands, Offers, Priorities, and Expectations

(Provide copy to Instructor before you start to negotiate)

Priorities	Demands or Offers	Expectations	Minimum Acceptable Contract Terms

List all team members:_____

Group:_____

PLEASE FILL OUT THIS FORM. To complete this form you can use additional pages. On this form you do not have to include proposed contract language. Agreed upon and proposed contract language has to be included with all your data submitted to your instructor at the end of your simulation.

FORM II Demands and/or Offers and Arguments Justifying Party's Position

Demands or Offers	Arguments

List all team members:————————————————

Group:—————————————————

PLEASE COMPLETE THIS FORM.

FORM III Demands and/or Offers and Arguments Justifying Opponent's Position

Opposition Demands or Offers	Revision of Demands	Arguments by Opposition

List all team members:_____

Group:_____

PLEASE COMPLETE THIS FORM.

FORM IV (Confidential) Demands, Offers, Priorities, and Expectations

(Provide copy to instructor before your last session)

Priorities	Demands or Offers	Expectations	Minimum Acceptable Contract Terms

List all team members: _____

Group: _____

PLEASE COMPLETE THIS FORM.

INSTRUCTIONS FOR FORMS V–X

1. Summarize newly negotiated provisions, if any, of the following contract clauses: union security, management rights, contracting out, severance pay, and medical insurance. See Form IX.
2. Compute the hourly cost of *each* old benefit under the newly negotiated average hourly rate.*
3. Calculate hourly wage, cost-of-living, and fringe benefit increases for each year of the newly negotiated contract.
4. Calculate the average hourly cost-of-wage, cost-of-living, and fringe benefit increases over the life of the contract.
5. Compute the average annual total cost of your new contract.
6. Compute the annual cost-of-wage, cost-of-living, and fringe benefit increases. Do it for each year of your newly negotiated contract.
7. Calculate the total percentage increases of wages, cost-of-living, and fringe benefits for each year of your contract.
8. Complete Forms V–X.

---

*Form V, Worksheets 1 and 2, indicate higher costs of old fringes under the newly negotiated wage rate. The forms reflect the rollup effect, which measures the impact of wage increases on cost of some wage related fringe benefits. Form V, Worksheet 2 does not reflect costs of newly negotiated improvements in holidays and vacations, if any.

FORM V WORKSHEET 1 WAGES AND BENEFITS

This worksheet is to be completed by each team. List all team members:

Wages
1st Year of Contract

NNAHW = Newly Negotiated
Average Hourly Wage at EDP

$_____ /hour

NNAHW _____ / × 150% = THWF _____

NNAHW = Newly Negotiated Average Hourly Wage at EDP

THWF = Total Hourly Wage and Fringe Benefit Costs or Total Hourly Payroll Cost

THWF $_____ − NNAHW $_____ = _____ [3]
Hourly Cost of Fringe Benefits

	A. Percentage of total base compensation, (under old contract) spent on each fringe benefit		B. Total Hourly Payroll Cost (THWF or NNAHW × 150%[2])		C. Hourly dollar cost of various existing fringe benefits under the newly negotiated wage rate[1]	D. Hourly dollar cost of various existing fringe benefits under the old contract (from Worksheet A)	E. Increased hourly dollar cost of various existing fringe benefits under the newly negotiated wage rate C − D = E
	A	×	B	=	C	D	E
Holidays	3%	×	$_____	/hr =	$_____	_____	_____
Vacations	5%	×	$_____	/hr =	$_____	_____	_____
Other fringe benefits: Medical insurance Pension Government payments Misc. insurance	25.33%	×	$_____	/hr =	$_____	_____	_____
TOTAL	33.3%	×	$_____	/hr =	$_____	_____	_____

Total annual cost (wages and existing fringes 1st year of contract) = THWF $_____ / × 2080 hours × 1000 workers = $_____ /.

[1]The dollar cost only covers the cost of old fringes under the newly negotiated wage rate. The parties agreed not to negotiate over improvements of holidays and vacations for the first year of the contract. The sum of this column equals 33.33% of the total hourly payroll cost.
[2]See previous section "Current Wages and Benefits, EDP, Inc."
[3]THWF − NNAHW = Hourly cost of fringe benefits, 1st Year of the Contract, e.g., If NNAHW were $4.40 and THWF were $6.60 ($4.40 × 150%), hourly cost of fringe benefits would be $2.20 ($6.60 − $4.40 = $2.20).

511

FORM V WORKSHEET 2 WAGES AND BENEFITS

This worksheet is to be completed by each team. List all team members:

Wages
2nd Year of Contract
NNAHW = Newly Negotiated Average Hourly Wage at EDP

$ _____ /hour

NNAHW _____ / × 150% = THWF

NNAHW = Newly Negotiated Average Hourly Wage at EDP

THWF = Total Hourly Wage and Fringe Benefit Costs or Total Hourly Payroll Cost

THWF $ _____ − NNAHW $ _____ = _____ [3] =
Hourly Cost of Fringe Benefits

	A. Percentage of total base compensation, (under old contract) spent on each fringe benefit		B. Total Hourly Payroll Cost (THWF or NNAHW × 150%[2])		C. Hourly dollar cost of various existing fringe benefits under the newly negotiated wage rate[1]	D. Hourly dollar cost of various existing fringe benefits under the 1st year of the contract (from Form V) Worksheet 1.	E. Increased hourly dollar cost of various existing fringe benefits under the newly negotiated wage rate $C - D = E$
	A	×	B	=	C	D	E
Holidays	3%	×	$ _____ /hr	=	$ _____	_____	_____
Vacations	5%	×	$ _____ /hr	=	$ _____	_____	_____
Other fringe benefits: Medical insurance Pension Government payments Misc. insurance	25.33%	×	$ _____ /hr	=	$ _____	_____	_____
TOTAL	33.3%	×	_____ /hr	=	$ _____	_____	_____

Total annual cost (wages and existing fringes) under 2nd year of contract = THWF $ _____ / × 2080 hours × 1000 workers = $ _____ /.

[1]Improvements in fringe benefits negotiated under the new contract (if any) are not included in this particular calculation. The dollar cost only covers the higher cost of old fringes under the newly negotiated wage rate. This is the roll-up effect.
[2]See previous section "Current Wages and Benefits," EDP, Inc.
[3]THWF − NNAHW = Hourly Cost of Fringe Benefits, e.g., If NNAHW were $4.40 and THWF were $6.60 ($4.40 × 150%), hourly cost of fringe benefits would be $2.20 ($6.60 − $4.40 = $2.20).

512

FORM V WORKSHEET 3

This worksheet is to be completed by each team. List all team members:

	A Hourly Increases First Year of Contract	B Cost of First Year Increases over A Two-Year Contract	C Hourly Increases Hourly Increases Second Year of Contract	D The Total Hourly Increases for the Full Term of the Contract (THIFTC) $B + C = D$
Hourly wage increases[1]	$ _____ × 2^2 =	$ _____ +	_____	= _____
Hourly cost increases of all existing fringe benefits under the newly negotiated wage rate from Worksheets 1 and 2	$ _____ × 2^2 =	$ _____ +	_____	= _____
Hourly cost of cost-of-living adjustments, if any	$ _____ × 2^2 =	$ _____ +	_____	= _____
Hourly cost of newly negotiated improvements in holidays if any, see Form V worksheet 4		_____	_____	_____
Hourly cost of newly negotiated improvements in vacations, if any, see For V worksheet 5		_____	_____	_____
Total hourly wage, cost-of-living and fringe benefit increases	$ _____ × 2^2 =	$ _____ +	$ _____	= THIFTC $ _____

(A) (C) (A+C) (D)
(A)

[1] To calculate the negotiated hourly wage increase of the 1st year of your contract subtract the original hourly wage (as per Form A) from the newly negotiated hourly wage of your 1st year contract (as per Form V, Worksheet 1). To calculate the negotiated hourly wage increase of the 2nd year of your contract subtract the 1st year negotiated hourly wage (as per Form V, Worksheet 1) from the negotiated hourly wage of your 2nd year contract (as per Form V, Worksheet 2).

[2] First year increases over a two-year contract. If a two-year contract provides for the following increases: $.71 per hour 1st year, $1.32 per hour 2nd year then the cost for the first year is $2.03 ($1.32 + .71) and the total hourly increase is $2.74 ($2.03 + .71).

The first year increase also has to be paid during the 2nd year of the contract.

FORM V WORKSHEET 4

Computation of Newly Negotiated Hourly Holiday Costs, if any

The parties agreed not to negotiate over improvements of holidays for the first year of the contract. Increased costs of holidays for the first year of the contract as shown on FORM V, WORKSHEET 1 and on FORM V, WORKSHEET 2 for the 2nd year of the contract are entirely the result of the roll-up effect.[7]

Indicate number of newly negotiated additional holidays, if any _____ .

Number of Employees[1]	×	NNAHW[2] as per Form V Worksheet 2	×	NEWLY NEGOTIATED HOLIDAY HOURS	=	Total Annual Cost for All Employees
_____	×	_____	×	_____	=	_____

Example:

1000 employees[1]	×	$7.06[2]	×	16[3]	=	112,960[4]

Total Annual Cost

$$\frac{TAC[8]}{Hours[6] \times Employees} = HCNNH[9] \text{_____}$$

Example:

$$\frac{112,960[4]}{2080[6] \times 1000[1]} = .05[5]$$

[1]*Number of employees; assume 1000.*
[2]*Newly Negotiated Average Hourly Wage (NNAHW), as per Form V Worksheet 2; for purposes of example assume $7.06. Although in our examples we used NNAHW totals, an argument can be made for utilizing Total Hourly Wage and Fringe Benefits Costs (THWF) since cost of holiday pay includes cost of fringe benefits. Both sides will compute the cost of any new holidays, if any, on the basis of any agreed upon method. Your team must negotiate whether to apply to holiday costing the NNAHW or the THWF method.*
[3]*Newly negotiated paid holiday hours; for purposes of example assume 16 hours.*
[4]*Total annual cost of newly negotiated holidays for all employees.*
[5]*Hourly cost of newly negotiated holidays.*
[6]*Assume that each employee works 2080 hours per year.*
[7]*Roll-up measures the impact of wage increases on costs of some wage-related fringe benefits.*
[8]*TAC = Total annual cost for all employees.*
[9]*HCNNH = Hourly cost of newly negotiated holidays.*

FORM V WORKSHEET 5

Computation of Newly Negotiated Hourly Vacation Costs, if any[9]

The parties agreed not to negotiate over improvements of vacations for the first year of the contract. Increased costs of vacations for the first year of the contract as shown on FORM V, WORKSHEET 1 and on FORM V, WORKSHEET 2 for the 2nd year of the contract are entirely the result of the roll-up effect.[10]

300 employees with less than 5 years of service	Newly negotiated vacation days	×	8 hours per day	×	NNAHW	=	Increased annual cost of vacation for employees with less than 5 years of service.
350 employees with 5–10 years of service	× Newly negotiated vacation days	×	8 hours per day	×	NNAHW	=	Increased Annual Cost of Vacation for employees with 5–10 years of service.
100 employees with 10–15 years of service	× Newly negotiated vacation days	×	8 hours per day	×	NNAHW	=	Increased Annual Cost of Vacation for employees with 10–15 years of service
100 employees with 15–20 years of service	× Newly negotiated vacation days	×	8 hours per day	×	NNAHW	=	Increased Annual Cost of Vacation for employees with 15–20 years of service.
50 employees with 20–25 years of service	× Newly negotiated vacation days	×	8 hours per day	×	NNAHW	=	Increased Annual Cost of Vacation for employees with 20–25 years of service.
100 employees with over 25 years of service	× Newly negotiated vacation days	×	8 hours per day	×	NNAHW	=	Increased Annual Cost of Vacation for employees with over 25 years of service.
	×			×		=	

Total Annual Cost of newly negotiated vacations. (TACV) = _____

$$\frac{TACV}{2080^7 \times 1000^8} = \frac{\text{Average Hourly Cost of Newly Negotiated Vacations per}}{\text{Employee}}$$

For example,

| 350 employees[1] | × | 5[3] | × | 8[4] | × | $7.06[2] | = | $98,840 |
| 100 employees[1] | × | 5[3] | × | 8[4] | × | $7.06[2] | = | $28,240 |

Total annual cost of newly negotiated vacations for employees with 5 to 10 years and those with 15 to 20 years of service. = $127,080[5]

$$\frac{\text{(TACV) } 127,080^5}{2080^7 \times 1000^8} = 0.6^6$$

[1] Number of employees affected, according to years of continuing service.
[2] Newly Negotiated Average Hourly Wage (NNAHW); assume $7.06.
[3] Newly Negotiated Vacation Days; assume 5 days.
[4] Assume each vacation day is equal to 8 hours.
[5] Total Annual Cost of Newly Negotiated Vacations for Two Groups of Affected Employees.
[6] Hourly Cost of Newly Negotiated Vacations.
[7] Assume that each employee works 2080 hours per year.
[8] Assume 1000 employees in the bargaining unit.
[9] Additional vacation days can be calculated by computing additional negotiated vacation days for each group of employees classified by years of continuing service. Multiply the number of employees in the group given the additional vacation days by the number of such additional days. Number of additional days for all groups are to be totaled, e.g., if employees with 20 to 25 years of service get an additional 5 days of vacation per year, and there are 250 employees in this group and those over 25 years of service get an additional 5 days per year and there are 200 employees in this group, and the other groups do not get any improvements in vacation, then the total number of additional vacation days is 2,250 [(250 × 5) + (200 × 5)]. 2,250 vacation days × 8 hours = 18,000 Newly Negotiated Vacation Hours (NNVH). To obtain total cost of NNVH, multiply hours times NNAHW[2]. Although in our examples we used NNAHW totals, an argument can be made for utilizing Total Hourly Wage and Fringe Benefits Costs (THWF) since cost of vacation pay includes cost of fringe benefits. Whether to apply to vacation costing the NNAHW or the THWF method is subject to negotiations. Both sides will compute the costs of any new vacation days, if any, on the basis of any agreed upon method.*
[10] Roll-up measures the impact of wage increases on costs of some wage-related fringe benefits.

*Instructions: Your team must negotiate whether to apply to vacation costing the NNAHW or the THWF method.

FORM VI

Calculate the average hourly cost of a wage, cost-of-living, and fringe benefit increase over the life of this contract.

To compute the average hourly cost of a wage, cost-of-living, and fringe benefit increase of a multi-year contract, arrive at the total hourly increase over the life of the new contract and then divide this sum by the length of the contract. SOURCE: Form V, Worksheet 3.

For example, assume a per-hour wage, cola, and fringe benefit increase of $2.74 over a two-year contract.

$$\frac{\$2.74}{2 \text{ years}} = \$1.37 = \text{average hourly cost of wage, cola, and fringe benefit increase.}$$

If per-hour wage, cost-of-living, and fringe benefit increase of two-year contract is W and the contract is in effect for n years then the average hourly cost of wage, cost-of-living and benefit increase per year is W/n. Compute your average *hourly* cost of wage, cost-of-living, and fringe benefit increases.

$ THIFTC from Worksheet 3 $ _____ : ___ 2 = _____

To compute the annual total cost increase of your new contract, multiply number of hours by number of employees by average hourly cost of wage, cost-of-living, and fringe benefit increase over life of a two-year contract.

For example,

Number of hours worked per year (2080) × number of employees (1000) × average hourly cost of wage, cost-of-living, and benefit increase over life of two-year contract (assume for purposes of example $1.37): 2080 × 1000 × $1.37 = $2,849,600 = annual total cost of a new contract.

Compute the average annual total cost of your new contract.

D	E	F	G
Number of hours worked per year	Number of employees	Average annual hourly cost-of-wage, cost-of-living, and benefit increase over life of a two-year contract	Average annual total cost increase of new contract (D) × (E) × (F) = G
2080 ×	1000 ×	_____	= _____

List all team members: _____
Group: _____

FORM VII

This form is to be completed by each team.
Compute your cost increases for first and second year of contract.

1st year of contract

H Total hourly wage,[1] cost-of-living and fringe benefit increase		I Number of hours worked per year		J Number of employees		K[1] Annual cost increase $H \times I \times J = K$
_____	×	2080	×	1000	=	_____

2nd year of contract

L Total hourly wage[1] cost-of-living and fringe benefit increase		M Number of hours worked per year		N Number of employees		O Annual cost increase $L \times M \times N = O$
_____	×	2080	×	1000	=	_____

Calculate your annual percentage increases for each year of the newly negotiated contract.

For example: If annual cost increase is $2 million and the old total annual cost was $40 million, then the percentage increase is 5%.

$$\frac{2 \text{ million}}{40 \text{ million}} \times 100 = 5\%$$

We multiply by 100 in order to express the result as a percentage.

$$\frac{1\text{st-year annual cost increase} (\quad)}{\text{Annual cost of old contract}[2] (\quad)} \times 100 = \underline{\quad} \quad \text{Annual percentage increase of 1st year contract}$$

$$\frac{2\text{nd-year annual cost increase} (\quad)}{\text{Total annual cost of 1st-yr contract}[3] (\quad)} \times 100 = \underline{\quad} \quad \text{Annual percentage increase of 2nd-year contract}$$

X Annual percentage increase of 1st-year contract		Y Annual percentage increase of 2nd-year contract		Z Percentage increase of a two-year contract
_____	+	_____	=	_____

To obtain the average percentage increase of a two-year contract divide Z by 2 _____

---

[1]SOURCE: Form V, Worksheet 3.
[2]SOURCE: Worksheet A.
To compute the total annual payroll cost of the existing contract multiply the number of hours worked per year (2080) time the number of employees in the bargaining unit (1000) times the total hourly payroll cost which consists of wages and fringe benefits (hourly wage rate times 150%).
[3]SOURCE: Worksheet 1.
List all team members:_____
Group:_____

FORM VIII SUMMARY OF FORMS V-VII

First Year of Contract; SOURCE: Form V, Worksheet 1.

Newly negotiated
average hourly wage _____

Increased hourly cost
of all existing fringe
benefits under the newly
negotiated wage rate _____

Total annual cost of the
first year of contract _____

Second Year of Contract; SOURCE: Form V, Worksheets 2 and 4.

Newly negotiated
average hourly wage _____

Increased hourly cost
of all *existing* fringe
benefits under the newly
negotiated wage rate _____

Annual cost of second year of contract
(Wages and *existing* fringes), does not include
cost of any newly negotiated fringes _____

Number of newly negotiated holidays, if any _____

Total annual cost of
newly negotiated holidays,
if any; SOURCE: Form V, Worksheet 4 _____

Increased annual cost of
vacations for all employees, if
any; SOURCE: Form V, Worksheet 5 _____

Form V, Worksheet 3, Column D

Total hourly wage
increases for the full term
of the contract _____

Total hourly increases
of all *existing* fringe benefits for
the full term of the contract _____

Hourly cost of newly
negotiated improvements
in holidays, if any _____

Total hourly cost-of-living adjustments, if any _____

Increased hourly cost of
newly negotiated improvements
in vacations, if any _____

Total hourly wage and
fringe benefit increases for
the full term of the contract _____

From Form VII

Annual percentage increase
of first year of contract _____

Annual percentage increase
of second year of contract _____

FORM IX   FINAL CONTRACT TERMS AND SEVERANCE PAY

At the conclusion of negotiations, this form is to be completed by each team. Indicate with an "X" your opinion of the final contract terms for union security, management rights, contracting out, severance clauses, and medical insurance.

Issues	Team	
	Union	*Management*

UNION SECURITY
No change of existing clause _____
Existing clause has been revised, explain _____
New clause favors management _____
New clause strongly favors management _____
New clause favors union _____
New clause strongly favors union _____

MANAGEMENT RIGHTS
No change of existing clause _____
Existing clause has been revised, explain _____
New clause favors management _____
New clause strongly favors management _____
New clause favors union _____
New clause strongly favors union _____

CONTRACTING OUT
No change of existing clause _____
Existing clause has been revised, explain _____
New clause favors management _____
New clause strongly favors management _____
New clause favors union _____
New clause strongly favors union _____

SEVERANCE PAY
No change of existing clause _____
Existing clause has been revised, explain _____
New clause favors management _____
New clause strongly favors management _____
New clause favors union _____
New clause strongly favors union _____

MEDICAL INSURANCE
No change of existing clause _____
Existing clause has been revised, explain _____
New clause favors management _____
New clause strongly favors management _____
New clause favors union _____
New clause strongly favors union _____

On the back of this page you are required to provide a rationale for your rating of any of the above contract clauses as either favorable to the union or to the management side, also provide the text of the above newly negotiated clauses, if any.

FORM X INDIVIDUAL EVALUATION FORM

Name _____

Confidental evaluation of your team members and your opponents, to be provided to your instructor at the end of the simulation.

Please use a *separate* sheet to evaluate each member of the management and the union team. In your evaluation apply the criteria and the format listed below. To each criterion respond in a very brief *separate* paragraph, consisting of one or more short sentences. Also assign to each criterion a *letter grade* on a scale of "A-F." No grade is necessary for evaluating weaknesses and strengths.

Format:

Individual Evaluation Form
Confidential

Name of person being evaluated: _____
Team No. _____
Union or Management _____

Criteria:	LETTER GRADE	COMMENT
Effectiveness	_____	_____
Contributions	_____	_____
Weaknesses	Describe	_____
Strengths	Describe	_____
Cooperation	_____	_____
Leadership	_____	_____
Initiative	_____	_____
Grasp of issues	_____	_____
Overall evaluation	_____	_____

Discuss the impact of time pressures and deadlines—particularly during the last 30 minutes of negotiations— on the behavior and reactions of the person being evaluated. Use the back page for further evaluation.

EVALUATION QUESTIONNAIRE*
FINAL SESSION

1. What were some of the tactics and strategies utilized by your team?
2. How successful were your tactics and strategies?
3. What did you think of the tactics and strategies utilized by your oppoonents?
4. Discuss all the changes that have been made in the agreement.
5. Evaluate management offers, demands, expectations, and final achievements.

_____

*The above questions are to be answered jointly by each union and management team. Submit the answers to your instructor at the end of the simulation. Some of these questions will also be discussed in class. You do not have to submit written answers to questions 4 and 9.

6. Evaluate union demands, expectations, and final achievements.

7. How successful were you in achieving your original goals?

8. What do you think of the agreement you negotiated? Would it be ratified in the "real world"? Would "real" management approve of such a settlement?

9. How did the personalities of your teammates influence the negotiations?

10. How did the personalities of your opponents influence the negotiations?

11. Any comments about working jointly as a team?

12. If you had to do it all over again, would you change your tactics and strategies? How?

13. Which contract terms were most difficult to negotiate? Why?

14. Evaluate the strengths and weaknesses of your team and of your opponents.

15. Discuss mistakes made by your team and by your opposition.

16. Evaluate the impact of time pressures and deadlines on your team members and on your opponent's behavior particularly during the last 30 minutes of negotiations.

TEAM COMPOSITION

Team I

Company		Union	
Industrial Relations Manager	_____	International Representative	_____
Plant Manager	_____	President of the Local Union	_____
Plant Controller	_____	Benefits Specialist	_____

Team II

Company		Union	
Industrial Relations Manager	_____	International Representative	_____
Plant Manager	_____	President of the Local Union	_____
Plant Controller	_____	Benefits Specialist	_____

Team III

Company		Union	
Industrial Relations Manager	_____	International Representative	_____
Plant Manager	_____	President of the Local Union	_____
Plant Controller	_____	Benefits Specialist	_____

ARBITRATION CASES

Goodyear Tire & Rubber Company, Point Pleasant Chemical Plant and United Rubber, Cork, Linoleum and Plastic Workers of America, AFL-CIO, Local Union 644

JONATHAN DWORKIN, Arbitrator. Hearing Held at Gallipolis, Ohio, September 10, 1984. Award issued October 30, 1984.

Bargaining Units—Jurisdiction—Assignment of Work Outside Unit—Work Formerly Contracted Out—*De Minimis* Doctrine

[Text of Award]

DWORKIN, Arbitrator; ISSUE: Article XI, Section 1(a)—Claim that work assignment to exempt guards violated Union's jurisdiction.

Background of Dispute

In June, 1984, the Company installed scales at its main gate to weigh incoming trucks. Weighing is an essential part of the Company's inventory control and record keeping functions. When polymers and raw materials are transported into the plant by truck, the quantity received is measured by weight, and the best method is to weigh the loaded truck at the time of delivery.

The weighing procedure is not something new that was instituted when the scales were purchased. It has always been done but, prior to June, 1984, it was performed off Company premises by a subcontractor. This controversy arose when the subcontracting was eliminated and the function was assigned to the exempt unit of guards. The Union protested, contending that this job is identical to work ordinarily performed by the represented workforce. In the Union's judgment, using guards to weigh trucks violates Article XI, Section 1(a) of the Agreement which recognizes that certain work belongs to the bargaining unit. The Section provides in part:

> (a) Non-bargaining unit employees will not perform work which would ordinarily be done by employees in the bargaining unit except in emergencies where damage to material or hazard to employee or equipment is involved, in instructing employees or instructing and training employees when methods are changed or work associated with technical difficulties when they develop in the production operation.

The Company resisted the Union's demand for the work, and this grievance was initiated. At the outset of the hearing, the parties stipulated that the Umpire was authorized to issue a conclusive award on the question of whether weighing trucks on Company premises is or is not bargaining unit work which is protected by Article XI, Section 1(a) of the Agreement.

Evidence and Arguments

[Quantity of Work Involved]

Most of the facts are in agreement. There are, however, a few areas of dispute. One concerns the time required to weigh trucks. The Company argues that the grievance is trivial because the work sought by the Union amounts to perhaps ten minutes per day. To support its contention, Management introduced the results of a study. Truck traffic

was monitored during the ten-day period of July 16 through July 26, and it was discovered that, on the average, 3.3 polymer trucks and .5 raw material trucks pass through the gate each day. The Company estimates that the time needed to weigh a polymer truck is less than three minutes, a raw material truck, less than two minutes.

The Union challenges Management's facts as well as its conclusion. According to Union witnesses, a truck cannot be weighed in fewer than fifteen minutes, and often more time is required. However, the Union does not rest on the position that its time estimates are better or more realistic than Management's. It contends that the number of trucks entering the plant today is not indicative of what is expected in the future. The Union reasons that the Company had a sound business motive for installing new scales, and that truck traffic unquestionably will increase to far more than the current level. The Union foresees the possibility that weighing trucks will become a full-time job. Although Management does not agree with the Union's projection, the Warehouse Section Head candidly admitted that a significant increase in truck deliveries is anticipated.

The Union maintains that the dispute over the time required to weigh trucks should not be regarded as substantive in this case. It contends that the critical issue is whether bargaining unit work is being eroded, not how much erosion is occurring. The Union points out that Article XI, Section 1(a) states plainly that exempt personnel shall not perform bargaining unit work. The prohibition is absolute. The Agreement contains no language suggesting that amount of violation is material to the Union's rights. Therefore, the Union maintains that the only question before the Umpire is whether weighing trucks conforms to the contractual definition, "work which would ordinarily be done by employees in the bargaining unit." If it does, the Union contends that the grievance must be sustained. This argument appears in the following portion of the Union's brief:

> [O]ur jobs like most everything in life are made up of many incidental items and if enough incidental items are deleted, a little here, a little there, pretty soon the original job or item or the need for the job or item no longer exists. Do not misunderstand us, we are not saying the job in question [is] an incidental part of the warehouse job because it could be a large job depending on how many trucks, trailers etc are required to be weighed in the future. What we are saying is, the integrity of the Bargaining Unit and the jobs covered by the . . . Agreement and we do not believe that this expansion of our work should be allowed to be transferred to non-bargaining unit employees because the Company would like to have it done that way or it would be a little more convenient for them.

[Functional Jurisdiction]

In the Union's judgment, the function of weighing trucks is indistinguishable from work bargaining unit employees currently perform and performed in the past. The Company receives raw materials by rail as well as by truck, and four years ago it installed scales to weigh rail cars. From the beginning, warehouse personnel who are members of the represented workforce have been assigned to operate those scales. Other measurements of delivered materials also are carried out by the bargaining unit. In the past, when trucks were weighed by the outside contractor, quantities were doubled-checked by a method known as "stocking." The process involved using a measuring stick to determine the volume of material in a receiving tank immediately before and after delivery. Stocking was always recognized as a bargaining unit function, and to the extent that it is still being performed, it continues to be the job of represented employees.

The Union regards railroad car weighing and stocking as substantively identical to weighing trucks primarily because all three functions share the same purpose—determining how much raw material is delivered to the Company in a shipment. The Company disagrees with the Union's conclusion. Its position centers upon the fact that bargaining unit employees have *never* weighed trucks. This is a completely new job in the plant, and it is argued, therefore, that it is not covered by Article XI, Section 1(a). The Section limits Union work jurisdiction to jobs "which would *ordinarily* be done by employees." The Company forcibly contends that a job never before performed by anyone at this plant cannot possibly fall within the contractual definition. In the Company's view, the only provision relevant to the dispute is Article III, which states:

Management Clause

Section 1. The management of the business and the operation of the plants and the authority to execute all of the various duties, functions and responsibilities incident thereto is vested in the Company. The exercise of such authority shall not conflict with this Agreement.

[Efficiency Considerations]

While the Company asserts that assignment of the work was a managerial prerogative, it acknowledges that unreasonable or discriminatory exercises of Management Rights may be open to arbitral intervention. In this case, it is contended, the decision to use guards to weigh trucks was completely reasonable; whereas using bargaining unit personnel would be extremely inefficient and costly. The Company supports its position with three arguments:

1. *The guardpost was the only feasible location for the scales.* Trucks do not

deliver materials to a single plant location. After passing the gate, they are dispatched to any of several areas. Obviously, it would be impracticable to install more than one set of scales and, therefore, the decision to place scales at the plant entrance was the only one that was reasonable. Moreover, the electronic printer mechanism must be housed in a controlled, air-conditioned environment. The guardhouse is the only existing structure which meets this requirement. The Company points out that it would have been wasteful to construct a special building for the scales.

2. *Weighing trucks has important security aspects which are consistent with the general responsibilities of the Company's security force.* The Company is vulnerable to possible theft whenever materials are delivered. According to the Company, a loss could easily occur through conspiracy between a truck driver and an employee assigned to weighing. The employee could purposely record a truck weight as being greater than it actually was. The driver could then deliver less than the full load without fear that the shortage would be discovered, because the true weight of the truck as it exited would indicate a greater delivery than had actually been made. The remaining material could then be sold to a different buyer, resulting in an illegal profit for the employee and the truck driver. Protecting property and ensuring against theft are primary functions of the guard unit. Polymers and raw materials are valuable commodities which the Company believes should be monitored by guards as part of their security responsibilities. In its brief, the Company explained its position as follows:

> It is advantageous to have a third party involved in weight control to avoid coverup of errors or schemes to unlawfully obtain the Company's materials. With our present setup the truck driver has the responsibility to deliver or haul away material, the bargaining unit employee has the responsibility to load or

unload the material and the guard has the responsibility to weigh and make sure the proper weight of material is delivered or shipped.

3. *Weighing trucks is similar to the routine work of the guards.* Guards have a specific responsibility to monitor incoming trucks. They are authorized to issue gate passes only after obtaining certain information. [Company Exhibit 1] is an illustration of the form which must be filled out for every truck entering the property [not reproduced].

The Company argues that recording weights of trucks is not perceptibly different from the other duties guards historically have performed.

The Company's concluding statement emphasizes the fact that assignment in no way diminished the scope of bargaining unit work. The represented employees still do the same jobs they performed before the scales were installed. Since the evidence confirms that Management's decision was founded upon sound business reasons which were not arbitrary, the Company urges that the grievance lacks merit and should be denied.

QUESTIONS

1. After reviewing the background, evidence, and arguments in this case, in your view which side is in a contractually stronger position? Explain.

2. Management claims that efficiency would be sacrificed if bargaining-unit members were to perform the weighing function. How much importance should the arbitrator attach to this argument? Evaluate.

3. If you were the arbitrator what would be your decision? Why?

SOURCE: Labor Arbitration Awards, Commerce Clearing House, Inc. Reproduced with permission from LABOR ARBITRATION AWARDS, published and copyrighted by Commerce Clearing House, Inc., Chicago, Illinois 60646

Pantry Pride Enterprises, Inc., and Bakery, Confectionery and Tobacco Workers International Union of America, AFL-CIO, Local Union No. 482

R.G. CARSON, JR., Arbitrator (FMCS No. 82K/14873). September 10, 1982.

Strikes, Slowdowns and Work Stoppages—Slowdowns—Definitions

[Text of Award]

CARSON, Arbitrator; [INTRODUCTION]: [P.], an employee in the Sanitation Department and a Union shop steward with about six years' seniority, was discharged on June 12, 1981. He filed a grievance protesting his discharge, but the employer responded that the matter was not subject to the grievance or arbitration procedure because he was terminated for inducing his fellow employees to engage in a work slowdown. The collective bargaining agreement provides that the Company may discharge without recourse an employee who engages in a slowdown. The Union's response was to file a second grievance on July 8, 1981, protesting the employer's refusal to entertain the first grievance or to arbitrate the dispute. This grievance was denied by the Company on the same grounds.

On July 13, the Union, on behalf of the grievant, filed unfair labor practice charges against the Company with the National Labor Relations Board. The NLRB Regional Director deferred the matter pending the Union's efforts to proceed with arbitration.

On December 13, 1981, a motion to compel arbitration was filed in the Circuit Court for the Fourth Judicial Circuit, Duval County, Florida. The court ordered that the parties proceed to arbitration according to the terms and procedures contained in the collective bargaining agreement.

[Issues]

The issues to be decided are:

1. Is the discharge of [P.] for allegedly being involved in a work slowdown an arbitrable issue under the collective bargaining agreement?
2. If the matter is arbitrable, was the discharge of [P.] for just cause under the terms of the collective bargaining agreement in effect at the time?
3. If the discharge was not just cause, what is the appropriate remedy?

[Pertinent Contractual Provisions]

Pertinent portions of the collective bargaining agreement are:

Purpose

Section 1. That the joint purpose of this Agreement is to secure industrial peace and efficiency, enabling the Company and the employees to provide as far as economic conditions may permit, security and continuity of employment, and to set forth a basic understanding relative to rates of pay, hours of work and conditions of employment.

Arbitration

Section 17. (a) Any unresolved dispute or grievance arising out of the interpretation of this Agreement, working condition hereunder or affecting the conduct or relationship between the parties shall upon notice from either party to the other be submitted to arbitration . . .

Management Rights

Section 19. The Management of the plant and the direction of the working force, including but not limited by the maintenance of discipline and efficiency of employees, the right to hire, transfer, suspend or discharge for proper cause, issue work instructions, and the right to relieve employees for lack of work or for other legitimate reasons is an exclusive Company function, provided that such will not be used for the purpose of discrimination against any employee of otherwise in conflict with terms of this Agreement.

Cause of Discharge

Section 20. Employees may be discharged or disciplined summarily for just cause, at any time. Just cause shall include but is not limited to, dishonesty, insubordination, incompetence, inefficiency, assault or battery, carrying concealed weapons, possession or use of intoxicating beverages or drugs, negligence, repeated absences or tardiness.

(c) In the event of a disagreement, the discharge shall be handled under the Grievance Procedure as previously set forth.

Work Stoppages

Section 21. During the term of this contract the Union agrees there shall be no strikes, slowdowns, or stoppages of work by the Union or its members and the Company agrees that there shall be no lockouts. The Company may discharge without recourse any employee involved in any strike, slowdown, or work stoppage in violation of this Agreement."

Background

The Company operates a bakery in Jacksonville, Florida as part of a chain of food outlets. Local 482 has been the exclusive bargaining agent for the bakery employees for over 24 years. In October, 1978, the Company filed for bankruptcy proceedings under Chapter XI of the Bankruptcy Act. A number of stores were closed and strenuous efforts were made to control costs. This information was imparted to the employees through meetings and periodic memoranda and employees were urged to contribute their best efforts. Many of them were acutely aware of the possibility that the bakery might close.

The grievant and a co-worker worked as crew mates in the Sanitation Department. The grievant also worked some of the time in the Shipping Department. Duties in the Sanitation Department consisted of cleaning up the machinery, overhead rails and exhaust ducts as well as other assigned jobs to be sure that sanitary conditions were maintained. Sanitation Department employees also performed other work when time permitted, such as painting the walls.

In the months prior to June 1981, several employees complained to Supervisor [K.] that the grievant was not pulling his share of the work load and that he was encouraging them to not do so much work. [K.] talked to all of the employees under his supervision in a group (including the grievant) about the need to maintain good work habits and stay on the job. In addition, he talked individually to the grievant several times about the grievant's work habits and about spending too much time away from his work. [K.] also passed information about the complaints on to his supervisor, the plant manager. It was determined that little could be done unless [K.] could get written statements from other employees.

[K.] asked several employees if they

would be willing to come forward with written complaints concerning the grievant. Several of them in previous talks with [K.] had indicated that while they complained of the grievant's work habits, they did not want to be quoted or drawn into a controversy. In June, however, several of them indicated their willingness to sign statements to the effect that the grievant had encouraged them to slow down. This information was relayed to the plant manager and to [E.], the Company's Director of Personnel and Labor Relations for the area including Jacksonville. [E.] and [L.] worded statements which [L.] typed and four employees signed. These statements, all dated June 9, 1981 and addressed To Whom It May Concern, read as follows:

> This is to certify that the statement given is given of my own free will and do swear that my shop steward Mr. [P.] requested and argued for me to effectuate a slow down regarding my work performance.
>
> This request was made of me by Mr. [P.] on Friday, 6-5-1981 when doing my assigned work of cleaning up the bakery, blowing down and mopping the floor to be exact.
>
> This request by Mr. [P.] has been made several times before. (Note: Signed by [R.] on June 9, 1981.)
>
> This is to certify that the statement given is given of my own free will and do swear that my shop steward Mr. [P.] requested and argued that I should effectuate a slow down regarding my work performance.
>
> This request was made more than one time, however the latest being on Saturday 6-6-1981 during the performance of doing my assigned job of blowing down and mopping the bakery. (Note: Signed by [H.] on June 9, 1981.)
>
> This is to certify that the statement given is given of my own free will and do swear that the shop steward Mr. [P.] requested and argued for me to effectuate a slow down regarding my work performance.
>
> This request was made quite some time back and I do not remember the exact date, however it was during the time that I

was mopping the floor of the bakery as I was part of the sanitation crew and that was one of my jobs. (Note: Signed by [W.] on June 9, 1981.)

> This is to certify that the statement given is given of my own free will and do swear that the shop steward Mr. [P.] requested and argued for me to effectuate a slow down regarding my work performance.
>
> This request by Mr. [P.] was made some time back prior to the time of my transfer from general helper to my present job of maintenance. (Note: Signed by [G.] on June 9, 1981.)

[K.] had the employees come one by one to his office to sign the statements. Information about the statements was relayed to [E.], and [E.] indicated that under the terms of the agreement he had no alternative except to terminate [P.]. Plant Manager [L.] called [P.] to his office and terminated him. The grievance charges and arbitration followed.

Position of the Company

The Company argues that the language of Section 21 of the agreement precludes arbitration. The article provides that the Company may discharge without recourse employees involved in a slow down. Without recourse means that no grievance or arbitration could result. Discharges under Article 20 may be carried through the grievance procedure for that right is specifically set forth, but the right is specifically excluded in Section 21.

Even if it were decided that the matter was arbitrable, the arbitrator would have no authority to alter the penalty. He would be limited solely to determining whether the employee engaged in the cited misconduct. Since Article 21 provides that there shall be no recourse if the employee is guilty of a slowdown, then discharge is the only penalty or discipline permitted.

The grievant engaged in a slowdown by dragging out his work, leaving his assignment periodically to talk with other employees and encouraging others to slowdown in their work. This was conclusively established by the statements and testimony of [R.], [G.], [W.] and [H.] who as a matter of credibility must be believed. They all worked with and had daily contact with the grievant. Statistical evidence in the form of pounds per man hours handled by the Shipping Department during the year after the grievant was terminated show how much work performance improved after the grievant left.

In addition, the grievant also violated Section 20. As a shop steward, the grievant should have been more conscientious about his work habits and should have tried to set a good example. Rather than that, he discouraged other people from working and engaged in poor work habits himself, all of which more than justified his termination.

Position of the Union

The Union contends that the matter is arbitrable. If it were not, the Company could discharge any employee by simply charging that he or she engaged in a slowdown. That would be totally illogical. Section 17 provides that *any* unresolved dispute may be submitted to final and binding arbitration. The section makes no exclusion for discharges that the Company might unilaterally determine to be a slowdown. Taking Sections 21 and 17 together, therefore, the issue of whether an employee has engaged in a slowdown is clearly subject to determination by arbitration. The "without recourse" phrase of Section 21 applies to the discipline that may be imposed once a determination of guilt has been made. Clearly, whether there was a slowdown and whether the grievant was involved in the slowdown has to be determined before a determination can be made that the grievant is to be discharged without recourse.

The question of arbitrability was submitted to the courts in Florida who decided that the matter should be arbitrated under the procedures provided in the contract, and this is what has occurred.

No work slowdown occurred at the bakery. Slowdown is a deliberate effort by employees to alter their work habits so as to impede the ultimate production of their employer's final product. This definition does not encompass the events that took place at the bakery. The only evidence concerning overall productivity was the table of pounds per man hour in the Shipping Department and general testimony that matters were better after the grievant's termination. None of this information was specific nor would it hold up under close scrutiny. No equipment was ever inoperative due to lack of work that should have been done by the grievant, nor was the next shift ever delayed.

The Company has the burden of proving that the grievant himself engaged in or encouraged a work slowdown with the deliberate intent to restrict production. It has failed to carry this burden. Most of the evidence related to the individual work habits of the grievant and does not support the Company's position of a decline in productivity connected to the grievant.

The statements provided by the four fellow employees do not constitute evidence of a slowdown. Most of their testimony at the hearing had to do with the grievant's work habits, not with efforts to encourage a slowdown. Many of the grievant's remarks were taken as jokes. Others were isolated comments. There were never arguments concerning doing less work or stretching the work out. The grievant was away from his work often because of his activities as a shop steward.

The Company has failed to show that the grievant engaged in or encouraged a slowdown or otherwise violated Section 21 of the agreement.

QUESTIONS

1. Under Section 20, "Employees may be discharged or disciplined summarily for just cause, at any time." Did the management have legitimate reasons in discharging Grievant [P] "for just cause"?

2. Is an employee necessarily engaging in a "slowdown" when he or she slows down or "takes it easy" on the job and successfully encourages others to do so also?

3. Can a "slowdown" consist of one employee?

4. During future contract negotiations, what changes should management attempt to make in Section 19 and Section 21, if any?

5. If you were the management in this case, how would you have handled the grievant's issue?

SOURCE: Labor Arbitration Awards Cited, Commerce Clearing House, Inc. Reproduced with permission from LABOR ARBITRATION AWARDS, published and copyrighted by Commerce Clearing House, Inc., Chicago, Illinois 60646

Century Papers, Inc., and United Paperworkers International Union, Local No. 768

SAMUEL J. NICHOLAS, JR., Arbitrator. Selected through FMCS, No. 84K/04754. Hearing held at Houston, Texas, April 25, 1984. Award issued June 6, 1984.

Lie Detector Tests—Refusal to Take, Effect— Second Test—Termination of Employment

[Text of Award]

NICHOLAS, Arbitrator; [GRIE-VANCE]: The parties to this dispute, Century Papers, Inc. ("Company") and the United Paperworkers International Union, Local #768 ("Union"), are signatories to a certain collective bargaining agreement, ("Agreement"). Under said Agreement, Union is recognized as the sole collective bargaining agent for all production and maintenance employees at Company's Houston, Texas plant (*See* Article I). Company, likewise, has retained certain Management Rights, including the right to manage the business and direct the working forces (*See* Article II).

This matter comes on to arbitration via a certain complaint ("grievance") filed by Union on behalf of one [R.] ("Grievant"). The grievance, as written by Union and dated September 30, 1983, reads as follows:

> I was fired unjustly for no reason. I want my job back with back pay and no seniority loss.

The grievance was properly filed and has been duly considered and processed through the various stages of the contractually provided grievance procedure (*See* Article XIV); however, with the parties having failed to reach a satisfactory resolution of the matter, the dispute was moved forward to arbitration.

[Pertinent Contractual Provisions]

This provisions of the Agreement, cited as relevant and pertinent to the instant case, are hereby noted:

Article II—Management Rights

Section 1. The management of the Company's business and direction of the working forces, including the right to plan, direct, expand, reduce, control and terminate operations, to hire, assign, transfer, suspend, or discharge for just cause, to relieve employees from duty because of lack of work or for any other bona fide reason, the right to introduce any new or improved methods or facilities, and to make such rules and regulations as may be necessary or desirable for the operation of the business (provided that such rules and regulations are reduced to writing by the Company and made available to the Union and the employees) shall be vested exclusively in the Company provided that such rules and regulations are not in conflict with the terms of this Agreement; provided, however, that the exercise of these functions shall not be applied so as to discriminate against any employee.

Article XIV—Grievance Procedure and Arbitration

Section 1. For the purpose of this Agreement, the term Grievance means any dispute between the Company and the Union or between the Company and any employee or employees concerning the effect, interpretation, application, claim of breach or violation of this Agreement, or any dispute which may arise between the parties.

Section 10. In any case where an employee is discharged or otherwise disciplined by the Company for any reason other than the infraction of a Company rule or regulation, and the grievance is submitted to arbitration, the Arbitrator's authority shall be limited as follows:

(a) To a determination of the question of whether or not the employee was discharged or otherwise disciplined for just cause. The Arbitrator shall not determine that the discipline imposed by the Company is too severe if just cause for disciplinary action exists.

(b) In the event the Arbitrator shall find that any employee was not disciplined or discharged for just case, the arbitrator shall not award back pay in any case for more than a period of sixty (60) days after the date of mailing of the panel of arbitrators by the Federal Mediation & Conciliation Service, or after the date of designating a mutually agreed upon arbitrator, as the case may be.

Section 11. The Arbitrator shall not have authority to alter, amend or change the terms or provisions of this Agreement in any way. If the Arbitrator's decision exceeds his authority as defined in this Article, the decision shall be null and void in its entirety. The decision of the arbitrator within the purview of his authority as herein confined shall be final and binding on the parties.

Article XV—Seniority

Section 4. Any employee guilty of any of the following offenses may be summarily discharged:

(a) Bringing intoxicants or narcotics into or consuming intoxicants or narcotics in the plant or upon the plant premises or while riding in or driving any of the Company's motor vehicles;

(b) Reporting for duty under the influence of intoxicating liquors;

(c) Willful or negligent destruction of property or Company's trucks or equipment;

(d) Any willful act omission which endangers property, health or life;

(e) Stealing;

(f) The use of profane, abusive and/or threatening language toward customers and supervisors or other employees;

(g) Falsification of any records or reports submitted to the Company;

(h) Willful disregard of Company safety practices;

(i) Becoming of unsound mind.

Article XVIII—Responsibilities

Section 1. The Union and its members recognize that it is to their best interest as well as to the best interest of the Company for the Company to produce a quality product.

Section 2. The parties recognize that the operation of the plant and the direction of the work force therein is the sole responsibility of the Company, which is in accordance with other provisions of this contract. Such responsibility includes among other things: (1) the right to discharge, discipline, demote, layoff or suspend for just cause; (2) the right to hire, schedule and assign work; (3) the right to transfer, promote, demote, layoff or recall employees.

Section 3. The Union and all members covered by this Agreement hereby pledge themselves to use every earnest and diligent effort to eliminate waste, inefficient operation, incorrect reporting of time on time cards and damage to materials and equipment and to cooperation in every possible way toward maintaining and advancing the employer's competitive position in the industry.

Article XXIV—Duration

Section 1. This Agreement, when executed, shall be deemed to define wages, hours and rates of pay and other terms and conditions of employment of the employees covered hereby for the term hereof, and no new or additional issues not included herein or covered hereby shall be subject to negotiations between the Company and the Union during the term of this Agreement, except by mutual agreement of the parties.

Section 2. It is agreed and expressly understood that this Agreement contains the entire understanding and contract between the Company and the Union and any prior or subsequent undertakings inconsistent with this Agreement shall be null and void."

[Facts]

This case turns on the matter of credibility; thus, there is considerable controversy over the relevant facts. Accordingly, the Arbitrator has attempted to reconcile the parties' conflicting representations and such is reflected in the following summary.

Company owns and operates a Warehouse Distribution Center in Houston, Texas, which employs approximately 29 bargaining unit employees. At this facility, Company warehouses paper products, cleaning products, supplies and the like, which are distributed to various customers throughout the Houston area.

Grievant is a truck driver within the bargaining unit, and one who is responsible for making deliveries to various locations on a given route. On a particular day in mid-

August, 1983 (the date is uncertain), Grievant made deliveries to a Palais Royal store in downtown Houston. This store—as with many on Grievant's route—deals in jewelry, perfume and other such expensive merchandise. Upon completing his delivery around 9:00 A.M., Grievant continued on his route as per his usual practice.

At some later date, perhaps a week or so after Grievant's delivery on the day in question, a complaint was made to Company by the Security Chief at Palais Royal, concerning a certain allegation by one of Palais Royal's employees. Specifically, the allegation charged that Grievant had proposed that Palais Royal employee secured some "Halston" brand perfume for Grievant (by stealing or some other means) so that he could "purchase" the perfume at a reduced price. Upon receipt of the complaint, Company decided that Grievant should take a polygraph examination to "clear the matter up." In that connection, on September 2, 1983, Grievant was given a polygraph examination by one [W.], a trainer examiner. [W.'s] analysis of the examination stated that conclusive results could not be reached due to "erratic physiological responses noted on this subject's charts." Grievant was charged with "deliberate failure to follow instructions given by this examiner."

Following his inconclusive polygraph test, Grievant was allowed to return to work until Company reached a final decision on the matter. In assessing the examiner's findings, Management surmised that Grievant had deliberately attempted to distort the results of the examination. Accordingly, company advised Grievant that he would be required to take another polygraph and that the second examination was to be paid for by him because of his tactics in deliberately disturbing the first test. Grievant refused to take another test, contending that he had been harassed by the examiner during the first test and that he could not afford to pay for another examination.

Grievant persisted in his refusal to take another test, notwithstanding an offer by Union and Company officials to jointly pay for the test. Finally, on September 28, 1983, Grievant was discharged for his refusal to take another polygraph examination; and it was at this point that the subject grievance was filed.

[Positions of the Parties]

The positions of the parties are summarized as follows:

Company

1. Grievant was justly discharged for his refusal to comply with his supervisor's request that he take another polygraph test; this refusal constituted insubordination. Furthermore, in refusing another polygraph, Grievant violated a well-known Company rule and practice which requires employees to take polygraph examinations upon demand by Management.

2. Under the Employee Agreement of 2/6/79, Grievant agreed to submit to polygraph tests "when requested at any time." Thus, in refusing to submit to such a test, Grievant has violated this agreement.

3. The request made by Grievant was a proper exercise of Management's Rights under Article II; and, his refusal to comply to Management's request constitutes proper grounds for summary discharge under Article XV, §4.

4. Grievant was *not* discharged for theft. Any determination on this question is outside the realm of the Arbitrator's jurisdiction in the instant case; it would be null and void under Article XIV, §11 of the Agreement.

5. After due consideration of the facts in this case, it should be clear that the discharge should stand as given; the grievance should, therefore, be denied in its entirety.

Union

1. The agreement signed by Grievant which required him to submit to polygraph examinations was a pre-employment agreement and should be viewed as effective only while Grievant was a probationary employee. The requirement of taking polygraphs upon demand of Company has not been made a part of the parties' Agreement.

2. Prospective and probationary employees are not Union members; they are not represented by Union when they sign the agreement to take polygraph tests. However, once they come under the Agreement, employees are not required to take polygraph examinations except on a voluntary basis.

3. Grievant has, in fact, actually complied with Management's request because he has already taken a polygraph test—in which he was harassed and badgered by the examiner. To be sure, he should not be required to take another examination simply because of the examiner's inability to make conclusive findings based on the first test.

4. The fact that Company offered to pay for the second polygraph is irrelevant, as this offer was made *after* Grievant had already been discharged.

5. The accusation that Grievant was forced to take a polygraph was based solely on hearsay evidence. No direct evidence was presented against Grievant to substantiate the so called accusation made by the phantom Palais Royal employee.

6. Grievant has an excellent work record, with no disciplinary action of any kind ever having been taken against him. Moreover, his supervisor recommended re-hiring him.

7. The grievance should be fully upheld: Grievant should be reinstated and

made whole for all lost back pay and seniority.

QUESTIONS

1. In addition to the contract language and the facts of the case, what may the arbitrator consider in deciding this case?
2. What effect should past practice have in this case, if any? Explain.
3. In an effort to strengthen their respective positions with regard to the poly-graph issue, what language do you suggest the parties attempt to insert in their next contract?
4. How should the arbitrator decide this case? Why?

SOURCE: Labor Arbitration Awards Cited, Commerce Clearing House, Inc. Reproduced with permission from LABOR ARBITRATION AWARDS, published and copyrighted by Commerce Clearing House, Inc., Chicago, Illinois 60646

Kroger Company and United Food and Commercial Workers International Union, Local 347

WILLIAM C. STONEHOUSE, JR., Arbitrator. Hearings held December 10, 1983, and January 11, 1984. Award issued at Johns Island, South Carolina, June 8, 1984.

Theft—Conspiracy to Steal—Company Property—Termination of Employment—Basis

[Text of Award]

STONEHOUSE, Arbitrator; ISSUE: The issue is: whether or not there was just cause for the termination of the Grievant, [P.].

Pertinent Portions of the Agreement

Article 4—Management Rights

The management of the business and direction of the working forces, including the right to plan, direct and control store operations, hire, suspend, or discharge for proper cause, relieve employees from duty because of lack of work or for other legitimate reasons, the right to study or introduce new or improved production methods and facilities, and the right to establish and maintain rules and regulations covering the operation of the stores, are vested in the Employer. Nothing contained herein shall deprive an employee of his rights as provided for by this Agreement.

Article 5

. . .

Section 5.9 "The Employer shall have the right to discharge for any good and sufficient cause. Any discharge shall be subject to the grievance procedure. If arbitration results in reinstatement, back pay shall be paid in accordance with the decision of the arbitrator."

. . .

Pertinent Portion of the "Basic Store Rules"

. . .

14. Dishonesty—Any act of dishonesty will lead to disciplinary action up to and including discharge, a violation of the rules listed under this heading will not be tolerated and will be considered to be discharge offenses.

a. Employees may not consume, remove, or cause to be removed, company property without a specific authorization.

Background

The Grievant, [P.], was employed at what is known as store 731 in Huntington, West Virginia, as a dairy clerk and has about 20 years service with the Company. He frequently substituted for the head dairy clerk when that employee was absent on vacations and the like, since at one time he had been a head dairy clerk.

During the summer of 1983 a lady who lived near the store noticed a man parked in a car at the rear of the store and on two occasions she saw him (once in a truck rather than a car) load boxes from the rear door of the store into his car or truck, assisted by a store employee who she later identified as the Grievant, [P.]. She testified that the boxes appeared to be heavy.

The lady had a son-in-law who worked at the store and she reported the incidents to him. He in turn reported this to the store manager and he reported it to the district manager, who had his headquarters at store 731.

On Monday, September 19, 1983, the Grievant asked the store manager if he could come to work early to clean out the milk cases and also asked him if he would be taking the day off. (The Grievant was filling in as head dairy clerk for the week.)

His suspicions aroused, the store manager contacted the district manager. The store manager agreed to go ahead and take the day off but it was arranged that if anything unusual occurred, the district manager would contact him.

The district manager came to work on Tuesday morning and noticed and spoke to a Kraft salesman, who was talking on the telephone. He then noticed three egg cartons laying on the floor and shortly thereafter he noticed them sitting on a pallet load of Kraft products which had been delivered that morning. He then called the store manager, who came to a place outside the store where he could observe the rear door, and the district manager also left the store to a point where he could observe from the outside the store.

The district manager returned to the store where he saw the salesman and the Grievant conversing, then left again. On the way out he mentioned to the salesman that he had a busy schedule and the salesman stated

that he did also. The manager drove away but returned to a point near the store.

The store manager saw the salesman leave the store and sit in his car for 20-30 minutes and then move it to an access road. Then he observed the Grievant come out the back of the store with three egg cartons on a stock cart and look around the corner of the store to the salesman's car, whereupon the salesman drove to the rear door of the store. The Grievant and the salesman then began loading the egg crates into the car.

The two managers then walked toward the back door, and as they approached, the district manager observed the Grievant write something on a piece of paper, which later turned out to be one sheet of a three-part form used to transfer products. He asked them what they were doing and the salesman stated several times that they were moving the product to store 717, until he was reminded that store 717 had been closed for a year. He then stated that they were moving it to store 724 in Russell, Kentucky, where a big display rack was available and the product could readily be moved.

The three egg crates each contained three 36 pound cartons of cheese, the total cost value of the lot being $730.08.

The district manager then brought the Kraft salesman and the Grievant to his office where he questioned them. The Grievant stated that he had received ten cases of cheese when he had ordered only one, and the salesman suggested he transfer the excess to store 724.

The salesman gave essentially the same story except that he said the Grievant had asked him to take the excess merchandise to store 724 which he had called in advance but the telephone line was busy.

The district manager then suspended the Grievant pending further investigation and subsequently terminated his employment for "removal of product from the store without proper authorization or documentation and for violating employer purchase policy."

The instant grievance was then filed, and, remaining unresolved, it has been appealed to arbitration hereunder.

Contentions of the Parties

Company Contentions

The Company contends that the Grievant clearly violated the Company rule forbidding removal of Company property from the premises without authorization to do so.

Grievant's defense that there were no management personnel available from whom to obtain approval at the time is without merit, according to the Company, and it notes that the Grievant spoke with both the store co-manager and the district manager on the morning in question after he had received the alleged overshipment of cheese and made no mention of the matter to them. His other defense that it was common practice to make such transfers is equally invalid according to the Company, and was refuted by the Union's own witnesses who testified that they always received permission from their manager or the receiving store before making such transfers.

Although the Company maintains that it is not necessary to prove intent to steal the cheese, it argues that that was the Grievant's intent as shown by the evidence and testimony presented.

It points to the neighbor's reports of suspicious activity behind the store by the salesman and the Grievant, and the loading of heavy boxes into the salesman's car and truck.

It asserts that the Grievant ordered the excess cheese, as is indicated by Company records, with the intent to steal it, made the transactions so that they occurred at a time when the head dairy clerk was on vacation and came to work an hour early on the day in question so as to assure a lack of supervision.

The Company further points to a similar suspicious transaction which occurred when the head dairy clerk was on a previous vacation and thirty cases of cheese were ordered and no one in the store noticed an overstock.

Also, the Company argues that the Grievant had no intention of completing a transfer form (form 40) which he claimed he was filling out to transfer the cheese. It notes that he had only one copy of the form which comes in sets of three, that the form was improperly filled out as to quantity and description and maintains that the Grievant did this hurriedly when he saw that the manager was approaching in order to cover his tracks.

The Grievant's entire story, as well as the salesman's, lacks credibility in its entirety according to the Company and it submits that there was just cause for the termination of the Grievant and that the grievance should be denied.

Union Contentions

The Union contends that the Company has failed to prove a violation of rule 14(a) or that the Grievant intended to steal the cheese and that there was not just cause for the termination of the Grievant.

Although it concedes that the rule is fairly clear, it maintains that the common practice was entirely different. It points out that various witnesses testified that they had transferred products to other stores without permission or even the knowledge of the store manager. As to the form 40 used to transfer products, it argues that these were sometimes filled out before loading the product, after loading the product and during the loading of the product and were sometimes signed by the sending store, sometimes by the receiving store, and sometimes not at all. It also notes that none of the employees received any training in the use of the forms and that the requirement that they be signed by the store manager was only instituted after the incident in which the Grievant, [P.], was involved occurred.

The Grievant did not order extra cheese in order to steal it, the Union argues, as shown by the fact that the regular head dairy clerk was at work on the day the cheese was ordered and that numerous witnesses testified that the warehouse frequently sent to stores more products than had been ordered.

The fact that the Grievant came to work early on the day in question and inquired as to whether the manager was taking the day off should be given no weight, according to the Union, since the regular clerk frequently came to work early with and without permission, and several other employees had also inquired about the manager's day off.

As to concealing the cheese in egg cartons, the Union argues that egg cartons were frequently used to transfer products, there were no tops on the cartons, and the Grievant was merely using a handy method to load the cheese in the salesman's car after the salesman had agreed to take the excess cheese to another store where it could readily be disposed of.

The Company's case is based entirely on circumstantial evidence without clear and convincing proof of any intent to violate company policy or to steal the cheese according to the Union, and it argues that a stricter standard of proof is required where such serious charges are made than in lesser ones. In this respect, it cites a prior arbitration award in this same Kroger district and published authorities on the matter.

The Company, having failed to show just cause, the Union submits that the grievance should be sustained and that the Grievant should be reinstated to his employment with full back pay and all other contractual benefits.

QUESTIONS

1. As the arbitrator, what evidence should you give most weight? Why?
2. How might the union or the employer present its arguments more effectively?
3. How should the arbitrator rule in this case? Why?

Macy's Midwest and International Brotherhood of Teamsters, Chauffeurs, Warehousemen and Helpers of America, Local Union No. 20

PETER DILEONE, Arbitrator. Selected through FMCS, No. 84K/10160. Award issued at Cleveland, Cuyahoga County, Ohio, May 23, 1984.

Alcoholism, Drinking and Intoxication— Lunch-Hour Drinking—Plant Rules— Penalty Undefined—Termination of Employment

[Text of Award]

DiLEONE, Arbitrator; BACKGROUND FACTS: Macy's Midwest is in the business of retail sales. It owns and operates three department stores and a distribution warehouse in the Toledo area.

Local No. 20 of the Teamsters represents the drivers and warehouse employees in the Toledo warehouse. Both grievants were drivers at the time they were discharged for "drinking while on the job."

The issue in this case is whether or not there was just cause for the discharges.

For some time prior to the effective date of the current labor agreement, reports filtered through to Management that there was some drinking on the job by some drivers on their routes. It was not made clear in the evidence whether or not any attempt was made to determine what was consumed or who among the drivers was doing the drinking on the routes during working hours.

During the last contract negotiations, leading to the current agreement dated August 1, 1983, Management's negotiator informed the Union people at the negotiating table that drinking on the job would not be tolerated.

One of the Union members of that negotiating team was the grievant, Henneman, who admitted under cross-examination that the Company was not going to tolerate drinking on the job.

As a result of those negotiations, the parties agreed to include in Article VIII, Section 1 a prohibition against drinking on the job, and it reads as follows:

Article VIII—Discharge or Suspension

Section 1. The Employer shall not discharge or suspend any employee without just cause. In respect to discharge or suspension the Employer shall give at least one warning notice of the complaint against such employee to the employee, in writing, and a copy of the same to the Union and job steward affected, except that no warning notice need be given to an employee before he is discharged if the cause of such discharge is dishonesty, or drinking while on the job. . . .

After the contract went into effect, reports of some drinking still filtered through to Management, and as a result, observations of driver conduct by the Security Department was ordered.

The evidence establishes that on Friday, October 14, 1983, three security employ-

541

ees of the Company were sent out on several routes to observe driver activities.

The two grievants, [H.] and [S.], were working together on a route on the above date and at about noon, the security employees found their Company delivery truck parked at a bar and grill. One of the security employees entered the restaurant and saw both of the grievants there.

The security employee testified that while he was in the bar, he saw the two grievants each drinking two cans of beer, and a report was made of this incident. No discipline of any kind was imposed.

On the following Monday, grievant [S.] was again observed with another driver drinking beer at another restaurant, and several days later, both of the grievants, [S.] and [H.], were again observed drinking beer during their lunch hour at a restaurant. In none of these cases was discipline imposed.

Following these and other incidents of drinking by drivers on the job, Management decided that a group warning to the drivers was in order.

On October 26, 1983, such a group warning was issued except that no mention was made as to what the penalties would be if a driver was found to be drinking on the job.

For a while thereafter, no drinking was observed. It was not clear whether any security observers were sent out, but when reports later on filtered through to the effect that drinking on the job was taking place, security people went on the lookout again.

On January 10, 1984, both grievants worked together on a delivery route covering several "out-of-town stops." They were followed by security personnel who testified that the two grievants, on this occasion, were observed drinking beer in a cafe in Findlay, Ohio. Upon interrogating the grievants, after identification was made, each admitted they drank two beers during their lunch period.

Following the report of this latest incident, serious action was deemed to be in or-

der. There followed the discharge of both grievants and immediately thereafter, the two grievances were filed. The said grievances charge the Company with the imposition of "far too severe" a penalty, and in both cases the Union asks reinstatement of [H.] and [S.] and "back pay for time lost above any reasonable disciplinary action."

[Positions of the Parties]

The Company contends that its action of discharge in both cases was justified. The grievants were fully aware of the provisions of the contract which specifically prohibits drinking while on the job, says the Company, and both knew the penalty for such improprieties.

The Company contends further that condonation of such conduct, as drinking on the job, would effectively destroy whatever purpose was intended in the placement of such a requirement in the contract, especially with drivers who are in the public eye.

The Union takes the view that the penalties imposed upon both grievants do not fit the crime, especially since no employee was ever informed that drinking a beer or two at lunchtime would result in capital punishment under the cited contract provision.

QUESTIONS

1. Why do you suppose the company imposed such harsh penalties on these employees?

2. How should the company have approached the problem of drinking employees?

3. If you were the personnel manager or the union president, what steps would you have taken to improve your chances of winning the grievance?

SOURCE: Labor Arbitration Awards, Commerce Clearing House, Inc. Reproduced with permission from LABOR ARBITRATION AWARDS, published and copyrighted by Commerce Clearing House, Inc., Chicago, Illinois 60646

Associated Truck Lines, Inc., and Chicago Truck Drivers, Helpers and Warehouse Workers Union (Independent)

SAMUEL EDES, Arbitrator. Hearings held on February 10, and March 9, 1984. Award issued at Chicago, Illinois, June 21, 1984.

Alcoholism, Drinking and Intoxication— Drinking Prior to Reporting—Accident— Refusal of Sobriety Test—Impaired Condition

[Text of Award]

EDES, Arbitrator; STATEMENT OF THE CASE: The grievance before me concerns the discharge of [P.] (hereinafter "Grievant") for events that occurred on April 24, 1983.

The Company is a carrier of general commodities freight. In April of 1983 it had five trucking terminals in the Chicago area. The Company employs two classes of truck drivers, each performing distinct duties and each represented by a different Union. City pick up and delivery drivers, represented by the Chicago Truck Drivers, Helpers and Warehouse Workers Union (Independent) (hereinafter "Union"), pick up and deliver general freight at various Company customers within a sixty-mile radius of the Chicago metropolitan area. Over-the-road drivers, on the other hand, travel between cities and generally cover greater distances than city drivers. They are represented by Local 710 of the International Brotherhood of Teamsters, Chauffeurs, Warehousemen and Helpers of America (hereinafter "Local 710"). Grievant was employed as a city driver.

Notwithstanding this division of labor, the Company has had occasion to employ city drivers in an over-the-road capacity. Generally, this occurs on weekends when over-the-road drivers are either unavailable or have run out of statutory driving time. When confronted with this situation the Company posts sign-up sheets on the Thursday before the weekend assignment, notifying city drivers of the opportunity. Qualified city drivers may sign the sheet, indicating their willingness to accept such an assignment. From the various sign-up sheets the Company compiles a master list, arranging the names by seniority. The Company then goes down the list and offers the drivers the over-the-road assignments. If the driver accepts, the Company will call him back within two hours of the scheduled run and inform him of the specific time he is supposed to go. Acceptance of an over-the-road run is purely voluntary on the part of the driver. Even after entering his name on the sign-up sheet he may thereafter reject any run that is offered him. If a city driver accepts the over-the-road run he is paid according to the rates set forth in the Company's collective bargaining agreement with Local 710, as opposed to those in the agreement with the Union.

The Grievant was discharged as a consequence of events that took place on Sunday, April 24, 1983, while he was making an over-the-road run. Grievant had put his name on the sign-up sheet the preceeding Thursday. On Sunday morning at 10:30 a.m. he received a telephone call at home offering him the opportunity to run a load of freight from the Company's South Holland terminal to East Moline. In East Moline he would drop off the freight, pick up a new load and return to South Holland. Grievant accepted the run.

Grievant punched in at South Holland at 12:25 p.m. and left for East Moline at 1:30 p.m. He arrived in East Moline at 5:00 p.m. and began the return trip at about 5:30 p.m. This trip proceeded without incident until approximately 9:50 p.m. At that time, while attempting to exit from the highway, he lost control of the truck and crashed through a guard rail. The location of the accident was four blocks from the South Holland terminal.

Shortly thereafter a State Trooper arrived at the scene of the accident and asked the Grievant to produce his driver's license, his driver's log and the vehicle registration card. Grievant was unable to find the registration card and told the Trooper he had left the log at home. The Trooper thereupon took the Grievant to the State Police barracks. Upon arriving at the barracks the Trooper requested that Grievant take a sobriety test. Grievant asked to speak to an attorney first. The Trooper did not permit him to do so at that time and instead began to write out four tickets against Grievant, telling him he could call his attorney when he was finished. The tickets were for driving while under the influence, improper lane usage, driving without a registration card and failure to keep the required logs. Grievant did not call an attorney at any time.

At approximately 11:30 p.m. Grievant contacted Central Dispatch, the Company's office in Grand Rapids, Michigan, and notified it of the accident. Central Dispatch then notified [S.], the Company's Regional Safety Supervisor. [S.] instructed Central Dispatch to contact the South Holland terminal and

have individuals there investigate the situation. [M.], a supervisor at the South Holland terminal, went to the scene of the accident that evening.

Grievant did not report to the South Holland terminal until approximately 1:00 a.m. on the morning of April 25. At the terminal he met with [M.] and [A.], another supervisor. By this time Grievant's truck had been towed from the scene of the accident by a private towing company. Grievant told [M.] and [A.] that he had left some personal belongings in the truck and wished to retrieve them. [M.] asked Grievant to remain at the terminal until [S.] arrived so that they could complete the necessary accident reports. [M.] testified that during the conversation he detected the odor of alcohol on Grievant's breath. Accordingly, [M.] asked the Grievant to submit to a sobriety test. Grievant refused, stating that if he would not take the test for the State Police, he was not going to take it for the Company. [M.] thereupon told Grievant he was discharged. On April 26, 1983, the Company sent Grievant a discharge letter, citing his refusal to submit to the sobriety test, "all indications, your actions and strong odor of alcohol on your breath."

The above narrative sets forth a skeletal outline of the events leading to the decision to discharge the Grievant. There was additional testimony pertaining to Grievant's actions on the weekend of April 24. This testimony, which in the main related to Grievant's physical condition while making the over-the-road run, is of critical importance in determining whether there is cause for Grievant's discharge.

The Grievant testified that on Saturday evening, April 23, he and his wife attended a party. Grievant did not leave the party until 4:30 a.m. Sunday morning, April 24. Grievant admitted to drinking "at least" ten beers at the party. Grievant had his wife drive him home from the party as he had had too much to drink. Once he arrived home Grievant did not go to bed. Instead he stayed up, reading the newspaper and talking with his father. Grievant denied having any more to drink after leaving the party.

Grievant, therefore, was still awake at 10:30 a.m. on April 24 when he received the Company's call offering him the run from South Holland to East Moline and back. Grievant accepted, although he knew he was under no obligation to do so. Grievant was asked why he accepted the run despite not having had any sleep and after consuming so much alcohol at the party. At the hearing before the Joint Grievance Committee Grievand stated, "I just took the chance because I lost so much time—." At the arbitration hearing, however, he stated that he felt he was in fit condition.

Grievant reported to the South Holland terminal and punched in at 12:25 p.m. on Sunday, April 24. He left for East Moline at 1:30 p.m. Grievant denied drinking any alcoholic beverages between the time he left the party on Sunday morning, 4:30 a.m., and the time of the accident, approximately 9:30 p.m. However, he did admit to consuming seven or eight ounces of NyQuil while driving because he had a cold. NyQuil has an alcohol content of twenty-five percent. The label on the bottle bears this warning: "This preparation may cause drowsiness. Do not drive or operate machinery while taking this medication." Further, the label indicates the recommended dosage as one ounce at bedtime or one ounce every six hours for people confined to bed. Grievant testified that the NyQuil did not make him drowsy.

As far as the accident is concerned, Grievant lost control of his vehicle while making a gradual right-hand turn on an exit ramp. While the ramp had a posted speed limit of 25 miles per hour, Grievant testified that he was travelling between 30 to 35 miles per hour at the time of the accident. The truck crashed through a guardrail. Forty feet of guardrail, two upright posts, a light pole and a traffic sign had to be replaced by the Illinois State Toll Highway Authority, which billed the Company $3,180.80.

Grievant did not report the accident to the South Holland terminal. He did notify the Company's Central Dispatch office in Michigan. After receiving the four tickets at the State Police barracks, Grievant telephoned his wife to have her pick him up. Grievant returned home, where he drank two beers to calm his nerves. While at home he grew concerned about personal belongings he had left in the truck and went to the South Holland terminal to find out the location to which the truck had been towed. Once there he had the conversation with [M.] and [A.] which resulted in his being asked to submit to a sobriety test and his refusal.

Twice on the evening of April 24, Grievant was asked to take a sobriety test, once by the State Police and once by his employer. He refused on both occasions. At the hearing in this matter Grievant was asked to give his reasons for doing so. With respect to the State Police request, Grievant stated that he did not flatly refuse to take the test. Instead, he merely asked to speak to an attorney first but was denied permission. As far as the Company's request is concerned, Grievant admittedly told [M.] that if he did not take the test for the State Police he was not going to take it for him.

Grievant has given two different explanations for refusing to submit to a sobriety test for the Company. At his appearance before the Joint Grievance Committee Grievant testified to his fear that his consumption of NyQuil would adversely affect his performance on the test. At the hearing in this arbitration he asserted as his reason the consumption of two beers at home after the accident. He acknowledged that this was the first time he had revealed this information.

Grievant retained an attorney to represent him on the traffic tickets. On August 9, 1983, he pleaded guilty to one of the charges—failure to keep the required logs—for which he was fined and placed under court supervision. The other three charges, including the DWI charge, were stricken off the call with leave to reinstate ("SOL"). SOL is a device which permits the prosecutor to deactivate criminal charges. If after a specified period of time the prosecutor has not moved to reinstate the charges, they are dismissed. The parties disagreed over the significance of this deposition. The Union presented the testimony of the attorney who represented Grievant on the tickets, who claimed that a disposition of SOL is, for all practical purposes, a dismissal of the charges. The Company has cited Illinois case law holding that an SOL'd charge is not dismissed but only dormant. In any event the time period for reinstating the charges has passed and there is nothing in the record suggesting that a motion to reinstate has been made.

Finally, as a consequence of not taking the sobriety test for the State Police Grievant's driver's license was suspended for six months.

[Issue]

The issue before me is whether the discharge of the Grievant was for just cause.

[Contentions of the Parties]

The Company advances two basic arguments in support of its position. First, it asserts that Grievant was under the influence of an intoxicant while making the over-the-road run on April 24, 1983, and that this clearly constitutes just cause. Second, it cites Grievant's refusal to submit to the sobriety test as grounds for discharge and as establishing a presumption of drunkenness.

The Union vigorously argues that there is no evidence tending to show that Grievant was intoxicated while making the run. There is no evidence that Grievant had anything to drink after 4:30 a.m. Sunday morning, some eight hours before he punched in. Further, it argues that the discharge of Grievant constitutes prohibited disparate treatment, as the Company in the past has commuted the discharges of its drivers for drinking to suspensions.

QUESTIONS

1. In your view, was the discharge of the grievant for just cause?

2. In your view should grievant's refusal to submit to the sobriety test be sufficient grounds for discharge? Explain.

3. Discuss the importance of past practice for this case.

4. What weight should be given grievant's claim that he was ignorant of the company's policy?

5. Why do you suppose the union pursued this grievance to the arbitration step?

6. How should the arbitrator decide this case?

SOURCE: Labor Arbitration Awards, Commerce Clearing House, Inc. Reproduced with permission from LABOR ARBITRATION AWARDS, published and copyrighted by Commerce Clearing House, Inc., Chicago, Illinois 60646

National Distillers Products Company and International Brotherhood of Firement Oilers, Local No. 73

EARL M. CURRY, Jr., Arbitrator. Selected through FMCS, No. 83K/21078. Award issued May 4, 1984.

Bumping—Restriction of Bumping Rights—Temporary Termination of Job—Choice of Available Positions—Chain Bumping

[Text of Award]

CURRY, Arbitrator; BACKGROUND: The instant grievance arose between the National Distillers Products Company (the "Company") and the International Brotherhood of Firemen and Oilers, Local No. 73, AFL-CIO (the "Union") when the Company, during a reduction in the work force, refused to allow the grievant, [P.], to bump into the job of his choice, but instead required him to bump the employee with the least seniority in the bargaining unit. The instant grievance was filed by [P.] on May 4, 1983 and was processed through the various steps of the parties' grievance procedure. When the parties were unable to resolve the matter between themselves it was referred to arbitration.

Statement of Facts

The Company operates a facility in Cincinnati, Ohio, in which it produces and bottles distilled spirits of various types. An integral part of this facility is the boiler room operation. A seasonal pattern exists with regard to the boiler operation. During the winter months, typically November through May, the boiler is in operation continuously, seven days a week. During this time period the boiler operation is staffed with one Fireman per shift, seven days per week. A Helper is also assigned on two shifts, seven days a week, and there is a single Fireman "A" assigned to the day shift who works on maintenance matters five days a week. Thus, the winter schedule for the boiler operation requires a total of 8 full-time positions: 4 Firemen, 3 Helpers and 1 Fireman "A."

The summer schedule is considerably less intense. The boiler is only operated five days a week and two shifts per day. As a result only 5 full-time positions are necessary: 2 Firemen, 1 Helper and the Fireman "A." While these seasonal schedules have been in effect for some time, this incident was the first time that employees were actually laid off. In the past, the implementation of the seasonal schedule was accomplished by rescheduling Fireman from night shifts to other types of Monday through Friday duties. In the instant case the grievant was one of the junior Firemen who was displaced when the Company moved from its winter schedule to its summer schedule. Since [P.] was sufficiently senior to remain in active employment, he was assigned to a vacancy created by the layoff of one of the junior employees—that of Fireman "A."

The layoffs were effected by choosing the junior employees of the unit, creating a vacancy in the Fireman "A" position but not a vacancy in the Helper classification. [P.] complains that the contract was violated when he was assigned to the next-highest-rated position, arguing that he was entitled to bump into the job of his choice. When the Company refused to allow him to do so the instant grievance was filed. As stated above, the grievant was placed in a higher rated position and suffered no loss of pay. Therefore, the only remedy requested by the parties is a clarification of the contract language in question.

Issue

Did the Company violate the terms of Article VI of the Collective Bargaining Agreement when it refused to allow the grievant to bump into the job of his choice?

Pertinent Contract Provisions

Article VI

Seniority of employees in said power plant shall mean the length of service and the ability of the individual. Seniority with the Company shall begin with the date the employee was first employed in the department where the employee now works. Ability being equal, seniority shall prevail. No employee shall have seniority in more than one plant. A seniority list will be posted upon the signing of this agreement, as soon as practicable, for the purpose of giving the employees ten (10) days in which to make any corrections or objections as to the date of their seniority. If there are no corrections or objections within ten (10) days from the date of posting, list will stand as posted.

After the expiration of the ten (10) days referred to in the above paragraph, employees will not be allowed to exercise their seniority until a vacancy occurs. In the event at any time or times, because of production considerations, fewer employees shall be needed,

they shall be laid off in the inverse order of the above. When the Company again adds to the number of employees, those laid off shall be again re-employed in the order of their lay off.

Within ten (10) days following the signing of this agreement, employees will have the opportunity to exercise their seniority for shift preference in their classification.

Upon the termination of any particular job, the employees affected will be given the opportunity to exercise their departmental seniority and ability to bump into classification, provided they are qualified.

In the event that employees are recalled to work after completing their scheduled day to perform a specific job, they shall receive pay for at least four (4) hours at the prevailing overtime rate. The employee(s) shall not perform any other work than emergency work.

Contentions of the Parties

Union's Contentions

The Union contends that the Company violated the provisions of Article VI of the Labor Agreement when the Company refused to allow the grievant to bump into the Helper classification and required him to bump the employee with the least seniority in the bargaining unit who had the Fireman "A" (maintenance) job. The parties agreed at the arbitration hearing that the grievant was qualified and experienced to perform the duties of either of these two jobs.

The Union relies upon the language of Article VI, Paragraph 4 which states that "[u]pon the termination of any particular job, the employee affected will be given the opportunity to exercise their departmental seniority and ability to bump into any classification, provided they are qualified."

The Company has contended that the job was not terminated and this was a temporary layoff of six months. The Union contends that the "particular job" was terminated and that it is not relevant whether it was permanently terminated or temporarily terminated.

The Union argues that the provision in question was incorporated into the Agreement in the parties' negotiations in 1973 at the request of the Union. The reason for this language, it argues, was that the Cincinnati Local was aware that the Company's Kentucky facilities were reducing the work force when they went from a winter to summer schedule. While this reduction had not occurred at the Cincinnati facility, it was believed that the Company would institute a layoff of Power House employees at a later date. Inasmuch as there had been recent misunderstandings within the bargaining unit on other provisions of the Agreement, the Union wished to clarify the contract language to eliminate any misunderstanding. It argues that the provision in question was discussed with the Company as a local issue and that the Company was in agreement with the Union's proposal. It argues that discussions as to the intent of the language were held and both parties agreed that an employee could bump to any classification if his job was terminated during the summer schedule. It asks, accordingly, that the grievance be sustained.

Company's Contentions

The Company denies that it has violated the Labor Agreement as alleged by the Union. It states that the layoffs were effected by choosing the junior employees of the unit, creating a vacancy in the Fireman "A" position but not a vacancy in the Helper classification. There is no dispute before the Arbitrator regarding the persons who were selected for the layoffs or even as to how those individuals were chosen. The instant dispute is more narrow: Do the individuals whose seniority and ability have kept them from being laid off have the right to select which of the remaining

jobs they will perform? The grievant's complaint in the instant case is that he preferred to be assigned to the lower-rated position of Helper, displacing the incumbent who would then move to the Fireman "A" position. The Union is relying upon Paragraph 4 of Article VI. This paragraph was inserted into the collective bargaining agreement in 1972 as the result of the Union's request in its contract proposals that "when an employee's job is *terminated*," he be permitted to exercise his seniority and bump to any classification. The Company agreed with that proposal and it was duly added to the next collective bargaining agreement. It is the meaning of that clause that is the issue here, it argues.

On its face, the meaning of the disputed provision is clear. When a particular position is "terminated," the employee whose job was terminated is permitted to bump into "any" classification so long as that employee is qualified to do so and a junior employee is holding the desired position. The word "terminated," proposed by the Union, has a clear meaning in the English language, it argues. To terminate something means to bring it to a final conclusion, to an end, to cease an activity on a permanent basis. *Webster's New International Dictionary*, Second Edition, defines the word "terminate" as follows:

> To put an end to; to make to cease; to end. . . . To have its end, final part, or outcome.

It argues that had Mr. [P.] been told that *he* was being terminated, he would have had no doubt that he was through at National Distillers on a permanent and final basis.

Thus, the phrase in the collective bargaining agreement read in its ordinary everyday meaning, provides that when a particular job is brought to an end, to its final outcome, the incumbent is entitled to bump into any job held by a junior member of the unit.

This seems fair and logical. The displaced employee is seeking a new permanent position. He is allowed to choose his new permanent job from among those held by junior employees. Sequential bumping, such as which occurs when a senior employee is permitted to bump any less senior employee, who would then bump another less senior employee, etc., is undesirable from the Company's standpoint because it introduces significantly more disruption and requires considerably more either retraining or at least refamiliarization than would take place if the senior bumped employee were only permitted to move into a vacant position. Nevertheless, when the senior employee's job is eliminated on a final basis, the senior employee will be given a wider range of choice to select a new "home."

A much different situation is presented when a job is only temporarily discontinued, as in a seasonal reduction, it argues. The senior employee will return later to his regular position. "Daisy-chain" bumping, unless clearly agreed to by the Company, is not necessary to redress the balance. Ordinarily, layoffs in which the recall of the employee is contemplated do not constitute job "terminations" in any sense. Seasonal layoffs are temporary by definition. The Company has switched from its winter schedule to its summer schedule since the building of the facility decades ago. When the Company goes to a summer schedule in May, the members of the bargaining unit know from years and years of experience that a winter schedule will begin next fall. A job which is stricken from the summer schedule will reappear—its discontinuance is only temporary, it argues.

The use of the word "terminate" in Article VI must be given clear and unambiguous meaning of final or permanent elimination, it argues. This is a universally accepted principle of contract construction, it argues, and it cites arbitral authority in accord.

It is apparent from the foregoing, it argues, that the clause on which the Union seeks to rely is inapplicable to the current situation. The grievant's job was not terminated, but simply temporarily discontinued with the undisputed expectation that his job would be reactivated a few months later. The claim of grievant [P.] is invalid when the word "terminated" is given, as it must be, its clear and unambiguous meaning, it argues.

The Union asserted that the word "terminated" was nevertheless intended to apply to situations such as seasonal layoffs. Union representative [R.] testified that he recalled that from the negotiations which took place over a dozen years ago, Mr. [A.], who was at those same negotiations for the Company, however, had notes which revealed that discussions concerning seniority at the Cincinnati plant did occur, but did not deal with this particular question at all. Mr. [R.'s] response to this was that the discussions he recalled must have taken place in a side room session. Sadly for the Company, the Company's participants in the side room discussions are in one instance deceased, and in the other, retired, and living far out of state.

Mr. [R.'s] recollection of those discussions cannot control this grievance, it argues. First of all, the plain language of the provision containing the phraseology proposed by the Union is clear and is entitled to its ordinary and plain meaning. Application of the parol evidence rule excludes [R.'s] post-facto explanation. Second, the fact that the language was proposed by the Union itself requires that if there were any ambiguities, those would be resolved against the Union, and it cites arbitral authority in support of its contentions.

Additionally, at no time during the discussions which took place in full session was this proposal advanced, even though there was discussion of seniority problems specifically related to the Cincinnati plant. Finally, it would be unwise and unfair to rely upon the uncorroborated memory of a single participant to a discussion which took place more than a dozen years ago who does not have any notes or documents to support his position.

As was stated to the Arbitrator, this is a matter of first impression. It was agreed that no layoffs have occurred since the addition of this clause to the collective bargaining agreement as a result of the implementation of seasonal schedules. In the past the implementation of the seasonal schedule was accomplished by rescheduling Firemen from night shifts to other types of Monday through Friday duties. Thus, no past practice exists to guide us.

The Company would agree that if it were, for example, to alter its method of operation by operating the boiler only 5 days a week all year, that any particular Fireman jobs affected would be "terminated" in the sense of Article VI. The incumbent would then have the right to bump any junior employees. Similarly, if new equipment were obtained that resulted in the elimination of particular Helper duties, a displaced Helper would be in a position to invoke Article VI bumping rights. These situations, however, are completely different from the mere seasonal layoffs which have traditionally permitted an employee to either take a vacant position or bump the junior remaining employee, it argues.

In conclusion, it argues that the Union's reliance upon this clause in Article VI is invalid and it asks, accordingly, that the grievance be denied.

QUESTIONS

1. What provision could be added to the contract to prevent similar misunderstandings in the future?
2. What weight should be given by the arbitrator to the company's citation of *Webster's Dictionary* definition of the word *terminate*?
3. In your view, what is the real reason for the arbitration of this grievance?
4. How should the arbitrator rule in this case?

SOURCE: Labor Arbitration Awards, Commerce Clearing House, Inc. Reproduced with permission from LABOR ARBITRATION AWARDS, published and copyrighted by Commerce Clearing House, Inc., Chicago, Illinois 60646

Standard Slag Company and United Steel Workers of America, Local No. 2956

THEODORE K. HIGH, Arbitrator. Selected through FMCS, No. 83K/18341. Hearing held at Southpoint, Ohio, August 26, 1983. Award issued October 21, 1983.

Severance Pay—Layoff—Loss of Contractor's Bid—Recall Unlikely

[Text of Award]

HIGH, Arbitrator; STATEMENT OF THE CASE: The Company is engaged in the business of carrying away, reprocessing, selling byproducts of slag produced by steel mills. It operates at a number of locations in Ohio, Pennsylvania, West Virginia, Kentucky and Illinois. Prior to March of 1983, it had such a location at the Ashland, Kentucky plant of Armco, Inc. At this plant, it took away the molten slag, allowed it to cool, and from it produced byproducts which are largely used in the manufacture of asphalt and other products for road building.

Prior to the 1st of March, 1983, Armco announced to the Company that it was going to take bids for a 7-year contract for the slag business. Thereafter, bids were submitted and the contract was awarded to another company, called Heckett, Division of Harsco Corporation (Heckett). After the award, the Company began to remove equipment from the location adjacent to the Armco plant. It appears that some of the Company's facilities were on Armco property and some were on property owned by it. Some of the equipment in question was taken away and other of the equipment was sold to Heckett. In addition, the Company sold some buildings on the premises in question to Heckett.

After March 1, 1983, Heckett succeeded the Company to the operation of the slag function at the Ashland plant of Armco. Thereafter, all of the employees working at the Armco plant for the Company were laid off. An exception to this were a few employees who were engaged in work in connection with the termination of the Company's operations. These employees were subsequently laid off also. After the termination of the Company's operations, the instant grievance was filed on March 18, 1983, demanding that the Company pay severance pay pursuant to the provisions of Section 20 of the Agreement. The Company declined to make severance payments on the grounds that its operations at Ashland were not permanently closed. The parties have been unable to resolve the grievance and it is before the Arbitrator for disposition.

[Issue]

The issue for disposition is whether the Company violated Section 20 of the Agreement by refusing to make severance pay payments to employees laid off on March 1, 1983 and thereafter.

[Relevant Contractual Provisions]

The relevant section of the Agreement is paragraph 20.01, which provides as follows:

Severance Allowance

20.01 Conditions of Allowance

When, in the sole judgment of the Company, it decides to close permanently a plant or discontinue permanently a department of a plant or a substantial portion thereof and terminate the employment of individuals, an employee whose employment is terminated either directly or indirectly as a result thereof because he was not entitled to other employment with the Company under the provision of seniority of this Agreement and subsection .02(b) below, shall be entitled to a severance allowance in accordance with and subject to the following provisions.

It should also be observed that Section 20.08 gives the employees who are terminated under the provisions of Section 20.01 the election to be placed on layoff status for thirty days (or continue on layoff status for an additional thirty days, if already laid off), on the one hand, or electing to be considered terminated and receive a severance allowance under the provisions of Section 20.

[Additional Background]

As can be seen from the above quoted language of Section 20.01, the question turns on the interpretation of the phrase "when, in the sole judgment of the Company," the Company decides to close the plant permanently. The Company takes the position that only it may decide when a plant has been closed permanently and that it has not so decided in this case. It, therefore, takes the position that the employees in question are only on layoff and are ineligible to make the election to receive severance allowance as provided in Section 20.08.

The Company, in support of its position, produced evidence to the effect that it has substantial ongoing operations in the Ash-

land, Kentucky area, although it does not contend that it is conducting operations at the Armco plant. It does point out, however, that the Armco plant does continue to operate and must be served by a slag processor. The Company also argues that Heckett has had no prior marketing presence in the Ashland, Kentucky area, whereas the Company continues to dominate the aggregate production and marketing in the area. The Company also takes the position that Heckett will not have enough storage space to process the amount of slag which will be produced when the Armco plant returns to full operation. Its evidence is to the effect that the two properties of the Company in the immediate vicinity of the Armco Ashland plant will be essential to a successful operation of the slag service by Heckett. Further, it points out that if Heckett fails to perform its contract with Armco satisfactorily, the latter has the option of terminating that Agreement at any time prior to its term. Otherwise, the contract between Heckett and Armco is for seven years from March 1, 1983. The Company argues that in the event of the termination of Heckett's operations, the Company would be the logical party to succeed to the slag operation.

The parties agreed to the admission into evidence of a letter from an official of Armco Inc., which confirms the fact that Heckett was the successful bidder on the slag operation and that the contract was effective, commencing March 1, 1983, and is to be effective for a period of seven years thereafter. It also indicates that the termination of the contract may be upon one of three contingencies: 1) the completion of the contract; 2) nonperformance to the contract specifications; and 3) the insolvency or bankruptcy of Heckett.

QUESTIONS

1. To what extent should an arbitrator take future probabilities into account in

rendering a decision, particularly if the evidence is substantial?

2. Technically, Standard Slag still owns the property on which Heckett operates. Does this mean that, technically, Standard Slag's plant is still operational? Potentially operational?

3. What is the probability any of the three contingencies mentioned at the end of the case will occur (i.e., (1) completion of the contract; (2) Heckett's failure to meet specifications; (3) Heckett's becoming insolvent)?

4. If Standard Slag Co. had documentation that Armco was dissatisfied with Heckett (i.e., a warning letter to Heckett, bid-letting by Heckett to subcontract work, verbal or other comments from Armco officials expressing concern with or disappointment in Heckett's delivery of services), should the arbitrator take this into consideration in formulating his or her decision?

SOURCE: Labor Arbitration Awards Cited, Commerce Clearing House, Inc. Reproduced with permission from LABOR ARBITRATION AWARDS, published and copyrighted by Commerce Clearing House, Inc., Chicago, Illinois 60646

Masonite Corporation and International Association of Machinists, District No. 34

THEORORE K. HIGH, Arbitrator (FMCS No. 79K/02980). May 29, 1979.

Insurance—Coverage—Nursery Service for Newborn Infants—Past Practice of Insurer v. Clear Agreement Language

[Text of Award]

HIGH, Arbitrator; STATEMENT OF THE CASE: Before 1974, the Agreement between the Company and Union provided for Blue Cross/Blue Shield coverage for sickness and accident benefits. Sometime during the term of the 1971 Contract (which immediately preceded the 1974 Contract), the Company proposed that the coverage be changed from Blue Cross/Blue Shield to Employers of Wassau. It made this proposal because it felt that the same coverage could be secured at a lower cost. Eventually, the Union agreed. That agreement was incorporated into the 1974 Agreement as "Exhibit C". Exhibit C defines covered dependents as children of employees from the age of 14 days to 18 years, with an exception not relevant here. Notwithstanding the exception for children less than 14 days of age, the insurance carrier, Employers of Wassau, continued to pay claims for nursery expenses for newborn children of employees.

Sometime early in 1978, the handling of the employees' claims was shifted from the Indianapolis office of the insurance carrier to its office in Wassau. The insurance carrier personnel at the Wassau office noticed the exception and indicated, in March of 1978, that the claims of two employees for nursery service for newborn children would be rejected. The Company prevailed upon the insurance carrier to pay those two claims, since the nonpayment represented a departure from that which the employees had expected under the coverage of Employers of Wassau and Blue Cross/Blue Shield. There is a dispute as to whether the Company then notified the Union that henceforth claims for nursery service would not be paid. In any case, the Company contends that it notified the Grievant prior to the birth of his child on May 26, 1978 that payments for nursery service would not be made.

Grievant was not reimbursed for nursery service following the birth of his child, nor did he pay the hospital bill for such services until legal action was brought by the hospital. The result was that the Grievant has filed the instant grievance.

Issue

The parties agreed that the issue for disposition is whether or not the Company violated the Collective Bargaining Agreement by refusing to pay for the nursery charges in the maternity case involving the Grievant.

Discussion

The facts are largely undisputed. It is undisputed that the nursery service was covered by the Blue Cross/Blue Shield coverage and that it was represented to the Union by the Employer that the coverage would remain the same when shifted, at a lower cost, to Employers of Wassau. The 1974 Agreement provides in Article XX, Paragraph 20.01 that the sickness and accident benefits are as set forth in Exhibit C. This same Exhibit C is carried forward to the current Agreement. The paragraph of Exhibit C entitled "Coverage for Employee and Dependents," contains the following definition of persons covered by the benefits:

> Dependents are defined as an employee's spouse and unmarried children fourteen (14) days to nineteen (19) years or to age twenty-three (23) if regularly attending school and dependent solely on the employee for support.

It is undisputed that the benefits sought by the instant grievance are for a person who was less than 14 days of age at the time the services were rendered.

[Positions of the Parties]

The Company contends that the language of Exhibit C makes it clear that there is no coverage. The Union admits that Exhibit C was made a part of the collective bargaining process in both 1974 and 1977, that it read that exhibit, and agreed to the provisions thereof. It relies, instead, on what is in effect a past practice. It relies upon the Company's representation that the benefits would be the same, or at least not less than, those benefits available under the previous Blue Cross/Blue Shield contract. It further relies upon the practice of making payments for nursery services since the beginning of the Employers of Wassau contract until the time of the shift of the claims office from Indianapolis to Wassau, Wisconsin, sometime in 1977.

QUESTIONS

1. Should the company bear the expense of the nursery benefits in question until the expiration of the present contract as a goodwill gesture to the union and to the employees?

2. Should the company have a specified procedure for notifying employees of a change in benefits which is agreed upon by management and the union?

3. Does the union have a justified complaint, based on past practice, against the employer concerning the issue of nursery service for infants prior to the age of fourteen days?

SOURCE: Labor Arbitration Awards "79-2 ARB, 1979, Commerce Clearing House, Inc. Reproduced with permission from LABOR ARBITRATION AWARDS, published and copyrighted by Commerce Clearing House, Inc., Chicago, Illinois 60646

Superwood Corporation and United Paperworkers International Union, Local 776

THOMAS P. GALLAGHER, Arbitrator. Selected through FMCS, No. 84K/00841. Hearing held at Duluth, Minnesota, March 20, 1984. Award issued June 8, 1984.

Demotions—Incompetence and Inefficiency—Nondisciplinary Demotion—Efficiency Motive

[Text of Award]

GALLAGHER, Arbitrator; FACTS: The Employer manufactures construction panels from pressed wood at its plant in Duluth, Minnesota. The Union represents about 240 employees of the Employer—those engaged in production and maintenance. The grievant was hired in October, 1970. He worked in several departments of the plant before he was assigned in 1975 to work in the Board Mill on the Grinder Deck. On June 15, 1983, just before the demotion that is the subject of this grievance, the grievant was classified as a Grinder Operator, and as such he received the highest hourly pay in the Board Mill.

On the Grinder Deck, the materials that are used to make the construction panels produced by the plant are mixed and pressed into the panels. These materials—wood chips and fiber, hot wax and several chemicals—are supplied to the Grinder Deck through a complex network of conveyors, pipes and tubing. It is the responsibility of the Grinder Operator to monitor and control the flow of these materials to the Grinder Deck.

In 1978, the Employer installed equipment that made possible the automated control of the flow of materials to the Grinder Deck. The new system permitted the monitoring on a cathode ray tube of such information as the rate of flow, the level of available supply and the percentage of each material in the mixture currently flowing to the Grinder Deck. With new electronic controls, the Grinder Operator could make a change in the mixture when the monitor showed a change to be necessary.

The Grinder Deck is kept in operation twenty-four hours per day, seven days per week. The Employer uses four production crews—one for each of three daily shifts, and one for relief—to keep it operating continuously. One Grinder Operator is assigned to each of the four production crews.

On June 15, 1983, the Employer reassigned the grievant from his classification as a Grinder Operator to that of Press Operator. As a result of the change in his classification, the grievant's pay was reduced by 93¢ per hour under the wage schedule then in effect; the reduction is slightly more under the current wage schedule.

[Union Contentions]

By the present grievance, the Union contends that the Employer's demotion of the grievant was discipline and that, because demotion is not one of the methods of discipline authorized by the agreement, such discipline violates the labor agreement. The Union seeks reinstatement of the grievant to his former position, and it seeks his reimbursement for lost pay.

The Plant Rules, contained in an addendum to the labor agreement, list the following three categories of "cause for disciplinary action.":

[1.] Violation of the following rules shall be cause for disciplinary action by a written reprimand after the first offense, layoff of three days after the second offense and discharge after the third offense:

> Failure to report to work when scheduled without acceptable reasons or sufficient notice.
> Chronic absenteeism or habitual tardiness.
> Sleeping while on duty.
> Tour workers leaving their jobs before properly relieved.
>
> . . .
>
> Neglect of duty.
> Continued unsatisfactory work.

[2.] Violation of the following rules shall be cause for disciplinary action by layoff of three days after the first offense and discharge after the second offense:

> Reporting for duty while under the influence of intoxicating liquors.
> Smoking in prohibited areas.

[3.] Violation of the following rules may be considered cause for immediate discharge:

> Theft.
> Drinking while on duty.
>
> . . .

The Union argues that the Employer may use only the methods of discipline that are stated in the Plant Rules. In support of its position, the Union cites the maxim that the expression of one thing is the exclusion of those things not expressed. According to the Union, the Employer may discharge, suspend or reprimand because those three methods of discipline are explicitly authorized by the rules, but it may not demote because, by the failure of the parties to list that method of discipline as one of those permitted, they have expressed their intention not to permit it.

[Employer Contentions]

Although the Employer recognizes the disciplinary effect of the change in the grievant's classification, it argues that it did not remove him from his position as a Grinder Operator in order to discipline him, but did so in order to eliminate production problems on the Grinder Deck caused by the grievant's tardiness, poor attendance and poor job performance.

The Employer relies on two provisions of the labor agreement that, the Employer argues, reserve its power to change the grievant's classification in order to increase the efficiency of operations. The first, Section III of the labor agreement, states the right of the Employer to manage its business in the following language:

> The operation of the business and all the procedures and methods of production, including the assignment of work to employees, shall remain in the Company, except as specifically modified by this Agreement.

The second provision of the agreement relied upon by the Employer is the following one, Section VIII, Paragraph E:

> The Company agrees to follow the principles of seniority as set forth herein,

provided the employees are capable and qualified and have the ability to perform the job in an efficient manner, but the Company shall not be required to place or retain any employee in a job for which he does not have the ability or qualifications or is not capable of performing the same efficiently.

The Employer argues that it must fill the position of Grinder Operator on each of the four production crews with a reliable worker. The continuation of production on the Grinder Deck depends upon the presence of a reliable and competent Grinder Operator to monitor and control the proper flow of materials to the press. If one of the four Grinder Operators is tardy or absent from his shift, the Employer must use one of the other three to fill his position. Frequent absence and tardiness cause inconvenience both to the Employer and to the other Grinder Operators.

The Employer agrees with the Union that the grievant is qualified to perform the job of Grinder Operator, *i.e.*, that he has the knowledge and skills to do so. Nevertheless, the Employer argues, the grievant does not meet the performance standards for the position because his absence and tardiness and, at times, his carelessness in performance make him unreliable.

QUESTIONS

1. In your opinion, is Section III of the labor agreement a strong management-rights clause? Explain.
2. In your view why did the union bring this grievance to arbitration even though grievant's work record was not particularly impressive?
3. As an arbitrator, how would you decide this case? Why?

SOURCE: Labor Arbitration Awards, Commerce Clearing House, Inc. Reproduced with permission from LABOR ARBITRATION AWARDS, published and copyrighted by Commerce Clearing House, Inc., Chicago, Illinois 60646

Louisiana Dock Company, Inc., Division of Texas Gas Transmission Company Corporation and United Industrial Workers Union of the Seafarers International Union of North America, AFL-CIO

BERNARD MARCUS, Arbitrator (FMCS No. 82K/03879). April 14, 1982.

Union Security—Checkoff—Expiration of Contract

[Text of Award]

MARCUS, Arbitrator; COLLECTIVE BARGAINING AGREEMENT: The most recent collective bargaining agreement between the parties was effective between August 19, 1976 and August 19, 1981, and expired by its terms on the latter date.

Article I of the collective bargaining agreement, "Recognition," provides in relevant part as follows:

Section 1. The Company recognizes the Union as the sole collective bargaining agent for wages, hours, and conditions of employment for all employees at its Harahan and Westwego, Louisiana fleeting and repair facility, its Cairo, Illinois fleeting and repair facility; and at its coal transfer facilities located at Hall Street, St. Louis, Missouri, Columbia Bottoms, St. Louis County, Missouri, and at Louisville, Kentucky, excluding all office and clerical employees, professional employees, guards and supervisors, as defined in the National Labor Relations Act.

Article II of the collective bargaining agreement provides in relevant part as follows:

Section 6. The Company agrees that as a condition of employment all present employees shall become members of the Union within thirty-one (31) days after the execution of this Agreement or thirty-one (31) days after hire, whichever is later, and all new employees hired subsequent to the execution of this Agreement shall become members of the Union while employed by the Company and during the life of this Agreement. The Company is not obligated to take steps to enforce this provision unless due notice is received from the Union to the effect that an employee is not in compliance therewith. This section will not go into effect in any state wherein these provisions are contrary to State Law.

Section 7. (a) If any provision of this Article is invalidated under Federal or State Law, such provision shall be renegotiated in good faith for the purpose of adequate replacement. If such negotiation shall not result in mutually satisfactory agreement, the differences between the parties shall be resolved by resorting to the grievance procedure.

(b) To the extent that amendments may become permissible under Federal and State Law during the life of this Agreement as a result of legislative, administrative or judicial determination, all of the provisions of this Article shall be renegotiated to embody the greater union security provisions permissible under such law or rulings.

Section 8. Nothing contained in this Agreement shall be considered as to require the Company to violate any applicable laws.

Article IV of the collective bargaining agreement, "Dues Check-Off," provides as follows:

Section 1. Upon a voluntary written authorization delivered to the Company, it shall deduct the regular quarterly Union dues of any employee covered by this Agreement from his wages and shall remit such deducted dues to the proper officer of the Union. Proper authorization for this deduction shall be made by the employee dating and signing the following authorization form which states the conditions controlling the deduction:

"DUES CHECK OFF AUTHORIZATION"

"I hereby authorize Louisiana Dock Company, Inc. to deduct from my first wage payment of each quarter the sum of $—, the amount of the membership dues in the United Industrial Workers Union of the Seafarers International Union of North America, Atlantic, Gulf, Lakes and and Inland Waters District, AFL-CIO. The sums thus deducted hereby assigned by me to the Union are to be remitted by the Company to the proper officer of the Union.

"I submit this authorization and assignment with the understanding that it will be effective and irrevocable for a period of one (1) year from this date, or up to the termination of the current collective bargaining agreement between the Company and the Union, whichever date occurs the sooner.

"This authorization and assignment shall continue in full force for yearly periods and beyond the irrevocable period set forth above, and each subsequent yearly period will be similarly irrevocable unless revoked by me within thirty (30) days prior to expiration of any irrevocable period hereof. Such revocation shall be effected by written notice to the Company and the Union within such thirty (30) day period."

> "Date:—— Name:——
> "SS#:——

"Please sign two copies; one to the Union; one to the Company."

Section 2. If an employee is permanently transferred to a job not covered by this Agreement, his dues check-off authorization shall be null and void.

In addition, the parties entered into an addendum to the foregoing described collective bargaining agreement. The addendum defines a grievance in the following terms:

A. Grievances are any disputes arising between the parties hereto relating to, arising out of or in connection with or involving questions of interpretation or any acts, conduct or relations between the parties hereto or their members. Should grievances, as defined herein, arise, there shall be no suspension of work and an earnest effort shall be made to settle such difficulties promptly in the manner hereafter outlined. . . .

(F) It is expressly understood and agreed that the arbitrator shall not have the power to amend, modify, alter, or in any way add to or subtract from this Agreement or any provision hereof; but nothing herein mentioned shall limit, in any way, the powers and duties of the arbitrator who may, as part of his award, issue any and all mandatory directions, prohibitions or orders directed to or against any party breaching this agreement or any part hereof.

Issue

Did the employer violate the collective bargaining agreement between the parties, which was effective by its terms through August 19, 1981 when it ceased checking off dues from and after August 31, 1981.

In connection with the foregoing formulation, the company contends that the grievance is not arbitrable because the collective bargaining agreement expired on August 19, 1981, dues were deducted through August 31, 1981, and the check off clause did not survive the expiration of the agreement.

Facts

The company and the union have had a collective bargaining relationship with each other for a number of years, represented by the most recent contract, which, as noted, expired by its terms on August 19, 1981. This agreement covered company operations at Harahan, Louisiana, herein involved, and also operations at Cairo, Illinois, St. Louis, Missouri, and Louisville, Kentucky.

It appears that a competing union, Teamsters Local 89, made a demand for recognition of the employees in the bargaining unit at the Louisville, Kentucky, installation, proved to the company that it indeed represented a majority of those employees, and secured recognition from the company as the bargaining representative for said employees.

The union demanded that the company bargain with it as the exclusive collective bargaining representative for all bargaining unit employees at all installations, including the Louisville, Kentucky, installation, in a single bargaining unit. The company offered to bargain with the union for all employees except those in the Louisville, Kentucky, operation.

Both company and union adhere to their respective positions. No realistic bargaining has taken place. Both parties have filed refusal to bargain and other charges with the National Labor Relations Board, and all NLRB cases are now pending with the office of the General Counsel of the NLRB in Washington for advice as to what to do.

In the meantime, because of the impasse, and because there has been no renewal or extension of the agreement which expired on August 19, 1981, the company, on September 1, 1981, put the union on notice that all dues checkoffs at the Harahan installation would terminate as of August 31, 1981.

The union responded on September 14, 1981, and contended that the dues checkoff agreement survived the bargaining agreement and that it was an unfair labor practice to terminate the checkoff absent timely revocation by individual employees, and demanded immediate reinstatement of the checkoff agreement.

There is indication of the exchange of correspondence that checkoff was also terminated at other company installations. However, the discussion at the arbitration hearing confined the issue to the Harahan installation.

While there has not been a large amount of administration by the union of the collective bargaining relationship at Harahan, I am satisfied from the testimony at the hearing that the union has continued to service the Harahan installation, has made visitations to monitor safety, and has held discussions with installation management with respect to potential problems which might have otherwise led to the filing of grievances. Thus [H.], Jr., manager of the Harahan operation, testified that he has spoken to union representatives since the contract expired concerning a vacation pay claim (which was denied), and that there have been regular visitations to the operation by a union business representative, and approximately three complaints which were handled by shop stewards. There was also one discharge for absenteeism which the company unilaterally reduced to a three day suspension. The union was informed of the company's action so that it could afford the employee representation if representation were desired.

On the basis of the foregoing showing, I find that the union has continued as the bargaining representative of the bargaining unit employees at Harahan at all times since August 19, 1981.

Contentions of the Parties

Company's Contentions

The company contends that the checkoff clause does not survive expiration of the collective bargaining agreement. The grievance arose at the earliest on September 1, 1981, following the expiration of the agreement, and therefore, unlike the situation in *John Wiley* v. *Livingston*, [49 LC ¶ 18,846] 376 US 543, the issue is not arbitrable even if there might have been survival, because grievances which arise subsequent to expiration of the collective bargaining agreement are not arbitrable.

As for the merits of the grievance, by its terms the checkoff authorization expired when the contract expired. Thus, the grievance must be denied because there are no valid authorizations extant.

Union's Contentions

The union contends that the company never raised the arbitrability issue, although it concedes that there was no formal processing of the grievance during which the company might have had opportunity to ventilate the issue of arbitrability.

The union contends on the merits of the grievance that the dispute does arise under the terms of the contract, that the contract language extends some of its terms beyond its expiration date, that the text of the dues checkoff authorization establishes that the checkoff continues in the absence of a timely revocation, that this language is designed to cover hiatus periods between successive collective bargaining agreements, and that the duty to arbitrate lives on.

QUESTIONS

1. Taking into account that the union and company have had a collective bargaining relationship for a number of years, does the expiration of a contract imply a de facto termination of the bargaining relationship? If the relationship is considered to be ongoing, what responsibilities does this place on the parties?

2. Does the recognition of the Union as the "sole collective bargaining agent" have a life separate from the collective bargaining agreement?

3. Is the language in the "Dues Check Off Authorization" form explicit in its reference to the current agreement or can it be interpreted as referring to the longterm bargaining relationship?

4. Is this grievance a result of ambiguous contract language? If so, how can the language of the contract be reworded to eliminate the problem?

5. What did the company have to gain by ceasing the "check-off dues" of the union?

6. With all evidence before you, what conclusion would you draw as an arbitrator?

SOURCE: Labor Arbitration Awards, Commerce Clearing House, Inc. Reproduced with permission from LABOR ARBITRATION AWARDS, published and copyrighted by Commerce Clearing House, Inc., Chicago, Illinois 60646

California Horse Racing Industry and Parimutuel Employees Guild of California, Local 280

JOSEPH F. GENTILE, Arbitrator. August 31, 1982.

Union Security—Fines—Working for Employer During Strike—Picket Lines—Breach of Amnesty Agreement

[Text of Award]

GENTILE, Arbitrator; ISSUES AND PROCEDURAL CONSIDERATIONS: After considerable discussion regarding the issue(s) in dispute, the parties stipulated to the following as the specific issue to be addressed and determined in this proceeding:

> Has Local 280 violated the amnesty clause set forth in the June 19, 1979 letter; if so, what is the remedy?

During the course of the hearing certain problems developed as to the availability of requested documents. This is simply noted without comment as the transcript of the hearing provides ample coverage.

Applicable Provisions of the Amnesty Agreement

That provision of the Amnesty Agreement having particular relevance to the issues in dispute was Paragraph One. Paragraph One stated in full text for the following:

> The Union agrees and promises that no present or former member of Local 280,

SEIU, shall in any manner be discriminated against including, *but not limited to fines, expulsion, suspension, or denial or revocation of, in whole or in part, any fringe benefits*, such as pension or group insurance, because they worked at Hollywood Park, Inc., Los Alamitos Race Course or Golden Gate Fields during the strike which commenced on 4/11/79.

> [italics supplied]

Factual Summary

As indicated in the Amnesty Agreement, there existed strike conditions at three race tracks in California: Hollywood Park, Los Alamitos Race Course and Golden Gate Fields. The strike condition commenced on April 11, 1979. The strike ended on or about May 8, 1979.

In the latter part of October, 1979, [R., Employer's Director of Labor Relations] was advised by several supervisors that the Union had threatened them with fines. Under the terms of the applicable Collective Bargaining Agreement certain supervisors were members of the bargaining unit. [R.] responded by letter dated November 2, 1979, to the Union protesting these fines as a violation of the Amnesty Agreement. Arbitration was also requested pursuant to the terms of the Amnesty Agreement quoted above.

Another letter was sent by [R.] to the Union dated November 13, 1979. In this communication the position of the Employer was stated as follows:

> . . . it is the position of the Industry that those union members who actively worked for the employers during the period of 4/11/1979 through 5/8/1979 are protected by the Amnesty Clause and should not be subjected to the actions taken by the union's Executive Board.

[R.] then stated that "[i]t is on behalf of these individuals that we officially protest such fines and request submission of said grievance to Arbitrator Gentile."

The Union did not respond to either of these letters from [R.] to [N., President of the Union].

The matter apparently rested in a dormant state until May, 1980. In May several supervisors showed [R's.] letters from the Union which charged them with violating various articles of the Union's Constitution because they worked during the strike. The letters were dated May 9, 1980, addressed to the affected employees, on the stationery of the Union, and over the signature of [S.], the Secretary-Treasurer of the Union.

In the text of these letters, [S.] charged that the affected employees and members violated Article XIX, Section 3(a), 11, Section 3(b) and Section (4) of the Union's Constitution and By-laws. Trial dates before the Union's Trial Board were also stated in these letters.

On behalf of the Employer, [R.] responded by letter dated May 14, 1980, to the Union's President, [N.]. In this letter, [R.] protested these charges, contended they violated the Amnesty Agreement and renewed his request that the matter proceed to arbitration. Shortly after this letter, the Arbitrator was notified of this dispute. The letter of notification was dated May 29, 1980.

The above narrative represents the evolvement of the instant dispute.

With reference to those Supervisors affected by the Union's actions as just described, the evidence indicated the following:

1. At Hollywood Park, Supervisors [F.], [D.], [T.], [M.], [H.] II and [A.] at some time crossed the Union's picket lines and reported to work. With the exception of [A.], the Union charged, tried and fined each of these named supervisors who worked during the strike. These fines were for allegedly failing to perform the required picket duty; however, no evidence was presented that those supervisors who did not cross the Union's picket line performed any picket duty.

2. At Los Alamitos Race Course, Supervisors [W.], [I.], [C.], [L.], [Z.], and [P.] at some time crossed the Union's picket lines and reported to work. These supervisors who worked during the strike were charged, tried and fined. The fines were for the same reasons as noted in paragraph "1" above.

3. At Golden Gate Fields, Supervisors [E.] and [G.] at some time crossed the Union's picket lines and reported to work. They were charged, tried and fined as the other supervisors identified above.

The Union required regular employees to picket two shifts per week for a total of eight for the four-week strike period [April 11, 1979 to May 8, 1979], and those who did not were fined $25. per missed shift. All of the named supervisors in numbered paragraphs 1, 2 and 3 above were fined with the exception of [A.]. According to the only documentation made available at the hearing, all of the fined supervisors were fined $200.00 for this missed 8 shifts. The only exception was [H.] II, who missed 7 shifts and was fined $150.000. This same document indicated that a number of the supervisors paid the fine while others were "suspended 2/1/80-non payment of dues."

Testimony from [T.] and [H.] II was that they picketed during the strike on more than one occasion. This testimony was unrebutted. It was noted parenthetically that no documents were made available as to picketing schedules and who picketed during the period of the actual strike.

With respect to the activities of [A.] during the strike, the testimony indicated that he worked a six-day schedule from 8:30 a.m. to 9:30 p.m. doing the TIM 300 training. [A.] was questioned as to why he was not picketing; however, he told the person making the inquiry about his responsibilities and nothing further was said. [O.], also a supervisor, joined in this activity and he was not fined by the Union.

Positions of the Parties

The respective positions of the parties were well developed in Post-Hearing Briefs. These arguments and contentions were considered, but will not be restated herein in detail form— only the essence will be noted:

Employer's Position

The fundamental thrust of the Employer's position was that the Supervisors in question were fined because they crossed the Union's picket lines and worked during the strike. In support of this position, the Employer noted the statement in the Union's own letter dated May 9, 1980 which stated in part that: "You are charged by Local 280 under Local 280 Constitution and By-Laws . . . Article XIX, Section 4, Any member who (1) knowingly goes to work or remains in the employment of any person, firm or corporation whose men are on strike or locked out, unless he has permission of the International or his Local Union, may be tried by the Special Trial Board of his Local Union." In the Employer's judgment, this was in direct viola-

tion of the Amnesty Agreement.

In response to three procedural arguments presented by the Union, the Employer took these positions: (1) the dispute was timely filed as there existed no time constraints under the Amnesty Agreement; (2) the Employer had standing to enforce the terms of the Amnesty Agreement in that it was a party to this document and (3) this proceeding was not interference with the internal operations of the Union as it was clearly made a part of the Amnesty Agreement which provided for arbitration of disputes as to its interpretation and application.

Union's Position

The essence of the Union's position was that the named persons were not fined because they worked behind the picket line during the strike, but were fined for "not picketing" during the strike. Such an approach was within the authority of the Union's internal control procedures and outside the inquiry of the Employer.

The Union further argued that the Employer failed to carry its burden of proof in establishing that the Union had knowledge that the named persons were working during the strike and that the Union discriminated against these same persons because they worked during the strike.

In further amplification of its "internal disputes" argument, the Union further noted that none of the affected persons brought a grievance in a timely manner or sought to exhaust their internal Union remedies by appearing before the Trial Board or by appealing to that body in writing.

QUESTIONS

1. In your view, was the amnesty clause violated by the union?

2. In your opinion is there some underlying motive that has caused the union to

sanction these particular supervisors?

3. Should an employer attempt to intervene in and regulate a union's internal dispute?

4. What recourse would the supervisors have if the company refused to file a grievance on their behalf?

5. As the arbitrator, how would you rule and what portions of the testimony and/or evidence would you use to support your decision?

SOURCE: Labor Arbitration Awards, Commerce Clearing House, Inc. Reproduced with permission from LABOR ARBITRATION AWARDS, published and copyrighted by Commerce Clearing House, Inc., Chicago, Illinois 60646

South Central Rural Telephone Cooperative Corporation, Inc., and International Brotherhood of Electrical Workers, Local 463

FRANCIS W. FLANNAGAN, Arbitrator. Selected through FMCS, No. 83K/19913. Hearing held at Cave City, Kentucky, July 21, 1983. Award issued September 12, 1983.

Bidding—Ability v. Seniority—Management Right to Evaluate Qualifications—Lack of Discrimination

[Text of Award]

FLANNAGAN, Arbitrator; STIPULATED ISSUE: Did the Company violate the collective bargaining agreement when it selected [G.] over [F.] in filling the job of Plant Engineer?

Labor Agreement Provisions

Article III—Management

Except to the extent expressly abridged or limited by a specific provision of this Agreement, the Union stipulates that the Employer reserves and retains, solely and exclusively, all of its inherent rights, functions and prerogatives of management as such rights, functions and prerogatives existed prior to the execution of this Agreement. Such rights, functions and prerogatives include, but are not limited to, the Company's right to . . . select and determine the number and types of employees required; to assign work to such employees in accordance with requirements determined by the Employer; . . . to transfer, promote or demote employees . . .

Article XIV—Job Bidding

Section 1. Vacancies, New Jobs, Job Bidding:

Permanent job vacancies and permanent new jobs which are in the bargaining unit will be filled according to the procedures set forth below. The Employer shall determine whether a vacancy or job is permanent.

A. Notice of such job or jobs showing job classification, pay, and shift shall be posted for five (5) work days. Any employee who desires to be considered for such job shall sign the posting. However, the company is under no obligation to award a job to any employee who has not performed his present job for at least twelve (12) months and, furthermore, the company is under no obligation whatsoever to award a downward bid unless, in the Employer's opinion, an extreme hardship would be placed on the employee by not allowing a downward bid, such as a medical problem. At the end of the fifth work day, the Employer shall remove the posting and will give consideration to bidders in the following manner. Where skill, work record, and ability of bidders are equal in the judgment of the Employer, then seniority shall prevail provided the employee is physically able to perform the work without endangering his health or safety or the safety of others. . . .

B. The successful bidder, shall be given a ten (10) working day period in which to prove his adaptability to the new job and to demonstrate his ability thereon.

Article V—Grievance and Arbitration

Section 4. . . . The Arbitrator shall have no power to add to, subtract from, change or modify any of the terms of this Agreement; or to modify or reduce disciplinary or discharge action taken by the Employer if he finds that cause exists for discipline unless such action is determined by the arbitrator to be arbitrary and capricious; or to determine wage rates for the parties, and his decision must be based upon the terms of this Agreement in order to be valid.

Facts

For many years [A.] had been traffic engineer for the Company. This job falls under the classification of Plant Engineer. Its negotiated job description is as follows:

Duties

1. In accordance with Company Standards, stakes, designs, tests, and obtains right-of way, on all outside plant installed, removed, or changed outside the Central Office.
2. Initiates, changes, and updates all engineering records such as; maps, staking sheets, cable schematics, etc.
3. Initiates and closes out plant work orders in accordance with South Central and REA procedures.
4. Periodically collects data for traffic studies, dial tone delay studies, quality control studies, and COE index studies.
5. Maintains by years, a current five year trunk and equipment forecast showing equipment required to meet service demands, compiled from traffic studies and standard engineering tables.

Minimum Requirements

1. High School Diploma
2. Must have satisfactorily completed a basic Electricity course or have demonstrated this knowledge by successfully passing a Basic Electricity test administered by the Company.
3. Must possess a valid driver's license.

In practice, however, this job is broken down into four categories:

1. Outside plant design.
2. Right-of-way acquisition.
3. New installation orders.
4. Traffic engineer.

There are six employees with the classification of plant engineer. Those working in categories 1 thru 3 are not required to do category 4 work and the one employee working in category 4 is not required to do work in categories 1 thru 3.

The duties of the traffic engineer were described as studying the usage of circuits within an office which includes local to local calls; calls that go to each type of trunk, that is circuits from town to town; and toll circuits.

From the data taken in the studies, and based upon the number of lines in each office, a projection is made as to what will be required to service its customers in five years. The traffic engineer, in recent years, with the advent of digital equipment, does indexing to show how each office is operating. The indexing is also supplied to the Public Service Commission. Records are also kept as to what equipment is out of service and how long it is out of service. Another duty is dial tone delay service study and call completion rate. The job requires a knowledge of basic electricity and basic math.

In October of 1981, in anticipation of the retirement of Albany, a new job, Traffic Clerk, was posted for bids. On the posting the general duties were described as:

> Responsible for recording traffic and quality control data on all COE and trunking equipment. The objective is to make sure that all equipment meets service standards set by the company.

[G.] was the only bidder and the job was awarded to her. [G.] remained in this job until the retirement of Albany, at which time a bid was posted for the vacancy of Plant Engineer. The posting listed the minimum requirements for the job. While the posting was for Plant Engineer, the job to be performed was that of traffic engineer. There were twelve bidders including Grievant and [G.]. The bid was awarded [G.]. Grievant, more senior, filed a grievance reading:

> I have been a loyal and dedicated employee of South Central R.T.C. for many years. I have worked in all areas of the work. I also meet the criteria set forth in the job description posted for the job of "Plant Engineer."
>
> Feel I did not *receive* fair consideration for this job, as set forth in Article 14 of the contract.

The Company replied:

> It was the judgment of the promotion committee that the Employee selected for the job vacancy was the most qualified of the Bidders. Therefore grievance denied.

In order to determine which bidder was to be awarded the job, the Company appointed a committee of nine supervisors. Each bidder's supervisor was on this committee. This committee reviewed the personnel files of the bidders. It reduced the bidders to four, the four it considered most qualified, and from the four selected [G.] as the most qualified. Grievant was not in the last four. All bidders met the minimum requirements. One only, [G.], had any college degrees. She

had B.A. and M.A. degrees. All had completed the basic math course offered by the Company. [G.] scored 79, the highest grade. Grievant scored 16. The committee also considered all work performance and duties of the twelve bidders. Grievant had completed a course in basic electronics in 1975 and a course in basic electricity in 1983.

The latest evaluation reports on [G.], while she was working as traffic clerk, showed quality of work and ability to get along with people as "average". The latter was also checked as "above average" and initialed by R.D. On quality of work, initiative and attitude towards job [G.] was rated "above average". The comments on the report were as follows:

> [G.] is trying very hard to do her job well & never complains if additional work is asked of her. If she doesn't understand something, she asks questions. She is very dependable.

Grievant's last evaluation report was rated as "average" for quality of work, attitude towards job, and ability to get along with people. She was rated "above average" on quantity of work. The comments were:

> [F.] works very hard at trying to do the things she needs to do in order to *fulfill* her job responsibilities. She puts out extra effort to do whatever she can do to help others and get the job done. The reference to the quantity of work below average is not a reflection on effort but solely to the amount of work she can do in comparison to how I feel the average is.

[J.], Chief Design Engineer, testified that for the last eight months to one year [G.] had been doing all the traffic clerk's work plus 50% of the traffic engineer's work. He stated that [A.] was more interested in the mechanical equipment, on which equipment he worked, and that [G.] did the traffic engineering work on the digital equipment. She also did all dial delays, COE and quality control work.

Grievant, the only witness other than [J.], testified in her own behalf. She is a 29 year employee classified as Service Center Clerk. When first employed in 1954 she was in the Engineering Department where she assigned the lines and cable repairs, prepared service orders, dispatched men to install telephones, and took trouble reports. In 1963 she was promoted to Service Representative. She took applications, talked with customers regarding complaints, advised of all installations and removals, kept directory and special orders. She testified that the work done in engineering "is a backup to what she is doing now. Of course, it is more sophisticated work now." At that time there were no data terminals. At the present time [G.] takes the trouble off the data terminals and transfers it into the Grievant's department where Grievant dispatches it to the men for repair and checking.

Grievant was elected as "Woman of Achievement 1976" by a Glasgow civic group.

Position of the Parties

The Union argues:

1. Grievant has equal or superior skill, work record and ability to [G.].
2. Grievant is senior to [G.].
3. Under Article XIV of the Labor Agreement the job should have been awarded to Grievant.

The Company argues:

1. Where skill, word record and ability are not equal, seniority is irrelevant.
2. The burden is on the Union to prove that Grievant's skill, work record and ability are equal to those of [G.].
3. [G.'s] skill, work record and ability are superior to Grievant's.
4. The arbitrator should not substitute his judgment for the Company has exercised its discretion in a reasonable and good faith manner.

QUESTIONS

1. If you were the union negotiator, what changes, if any, would you try to make in Article XIV, Section 1 of this contract? Why?
2. Should the union attempt to revise the future contract regarding job bidding and job vacancies? Explain why or why not.
3. If you were the human resource manager for the company, what action would you take, if any, to prevent or reduce grievances in the future? Explain.
4. If you were the arbitrator in this case, what would be your award? Why?

Air Buensod, Inc., and Sheet Metal Workers International Association, Local 194

THOMAS J. DiLAURO, Arbitrator. Selected through AAA, No. 14-30-0017-84R. Hearing held May 4, 1984. Award issued June 1984.

Seniority—Ability v. Seniority—Bidding— Qualifications—Tests

[Text of Award]

DiLAURO, Arbitrator; BACK-GROUND: In November, 1983, the Employer, Air Buensod-Agitar Division, posted for bid the position of Punch Press Set Up Operator—a fairly skilled Class 2 job. The Company tested all employees who bid for the position including the Grievant, [H.], prior to awarding the bid. The job was awarded to the more senior of the two employees who scored the highest on the test. The Grievant, the most senior of the employees bidding, was not offered the position.

The Grievant had previously bid for the same position in 1979. He was the most senior bidder at that time as well. In that instance, however, none of the bidding employees was deemed qualified by the Employer and someone from outside the Company was hired to fill the position. No grievance was filed at that time. When the Employer again refused to accept Mr. [H.'s] bid in November of 1983, he filed the instant grievance asking to be awarded the position of Punch Press Set Up Operator with all appropriate retroactive back pay and benefits. The Union has also grieved,

claiming that the Employer has violated the Collective Bargaining Agreement and requested clarification of the Contract provisions.

Contract Language

Article XIV (4)

In making job assignments within a classification or from one classification to another, the most senior employees shall be given preference providing they have the necessary qualifications. When qualifications are reasonably equal, seniority shall be the deciding factor. The Company shall have the right to make job assignments within a classification by assigning employees to work where and when needed in the same classification.

Article XIV (6)

Whenever a vacancy occurs in a classification, the job opening shall be posted on the plant bulletin board for a period of three (3) days. Such jobs shall be filled on the basis of seniority and qualifications. Employees with the most seniority shall be given a reasonable opportunity to qualify for the job openings (Class 1 through 2 maximum of 90 days; Class 3 through 6 maximum of 30 days) before employees with less service are considered. If an employee is fired or quits and a temporary man is put in the job then the job shall be posted within one (1) week. Assignments shall be made for qualification within five (5) working days after close of the three (3) day posting period.

Article XIV (6)(e)

The Union will be presented with a copy of all test results from the bidding procedure.

Issues

1. Did the Employer violate the terms of the Collective Bargaining Agreement by failing to award the position of Punch Press Set Up Operator to the bidder with the most seniority?
2. Did the Employer violate the terms of the Collective Bargaining Agreement by pretesting bidding employees and giving qualifications, as determined by the testing, priority over seniority in awarding the bid?

Position of the Company

The Company asserts that it acted within the guidelines established by the Collective Bargaining Agreement by providing the employees bidding for the job of Punch Press Set Up Operator with an opportunity to qualify for the position through preaward testing. Ms. [R.], Manager of Production Control for the Agitar Division of Air Buensod and spokesperson for the Employer, stated that when bidding employees have equal or similar qualifications *and* seniority, it is Company policy to award the bids strictly on the basis of seniority. However, in cases where these two factors do not coincide, qualifications will prevail as the determinative criteria.

The Employer cited Article XIV (6)(e), which provides that the Union shall receive a copy of all test results from the bidding procedure, as authorization for the administration of pre-award testing. In support of its position, the Employer emphasizes the need to place qualified employees in skilled positions.

The Company also claims that the job in question here is vital to plant operations and, therefore, it is essential that the best qualified bidder be awarded the position. Furthermore, the Company points out that since no on-the-job training was available in the instant case, awarding the bid on the basis of seniority alone would have had an adverse effect on proper functioning of the plant and, consequently, the Employer had no choice but to place the most qualified applicant in the position of Punch Press Set Up Operator.

Relying on the pre-award test results of the applicants, including Grievant's, the Company claims that Mr. [H.] was unable to perform the most important function of a Punch Press Set Up Operator, i.e., read a blueprint accurately. The Employer also points out that of the two applicants with equal qualifications, the bid was awarded to the most senior employee. The Company also relies on Article XIV (4) as justification for the proposition that, as a threshold matter, qualification should be the prevailing criteria. With regard to the Grievant, the Company notes that despite the five-year gap between his initial bid for the position in 1979 and the Employer's denial of his second application which gave rise to the instant grievance, Mr. [H.] had failed to acquire the requisite skills. The Company asserts, without citing any specific provision of the Contract, that an employee is not eligible to bid twice for the same job within a six-month period unless he has obtained the necessary qualifications during the interim.

In sum, it is the Employer's position that Article XIV (6) establishes both seniority and qualifications as appropriate criteria in awarding bids. Additionally, an applicant must first demonstrate that he has the minimum skills necessary to perform the job before being given an opportunity (in this case, ninety days) to learn the job.

Position of the Union

The Union asserts that the Employer has violated the Collective Bargaining Agreement in two ways. First, by pre-testing the bidding employees; and secondly, by utilizing qualifications rather than seniority as the prevailing factor in awarding the bid. It is the Union's position that, pursuant to Article XIV (6), the Grievant, as the most senior bidder, should have automatically been awarded the job of Punch Press Set Up Operator. Thereafter, Mr. [H.] should have had ninety days within which to qualify in accordance with the Company's requirements. The Union points out that the Contract does not provide for pre-award testing and contends that the Employer's reliance on Article XIV (6)(e) is misplaced, in that, that term refers only to post-award procedures.

Mr. [S.], Business Mgr., Financial Secretary and Treasurer for Union Local 194, Sheet Metal Workers, testified on behalf of the Union. Mr. [S.] stated that it is his function to negotiate and administer the Collective Bargaining Agreements between the parties and that he was an active participant in negotiations for the last two contracts. The witness indicated that the parties had engaged in extensive discussions concerning the bidding procedure during the 1980 contract negotiations and that the Company had strenuously objected at that time to seniority being established as the prevailing factor in awarding bids. The Union, however, had succeeded in negotiating contract language which provided that, initially, seniority would be the determinative criteria. Mr. [S.] noted further that the current Agreement made no significant change in the relevant contract terms.

The Company's need for skilled employees was accommodated in the Contract by providing for a post-award qualification period which varies according to the complexity of the job involved. Upon both direct and cross-examination, Mr. [S.] insisted that the contract requires only that the most senior bidder qualify within the stated period *while on the job*, and that the Company must initially award the bid on the basis of seniority alone.

Mr. [S.'s] testimony also confirmed the Union's contention that Article XIV (4) is not applicable to the bidding process.

Mr. [Y.], long-term employee and Chairman of the Shop Committee for the past eleven years, corroborated Mr. [S.'s] interpretation of Article XIV (4) and (6). In addition, Mr. [Y.] testified that past practice has consistently supported the Union's position that seniority must be the prevailing factor in awarding job bids. The witness stated that, with one exception, he does not know of any instance where the Company failed to award a bid to the most senior applicant and the Union did not grieve. Mr. [Y.'s] testimony was supported by Exhibits U-2—U-5, inclusive.

Regarding the Grievant's prior bid for the position of Punch Press Set Up Operator in 1979, where none of the bidders qualified in pre-award testing administered by the Company and the job was ultimately filled by an outside applicant, the witness stated that while the Union objected to the procedure, no grievance was instituted because the job was withdrawn and contract negotiations were pending.

The Union contends that the language of Article XIV (6) is controlling in the instant matter. Moreover, it is argued that the application of any other Contract term in this case would render the provisions of Article XIV (6) meaningless. In response to the Employer's reliance on Article XIV (4) and (6)(e), the Union asserts that Article XIV (4) is only relevant with regard to lateral job assignments and Article XIV (6)(e) refers solely to post-award procedures. The Union also emphasizes that the Employer failed in its attempts to alter the provisions of Article XIV (6) during prior contract negotiations and that the Union has vigorously and successfully defended its interpretation of the Collective Bargaining Agreement by grieving virtually all deviations from established procedure.

The Union requests that the Arbitrator support its interpretation of the Contract and provide relief to the Grievant by directing that Mr. [H.] be placed in the position of Punch Press Set Up Operator and afforded an opportunity to qualify within the mandated ninety-day period. The Union also requests that the Grievant be awarded all appropriate back pay and benefits, retroactive to the date of the original award.

QUESTIONS

1. Why would the company pretest employees for available positions?

2. On the basis of the contract language, do you think the union is a strong bargaining agent? Explain?

3. In your view, did the employer violate the terms of the collective bargaining agreement by failing to award the position of punch press set up operator, the bidder with the most seniority?

4. Did the employer violate the terms of the collective bargaining agreement by pre-testing bidding employees and giving qualifications, priority over seniority in awarding the bid?

SOURCE: Labor Arbitration Awards Cited, Commerce Clearing House, Inc. Reproduced with permission from LABOR ARBITRATION AWARDS, published and copyrighted by Commerce Clearing House, Inc., Chicago, Illinois 60646

Schaibles Bakery and Bakery, Confectionery and Tobacco Workers International Union, Local 6

THOMAS J. DiLAURO, Arbitrator. Selected through AAA, No. 14-30-0967-830. Hearing held October 24, 1983. Award issued November 8, 1983.

Bidding—Denial of Bid—Qualifications—Poor Attendance

[Text of Award]

DiLAURO, Arbitrator; FACTS: The factual background of this case is undisputed. In February, 1983 the Company posted a bidding notice for the position of Vacation Relief worker. This job, the highest paid position in the production unit at the bakery, requires the employee to fill-in for various skilled workers during vacation periods. Uncontradicted testimony presented at the hearing indicted that there are a total of 19 skilled positions and 3 Vacation Relief Workers. Most of the skilled jobs are held by senior employees whose vacation periods range from 3 to 6 weeks per year. The Personnel Manager testified that most of the time, all three Vacation Relief workers are needed. The Company also employs a number of "helpers" or "floaters" who provide coverage for the unskilled jobs on an as needed basis.

Three employees, including the Grievant, Mr. [F.], placed bids for the posted position. The Grievant had the least seniority and, therefore, was the last in line for the job. The two more senior employees, however, declined the placement leaving the Grievant as the only available bidder at that time. It is not disputed that the Grievant has the requisite skills to perform the various jobs involved. In fact, the Grievant had actually held the position in question previously but was "demoted" to floater in August, 1982 because of chronic absenteeism and tardiness. The Company has refused to honor the Grievant's bid and offer him the position because of his poor attendance record. Consequently, Mr. [F.] filed the instant greivance.

Contractual Provisions

Article II—Temporary Transfers and Posting Vacancies

5. An employee who bids in a job shall be entitled to a trial period of up to two (2) weeks, or such longer period as the Company and the Union shall agree, if the Company or the Union feels that the employee is otherwise qualified for the job, except that in the case of plant and garage maintenance jobs the Company will administer skill and job knowledge tests to employees interested in these positions in order to determine if such employees have the qualifications to begin a trial period. A disagreement concerning a Company's determination that an individual is not entitled to a trial period because of the results of the testing is subject to the grievance-arbitration procedure. Should any wage rate change be involved, the new rate will take effect when the employee accepts the job and assumes the responsibility for said job. However, should the employee accept the job but

doesn't have the responsibility due to the necessity of training with another employee, the rate will go into effect at the end of the two (2) week trial period.

Issue

Can the Company, pursuant to the Collective Bargaining Agreement, properly consider an employee's attendance record in determining the award of a job bid? If not, the Union requests that the Grievant be placed in the Vacation Relief worker position and he be awarded, as back pay, the salary differential between his current position and that of the Vacation Relief worker.

Position of the Union

It is the Union's position that, under the Agreement, the Company may not consider an employee's attendance record in determining whether or not to place him in a position for which he is otherwise qualified. In the instant case, the Union admits that the Grievant has a chronic attendance problem but contends nevertheless that his attendance record has no bearing on his ability to perform the job in question and, therefore, should not be considered in a job skills determination. The Union asserts that the bidding procedure established by the Contract is not designed to deal with absenteeism, especially in light of the Company's comprehensive attendance policy. It is claimed that this program of progressive discipline provides an exclusive method for treating such problems. The Union argues further that the Company's refusal to award the Grievant the job of Vacation Relief worker based on his poor attendance record constitutes a form of disciplinary action, thereby placing the Grievant in a position of "double jeopardy" since appropriate discipline has already been imposed pursuant to the Company's absentee policy. The Union

emphasizes that since the Grievant held the position of Vacation Relief worker previously, he has proven his ability to do the job. Moreover, the Union points out that upon award of his bid, the Grievant would be required to complete a two-week trial period which would provide the Company with ample opportunity to assess his qualifications.

It is the Union's claim that since the Grievant obviously possesses the requisite seniority and skills, he has fulfilled every condition set forth in the Contract and, therefore, his attendance record is irrelevant to this proceeding. Consequently, the Union requests that the Grievant be assigned the position of Vacation Relief worker and be awarded, as back pay, the salary differential between his current position and that of a Vacation Relief worker from the time the bid was awarded to the date of the Grievant's placement.

Position of the Company

The Company contends that good attendance and punctuality is a critical qualification for the position of Vacation Relief worker since there are a limited number of employees able to perform the required tasks. The Personnel Manager testified that the job in question is a highly skilled position requiring training in the various jobs over a period of several months. He further stated that the primary responsibility of a Vacation Relief worker is to fill-in for vacationing employees. If the relief worker is absent or late, it is unlikely that a replacement would be available because all 3 Vacation Relief workers in the production unit are usually scheduled to work at the same time. He also testified that while "helpers" or "floaters" are also available for relief work, these employees are only qualified to provide coverage for low skilled jobs.

The Company argues further that although the Grievant possesses the necessary job skills, his past performance in the position was unsatisfactory because of his absentee problem and he is, therefore, not qualified to fill the position. The Company also emphasizes that since the Grievant has shown no improvement in his attendance record, the Employer is justified in refusing to award the bid to him.

The Company noted that the Contract provides that an employee who bids for a job shall be entitled to a trial period if that employee is otherwise qualified for the position, and argues that the phrase "otherwise qualified" offers the Company sufficient authorization to disqualify the Grievant because of poor attendance. This is based on the Company's assertion that the position of Vacation Relief worker is particularly sensitive to matters of attendance and punctuality and the Company is, therefore, entitled to consider this crucial factor in determining how to award the bid.

QUESTIONS

1. In view of this case, if you were the labor-relations manager, would you attempt to revise the contract in the future? Explain, why or why not?

2. In your opinion, could a revision of the company absenteeism policy and procedures prevent similar grievances in the future? Explain.

3. If you were representing the union at the arbitration hearing, in order to strengthen your case, what could be some of the arguments and evidence that you could present at the hearing?

4. In your view, can the employer, pursuant to the agreement, properly consider an employee's attendance record in determining the award of a job bid?

5. If you were the arbitrator, what award would you make?

SOURCE: Labor Arbitration Awards, Commerce Clearing House, Inc. Reproduced with permission from LABOR ARBITRATION AWARDS, published and copyrighted by Commerce Clearing House, Inc., Chicago, Illinois 60646

Tell City Chair Company and International Brotherhood of Pottery & Allied Workers, AFL—CIO

THEODORE K. HIGH, Arbitrator. Selected through FMCS, No. 82K/16783. Hearing held at Tell City, Indiana, September 23, 1982. Award issued December 3, 1982.

Layoffs—Temporary—Mandatory Assignment of Available Work to Senior Employees

[Text of Award]

HIGH, Arbitrator; STATEMENT OF THE CASE: The Company is a manufacturer of hardwood early American furniture at its Tell City, Indiana Plant. It is approximately 100 employees below its usual complement of 600—630. In the instant Grievance, filed by a shop steward, the Union claims that a past practice has developed, in cases of short term layoffs where some employees are required in a given department of offering the available work to the most senior employee in the classification, with that employee having the right to refuse. In other words, the Company, the Union contends, should go down the seniority roster allowing refusals and come up from the bottom with the mandatory assignment. On the occasions in question, the Company assigned the work, mandatorily, to the senior employees in the classification. The parties have been unable to resolve the grievance and it is before the Arbitrator for disposition.

Issue

The issue for disposition is whether there is a past practice which can cause Section 12 of the Agreement to be read as permitting senior employees to decline work assignment where there is to be a layoff of less than all of a classification for five days or less.

[Facts]

The facts of this case are largely undisputed. The Grievance arose in the Shipping and Warehouse Department, Plant 3. It appears that the plant which produces tables for dining room sets frequently is behind the plant producing the chairs. Therefore, on some days less than a full complement is required in that department.

It appears that for the week ending Christmas Day 1981 and the week ending New Year's Day 1982, the Chair Plant was shut down. The Company had need of two employees in the Shipping and Warehouse Department for the first four days of those weeks and, sometime before December 18, 1981, scheduled the two most senior employees in the department to work. The most senior employee in the department raised the question with his steward-elect of whether his refusal to work would deprive him of unemployment compensation benefits. Upon receiving an affirmative reply, he decided to work and the two senior employees worked the days in question. On December 17, 1981, a negotiation meeting, looking toward the present Agreement, was held and the question was raised by the union. It appears that the Company stood by its position that it would assign (rather than offer the choice) the

579

work to the senior employees. It appears that the matter did not come up again in the negotiations and the parties stipulated that the relevant contractual provision, Section 12, remained unchanged in the new Agreement, effective January 25, 1982.

For weeks January 15, January 22, and January 29, 1982, the Company scheduled the Chair Factory for four days, closing each Friday. It decided, however, to schedule two employees for each of the Fridays from the 85 classification of the Shipping and Warehouse Department, with the result that the two senior employees in the 85 classification were assigned, without choice, to work the three Fridays.

It is undisputed that prior to December, 1981, there were a number of occasions when less than a full crew was required in the 85 classification for one day and the most senior employees were given the choice of accepting or declining the assignment (apparently, the most senior 85 frequently declined extra work). The steward who filed the grievance testified that this practice was followed when he worked as a forklift driver in Department 301.

[Position of the Parties]

The Company's evidence is that prior to July, 1981, at least four methods of assigning the work existed. There were: (1) allowing the senior employees the choice, as in the Shipping and Warehouse Department; (2) assignment to the crew of the machine which had the work and laying off entire crews without regard to seniority; (3) involuntary scheduling of the most senior employees; and (4) in some cases, simply asking for volunteers.

According to the Company, its present policy derived from the settlement of a grievance by an employee named [O.]. The evidence shows that [O.] was a member of one of only two crews which operate a certain type of

machine. The grievance arose because there was insufficient work for both machines one day and because the other machine was already working on the work in question that crew was assigned the work, notwithstanding that [O.] had superior seniority to some, or all, of the members of the other crew. [O.] filed a grievance, which was resolved at the third step with the following Answer:

> The resolution of this grievance is that the Company shall follow Section 12 of the current contract where there are work crews with the same classifications. Example: the double end tenoner and offbearer at Plant #2, recognizing that the offbearer classification goes with the machine and this applies to full days of work only. Partial days are excluded. This resolution shall apply throughout the Company. The grievant shall receive 4 hours of day work pay in the settlement of this grievance. The one day extension to the Company is appreciated.

The Company emphasizes the language, "shall apply throughout the plant." Section 12 of the Agreement provides, in pertinent part:

> 12. Seniority shall be on a departmental basis by job classification and shall govern all permanent layoffs and rehirings. When a layoff occurs at a time when the Company anticipates a temporary layoff of less than five (5) days, it shall be made by seniority on a job classification basis, in that department. Here, the Company emphasizes the "shall be made by seniority on a job classification basis . . ." language, arguing that this compels the assignment to senior employees (not permitting a choice to the senior employees).

The Union argues that its position is consistent with both the mandate of Section 12 and the settlement of the [O.] grievance. Its position is that while Section 12 requires that the Company offer work during a partial layoff of five days or less to the senior employees in the classification, the past practice upon which it relies establishes a right on the part of the senior employees to waive that right.

The Company's position is that the past practice was not uniform, but, in any case, was terminated by the [O.] settlement. It points out that it defended the [O.] grievance on precisely the same grounds as the Union raises in this case; namely, that the past practice in [O.'s] department called for assignment of work during temporary layoff depending upon which crew was doing the work, not the seniority of individual employees. Its evidence is to the effect that it decided it would lose the [O.] grievance if it went to arbitration, given the language of Section 12, and that it, accordingly, decided it should settle that grievance, but that it should insist upon language in the settlement agreement which would ensure uniformity throughout the Company's operations. As can be seen from the language of the settlement agreement, the agreement was made applicable "throughout the Company."

QUESTIONS

1. Evaluate the issue in this case.
2. Explain the concept of past practice and its importance for labor-management relations.
3. Discuss the importance of past practice for this case.
4. How should the arbitrator rule in this case? Why?

SOURCE: Labor Arbitration Awards, Commerce Clearing House, Inc. Reproduced with permission from LABOR ARBITRATION AWARDS, published and copyrighted by Commerce Clearing House, Inc., Chicago, Illinois 60646

BIBLIOGRAPHY*

BIBLIOGRAPHIES AND DICTIONARIES

AZEVEDO, ROSS E.   *Labor Economics: A Guide to Information Sources.* (Economics Information Guide Series, Vol. 8.) Detroit: Gale Research Co., 1977. 261 pp.

CORNELL UNIVERSITY.   Libraries. Industrial and Labor Relations Library. *Library Catalog of the New York State School of Industrial and Labor Relations.* Boston: G.K. Hall, 1967–1981. 12 vols. with supplements.

*This bibliography was compiled by Philip R. Dankert, Collection Development Librarian, Martin P. Catherwood Library, New York State School of Industrial and Labor Relations, Cornell University, Ithaca, New York 14851-0952.

Space limitations prevented a more complete listing. (Thus, it is to be hoped that omissions were intentional.) Certain subject areas are excluded—for example, organizational behavior and personnel management, except for journals.

For such categories as *Bibliographies, Journals/Serials, Selected Loose-Leaf Reporting Services and Related Publications*, and *Statistics*, the reader would be advised to consult further Soltow and Sokkar and Herman and Lloyd (under bibliographies component).

Not all titles included are still in print. (No designation has been supplied to so indicate.)

We wish to express our appreciation to Carla Weiss for suggesting valuable additions; to Patricia Randorf for verifying that later editions to certain titles have been published since the first edition of *Collective Bargaining and Labor Relations* was published in 1981; and especially to Helen Hamilton for her tireless efforts typing and checking the accuracy of the various entries in this bibliography.

DOHERTY, ROBERT E. *Industrial and Labor Relations Terms: A Glossary.* (ILR Bulletin, No. 44) 4th ed. rev. Ithaca: New York State School of Industrial and Labor Relations, Cornell University, 1979. 34 pp.

FOX, MILDEN J., and PATSY C. HOWARD. *Labor Relations and Collective Bargaining: A Bibliographic Guide to Doctoral Research.* Metuchen, N.J.: Scarecrow Press, 1983. 281 pp.

HERMAN, GEORGIANNA, and GWENDOLYN LLOYD. "PAIR Literature: Keeping Up To Date." In *ASPA Handbook of Industrial Relations, Vol. 8: Professional PAIR.* Edited by Dale Yoder and Herbert G. Henemen, Jr., pp. 8–113—8–248. Washington, D.C.: Bureau of National Affairs, 1979.

Labor in America: An Historical Bibliography. Santa Barbara, Calif.: ABC-Clio Information Services, 1985. 307 pp.

MCBREARTY, JAMES C. *American Labor History and Comparative Labor Movements; A Selected Bibliography.* Tucson: University of Arizona Press, 1973. 262 pp.

NEUFELD, MAURICE F., DANIEL J. LEAB, and DOROTHY SWANSON. *American Working Class History: A Representative Bibliography.* Rev. ed. New York: Bowker, 1983. 356 pp.

ROBERTS, HAROLD S. *Roberts' Dictionary of Industrial Relations.* (3rd ed.) Washington, D.C.: Bureau of National Affairs, 1986. 811 pp.

SEIDE, KATHARINE, ed. *The Paul Felix Warburg Union Catalog of Arbitration: A Selective Bibliography and Subject Index of Peaceful Dispute Settlement Procedures.* Totowa, N.J.: Published for the Eastman Library of the American Arbitration Association by Rowman and Littlefield, 1974. 3 vols.

Selected References. Princeton, N.J.: Princeton University, Industrial Relations Section, 1945—[Irregular].

SHAFRITZ, JAY M. *Facts on File Dictionary of Personnel Management and Labor Relations.* (2nd ed.) Rev. and expanded. New York: Facts on File, 1985. 534 pp.

SOLTOW, MARTHA JANE, and JO ANN S. SOKKAR. *Industrial Relations and Personnel Management: Selected Information Sources.* Metuchen, N.J.: Scarecrow Press, 1979. 286 pp.

SOLTOW, MARTHA JANE, and MARY K. WERY. *American Women and the Labor Movement, 1825–1974: An Annotated Bibliography.* (2nd ed.) Metuchen, N.J.: Scarecrow Press, 1976. 247 pp.

SOLTOW, MARTHA JANE, and SUSAN GRAVELLE. *Worker Benefits; Industrial Welfare in America 1900–1935: An Annotated Bibliography.* Metuchen, N.J.: Scarecrow Press, 1983. 230 pp.

United States. Department of Labor. Library. *United States Department of Labor Library Catalog.* Boston: G.K. Hall, 1975. 38 vols.

BIOGRAPHIES

The American Labor Who's Who. Solon DeLeon, ed. New York: Hanford Press, 1925. 374 pp.

Directory of Labor Arbitrators. Fort Washington, Pa.: Labor Relations Press, 1982– [Loose-leaf].

FINK, GARY M., ed.   *Biographical Dictionary of American Labor* (2nd ed.) Westport, Conn.: Greenwood Press, 1984. 767 pp.

GIFFORD, COURTNEY D., and WILLIAM P. NOBGOOD. *Directory of U.S. Labor Arbitrators: a Guide for Finding and Using Arbitrators.* Washington, D.C.: Bureau of National Affairs, 1985, 445 pp.

Industrial Relations Research Association. *Membership Directory Handbook.* Madison, Wis., 1949– [Irregular].

National Academy of Arbitrators. *Membership Directory.* Washington, D.C., 1947– [Annual].

ROBERTS, HAROLD S.   *Who's Who in Industrial Relations.* Honolulu: University of Hawaii, Industrial Relations Center, 1966–1967. 2 vols.

Who's Who in Labor. New York: Dryden Press, 1946. 480 pp.

Who's Who in Labor. New York: Arno Press, 1976. 807 pp.

JOURNALS/SERIALS

Academy of Management Journal. Mississippi State, Miss.: Academy of Management, 1958– [Quarterly].

Administrative Science Quarterly. Ithaca, N.Y.: Graduate School of Management, Cornell University, 1956– [Quarterly].

Advances in Industrial and Labor Relations. Greenwich, Conn.: JAI Press, 1983– [Annual].

American Economic Review. Nashville, Tenn.: American Economic Association, 1911– [Quarterly].

Arbitration Journal. New York: American Arbitration Association, 1946– [Quarterly].

British Journal of Industrial Relations. London: London School of Economics and Political Science, 1963– [Traditional].

Directory of U.S. Labor Organizations. Washington, D.C.: Bureau of National Affairs, 1982/1983– [Biennial].

Economic and Industrial Democracy. London: Sage Publications, Ltd., 1980– [Quarterly].

Employee Relations Law Journal. New York: Executive Enterprises Publications, 1975– [Quarterly].

Harvard Business Review. Cambridge, Mass.: Graduate School of Business Administration, Harvard University, 1922/1923– [Bimonthly].

Human Resource Management. Ann Arbor, Mich.: Graduate School of Business Administration, University of Michigan, 1962– [Quarterly].

Human Resource Planning. New York: Human Resource Planning Society, 1978– [Quarterly].

Industrial and Labor Relations Review. Ithaca, N.Y.: New York State School of Industrial and Labor Relations, Cornell University, 1947– [Quarterly].

Industrial Relations: A Journal of Political Economy. Berkeley: Institute of Industrial Relations, University of California, 1961– [Triannual].

Industrial Relations Law Journal. Berkeley: School of Law, University of California, 1976– [Quarterly].

International Labor and Working Class History. New Haven, Conn.: Study Group on Labor and Working Class History, Dept. of History, Yale University, 1972– [Semiannual].

International Labour Review. Geneva: International Labour Office, 1921– [Bimonthly].

Journal of Collective Negotiations in the Public Sector. Farmingdale, N.Y.: Baywood Publishing Co., 1972– [Quarterly].

Journal of Human Resources: Education, Manpower, and Welfare Policies. Madison, Wis.: University of Wisconsin Press, 1966– [Quarterly].

Journal of Labor Economics. Chicago: University of Chicago Press, 1983– [Quarterly].

Journal of Labor Research. Fairfax, Va.: Department of Economics, George Mason University, 1980– [Quarterly].

Journal of Occupational Psychology. Leicester, England: British Psychological Society, 1922– [Quarterly].

Labor History. New York: Tamiment Institute, New York University, 1960– [Quarterly].

Labor Law Journal. Chicago: Commerce Clearing House, 1949– [Monthly].

Labor-Management Relations Service Newsletter. Washington, D.C., 1979– [Monthly].

Labor Relations Yearbook. Washington, D.C.: Bureau of National Affairs, 1965– [Annual].

Labor Studies Journal. New Brunswick, N.J.: Transaction Periodicals Consortium, Rutgers University, 1973– [Triannual].

Monthly Labor Review. Washington, D.C.: G.P.O., 1915– [Monthly].

National Productivity Review. New York: Executive Enterprises Publications Co., Inc., 1981-82– [Quarterly].

Organizational Dynamics. New York: AMACOM, 1972/1973– [Quarterly].

Personnel Administrator. Berea, Ohio: American Society for Personnel Administration, 1956– [Monthly].

Personnel Psychology: A Journal of Applied Research. Columbus, Ohio, 1948– [Quarterly].

Public Productivity Review. New York: Center for Productive Public Management, John Jay College of Criminal Justice, City University of New York, 1975– [Quarterly].

Research in Labor Economics: Greenwich, Conn.: JAI Press, 1977– [Annual].

Research in Organizational Behavior. Greenwich, Conn.: JAI Press, 1979– [Annual].

Research in Personnel and Human Resources Management. Greenwich, Conn.: JAI Press, 1983– [Annual].

Social Security Bulletin. Washington, D.C.: G.P.O., 1938– [Monthly].

TROY, LEO, and NEIL SHEFLIN. *Union Sourcebook: Membership, Structure, Finance, Directory.* West Orange, N.J.: IRDIS, 1985– [Annual].

U.S. National Labor Relations Board. *N.L.R.B. Election Report.* Washington, D.C., 1962– [Monthly].

PROCEEDINGS OF PROFESSIONAL ORGANIZATIONS

Conference on Labor, New York University, *Proceedings, 1st–*. New York: Matthew Bender, 1948– [Annual].

Industrial Relations Research Association (IRRA), *Proceedings of the Annual Spring Meeting, 1st–*. Madison, Wis., 1958–.

Industrial Relations Research Association (IRRA), *Proceedings of the Annual Winter Meeting, 1st–*. Madison, Wis., 1948–.

National Academy of Arbitrators, *Proceedings of the Annual Meeting, 1st–*. Washington, D.C.: Bureau of National Affairs, 1955–.

Society of Professionals in Dispute Resolution (SPIDR), *Proceedings of the Annual Convention.* Washington, D.C., 1973–.

Southwestern Legal Foundation. Institute on Labor Law, *Proceedings, 1st–*. New York: Matthew Bender, 1949– [Annual].

SELECTED LOOSE-LEAF REPORTING SERVICES AND
RELATED PUBLICATIONS

BNA Pension Reporter. Washington, D.C.: Bureau of National Affairs, 1974– [Loose-leaf].

BNA Policy and Practice Series. Washington, D.C.: Bureau of National Affairs, 1950– [Loose-leaf].

BNA's Employee Relations Weekly. Washington, D.C.: Bureau of National Affairs, 1983–.

Collective Bargaining Negotiations and Contracts. Washington, D.C.: Bureau of National Affairs, 1951– [Loose-leaf].

Daily Labor Report. Washington, D.C.: Bureau of National Affairs, 1941–.

Employee Benefit Plan Review; Research Reports. Chicago: Charles D. Spencer & Associates, 1957– [Loose-leaf].

Employment Coordinator. New York: Research Institute of America, 1984– [Loose-leaf].

Employment Practices Guide. Chicago: Commerce Clearing House, 1965– [Loose-leaf].

Federal Labor Relations Reporter. Fort Washington, Pa.: Labor Relations Press, 1970– [Loose-leaf].

Federal Merit Systems Reporter. Fort Washington, Pa.: Labor Relations Press, 1981– [Loose-leaf].

FEERICK, JOHN D., HENRY P. BAER, and JONATHAN P. ARFA. *NLRB Representation Elections: Law, Practice and Procedure*. (2nd ed.) New York: Law and Business; Washington, D.C.: Harcourt Brace Jovanovich, 1985– [Loose-leaf].

Government Employee Relations Report. Washington, D.C.: Bureau of National Affairs, 1963– [Loose-leaf].

Industrial Relations Guide. Englewood Cliffs, N.J.: Prentice-Hall, 1970– [Loose-leaf].

KHEEL, THEODORE W. *Labor Law*. New York: Matthew Bender, 1972– [Loose-leaf; 10 vols. plus consolidated table of cases and index].

Labor Arbitration Awards. Chicago: Commerce Clearing House, 1961– [Loose-leaf].

Labor Arbitration Information System. Fort Washington, Pa.: Labor Relations Press, 1981– [Loose-leaf].

Labor Law Reporter. Chicago: Commerce Clearing House, 1960– [Loose-leaf].

Labor Relations Reporter. Washington, D.C.: Bureau of National Affairs, 1947– [Loose-leaf].

LARSON, ARTHUR. *Employment Discrimination.* New York: Matthew Bender, 1975– [Loose-leaf; 4 vols.].

National Public Employment Reporter. Fort Washington, Pa.: Labor Relations Press, 1979– [Loose-leaf].

NLRB Advice Memorandum Reporter. Fort Washington, Pa.: Labor Relations Press, 1976– [Loose-leaf].

Occupational Safety and Health Reporter. Washington, D.C.: Bureau of National Affairs, 1971– [Loose-leaf].

Pennsylvania Public Employee Reporter. Fort Washington, Pa.: Labor Relations Press, 1971– (Labor Relations Press also publishes state reporters for California, Florida, Indiana, New Jersey, New York and Ohio.) [Loose-leaf].

Public Employee Bargaining. Chicago: Commerce Clearing House, 1970– [Loose-leaf].

Public Personnel Administration: Labor-Management Relations. Englewood Cliffs, N.J.: Prentice-Hall, 1972– [Loose-leaf].

STESSIN, LAWRENCE, AND LEN SMEDRESMAN. *Encyclopedia of Collective Bargaining Contract Clauses.* New York: Business Research Publications, 1984– [Loose-leaf].

Union Labor Report. Washington, D.C.: Bureau of National Affairs, 1954– [Loose-leaf].

U.S. National Labor Relations Board. *Decisions and Orders, Vol. 1– Washington, D.C.: GPO, 1935/36– .*

West's Social Security Reporting Service. St. Paul, Minn.: West, 1983– .

STATISTICS

American Statistics Index. Washington, D.C.: Congressional Information Service, 1973– [Monthly, cumulates quarterly and annually].

Statistical Reference Index. Washington, D.C.: Congressional Information Service, 1980– [Monthly, cumulates quarterly and annually].

U.S. Bureau of Labor Statistics. *Area Wage Survey.* Washington, D.C.: GPO, 1950– [Irregular].

——. *Bargaining Calendar.* Washington, D.C.: GPO, 1978– [Annual].

——. *Current Wage Developments, No. 1– Washington D.C.: GPO, 1948–* [Monthly].

——. *Employment and Earnings, Vol. 1– Washington, D.C.: GPO, 1954–* [Monthly].

————. *Employment, Hours and Earnings, States, and Areas, 1939–1982–*. Washington, D.C.: GPO, 1963– [Annual].

————. *Geographic Profile of Employment and Unemployment*. Washington, D.C.: GPO, 1971– [Annual].

————. *Handbook of Labor Statistics*. Washington, D.C.: GPO, 1926– [Annual].

————. *Industry Wage Survey*. Washington, D.C.: GPO, 1950– [Irregular].

————. *Labor Force Statistics Derived From the Current Population Survey: A Databook*. Washington, D.C.: GPO, 1982 [2 vols.].

U.S. Bureau of the Census. *Historical Statistics of the United States, Colonial Times to 1970*. Washington, D.C.: GPO, 1976 [2 vols.].

————. *Statistical Abstract of the United States*. Washington, D.C.: GPO, 1879– [Annual].

ARBITRATION/MEDIATION

AARON, BENJAMIN, and others, *The Future of Labor Arbitration in America*, edited by Joy Correge, Virginia A. Hughes, and Morris Stone. New York: American Arbitration Association, 1976. 304 pp.

BAER, WALTER E., *The Labor Arbitration Guide*. Homewood, Ill.: Dow Jones-Irwin, 1974. 191 pp.

BERNSTEIN, IRVING, *Arbitration of Wages*. (California. University. Institute of Industrial Relations Publications.) Berkeley: University of California Press, 1954. 125 pp.

ELKOURI, FRANK, and EDNA A. ELKOURI, *How Arbitration Works*. (4th ed.) Washington, D.C.: Bureau of National Affairs, 1985. 850 pp.

FAIRWEATHER, OWEN, *Practice and Procedure in Labor Arbitration*. (2nd ed.) Washington, D.C.: Bureau of National Affairs, 1983. 789 pp.

FLEMING, ROBBEN W. *The Labor Arbitration Process*. Urbana: University of Illinois Press, 1965. 233 pp.

GROSSMAN, MARK M., *The Question of Arbitrability: Challenges to the Arbitrator's Jurisdiction and Authority*. Ithaca, N.Y.: ILR Press, New York State School of Industrial and Labor Relations, Cornell University, 1984. 122 pp.

————, *Evidence in Arbitration*. Washington, D.C.: Bureau of National Affairs, 1980. 201 pp.

HILL, MARVIN F., and ANTHONY V. SINICROPI, *Remedies in Arbitration*. Washington, D.C.: Bureau of National Affairs, 1981. 355 pp.

KOLB, DEBORAH M., *The Mediators*. (MIT Press Series on Organization Studies.) Cambridge, Mass.: MIT Press, 1983. 230 pp.

MCKELVEY, JEAN T., ed.,   *The Changing Law of Fair Representation*. Ithaca, N.Y.: ILR Press, New York State School of Industrial and Labor Relations, Cornell University, 1985. 298 pp.

MCPHERSON, DONALD S.,   *Resolving Grievances: A Practical Approach*. Reston, Va.: Reston, 1983. 171 pp.

POPS, GERALD M.,   *Emergence of the Public Sector Arbitrator*. Lexington, Mass.: Lexington Books, 1976. 136 pp.

PRASOW, PAUL, and EDWARD PETERS,   *Arbitration and Collective Bargaining: Conflict Resolution in Labor Relations*. (2nd ed.) New York: McGraw-Hill, 1983. 536 pp.

TROTTA, MAURICE S.,   *Arbitration of Labor-Management Disputes*. New York: AMACOM, 1974. 499 pp.

UPDEGRAFF, CLARENCE M.,   *Arbitration and Labor Relations*. Washington, D.C.: Bureau of National Affairs, 1970. 454 pp.

ZACK, ARNOLD M., ed.,   *Arbitration in Practice*. Ithaca, N.Y.: ILR Press, New York State School of Industrial and Labor Relations, Cornell University, 1984. 256 pp.

COLLECTIVE BARGAINING/NEGOTIATION

AARON, BENJAMIN, JOSEPH R. GRODIN, and JAMES L. STERN, eds.,   *Public-Sector Bargaining*. (Industrial Relations Research Association Series.) Washington, D.C.: Bureau of National Affairs, 1979. 327 pp.

ATHERTON, WALLACE N.,   *Theory of Union Bargaining Goals*. Princeton, N.J.: Princeton University Press, 1973. 168 pp.

BACHARACH, SAMUEL B., and EDWARD J. LAWLER.,   *Bargaining, Tactics, and Outcomes*. San Francisco: Jossey-Bass, 1981. 234 pp.

BARTOS, OTOMAR J.,   *Process and Outcome of Negotiations*. New York: Columbia University Press, 1974. 451 pp.

BEGIN, JAMES P., and EDWIN F. BEAL,   *The Practice of Collective Bargaining*. (7th ed.) Homewood, Ill.: R.D. Irwin, 1985. 560 pp.

BERENDT, GERALD E.,   *Collective Bargaining*. (Contemporary Litigation Series.) Charlottesville, Va.: Michie, 1984. 340 pp.

BERNSTEIN, IRVING,   *The New Deal Collective Bargaining Policy*. (Franklin D. Roosevelt and the Era of the New Deal, 1950, Reprint.) New York: Da Capo Press, 1975. 178 pp.

CARPENTER, JESSE T.,   *Competition and Collective Bargaining in the Needle Trades, 1910–1967*. (Cornell Studies in Industrial and Labor Relations, 17.) Ithaca: New

York State School of Industrial and Labor Relations, Cornell University, 1972. 910 pp.

CHAMBERLAIN, NEIL W., and JAMES W. KUHN, *Collective Bargaining.* (3d ed.) New York: McGraw-Hill, 1986. 493 pp.

CHERNISH, WILLIAM N., *Coalition Bargaining: A Study of Union Tactics and Public Policy.* (Pennsylvania. University. Wharton School of Finance and Commerce. Industrial Research Unit. Research Studies, no 45.) Philadelphia: University of Pennsylvania Press, 1969. 286 pp.

CROSS, JOHN G., *The Economics of Bargaining.* New York: Basic Books, 1969. 247 pp.

DAVEY, HAROLD W., MARIO F. BOGNANNO, and DAVID L. ESTENSON, *Contemporary Collective Bargaining.* (4th ed.) Englewood Cliffs, N.J.: Prentice-Hall, 1982. 472 pp.

DE MENIL, GEORGE, *Bargaining: A Monopoly Power Versus Union Power.* Cambridge, Mass.: MIT Press, 1971. 123 pp.

DUNLOP, JOHN T., *Dispute Resolution: Negotiation and Consensus Building.* Dover, Mass.: Auburn House, 1984. 296 pp.

FOURAKER, LAWRENCE E., and SIDNEY SEIGEL, *Bargaining Behavior* (1963, Reprint). Westport, Conn.: Greenwood Press, 1977. 309 pp.

GIBBONS, MURIEL K., and others, *Portrait of a Process: Collective Negotiations in Public Employment.* Fort Washington, Pa.: Labor Relations Press, 1979. 463 pp.

GRANOF, MICHAEL H., *How to Cost Your Labor Contract.* Washington, D.C.: Bureau of National Affairs, 1973. 147 pp.

HOLOVIAK, STEPHEN J., *Costing Labor Contracts and Judging Their Financial Impact.* New York: Praeger, 1984. 194 pp.

KARRASS, CHESTER L., *Give and Take: The Complete Guide to Negotiating Strategies and Tactics.* New York: Crowell, 1974. 280 pp.

KOCHAN, THOMAS A., *Collective Bargaining and Industrial Relations: From Theory to Policy and Practice.* Homewood, Ill.: R.D. Irwin, 1980. 523 pp.

MORLEY, IAN E., and GEOFFREY M. STEPHENSON, *The Social Psychology of Bargaining.* London: G. Allen and Unwin, 1977. 317 pp.

MORSE, BRUCE, *How to Negotiate the Labor Agreement: An Outline Summary of Tested Bargaining Practice Expanded From Earlier Editions.* (10th ed.) Southfield, Mich.: Trends Publishing Co., 1984. 83 pp.

MOSKOW, MICHAEL H., J. JOSEPH LOEWENBERG, and EDWARD C. KOZIARA, *Collective Bargaining in Public Employment.* New York: Random House, 1970. 336 pp.

NIERENBERG, GERALD I., *The Art of Negotiating: Psychological Strategies for Gaining Advantageous Bargains.* New York: Hawthorne Books, 1968. 195 pp.

RICHARDSON, REED C., *Collective Bargaining by Objectives: A Positive Approach.* (2nd ed.) Englewood Cliffs, N.J.: Prentice-Hall, 1985. 326 pp.

ROSS, PHILIP, *The Government as a Source of Union Power; The Role of Public Policy in Collective Bargaining.* Providence, R.I.: Brown University Press, 1965. 320 pp.

ROTHSCHILD, DONALD P., LEROY S. MERRIFIELD, and HARRY T. EDWARDS, *Collective Bargaining and Labor Arbitration: Materials on Collective Bargaining, Labor Arbitration and Discrimination in Employment.* (Contemporary Legal Education Series.) (2nd ed.) Indianapolis: Bobbs-Merrill, 1979. 1075 pp.

ROWEN, RICHARD I., ed., *Collective Bargaining: Survival in the 70's? Proceedings of a Conference.* (Labor Relations and Public Policy Series, Report no. 5.) Philadelphia: Industrial Research Unit, Department of Industry, Wharton School of Finance and Commerce, University of Pennsylvania, 1972. 481 pp.

RUBIN, JEFFREY Z., and BERT R. BROWN, *The Social Psychology of Bargaining and Negotiation.* New York: Academic Press, 1975. 359 pp.

SIEGEL, ABRAHAM J., ed., *The Impact of Computers on Collective Bargaining.* Cambridge, Mass.: MIT Press, 1969. 294 pp.

SLITCHER, SUMNER H., JAMES J. HEALY, and E. ROBERT LIVERNASH, *The Impact of Collective Bargaining on Management.* Washington, D.C.: Brookings Institution, 1960. 982 pp.

STEVENS, CARL M., *Strategy and Collective Bargaining Negotiation.* New York: McGraw-Hill, 1963. 192 pp.

STRAUSS, ANSELM L., *Negotiations: Varieties, Contexts, Processes, and Social Order.* San Francisco: Jossey-Bass, 1978. 275 pp.

TWENTIETH CENTURY FUND. Labor Committee, *How Collective Bargaining Works, A Survey of Experience in Leading American Industries,* edited by Harry A. Millis. (American Labor: From Conspiracy to Collective Bargaining, 1942, Reprint.) New York: Arno Press, 1971. 986 pp.

WALTON, RICHARD E., and ROBERT B. MCKERSIE, *A Behavioral Theory of Labor Negotiations; An Analysis of a Social Interaction System.* New York: McGraw-Hill, 1965. 437 pp.

WEBER, ARNOLD R., ed., *The Structure of Collective Bargaining.* (Chicago University. Graduate School of Business Publications. Third Series: Studies in Business.) New York: Free Press, 1961. 380 pp.

WEITZMAN, JOAN P., *The Scope of Bargaining in Public Employment.* New York: Praeger, 1975. 384 pp.

YOUNG, ORAN R., ed.,   *Bargaining: Formal Theories of Negotiation*. Urbana: University of Illinois Press, 1975. 412 pp.

ZACK, ARNOLD,   *Public Sector Mediation*. Washington, D.C.: Bureau of National Affairs, 1985. 200 pp.

DISCRIMINATION IN EMPLOYMENT

BECKER, GARY S.,   *The Economics of Discrimination*. (Chicago. University. Economics Research Center. Economic Research Studies.) (2nd ed.) Chicago: University of Chicago Press, 1971. 167 pp.

FASMAN, ZACHARY D.,   *Equal Employment Audit Handbook*. New York: Executive Enterprises Publications, 1983. 452 pp.

FULLINWIDER, ROBERT K.,   *The Reverse Discrimination Controversy: A Moral and Legal Analysis*. Totowa, N.J.: Rowman and Littlefield, 1980. 300 pp.

HARTMANN, HEIDI I.,   *Comparable Worth: New Directions for Research*. Washington, D.C.: National Academy Press, 1985. 178 pp.

HILL, HERBERT,   *Black Labor and the American Legal System*. Washington, D.C.: Bureau of National Affairs, 1977. 2 vols.

LLOYD, CYNTHIA B., and BETH T. NIEMI,   *The Economics of Sex Differentials*. New York: Columbia University Press, 1979. 355 pp.

MARSHALL, RAY, and others, *Employment Discrimination: The Impact of Legal and Administrative Remedies*. New York: Praeger, 1978. 153 pp.

MINER, MARY G., and JOHN B. MINER,   *Employee Selection Within the Law*. Washington, D.C.: Bureau of National Affairs, 1978. 568 pp.

NORTHRUP, HERBERT R., and others,   *Negro Employment in Basic Industry: A Study of Racial Policies in Six Industries*. (Studies of Negro Employment, Vol. 1; Recent Industrial Research Unit Studies No. 46.) Philadelphia: Industrial Research Unit, Department of Industry, Wharton School of Finance and Commerce, University of Pennsylvania, 1970. 769 pp.

PARCEL, TOBY L., and CHARLES W. MUELLER,   *Ascription and Labor Markets: Race and Sex Differences in Earnings*. New York: Academic Press, 1983. 315 pp.

PERRIN, SUZANNE M., *Comparable Worth and Public Policy: the Case of Pennsylvania*. (Labor Relations and Public Policy Series, No. 29.) Philadelphia: Industrial Research Unit, The Wharton School, University of Pennsylvania, 1985. 123 pp.

PLAYER, MACK A.,   *Employment Discrimination Law: Cases and Materials*. (2nd ed.) (American Casebook Series.) St. Paul, Minn.: West, 1984. 782 pp.

REMICK, HELEN, ed., *Comparable Worth and Wage Discrimination: Technical Possibilities and Political Realities.* (Women in the Political Economy.) Philadelphia: Temple University Press, 1984. 311 pp.

ROSEN, BENSON, and THOMAS H. JERDEE, *Older Employees: New Roles for Valued Resources.* Homewood, Ill.: Dow Jones-Irwin, 1985, 201 pp.

SCHLEI, BARBARA L., and PAUL GROSSMAN, *Employment Discrimination Law.* (2nd ed.) Washington, D.C.: Bureau of National Affairs, 1983. 1661 pp.

————. *Employment Discrimination Law: 1983 Supplement.* (2nd ed.) Washington, D.C.: Bureau of National Affairs, 1984. 240 pp.

SMITH, ARTHUR B., CHARLES B. CRAVER, and LEROY D. CLARK, *Employment Discrimination Law: Cases and Materials.* (2nd ed.) (Contemporary Legal Education Series.) Indianapolis: Bobbs-Merrill, 1982. 1041 pp.

WILLBORN, STEVEN L., *A Comparable Worth Primer.* Lexington, Mass.: Lexington Books, 1986. 129 pp.

INDUSTRIAL RELATIONS

AARON, BENJAMIN, and others, *The Next Twenty-Five Years of Industrial Relations,* edited by Gerald G. Somers. (Industrial Relations Research Association Series.) Madison, Wis.: Industrial Relations Research Association, 1973. 207 pp.

ADAMS, ROY J., and others, *Industrial Relations in a Decade of Economic Change.* (Industrial Relations Research Association Series.) Madison, Wis.: Industrial Relations Research Association, 1985. 407 pp.

ALLEN, ROBERT E., and TIMOTHY J. KEAVENY, *Contemporary Labor Relations.* Reading , Mass.: Addison-Wesley, 1983. 666 pp.

BARBASH, JACK, *The Elements of Industrial Relations.* Madison, Wis.: University of Wisconsin Press, 1984. 153 pp.

BAROCCI, THOMAS, and others, *Industrial Relations Research in the 1970's; A Review and Appraisal.* Madison , Wis.: Industrial Relations Research Association, 1982. 314 pp.

BEAN, RON, *Comparative Industrial Relations: an Introduction to Cross-National Perspectives.* New York: St. Martin's Press, 1985. 261 pp.

BLOCK, RICHARD, and others, *U.S. Industrial Relations, 1950–1980: A Critical Assessment.* Madison, Wis.: Industrial Relations Research Association, 1981. 361 pp.

BLUM, ALBERT A., ed., *International Handbook of Industrial Relations: Contemporary Developments and Research.* Westport, Conn.: Greenwood Press, 1981. 698 pp.

Bok, Derek C., *Labor and the American Community*. New York: Simon & Schuster, 1970. 542 pp.

Bradley, Keith, and Alan Golb, *Worker Capitalism: the New Industrial Relations*. Cambridge, Mass.: MIT Press, 1983. 186 pp.

Brandes, Stuart D., *American Welfare Capitalism, 1880–1940*. Chicago: University of Chicago Press, 1976. 210 pp.

Carter, Michael J., and William H. Leahy, eds., *New Directions in Labor Economics and Industrial Relations*. Notre Dame, Ind.: University of Notre Dame Press, 1981. 214 pp.

Chamberlain, Neil W., Donald E. Cullen, and David Lewin, *The Labor Sector*. (3rd ed.) New York: McGraw-Hill, 1980. 669 pp.

Derber, Milton, *The American Idea of Industrial Democracy, 1865–1965*. Urbana: University of Illinois Press, 1970. 553 pp.

Dilts, David A., and Clarence R. Deitsch, *Labor Relations*. New York: Macmillan, 1983. 476 pp.

Doeringer, Peter B., *Industrial Relations in International Perspective: Essays on Research and Policy*. New York: Holmes and Meier, 1981. 425 pp.

Dunlop, John T., *Industrial Relations Systems*. (1958, Reprint.) Carbondale: Southern Illinois University Press, 1977. 399 pp.

Fossum, John A., *Labor Relations: Development, Structure, Process*. (3rd ed.) Plano, Tex.: Business Publications, 1985. 501 pp.

Hagburg, Eugene C., and Marvin J. Levine, *Labor Relations: An Integrated Perspective*. St. Paul: West, 1978. 390 pp.

Hamermesh, Daniel S., ed., *Labor in the Public and Nonprofit Sectors*. Princeton, N.J.: Princeton University Press, 1975. 272 pp.

Harris, Howell J., *The Right to Manage: Industrial Relations Policies of American Business in the 1940s*. Madison, Wis.: University of Wisconsin Press, 1982. 290 pp.

Juris, Harvey A., and Myron Roomkin, eds., *The Shrinking Perimeter: Unionism and Labor Relations in the Manufacturing Sector*. Lexington, Mass.: Lexington Books, 1980. 223 pp.

Kilgour, John G., *Preventive Labor Relations*. New York: AMACOM, 1981. 338 pp.

Kochan, Thomas A., ed., *Challenges and Choices Facing American Labor*. Cambridge, Mass.: MIT Press, 1985. 356 pp.

Mills, Daniel Q., *Labor-Management Relations*. (2nd ed.) New York: McGraw-Hill, 1982. 644 pp.

MILLS, DANIEL Q., and JANICE MCCORMICK,   *Industrial Relations in Transition: Cases and Text*. (3d ed.) New York: McGraw-Hill, 1986, 604 pp.

MOORE, WILBERT E.,   *Industrial Relations and the Social Order*. (Work, Its Rewards and Discontents, 1951, Rev. reprint.) New York: Arno Press, 1977. 660 pp.

REYNOLDS, LLOYD G., STANLEY H. MASTERS, and COLLETTA H. MOSER,   *Labor Economics and Labor Relations*. (9th ed.) Englewood Cliffs, N.J.: Prentice-Hall, 1986. 635 pp.

SCHUSTER, MICHAEL H.,   *Union-Management Cooperation: Structure, Process, Impact*. Kalamazoo, Mich.: W. E. Upjohn Institute for Employment Research, 1984. 235 pp.

SIEGEL, IRVING H., and EDGAR WEINBERG,   *Labor-Management Cooperation: The American Experience*. Kalamazoo, Mich.: W.E. Upjohn Institute for Employment Research, 1982. 316 pp.

SLOANE, ARTHUR A., and FRED WITNEY,   *Labor Relations*. (5th ed.) Englewood Cliffs, N.J.: Prentice-Hall, 1985. 542 pp.

SOMERS, GERALD G., ed.,   *Essays in Industrial Relations Theory*. Ames: Iowa State University Press, 1969. 200 pp.

———,   *Labor, Management, and Social Policy: Essays in the John R. Commons Tradition*. Madison: University of Wisconsin Press, 1963. 303 pp.

THURLEY, KEITH, and STEPHEN WOOD, eds.,   *Industrial Relations and Management Strategy*. (Management and Industrial Relations Series, 4.) New York: Cambridge University Press, 1983. 242 pp.

WELLINGTON, HARRY H.,   *The Unions and the Cities*. (Studies of Unionism in Government.) Washington, D.C.: Brookings Institution, 1971. 226 pp.

LABOR ECONOMICS

BLOOM, GORDON F.,   *Economics of Labor Relations*. (9th ed.) Homewood, Ill.: R.D. Irwin, 1981. 860 pp.

BOWEN, WILLIAM G., and ORLEY ASHENFELTER, eds.,   *Labor and the National Economy*. (Rev. ed.) New York: Norton, 1975. 206 pp.

CARTTER, ALLAN,   *Theory of Wages and Employment*.   Homewood, Ill.: R.D. Irwin, 1959. 193 pp.

DARITY, WILLIAM, ed.,   *Labor Economics: Modern Views*. Boston, Kluwer-Nijhoff, 1984. 296 pp.

DOERINGER, PETER, and MICHAEL J. PIORE,   *Internal Labor Markets and Manpower Analysis*. Lexington, Mass.: Heath, 1971. 214 pp.

DUNLOP, JOHN T.,   *Wage Determination Under Trade Unions* (1944, Reprint.) New York: A.M. Kelley, 1966. 230 pp.

EHRENBERG, RONALD G., and ROBERT S. SMITH, *Modern Labor Economics: Theory and Public Policy.* (2nd ed.) Glenview, Ill.: Scott, Foresman, 1985. 580 pp.

FLANAGAN, ROBERT J., ROBERT S. SMITH, and RONALD G. EHRENBERG, *Labor Economics and Labor Relations.* Glenview, Ill.: Scott, Foresman, 1984. 653 pp.

FLEISHER, BELTON M., and THOMAS J. KNIESNER, *Labor Economics: Theory, Evidence, and Policy.* (3rd ed.) Englewood Cliffs, N.J.: Prentice-Hall, 1984. 536 pp.

FOGEL, WALTER, ed., *Current Research in Labor Economics.* (Monograph and Research Series, 38.) Los Angeles: Institute of Industrial Relations, University of California, Los Angeles, 1984. 159 pp.

GINZBERG, ELI, *The Human Economy.* New York: McGraw-Hill, 1976. 274 pp.

GITLOW, ABRAHAM L., *Labor and Manpower Economics.* (3rd ed.) Homewood, Ill.: R.D. Irwin, 1971. 555 pp.

HAMERMESH, DANIEL S., and ALBERT REES, *The Economics of Work and Pay.* (3rd ed.) New York: Harper and Row, 1984. 402 pp.

HICKS, JOHN R., *The Theory of Wages.* (2nd ed.) New York: St. Martin's Press, 1963. 388 pp.

HILDEBRAND, GEORGE H., *American Unionism: An Historical and Analytical Survey.* (Perspectives on Economics Series.) Reading, Mass.: Addison-Wesley, 1979. 132 pp.

HOFFMAN, SAUL D., *Labor Market Economics.* Englewood Cliffs, N.J.: Prentice-Hall, 1986. 354 pp.

KREPS, JUANITA, and others, *Contemporary Labor Economics and Labor Relations: Issues, Analysis, and Policies.* (2nd ed.) Belmont, Calif.: Wadsworth, 1980. 478 pp.

LEVINSON, HAROLD M., *Determining Forces in Collective Wage Bargaining.* New York: John Wiley, 1966. 283 pp.

LEVITAN, SAR, GARTH L. MANGUM, and RAY MARSHALL, *Human Resources and Labor Markets: Employment and Training in the American Economy.* (3rd ed.) New York: Harper & Row, 1981. 551 pp.

LLOYD, CYNTHIA B., EMILY ANDREWS, and CURTIS L. GILROY, eds., *Women in the Labor Market.* New York: Columbia University Press, 1979. 393 pp.

MARSHALL, F. RAY, VERNON M. BRIGGS, and ALLAN G. KING, *Labor Economics: Wages, Employment, Trade Unionism, and Public Policy.* (5th ed.) Homewood, Ill.: R.D. Irwin, 1984. 676 pp.

MCCONNELL, CAMPBELL R., and STANLEY L. BRUE, *Contemporary Labor Economics.* New York: McGraw-Hill, 1986. 607 pp.

MCNULTY, PAUL J., *The Origins and Development of Labor Economics: A Chapter in the History of Social Thought.* Cambridge, Mass.: MIT Press, 1980. 248 pp.

MIERNYK, WILLIAM H., *The Economics of Labor and Collective Bargaining.* (2nd ed.) Lexington, Mass.: Heath, 1973. 531 pp.

MILLS, DANIEL Q., *Government, Labor, and Inflation: Wage Stabilization in the United States.* Chicago: University of Chicago Press, 1975. 311 pp.

MULVEY, CHARLES, *The Economic Analysis of Trade Unions.* New York: St. Martin's Press, 1978. 159 pp.

PERLMAN, RICHARD, *Labor Theory.* New York: John Wiley, 1969. 237 pp.

REES, ALBERT, *The Economics of Trade Unions.* (2nd rev. ed.) Chicago: University of Chicago Press, 1977. 200 pp.

ROSS, ARTHUR N., *Trade Union Wage Policy.* Berkeley: University of California Press, 1948. 133 pp.

ROTHSCHILD, KURT W., *The Theory of Wages.* Oxford: Blackwell, 1954. 178 pp.

SMITH, RALPH E., ed., *The Subtle Revolution: Women at Work.* Washington, D.C.: Urban Institute, 1979. 279 pp.

TAYLOR, GEORGE W., and F. C. PIERSON, eds., *New Concepts in Wage Determination.* New York: McGraw-Hill, 1957. 336 pp.

Universities-National Bureau Committee for Economic Research. *Aspects of Labor Economics; A Conference of the Universities-National Bureau Committee for Economic Research.* A Report of the National Bureau of Economic Research. (National Bureau of Economic Research. Special Conference Series, 14; National Bureau of Economic Research Publications in Reprint; 1962, Reprint.) New York: Arno Press, 1975. 349 pp.

LABOR LAW

BIOFF, ALLAN L., and others, eds., *The Developing Labor Law: the Board, the Courts, and the National Labor Relations Act.* (2nd ed.) Editor in chief, Charles J. Morris. Washington, D.C.: Bureau of National Affairs, 1983. 2 vols. [Kept up to date by annual supplements].

CABOT, STEPHEN J., *Labor Management Relations Act Manual: A Guide to Effective Labor Relations.* Boston: Warren, Gorham and Lamont, 1978–.

———, *Labor Management Relations Act Manual: A Guide to Effective Labor Relations. 1984 Supplement.* Boston: Warren, Gorham and Lamont, 1984. (Various pagings.)

Commerce Clearing House, *Labor Law Course, 1st–.* Chicago, 1947– [Irregular].

COX, ARCHIBALD, DEREK C. BOK, and ROBERT A. GORMAN, *Cases and Materials on Labor Law.* (University Casebook Series.) (9th ed.) Mineola, N.Y.: Foundation Press, 1981. 1215 pp.

————, *Cases and Materials on Labor Law. 1983 Case Supplement.* (University Casebook Series.) (9th ed.). Mineola N.Y.: Foundation Press, 1983. 219 pp.

EDWARDS, HARRY T., R. THEODORE CLARK, and CHARLES B. CRAVER, *Labor Relations Law in the Public Sector: Cases and Materials.* (2nd ed.) Indianapolis: Bobbs-Merrill, 1979– [Kept up to date by annual cumulative supplement].

Federal Labor and Employment Laws. Washington, D.C.: Bureau of National Affairs, 1983. 298 pp.

FELDACKER, BRUCE S., *Labor Guide to Labor Law.* (2nd ed.) Reston, Va.: Reston, 1983. 527 pp.

GETMAN, JULIUS G., and JOHN D. BLACKBURN, *Labor Relations: Law, Practice, and Policy.* (2nd ed.) Mineola, N.Y.: Foundation Press, 1983. 756 pp.

GETMAN, JULIUS G., STEPHEN B. GOLDBERG, and JEANNE B. HERMAN, *Union Representative Elections: Law and Reality.* New York: Russell Sage Foundation, 1976. 218 pp.

GOLDMAN, ALVIN L., *Labor Law and Industrial Relations in the United States of America.* (2nd ed.) Washington, D.C.: Bureau of National Affairs, 1984. 373 pp.

————, *The Supreme Court and Labor-Management Relations Law.* Lexington, Mass.: Lexington Books, 1976. 191 pp.

GORMAN, ROBERT A., *Basic Text on Labor Law, Unionization, and Collective Bargaining.* St. Paul, Minn.: West, 1976. 914 pp.

GOULD, WILLIAM B., *Japan's Reshaping of American Labor Law.* Cambridge, Mass.: MIT Press, 1984. 193 pp.

————, *A Primer on American Labor Law.* Cambridge, Mass.: MIT Press, 1982. 242 pp.

————, *Strikes, Dispute Procedures, and Arbitration: Essays on Labor Law.* (Contributions in American Studies, No. 82.) Westport, Conn.: Greenwood Press, 1985. 313 pp.

GREGORY, CHARLES O., and HAROLD A. KATZ, *Labor and the Law.* (3rd ed.) New York: Norton, 1979. 719 pp.

JUSTICE, BETTY W., *Unions, Workers and the Law.* Washington, D.C.: Bureau of National Affairs, 1983. 291 pp.

MCLAUGHLIN, DORIS B., and ANITA W. SCHOOMAKER, *The Landrum–Griffin Act and Union Democracy.* Ann Arbor: University of Michigan Press, 1979. 288 pp.

MELTZER, BERNARD D., *Labor Law: Cases, Materials, and Problems.* (2nd ed.) (Law School Casebook Series.) Boston: Little, Brown, 1977. 1300 pp.

————, *Labor Law: Cases, Materials, and Problems. 1982 Supplement.* Boston: Little, Brown, 1982. 242 pp.

————, *Appendix to Labor Law: Cases, Materials, and Problems.* (2nd ed.) (Law School Casebook Series.) Boston: Little, Brown, 1977. 169 pp.

MILLER, EDWARD B., *Antitrust Laws and Employee Relations: an Analysis of Their Impact on Management and Union Policies.* (Labor Relations and Public Policy Series, No. 26.) Philadelphia: Industrial Research Unit, The Wharton School, University of Pennsylvania, 1984. 144 pp.

MILLS, HARRY A., and EMILY C. BROWN,   *From the Wagner Act to Taft-Hartley; A Study of National Labor Policy and Labor Relations.* Chicago: University of Chicago Press, 1950. 723 pp.

OBERER, WALTER E., KURT L. HANSLOWE, and JERRY R. ANDERSON,   *Cases and Materials on Labor Law: Collective Bargaining in a Free Society.* (2nd ed.) (American Casebook Series.) St. Paul, Minn.: West, 1979. 1168 pp.

————, *Cases and Materials on Labor Law: Collective Bargaining in a Free Society. Statutory Supplement.* (2nd ed.) (American Casebook Series.) St. Paul, Minn.: West, 1979. 157 pp.

PERRY, CHARLES R., ANDREW M. KRAMER, and THOMAS J. SCHNEIDER,   *Operating During Strikes: Company Experience, NLRB Policies, and Governmental Regulation.* (Labor Relations and Public Policy Series, no. 23.) Philadelphia: Industrial Research Unit, Department of Industry, Wharton School of Finance and Commerce, University of Pennsylvania, 1982. 163 pp.

SCHLOSSBERG, STEPHEN I., and JUDITH A. SCOTT,   *Organizing and the Law.* (3rd ed.) Washington, D.C.: Bureau of National Affairs, 1983. 433 pp.

SMITH, RUSSELL A., and others,   *Labor Relations Law: Cases and Materials.* (7th ed.) (Contemporary Legal Education Series.) Charlottesville, Va.: Michie, 1984. 1102 pp.

————, *Labor Relations Law. Statutory Appendix: Cases and Materials.* (7th ed.) (Contemporary Legal Education Series.) Charlottesville, Va.: Michie, 1984. 173 pp.

TAYLOR, BENJAMIN J. and FRED WITNEY,   *Labor Relations Law.* (4th ed.) Englewood Cliffs, N.J.: Prentice-Hall, 1983. 914 pp. [Kept up to date by cumulative supplements].

TOWNLEY, BARBARA, *Labor Law Reform in U.S. Industrial Relations.* Brookfield, Vt.: Gower, 1986. 263 pp.

TWOMEY, DAVID P.,   *Labor Law and Legislation.* (7th ed.) Cincinnati: South-Western, 1985. 634 pp.

WELLINGTON, HARRY H.,   *Labor and the Legal Process.* New Haven: Yale University Press, 1968. 409 pp.

LABOR/LABOR UNIONS—HISTORY

ARONOWITZ, STANLEY, *False Promises: The Shaping of American Working-Class Consciousness*. New York: McGraw-Hill, 1973. 465 pp.

BEARD, MARY R., *A Short History of the American Labor Movement*. (1924, Reprint.) Westport, Conn.: Greenwood Press, 1968. 206 pp.

BERNSTEIN, IRVING, *The Lean Years; A History of the American Worker, 1920–1933*. New York: Da Capo Press, 1983. 577, 16 pp.

———, *Turbulent Years; A History of the American Worker, 1933–1941*. Boston: Houghton Mifflin, 1969. 873 pp.

BROOKS, ROBERT R. R., *When Labor Organizes*. (American Labor: From Conspiracy to Collective Bargaining, 1937, Reprint.) New York: Arno Press, 1971. 361 pp.

BROOKS, THOMAS R., *Toil and Trouble; A History of American Labor*. (2nd ed. rev. and enl.) New York: Delacorte Press, 1971. 402 pp.

COMMONS, JOHNS R., *History of Labor in the United States*. (Reprints of Economic Classics, 1918, Reprint.) Fairfield, N.J.: Kelley, 1966. 4 vols.

COMMONS, JOHN R., and others, *A Documentary History of American Industrial Society*. (1909–1911, Reprint.) New York: Russell and Russell, 1958. 10 vols.

Correspondence of Mother Jones. (Pittsburgh series in Labor History.) Edited by Edward M. Steel. Pittsburgh: University of Pittsburgh Press, 1985, 360 pp.

DUBOFSKY, MELVYN, *Industrialism and the American Worker, 1865–1920*. (2nd ed.) Arlington Heights, Ill.: Harlan Davidson, 1985. 167 pp.

———, *We Shall Be All; A History of the Industrial Workers of the World*. Chicago: Quadrangle Books, 1969. 557 pp.

DUBOFSKY, MELVYN, and WARREN VAN TYNE, *John L. Lewis: A Biography*. New York: New York Times Book Co., 1977. 619 pp.

DULLES, FOSTER R., and MELVYN DUBOFSKY, *Labor in America: A History*. (4th ed.) Arlington Heights, Ill.: Harlan Davidson, 1984. 425 pp.

ESTEY, MARTIN S., *The Unions: Structure, Development, and Management*. (3rd ed.) New York: Harcourt Brace Jovanovich, 1981. 153 pp.

FILIPPELLI, RONALD L., *Labor in America: A History*. New York: Alfred A. Knopf, 1984. 315 pp.

FONER, PHILIP S., *History of the Labor Movement in the United States*. New York: International Publishing Co., 1947–1980. 5 vols.

————, *First Facts of American Labor: A Comprehensive Collection of Labor Firsts in the United States*. New York: Holmes and Meier, 1984. 237 pp.

FREEMAN, RICHARD B., and JAMES L. MEDOFF, *What Do Unions Do?* New York: Basic Books, 1984. 239 pp.

FRISCH, MICHAEL H., and DANIEL J. WALKOWITZ, eds., *Working-Class America: Essays on Labor, Community and American Society*. (The Working Class in American History.) Urbana: University of Illinois Press, 1983. 313 pp.

FULMER, WILLIAM E., *Union Organizing: Management and Labor Conflict*. New York: Praeger, 1982. 228 pp.

GALENSON, WALTER, *The United Brotherhood of Carpenters: The First Hundred Years*. (Wertheim Publications in Industrial Relations.) Cambridge, Mass.: Harvard University Press, 1983. 440 pp.

GARLOCK, JONATHAN, comp., *Guide to the Local Assemblies of the Knights of Labor*. Westport, Conn.: Greenwood Press, 1982. 682 pp.

GARNEL, DONALD, *The Rise of Teamster Power in the West*. Berkeley: University of California Press, 1972. 363 pp.

GINZBERG, ELI, and HYMAN BERMAN, *The American Worker in the Twentieth Century, A History Through Autobiographies*. New York: Free Press, 1963. 368 pp.

GOMPERS, SAMUEL, *Seventy Years of Life and Labour; An Autobiography*. (Library of American Labor History, Reprints of Economic Classics, 1953, Reprint.) New York: A.M. Kelley, 1967. 2 vols.

GOULDEN, JOSEPH C., *Meany*. New York: Atheneum, 1972. 504 pp.

GROB, GERALD N., *Workers and Utopia: A Study of Ideological Conflict in the American Labor Movement, 1865–1900*. New York: Quadrangle Books, 1976. 220 pp.

JACKSON, ROBERT M., *The Formation of Craft Labor Markets*. (Studies in Social Discontinuity.) New York: Academic Press, 1984. 353 pp.

JACOBY, SANFORD, M., *Employing Bureaucracy: Managers, Unions, and the Transformation of Work in American Industry, 1900–1945*. New York: Columbia University Press, 1985. 377 pp.

KAUFMAN, STUART, B., ed., *The Samuel Gompers Papers*. Urbana: University of Illinois Press, 1986–.

Labor Unions, ed. Gary M. Fink (The Greenwood Encyclopedia of American Institutions). Westport, Conn.: Greenwood Press, 1977. 520 pp.

LEAB, DANIEL J., ed., *The Labor History Reader*. (The Working Class in American History.) Urbana: University of Illinois Press, 1985. 470 pp.

MILLIS, HARRY A., and ROYAL E. MONTGOMERY, *Organized Labor*. (The Labor Movement in Fiction and Nonfiction, 1945, Reprint.) New York: AMS Press, 1976. 930 pp.

MILTON, DAVID, *The Politics of U.S. Labor: From the Great Depression to the New Deal*. New York: Monthly Review Press, 1982. 189 pp.

MONTGOMERY DAVID, *Workers' Control in America: Studies in the History of Work, Technology, and Labor Struggles*. New York: Cambridge University Press, 1979. 189 pp.

MORRIS, JAMES O., *Conflict Within the AFL: A Study of Craft Versus Industrial Unionism 1901–1938*. (Cornell Studies in Industrial and Labor Relations, Vol. 10, 1958, Reprint.) Westport, Conn.: Greenwood Press, 1974. 319 pp.

MORRIS, RICHARD B., *The U.S. Department of Labor Bicentennial History of the American Worker*. Washington, D.C.: GPO, 1976. 327 pp.

PELLING, HENRY, *American Labor*. Chicago: University of Chicago Press, 1960. 247 pp.

PERLMAN, SELIG, *A History of Trade Unionism in the United States*. (1922, Reprint.) Fairfield, N.J.: Kelley, 1950. 313 pp.

PESSEN, EDWARD, *Most Uncommon Jacksonians: The Radical Leaders of the Early Labor Movement*. Albany: State University of New York Press, 1967. 208 pp.

REUTHER, VICTOR G., *The Brothers Reuther and the Story of the UAW: A Memoir*. Boston: Houghton Mifflin, 1976. 523 pp.

REYNOLDS, MORGAN O., *Power and Privilege: Labor Unions in America*. New York: Universe Books, 1984. 309 pp.

ROBINSON, ARCHIE, *George Meany and His Times, A Biography*. New York: Simon and Schuster, 1961. 445 pp.

SEIDMAN, JOEL I., *American Labor from Defense to Reconversion*. Chicago: University of Chicago Press, 1953. 307 pp.

STEIN, LEON, and PHILIP TAFT, eds., *Wages, Hours, and Strikes: Labor Panaceas in the Twentieth Century*. (American Labor: From Conspiracy to Collective Bargaining.) New York: Arno Press, 1970. 1 vol. [various pagings].

TAFT, PHILIP, *Organized Labor in American History*. New York: Harper and Row, 1964. 818 pp.

TOMLINS, CHRISTOPHER L., *The State and the Unions: Labor Relations, Law, and the Organized Labor Movement in America, 1880–1960*. (Studies in Economic History and Policy.) New York: Cambridge University Press, 1985. 348 pp.

ULMAN, LLOYD, *The Rise of the National Trade Union: The Development and Significance of Its Structure, Governing Institutions, and Economic Policies*. (2nd ed.) (Wertheim Publications in Industrial Relations.) Cambridge, Mass.: Harvard University Press, 1966. 639 pp.

Unions Today: New Tactics to Tackle Tough Times. (BNA Special Report.) Washington, D.C.: Bureau of National Affairs, 1985. 140 pp.

WOLMAN, LEO,   *The Growth of American Trade Unions, 1880–1923.* (1924, Reprint.) New York: Arno Press, 1975. 170 pp.

ZEITLIN, MAURICE, ed.,   *How Mighty a Force?: Studies of Workers' Consciousness and Organization in the United States.* (Monograph and Research Series, 35.) Los Angeles: Institute of Industrial Relations, University of California, Los Angeles, 1983. 369 pp.

ZIEGER, ROBERT H.,   *American Workers, American Unions, 1920–1985.* Baltimore: Johns Hopkins University Press, 1986. 233 pp.

NATIONAL LABOR RELATIONS BOARD

ABODEELY, JOHN E., RANDI C. HAMMER, and ANDREW L. SANDLER,   *The NLRB and the Appropriate Bargaining Unit.* (Rev. ed.) (Labor Relations and Public Policy Series, No. 3.) Philadelphia: Industrial Research Unit, The Wharton School, University of Pennsylvania, 1981. 359 pp.

ABODEELY, PAUL A.,   *Compulsory Arbitration and the NLRB, A Study of Congressional Intent and Administrative Policy.* (Labor Relations and Public Policy Series, Report No. 1.) Philadelphia: Industrial Research Unit, Department of Industry, Wharton School of Finance and Commerce, University of Pennsylvania, 1968. 96 pp.

BOYCE, TIMOTHY J., and RONALD TURNER,   *Fair Representation, the NLRB and the Courts.* (Rev. ed.) (Labor Relations and Public Policy Series. Report No. 18.) Philadelphia: Industrial Research Unit, Department of Industry, Wharton School of Finance and Commerce, University of Pennsylvania, 1984. 194 pp.

DERESHINSKY, RALPH M., ALAN D. BERKOWITZ, and PHILIP A. MISCIMARA,   *The NLRB and Secondary Boycotts.* (Rev. ed.) (Labor Relations and Public Policy Series, Report No. 4.) Philadelphia: Industrial Research Unit, Department of Industry, Wharton School of Finance and Commerce, University of Pennsylvania, 1981. 349 pp.

GROSS, JAMES A.,   *The Making of the National Labor Relations Board; A Study in Economics, Politics, and the Law.* Albany: State University of New York Press, 1974–1981. 2 vols.

HUNSICKER, J. FREEDLY, JONATHAN A. KANE, and PETER D. WALTHER, *NLRB Remedies for Unfair Labor Practices.* (Rev. ed.) (Labor Relations and Public Policy Series, No. 12.) Philadelphia: Industrial Research Unit, The Wharton School, University of Pennsylvania, 1986. 266 pp.

KEELINE, THOMAS J.,   *NLRB and Judicial Control of Union Discipline.* (Labor Relations and Public Policy Series, Report No. 5.) Philadelphia: Industrial Research Unit, Department of Industry, Wharton School of Finance and Commerce, University of Pennsylvania, 1976. 105 pp.

MILLER, EDWARD B.,   *An Administrative Appraisal of the NLRB.* (2nd rev. ed.) (Labor Relations and Public Policy Series, No. 16.) Philadelphia: Industrial Research Unit, The Wharton School, University of Pennsylvania, 1980. 169 pp.

MODJESKA, LEE,   *NLRB Practice.* Rochester, N.Y.: Lawyers Cooperative Publishing Co., 1983. 676 pp.

MURPHY, BETTY S., and ELLIOT S. AZOFF,   *Practice and Procedure Before the National Labor Relations Board.* (Corporate Practice Series, No. 41.) Washington, D.C.: Bureau of National Affairs, 1984. 1 vol.

SWIFT, ROBERT A.,   *NLRB and Management Decision Making.* (Labor Relations and Public Policy Series, Report No. 8.) Philadelphia: Industrial Research Unit, Department of Industry, Wharton School of Finance and Commerce, University of Pennsylvania, 1974. 146 pp.

WILLIAMS, ROBERT E.,   *NLRB Regulation of Election Conduct.* (Rev. ed.) (Labor Relations and Public Policy Series, No. 8.) Philadelphia: Industrial Research Unit, The Wharton School, University of Pennsylvania, 1985. 539 pp.

GLOSSARY*

Agency Shop—A bargaining unit covered by a union security clause in the collective bargaining agreement which states that all employees in the unit must pay the union a sum equal to union fees and dues as a condition of continuing employment. Nonunion employees, however, are not required to join the union as a condition of employment.

Apprentice—A method of perpetuating the skills of a trade as well as of regulating the entrance of craftsmen into the trade. It is designed to maintain standards of workmanship and skill.

Arbitration—A method of settling a dispute which involves having an impartial third party, known as an arbitrator, render a decision that is binding on both the union and the employer.

Authorization Card—A statement obtained from each employee by a union during an organization drive. The statement authorizes the union to represent the employee for purposes of collective bargaining.

Bargaining Power—The relative power positions of management and labor during the negotiating process.

*This glossary was compiled by: Philip R. Dankert, Collection Development Librarian, Martin P. Catherwood Library, New York State School of Industrial and Labor Relations, Cornell University, Ithaca, New York 14851-0952.

The compiler gratefully acknowledges his reliance on *Industrial and Labor Relations: A Glossary* by Robert E. Doherty (ILR Press, 1979) from which many of these definitions were drawn.

Bargaining Unit—A group of employees (or jobs) in a plant or industry with sufficient commonality to constitute the unit represented in collective bargaining by a particular bargaining agent.

Blacklist—A list of workers circulated among employers containing the names of "undesirable" employees. Workers whose names are listed are often fired from their jobs or not hired in new ones. It was declared an unfair labor practice by the *National Labor Relations Act* in 1935.

Boulwarism—A collective bargaining approach in which the employer attempts to persuade his employees that his or her initial offer is in their best interests, thus bypassing the union, and changes this offer only if new information or persuasive arguments are received from the union. It was originally named after Lemuel Boulware, a former vice president for employee and public relations at the General Electric Company.

Business Agent—A full-time local union officer who handles the union's financial, administrative and labor-relations problems.

Certification—Official recognition by the National Labor Relations Board or an appropriate state agency, that a particular union is the majority choice, and thus the exclusive bargaining agent of all employees in a particular bargaining unit.

Checkoff—A procedure under which the employer deducts from the pay of all employees who are union members union dues, assessments and initiation fees and turns these funds over to the union.

Closed Shop—A union-security arrangement under which the employer is required to hire only employees who are members of the union. Membership in the union is also a condition of continued employment. The closed shop was declared illegal by the *Taft—Hartley Act* in 1947.

Coalition Bargaining—A form of collective bargaining in which several different unions representing several different categories of employees of a single employer attempt to coordinate their bargaining.

Collective Bargaining—A method of determining terms and conditions of employment by negotiation between representatives of the employer and union representatives of the employee.

Company Union—An organization of employees, usually of a single company, that is either dominated or strongly influenced by management. The *National Labor Relations Act* of 1935 declared that such management interference is an unfair labor practice.

Conciliation—A process under which a third party acts as the intermediary in bringing together the parties to an industrial dispute but does not take an active part in the settlement process.

Cost of Living Adjustment (COLA)—A provision found in collective bargaining agreements that *ties* wage increases to the cost of living during the term of the agreement. Sometimes referred to as an "escalator clause."

Craft Union—A union that limits its membership to those workers in a particular craft. Many craft unions have enlarged their jurisdiction to include as members many occupations and skills not closely related to the originally designated craft.

Decertification—The procedure for removing a union as the certified bargaining representative of employees in a bargaining unit. This is done after petition alleging that the union no longer represents the majority of the employees.

Economic Strike—A work stoppage that results from a dispute over wages, hours, and other terms of employment. Economic strikers retain employee status, but they may be permanently replaced and are not entitled to bump their replacements when the strike has been terminated.

Emergency Dispute—A labor-management dispute believed to endanger the public's health or safety.

Fact-finding—The investigation of a labor-management dispute by a board or panel or an individual usually appointed by the head of a government agency that administers a labor relations law. These boards or, in the case of an individual, fact-finders issue reports that describe the issues in a dispute and frequently make recommendations for their solution.

Featherbedding—Labor practices on the part of some unions to make work for their members that are inefficient or unprofitable for the employer. These include payment for work not performed and the creation of nonessential jobs.

Grievance—Any complaint usually by an employee, but sometimes by the union or management, concerning any aspect of the employment relationship.

Hot Cargo Provisions—Contract provisions that allow workers to refuse to handle or process "hot cargo" goods coming from a plant where there is a labor dispute.

Impasse—In negotiation, a state in which no further progress in reaching agreement can be made. Either party may determine when an impasse has been reached.

Industrial Union—A union representing all workers, both skilled and unskilled, in a plant or industry.

Injunction—A court order that restrains an individual or a group from committing acts that it has determined will do irreparable harm. There are two types of injunctions: temporary restraining orders and permanent injunctions.

Jurisdictional Strike—A strike resulting from a dispute over representation rights by two rival unions.

Just Cause—Provocation found by an arbitrator to be sufficient to substantiate an employer's disciplinary action.

Maintenance of Membership—A provision in a collective bargaining agreement stating that no worker must join the union as a condition of employment, but all workers who voluntarily join must maintain their membership for the duration of the contract in order to keep their jobs. Most include an escape clause setting aside an interval, usually ten days or two weeks, during which members may withdraw from the union without penalty.

Management Prerogatives—Rights that management believes are exclusively its own and thus are not subject to collective bargaining. Such rights may include production, scheduling, determining process of manufacture and so forth.

Mandatory Issue—A bargaining issue upon which the union and management are free to bargain to impasse and are required to bargain in good faith.

Mediation—An attempt by a third party, usually a government official, to bring together the parties in an industrial dispute. The mediator does not have the power to force a settlement. Although often used interchangeably with "conciliation," there is a distinction. Whereas conciliation merely attempts to bring the two sides together, mediation involves the suggesting of compromise solutions by the third party.

Multiemployer Bargaining—Collective bargaining which involves more than one company in a given industry. It takes such forms as area-wide bargaining and industry-wide bargaining.

Multiplant Bargaining—Collective bargaining in which the employer negotiates and bargains with more than one plant.

Negotiation—The process by which representatives of labor and management bargain to set terms and conditions of work, that is, wages, hours and benefits.

Open Shop—A factory or business establishment in which there is no union. It is also sometimes applied to places of work in which there is no union or where union membership is not a condition of employment.

Pattern Bargaining—A procedure in collective bargaining under which key terms reached in a settlement in one company are closely followed by other companies.

Permissive Issue—A bargaining issue that may be placed on the table by either party, but the other party is not required to bargain over the issue.

Picketing—The actual patrolling at or near the employer's place of business during a strike or other dispute to give notice of the existence of a labor dispute, to publicize it, or to persuade workers to join the union and to discourage or prevent persons from entering or going to work. Informational picketing occurs when off-duty employees picket to inform the public of the union's position in a dispute. Organizational or recognition picketing is an attempt on the part of a union to force the employer to recognize the union.

Ratification—The process of approval of a newly negotiated collective bargaining agreement by the union membership.

Recognition—Acknowledgment by an employer that the majority of his or her employees in a given bargaining unit want a specific union to represent them in collective bargaining.

Reopening Clause—A provision in a collective bargaining agreement that permits either side to reopen the contract during its term, generally under specific circumstances, to reconsider economic and other issues. Often called a "reopener".

Right-to-Work Laws—Provisions in state laws that prohibit the union shop, maintenance of membership, preferential hiring, or any other union-security provisions calling for compulsary union membership.

Roll-up, Impact, Creep, Add-on—Terms commonly used to describe the costs of non-wage contractual items linked to wage rates which must be added to the total cost of a negotiated wage-and-benefit settlement in order to accurately reflect the ultimate labor cost for a given contract term.

Scab—An individual who continues to work while a strike is in progress. Also, a worker who is hired to replace one who is on strike.

Secondary Boycott—Pressure exerted on employers who are not directly involved in a dispute. It may involve the refusal to handle or work on products of a company that is dealing with an employer with whom the union has a dispute.

Seniority—The length of continuous employment an employee has in the plant.

Shop Steward—A representative of the union who carries out union duties in the plant or shop. Included here are handling grievances, collecting dues, and recruiting new members. He or she can be either elected by other union members in the plant or appointed by higher union officials.

Slowdown—A concerted and deliberate effort by workers to reduce output and efficiency in order to obtain concessions from an employer.

Strike Fund—Money put aside, generally by the international union, to defray the expenses of a strike. Strike expenses cover strike benefits to individual members, legal fees, publicity and other miscellaneous expenses.

Struck Work—A situation where work done is for an employer or company whose employees are on strike.

Sympathy Strike—A strike by workers not directly involved in a labor dispute; an attempt to demonstrate labor solidarity.

Unfair Labor Practice—Actions of either union or management that violate provisions of national or state labor relations acts. Failing to bargain in good faith is an example of an unfair labor practice on the part of either management or a union.

Union Dues—Periodic payments, usually on a monthly basis, paid by members to the union in order to defray the costs of the organization. Their amount is set by either the constitution or by-laws and is subject to revision by the membership.

Union Security Clauses—Provisions in collective bargaining agreements designed to protect the union against employers, nonunion employees, and/or raids by competing unions.

Union Shop—A form of union security that allows the employer to hire whomever he or she pleases but requires all new employees to become members of the union within a specified period of time (by law, not less than thirty days) after being hired and to retain membership as a condition of continuing employment.

Wildcat Strike—A work stoppage that violates the contract and is not authorized by the union.

Yellow-Dog Contract—An agreement between an employer and a worker, which provides that as a condition of employment the worker will refrain from joining a union or, if a member, will leave the organization. The *Norris–LaGuardia Act* of 1932 nullified the yellow-dog contract by declaring it unenforceable in the courts.

INDEX

Labor practices, unfair, 45
  freedom of speech and, 42−45
  jurisdictional disputes and, 48
  public sector and, 421−22
  Wagner Act and, 37−38
Laborer's International Union, 415
Landrum−Griffin Act, 40, 49
  employment discrimination and, 82
Leadership, psychology and politics in, 121−22
Leon, Daniel de *see* de Leon, Daniel
Lewis, John L., 13, 14, 122, 293, 356
Lincoln Mills case, 46, 69
Linden Lumber Division, Summer and Company versus NLRB, 145
Lining Up the Facts, 174, 175
Livernash, Robert, 310
Living wage criteria, 305
Lloyd−LaFollette Act, 406
LLRB *see* Labor Law Reform Bill
LMRA *see* Labor Management Relations Act of 1947
LMWPR *see* Office of Labor-Management and Welfare-Pension Reports
Local 12, Rubber Workers versus NLRB, 83
Local 189, United Papermakers & Paperworkers versus the United States, 90
Local union, 110−12
Lockouts,
  law and, 62
  legal status of, 60−61
Loew versus Lawler, 32
Lowry versus Whitaker Cable Corporation, 95
Ludlow Massacre, 12

M

McBride, John, 10
McDonnell Douglas Corp. versus Green, 94
McKersie, Robert, 438
Maintenance of membership, 377, 378
Major Collective Bargaining Agreements, 197
Mallinckrodt Chemical Works case, 151−53
Mallinckrodt doctrine, 152
Management,
  antiunion activity and, 381−84
  bargaining teams, 171−72
  concession bargaining and, 437−38
  development of, 358−59
  environment and thinking of, 128
  internal aspects of, 128−30
  proposal formulation for bargaining, 185−86
  proposals, financial dimensions of, 205−6
  restrictions on rights, 366
  rights provisions, 365
  secure, versus insecure, 360−63

security, 73, 352−69
  ability, decision making, and, 357−58
  allocation of prerogatives, 358−60
  background factors in, 364−66
  defense of, 361−62
  defined, 352
  freedom and the problem of prerogatives, 354
  interest criterion and, 356−27
  legal and practical aspects of, 368−69
  nature and status of, 352−54
  unilateral control of, 355−56
  union representation on corporate boards and, 366−68
  types of, 130−33
  union security and, 375−76
  unique property in relations with unions, 245−47
  worker owned plants and, decision making in, 358−60
  see also Employers
Massachusetts Labor Relations Commission, 420
Meadows versus Ford Motor Company, 91
Meany, George, 16, 17
Mediation, 69
Mediators, 284−85
Medicaid, 410
Medicare, 410
Medoff, James, 308
Midland National Life Insurance case, 45
Miranda Fuel Co. case, 82
Mitchell, Daniel J. B., 300, 422, 430, 435, 438
Molly Maguires, 11
Monthly Labor Review, 21, 197, 316
Moore Dry Dock case, 68
Multiemployer bargaining,
  future of, 160
  units, 154−60
    bargaining power in, 156−57
    effects of on employers and unions, 154−56
    labor law and, 159−60
    pros and cons of, 157−59
Multi-industrial unions, 109
Multinationals, industrial relations and, 134
Murphy, Frank, 15
Murphy, T. A., 366
Murray, Philip, 16

N

NALC *see* National Association of Letter Carriers
NAM *see* National Association of Manufacturers
National Association of Letter Carriers (NALC), 215, 410